Complexity and Entrepreneurship

Andreas Liening

Complexity and Entrepreneurship

Complexity Research and Its Implications on Entrepreneurship Processes

Springer

Andreas Liening
Fakultät Wirtschaftswissenschaften, Lehrstuhl
Entrepreneurship und Ökonomische Bildung
Technische Universität Dortmund
Dortmund, Germany

ISBN 978-3-658-44031-2 ISBN 978-3-658-44032-9 (eBook)
https://doi.org/10.1007/978-3-658-44032-9

This book is a translation of the original German edition "Komplexität und Entrepreneurship" 2nd edition, by Andreas Liening, published by Springer Fachmedien Wiesbaden GmbH in 2023. The translation was done with the help of an artificial intelligence machine translation tool. A subsequent human revision was done primarily in terms of content, so that the book will read stylistically differently from a conventional translation. Springer Nature works continuously to further the development of tools for the production of books and on the related technologies to support the authors.

This Springer imprint is published by the registered company Springer Fachmedien Wiesbaden GmbH, part of Springer Nature.
The registered company address is: Abraham-Lincoln-Str. 46, 65189 Wiesbaden, Germany

Paper in this product is recyclable.

Preface to the Second Edition

Yes, just make a plan!
Just be a great light!
And then make a second plan
Neither of them will work. (Brecht, 1928)

The world in which we live is perceived as increasingly complex. We often feel as if we are in a fog. Complexity is more than just a "feeling", it is an empirical fact. And yet, we are constantly surprised by developments that we have not even remotely anticipated. This applies to events on the world stage, where financial crises, climate crises, state crises, and other escalations up to and including military conflicts catch us unprepared. Nevertheless, major events that begin as perceived crises can also be positive, as the "fall of the Berlin Wall" shows, which no one had anticipated.

However, complex, unpredictable events exist not only on a large scale, but also on a small scale, as in the context of one's own individual experiences:

Everyone, for example, writes a "CV", a Curriculum Vitae, which, when viewed as a reader, reveals a "common thread". In retrospect, much can be interpreted sensibly and you can assign a meaning to the developments of life. However, if you are at the beginning of those developments that later appear so sensible and logical, you may well have the impression that this supposed "common thread" does not exist at all.

Often, it is rather the small coincidences, but of course also a lot of hard work and perseverance, close friends who have supported and accompanied you, decisions that you made in a certain situation, but certainly not a long-term plan, which could be assumed from the example of the curriculum vitae, that characterises one's professional career.

Quite the contrary: Particularly significant, major events in one's own life often happen unplanned and seemingly randomly, and are rarely the result of a sophisticated plan. And this applies not only to your profession: For example, you may have met your life partner because you happened to "end up" in a certain club with a few friends; you contemplate at a fork in the road whether to turn left or right, spontaneously decide for one direction and against the other, and encounter an interesting person, and your life is steered in a completely new direction, etc.

Often, we can only make sense of developments in retrospect, and then we speak of a "red thread". Ex post, everything can be explained, but ex ante, it is often much more difficult to find an explanation.

If, on the one hand, we experience a negative event, for example, we often speak of "bad luck" or "fate" to indicate that it was beyond our control.

We often overlook the fact that much of what "happens" to us was brought about by ourselves, and even when we admit our own mistakes as such, we often overlook the fact that it is precisely these mistakes that make us stronger and more confident in mastering life.

On the other hand, if the experiences are positive, we tend to attribute the success much more to ourselves alone, rather than remembering who and what, but also which unforeseen circumstances, helped us to achieve this success. Only sometimes are the experiences of such great importance to us that we elevate them and speak of "providence", "fate" or "destiny".

In English, the idea that positive experiences sometimes have to be attributed to things that are beyond our control and may not even have been intended finds expression in the beautiful word: *Serendipity*—Fortunate coincidence.

Both belong together, the negative as well as the positive, only in the interplay of the two poles is balance achieved: Hard and soft—*Go* and *Ju*—*Goju,* as karateka of a certain style would describe their way of life, the Karate-Do, where the path (Do) itself, which one bravely takes step by step, is the actual goal.

But it's not just in our personal lives and on a small scale; many things can't be planned, especially in public and on a larger scale. Let's take the German national economy as an example and the enormous task of coordinating supply and demand, which affects millions of individuals in Germany every day. Those who thought they could plan this centrally for decades were not only mistaken, their whole (political and economy) system ultimately failed. How can a central authority possibly know *which* goods or services should be provided individually, *when* and *where*, in which *quantity* and in which *quality* should be provided to each individual?

However, despite the limitations that plans obviously have, we cannot do without plans.

For example, macroeconomic coordination and other related issues can only be solved with the help of the decentralised knowledge of hundreds of thousands of entrepreneurs, managers, and merchants "on the spot". This requires meticulous planning at the decentralised level, which ultimately represent tools for solving a factual problem. But plans also have important functions beyond that as they

- … are *communicative:* They make the intentions of the planner and his approach clear to other people.
- … enable *coordination:* Thus, the activities of several people can be coordinated with each other using a plan against the backdrop of a common goal.
- … *commit:* By trusting that we will adhere to our plans, we allow others to rely on the outcomes of our planned projects. Thus, plans create certainty of action.

- … ensure *transparency:* They make goals and procedures clear and discussable, they enable an improvement of action frameworks, possibly even a change of goals.
- … *relieve:* Once a plan is in place, you don't have to constantly recall all the details or rethink them over and over again (Strohschneider, von der Weth et al., 2001, p. 12 ff.).

Predictability from the perspective of startups can, for example, include knowledge of the supply and demand situation in existing markets. In this context of an existing market in which new start-ups are emerging, we speak of a *Red Ocean.* The ocean turns red because suddenly new fish appear in the sea that eat the others. But plans have their limits. This is always the case when situations, processes, etc. no longer move "in calm waters", when past data no longer helps us to develop solutions for the future, but when we get into complex situations, when turbulence, dynamic leaps, and chaos occur.

Of all entrepreneurial fields of action, entrepreneurship is particularly affected by these boundaries. Especially in startups, the limits of plans become apparent very quickly. Especially in uncertain times like these, where also the resurgence and advancement of artificial intelligence (AI), coupled with an explosive increase in its usage, enable entirely new business models, the limitations of traditional planning become more than apparent. No wonder that the founder of Amazon, Jeff *Bezos,* says that a business plan will not survive its first encounter with reality. It will always be different. Reality will never match the plan, according to *Bezos* (Mochere, 2022). After all, startups have little chance of foresight, especially since they are often the cause of unpredictable changes and disruption themselves.

Newly emerging markets cannot possess a past. Before the invention of significant innovations—from steam power to smartphone technology—no one could have obtained detailed information about demand or supply—they simply did not exist. The tearing down of old markets, the creation of new markets, in short—as *Schumpeter* once said—*creative destruction,* is indeed a hallmark of a startup.

The chaos that we encounter in the environment of a startup is therefore rather positive for the startup itself: As chaos and complexity are signs of great uncertainty and only enable the development of the startup, enable creative destruction, while order only generates habit and relies on what has been proven so far, which is swept away by the startup. Here we speak of the *Blue Ocean,* the blue ocean, which still wants to be explored. Creating new markets is like sailing over the blue ocean to an undiscovered land that is not marked on any map. In this process, a classic business administration, which is oriented towards existing companies, often fails because it needs past data to predict the future. However, startups that have just been founded do not have any past values.

Furthermore: Even if numerous (past) data are available, they do not help us if we venture into complex waters. The *Laplacian Demon,* who can predict everything because he knows all initial conditions and has all necessary information, and who also permeates our thinking, must fail in complex phases, as is explained and justified in great detail in this book. One could say: In the realm of complexity, the future lies between chance and order like in a fog.

Yes, even more so, complexity itself *is*, figuratively speaking, like fog: Short-term forecasts are indeed possible, but then the so-called butterfly effect sets a clear limit to predictability.

Complex phenomena are often popularly described with this *'butterfly effect'*, which states that the flap of a butterfly's wings in Brazil could, after some time, trigger a tornado in Texas.

And with that, we do not see the turbulence coming, we cannot predict it. The classic methods are blind to complexity: And even if we could capture all the smallest snippets of information, the collection, analysis, and evaluation would still take more time than it would take to get the results in time, so that the events would roll over us one way or another. Certainly, one can analyse the fog with classic methods. But, to stay with this image, even after the most thorough analysis, the fog is still there.

But there is hope—There are indeed scientific answers to the question of how we can walk safely step by step through the fog:

For several decades, there have been established quantitative, respectively mathematical-empirical methods that can be successfully applied to questions of complexity between order and randomness. And it becomes clear: Chaos is not a coincidence on the one hand, and on the other hand, chaos and order belong together, like two sides of a coin, just as *Ying* and *Yang* are inconceivable without each other and condition each other.

While the first edition of this book focussed on theory, the second edition places particular emphasis on the integration of empirical approaches, whether to better understand behavioural anomalies in simple, complicated, and also complex systems through case studies, or to make the different levels of the "Synergetic Entrepreneurship Model (SEM)" developed in this book, which considers both the individual, organisational, and macroeconomic phenomena of entrepreneurship, accessible for empirical investigation through complexity science analyses of concrete time series.

For example, abrupt changes in system behaviour, which are described as phase transitions, can be diagnosed and investigated in complex processes by including the calculation of *Lyapunov* exponents, (fractal) dimensions, permutation entropies, *Recurrence* plots, and other methods, whereby these methods are previously described and analysed in detail theoretically. This makes it possible to investigate complex processes of structure genesis, as can be observed in the development of business models up to entire entrepreneurial ecosystems.

Often, entrepreneurs stand as if in front of a fog wall, where they need to test or realign their thinking. There is probably no "red thread" that they can cling to, no 'Business Plan' that could last five years. For a long time, people oriented themselves towards a mechanistic model, whose mathematics successfully shaped economics for many years, but reaches its limits in complex phases. Some economists therefore advocate a departure from mathematics in economics. However, this is not necessary, because “Where there is danger, the saving power also grows,” writes the poet (Hölderlin, 2015). And so the established quantitative, empirical-mathematical methods of complexity sciences, which are increasingly also making their way into economics, help us find a path through the complex tangle and safely shape our startup: The fog is lifting.

Dortmund
January 2024

Univ.-Prof. Dr. Andreas Liening

Reference

Brecht, B. (1928). *Ballad of the insufficiency of human planning*. Threepenny Opera.

Hölderlin, F. (2015). *Poems*. CreateSpace Independent Publishing Platform.

Mochere, V. (2022). *Best quotes from Jeff Besoz*. Retrieved March 10, 2022.

Strohschneider, S., et al. (2001). Ja, mach nur einen Plan! - Pannen und Fehlschläge - Ursachen, Beispiele, Lösungen. Hogrefe AG.

Preface

For a long time, economics had a perhaps silent, but certainly large role model: Physics with its Newtonian mechanics. It allows us to calculate the trajectory of a rocket to the moon, or even to land instruments precisely on a distant tiny asteroid. The basis is the famous Newtonian law: Force = Mass times Acceleration. The force is the *cause* for a very specific *effect:* The acceleration, i.e., the force determines the latter. Even more: A double force produces a twice as large acceleration, i.e., a *linear* relationship applies. It is more than evident how tempting it is to transfer this reaction to economic events. For example, predictability means complete planning, which found its expression in Marxist economic theory and large-scale practice with its devastating consequences.

Now, this "worldview" of physics, just presented, has experienced two severe shocks in the last century:

1. Quantum physics, without which the entire information technology we use daily would not exist, but whose fundamental processes are not at all deterministic.
2. The second, probably more in the spotlight and brought to a wider audience, is the theory of chaos. However, the sensational term "chaos" used by scientists is not accurate: it refers to aesthetically highly appealing and *highly ordered* structures generated on computers. But this also obscures a fundamental aspect of chaos research: Although their equations are strictly deterministic, the smallest inaccuracy grows enormously in the course of the calculation process, so that predictability is fundamentally not possible. The failure of weather forecasting beyond several days is the glaring example almost inevitably cited in this context.

Around the same time as the emergence of chaos theory, I founded synergetics—the study of interaction. How do the individual parts of a complex system manage to interact in such a way that ordered structures or functions are created? Even with a system from physics, the then novel light source laser, it turned out that entirely new concepts were needed to represent the self-organisation of laser light that occurs here. Determinism is replaced by a strange combination of certainty and chance, linearity is replaced by non-linearity, causality is replaced by "circular causality", and finally: instead of direct control, indirect influence. I do not want to anticipate the author's explanations, Prof. Andreas Liening. However, it is clear that new perspectives on economics emerge from here, with only an economist being able to draw and present the appropriate conclusions. These are vital for the entrepreneur in an increasingly complex world. I am pleased that Prof. Liening mentions the significant economists Robert Solow and Friedrich August von Hayek in his conclusion. I have met both scientists several times. As I learned from Solow, he dealt with synergetics. Hayek advocated the concept of market self-organisation with its collective intelligence, which could not be predicted. So, with both scientists, Prof. Liening is "in good company". I am sure that the comprehensive work of Prof. Andreas Liening will not only be groundbreaking for entrepreneurs, but will also have a significant influence on the further development of economics.

Stuttgart, Germany
February 2016

Univ.-Prof. Dr. rer. nat. Dr. h.c. mult. Hermann Haken

Greetings

None other than *Seneca* once said:

> "Reading is, I believe, absolutely necessary for me:
> Firstly, so that I do not have to be content with myself alone, secondly, to become acquainted with the knowledge of others, thirdly, so that I can form an opinion about what they have discovered and think about the questions that still need to be answered." (Seneca, approx. 4 BC–65 AD)

In this regard, I thank the research team at my chair for the tremendous support. Special thanks go to Hermann *Haken* for his foreword and the inspiration through his life's work.

I wish the readers much joy in reading, interesting insights, and hopefully many ideas and questions about the complexity between order and randomness and their significance for entrepreneurship research!

Your

Prof. Dr. Andreas Liening

Contents

1 Introduction 1
1.1 About the Presumption and Limits of Knowledge 2
1.2 Economy and its Subsectors as Complex Systems 5
1.3 Scientific Approaches—Complexonomics 6
1.4 Complexity Science Substantiates Entrepreneurship as an Independent Business Discipline 8
1.5 Objectives and Content—'Run Through' 14
1.5.1 The Fourfold Objective 14
1.5.2 On the Structure and Contents 15
1.6 About the Approach: On Mathematics, Simulations, and the *Papillon* Spiral 17
1.6.1 About Mathematics 17
1.6.2 About Visualisations and Simulations 18
1.6.3 The *Papillon* Spiral 18
References 19

Part I Background and History

2 How do we Respond To Complexity?—A (not only) Behavioural Economic Consideration for Entrepreneurs 23
2.1 Crises, Chaos, Opportunities—Demands on our Thinking 24
2.1.1 'Time of Crisis'—'Time of Opportunity'—The World is Becoming More Complex... 24
2.1.2 How Rational is Man? 32
2.2 Behaviour in Simple Situations—Behavioural Anomalies are Observable 34
2.2.1 Anomalies in the Information Process 34
2.2.2 Information Perception 35
2.2.2.1 'Selective Perception'—Selective Perception of Information 35

2.2.2.2 'Availability'—Availability of Information 36
2.2.2.3 'Framing'—Presentation of Information 38
2.2.3 Information Processing 40
2.2.3.1 'Mental Accounting'—Mental Account Management in Information Processing 40
2.2.3.2 'Anchoring'—Anchoring of Information Processing 40
2.2.3.3 'Representativeness'—Representativeness in Information Processing 42
2.2.3.4 'Information-Sources-Effect'—Information Source Effect in Information Processing 43
2.2.4 Information Evaluation 43
2.2.4.1 'Reference-Point'—Reference Point in the Context of Information Evaluation 43
2.2.4.2 'Loss Aversion'—Loss Aversion in Information Evaluation 44
2.2.4.3 'Weighting of Probabilities'—Probabilities in Information Evaluation 45
2.2.4.4 'Survivorship Bias'—Bias in Favour of the Survivors 48
2.2.5 Control Behaviour 49
2.2.5.1 Anomalies due to the Need for Control 49
2.2.5.2 'Overconfidence'—Overestimating One's Own Abilities 50
2.2.5.3 'Regret Aversion' 51
2.2.5.4 'Illusion of Control' 51
2.2.5.5 'Home Bias'—Preferring the Familiar 53
2.2.5.6 'Herding'—The J-Pattern 53
2.3 Behaviour in Complex Situations 55
2.3.1 Four Observable Strategies 55
2.3.1.1 'Trial and Error'—Experimentation 55
2.3.1.2 'Fading Out' 57
2.3.1.3 'Rational Behaviour'—Rational Approach. 59
2.3.1.4 'Simplicity'—Reduction to Simple Factors 60
2.3.2 The Oil Spot Theory—"Recursive Consequences Spiral Out of Control" 61
2.3.3 Intuition as a Successful Strategy for Coping with Complex Challenges? 63
References................................ 65

3 Canvas—From the Mechanistic to the Complex View of the World 69
3.1 A Brief Look into History—About Newtonian Physics and Analogies in Economics 71
3.1.1 A Brief Look into the History of Economics and the Worldview at the Beginning of the Modern Era 71
3.1.1.1 Physiocracy and the Mechanical Man 71
3.1.1.2 The Classical National Economy 76
3.1.1.3 The Neoclassicism and its Image of Man 77
3.1.1.4 The Historical Human Image of Economics: Controversial Receptions of the Entrepreneur 80
3.1.2 About Classical Mechanics and Newtonian Physics—'natura non facit saltus' 82
3.1.2.1 From the Principle of Mimesis to the Modern Understanding of Science (Liening, 1996) 83
3.1.2.2 The "Laplacian Demon" as a Symbol of Determinism 86
3.1.2.3 "Everything is reversible"—Reversibility 87
3.1.2.4 "From a follows b"—(strong) Causality 88
3.1.2.5 Systems are Decomposable—Summativity 88
3.1.3 Analogy between Classical Mechanics and Economics 89
3.1.3.1 The Influence of Classical Mechanics on Economics 89
3.1.3.2 An Illustrative Linear, Static Supply-Demand Model: Multicopter Engineers Wanted for a Startup 91
3.1.3.3 The Cobweb Model—Dynamisation of a Linear Supply-Demand Model: "Multicopter engineers wanted for a startup" 95
3.1.3.4 Background Information: Mathematical Considerations on a Linear Cobweb Model 100
3.1.3.5 Philosophical Consideration of the Analogy Formation between Classical Mechanics and Economics—The Danger of Knowledge in the Essential Spell of Technology 103
3.2 The Collapse of the Laplacian Worldview 107
3.2.1 First Doubts 107
3.2.2 The Weather Forecast and the Butterfly Effect 110
3.3 A Paradigm Shift is Announced—Characteristics of the New Approach 113
3.3.1 Paradigm Shift in Economics 113

3.3.2 Describing the World with Systems and Models—What is a System, What is a Model? 115
3.3.2.1 Historical. 115
3.3.2.2 The Concept of System. 119
3.3.2.3 Basic Characteristics of Systems 122
3.3.2.4 What are Models? 140
3.4 Modeling and Simulation of Complex Systems 141
3.4.1 Systems Dynamics—The 'new' Language 141
3.4.2 Simulations with Counterintuitive System Behaviour 143
3.4.2.1 Positive Feedback Loops 144
3.4.2.2 Negative Feedback Loops 148
3.4.2.3 Double Feedback Loops 154
3.4.3 System Archetypes—Dealing with Complexity 156
3.4.3.1 Equilibrium Process with Delay 157
3.4.3.2 Limits of Growth. 158
3.4.3.3 Problem Shifting 159
3.4.3.4 Eroding Goals 162
3.4.3.5 Escalation 164
3.4.3.6 Success to the Successful 166
3.4.3.7 Tragedy of the Commons 167
3.4.3.8 Error Corrections 169
3.4.3.9 Growth and Underinvestment 171
3.4.4 Why are Simulations so Important?. 174
3.4.5 Simulation of a 'Complex System' Using the Example of a Supply-demand Model—"Multicopter Engineers Wanted for a StartUp" 177
3.4.6 First Steps to Understanding Complexity 182
3.4.6.1 On the Irreversibility of Time and Catallaxy 182
3.4.6.2 What does Complexity Mean?—The End of Reductionism?. 187
3.4.7 Consequences for the Example of the Supply-Demand Model 194
3.5 First Conclusion—Summary of Important Aspects and a Brief Plea for a (Free) Market Economy and the Consideration of Entrepreneurship as a Complex Phenomenon 197
3.5.1 Complexity and Behavioural Economics. 197
3.5.2 Complexity, the Laplacian Demon, and Economics 197
3.5.3 Complexity and (Free) Market Economy. 198
3.5.4 Complexity and Entrepreneurship 199
3.5.5 Outlook. 200
References. 200

Part II Theory and Empiricism—Recent Developments in Complexity Research

4 Theory—Theoretical Approaches to Complexity 211
4.1 (Strange) Attractors and Fractals 213
4.1.1 Attractors of All Kinds 213
4.1.1.1 What is a Phase Space? 213
4.1.1.2 What is Meant by an Attractor? 215
4.1.1.3 'Benign' Attractors 216
4.1.1.4 Background Information: The Ratio and the Recurrence—Rational Numbers 224
4.1.1.5 Background Information: Excursion to "Square Root of 2" (Liening, 2005, p. 40 ff.) 225
4.1.1.6 'Strange' or 'Chaotic' Attractors 229
4.1.2 Fractals for Describing Deterministic Chaos 231
4.1.2.1 Self-similarity or Scale Invariance as a Characteristic of a Fractal 231
4.1.2.2 The Tree as an Analogy to the Fractal 231
4.1.2.3 The 'Mandelbrot Set' or: About the Emergence of Self-Similar Structures 231
4.1.2.4 About the Length of a Fractal Edge—'How long is the Coast of Britain'?—Koch Curves and Similar Considerations 235
4.1.2.5 Background Information: Calculation of the Area of the Koch Island 237
4.1.2.6 The Oddity of Fractional Dimensions 240
4.1.2.7 Background Information: (Box-)Dimensions 242
4.2 Bifurcations 248
4.2.1 Bifurcations in Dynamic Systems 248
4.2.1.1 What are Bifurcations? 248
4.2.1.2 The Discovery of Bifurcations 249
4.2.1.3 Bifurcation Scenario Using the Example of the Logistic Function 249
4.2.1.4 Intermittency and Bifurcations 256
4.2.2 Evidence of Erratic Behaviour 257
4.2.2.1 The *Li/Yorke* Theorem 257
4.2.2.2 *Lyapunov* Exponents 259
4.2.2.3 Background Information: Basic Calculation of the *Lyapunov* Exponent 260
4.3 Catastrophe Theory 263
4.3.1 René *Thom's* Theory 263
4.3.1.1 'Catastrophes' from a Scientific Perspective 263

4.3.1.2 About Singularities, Manifolds and Catastrophe Sets . . . 263
4.3.2 Hermann *Haken's* Criticism. . . . 266
4.4 Synergetics—The Theory of Self-Organisation. . . . 266
4.4.1 The Basic Idea of Synergetics 266
4.4.1.1 Explaining Self-Organisation Phenomena 266
4.4.1.2 About the Laser. . . . 267
4.4.1.3 Swarm Intelligence—The Migration of Birds (Liening & Mittelstädt, 2008, pp. 41–43). . . . 270
4.4.2 Interpreting Companies and Innovations Synergistically 270
4.4.2.1 Partial and Total Systems in Synergetics 270
4.4.2.2 The Mathematical Trick: The 'Slaving Principle'. . . . 271
4.4.3 Critical Remark 272
4.5 Order and Chaos only in the Computer? About Definitions, Bolzano-Weierstraß and 'Controlling Complexity'. . . . 273
4.5.1 'Working definitions' 273
4.5.1.1 The Genesis of the Term 'Chaos'—Sharpening of the Complexity Concept. . . . 273
4.5.1.2 Preliminary Interpretation of the Concept of Chaos. . . . 277
4.5.1.3 Definitions of Chaos and Complexity. . . . 277
4.5.1.4 'Order' as a Counter-concept to 'Chaos'?. . . . 281
4.5.2 Does Chaos Only Exist in the Computer? 282
4.5.2.1 Ignis Fatuus?—Does the Computer Generate Chaos?. . . . 282
4.5.2.2 The First Argument: Increased Computational Accuracy in Complex Systems Does Not Lead to More Accurate Results 283
4.5.2.3 The Second Argument: The 'Shadow Lemma'. . . . 285
4.5.2.4 Third Argument: The 'L-Density Argument' 287
4.5.2.5 Background Information: The Proof of the Purely Algebraic "Butterfly Effect" in the Logistic Equation: The L-Density Argument 288
4.5.3 'Controlling Complexity'—Can Chaos be Controlled?. . . . 292
4.5.3.1 Chaotic Systems and Control—A Contradiction? 292
4.5.3.2 A Little Hope—Influence Possibilities in Chaotic Systems 293
4.5.3.3 An Alternative (synergetic) Approach: Complexity as an Opportunity 295
4.5.3.4 'Nudges' and the Emergence of *Desired* Order Parameters. . . . 300

4.5.3.5 Measuring Complexity to Determine the Placement of 'Nudges' ... 302
4.5.3.6 There is Even a Predictable Path in Chaos—At Least Theoretically (Theorem of *Bolzano-Weierstraß*) ... 303
4.5.3.7 Background Information: There must be a Predictable Path in Chaos!—The Theorem of *Bolzano-Weierstraß* ... 304
4.6 Second Conclusion—Summary of Important Aspects and the (Heuristic) Value of a Science of Complex Systems for Economics in General and the Topic of Entrepreneurship in Particular ... 307
4.6.1 Brief Summary of Important Aspects ... 307
4.6.2 What can a Science of Complex Systems do for Economics? ... 308
4.6.2.1 Complex versus Mechanistic Viewpoint ... 308
4.6.2.2 Methods of the Science of Complex Systems as Heuristic Analysis Tools ... 309
4.6.2.3 Economic Significance from a Macroeconomic Perspective ... 309
4.6.2.4 Economic Significance from an Entrepreneurship Perspective ... 310
4.6.3 Outlook: Predictions—Even at the Company Level—Are not Trivial in Complex Situations, Processes or Structures, Empirical Studies are Nevertheless Useful and Necessary ... 310
References ... 311

5 Empiricism—Empirical Methods of Complexity Measurement ... 317
5.1 Complexity Measures in Discourse—Are *Lyapunov* Exponents and Fractal Dimensions Suitable? ... 319
5.1.1 On the Relationship Between Theory and Practice ... 319
5.1.1.1 The Inductive Perspective ... 319
5.1.1.2 The Deductive Perspective ... 320
5.1.1.3 Science as a Social Process ... 321
5.1.1.4 Sophisticated Falsification ... 322
5.1.1.5 Allowing Contradictory Theories ... 323
5.1.1.6 The Importance of Methods ... 324
5.1.2 Time Series in Empirical Analysis ... 325
5.1.2.1 Time Series as a Result of Non-linear Dynamic Processes ... 325
5.1.2.2 Preparation of Time Series for Complexity Science Investigations ... 329

5.1.3 Fractal Dimension, *Lyapunov* Exponents and other 'classic' Methods 335
5.1.3.1 An Initial Overview of Determining Complexity in Time Series 335
5.1.3.2 Reconstruction of a System's Phase Space 339
5.1.3.3 Special Features in the Reconstruction of Phase Spaces—The Determination of Time-Lag 347
5.1.3.4 Background Information: Correlation Coefficient—Autocorrelation 350
5.1.3.5 Background Information: Expected Value of a Random Variable & 'Mutual Information' 352
5.1.3.6 Special Features in the Reconstruction of Phase Spaces—The Determination of the Attractor Dimension: D_2 356
5.1.3.7 Special Features in the Reconstruction of Phase Spaces—Non-Overlap and Orthogonality 358
5.1.3.8 Special Features in the Reconstruction of Phase Spaces—Surrogate Test 360
5.1.3.9 About the Use of *Lyapunov* Exponents for Empirical Research: D_2, PD_2, *Wolf*-, *Briggs*-, *Kantz*- and other Algorithms 361
5.1.3.10 Background Information: Complexity Measurement 364
5.1.4 Examples of the Application of 'Classical' Methods in the Context of Empirical Studies 372
5.1.4.1 Macroeconomic Time Series, Such as GDP Time Series 372
5.1.4.2 Price Developments 373
5.1.4.3 Exchange Rate Fluctuations 373
5.1.4.4 Stock Price Fluctuations 373
5.1.5 Critical Examination of the 'Classical' Methods 376
5.1.5.1 Reconstruction of the Phase Space 376
5.1.5.2 Fractals and Reality 377
5.1.5.3 Lyapunov Exponents Under Criticism 378
5.2 Algorithmic Encodings as Alternative Complexity Measures?—Entropy Encodings and Other Measures 379
5.2.1 Resignation or Opportunity? 379
5.2.1.1 Sorting Algorithms: From 'Bubble' to 'Quick' Sort 379
5.2.1.2 Compression Algorithms—Much Better 381

5.2.2 Entropy as a Measure of Complexity 384
5.2.3 Entropy in Information Theory—'Information Entropy' 386
5.2.3.1 Introduction to *Shannon* Entropy 386
5.2.3.2 'Variable Length Coding' (VLC) and the *Shannon* Entropy 389
5.2.3.3 Huffman Encoding for Generating Optimal Variable Length Codes 392
5.2.3.4 Entropy Encoding and Complexity 399
5.2.4 'Permutation entropy' Versus 'Information Entropy' 400
5.2.5 'Grammar Complexity' as an Inverse Alternative to 'Permutation Entropy' 403
5.2.6 'Recurrence Plots'—Return Diagrams 404
5.3 JPEG as a Solution?—Transformation Encodings 416
5.3.1 *LZW*-Compression Algorithm (Lempel, *Ziv, Welch*) 416
5.3.2 Transformation Encodings 417
5.3.2.1 (Discrete) *Fourier* Transformation (FT and DFT) 417
5.3.2.2 Discrete Cosine Transformation (DCT) 421
5.3.2.3 The JPEG Compression Algorithm 422
5.3.2.4 Audio Compression 423
5.3.2.5 Background Information: Transformation Encoding 425
5.3.3 Complexity Studies 438
5.3.3.1 Application of Image Compression Methods 438
5.3.3.2 Application of Audio Compression Methods 438
5.3.3.3 Application of Text Document Compression Methods 439
5.4 Third Conclusion—Numerous Methods for Determining Complexity 439
5.5 Outlook 441
References 441

Part III Multiperspective—Entrepreneurship and Complexity

6 Entrepreneurship and Complexity 449
6.1 What is Entrepreneurship?—Trends and Controversies 450
6.1.1 What is Entrepreneurship? 450
6.1.1.1 On the Origin of the Term 450
6.1.1.2 Entrepreneur versus Manager 455
6.1.1.3 Entrepreneur—"Born or Made"? 459
6.1.1.4 Different Entrepreneurship Classifications 459

6.1.2 Current Trends and Controversies 461
6.1.2.1 The Deterministic Belief in Feasibility and the *Laplacian* Demon 461
6.1.2.2 Entrepreneurs between a Simple and Complex World. 463
6.1.2.3 *'Discovery-'* versus *'Creation-Theory'*. 465
6.1.2.4 The *Effectuation* Approach 469
6.1.2.5 The *Bricolage* Approach. 471
6.2 Development of a 'Synergetic Entrepreneurship Model' (SEM). 474
6.2.1 Basics: Lineality versus Non-Lineality 474
6.2.2 Synergetics as the Basis for the Complexity Science Discussion of Entrepreneurship 476
6.2.3 The Extended Synergetic Model 479
6.2.4 Basic Explanation of the Model. 482
6.2.4.1 The Embedding of the Analysis of Entrepreneurial Founding Processes in a Multi-Level Structure 482
6.2.4.2 Closer Examination of the Three Levels of an Entrepreneurial Founding Process 485
6.2.4.3 The Economic Perspective—Three Perspectives on Entrepreneurial Founding Processes 487
6.2.4.4 Three Submodels, the Multi-Level Model, and Synergetics 488
References. 490

7 The '*S*ynergetic *E*ntrepreneurship *M*odel' *(SEM)* 497
7.1 The Individual Level: Focus on Entrepreneurship Education *(SEM1)* . . . 498
7.1.1 Rough Sketch of the 'Synergetic Entrepreneurship Model 1': The Individual Level from an Economic Didactic Perspective *(SEM1)* 498
7.1.2 The Elements of the System. 503
7.1.2.1 Control Parameters 503
7.1.2.2 The Microscopic Level 515
7.1.2.3 The Macroscopic Level—Order Parameters. 516
7.1.2.4 Limitations 516
7.1.2.5 Environment 517
7.1.3 The Circular Causal Process 518
7.1.3.1 General Explanation of the Circular Causal Process 518
7.1.3.2 Order Parameters Arise through Self-Organisation and Synchronsation—The Importance of Phase Transitions. 520

7.1.3.3 *'Nudges'* Can Support the Emergence of Appropriate Order Parameters that Favour a Justified Entrepreneurial Attitude . . . 524
7.1.3.4 Measuring Complexity for Targeted Initiation of *'Nudges'* . . . 526
7.2 The Organisational Level: Focus on Entrepreneurial Founding Processes *(SEM2)* . . . 527
7.2.1 Rough Sketch of the 'Synergetic Entrepreneurship Model 2': The Organisational Level from a Business-Entrepreneurial Perspective *(SEM2)* . . . 527
7.2.2 The Elements of the System . . . 528
7.2.2.1 Control Parameters . . . 528
7.2.2.2 The Microscopic Level . . . 529
7.2.2.3 The Macroscopic Level—Order Parameters . . . 530
7.2.2.4 Limitations . . . 541
7.2.2.5 Environment . . . 542
7.2.3 The Circular Causal Process . . . 542
7.3 The Macroeconomic Level: Focussing on Market, Business Cycle, and Growth *(SEM3)* . . . 543
7.3.1 Rough Sketch of the 'Synergetic Entrepreneurship Model 3': The Macroeconomic Level from a Predominantly Economic Perspective *(SEM3)* . . . 543
7.3.2 The Elements of the System . . . 550
7.3.2.1 Control Parameters . . . 550
7.3.2.2 The Microscopic Level . . . 550
7.3.2.3 The Macroscopic Level—Order Parameters . . . 551
7.3.2.4 Limitations . . . 552
7.3.2.5 Environment . . . 552
7.3.3 The Circular Causal Process . . . 553
7.3.3.1 Business Cycle . . . 553
7.3.3.2 Dynamic Growth . . . 554
7.3.3.3 A Growth Model with Endogenised Human Capital Formation—Transmission Effects through Entrepreneurial Attitude . . . 561
7.4 Fourth Conclusion: Synergetic View of Entrepreneurship from Multiple Perspectives . . . 566
7.4.1 Brief Summary of the *SEM* Model and the Theories and Views Behind It . . . 566
7.4.2 *SEM1*—The Individual Level: Entrepreneurship Education as a Self-Organising, Complex Process . . . 570

7.4.3 *SEM2*—The Organisational Level: StartUp Foundations as a Synergetic Process Involving Specific, Ordering Business-Economic-Entrepreneurial Methods 571
7.4.4 *SEM3*—The Macroeconomic Level: StartUps Support the Macroeconomic Growth Process through an Entrepreneurial Transmission Effect 571
References 572

8 Empirical Studies—The "Synergetic Entrepreneurship Model" in Practice 579
8.1 Studies Using Complexity Science Methods within the Framework of the "Synergetic Entrepreneurship Model" 580
8.2 Studies on Phase Transitions and Complexity Measurements in the Context of SEM1 582
8.2.1 The 'Entrepreneurship Academy' as a Practical Implementation of *SEM1* 582
8.2.2 The 'Synergetic Entrepreneurship Model' (*SEM*) and the Problem of Phase Transitions 585
8.2.3 *'Business Gaming'* as a Practical Control Parameter of the 'Entrepreneurship Academy' 586
8.2.4 Complexity Measurement for Determining Phase Transitions and Their Practical Consequences 589
8.2.4.1 Learning Processes, Crises, and Complexity Measurements 589
8.2.4.2 A Study from the Field of Business Gaming: "Learning from Crises—Complexity Measurements" 589
8.2.4.3 Critical Examination of the Study Results 598
8.2.5 Another Study from the Field of *Business Gaming* (Complex Stock Market Simulation)—in the Context of SEM1 599
8.3 Complex Dynamics of StartUps within the Framework of SEM2 603
8.3.1 The Business Game as an Environment for Observing Learning Processes at the Organisational Level 603
8.3.2 An Example of Observing a Real Startup in the Founding Process 604
8.4 Complexity Investigations within the Framework of SEM3 605
8.4.1 Complexity Science Investigations of Entrepreneurial Ecosystems 605
8.4.1.1 Entrepreneurial Ecosystems in Research 605
8.4.1.2 Objectives of the Study 606
8.4.1.3 Approach to Complexity Science Data Analysis 606

8.4.1.4 Results of the Complexity Science Analysis 608
8.4.1.5 Conclusions from the Results of the Complexity Science Analysis 609
8.4.2 Development of Business Start-ups in Germany 612
8.4.2.1 Company Founding in Germany 612
8.4.2.2 On the Empirical Methodology and Procedure 613
8.4.2.3 Results: Federal 613
8.4.2.4 Results: Federal States 614
8.4.2.5 Plausible External Events 619
8.5 Fifth Conclusion—Limitations in the Explanation of the Study Results and Perspectives 622
References 624

Part IV Final Considerations

9 Conclusion 629
9.1 About the First Part of the Book 630
9.2 About the Second Part of the Book 631
9.3 About the Third Part of the Book 632
9.4 Concluding Remarks 635
References 636

10 Outro—Excerpt from a Travel Report 637
References 640

List of Figures

Fig. 1.1	About the tasks of an entrepreneur, a leader, a manager, an employee in a complex world	4
Fig. 1.2	Important representatives of the fundamentals of a complexity science in different disciplines. *Source* Bandte (2007, p. 50)	8
Fig. 1.3	The Papillon Spiral	18
Fig. 2.1	The information process. (Based on: Mazanek, 2006, p. 71)	35
Fig. 2.2	Need for Control	50
Fig. 2.3	Example of a tilt image. (The illustration was designed by W. E. *Hill* and first published in Puck Magazine (1915) (Attneave, 1971, p. 66))	58
Fig. 3.1	Economic Schools of Thought. (It should be noted that the diagram with its links between the listed economic schools of thought represents only a *rough* simplification. It includes significant model-theoretical schools of thought that are essentially in an 'institutional vacuum'. This means that, for example, directions of thought of the New Political Economy, the New Institutional Economics etc. are not listed. Since this does not further hinder the argumentation, this simplification is justified.)	72
Fig. 3.2	The Writer by Pierre Jaques-Droz (1773)	73
Fig. 3.3	The 'Chess Automaton' by Kempelen, copper engraving by Windisch. (Note: The images shown here are in the public domain, as their copyright protection period has expired.)	74
Fig. 3.4	Tableau Economique. *Source* Schmidt (1994, p. 53)	75
Fig. 3.5	Linear supply curve	92
Fig. 3.6	Linear demand curve	94
Fig. 3.7	Linear supply and demand curve	95
Fig. 3.8	Converging Cobweb Model. *Source* Liening (2012)	96
Fig. 3.9	Convergent price model. *Source* Liening (2012)	98
Fig. 3.10	Cyclic price model. *Source* Liening (2012)	99
Fig. 3.11	Divergent price model. *Source* Liening (2012)	99

Fig. 3.12 Lineal cause-effect chain 105
Fig. 3.13 The Lorenz Attractor 112
Fig. 3.14 Representation of a system 121
Fig. 3.15 Stability Act: Interactions of individual goals 135
Fig. 3.16 Complementary relationships. (Based on: Gharajedaghi, 2005, p. 40) 136
Fig. 3.17 Leadership typologies. (Adapted from: Cope, 2003, p. 354). 137
Fig. 3.18 Questioning technique for model building. *Source* Figure provided by Consideo. www.consideo.de 143
Fig. 3.19 Lineal relationship 144
Fig. 3.20 Positive Feedback 145
Fig. 3.21 Linear Growth 145
Fig. 3.22 Exponential Growth 146
Fig. 3.23 Positive feedback with target-actual comparison or control variable (discrepancy) 148
Fig. 3.24 Positive feedback with delay 149
Fig. 3.25 Negative Feedback 150
Fig. 3.26 Negative Feedback 150
Fig. 3.27 Negative feedback with target-actual comparison or control variable (discrepancy) 151
Fig. 3.28 Negative feedback with delay 152
Fig. 3.29 Negative feedback using the example of a heating system (thermostat) 153
Fig. 3.30 Simulation of room temperature—negative feedback 153
Fig. 3.31 Double feedback loop 154
Fig. 3.32 Decreasing marginal returns: "Feedback" 155
Fig. 3.33 Increasing marginal returns: "Feedback". 155
Fig. 3.34 Archetype 1—Model—Equilibrium process with delay 157
Fig. 3.35 Archetype 1—Simulation—Equilibrium process with delay: "Surplus demand" 157
Fig. 3.36 Archetype 2—Model—Limits of Growth 159
Fig. 3.37 Archetype 2—Simulation—Limits of Growth: "Product volume produced and sold" 160
Fig. 3.38 Archetype 3—Model—Problem Shifting 161
Fig. 3.39 Archetype 3—Simulation—Problem Shifting: "Stress Development" 161
Fig. 3.40 Archetype 4—Model—Eroding Goals 162
Fig. 3.41 Archetype 4—Simulation—Eroding Goals: "Target/actual deviation" 163
Fig. 3.42 Archetype 5—Model—Escalation. 164
Fig. 3.43 Archetype 5—Simulation—Escalation: "Price reduction escalates" 165

Fig. 3.44 Archetype 6—Model—Success to the Successful. 166
Fig. 3.45 Archetype 6—Simulation—Success of Product A – Failure of Product B – Success to the Successful 167
Fig. 3.46 Archetype 7—Model—Tragedy of the Commons. 168
Fig. 3.47 Archetype 7—Simulation—Tragedy of the Commons: “Fish stock” – Long-term decline in catch quotas despite increasing efforts 169
Fig. 3.48 Archetype 8—Model—Error Corrections 170
Fig. 3.49 Archetype 8—Simulation—Error Corrections: “Liquidity shortfalls” 171
Fig. 3.50 Archetype 9—Model—Growth and Underinvestment 172
Fig. 3.51 Archetype 9—Simulation a)—Effect of an investment without delay . . . 173
Fig. 3.52 Archetype 9—Simulation b)—Effect of an investment with delay 173
Fig. 3.53 Double-loop-learning. (Based on: Sterman, 2000) 174
Fig. 3.54 Idealised learning process involving virtual worlds. (Based on: Sterman, 2000). 176
Fig. 3.55 Systemic Model—Logistic Equation. 178
Fig. 3.56 Fixed point attractor in the price system. *Source* Liening (2012) 179
Fig. 3.57 Fixed point attractor in the price system—Simulation – (starting price, lambda, price development). 180
Fig. 3.58 Two-cycle attractor in the price system. *Source* Liening (2012) 181
Fig. 3.59 Two-cycle in the price system—Simulation – (starting price, lambda, price development). 181
Fig. 3.60 Chaos in the price system. *Source* Liening (2012) 182
Fig. 3.61 Chaos in the price system—Simulation - (starting price, lambda, price development). 183
Fig. 3.62 Maximum and minimum prices. 195
Fig. 4.1 Roller coaster ride 214
Fig. 4.2 Pendulum movements 216
Fig. 4.3 Pendulum motion—sine curve. 217
Fig. 4.4 Pendulum motion—location and momentum curve 217
Fig. 4.5 Two-dimensional phase space, part 1 217
Fig. 4.6 Two-dimensional phase space, part 2 218
Fig. 4.7 Two-dimensional phase space, part 3 218
Fig. 4.8 Two-dimensional phase space, part 4 219
Fig. 4.9 Two-dimensional phase space with point attractor 220
Fig. 4.10 Two-dimensional phase space with limit cycle attractor 221
Fig. 4.11 Torus. 222
Fig. 4.12 Number line 226
Fig. 4.13 Tree—Fractal 232
Fig. 4.14 Tree crown—Fractal 232
Fig. 4.15 Branches—Fractal 233

Fig. 4.16 The *Mandelbrot* set ('apple man') 234
Fig. 4.17 The *Mandelbrot* set—enlargement of a section ('apple man') 235
Fig. 4.18 Coastline length of Great Britain. *Source* Peitgen et al. (1994, p. 233) 236
Fig. 4.19 Development of the *Koch*-curve of order 1-5 238
Fig. 4.20 *Koch*-Island 239
Fig. 4.21 *Hilbert* curves 240
Fig. 4.22 Point attractor 250
Fig. 4.23 Point attractor 250
Fig. 4.24 Limit cycle attractor on the time axis 251
Fig. 4.25 Limit cycle attractor 251
Fig. 4.26 Four-cycle on the time axis 252
Fig. 4.27 Four-cycle 252
Fig. 4.28 Chaotic or strange attractor on the time axis 253
Fig. 4.29 Chaotic or strange attractor 254
Fig. 4.30 Bifurcation diagram 254
Fig. 4.31 Bifurcation diagram 256
Fig. 4.32 *Lyapunov* Diagram 260
Fig. 4.33 *Lyapunov* and Bifurcation Diagram 261
Fig. 4.34 Bifurcation 264
Fig. 4.35 Fold catastrophe 265
Fig. 4.36 The Synergetic Concept. (Based on: Strunk and Schiepek 1994, p. 27, see also: Strunk and Schiepek 2006, p. 81) 269
Fig. 4.37 Dynamics and complexity. *Source* Strunk and Schiepek (2014, p. 79) 274
Fig. 4.38 Higher computational accuracy does not yield better results (17 decimal places) 284
Fig. 4.39 Higher computational accuracy does not yield better results (100 decimal places) 285
Fig. 4.40 Higher accuracy provides more accurate results for root of 2 286
Fig. 4.41 The Shadow Lemma 287
Fig. 4.42 Logistic function after different iteration stages 289
Fig. 4.43 Stable situation—'Ball in the valley' 296
Fig. 4.44 Change—'Pushing the ball out of the valley' 297
Fig. 4.45 'Rolling back the ball'—Hysteresis effects in the stable attractor 297
Fig. 4.46 Tilt image—'Frog—Horse' 298
Fig. 4.47 Phase transition 299
Fig. 4.48 Phase transition—'Nudges'—Butterfly effect 301
Fig. 5.1 (problematic) Induction 320
Fig. 5.2 (problematic) Deduction 321
Fig. 5.3 Number sequence A 326
Fig. 5.4 Number sequence B 326

Fig. 5.5 Number sequence C . . . 326
Fig. 5.6 Logistic Function . . . 328
Fig. 5.7 Attractor based on the logistic function . . . 329
Fig. 5.8 Raw data . . . 330
Fig. 5.9 Return . . . 331
Fig. 5.10 Relative Return . . . 331
Fig. 5.11 Natural logarithm . . . 334
Fig. 5.12 Logarithmic Return—LogReturn . . . 335
Fig. 5.13 Characterisation of various attractor types in three-dimensional phase space. *Source:* Argyris et al., 2010, p. 307 . . . 340
Fig. 5.14 Pendulum movements . . . 341
Fig. 5.15 Pendulum—(discrete) impulse curve. (The points A, B, C and D have already been explained in the context of the pendulum.) . . . 342
Fig. 5.16 Pendulum: 'time-delay' coordinates with $\tau = 1$ . . . 343
Fig. 5.17 Pendulum: 'time-delay' coordinates with $\tau = \pi/2$ . . . 344
Fig. 5.18 Sine and cosine in the unit circle . . . 345
Fig. 5.19 Points in the coordinate system. *Source:* Fahrmeir et al., 2007, p. 137 . . . 352
Fig. 5.20 The *Wolf* algorithm for determining *Lyapunov* exponents . . . 366
Fig. 5.21 *Kantz* algorithm for determining the *Lyapunov* exponent . . . 370
Fig. 5.22 *Rosenstein* algorithm for determining the *Lyapunov* exponent . . . 370
Fig. 5.23 *Wolf*-, *Rosenstein*- and *Kantz*-algorithm comparison . . . 371
Fig. 5.24 Relative frequencies of the occurrence of characters in a string . . . 393
Fig. 5.25 *Huffman*-Tree 1st level . . . 393
Fig. 5.26 *Huffman*-Tree 2nd level . . . 394
Fig. 5.27 *Huffman* Tree 3rd level . . . 394
Fig. 5.28 Encoding of the character a . . . 395
Fig. 5.29 Encoding of the character d . . . 395
Fig. 5.30 Encoding of the character c . . . 396
Fig. 5.31 Encoding of the character b . . . 396
Fig. 5.32 Equally distributed, but random . . . 397
Fig. 5.33 Unequally distributed and random . . . 398
Fig. 5.34 Pendulum cycle sine curve . . . 407
Fig. 5.35 Recurrence plot for the pendulum cycle—sine curve . . . 408
Fig. 5.36 Randomness—White Noise . . . 409
Fig. 5.37 Recurrence Plot for Randomness—White Noise . . . 410
Fig. 5.38 Two Coupled Oscillations . . . 411
Fig. 5.39 Recurrence Plot: Coupled Oscillation . . . 412
Fig. 5.40 Trend—Logistic Function . . . 412
Fig. 5.41 Recurrence Plot for the Trend—Logistic Function . . . 413
Fig. 5.42 *Lorenz* System—Data Series . . . 413
Fig. 5.43 *Lorenz* System—Recurrence Plot . . . 414

Fig. 5.44 8x8 pattern . . . 430
Fig. 5.45 Pattern—'1:1:1' . . . 432
Fig. 5.46 Pattern—'2:1:1' . . . 432
Fig. 5.47 Pattern—'4:1:1' . . . 432
Fig. 5.48 Zigzag Order . . . 435
Fig. 5.49 Characterisation of different attractor types in three-dimensional phase space. (*Sources:* Loistl & Betz, 1993, p. 63; Argyris et al., 2010, p. 307) . . . 440
Fig. 5.50 Characterisation of different arrangements of root 2 in two-dimensional phase space . . . 440
Fig. 6.1 Lineal phase model of a startup process. (Based on: Volkmann & Tokarski, 2006, p. 402) . . . 464
Fig. 6.2 Randomness, complexity, and simplicity . . . 465
Fig. 6.3 Effectuation approach. (Based on: Sarasvathy, 2009) . . . 470
Fig. 6.4 Lineal-causal founding phases . . . 475
Fig. 6.5 Non-lineal founding phases . . . 476
Fig. 6.6 Synergetic model. (Based on: Strunk & Schiepek, 1994, p. 27, see also: Strunk & Schiepek, 2006, p. 81) . . . 479
Fig. 6.7 Extended synergetics model. (Based on: Strunk & Schiepek, 2006, p. 81, see also Haken & Schiepek, 2010) . . . 480
Fig. 6.8 Scientific perspectives on the three levels . . . 485
Fig. 6.9 The three levels of a linear entrepreneurial process . . . 486
Fig. 6.10 The three levels of a non-linear entrepreneurial process . . . 487
Fig. 6.11 Non-linear, abrupt course of the entrepreneurial process . . . 488
Fig. 7.1 The 'Synergetic Entrepreneurship Model 1': The economic didactic dimension of individual learning *(SEM1)* . . . 499
Fig. 7.2 Multimedia learning environment as control parameter . . . 504
Fig. 7.3 Double-loop-learning. (Based on: Sterman, 2000) . . . 519
Fig. 7.4 'White noise' versus 'order': Microlevel . . . 521
Fig. 7.5 Stable situation—'ball in the valley' . . . 521
Fig. 7.6 Change—'pushing the ball out of the valley' . . . 522
Fig. 7.7 Change—'Without permanent energy supply, the ball rolls back' . . . 522
Fig. 7.8 Phase transition . . . 523
Fig. 7.9 Phase transition—'Nudges'—Butterfly effect . . . 524
Fig. 7.10 The 'Synergetic Entrepreneurship Model 2': the Founding Dimension *(SEM2)* . . . 529
Fig. 7.11 Build-measure-learn feedback loop. (Based on: Ries 2011, p. 75) . . . 532
Fig. 7.12 Customer development process. (Based on: Blank & Dorf, 2012, p. 23) . . . 534
Fig. 7.13 Template of the business model canvas. (Source: https://strategyzer.com/, Osterwalder & Pigneur, 2011) . . . 538

Fig. 7.14 The 'Synergetic Entrepreneurship Model 3': *An* example for the market dimension *(SEM3)* 549
Fig. 7.15 Business cycle 553
Fig. 7.16 Business cycle and growth. 555
Fig. 7.17 Endogenous law of returns growth of human capital 559
Fig. 7.18 Two-cycle attractor in the growth model with endogenised human capital formation 561
Fig. 7.19 Cyclical development of capital intensity in a growth model with endogenous human capital formation 563
Fig. 7.20 Bifurcation diagram—growth model with endogenised human capital formation 563
Fig. 7.21 Strange attractor—development of capital intensity in the growth model with $\beta = 0.55$ 564
Fig. 7.22 Complex development of capital intensity in the growth model with $\beta = 0.55$ 564
Fig. 7.23 *Lyapunov* diagram for the growth model with endogenous human capital formation 565
Fig. 7.24 Complex growth cycles—$Y(t) = F(K(t),\ L(t)\ \cdot\ A(t))$. 565
Fig. 7.25 S*ynergetic* E*ntrepreneurship* M*odel* (*SEM*). (The final structure of the *SEM* presented here was critically questioned and refined in numerous workshops with the participation of Jan-Martin *Geiger*, Ronald *Kriedel*, Till *Sender* and Waldemar *Wagner*, the author's research team. For example, the creation of the *SEM1* was critically and constructively accompanied by *Sender*. The variants of the micro level of the *SEM2* are the result of extensive discussions with *Geiger*. The selection of entrepreneurial methods as order parameters of the *SEM2* are largely due to the numerous discussions with *Kriedel*. In particular, details of the *SEM3* were repeatedly critically questioned by *Kriedel* and *Wagner*, so that overall the results of the numerous discussions of the research team have flowed into the *SEM*. The graphic itself was implemented by Maximilian *Schimanski*, like many other graphics in this book). 569
Fig. 8.1 "StartUp Cockpit" of the business game 588
Fig. 8.2 Change in complexity and phase transitions-bifurcations 593
Fig. 8.3 Permutation entropy in the Business Game (in Bit). (Source: Liening et al., 2012: p. 45) 596
Fig. 8.4 Research design 600
Fig. 8.5 Descriptive results 601
Fig. 8.6 Hypothesis tests and results. 602
Fig. 8.7 Recurrence Plot for the number of founding activities (fortnightly) of HealthInfo. (Figure created with tool by Arwan et al., 2007). 605

Fig. 8.8 Raw time series of the establishment of new companies, 1970/1 to 2018/5 (Haarhaus et al., 2020: p. 3) 607
Fig. 8.9 Time series of logarithmic returns (Haarhaus et al., 2020: p. 4) 607
Fig. 8.10 Development of PD_2 over time (Haarhaus et al., 2020: p. 5) 609
Fig. 8.11 LLLE over time (Singapore) (Haarhaus et al., 2020: p. 7) 610
Fig. 8.12 BDS over time including peaks (Singapore) (Haarhaus et al., 2020: p. 6) 610
Fig. 8.13 LLLE over time (Singapore)—Peaks 611
Fig. 8.14 Business registrations in Germany (01/20) 614
Fig. 8.15 Log-Returns of business registrations in Germany 614
Fig. 8.16 PD_2 over time (Federal) 615
Fig. 8.17 LLLE over time (Federal) 615
Fig. 8.18 Business registrations in NRW, Bavaria, Baden-Württemberg, Hesse 616
Fig. 8.19 PD_2 over time (NRW, Bavaria, Baden-Württemberg, Hesse) 616
Fig. 8.20 LLLE over time (NRW, Bavaria, Baden-Württemberg, Hesse) 616
Fig. 8.21 Business registrations in Lower Saxony, Berlin, Rhineland-Palatinate, Saxony 617
Fig. 8.22 PD_2 over time (Lower Saxony, Berlin, Rhineland-Palatinate, Saxony) 617
Fig. 8.23 LLLE over time (Lower Saxony, Berlin, Rhineland-Palatinate, Saxony) 617
Fig. 8.24 Business registrations in Schleswig-Holstein, Brandenburg, Hamburg, Thuringia 618
Fig. 8.25 PD_2 over time (Schleswig-Holstein, Brandenburg, Hamburg, Thuringia) 618
Fig. 8.26 LLLE over time (Schleswig-Holstein, Brandenburg, Hamburg, Thuringia) 618
Fig. 8.27 Business registrations in Saxony-Anhalt, Mecklenburg-Western Pomerania, Saarland, Bremen 619
Fig. 8.28 PD_2 over time (Saxony-Anhalt, Mecklenburg-Western Pomerania, Saarland, Bremen) 619
Fig. 8.29 LLLE over time (Saxony-Anhalt, Mecklenburg-Western Pomerania, Saarland, Bremen) 620
Fig. 8.30 Interpretation of PD_2 over time (federal) incl. peaks 620
Fig. 8.31 Interpretation of LLLE over time (federal) incl. peaks 621
Fig. 9.1 The Papillon Spiral. (Since we are on the last pages of this book, it can be mentioned at this point that the term "complex" in the context of a book should rather be put in quotation marks.) 630

List of Tables

Table 2.1 Example Guessing Game 1 46
Table 2.2 Example Guessing Game 2 47
Table 3.1 Cumulative supply of 'Multicopter' engineers 92
Table 3.2 Cumulative demand for 'Multicopter' engineers.................... 94
Table 4.1 Dimension of a line, a surface, and a cube 245
Table 4.2 Calculation of the Feigenbaum constant 255
Table 4.3 Dynamic behaviour at selected bifurcation points.................. 257
Table 4.4 Logistic function with minimal changes in initial conditions 295
Table 4.5 Accuracy—logistic function: Assumed result 303
Table 4.6 Accuracy—logistic function: Actual result 304
Table 5.1 Number sequences 327
Table 5.2 Various Returns—Price is at 50, rises by 50, falls by 5.............. 333
Table 5.3 Various Returns—Slight Price Fluctuations 333
Table 5.4 relative, logarithmic, and absolute returns 333
Table 5.5 Various returns—data close to zero 333
Table 5.6 Recurrence Plots and their interpretations. *Source:* http://www.recurrence-plot.tk/glance.php?show_intro=1 415
Table 5.7 Graphic format—GIF.. 423
Table 5.8 Graphic format—PGN.. 424
Table 5.9 Graphic format—JPEG 424
Table 5.10 Graphic format—TIFF... 425
Table 6.1 Seven perspectives on entrepreneurship............................ 453
Table 6.2 Distinguishing between Managers and Entrepreneurs............... 455
Table 6.3 Entrepreneurship schools. 460
Table 6.4 'Discovery-' versus 'Creation-Theory'........................... 466
Table 7.1 Basic variants of case studies....................................... 506
Table 8.1 Key figures in Phase 1 and Phase 2. (Source: Liening et al., 2012: p. 45) 595
Table 8.2 Stepwise multiple regression for the ROI in Phase 3. (Source: Liening et al. 2013: p. 534)............................ 598

Introduction 1

Contents

1.1 About the Presumption and Limits of Knowledge . . . 2
1.2 Economy and its Subsectors as Complex Systems . . . 5
1.3 Scientific Approaches—Complexonomics . . . 6
1.4 Complexity Science Substantiates Entrepreneurship as an Independent Business Discipline . . . 8
1.5 Objectives and Content—'Run Through' . . . 14
1.5.1 The Fourfold Objective . . . 14
1.5.2 On the Structure and Contents . . . 15
1.6 About the Approach: On Mathematics, Simulations, and the ***Papillon*** Spiral . . . 17
1.6.1 About Mathematics . . . 17
1.6.2 About Visualisations and Simulations . . . 18
1.6.3 The ***Papillon*** Spiral . . . 18
References . . . 19

A. Liening, *Complexity and Entrepreneurship*,
https://doi.org/10.1007/978-3-658-44032-9_1

1.1 About the Presumption and Limits of Knowledge

The peculiar task of economics is to show mankind how little they know about something they believe they can shape.
(Hayek, 1996a, p. 76)

"What can we know?"[1] This question has occupied not only philosophers around the world since Immanuel *Kant* dedicated himself to it in the 'Critique of Pure Reason' (Kant, 1995). In a time when economic disasters are shaking the globalised world, this question is also being asked of economists, who apparently were partly wrong with their forecasts and have to constantly adapt their predictions to the new factual situations.

As long as development is steady and uniform in a certain way, the forecasts are often very close to the real situation that then arises.[2] This applies to weather forecasts as well as to the forecasts of the major economic research institutes, which can generally be relied upon very well. And the same applies at the corporate level: the development of a company can be planned well to a certain extent—as long as it is steady and uniform. And crises can usually be dealt with using proven methods. If a certain solution algorithm has proven to be reliable, it can usually also be successfully applied to similar problems; one must qualify the employees accordingly within the framework of personnel development and implement the known measures.

Someone who wants to start a company, because, for example, he wants to introduce an Invention (invention) as a new product into the market (Innovation), usually needs a so-called 'Business Plan'. Such a plan includes, among other things, a market entry strategy with concrete advertising and sales considerations and financial planning up to medium-term development plans including risk assessments. The Entrepreneur, who is by definition risk-taking and responsible at the same time, can rely on his 'Business Plan' in such a phase, provided it was created with care and appropriate competence. The individual steps are well thought out and can be successfully completed. The lineal character of such a business plan is in line with the lineal, steady development of the economic environment in which the company is embedded.

But does this correspond to reality? Can the future be predicted, for example, over a period of five years, as is often expected in business plans? Hardly, must be the intuitive

[1] The equally significant *Kantian* question: "What should we do?", which hits the level of morality, cannot be addressed here, but should be modified into "What can we (at all) do?" at the end of the book in view of the results of the complexity science analysis as an outlook. Although the should is not yet addressed, at least potentials of conceivable action are shown. Much more can hardly be achieved by a science that has committed itself to value-free judgement, although the difference and thus also the deficit between science and individual action becomes apparent here.

[2] As the author writes these lines, he is in a cell of the Himmerod monastery, where the Cistercian monks have been performing the same rites and procedures between Ora and Labora every day for over 900 years. The probability that tomorrow morning at 04.30 a.m. the day will start with the vigils and end at 19.30 p.m. with the Compline is very high; only on Sundays and holidays will they start already at 04.15 a.m., this is also very likely, as nothing has changed since the monastery was founded here in 1134.

answer. The world's development is anything but lineal, it develops rather in leaps and entanglements, one could say: non-lineal. We are not even able to predict the weather for the coming week, let alone for a longer period.

And what about the beginning of a founding phase?

Perhaps at least at the beginning everything is lineal, one might hope: A market study shows where the need is; one finds an idea for it, works it out, creates a five-year plan, convinces the bank, which provides the necessary capital etc.

Or is it often quite different already here, rather non-lineal; like in the former 'carriage business'.

Example 'Carriage Business'

Customer analyses in the late nineteenth century may have shown that people wanted to travel faster over long distances. They desired faster horses, a better network for changing horses, more horses in front of a carriage, better trained coachmen, etc. But suddenly, two clever individuals from a completely different field, who were not experts in carriages at all, but worked in an engine factory, came along. They tinkered in the converted garden house of their home villa with an idea that improved the (co-)invention of their boss, a certain Mr. *Otto,* and built it into a carriage to rely on engines instead of horses. They founded their own company and thus, these then completely unknown gentlemen, whose names were *Maybach* and *Daimler*, eventually triggered a revolution in the transport industry that the market for carriages and their protagonists could never have foreseen and that made carriages disappear into insignificance and ushered in a new era of mobility worldwide.[3] ◄

When change processes are abrupt and leap-like in nature, the known solutions often fail, so that even the best market study and the most thoroughly tested 'business plan' can fail. Even the most sophisticated mathematical models of economists, whose systems of equations—to show a high degree of realism—have always been supplemented by heuristics that include past values, no longer work. The half-life of forecasts is reduced to the smallest periods in such seemingly chaotic phases, and what previously seemed successful fails. As early as 1967, the later Nobel laureate in economics, *Friedrich August von Hayek*[4] stated in his treatise on the 'Theory of Complex Phenomena':

[3]This example may not represent a historically verifiable development in detail, as the role that Nicolaus August *Otto* actually played at the time, or the fact that other competitors like Carl Gustav *Benz* etc. would also have to be mentioned here. Thus, *Benz*'s three-wheeled patent motor car from 1885 is considered the first truly practical automobile. However, the above example of the development of the "motor carriage" by *Daimler* and *Maybach* vividly illustrates the fundamental challenge when innovations unexpectedly penetrate markets and have the power to overrun them.

[4]The economist Friedrich August *von Hayek* received the Nobel Prize in Economic Sciences in 1974. He can be considered a representative of liberalism, who critically engaged with the statements of his contemporary John Maynard *Keynes*, whose demand-oriented concepts of global control he questioned.

"So far, no economist has succeeded in acquiring a fortune by buying or selling goods on the basis of his scientific prediction of future prices," and added slightly sardonically: "although some may have succeeded in selling such predictions." (Hayek, 1996b, p. 298)

So what can we know at all? How can we understand the economy and its development? How can we successfully manage a company, especially in the start-up and first growth phase? What measures need to be taken in personnel development, controlling, marketing, production, etc. to shape a company in such a complex situation? Do the proven methods of the past still help?

If we consider the tasks of entrepreneurs, but also more generally of executives, managers, or responsible employees in companies, whether private or public, a whole range of competencies are expected that enable them to deal adequately with processes, situations, or structures in our complex world. Executives, managers, employees must primarily be able to analyse processes, structures, or specific situations, identify the challenges that arise from them, then develop solutions or design options, evaluate and assess them, in order to finally make decisions and put them into action, and then or also parallel again to analyse etc. Ultimately, one could derive a circular causal chain from this, which presupposes analytical ability, problem-solving ability, value judgement ability, decision-making ability, and action ability in those responsible. This chain is circular causal because the individual steps can be repeated arbitrarily and also the beginning could start at any of these nodes. Fig. 1.1 shows this conception of tasks and abilities.

And what about the state level? Can the state successfully intervene in an economy if apparently not even the experts can make meaningful predictions about economic events in times of crisis?

Ultimately, these are all questions for science, because it applies: No good practice without good theory. So what can we learn from economics? What contribution can it make?

First of all, it seems that due to an economy characterised by increasing complexity, many traditional economic explanatory models are increasingly losing their persuasive

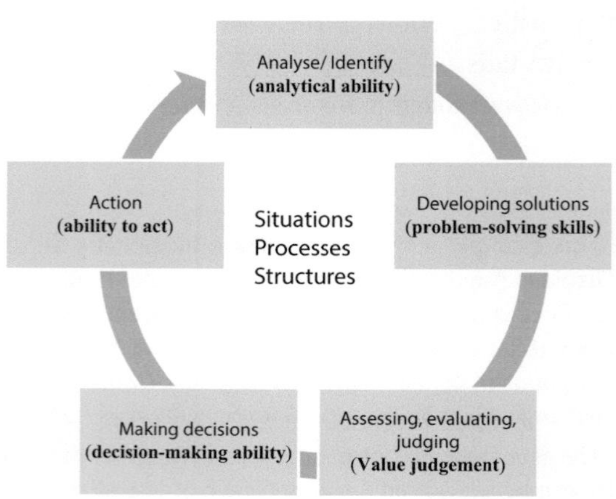

Fig. 1.1 About the tasks of an entrepreneur, a leader, a manager, an employee in a complex world

power. The developments in the economy as a whole or in individual areas such as the corporate sector, are not always characterised by smooth transitions, as suggested by numerous traditional models. Discontinuities, jumps, and turbulences often occur. The seemingly abrupt emergence of the financial crisis in 2008, followed by the global economic crisis from 2009, which abruptly ended the previous years of economic upswing, may serve as credible examples here.

1.2 Economy and its Subsectors as Complex Systems

Economic and economic-related subsectors can, as described above, thus be understood as non-linear, dynamic systems. In this context, we also speak of complex systems.

Therefore, it is fundamentally appropriate to research new concepts and procedures in the field of complex dynamic systems. The research approaches of this domain are increasingly making their way into economics in order to better understand complex order patterns, such as those produced by market economic systems.

If one follows, for example, *von Hayek*, it becomes clear that orders do not have to be seen as the result of planning. In this context, he even postulates a constructivist error (Hayek, 1996b, p. 17 f.). In this context, *von Hayek* writes:

> It is therefore paradoxical and based on a complete misunderstanding of these relationships when it is often said today that we consciously plan modern society because it has become so complex. In reality, we can only maintain an order of such complexity if we do not handle it according to the method of the plan, i.e., not by commands, but aim for the formation of a spontaneous order based on general rules (Hayek, 2003, p. 16).

Following *von Hayek*, such an order cannot be adequately investigated using the classical models[5] that are still widely used. For these are largely based on mechanistic, lineal[6] cause-effect chains and thus postulate the claim of predictability.

To model the complex developments encountered in reality, traditional methods rely on exogenous disturbances or random variables. Irregular and abrupt developments are ultimately examined with methods that only seem suitable for linear, respectively lineal conditions or only for continuous processes. For a long time, economics was under the regulation of the mechanistic worldview, which, for example, relied on models whose

[5] Models can be interpreted as material or immaterial systems that represent other systems, so that experimental manipulations of the depicted structures and states become possible. See Niemeyer (1977, p. 57).

[6] Lineal systems are conceptions in which the elements of the system are arranged in a chain one after the other. Since such a structure lacks feedback loops in contrast to non-lineal systems, a predefined behaviour is processed without reacting to endogenous or exogenous events. Lineal systems are often mathematically lineal, non-lineal systems, on the other hand, are often non-linear.

trajectories[7] tending towards equilibrium appeared predictable and graspable with partial analyses.

However, economic reality is often much more intricate and complex than linear models suggest. For example, self-organising processes far from equilibrium cannot be explained using linear perspectives. *Nijkamp* and *Poot* therefore rightly state:

> Our economic world is highly dynamic and exhibits a wide variety of fluctuating patterns. This forms a sharp contrast with our current economic toolbox, which is largely filled with linear and comparative static instruments (Nijkamp & Poot, 1993, p. 25).

Dealing with non-linear, complex systems can play a central role in the search for an extension of the 'economic toolbox'. With them, a very wide range of economic behaviours and explanatory patterns can be depicted. Complexity can be described, analysed, and understood where, for example, traditional statistical methods must fail completely.[8]

1.3 Scientific Approaches—Complexonomics

> *Knowledge and ignorance are inseparably linked like Siamese twins,*
> *but they are in a state of chaos. Chaos. Chaos.*
> (Murakami, 2004, p. 13)

In addition to the theory of self-organisation (synergetics), catastrophe theory, thermodynamics, and fractal geometry, the chaos theory is particularly noteworthy in this context, which, methodically flanked by the systems theory or the systems dynamics, will represent a central building block in our discussion. As different as these approaches may be: they all primarily deal with questions of the emergence and analysis of complex order patterns, which is why they can rightly be subsumed as sub-disciplines under a conceptual superstructure that we want to refer to here as *'complexity sciences'*[9]*resp. 'science*

[7] A trajectory is the line of development of a dynamic system. It describes the trajectory that a system takes over the course of starting from a specific starting point its dynamic development in phase space. The phase space is the space which is spanned by the time-varying variables of a dynamic system. If the trajectory moves into an 'attractive' dynamic state, this is also referred to as an attractor as a subset of a phase space. There are four types of attractors: which are called fixed point, limit cycle, torus and chaotic or strange attractor become.

[8] See, for example, the explanations on Grammar Complexity in: Strunk and Schiepek (2006, p. 203 ff.).

[9] The author previously spoke of a theory instead of science. However, because a theory is much more concrete, at the same time more consistent and coherent than the term 'science' suggests, we now speak of complexity sciences. We thus agree with Henning Bandte, who emphasises: "Despite numerous authors who already speak of a complexity theory (mea culpa, the author), it should be checked, especially against the background of the inconsistent use of terms (…), whether it is not premature to speak of a mature established (…) theory" (Bandte, 2007, p. 79).

of complex systems' and whose application to economics we want to label with the term *'complexonomics'*[10].

Looking at chaos theory, one finds that during its popular scientific boom in the nineties, it led some to the theory of a new, unified explanation of the world—or should one better say world glorification?[11]; others insulted the representatives of chaos theory as shamans.[12] Thus, even today, proponents of chaos theory are looking for the power of chaos in the structures of distant galaxies or in the smoke rising from a cigarette; opponents are eager to find new arguments as to why chaos exists only in the computer, and why the 'spook' is over as soon as the computer is turned off.

Many misunderstandings arose. It is a widespread view that chaos theory is a theory about disorder. As will become clear in the course of this paper, this is a completely misleading idea. Chaos theory neither refutes determinism nor does it consider ordered systems impossible. Although chaos theory suggests that the current state of a system may not be predictable, it shows that it is generally possible to model the overall behaviour of such a system. Thus, chaos theory does not emphasise disorder, the inherent unpredictability of a system state, but rather the system-immanent order structures—the universal properties of similar systems—or as *Nijkamp* and *Reggiani* note:

> There is 'order in chaos' (Nijkamp & Reggiani, 1993, p. 12).

It is true that the possibility of researching 'chaos' and associated order structures in complex systems only became conceivable with the development of modern computer technology. The multitude of calculations and the different visualisation types of complex structures were previously not feasible. Therefore, it is not surprising that this theory gained popularity at the beginning of the nineties of the last century.

Meanwhile, the euphoria associated with chaos theory has subsided and the number of popular scientific new releases has decreased. At the same time, however, the number of scientific publications is growing, which are trying to transfer important aspects of chaos theory to other scientific areas. This also increases the importance of complexity sciences for other scientific fields, and numerous representatives can be found in different scientific disciplines, as Fig. 1.2 shows.

Economics is not excluded from this, as it is hoped that chaos theory will provide a different, better approach to economic reality than, for example, the neoclassical paradigm can offer.[13] In particular, the application of complexity science to entrepreneurship,

---

[10] The term was first used by the author in the eponymous essay in 2009 (Liening, 2009).

[11] For popular scientific literature, see, for example, Bestenstreiner (1991).

[12] At this point, reference should be made to the series of essays in SPIEGEL, which is popularly known under the motto 'Cult of Chaos—Superstition or Explanation of the World' (Brügge, 1993a, b, c).

[13] See the explanations and literature references in: Liening (2007). In recent years, particularly in the field of business administration, relevant publications have appeared: See, for example, Bandte (2007), Warren (2008), Morecroft (2009) or Strunk (2009).

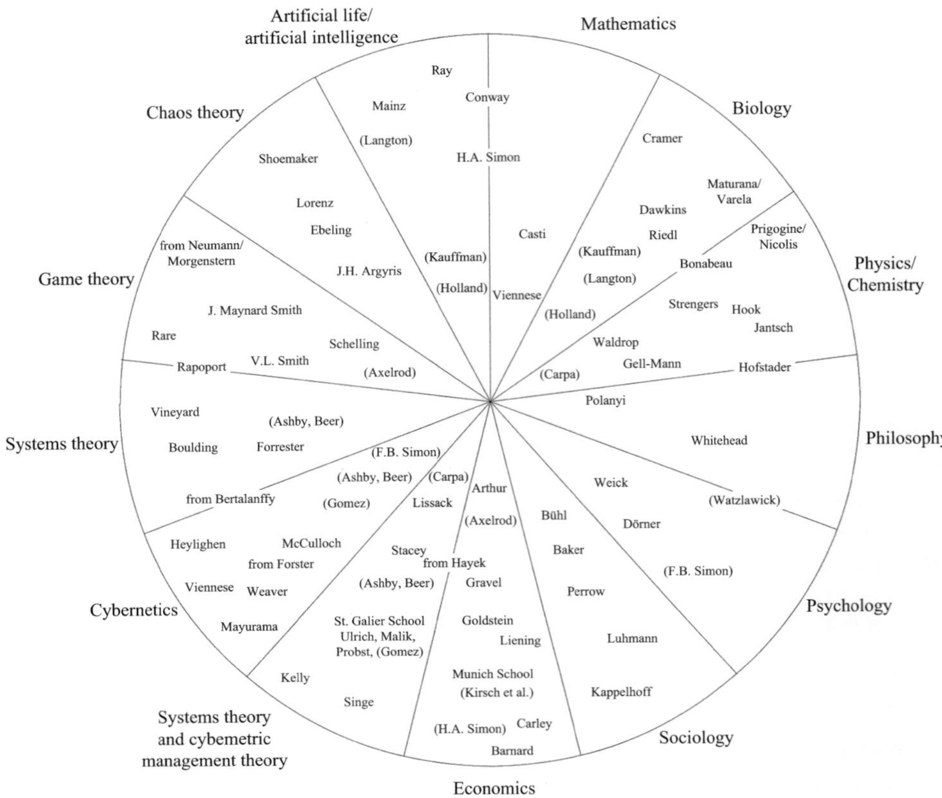

Fig. 1.2 Important representatives of the fundamentals of a complexity science in different disciplines. *Source* Bandte (2007, p. 50)

which is associated with keywords such as uncertainty, unpredictability, disruption, and much more, is to be of central importance in this book.

However, the literature lacks comprehensive presentations of this new field of research, not only in entrepreneurship, but in the field of economics in general. Furthermore, the current developments largely come from the Anglo-American area, as a look at the bibliographies shows, so that German-language contributions are rather scarce.

1.4 Complexity Science Substantiates Entrepreneurship as an Independent Business Discipline

All previous considerations suggest that the young discipline of entrepreneurship is increasingly establishing itself as an independent business discipline, although different currents exist that could be captured as follows or even further and partly differently (Stern, 2003: 4; Harms & Grichnik, 2008: 30 ff.).

On the one hand, entrepreneurship is seen as a *support function within universities* with regard to transfer activities, with teaching, consulting, and concrete support being at the forefront of activities. Increasingly, universities are consciously developing transfer as a third pillar alongside research and teaching, more or less intensively. NRW is taking a pioneering role in this respect from a state perspective, as the Ministry of Economic Affairs of the state of NRW announced a competition worth €150 million on the topic of "Excellence Start-up Centre.NRW", in which all universities in NRW participated. In 2019, six universities received the coveted excellence award, along with a huge funding sum between 15 and 30 million euros per university, which is intended to help transfer inventions from the universities into innovations through entrepreneurship.[14]

Secondly, a current can be diagnosed that interprets entrepreneurship as a kind of *cross-sectional function in business administration*, which cuts across various business administration subjects such as controlling, investment and financing, marketing, corporate management, production and logistics, human resources, etc., so that the contents related to company foundations are discussed in each of these areas.

In a third orientation, entrepreneurship can be perceived as a reduced or focussed application of classic business administration to founding processes. Here, entrepreneurship is not in the classic areas of business administration, but itself represents a *"small" business administration* with regard to start-ups, where cost accounting, marketing, etc. for start-ups are discussed.

Fourthly, entrepreneurship can be seen as a discipline consisting at its core of a seemingly arbitrary *collection of different scientific domains* such as psychology, economics, sociology, commercial and corporate law, business administration, etc.

Despite the different directions, there is much to suggest that entrepreneurship is increasingly establishing itself as an independent discipline alongside the classic business disciplines. However, what has been lacking so far is a scientific justification for this, which, in the author's view, can be provided with the help of complexity science approaches, as we will see in the introduction below.

Almost all classic sub-disciplines of business administration can be subsumed under the term "managerial" to facilitate a demarcation within business administration (BWL).

What does this mean?

If you consider that a business is a purposefully organised economic unit in which the production of goods and/or services, distribution, storage, and associated administrative

[14]Although the value and content of the federal government's concept of excellence differ significantly from that of the state of NRW, they are united by the attestation of outstanding performance, e.g. in the case of TU Dortmund concerning the interlocking of research, teaching, and transfer. "Excellence" can therefore be understood as a 'brand' for outstanding achievements. The fact that the concept of excellence is by no means subjected to arbitrary or inflationary use is manifested by the fact that it is first awarded by state authorities (BMBF, NRW-MWIDE) and secondly its award is associated with high funding sums. As carriers of this concept of excellence, the NRW universities that were successful here also benefit from the international reputation of the German "Excellence" brand.

activities take place, and a company ultimately represents the legal unit of one or more businesses, which within this company represent technical-organisational production units, then it becomes clear what is meant by managerial.

Managerial primarily means that the different traditional sub-areas of business administration work with analysis and planning tools[15] that ultimately are based on past values to extract aspects for further analysis and to derive forecasts for future developments. For this, more or less long time series of data or comprehensive information from the company and its environment, the market, are needed, which lead to a solid (calculation) basis, for example in the area of accounting in full or partial cost accounting or in standard cost accounting, or for example, to develop marketing strategies. And the more information is available, the more reliable the analyses and forecasts become.

Primarily, this is about the management of more or less extensive information, but then of course also about technologies, innovations etc., where classic cause-and-effect mechanisms come into play. It is always assumed that similar causes have similar effects, as no situation and no process is exactly like another. We are here in the world of the simple, at most the complicated, as we will examine more closely later (see Part I, Chap. 2). In the worst case, one is confronted with coincidences, but the associated risks often appear calculable, either based on empirical data (the author here calls them risk calculations "a posteriori"), or based on good theories (risk calculations "a priori").

To grasp the concept of entrepreneurship as an independent discipline a little more clearly, one could define it as follows:

▶ Entrepreneurship (Discipline)

Entrepreneurship is a scientific sub-discipline of business administration,

- which deals with the analysis of entrepreneurship processes (such as the identification of market opportunities, the development of business ideas and their implementation) as well as
- the development, research and evaluation of innovative, entrepreneurial methods.

A precise derivation, discussion and justification will be examined intensively later (see Part III of the book). However, we want to shed some light on some introductory thoughts on this:

In the field of entrepreneurship, in contrast to classical business administration, complexity prevails everywhere. And this means that one can ultimately derive little from past values, especially since in the early founding phase hardly any actual or past values can be available. Planning methods are of little use here. Or as the founder of Amazon Jeff *Bezos* once said about the meaningfulness of business plans, in which one

---

[15] These tools, instruments or methods vary greatly in their function, objective and application. They range from methods of financial mathematics, investment calculations, supply chain methods to various cost accounting methods, etc.

sometimes also makes forecasts of up to five years about the planned development of a company to be founded:

> You know the business plan won't survive its first encounter with reality. It will always be different. The reality will never be the plan … (Bezos, quoted in Robinson, 2010)[16]

Behaving or moving in complex systems, such as during a founding phase, is rather like a hike through a dark forest. But since the darkness and the multitude of trees etc. are part of or rather characteristics of the forest system, the darkness will not lift even if you have more information about the forest. The forest remains dark, and you can only grope your way forward slowly. But so that you don't get lost and can plan your way a little in advance, there are tools like a flashlight or compass, with which it is better than without them. The actual path you take is often not there before, it emerges as you go! And just like in a dark forest, you also need the right and other tools in entrepreneurship, new and other methods, to meet the complexity of a founding process with all its facets and to design it successfully. As soon as you reach a clearing in the forest, where the darkness or the complexity decreases, the known, traditional tools can be used. Bright clearings and dark forest areas alternate during the hike. Therefore, the thesis should be put forward here that entrepreneurship represents an independent business discipline due to the complexity of the processes and situations that need to be considered in entrepreneurship.

Newer approaches within entrepreneurship, such as the *Effectuation* concept by *Sarasvathy* emphasise uncertainty in the *Knightian* sense, so that causal approaches, which are based on predictability and forecasting possibilities, appear less successful. The *Knightian* considerations are usually translated in the Effectuation approach with risk, uncertainty, and *Knightian* uncertainty (Strunk, 2019: 81).

Risk is referred to by *Knight* as "a priori probability", so that probabilities can be calculated theoretically (risk a priori). He calls uncertainty "statistical probability" and means by this the term we use here, "risk a posteriori", i.e., the calculation of probability based on empirical studies (Knight, 1921, republished 2006). The third case, which *Sarasvathy* particularly emphasises in the field of Effectuation, is that of *Knightian* uncertainty ("true uncertainty"), which *Knight* assumes cannot be determined. However, for *Sarasvathy*, the three types are not objectively verifiable facts, but rather assumptions or beliefs of entrepreneurs about "how well or poorly the future can be predicted in their

---

[16] Although *Bezos* says, "The reality will never be the plan", he also adds "but the discipline of writing the plan forces you to think through some of the issues and to get sort of mentally comfortable in the space. Then you start to understand, if you push on this knob this will move over here and so on. So, that's the first step." This means, if you follow the advice of *Bezos,* it is nevertheless useful to create a plan for your own business, but you should not stick to such a plan under all circumstances, but it only represents a first step. Develop the plan, then proceed step by step, and always question, change and rethink. A high degree of flexibility is required in complex systems!

field of work." According to her studies, the views of entrepreneurs suggest that those who assume *Knightian* uncertainty "have more founding experience and are likely more successful." (Strunk, 2019: 82)

Effectuation thus challenges traditional business thinking. Or as *Strunk* rightly notes:

> The central basic position of the approach is based on a dissertation from 1921, which postulates a fundamental gap in the future prediction of entrepreneurial action (Strunk, 2019: 79).

While a corresponding traditional business economist would try to predict and plan an (uncertain) future using traditional business methods, a protagonist of the Effectuation approach would try to shape an unpredictable, complex future, consciously considering recursive structures, feedback loops, and turbulence (Dew et al., 2009; Sarasvathy, 2009).

Sarasvathy, as mentioned, refers to Frank *Knight,* who in his 1921 dissertation distinguishes between risks and two types of uncertainties. However, *Knight* ultimately provides no justification for his (third) concept of uncertainty. Or as *Strunk* accurately says:

> Therefore, it is not even certain whether the third form actually has a correspondence in reality. Just because this form is conceivable, it does not automatically exist. Or put another way: It is common that before a scientific explanation it is unclear how a phenomenon occurs and what the rules are by which something happens. The third form is thus "normal" as a starting point before a scientific investigation (Strunk, 2019: 83).

For *Strunk*, however, it is clear that *Knight* could not provide convincing arguments at that time.

> The justification for this could not succeed in 1921. Important scientific discoveries have not yet been made. (Strunk, 2019: 79)

Although the criticism is harsh, perhaps too harsh, it does fundamentally highlight a problem that must be addressed:

> The theoretical justification of the Effectuation approach is therefore not very convincing, and it appears mysterious that a work from 1921 is used to explain something that has been recognised as the state of research for decades, but was completely unknown in 1921. (Strunk, 2019: 79)

Knight does assume that it will fundamentally not be possible to ever solve certain problems. However, he indeed does not provide a viable justification. The complexity science findings of the past thirty years, however, show that under certain conditions there can indeed be fundamental limits to predictability in deterministic systems. These were not known in 1921, so it is not surprising that *Knight* himself could not provide a justification. But it is precisely complexity science that for the first time allows a scientifically substantiated underpinning of the *Knightian* assumption (Strunk, 2019).

This has three consequences:

Firstly:
If it is assumed that entrepreneurial processes often represent processes in complex systems or are complex themselves, a foundation can thus be provided for a justification for the independence of the entrepreneurship discipline, as its basis significantly deviates from the usual foundations of business thinking, which assume certainty to whatever kind of calculable risks. Complexity science can then contribute to theoretically substantiating the different entrepreneurial approaches and thus contribute to a coherent theory of entrepreneurship.

Secondly:
Also, the results of complexity science research for the first time provide the opportunity to provide empirically quantifiable methods for the field of entrepreneurship in terms of uncertainty or complexity. This allows not only qualitative but also quantitative empirical investigations to be carried out in such a conceived discipline of entrepreneurship, thus providing the necessary empirical foundation for a coherent theoretical structure in a real science.

Thirdly:
Furthermore, the findings of complexity science make it possible to empirically substantiate theoretical approaches. In addition, they provide methods that contribute to comprehensively investigating entrepreneurship in various practical situations, processes, and structures and to successfully carry out the corresponding "forest walks in complete darkness".

Complexity science thus substantiates and enriches the field of entrepreneurship in theory and empiricism. All of this needs to be further explored, justified, and applied in this book.

However, this does not mean that one should abandon managerial approaches and rely solely on entrepreneurial methods. As in the above forest walk metaphor, the use and research of methods in entrepreneurship ultimately depend on the complexity of the processes. These processes not only allow a interplay of traditional business administration and entrepreneurial approaches, but do not necessarily make the path to be taken appear as a predetermined path. Rather, this path is a path based to the greatest extent on happy coincidences—on serendipity, as the English say—which is shaped by opportunities that one seizes or discards, or that one even creates and develops anew.

And so, overall, against the background of the complexity of entrepreneurial processes, it makes sense to divide business administration into two areas: the diverse, classic business administration and the new business administration discipline of entrepreneurship.

1.5 Objectives and Content—'Run Through'

The summit is only the goal,
but the way there shapes and marks those,
who walk it.
(Stock Rupert)

1.5.1 The Fourfold Objective

Taking into account the above remarks, this book follows a fourfold objective:

- First of all, a contribution should be made to provide a new theoretical perspective for entrepreneurial analysis, solution, evaluation, decision-making, and action for entrepreneurs, but also for executives, managers, and employees in general.
- The discussion about terms like 'chaos', 'complexity' and 'complex systems' should be objectified or located. An attempt is made to return chaos theory as a subfield back to where it belongs as a theory: into the *science*. It should be stripped of its myth and opened to intersubjective verifiability, with special attention being paid to important concepts such as synergetics.
- Every real science, and thus also economics, is based not only on coherent theories and models, but also on the empirical verifiability of these theories and models. Furthermore, appropriate methods can represent a 'toolbox' that can support concrete decisions empirically. Therefore, thirdly, the question should be pursued whether it is possible at all, and if so, which credible methods exist to empirically investigate complexity and what consequences one might derive from it, for example, for the entrepreneurship area.
- Fourthly, the view is opened for the still relatively young research field 'Entrepreneurship'. For this purpose, the complexity science approaches presented here are applied to entrepreneurship and the possibilities that the new theories bring with them for different sub-aspects are discussed and subjected to a critical analysis. This also raises the question, for example, of how the willingness to start a business can be increased and how successful entrepreneurship education can be achieved in this context. Furthermore, the question is raised as to which credible complexity science methods are available to support entrepreneurs in the context of complex business start-ups. Also, the question of which empirical complexity 'toolbox' can successfully promote the management and design of young growth companies in a complex economic world is discussed.

So this contribution is not a traditional entrepreneurship book. Rather, the book focusses on the topic of complexity. The corresponding historical backgrounds in the context of economics, the theories and empirical approaches underlying the topic of complexity are presented, analysed, and critically discussed. Furthermore, selected examples from the field of entrepreneurship are used to show how the complexity issue can enrich the field of entrepreneurship in research and practice.

1.5.2 On the Structure and Contents

In terms of content, this book is divided into four parts, each of which includes a number of central chapters.

In **Part I** of the book, the backgrounds and history of the complexity topic are discussed in more detail in two chapters.

Economics deals with human behaviour. However, it does not consider groups or the like, but focusses on the individual due to its approach. It does not examine selected real individuals, but studies the behaviour of average people. It does not consider heroes, nor cowards, it examines *'Kreti and Pleti'*. In Chap. 2, the question is first pursued of how average people analyse certain situations, evaluate them, develop solutions, and finally act. Initially, action in lineal systems is examined and it is illustrated that even in seemingly simple systems, humans can be subject to a multitude of (systematic) errors, and that this places a multitude of demands on thinking. If the pitfalls are already so diverse here, what does the whole thing look like in non-lineal, complex systems?

But what are complex systems at all? Before a well-founded answer can be given, a systematic review is first ventured here, which in Chap. 3 provides an explanation of why we cling so much to lineal, mechanically appearing ways of thinking and how much this way of thinking has shaped economics for many decades up to the present day. But it also shows the change in thinking that is changing traditional economics, and what causes and consequences there are in this context. In particular, the consequences that result from a non-linear, chaos-theoretical perspective, which expand the horizon of the neoclassical linear view and partly contradict it, are worked out here.

Part II is dedicated to theory and empiricism in order to present and explain the newer developments in complexity research.

In addition to chaos theory, which needs to be scientifically presented and analysed, similarly structured theories are considered, with the focus on synergetics, which as a theory of self-organisation is of particular importance in the context of economic questions. However, all three theories have in common that they deal with complex systems. So in the context of these three domains, we speak of 'Science of Complex Systems' or 'Complexonomics'. Therefore, in Chap. 4, the theoretical approaches to complexity are described and analysed. Only these enable a well-founded answer to the question of what complexity actually is.

Chapter 5 addresses the empirical perspective with regard to the question of the meaningful methods for investigating complexity. The empirical methods that have been available so far to investigate complexity were very modest until the new millennium. Only now are methods emerging that allow meaningful research results to be achieved, which are critically presented and illustrated in this chapter.

In **Part III** of the book, different perspectives are taken under the keyword "Multiperspective—Complexity and Entrepreneurship".

In this part of the book, a so-called '*S*ynergetic *E*ntrepreneurship *M*odel' *(SEM)* is presented and discussed, which is based on the complexity science considerations of the other two parts and includes three levels—an individual, an organisational, and an economic one.

Chapter 6 deals with an introduction to the topic of entrepreneurship, taking into account the different trends and controversies as well as a first sketch of ideas of *SEM.*

Chapter 7 is about the concretisation of the *SEM.* First, the individual level of the model is developed. It deals with individual questions, decisions, and actions in relation to entrepreneurship and a corresponding entrepreneurship education. Here, an economic-didactic concept is presented, which is based on Synergetics as one of the essential theories of complex systems and shows a specifically complexity science approach to the theory of Entrepreneurship Education.

The business field of entrepreneurship is intended to serve as one of the innovative areas of business administration to open up newer approaches in the second level of the *SEM*. This is about the organisational level in the context of founding processes, with synergetics also providing the basis here.

Furthermore, in this chapter, companies are looked at after the founding phase, especially in the context of an overall economic context. Young growth companies with their innovative power are examined in detail from the economic perspective of an endogenous growth theory and the influence of the science of complex systems in the context of the third levels of the *SEM* is explained, which in turn is based on synergetics. An attempt is made to present the insights of complexity science not as a contrast to traditional neoclassical economics, but as a fruitful complement to it.

In Chap. 8 the empirical perspective in the context of entrepreneurship is in the foreground. Here, two studies are presented at all levels of the Synergetic Entrepreneurship Model (SEM), i.e., at the individual level (SEM1), the organisational level (SEM2), and the macroeconomic level (SEM3), in which selected complexity science methods such as PD_2, LLLE, permutation entropy or recurrence plots are used and their effectiveness is illustrated.

To conclude this book (**Part IV**), a conclusion is drawn and an outlook is sketched (Chap. 9). Here, the individual parts of the book and their central chapters are briefly recalled and essential findings are summarised. Finally, entrepreneurship is once again highlighted as an innovative business discipline in response to the challenges in a complex economic world. At the end of the book, there is finally a 'credits' section, which is formulated as an excerpt from a travel report (Chap. 10).[17]

1.6 About the Approach: On Mathematics, Simulations, and the *Papillon* Spiral

1.6.1 About Mathematics

At the end of the introduction, a few hints are given:

The science of complex systems and their applications in economics represent mathematically oriented facts. Therefore, this book cannot do without mathematical considerations.

If you as a reader do not bring a strong mathematical background: Do not be afraid!

Although it is not possible without mathematical formalism, the goal is for you to primarily strengthen your intuition and conceptual understanding of complex phenomena.

If you bring a strong mathematical background: Do not be afraid!

Whenever mathematical precision is helpful, these will be comprehensively presented in their own specially marked sections. This emphasis on mathematical explanations is also intended to show the less mathematically interested which passages can be skipped without significantly disturbing the meaningful flow of reading.

However, the mathematically interested reader must be aware that economists always talk and write about people and their behaviour in the end. Modeling human behaviour differs from physical systems. For example, it is difficult to 'put' entrepreneurs into a laboratory and experiment with them to see how they function, in order to model their behaviours. But with the help of mathematics, we at least get a more precise idea of what complexity actually is and how it could be measured. The transfer to the world of Entrepreneurship requires a high degree of analogy ability. This book is intended to help you gain this understanding.

---

[17] Some sections such as parts of the historical chapter (Chap. 3) or the theory part (Chap. 4) were written over twenty years ago and first published in Liening (1998). They have not lost their relevance to this day, but have been clarified, deepened and supplemented here. However, since these relevant passages have not lost their validity, it does not seem sensible to express them again in different words. Thus, the processed older aspects on the one hand form the basis for the description and development of the new empirical methods and on the other hand they are made accessible to a new audience within a completely different field of application than before. In the context of this book, these sections also give a more rounded picture overall than in their first publication. In recent years, synergetics has been particularly taken up again and used in publications (Liening, 1998, 2006, 2007, 2009, 2013, 2015). In this book, the findings from over twenty years of research and publication activity lead to a synergetic overall concept, which is presented here for the first time and with a content focus on entrepreneurship.

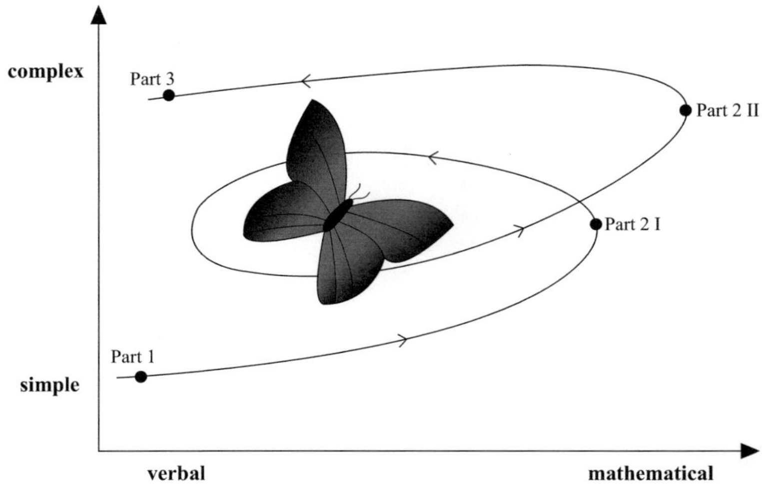

Fig. 1.3 The Papillon Spiral

1.6.2 About Visualisations and Simulations

Furthermore, this book contains a multitude of visualisations of complex systems. For this purpose, a special simulation software was developed. The software was designed using the object-oriented concept of software engineering in the computer language C++. The software ensures that the models can be viewed with various parameter values, variables, etc. In addition, the iModeler from *Consideo* was used for the visualisation of relationships. For the complexity science evaluations, the *GChaos* software from *Strunk* was used.

1.6.3 The *Papillon* Spiral

Many terms in this book are built up in the sense of a twisted spiral.

The spiral approach will be briefly explained using the example of the butterfly effect, which gave this spiral its name, and illustrated in Fig. 1.3:

1. Simple level: Verbal introduction of the terminology
   For example, the term 'butterfly effect' is introduced and explained verbally as a description of complexity in the first part of the book.
2. First turn: Mathematical precision of the terminology
   The term 'butterfly effect' appears again and again in the texts in its verbally formulated meaning and is first provided with a mathematical formula for precision in the second part of the book in the chapters on theory.

3. Second turn: Mathematical branching of the terminology
   In the following chapters on empirical methods, the term 'butterfly effect' is then taken up again, but this time with a whole series of mathematical methods. These mathematical methods all describe the same fact, but each try to get closer to the empirical reality of the described effect through differently situated approaches.
4. Third turn: Verbal transfer of the terminology
   In the third part of the book, the term 'butterfly effect' is taken up and used again. However, this time it is used purely verbally, knowing full well that the reader has now gained a comprehensive understanding of the term. He knows a verbal definition, a mathematical precision of the term, and can possibly apply several mathematical methods to quantify the term in a concrete situation. Thus, the reader uses the term, which is now only used verbally, at a high level of abstraction and understanding.

This *Papillon* spiral, which is recognisable in the approach of the book, can be aptly described with the quote of a ZEN master:

> Before I was enlightened, rivers were rivers and mountains were mountains. When I embarked on the path of enlightenment, rivers were no longer rivers and mountains were no longer mountains. Now that I am enlightened, rivers are again rivers and mountains are again mountains. (a ZEN master, quoted n. Fromm, Martino et al., 2011, p. 151).

References

Bandte, H. (2007). *Komplexität in Organisationen*. Deutscher Universitätsverlag.

Bestenstreiner, F. (1991). *Der phantastische Spiegel. Quanten, Quarks, Chaos – Oder vom Trost, der aus der Formel kommt*. Fischer-Taschenbuch.

Brügge, P. (1993a). Mythos aus dem Computer, Teil 1. *SPIEGEL, 39*, 156–164.

Brügge, P. (1993b). Mythos aus dem Computer, Teil 2. *SPIEGEL, 40*, 232–241.

Brügge, P. (1993c). Mythos aus dem Computer, Teil 3. *SPIEGEL, 41*, 240–252.

Dew, N., et al. (2009). Effectual versus predictive logics in entrepreneurial decision-making: Differences between experts and novices. *Journal of Business Venturing, 24*(4), 287–330.

Fromm, E., Martino, R. de, & Suzuki, D. T. (2011). *Zen-Buddhismus und Psychoanalyse*. Suhrkamp.

Harms, R., & Grichnik, D. (2008). Entrepreneurship als eigenständige Disziplin – Trendwende im Selbstverständnis der dt. Forschungsszene? In S. Kraus & K. Gundolf (Eds.), *Stand und Perspektiven der deutschsprachigen Entrepreneurship- und KMU-Forschung*. ibidem.

Hayek, F. A. von. (1996a). *Die verhängnisvolle Anmaßung: Die Irrtümer des Sozialismus*. Mohr Siebeck.

Hayek, F. A. von. (1996b). *Die Anmaßung von Wissen*. Mohr Siebeck.

Hayek, F. A. von. (2003). Arten der Ordnung (1963). In F. A. von Hayek (Ed.), *Rechtsordnung und Handelsordnung – Aufsätze zur Ordnungsökonomik* (pp. 15–29). Mohr Siebeck.

Kant, I. (1995). Kritik der reinen Vernunft. In I. Kant (Hrsg.), *Werke in sechs Bänden* (Vol. 2). Könemann.

Knight, F. H. (2006). *Risk, uncertainty and profit*. Dover Publications (Ersteveröffentlichung 1921).

Liening, A. (1998). *Komplexe Systeme zwischen Ordnung und Chaos*. LIT.

Liening, A. (2006). iLearning – Ein synergetischer Ansatz zum selbstorganisierten Lernen im Rahmen ökonomischer Bildung. In E. Brunner & T. Meynhardt (Eds.), *Selbstorganisation Managen. Beiträge zur Synergetik der Organisation* (pp. 179–205). Waxmann.

Liening, A. (2007). Ökonomische Chaostheorie. In H. May (Ed.), *Lexikon der Ökonomischen Bildung*. Oldenbourg.

Liening, A. (2009). Complexonomics – Über den Zusammenbruch des Laplaceschen Weltbildes und die Anmaßung des Wissens in der Ökonomie. In J. Weyer & I. Schulz-Schaeffer (Eds.), *Management komplexer Systeme – Konzepte für die Bewältigung von Intransparenz, Unsicherheit und Chaos* (pp. 91–118). Oldenbourg.

Liening, A. (2013). Econoplexity: About the breakdown of Laplace's world view and the pretence of knowledge in economics. *Modern Economy, 4*(4), 305–319.

Liening, A. (2015). *Ökonomische Bildung – Grundlagen und neue synergetische Ansätze*. Springer-Gabler.

Morecroft, J. (2009). *Strategic modelling and business dynamics*. Wiley.

Murakami, H. (2004). *Sputnik Sweethart*. Dumont.

Niemeyer, G. (1977). *Kybernetische System- und Modelltheorie: System Dynamics*. Vahlen.

Nijkamp, P., & Poot, J. (1993). Lessons from nonlinear dynamics economics. In P. Nijkamp & A. Reggiani (Eds.), *Nonlinear evolution of spatial economic systems* (pp. 25–57). Springer.

Nijkamp, P., & Reggiani, A. (1993). Nonlinear evolution of socioeconomic and spatial systems. In P. Nijkamp & A. Reggiani (Eds.), *Nonlinear evolution of spatial economic systems* (pp. 1–21). Springer.

Robinson, T. (2010). *Jeff Bezos: amazon.com architect*. ABDO Publishing Company.

Sarasvathy, S. D. (2009). *Effectuation – Elements of Entrepreneurial Expertise*. Elgar.

Stern, S. (2003). *Organisationentstehungen in innovativen Neugründungen*. Deutscher Universitätsverlag.

Strunk, G. (2009). Die Komplexitätshypothese der Karriereforschung. In A. Liening (Ed.), *Komplexe Systeme und Ökonomie* (Vol. 2). Lang.

Strunk, G. (2019). Entrepreneurship als Management von Komplexität – Versuch einer begrifflichen Klärung mit praktischen Implikationen. In T. Bijedić, I. Ebbers, & B. Halbfas (Eds.), *Entrepreneurship Education* (pp. 79–96). Springer.

Strunk, G., & Schiepek, G. (2006). *Systemische Psychologie – Eine Einführung in die komplexen Grundlagen menschlichen Verhaltens*. Elsevier – Spektrum Akademischer Verlag.

Warren, K. (2008). *Strategic management dynamics*. Wiley.

Part I
Background and History

How do we Respond To Complexity?—A (not only) Behavioural Economic Consideration for Entrepreneurs

2

If the only tool you have is a hammer, you tend to see every problem as a nail.

(Paul Watzlawik)

Contents

2.1 Crises, Chaos, Opportunities—Demands on our Thinking . . . 24
 2.1.1 'Time of Crisis'—'Time of Opportunity'—The World is Becoming More Complex . . . 24
 2.1.2 How Rational is Man? . . . 32
2.2 Behaviour in Simple Situations—Behavioural Anomalies are Observable . . . 34
 2.2.1 Anomalies in the Information Process . . . 34
 2.2.2 Information Perception . . . 35
  2.2.2.1 'Selective Perception'—Selective Perception of Information . . . 35
  2.2.2.2 'Availability'—Availability of Information . . . 36
  2.2.2.3 'Framing'—Presentation of Information . . . 38
 2.2.3 Information Processing . . . 40
  2.2.3.1 'Mental Accounting'—Mental Account Management in Information Processing . . . 40
  2.2.3.2 'Anchoring'—Anchoring of Information Processing . . . 40
  2.2.3.3 'Representativeness'—Representativeness in Information Processing . . . 42
  2.2.3.4 'Information-Sources-Effect'—Information Source Effect in Information Processing . . . 43
 2.2.4 Information Evaluation . . . 43
  2.2.4.1 'Reference-Point'—Reference Point in the Context of Information Evaluation . . . 43
  2.2.4.2 'Loss Aversion'—Loss Aversion in Information Evaluation . . . 44
  2.2.4.3 'Weighting of Probabilities'—Probabilities in Information Evaluation . . . 45

A. Liening, *Complexity and Entrepreneurship*,
https://doi.org/10.1007/978-3-658-44032-9_2

2.2.4.4 'Survivorship Bias'—Bias in Favour of the Survivors 48
2.2.5 Control Behaviour 49
2.2.5.1 Anomalies due to the Need for Control 49
2.2.5.2 'Overconfidence'—Overestimating One's Own Abilities 50
2.2.5.3 'Regret Aversion' 51
2.2.5.4 'Illusion of Control' 51
2.2.5.5 'Home Bias'—Preferring the Familiar 53
2.2.5.6 'Herding'—The J-Pattern 53
2.3 Behaviour in Complex Situations 55
2.3.1 Four Observable Strategies 55
2.3.1.1 'Trial and Error'—Experimentation 55
2.3.1.2 'Fading Out' 57
2.3.1.3 'Rational Behaviour'—Rational Approach 59
2.3.1.4 'Simplicity'—Reduction to Simple Factors 60
2.3.2 The Oil Spot Theory—"Recursive Consequences Spiral Out of Control" 61
2.3.3 Intuition as a Successful Strategy for Coping with Complex Challenges? 63
References 65

2.1 Crises, Chaos, Opportunities—Demands on our Thinking

2.1.1 'Time of Crisis'—'Time of Opportunity'—The World is Becoming More Complex...

' Turning Point', 'the turning point', is what *Capra* calls his famous work (Capra, 1988). However, if one considers the headlines of recent years, one might be more inclined to say that we live in a 'time of crisis', in which one crisis follows the next; in a time when crises occur in parallel all over the globe, disappear, only to reappear somewhere with even more devastating effects.[1] *Capra* saw in the nineteen eighties rather a perception crisis of the Western world, today, however, one gets the impression that these are empirical events:

'Stock market chaos', 'raw material crisis', 'chaos instead of Arab Spring', 'democracy crisis', 'impending collective old-age poverty', 'energy chaos', 'earthquake disasters', 'euro crisis', 'financial crisis', 'refugee crisis', 'globalisation trap', 'hunger disasters', 'climate catastrophe', 'Middle East conflict', 'war', 'political trust crisis', 'reactor disasters', 'revolutions', 'debt crisis', 'tsunami chaos', 'economic crisis' etc.

A typical headline in 2022, for example, read: "Energy chaos in Germany..." (Schweinfurth, R., 2022).

Even in the context of business start-ups, the change from times of growth to subsequent growth crises is discussed. In each phase, a crisis is discovered. Depending on the

[1] Nevertheless, the term turning point is quite interesting in the context of crises, as the original Greek term κριστς implies a decision-making situation associated with a turning point.

phase, one speaks of a leadership crisis, autonomy crisis, control crisis, staff-line crisis etc. (Volkmann & Tokarski, 2006, p. 404 ff.).

The headlines in the media landscape about crises, disasters, chaos and dramatic changes in our world seem to be exploding. Everywhere in the world, a new crisis, a new fundamental change appears, and no one seems to really have a solution for all the associated problems.

Change and transformation are fundamental categories of economy and society.

Especially the dynamic changes of the last decades are often perceived as crises, both socio-politically and economically, both at the macro level of a national economy and at the micro level of companies and individuals.

The crisis susceptibility of systems has an objective and a subjective side:

- Technological Innovations make systems very efficient on the one hand, but on the other hand, errors cannot be excluded and depending on the technology, they can have serious, if not catastrophic consequences. Since *Descartes*, we know that in order to "establish the undeniably true (…), we should equate everything somehow doubtful with the proven false (author's note)" (Jonas, 1984, p. 81). However, if we consider technologies whose risks are so great that they could endanger humanity as a whole, we should perhaps deviate from this traditional thinking and, as *Jonas* already admonished in the nineteen eighties, "treat the doubtful but possible (…) for decision-making purposes as certainty" (Jonas, 1984, p. 81).
- Economic structures are gradually being broken up and questioned: Primarily demographic change, but also other developments lead to the fact that so far well-functioning social security systems such as the pension system or the health system will no longer be financeable without comprehensive reforms. A further increase in the retirement age, greater necessary efforts in terms of private and corporate provision are just the tip of the iceberg of the emerging change. And also on the economic parquet we see that speculation bubbles are forming and bursting at the stock exchanges, financial markets are collapsing, 'systemic' banks are on the brink of ruin and even currency systems apparently are no longer immune to the danger of failure, even state bankruptcies seem conceivable.[2]

People who have experienced their lives as relatively safe and continuous are nowadays confronted with various risks and breaks, as Ulrich *Beck* first pointed out in his work 'Risk Society' in the nineteen eighties (Beck, 1986).

The often demanded flexibility and increasing individualisation by each individual, with all its dangers, risks, and contingencies, is also associated with new opportunities.

[2]One only has to remember Argentina in 2001, 2014, Iceland in 2008 or Greece in 2012, 2015, where the respective government almost or actually had to declare a state bankruptcy because it was no longer able to meet its state debt obligations.

Ultimately, flexibility and individualisation are an achievement (sic!) of the bourgeoisie, which freed itself from the constraints of the estate society towards the end of the eighteenth century. They are characteristics of self-determination and development opportunities as well as the basis of freedom and equal opportunities. In this respect, the equality of people has never been as great as it is today, where the only remaining criterion of differentiation is money. No church, no profession, and therefore no prince, no pastor, no large landowner or anyone else dictates how we should live and defines the differences and inequality already at birth. In pre-bourgeois times, personal status, such as profession, income, place of residence, etc., was predetermined, and the roles of men and women were indeed determined at birth and not questionable. And even childhood as a social category, in which the growing individuals are perceived as such and can playfully discover their world and their respective abilities, did not exist as such, as it was only invented with the emergence of the bourgeoisie (Rosenbaum, 1982; Aries, 2011).

Despite the far-reaching process of individualisation, bourgeois life also had a recognisable order, there were irrefutable laws that one could rely on: A marriage lasted a lifetime, one sought and found a *life* partner instead of a *life section* partner. Until then, the nuclear family was largely unrivaled. There were no 'patchwork' families etc. (Beck & Beck-Gernsheim, 1990, 1994). Those who had a good education also got a well-paid job, the employer was usually the same from education to retirement etc.

Life in Europe is no longer a slow, sluggish, continuous flow as in the sixties, seventies up to the nineteen eighties; the orders valid until then are being broken up and are gaining a complex character:

Examples: The individual level

In private, people were also in the bourgeoisie "other directed" or "traditional directed", as David *Riesman* (2001) formulated it. The church, the employer down to the immediate neighbourhood determined how the individual had to behave. Today, the individual often looks desperately into himself because no one from the outside gives a guideline or orientation anymore. The modern man is rather "inner directed", he is the inner-guided man, who, looking at himself, also runs the risk of losing himself in consumption and leisure focus, oriented towards money, power, and fame. In the past, there was something like value conservatism. Today, the world is rather existentialist. While the individual represented clear traditional values over a long period of the bourgeoisie, these have given way to a diffuse value plurality. This diversity of values makes a mandatory claim impossible. So it is not surprising that for example for *Sartre* morality does not lie in the obligation of a should, but at most, as he says, "in enduring existence out of nothing" (Sartre, 1989, p. 16). ◀

Examples: School, University, and Profession

- We feel the changes everywhere in the areas of school and profession: Until the nineteen seventies, there was a fixed learning phase that ended after school, for

example, with an apprenticeship. It was quite common to ask a young person "When have you finished learning?" to find out when the training is over. Until then, a working life followed the training, which lasted forty years or more, and in which one was usually active in one, perhaps two companies. Professional developments and careers were far less complex than today (Strunk, 2009).
The current situation can be described with the term 'lifelong learning'. It characterises a time when one never 'finishes learning' and must be highly flexible in changing jobs and employers to meet today's requirements.

- But also the institutions in which we learn are constantly being reformed. Centralised high school diplomas are introduced, school times are shortened, then extended again, types of schools are merged or separated. This leads on the one hand to more equality, but on the other hand to greater disorientation. If almost everyone can now show a high school diploma with good grades in every subject at the end of school, how can a suitable choice for a certain profession or a certain study be derived from this? How should one recognise who is particularly well or poorly suited for a certain task? This kind of equality, or—let's say provocatively—leveling, is extremely unsocial, because for example the young people predestined for a certain university study can no longer be identified.
- Even the university landscape as such is subject to a permanent reform process: Successful internationally competitive degrees, such as the German diploma, are abolished for the purpose of EU-wide standardisation in favour of (partly very inconsistent) Bachelor's and Master's degrees etc. At first glance, the differences between universities of applied sciences and universities disappear, even though they grow enormously due to the structural conditions[3] and the increasing internationalisation of universities, especially in terms of research.
- And also on an individual level, there are a multitude of learning variants that accompany lifelong learning: You learn at school, university, at work, in your free time, at home, alone or in groups, offline or online, in the morning, at noon or in the evening, during the week or at the weekend.
The new technologies enable 'social media' products such as WhatsApp, Facebook, Instagram, Skype, Beluga etc. in addition to email programmes, thus helping to achieve high individual flexibility. But with it also disappears a clear separation of work and leisure, of workplace and own flat, as it was once brought about by the bourgeoisie and where previously the idea of the 'whole house' (Rosenbaum, 1982) applied, to whose basic idea we apparently return, whereby the previous clearly dichotomous order turns into supposed or actual chaos. ◀

[3] Consider, for example, the significantly higher teaching load of professors at universities of applied sciences compared to university professors and the significantly different requirements for the appointment of professors in relation to the two types of universities, which each lead to very different research output: While the practical relevance plays an important role in the selection of a candidate for a professorship at universities of applied sciences, the proof of high-ranking international publications plays a central role at the university.

Examples: Political Conditions

A look at history shows how little permanence there is in states that seem to be designed for eternity: Consider the "eternal" Roman Empire, the rise and fall of the Soviet Union, or Germany's development over the last 200 years.

Nevertheless: In the old Federal Republic, political systems and conditions promised permanence and continuity: East versus West, Communism versus Democracy; the fronts were clear; one knew who the 'good' and who the 'evil' was—on both sides.

For example, the behaviour of voters in the democracy of the post-war years in the Federal Republic was predictable, there was a high party loyalty. The pollsters rarely erred with their predictions. And in the dictatorial states of the Eastern Bloc, one could rely on the political rulers, although one could feel abandoned.

In short: The political systems—regardless of their ideological and human (un) dignified colour, or whether they followed a liberal human image—had one thing in common: They seemed to be predictable.

In the West, the continuous, steady increase in prosperity despite economic fluctuations and stagflation problems[4], the growth of social security etc. was partly an unwritten law until the late nineteen eighties.

In the East, the propaganda about the increase in prosperity etc. while the opposite was happening was just as reliable (Liening, 2009). All of this has collapsed, as we know, and uncertainty up to the rejection of the Euro and Europe is spreading, even though the former President of the Bundestag *Lammert* rightly described Europe in a 2015 speech as the "most ambitious, demanding and intelligent design in response to the challenge of globalisation"[5] ◄

Examples: Companies and Industries

- Large companies in particular are often seen as permanent institutions from the outside, but also from the inside. However, if you look at history, even companies that—like the 'British East India Company' founded on 31.12.1600—seemed to be designed for eternity, are already forgotten by many today. For example, the 'East India Company' had a complete trade monopoly in several countries in the eighteenth century, which would sound like a fairytale to any entrepreneur today.

[4] In theory, inflation should develop along with the economic cycle. That is, during an economic downturn, inflation is declining, during an upswing, inflation is also increasing. However, in the nineteen seventies, it was observed that despite an economic downturn, inflation remained at a high level, so that it rose even further with the next upswing (stagflation = economic stagnation with simultaneous inflation). The cause of this was, among other things, structural economic problems and the anticipation of inflation, for example, by the wage policy of the trade unions, which no longer "fell for" the real wage reductions associated with inflation for the purpose of stimulating the economy.

[5] http://www.wiso.tu-dortmund.de/wiso/leo/de/einrichtung/aktuell/meldungen/150212/index.html.

It traded worldwide with coffee, wool etc., even had its own soldiers, its own navy and the British Empire allowed it to wage wars itself. In the end, the Company ruled over a fifth of the world's population. However, the competitive advantage disappeared due to new developments and competitors. Other events such as the mutiny of the Indian soldiers were added, and finally, on 01.01.1887, this 'global player' equipped with incredible privileges was liquidated.

- But one does not have to look back so far to have the downfall of large companies in mind: Think of the structural change in the coal and steel industry in the Germany's Ruhr area. Until the end of the nineteen eighties, Dortmund was a significant steel location, for example. The combination of steel, coal and breweries seemed to guarantee work and prosperity for many generations. But where the blast furnaces once dominated the cityscape, there is now a chic lake for sailing and relaxation, surrounded by numerous restaurants, city villas and other unitary facilities. Nothing, except some exhibits that are under monument protection, reminds of that time.
- No less significant, although accompanied by less media attention, is the change in Germany's Münsterland. Until the nineteen eighties, the textile industry shaped the entire life in Münsterland. There was no place that was not dominated and shaped by one or more textile companies and their entrepreneurs: The company owners of the large textile companies not only gave people in Münsterland work, they built houses for them, consumer shops for supply and leisure facilities. And today, only a few manufacturing companies from this industry have remained in Münsterland. Textiles still play a major role in Münsterland: But where the deafening noise of the weaving machines used to sound, there are now stylish outlet centres where textiles are sold in enormous quantities, but their actual production only takes place far away in East Asia etc. ◄

Large companies, even entire industries, change dramatically over longer periods of time, or even disappear after a great rise, as the examples mentioned show. Let's consider another example.

Example: World's Largest Companies

If one analyses the list of the world's largest companies according to Bloomberg, Datastream, DWS, Goldman Sachs, it is noticeable that only two companies, namely Exxon Mobil and Royal Dutch Shell, are still among the top 15 companies of 1980. Particularly striking in their development are the companies Halliburton and Eastman Kodak, which fell from 10th to 229th place and even from 9th to a rank beyond 500, respectively. Furthermore, it is noteworthy that at the end of 1980, 13 of the 15 largest companies were American. In 2010, the picture of the top 15 companies has changed significantly, and the USA has lost its dominance. Only 6 of the 15 companies are from the United States, while 5 companies are from China, indicating that Asian companies have gained importance. Furthermore, it is noticeable that the importance of oil companies in the list of the world's largest companies has decreased. The number of oil companies fell from 7 in 1980 to 4 in 2010, while the number of technology companies and banks has increased (Kempe, 2011). ◀

In short: If we look at longer periods of time, we do not find sustainable competitive advantages or permanent peak performances in companies, but rather great dynamics, transience of market advantages, rise and fall.

Based on these examples, it can be assumed that at least compared to the old Federal Republic of Germany, everything appears much more uncertain, unpredictable, and risky today. The multitude of challenges that arise from this is great. And many of us hope for simple answers. *Dahrendorf* states

> Today we face problems for which there are no simple answers (Dahrendorf, 2003, p. 116).

And he adds a warning:

> And when a political leader claims that he can simplify this complexity with the power of his will, then the moment has come to protest and teach him a lesson (Dahrendorf, 2003, p. 116).

Complexity is a buzzword that is booming. If you enter this term in German language "Komplexität" into the internet browser *Google*, you get (24/03/) over 22 million entries on this topic, in 2011 (10/2011) there were already 4.3 million findings. In 2005 there were 'only' 625,000, in 2001 only about 6,000 results (Pruckner, 2005, p. 21). *Pruckner* is probably right when she writes:

> The problem of complexity has not just been haunting humanity for a few years. The world and man have always been complex. We just feel it more and more today (Pruckner, 2005, p. 22).

She sees the reason for this in the fact that "we can produce, transmit and experience more and more data, signals and information" (Pruckner, 2005, ibid.). "This leads," according to *Pruckner,* "to a remarkable acceleration of processes, which more and more people can hardly keep up with" (Pruckner, 2005, ibid.).

Another aspect is the fact that many things in our life have become more diverse, versatile, and interconnected. Networking is an important buzzword here.[6] People say: We live in a complex world. In this, we observe a high degree of networking *in* and *between* systems: *In* and *between* companies, states, globalised markets etc., with the constantly increasing networking due to communication structures (Internet/Intranet, telephone, television etc.) playing an important role.

---

[6] It should be noted that *Pruckner* sees the increasing networking as less crucial for the fact that the issue of complexity is becoming more and more noticeable. She sees the actual cause, as noted above, in the data, signals and information that are being produced and disseminated worldwide at an ever faster rate (Pruckner, 2005, p. 22).

The often and also above-mentioned negative connotation with the term complexity is only one side of the coin. As we have also seen, increasing complexity is ultimately a consequence of increased individualisation and flexibility as an expression of greater freedom. This freedom, which allows for very different, self-determined life plans, naturally carries greater risks than a paternalistic system, which depending on its form, is conceivable in both dictatorships and democracies, would impose on each individual. But this imposition is an act of liberation, which—with 'healthy' risk-taking and simultaneous responsibility—makes *everything* seem possible. It is therefore the basis for educated people; that is, for those who are capable of judging, deciding and acting in a responsible and appropriate manner. It is the time for all those who can and want to shape their lives confidently and self-determinedly. It is the time for entrepreneurs, that is, for those who have the courage and ability to want to "undertake" something. The risk of failure is of course always present. If one looks at the different 'cultures' that have developed in this context in different countries, one finds, for example, a significantly different approach to the risk of failure in the USA than in Germany. Here, the person who has to go through bankruptcy is portrayed as a final failure, who is rather punished with ostracism for his failure than respected for his courage to have taken a risk. But: The one who fails has already "undertaken" something, has not capitulated in the face of the complexity of the world, but has seen the opportunities and tried to seize them.

> In a complex world, one must experiment, try out, dare to try. Soberly considered, every day is a bit of Waterloo: We fail our way forward (Lotter, 2014, p. 35).

The successful entrepreneur Max *Levchin* once noted:

> The first company I founded failed with a big bang. The second company failed a little less badly, the third company also failed decently, but that was somehow okay. I recovered quickly, and the fourth company already survived. Number five was then Paypal (Lotter, 2014, p. 35).[7]

Campaigns that counter the existing mentality are increasing. For example, in November 2015, the founders' fair "Die Initiale—Start, Found, Grow" tried to address exactly this topic with the motto formulated in 'youth slang': "Fuck Up, Stand Up, Start Up".

Complexity not only causes crises, but also opportunities. If complexity, due to a high degree of networking, growing information diversity, increasing individualisation etc., leads to an increase in complexity in systems and this complexity thus obviously becomes of great importance for shaping our lives in economy and society, then the question arises whether this high complexity, which is perceived more as a threat than an

[7] Two years after its founding, *Levchin* sold the company, which he had founded in 2000 with his colleagues Peter *Thiel* and Elon *Musk* and quickly became the world's most important online payment system, for 1.5 billion US$ to Ebay. Currently (as of 2014), there are about 240 million registered user accounts at Paypal (Lotter, 2014, p. 35).

opportunity due to traditional thinking and corresponding approaches, does not require a different, perhaps a systemic, a networked, but at least a thinking that meets this increasing complexity?

And if this were the case, would this mean that we need a rethink in existing theories, a rethink in practice?

An apparent cause for complexity, beyond political power issues, is apparently to be seen in the diversity of information. Do we ultimately have too much information? Or is it the wrong information on the basis of which we make decisions? Do we have too little knowledge? Information is far from being knowledge. Only structuring, evaluating and classifying turns information into knowledge. Are we perhaps not generating enough knowledge from information? Or should the information be more precise? Is there therefore a lack of measuring points? Or are we using too few equations in the mathematical models with which we capture the world? Do we conduct too few or perhaps the wrong surveys and conversations to get to the bottom of the problems or the solutions? Are we working with too small databases when determining the facts? Or is it ultimately a moral disorientation that prevents the 'right' handling.

Perhaps we also confuse the term "complex" with another term in the whole discussion about complexity: "complicated"? Or is one word a synonym for the other?

Often, we assess a problem that we previously considered complicated as actually quite simple after solving it. In hindsight, we are always wiser. With the term 'complicated', we associate words like 'arduous', 'unclear', 'convoluted', 'tedious', 'difficult', 'not easy', 'hard to understand', etc. Complicated appear to us those tasks whose solution we initially do not consider trivial. But does this also sufficiently describe the concept of Complexity? Or does it hide a completely different quality of existence, of the systems in which we live, which we obviously do not understand with the current methods, because they were not developed to deal with the challenge of complexity and are therefore not suitable?

We often describe as complex—pre-scientifically—indeed things or relationships that we do not understand, that we seemingly and actually cannot influence according to our will, that do not appear comprehensible to us.

2.1.2 How Rational is Man?

But how do we react to the increasingly complex world we perceive, and do we still have control or the ability to control? This question affects each of us, but especially those in our complex economy who want to make a difference, change something or build something and take risks for it. Entrepreneurs are particularly addressed here.

The economic image of man assumes rational action. We will get to know this concept more closely later on, especially as it gives us courage that we can grasp the world rationally, think it through and find optimal solutions. However, it should be said already now, and it will not surprise any reader, that unfortunately man does not have unlimited intellectual resources, but only limited rationality and perhaps also limited willpower. Man is impatient, he often tends to deceive himself, he lets his actions be guided by the need for fairness and justice. These needs can be proven by experiments; however, it turns out that actors do not always behave fairly and cooperatively (Liening & Mittelstädt, 2010, p. 10). People who deceive themselves often reinterpret decision situations through 'normative reframing' so that their self-esteem is not questioned.

Limited rationality, weakness of will, impatience, and preferences for fairness also shape the image of man in modern economic research and challenge the classical or neoclassical image of the Homo oeconomicus. However, there is no general theory that brings all this together!

Imperfect foresight, emotionality, and low risk tolerance, which become more apparent in complex situations, apparently shape human behaviour.

Example: Acquisition of a Car for the Fleet

Let's consider the example of acquiring a car for the new startup company, whose parameters and variables can seem quite complex to us: New or used car, age, planned running time, purposes of use, hundreds of brands, hundreds of options, from colour to equipment, special requests, test results, and payment method (buying, hiring, leasing, etc.) would actually have to be thought through and systematically weighed against each other and economically evaluated if the buyers wanted to make a rational decision.

Even the professional buyer can hardly do this, let alone the private buyer: If we are honest, buying a car is often an emotional affair that we justify rationally afterwards. ◀

It is easy to admit that there are far more complex problems than buying a car. Studies show that people struggle to deal with complex problems. *Halford* et al. write about their experimental findings:

> These findings suggest that a structure defined on four variables is at the limit of human processing capacity (Halford et al., 2005, p. 70).

It appears that the number of variables that people can handle when solving problems is not much more than four, rarely five.[8]

---

[8] In an experiment, thirty academics were shown descriptions of a statistical interplay of several variables. These descriptions were underpinned with graphics. The relationships between the variables varied in complexity. It was measured how long the participants took to solve the respective tasks. Afterwards, they were asked how confident they were in their solutions. It turned out that the academics performed worse and became more uncertain as complexity increased. "At the level of the four-way interactions, participants made comments such as 'Everything fell apart and I had to go back'", *Halford* et al. state. Solutions for tasks that operated with five variables were in the random range. The conclusion from the results was that people cannot process more than four variables at the same time (Halford et al., 2005).

So if we are not so rational and our handling of complexity ends at four variables, if we are not the rational beings that the classical ideas of the economic image of man hope for, the question arises whether we are at all capable of coping with complex situations, whether we are able to respond appropriately to complexity?

First, however, we need to clarify how we actually react to complex situations in order to decide whether these reactions are suitable for satisfactorily solving the questions that have arisen with complexity.

If *Pruckner* is right and the increasingly perceived complexity of the world is related to the ever faster and ever stronger flood of information, we can also ask more generally:

> How do we perceive information, how do we process it, and how do we finally evaluate it?

Perception, processing, and evaluation can be seen as the three decisive steps in the information process.

Perhaps there are no guaranteed and clear solutions in complex situations. It would then be all the more important to (re)know and profitably use the typical behaviours and mistakes that can be made in the analysis of complex problems and the search for corresponding solutions. If the mistakes we make arise from chance, they are beyond our control. However, mistakes that are systematically made can usually be avoided if they have been recognised as such. This is often referred to as behavioural anomalies. Anomalies refer to behaviours that are not rational. The surprising thing is: These behavioural anomalies are already observed in simple, non-complex situations. What behaviour might then be observed in complex situations?

2.2 Behaviour in Simple Situations—Behavioural Anomalies are Observable

2.2.1 Anomalies in the Information Process

Complicated-seeming events that challenge us intellectually, but even simple events, can lead to so-called behavioural anomalies.[9] Figure 2.1 provides an overview of anomalies that can occur in the context of the information process.

These behavioural anomalies often prevent us from making correct decisions even in seemingly simple situations. Let's first consider perception.

[9]The following examples are essentially taken from: Liening and Mittelstädt (2010).

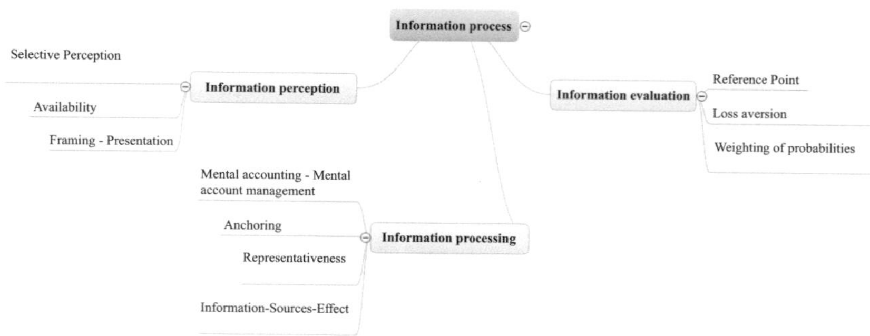

Fig. 2.1 The information process. (Based on: Mazanek, 2006, p. 71)

2.2.2 Information Perception

2.2.2.1 'Selective Perception'—Selective Perception of Information

A typical behaviour that can occur in the perception of particularly complex problems is 'blurring', 'repressing' or 'looking away'. The problems appear to us in such a way that we do not want to acknowledge them and the associated pressure for change. Wait and see, and if action must be taken, trust that the old strategies will somehow work. It doesn't even matter what new things could be conceivable, one sticks to one's old pattern and continues as before. We will examine this behaviour more closely in the context of complex situations. In this context, one also speaks of ***'selective perception'*** (selective perception).

Example: Selective Perception

Mr. *Lahmes*[10] has heard of the innovative trend drink 'Bubble Tea', which is made from green or black tea and sugar. The special feature is that small beads are added to the drink, which burst in the mouth when bitten—children are thrilled! The drink has been very popular in Southeast Asian countries for years. Mr. *Lahmes* sees his chance to conquer the German market with Bubble Tea. From then on, he reads one media report after another praising the success of 'Bubble Tea'. He completely ignores criticism of the harmful ingredients. Enthusiastically, Mr. *Lahmes* works on his business plan and shortly afterwards enthusiastically opens a 'Bubble Tea' café in Dortmund. And so it finally happens as it must: Due to the growing criticism of 'Bubble Tea', the product is less in demand: Mr. Lahmes has to close his café again. If only he had noticed the negative media echo beforehand! ◄

---

[10] Many of the following fictional startup examples are the result of several brainstorming workshops that reflect the ideas of Deniz *Madanoglu* and Cornelius *Lahme,* former members of the author's chair team.

Real Example: Selective Perception

The American startups *Lyft* and *Uber* revolutionised modern human transportation in the American market. Drivers and passengers can communicate with each other via a brokerage platform. Any car driver can essentially become a "chauffeur" with a registration via the application. The San Francisco-based startup *Shyp* also had a similar innovative business idea, with the difference that objects were to be transported in the future instead of people. With just a few button presses, products could be shipped internationally. A trip to the post office was no longer necessary, as Shyp took over the complete packaging and shipping labeling. This service was also supposed to be offered at better price conditions and lead to a modernisation of the postal industry.

After only a short market introduction phase, the young company attracted a lot of attention and aroused the interest of many major investors. Shyp achieved high growth early on. Excited about the growth rate, Shyp decided on further growth strategies: increasing venture capital, increasing the number of employees, building a physical infrastructure, and expanding the target group segment.

While Shyp continued to grow in terms of personnel and space, the number of their actual customers shrank. Instead of aiming for a reduction in the growth rate and an adjustment of previous strategies, the company intensified its growth goals.

Many young startups are influenced by the so-called "hockey stick effect" and continue to steer towards growth. A typical behavioural anomaly of the startup scene—steep increase in growth rate, but low stability. The selective perception led to the other relevant data being ignored. In 2018, Shyp announced the closure of the company. Looking back, founder Kevin Gibbon states: *"Picking the right things to work on at the right time was our biggest failure."* (Hochman, 2016; McCracken, 2018) ◀

2.2.2.2 'Availability'—Availability of Information

To avoid misinterpretations as much as possible, it is important to receive meaningful information. However, there are differences in the availability of information. For example, in a company, insider information is not accessible to every group of people, but only to those who come from the direct environment of the insider. Other employees do not have this privilege and rely on reports, e.g., from the management or the newspaper. This consequently leads to different information procurement and thus also to different efficiency considerations. Since information procurement often involves high costs, many resort to easily obtainable information. They often rely on information from direct colleagues, rely on rumors, or perhaps use the internet. These are more present and easier to access for them. Many then trust 'the hot tip', hope for a good result from it, and thus believe they are better informed than average. However, it should be noted that even the professional colleague cannot predict the future and the magazine often wants to lure with an exaggerated headline and a so-called insider tip. An insider tip? If it is published in the magazine, the supposed insider tip is already based on positive returns and is accessible to a large number of people. Each of us knows this, for example, from tour operators who advertise with insider tips. The fact that thousands of potential customers read and possibly use this insider tip quickly makes the term 'insider tip' absurd here.

No matter where you get the information, availability is characterised by the following four factors: *timeliness, conspicuousness, vividness* and *affective congruence.*

- The more current the information is, the more present it is for the person who is informed and thus influences his perception.
- The more conspicuously the information is presented, the faster it enters the memory of the person to be informed.
- The more vivid the information is, the better it can be used.
- The more positive the mood of the individual is, for example, due to a previous win, the more the informant overestimates himself in his subsequent decision.

The four factors mentioned, but also the different prerequisites for information procurement, lead to distortions of perception already in seemingly normal situations, which could potentially increase in complex, chaotic situations. These distortions make it difficult to make sensible decisions. This aspect is also called the ***'Availability',*** i.e., the aspect of the availability of information in the context of perception.

How much should one worry, for example, about issues such as inflation, bird flu, nuclear energy, BSE, unemployment, insolvency, etc.? People often estimate the probability of risks depending on how many examples they can think of. Someone who lives in a flood-prone area is more likely to take out insurance against flood damage if the last flood was experienced recently than if it was a long time ago. And someone who knows someone who has experienced a flood is more likely to take out appropriate insurance than other people, regardless of the actual level of risk (Thaler & Sunstein, 2012, p. 42 ff.).

Example: Availability—Availability of Information

Germany 1993: The country is reunified. Investors lure investors into the new federal states. After Mrs. *Denising* from the western Münsterland feels addressed by an advertisement for a real estate project in Güstrow in Mecklenburg-Vorpommern, she contacts a real estate company to discuss the offer. A GbR is quickly founded and Mrs. *Denising* invests 500,000 DM in a multi-family house. The real estate company is pleased, as it has just learned that a sugar factory, the largest employer in the small town, is closing. Finally, it gets rid of the real estate project. Who knows how the demand for housing will develop in Güstrow in the future. According to the *Wagner* Foundation, development forecasts regarding the number of inhabitants look bad. Mrs. *Denising* cannot be blamed: Only insiders knew about the closure of the sugar factory. ◄

2.2.2.3 'Framing'—Presentation of Information

Another difficulty that can arise in the context of perception is the so-called ***'Framing',*** the presentation of information. This stands for the different ways of presenting an event. Since there are several ways to present and present the same result or event, differing decisions can occur in information perception.

For example, the vast number and possibilities of financial products are often perceived as at least a complicated topic. *Weber* found in a study, in which 120 test persons each participated and in which three variants of risk representation were chosen by investors in the DAX, that investors significantly underestimate the risk of an investment due to a verbal explanation. The same applies to the representation using a bar chart, but in a weaker form. If the risk is represented using a distribution function, the risk is even overestimated. This is probably also due to the fact that this type of representation seems rather unfamiliar to investors. And the riskier the investment under consideration is, the more investors are off with their assessment. "The degree of misjudgement thus increases with the risk of the investment alternative, so that the misjudgements are most pronounced for very risky investments" (Weber, 2007, p. 159) Different forms of presentation do not necessarily bring clarity. For example, this 'framing' effect is very popular in advertising, as it can very easily control purchasing behaviour.

Example: Framing—Presentation of a Statistic

Suppose a doctor advises a patient to have surgery due to an illness. How should he decide?

If the doctor's statement is: "Of 100 patients who have undergone this operation, 90% are still alive after 5 years.", then the patient will tend to decide for the operation based on this presentation of the information. However, if the doctor's statement is: "Of 100 patients who undergo this operation, 10 die in the first 5 years.", he will tend to say 'no' based on this presentation of the same facts (Thaler & Sunstein, 2012, p. 57). ◄

"Framing works," according to *Thaler* and *Sunstein,* "because people often make their decisions thoughtlessly and rather passively" (Thaler & Sunstein, 2012, p. 58). So it depends very much on how information is presented if you want to achieve a certain goal. Let's look at another example.

Example: Framing—Presentation of Information

Franz *Krietel* is an enthusiastic athlete, fitness is his life. His dream: to offer people the opportunity to train in a high-quality gym for little money. He invests his saved capital in good fitness equipment and looks for suitable premises. In Marburg, Mr. *Krietel* finally finds what he is looking for! He is about to realise his dream. But how can he attract customers? Especially since there are already some gyms in Marburg! Franz *Krietel* is clever, he designs flyers with the slogan "Check Fit—now also in Marburg". This suggests to customers that the gym is already a successful chain. Because Mr. *Krietel* presents the event of the gym opening in a certain way, it is perceived differently by potential customers: The customers who read the flyer have become curious and storm the shop. If Franz *Krietel* had only referred to a new opening, who knows if he would have been so successful. ◀

Real Example: Framing—Presentation of Information

"Starting a company is like eating glass," describes Sean *Parker,* Napster co-founder, his founding experience. Similarly, serial founder Elon *Musk* describes founding: "Running a start-up is like chewing glass and staring into the abyss. After a while, you stop staring, but the glass chewing never ends." Founders operate in a difficult environment that is prone to failure. Thus, several statistical surveys show a high rate of start-up discontinuation. According to domestic surveys of the KfW start-up monitor, 30% of all start-ups discontinue their founding after three years. This number correlates positively with the number of founding years. After five years, the discontinuation rate increases to 50%, and after ten years, the rate is 80%. Comparable numbers are provided by the media company Forbes, which even reports a failure rate of 90%. Reasons for failure are numerous: from lack of market need to financial and personnel difficulties.

Despite the tragic discontinuation rate, founding activities fulfil central economic, social, and societal tasks. Teachers of entrepreneurship education are aware of the advantages and disadvantages of starting a business. In addition to the qualification and sensitisation objectives of entrepreneurship education, ideally, founding activities should be increased by encouraging and supporting those willing to start a business.

Framing plays an important role for the teacher in this context. Depending on the communication or presentation ("framing") of the information, the founding intention of the listeners can change. Here is a small example:

Variant A: 70% of all start-ups are still on the market after three years.
Variant B: 30% of all start-ups fail after three years.

Most likely, most people interested in founding would be more confident about their founding survival in variant A, and thus the founding intention would be more pronounced than in variant B. Because the second statement would probably deter most people interested in founding. This would in turn influence the fear of failure and lead to a negative evaluation of the founding inclination (Patel, 2015; Metzger, 2018). ◀

In the following chapter, we will look at information processing.

2.2.3 Information Processing

2.2.3.1 'Mental Accounting'—Mental Account Management in Information Processing

In information processing, not only companies but also individuals create a so-called account system and conduct proper accounting. For each individual event, there is a separate account to be able to book each event separately. Mutual influences or overlays are simply ignored.

Let's consider the following example, which clarifies from its description that we are still far from a complex context:

Example: Mental Accounting—Ticket Purchase—Ticket Loss

How would one act in the following situations?

- "*Situation A:* You have purchased a concert ticket for the price of 150 DM. Upon arriving at the concert hall, you realise that you have lost your ticket. There are still tickets of the same price category at the box office. Do you buy a new ticket?
- *Situation B:* You have reserved a concert ticket for 150 DM at the box office. Upon arrival, you realise that you have lost 150 DM from your wallet. Do you buy the ticket if you still have enough money with you?" (Goldberg & Nitsch, 2000, p. 54) ◀

Both situations involve a loss of 150 DM. Would one have reacted the same way? *Tversky* and *Kahneman* found in their study that respondents reacted differently despite the same event. While in situation A most respondents would have refrained from attending the concert, in situation B almost 50% would have been willing to buy a ticket. This problem, which can occur in information processing, is referred to as ***'Mental Accounting'.***

2.2.3.2 'Anchoring'—Anchoring of Information Processing

People often use a randomly determined number as an anchor point for their estimates ***('Anchoring').*** This was demonstrated in an experiment by Amos *Tversky* and Daniel *Kahneman.*

Example: Anchoring—Estimation of African Member States in the UN

In this case, a group of participants was asked about the percentage of African member states in the UN. First, each group spun a wheel of fortune with a number range from 1 to 100. Group 1 spun the number 10, group 2 the number 65. Next, the participants were asked whether the correct answer was above or below the randomly spun number. And finally, the participants were asked for the correct percentage. Group 1, which had spun the number 10, answered the question about the proportion of African UN member states on average with 25. Group 2, which had spun the number 65, answered the question on average with 45. ◀

This example suggests that people are influenced by randomly determined numbers and use them for their estimates.

Example: Anchoring—Car Inspection

Remember the last car inspection: The mechanic calls and says he has found a problem, the repair of which is estimated to cost 1000,-. We ask for time to think. After we have already come to terms with the inevitable, he calls again and says that thanks to his research he can get spare parts cheaply and can carry out the necessary repairs for only 700,-. We immediately agree, satisfied, as we have already committed to the anchor (1000,-). ◀

Example: Anchoring—Purchase of a Piece of Art

An American art lover had noticed a painting by a young German artist at an exhibition, who had just become self-employed with his painting. There was a lot of discussion and finally the price came up. The American understood 60,000,- and accepted the price. When it came to payment, the buyer was surprised by the invoice, which 'only' showed 16,000,-. Apparently there was a language problem here, but the artist assured that he only wanted this 16,000,- and no more for the picture. The American indignantly refused to buy such a cheap picture. He doesn't buy pictures for less than 60,000,-. A classic anchor situation! ◀

This cognitive bias is typical. The anchor just needs to be given enough attention. Distortions occur even with simple questions, as the examples show.

Example: Anchoring—Donation

The kindergarten's support association asks for annual donations, which are to be collected by direct debit. When asked what one would usually donate, the chairman says some donate 50,- per year, some 100,-. In this case, the parents donate more than if the chairman had answered: Many donate 10,- per year, but there are also higher donations. ◀

Thaler and *Sunstein* note that this "effect—the more you ask for, the more you get—(…) can be demonstrated in many areas" (Thaler & Sunstein, 2012, p. 41).

How difficult will it then be for us to assess a complex development, such as the economic development of the global economy next year, if we are influenced by an anchor. It is therefore deceptive to think that one always thinks or acts rationally, especially not in complex situations.

Such anchors do not even have to be of a quantitative nature. "Rather," says *Merath,* "an anchor can also be justified by personal or external opinions or attitudes" (Merath, 2006, p. 14). Such anchors can already solidify early in the management team and thus influence the development of the company in the long term. This poses, for example, the risk that the Entrepreneur misjudges his own crisis-ridden development of the company because he has firmly internalised or anchored the 'successful company'.

2.2.3.3 'Representativeness'—Representativeness in Information Processing

In everyday life, a perception of information is often observed that expresses a specific relationship from an object to an object class ***('Representativeness').*** It means something like a schema or thought pattern. The better something matches a schema, the higher its representativeness. This is significant for the assessment and evaluation of examples, events, or probabilities. Similarity is of central importance. It makes it possible to classify and evaluate events, people, or states. However, assessment based on similarities ultimately leads to misjudgements. Let's consider the following two course progressions as an example:

Example: Representativeness—Course Progressions

- Stock A: 90, 93, 92, 103, 109, 106 and
- Stock B: 101, 102, 103, 104, 105, 106.

Due to representativeness, most people will consider the course progression of stock A to be more likely. This fits better with a realistic course progression than that of stock B. This leads to a judgement bias. ◄

Example: Representativeness—Future Forecast

Cornelius *Sieber* is 30 years old, lives alone, is culturally interested, intelligent, and has studied sociology, specifically dealing with peace issues and issues of social justice. Several people are asked to make a future forecast as observers of Cornelius *Sieber*. The options are: a) "Mr. *Sieber* will become a company founder" or b) "Mr. *Sieber* will become a company founder, and he will be active in the peace movement".

Many observers will consider b) to be more likely.

However, such a judgement involves a logical error. It is unlikely that two (independent) events are more probable than one event. The representativeness heuristic suggests that Cornelius *Sieber* must also be active in the peace movement in addition to being a company founder. However, being a "company founder" does not exclude him from also being active in the "peace movement", as all pacifist company founders are undoubtedly company founders. However, case b) excludes that Cornelius *Sieber* does not pursue one of the two activities. This means that a) is more likely than b). See also Thaler and Sunstein (2012, p. 44 f.). ◄

Such judgement biases can be found in the three manifestations *overestimation of probabilities, overestimation of empirical correlations, and overestimation of causal correlations*.

2.2.3.4 'Information-Sources-Effect'—Information Source Effect in Information Processing

The ***'Information-Sources-Effect'*** is a perception problem where the observer only develops trust in information when it comes from multiple information sources. Without checking the reliability of the source, their decision is strongly influenced by the multiple confirmation of the information. Thus, other information is disregarded. This can, for example, lead to inefficient decisions.

Example: Information-Sources-Effect—Reliability of Information

The rumor mill is churning. Gelsenkirchen is supposed to get the DFB—Football Museum. "Currywurst and football-that belongs together!" thinks Peter *Sönderlin* and already hears the cash register ringing. It is supposed to be built near the Eichholz, so the numerous voices whisper. The early bird Mr. *Sönderlin* wants to have a piece of the cake too. He invests in a piece of land near the supposedly planned museum before prices threaten to rise. There he sees the highest customer frequency, namely when the fans pass by his currywurst stand on their way to the museum—he thinks! But his currywurst project fails before it has really started. Although Peter *Sönderlin* had numerous and different information sources that suggested the construction of the football museum. But could he rely on these sources without further ado? No way. He should have taken the trouble to check them: The museum goes to the neighbouring city. Unfortunately, Peter had invested before the final decision was made. ◄

The third and final step of the information process is information evaluation. After the information has been perceived and processed, it is finally evaluated.

2.2.4 Information Evaluation

2.2.4.1 'Reference-Point'—Reference Point in the Context of Information Evaluation

The ***'Reference Point'*** is translated as "reference or reference point" and thus represents a kind of normal state, the so-called status quo, to which the respective events are related. In the financial market, a reference point can, for example, be the entry price of a share. If the price is higher than the reference point, it is considered a profit; if the price is lower, it is considered a loss. The reference point is also crucial for sensitivity. The closer a value approaches the reference point, the higher the sensitivity. In the *Prospect Theory* by *Kahneman* and *Tversky* within the value function, the reference point and decreasing sensitivity are very significant. Depending on the starting point, the respective events are evaluated differently by individuals. For an investor who has a lower reference point, a loss of another investor can mean a profit. For example, if the price of a share is 50 €, it makes a significant difference whether my entry price and thus the reference point is 45 € (profit) or 55 € (loss). Consequently, the reference point is very decisive for the evaluation of information.

Example: Reference Point

She has always been skilled in crafts, but she has never been good with numbers. Beate *Mozzik,* 22 years old and a student at the Technical University in Clausthal-Zellerfeld, has been her own boss for a year: She produces customised umbrella stands for the hip urban bohème in the Federal Republic. Anyone who values themselves needs such an umbrella stand. Ms. *Mozzik's* business seems to be booming. She sells her products in her own online shop on a well-known e-commerce platform. After a year, she wants to take stock—but how? She lacks the comparative value to assess her success. A year later, she no longer has this problem: She can now evaluate her sales based on the previous year's figures and evaluate accordingly. The slight increase in sales excites her. However, this might be "comparing sloppiness with sloppiness," as *Schmalenbach* would say, since a comparison with the competition might reveal a completely different result. ◀

2.2.4.2 'Loss Aversion'—Loss Aversion in Information Evaluation

'Loss Aversion' is an anomaly where gains and losses are evaluated differently. Losses are valued more than gains, i.e., the frustration of a loss of 200 € is greater than the joy of a gain of 200 €. This phenomenon can be explained with the dissonance theory (Festinger et al., 1978). People try to reduce the dissonance, which leads to an uncomfortable feeling due to a negative result, and achieve a nicer feeling. For this reason, an alternative action with negative consequences weighs more heavily than one with positive consequences. An alternative action is always chosen that leads to less dissonance. By avoiding dissonance, which leads to loss aversion, it is not possible to make a rational evaluation between the gains and the losses. Adam *Smith* recognised this problem as early as 1776, when he wrote:

> … the chance of loss is frequently undervalued … (Smith, 1776, p. 125).

Example: Loss Aversion

After 365 days, he is back—Frieder *Wilkens* the globetrotter. What hasn't he experienced on his world tour! One thing particularly appealed to him: Goa, the dream of all dropouts! After a two-week Ayurveda cure with Bikram yoga, Mr. *Wilkens* wants to bring this feeling of life to Germany and open his own studio. Bikram yoga is a Hatha yoga method that takes place in a room heated up to 40° and serves the purpose of physical detoxification. The muscles are supposed to be relaxed by infrared heat. 40°? He needs a heater! Frieder *Wilkens* is surprised at how expensive such an investment is. And not only that: Of course, the new yoga studio should make a good impression. He needs various furniture and furnishings. Spend all his savings at once? The risk-averse Mr. *Wilkens* can't imagine that! It comes in handy that he gets an attractive offer from an electrical retailer in his neighbourhood: He can pay for the radiators in installments without interest and is also assured of free maintenance for the next five years. The fact that this is an installment credit agreement, in which, among other things, the prices for the maintenance service were added, does not occur to him. Regularly high costs seem more attractive to Mr. *Wilkens* than making a high investment at once. ◀

2.2.4.3 'Weighting of Probabilities'—Probabilities in Information Evaluation

In the anomaly ***'Weighting of Probabilities'***, predetermined probabilities are assigned subjective decision weights for events. Often, high probabilities are underestimated and low probabilities are overestimated. In the case of a high probability, e.g., of making a profit, the safe option is chosen. With low probabilities, on the other hand, people take a higher risk. These probabilities are overestimated and lead to people, for example, participating in lottery games and taking out various insurances.

Example: Weighting of Probabilities—Lottery Game

The chance of winning the lottery jackpot in a 6 out of 49 draw is approximately 1 in 14 million, more precisely:

$$Lotto\_6\_aus\_49 := \frac{1}{\binom{49}{6}} = \frac{1}{\frac{49!}{6!(49-6)!}} = \frac{1}{13.983.816} \approx 7{,}151123842 \cdot 10^{-8}.$$

This results in a probability of approximately 0, i.e., it is almost impossible to get 6 correct numbers in the lottery. Nevertheless, many people participate in the lottery and spend a lot of money on participation. Or they repeat the same numbers every week, although mathematically speaking, the draws are independent, so the probability of a particular number combination being drawn does not depend on what was drawn the week before. ◀

Here too, we can quote Adam *Smith*, who stated:

> That the chance of gain is naturally over-valued, we may learn from the universal success of lotteries (Smith, 1776, p. 124).

Table 2.1 Example Guessing Game 1

Gate 1	Gate 2	Gate 3	Game No.	Candidate chooses	Host opens	Candidate switches to	Win?
Convert-ible	Stuffed bear	Stuffed bear	1	1	2	3	No
Convert-ible	Stuffed bear	Stuffed bear	1	1	3	2	No
Convert-ible	Stuffed bear	Stuffed bear	2	2	3	1	Yes
Convert-ible	Stuffed bear	Stuffed bear	3	3	2	1	Yes

The idea that we can usually make good decisions using our gut feeling can sometimes hold true, but can also be easily refuted if we look at the following example, the solution of which contradicts the intuitive solution, as the reader can verify for themselves:

Example: Guessing Game

Last Saturday, Mr. *Lüning,* here briefly referred to as Mr. *L*, appeared in the well-known "What do I choose…" show on regional television. Mr. *L* is about to start his startup, which wants to produce special multimedia travel teddy bears that will make holiday trips by car easier for parents of children unwilling to travel, and he hopes to raise the last necessary funds in this unusual way. Although the first prize is a convertible, selling the car would be worth it for him. However, if he loses, he curiously receives a teddy bear…

The host, Mr. *Markis,* here referred to as Mr. *M*, greeted him particularly warmly. Mr. *L* was integrated directly into the quiz show after a short selection interview.

Mr. *M* presented the candidate *L* with three colourful garage doors. One door was red, the second yellow, and the third black.

"Behind one of these doors is a chic and expensive convertible from a well-known car brand, which," said host *M*, "you will surely like." Amidst great applause from the audience, Mr. *M* added: "Behind the other two doors is a small brown teddy bear. So they are duds. Your task now is to choose one of the three garage doors to try to win the great car."

With courage and determination, candidate *L* now—randomly—chose the red door amidst the cheers of the audience.

Now, host *M*, knowing what was behind the garage doors, opened one of the doors that the candidate had not chosen. Of course, there was a small brown teddy bear behind it, a dud.

Now, therefore, a door with a dud was opened. Mr. *M* then offered candidate *L* the opportunity to reconsider his decision and choose the other still closed door.

Table 2.2 Example Guessing Game 2

Gate 1	Gate 2	Gate 3	Game No.	Candidate chooses	Host opens	Cand. keeps	Win?
Convert-ible	Stuffed bear	Stuffed bear	1	1	2	1	Yes
Convert-ible	Stuffed bear	Stuffed bear	1	1	3	1	Yes
Convert-ible	Stuffed bear	Stuffed bear	2	2	3	2	No
Convert-ible	Stuffed bear	Stuffed bear	3	3	2	3	No

Mr. *L* did not want to switch because he saw no point in it. From his point of view, it was equally likely that the beautiful convertible was now behind his selected red door or the remaining second door.

The red door was opened and… a small brown teddy bear appeared. Mr. *L* had lost.

The host now tried in vain to explain to Mr. *L* that before the second opening of a door, it would have been more sensible for any candidate to switch, even if the candidate did not know where the beautiful car was. Neither the audience nor candidate *L* wanted to believe host *M*.

However, Mr. *M* had studied mathematics before he became a host and had conducted stochastic studies some time ago, which made the expressed knowledge appear plausible to him.

What had Mr. *M* worked out in his studies? First, he had made a claim or a thesis.

Thesis by Mr. M. Even though the vast majority of people tend to assume that it makes no difference whether to switch from the chosen door to the remaining second door or to stick with the initial decision, this assumption is incorrect. This thesis was justified by Mr. *M*:

Justification by Mr. M. Let's consider the initial situation. The total probability that a convertible is behind one of the doors is 1. This means that one can be 100% certain to find the car behind one of the doors. With three doors, the probability for each door is therefore 1/3. (1/3 + 1/3 + 1/3 = 1). The probability is evenly distributed, as it is a fair game.

The probability that the car is behind the door chosen by the contestant is therefore 1/3. The probability that it is behind one of the other two doors is thus 2/3.

The host now opens a door behind which the convertible definitely is not. (He can do this because he has looked behind all the doors in advance.)

Once it is clear which door the car is not behind, the 2/3 automatically falls on the other door. By switching, the contestant therefore doubles his chances of getting the car!

To ultimately understand the problem, one must realise that the contestant gets additional information from the host about the two doors not chosen by him, but he gets no additional information about his chosen door!

With a change of decision, the contestant wins 2 out of 3 games (see Table 2.1). Without a change of decision, he only wins 1 out of 3 games (see Table 2.2).

Ultimately, this problem is a problem of so-called "conditional probability". We do not want to delve deeper into this here. We will discuss this topic in more detail later on.

Instead, a slightly different variant of this game will be presented, which makes the solution even more obvious:

Another attempt at explanation The whole thing becomes more intuitive if you imagine that there are, for example, 3000 gates instead of 3. The probability that the first choice is correct is therefore 1/3000. The probability that the car is behind any of the other 2999 doors, on the other hand, is 2999/3000, i.e., 'almost' 1 or 'almost certain'. Now the host opens 2998 of the unselected gates, behind which are duds. Two gates remain: There is the one gate out of 3000 chosen by the candidate and the one gate that remained when the host—who definitely knows where the prize is—opened 2998 out of 2999 gates.

Wouldn't you now be inclined to switch from the first chosen gate to the second remaining gate? Does the candidate believe that he chose correctly right away, or could the car not also have been behind one of the 2999 other gates and thus behind the second gate deliberately left by the host? The answer is now obvious ... ◀

Smith discussed an example from 1776, comparing the risk of a house fire to the risk of a shipwreck. He found that 99 out of 100 did not insure their house against fire, whereas ship risks were significantly more insured. This was because, according to his explanation, potential shipwrecks were "more alarming to the greater part of people". Regarding fire insurance, he noted: "... many people despise the risk too much to care to pay it" (Smith, 1776, p. 125).

2.2.4.4 'Survivorship Bias'—Bias in Favour of the Survivors

The term ***'Survivorship Bias'*** refers to an anomaly that suggests we often only perceive the survivors, not those who have failed, leading to misconceptions due to the overvaluation of what is perceived.

Real Example: Survivorship Bias

During World War II, the English flew many attacks on Germany and its allies. Numerous planes did not return. British engineers examined the returned planes to find a solution that could increase the chances of survival. They repeatedly found the same spots where bullet holes were located and decided to armor these areas on the planes more heavily. Unfortunately, the expected result did not materialise, and it was thought that perhaps the heavy armor made the planes too cumbersome, possibly even increasing the risk of being shot down. Finally, a mathematician named Abraham *Wald* made a seemingly strange suggestion: He advised the engineers to armor the planes not where the bullet holes were and accumulated, but the spots where no bullet holes were found. The idea was that planes that came back and showed bullet holes apparently had no problems not returning, so they had only been hit where the shots had caused little damage. The planes that did not return must therefore have been hit in other places, namely where no bullet holes were found on the returned ones. The engineers had previously fallen into a fatal error (Beck, 2012). ◄

One could say that one should not only orient oneself towards the successful ones, but also keep an eye on those who have failed and failed. This applies, for example, to the stock market as well as to the question of the strategic orientation of companies, etc. In short: If you want to be successful, you should also deal with the losers (Beck, 2012).

For example, in the context of entrepreneurship education, it is important not only to use successful founders as "best-practice" examples in practical examples, but also to deliberately let those who have failed with their company have their say. Failure is ultimately indispensable for success. Lars P. *Feld*, a member of the Council of Experts for the Assessment of Overall Economic Development, says that the successes of the market economy system "are based on the learning effects" that failure provides, "on the effort not to accept failure. Risk and opportunities promise a profit—and they imply the possibility of failure" (cited according to Lotter, 2014, p. 35).

The above examples show how much one can sometimes be misled, how much the supposedly intuitively true, the presumed 'logical', is anything but logical.

Often our intuition is more than just a hindrance to finding solutions to problems.

2.2.5 Control Behaviour

2.2.5.1 Anomalies due to the Need for Control

In addition to the information problems described above, anomalies occur that are caused by a need for control and some of which are briefly mentioned in Fig. 2.2.

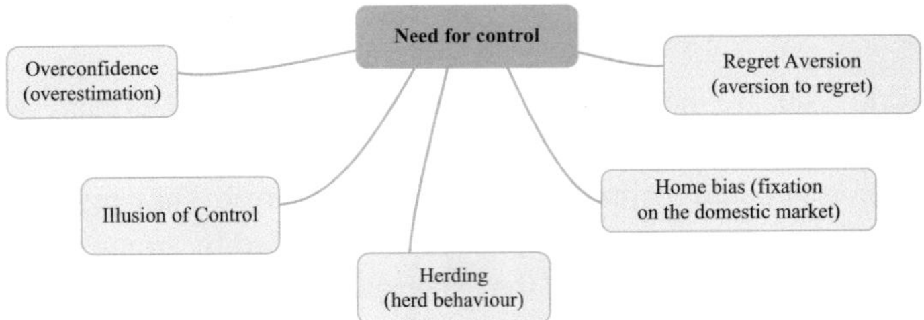

Fig. 2.2 Need for Control

2.2.5.2 'Overconfidence'—Overestimating One's Own Abilities

A typical psychological phenomenon is that many individuals constantly overestimate their actual knowledge. For example, if you ask drivers "How do you rate your driving skills", about 80% see themselves among the top 30%, which is not possible at all. Such a phenomenon of self-overestimation, which can be found especially in complex situations, is titled in the field of psychology as ***'Overconfidence Bias'***.

But why don't we learn from our mistakes? This phenomenon is referred to as ***'Hindsight Bias'***. It means that people overestimate their knowledge or intuition about an event. It is the "I knew that beforehand" effect. This can be observed, for example, with stockbrokers who explain the course of market movements at the end of a trading day as if they could not have gone any other way. This phenomenon explains why we do not learn enough from our mistakes: We overestimate our knowledge and abilities. In addition, we tend to remember past successes rather than failures. Moreover, we attribute successes to our own abilities, while failures are often attributed to external influences or other factors, rarely to ourselves.

Three facets must be distinguished in the 'Overconfidence Bias':

- We usually rate ourselves better compared to the average.
- We overestimate our knowledge compared to our actual abilities.
- We are convinced that we are correct with our statements and assessments.

Example: Overconfidence Bias—Professors and Entrepreneurs

According to a survey at a large university, about 94% of professors believed that they were better in research and teaching than the average of their colleagues.

Comparable overestimations can also be found, for example, in the field of business start-ups. The risk of failure is at least 50%. In a survey among entrepreneurs, they were asked how high their personal chances of success were in starting a business. 90% assessed the situation positively, which, based on empirical evidence, represents completely unrealistic optimism. See also Thaler and Sunstein (2012, p. 52 f.). ◄

Ultimately, one could follow *Schopenhauer*, who spoke of life as "being fooled by hope to dance into the arms of death" (Schopenhauer, 1851/1980).

Especially those who feel confident in their decision are often wrong. Therefore, it would be more sensible to toss a coin, as the probability of making the right choice is at least 50%.

2.2.5.3 'Regret Aversion'

The ***'Regret Aversion'*** is an anomaly that triggers an aversion to regret. The regret can occur both with decisions made and decisions not made. For example, if a stock is not bought despite a good tip, a feeling of regret arises when the stock rises over time. Although no action was taken at this point, the decision not to act is seen as a wrong "action". Consequently, people try to avoid decision situations that cause discomfort due to regret. This behaviour can lead to investors holding their stocks for too long. They fear a rise shortly after their sale. But even with already falling stocks, investors will not sell their stocks so quickly, as they do not want to realise this loss and thus do not want to suffer the regret of the loss. The aversion to regret and the strategy of avoidance can lead to investors acting non-rationally.

Let's look at an example from the field of entrepreneurship for a better understanding:

Example: Regret Aversion

Jan *Tender* and Martina *Palme* agree: Mobile dating apps are the future! On the other side of the big pond, the programme "Love me Tender" is booming. Singles can easily and freely find a partner in the region. Germany needs something like this too! They quickly code the programme—a few weeks later, the programme "L'Amour" is ready to go. Through word-of-mouth, the app becomes a hit and Germany has thousands fewer singles. But the American competition is not sleeping and wants to eliminate its competition: "Love me Tender" makes Mr. *Tender* and Ms. *Palme* a purchase offer, which they—rationally considered—cannot refuse! But they believe in their app and consider the offered price to be far too low. Out of fear of regretting the decision to have sold the app in the end, they reject the offer. They are sure that a better offer will come. Shortly afterwards, the original enters the German market: original beats copy. If only Mr. *Tender* and Ms. *Palme* had sold earlier! After the users have now switched to the original version from the USA, nobody wants to buy "L'Amour" anymore. The value of the once star of the German app sky has fallen. Now Mr. *Tender* and Ms. *Palme* deeply regret that they did not act due to the fear that they might regret the decision. ◀

2.2.5.4 'Illusion of Control'

Another phenomenon is the belief that we can influence the outcomes of decisions. This is referred to as ***'Illusion of Control'***. Investors believe they can apply fail-safe strategies in the market and thus possess a form of control. They believe they can predict and influence stock prices. However, the future is uncertain, and we can only learn to master dealing with uncertainty. Shareholders, on the other hand, try to suppress uncertainty or are confident in their actions. This illusion of control can thus lead to judgement distortions.

Example: Illusions of Control

Wilfred *Spis,* manager of the best Formula 1 driver, is a successful and confident man. For years, the driver Ronald Rennmeister has been winning one season after the next. The market for racing is huge. Mr. *Spis* has been observing the revenues generated in the merchandising industry for some time. He is a businessman through and through, indeed a born Entrepreneur. Why shouldn't he also get involved in the market? Especially since he, as a member of Team Ronald, has a direct influence on the success of his team. His dream is to make money with great miniatures and other licenced products. Wilfred *Spis* is ambitious. He uses his know-how and tinkers with a business plan to copy the successful concept. His company launches just in time for the start of the season. Mr. *Spis* had regularly observed how his merchandising competitors got into trouble at the end of the racing season, as they could only decide which face to print on the cups after the winner was determined. Wilfred *Spis,* the fox, wanted to be smarter. He "knew" who would win! So he bet everything on victory, specifically on his team around Ronald Rennmeister. Even before the championship decision, he put his merchandising items with the name of the winner Rennmeister, whom he assumed, into production. Mr. *Spis* hoped to gain a time advantage over his competitors. What an illusion! As if one could predict the future based on the past. Now Wilfred *Spis:* knew: One should never indulge in the illusion of being able to control everything and make decisions based on this. ◀

Of course, the market lives on the illusion of control, otherwise there would be no trade. The following factors, which cannot be controlled at the stock exchange, even though many investors see it differently, are part of the illusion of control:

- Influenceability
- Predictability
- Cognitive control (e.g., reinterpretation or denial)
- Retrospective explainability (i.e., explanation of, for example, previous price fluctuations)

Here, the connection to the ***'Overconfidence Bias'*** can be seen, as an exaggerated self-confidence, for example in the context of a company foundation, favours the illusion of control.

2.2.5.5 'Home Bias'—Preferring the Familiar

Home Bias stands for the anomaly that people tend to, for example, only purchase familiar products, especially those of domestic companies.

This anomaly can also be traced back to a need for control. The consumer, for example, believes that they can better obtain information about domestic products, determine transaction costs, and more easily evaluate or even influence the price. However, this is often not the case. The risk and expectations are thereby perceived and assessed in a distorted manner.

Do you always buy the product you really need, or do you buy it just because it is being advertised or because it is already known or familiar to you? The person who buys their own company's stock does not necessarily prove their talent as a savvy investment decision-maker!

Conversely, one can also imagine that as an entrepreneur, one might not want to enter the foreign market, less because of the sales prospects there, but because of the assumption that one would not feel as comfortable there as at home.

Example: Home Bias

Aurelie *Noglu* from Poitiers is successful. Having trained at La Moitié, the traditional patissier, she has been standing on her own two feet for three years. And how! Numerous renowned Grand Hotels are clamoring for her macarons. But the growth in haute patisserie is slowly reaching its limits. To increase her profits, Madame *Noglu* would finally have to venture abroad. After all, the French sweet pastry is also in high demand there. Analyses show that the sales potential is even significantly greater than at home. Aurelie *Noglu* has doubts. Although she knows about her chance abroad, she feels comfortable in her native France. Here she knows the market and the language. The customs abroad are foreign to her. Madame *Noglu* refrains from entering foreign markets and thereby wastes the potential for significantly higher profits. ◀

2.2.5.6 'Herding'—The J-Pattern

From childhood, we orient ourselves based on the behaviour and experiences of others ***('Herding')***. We often analyse the behaviour of others, try to figure out to what extent this behaviour has led to the goal, and imitate obviously promising strategies and methods. The more complicated a task seems, the more it is imitated. In doing so, we behave like sheep in a herd. We try to do the same as others and hope for the same positive results. This behaviour already occurs in very simple situations:

Let's consider the following examples, whose generalisation the author calls the J-pattern. At the centre of the following examples is Mrs. J., who is already considering generating a business idea from her attractiveness, which apparently affects every situation, in order to make money with it:

Examples: Herding

- Mrs. J. wants to go out to eat with her husband and discovers a nice restaurant at the holiday location with an appealing menu and a beautiful ambiance, which is apparently still without customers. Since Mrs. J. doesn't like it when people are crowded in the restaurant, she is very pleased about the empty restaurant, and the couple spontaneously decides to enter the restaurant. However, as soon as the two have taken their seats, more guests follow into the restaurant where Mrs. J. is already dining with her husband. Surprisingly, the new guests choose tables that are in the immediate vicinity of the diners, even though the entire restaurant still has free tables with undoubtedly beautiful views. Gradually, the restaurant fills up until the last table is occupied.
  Is it a coincidence that just shortly after Mrs. J. has taken her seat, the restaurant fills up and the new guests, despite free table selection, purposefully sit down at the neighbouring tables of Mrs. J. and her husband?[11]
- Mrs. J. discovers an empty ice cream stand. As soon as she orders an ice cream there, another customer comes and shortly after the ice cream stand is surrounded by people. Mrs. J. suspects that the ice cream seller is considering hiring her for marketing purposes. Or is it pure coincidence that Mrs. J. apparently boosts the ice cream sales?
- A department store offers interesting trousers, but apparently no one is interested. As soon as Mrs. J. has tried on one of the trousers and looked at it in the mirror, more interested customers come. Before the sales manager can encourage Mrs. J. to shop daily, she has already left the department store. ◀

Indeed, these are not just random observations that the author has (co-)experienced and titled as 'J-pattern'. Rather, *Shiller* examined this behaviour, which he describes as typical and refers to as 'Herding' (Shiller, 2000). This described herd behaviour is very widespread. People are influenced not only by what they see, but also by hearsay and especially by personal contacts (Akerlof & Shiller, 2009).

Example: Herding

After the market for long-distance buses was liberalised at the beginning of 2013, business is booming. The long-distance bus network is growing rapidly. Everyone wants to be part of it. Young entrepreneurs hope for big profits in the now finally opened market. Tom *Schimanski* and two fellow students also want to get involved when they see how many have already entered the market. They orient themselves

[11] A similar example, but with two identical, adjacent, empty restaurants instead of one, where the restaurant that a guest randomly chose first fills up, is also described by *Shiller* and is also taken up by *Brost and Rohwetter* (Brost & Rohwetter, 2004, p. 37).

to the numerous providers who transport people through the Federal Republic with their line buses. Mr. *Schimanski* and his friends can now call themselves entrepreneurs and company founders: With their new company "StudiBUS" they are now part of the game. After a few months, however, the rude awakening comes: The long-distance bus market is fiercely contested. Many providers who entered the market at the beginning of the liberalisation cannot withstand the price war. In addition, mergers of individual providers hinder the operational competence of smaller companies like StudiBUS. The market is becoming more and more concentrated. The largest provider holds about three quarters of the entire market. Fortunately, Tom *Schimanski* and his friends did not rely solely on the new business idea: You can now see the three of them more often in the lecture. That's just the way it is: Relying on the imitation of others' behaviour leading to similar success provides no guarantee. ◀

However, it must be stated that herd behaviour can indeed also have rational causes. *Garber* even emphasises:

> Of course, herding is not an irrational act. If it is known that someone is good at analysis and that person makes a move, it's reasonable to follow (Garber, 2000, p. 5).

The examples and typifications listed show that people can exhibit observable and systematically committed anomalies even in simple situations.

The question arises, can such anomalies be observed even more so when the situations are anything but normal and simple, but rather complex, dynamic, or even chaotic? To answer the question, we would first need to clarify what is meant by complexity, chaos, etc. And as we will see, the answer is anything but trivial. Nevertheless, using our pre-scientific understanding of complexity, which we have described above, some observations can be diagnosed, which we want to consider in the following.

2.3 Behaviour in Complex Situations

2.3.1 Four Observable Strategies

The more complicated, one might almost—at least pre-scientifically—say, the more complex the respective decision-making situation is, the more clearly several behavioural patterns crystallise, which can be observed and are presented here. These behavioural patterns can be found at every societal level, including in everyday life in and outside of the company, where one can experience them firsthand:

2.3.1.1 'Trial and Error'—Experimentation

The simplest and probably most naive strategy is that of "experimentation". Without even having a clue about a functioning solution strategy, let alone knowing what could actually help, one tries to test possible solutions one after the other according to the 'Trial-And-Error' principle to solve complex problems.

Without going into detail, it is obvious that this is not a good strategy if one is essentially trying out solutions at random.

Sometimes this may work, other times not. Finding a solution becomes a lottery. We never know if it can work, and if it does, we don't know why.

Example: 'Trial and Error'

The year is 2003: The entire mobile phone market is served by a Northern European manufacturer. Competitors have little chance of gaining market share. Many competing companies have resigned themselves to this, but not the Bavarian industrial conglomerate "Colibri". Its creative department is working hard to offer the market leader a run for its money with innovations. First attempt: A stylish mobile phone series for the fashion-conscious consumer, in unusual shapes and designs. The management is thrilled and sees a great opportunity—the series is launched! Several months pass, but sales are almost zero. The ambitious CEO Carlos *Lahmenda* sees himself as an Entrepreneur and has set himself the goal of shaking up the market with his innovative ideas. So the creative team is urged to make a second attempt. This time, the unique selling point of the innovation is an underwater function that allows end consumers to use the mobile phone even on deep dives. This attempt also fails! The team is not discouraged, a short time later innovation number three is introduced: The "Senses" mobile phone series is supposed to offer the consumer a sensory experience beyond the mere telephone function. The mobile phone case is tactilely covered with a fluffy fabric, olfactorily the device impresses with a perfume sensor that can be filled with the owner's favourite scent. The creative team is convinced of its product and expects the long-awaited sales boom. Unfortunately, they are disappointed again: Nobody wants the "Senses" mobile phone. Nothing seems to work! Frustrated, Carlos *Lahmenda* and his creative team give up after numerous attempts. The creative team lacked a crucial factor: They failed to conduct market analyses and consumer surveys. With their "trial and error" concept, they produced past the market. A few years later, the innovative company Banana manages to completely break open the market. Their recipe for success? A well-thought-out concept that even anticipates customer needs: The smartphone. ◀

Real Example: 'Trial-and-Error'—*NACA and the Aircraft Wings*

The National Advisory Committee for Aeronautics (NACA) used this method, for example, for the development of airfoil profiles for aircraft wings. In 1933, 78 airfoil profiles were examined in the wind tunnel with regard to profile thickness and profile curvatures. Since there was a lack of theoretical foundations and calculation possibilities, the selection of profiles was quite arbitrary. The collected test data were then recorded in a table and made available to aircraft manufacturers. These so-called NACA profiles were used for aircraft construction until 1955 and then replaced by computer technology. Nowadays, profiles are no longer selected from a table, but individually, using three-dimensional calculations, adapted to the given performance data. The progress of computing power has thus led to the *Trial-and-Error principle* becoming obsolete in most areas, as precise calculations can be made. At the same time, however, the increased computing power also allows an extreme form of *Trial and Error* to be applied. In this case, a problem is solved by calculating or going through all possible options until a solution is found. This approach is used, for example, in IT. Hackers have often used the so-called *Brute-Force method* to crack passwords. An algorithm goes through all possible options of number and letter combinations until the actual password and the combination that was tried match.

For companies, trying out all possible options is often not possible, yet sometimes *Trial-and-Error* in the classic sense is applied. Various options are tried out and failures are accepted. Companies known for such behaviour include those led by Elon Musk. Musk accepts failures and often just tries out various options. In an interview, he once said "it is better to make many decisions with a higher error rate than fewer decisions with a lower error rate, because a future correct decision can make up for a wrong decision [...]". Nevertheless, this method is very resource-intensive, as failures often come with high costs and trying out all possibilities also consumes high resources in terms of data, time and computing power (Pressman, 2018; O. V., 2021a, b). ◄

2.3.1.2 'Fading Out'

Another very popular strategy is "fading out". In this case, one relies on the old strategies working. It doesn't matter what new possibilities could be considered, one sticks to the old pattern and continues as before. However, this strategy also doesn't help in the end, as it seems to be a characteristic of complexity that traditional solution strategies often fail in complex novel change processes, as we will learn to understand later. 'Yes, we can change'[12] is often heard in political campaigns from the candidate, but one does not want to move oneself and rather suppresses the necessity for change.

Example: Fading Out

Heinrich *Arndt* is a marketing consultant, specialising in marketing consulting for young companies in the e-commerce sector, and one of the best! His marketing mix of SEM, guerilla actions, and viral visibility has proven successful. This time it's Anna *Block,* a friend of Mr. *Arndt,* who needs his advice. Since her divorce from her husband, she has radically changed her life and is part of the straight-edge scene. Her complete renunciation of alcohol, sex, and meat, she even no longer consumes caffeine, has reinforced her desire to start a vegan kebab snack bar. In the city centre

[12] The slogan that summarised the campaign of US President Obama, who was inaugurated on January 20, 2009, was: 'Yes, we can change' and later just 'Yes, we can'.

Fig. 2.3 Example of a tilt image. (The illustration was designed by W. E. *Hill* and first published in Puck Magazine (1915) (Attneave, 1971, p. 66))

of Tübingen, she opens the "Salad Pouch". To make this public, she turns to Mr. *Arndt,* who doesn't hesitate and as an old hand in the business unpacks his marketing tools. He quickly places a few ads for her on the proven sites and her "Salad Pouch" even appears in the search engines at number one. Mr. *Arndt* is satisfied, these tried and tested strategies have always worked wonderfully in all cases. However, the customers stay away and the cash registers remain empty. Mr. *Arndt* has made a crucial mistake: He simply transferred his usual strategy to a situation where completely different initial conditions prevail: Previously, Mr. *Arndt* advised companies in the online sector, in the gastronomy sector, of course, completely different requirements exist! His usual strategy simply no longer fits the "changed initial situation". Frustrated, Ms. *Block* closes her snack bar and goes to the currywurst stand next door. ◀

This strategy of holding on and fading out is known from synergetics, which we want to discuss in more detail later.[13] Here, the concept of hysteresis or "status quo bias" plays an important role, a physical system inertia that we also find in pattern formation in our brains (cognitive set). In a self-experiment, this can easily be demonstrated with so-called 'tilt images'. When viewing a tilt image, one viewer sees a specific image, e.g. an old woman, as in Fig. 2.3. Another viewer of this flip image sees not an old, but e.g. a young woman. The more the viewer focusses on the first recognised (old or young woman), the more difficult it is for him to recognise the other image. However, it is

[13] See in detail Part II, Sect. 4.4.

hardly possible to see both interpretations at the same time. When one leaves the view of one image, this does not happen successively, but abruptly and one recognises e.g. instead of the old woman the young woman. It is then initially difficult to recognise the previously recognised image again.

2.3.1.3 'Rational Behaviour'—Rational Approach

A third strategy is the rational approach that has been valid since the Enlightenment. One tries to get to the bottom of things, to penetrate them rationally and to look for a logical and generally understandable solution.[14]

But even such a seemingly simple undertaking, like the purchase of computers by a skilled purchasing employee, already shows the difficulty. There are countless parameters that one can consider, from technical parameters (processor type, -kind, -number, memory, memory modules, hard drives, -types) to brands or design, test results, price etc., so that it will hardly be possible for an employee in purchasing to come to a sales decision rationally by weighing all factors. How will the purchasing employee decide? Probably by ignoring most factors and focusses only on price and hard drive capacity.

Fictional Example: Limited Rationality

The hard-nosed Kordula *Brouwer,* a fashionista par excellence, lives in Düsseldorf, the fashion metropolis of North Rhine-Westphalia. As an Entrepreneur she plans her market entry into the clothing industry. As the 'It-Girl' of Düsseldorf's 'who-is-who', she knows about designs, after all, she is a graduate of a well-known fashion design school. After Mrs. *Brouwer* took a two-year break after her strenuous studies, she has been back from Marbella, the final stop of the trip, for a few months now. Her new project is the big business with handbags! During her world trip, she met a potential manufacturer of leather goods in Bangladesh, who, according to her research, offers the cheapest prices on the market. Admittedly, he does not take child labour and human rights in general very seriously. In her opinion, this is the only logical production site. But has Mrs. *Brouwer* really made the right decision, has she really decided rationally in the end? The basis of her decision was only the price. She ignores, for example, how Bangladesh as a production location in connection with possible precarious working conditions affects the image of her company, and thus also her sales. Also, it is not possible for her to carry out regular checks from Germany, and these are just two factors! In the end, it is impossible for her to perceive and process all relevant information, so that a truly rational decision is hardly possible for her in consequence. ◀

[14] Here we have arrived at a fundamental principle of science. The challenges that arise, however, will be discussed in more detail in the chapter on empirical methods (Part II, Chap. 5).

Real Example: 'Limited Rationality'—The Takeover of Monsanto by Bayer

With the takeover of the US corporation Monsanto, the pharmaceutical and agrochemical corporation Bayer has made the most expensive takeover of a German company and has entangled itself in a whirlpool of problems. Monsanto had a negative image from the start and had to deal with legal disputes because the company worked with health-damaging substances that increase the risk of cancer, among other things. Furthermore, it had to answer for allegations of bribery and extortion.

Despite Monsanto's negative reputation and many pending lawsuits, Bayer AG made and executed an offer to take over Monsanto. Since it was impossible for Bayer AG to estimate the extent of the lawsuits, they underestimated the risk and did not have access to internal data, they focussed their takeover considerations on some key factors, such as market dominance in the industry. The additional time pressure, due to the presence of other bidders, made it impossible for Bayer to perceive and process all relevant information. Based on a rational view of the information available to them, Bayer AG decided to take over Monsanto and now has to face the consequences: The company has to deal with several thousand lawsuits, pay pain and suffering and compensation, and explain the lowest low of the share price to shareholders (Dummer & Salz, 2016). ◀

Economists also speak in this context of 'bounded rationality' (Simon, 1955), that people only have limited rationality, as it is impossible for them to perceive and process all relevant information.

2.3.1.4 'Simplicity'—Reduction to Simple Factors

Thus, a fourth strategy often comes into play: not to suppress or experiment, but to approach the problem rationally by focussing or reducing to simple factors. "Simplicity" is the title of a book that indeed propagates this approach "The simple rules of a Complex World" (Kluger, 2007). Perhaps not exactly in this book, but often those who advocate "Simplify your life" (Küstenmacher & Seiwert, 2006) ultimately mean, maliciously formulated, trivialisation, benevolently formulated, reduction of complexity. The problem is that complex systems are treated like complicated systems that can be broken down and analysed in aspects. Complicated systems are initially systems that we do not understand because we do not have enough information. However, complicated systems are not necessarily complex systems, as we will only guess here, but analyse more precisely later. They are, to reveal in advance, of a completely different nature: No matter how much information does not necessarily help to understand them better or to predict their behaviour, and if we try to break them down, they are destroyed. In other words: Reduction does not work in complex systems. Nevertheless, the organisational psychologist *Kruse*[15] states:

[15] *Kruse* applies findings from neuroscience and the science of complex systems to processes in companies in his work (Kruse, 2010).

> The individual human brain is still nature's best response to complexity and dynamics (Kruse, 2010, p. 16).

Especially in complex systems, however, one is inclined to think in black-and-white categories due to the great confusion and to divide the world (inadequately) into 'true and false' or 'good and evil', as the last aspect of the previous section illustrates. In this process, well-intentioned intentions are often quickly reversed. One could also ask: What brings more harm to the world? Good intentions and alleged stupidity or bad intentions and alleged intelligence? To pursue this question with an example, a look at the macro level of societal decisions will be taken.

Real Example: 'Simplicity'

The technical expertise of Noah *Kraft* and Fritz *Lanman* was undisputed even before their joint company foundation. The former employees of Google and Microsoft could be described as real experts in the entertainment industry. In 2013, they founded their company Doppler Labs with a highly innovative product:

They developed wireless headphones, which were not only capable of playing music and receiving phone calls, but the headphones could also block out certain noise and were supposed to provide a real-time translation function in the future.

Kraft and *Lanman* could hardly keep up with inquiries from interested investors. The innovative technology would ensure a corresponding sales in the market; what could possibly go wrong?—the founders thought. But selling the headphones was not going to be that easy. The production turned out to be much more complicated than expected. The design of the products did not meet the taste of the customers and delivery dates could not be met. To make matters worse, the big players in the entertainment industry, Apple, Google and Microsoft, entered the market with their products and pushed out Doppler Labs. In the end, the startup had to close in 2017. Despite the innovative product, the founders had imagined the market entry to be easier than it turned out to be and approached it too simply (Pierce, 2017). ◄

2.3.2 The Oil Spot Theory—"Recursive Consequences Spiral Out of Control"

> *And it will fall out as in a complication of diseases, that by applying a remedy to one sore,*
> *you will provoke another; and that which removes the one ill symptom produces other…*
> (Sir Thomas More)

Let's look at a seemingly simple problem of market intervention, which due to recursive consequences, however, leads to more and more interventions and increases complexity instead of reducing it, so that in the end the initially simple problem has become so complex that it hardly seems solvable:

These difficulties and the resulting consequences are described by the economist Ludwig *von Mises* with the term oil spot theory. *Von Mises* suspects that a state intervention in a market leads to follow-up effects, which in turn call for state interventions, which in turn call for further interventions, etc. He compares this intervention with an oil spot on the water, which spreads more and more and ultimately spoils the entire water fauna.

Blankart, for example, has applied the oil spot theory to the area of statutory health insurance and writes:

Real Example: Health Insurance and the Oil Spot Theory

"To recognise the oil spot theory in statutory health insurance, it is best to start with the tariffs. The Bismarckian health insurance of 1883 was based on an income-dependent tariff. This was reasonable insofar as the loss of wages due to illness was to be insured, while the treatment costs were of secondary importance at that time. Today, treatment costs are the main burden of health insurance, while health insurance only provides subsidiary coverage for continued wage payment. Nevertheless, the premiums are still income-dependent. This does not match. If income-dependent premiums are maintained *(first intervention),* a further intervention must prevent health insurance companies from only contracting high-income earners and discriminating against low-income earners. For this, health insurance companies must be subjected to a contracting obligation *(second intervention).* Health insurance companies that want to survive financially will cope by offering lower service to low-income earners. Because this is also politically undesirable, it is necessary to prescribe a fixed service catalogue for insurance companies *(third intervention).* But this could endanger the financial stability of insurance companies with income-dependent tariffs. Therefore, a risk structure compensation must be established between insurance companies with different populations of income earners *(fourth intervention).* This forces health insurance companies to subsidise their competitors, which reduces their incentive to keep administrative costs low. This in turn requires special programmes for administrative rationalisation *(fifth intervention).* But the health insurance will also pay less attention to treatment costs. Therefore, official prevention and cost damping as well as cost capping programmes must be introduced *(sixth and further interventions).* An end to the interventions is not in sight. All in all, the oil spot theory is confirmed." (Blankart, 2008, p. 400) ◀

Of course, it is not irrelevant which of the four listed action strategies one ultimately follows, but none of the listed strategies will help in the end to act successfully in complex systems. If we have understood what complexity is and if we have understood what systems are, an important step has been taken to better understand these action strategies and to recognise and learn the consequences. Therefore, we will have to look at these things scientifically in the following. But one thing seems clear from the outset: To resign and in case of doubt only rely on the gut feeling will be of little help in complex situations, as the following section shows.

2.3.3 Intuition as a Successful Strategy for Coping with Complex Challenges?

The opposite of good is not evil, but well-intentioned.
(Kurt Tucholsky)

As a seemingly sensible alternative to the four mentioned, not very helpful strategies, the return to intuition, to gut feeling, is often cited recently. Trusting one's own intuition is widely promoted by consulting companies today to solve management tasks in complex situations. But some scientists also see a possible solution here and advocate this reflection on intuition (Kruse, 2010). A fundamental characteristic of intuition is that it is based on a high degree of experience to deliver useful results. Ultimately, intuitions, as *Gigerenzer* believes, come about in the same way as perceptual assumptions: "When the information is not sufficient, the brain invents something based on assumptions about the world" (Gigerenzer, 2008, p. 52). We are not aware of the assumptions and certainly do not know what they are. *Dörner* refers to this as implicit knowledge, which is usually called intuition (Dörner, 2007, p. 65). He cites as an example the musician who, upon hearing a piece of music, says: 'I don't know this, but it's Mozart.', without the musician being able to describe exactly how he recognises the composer of the piece (Dörner, 2007, p. 65). An experienced driver drives confidently through the densest traffic in the city. He brakes, accelerates, changes lanes, turns, shifts gears up or down, etc., without having to think about it and without being able to consciously describe in every situation why he acts this way and not differently. In this process, according to *Dörner*, a perceptual image is compared with an expectation image. However, similar things must be present in order to be compared. On the other hand, the perceptual image is then enriched with information that we have collected from experience, for example, and further developed in thought. "In this way," says *Dörner*, "the horizon of expectation is created as an anticipation of the near and distant future" (Dörner, 2007, p. 195).

Fictional Example: Intuition as a Successful Strategy?

Hans *Löhrwald* lives in Hebertshausen, Bavaria, and hairdressing is his hobby. In his circle of friends, he always takes on the role of hair stylist before celebrations and the results are impressive. It is even said that due to his immense experience, he is actually a professional. Since Mr. *Löhrwald* has now also got a long-haired Puli (Pulis are Hungarian herding and driving dogs and are characterised by their typical floor-length fur, which resembles cords), he is expanding his skills to the animal kingdom. After all, dogs with adequate fur are currently a hype in his clique! The dog-friendly Hans *Löhrwald* spends hours sprucing up his friends' little yappers. Whether poodles, Pekingese or Afghan hounds—the enthusiasm for hairdressing-capable four-legged friends knows no bounds! Why not approach the matter professionally, he thinks? Mr. *Löhrwald* has the intuition, based on his experience, that a dog grooming salon could become a successful business idea. A short time later, it happens: "Hansi's Dog Salon" opens. However, the supposed entrepreneur Hans *Löhrwald* has overestimated himself: The transition from hobby to profession, with a new type of customer (dog fur instead of human hair), is complex. Relying on experiences that apparently no longer fit here is not very helpful for acting in such complex situations. ◀

The problem for the case of complex systems now lies in the following:

When we consider complex situations, they are particularly characterised by the fact that they show other more surprising results than those we would have expected in times of uniform development strands. We will examine this in more detail later. Therefore, our experiential knowledge and ultimately our gut feeling does not help us. As we have seen in the previous section under the keyword 'Weighting of Probabilities', our own intuition can already be problematic in relatively simple situations. Dealing with non-linear systems, which also include complex systems, is even more difficult for us. Let's look at a very simple and perhaps surprising example.

Example: The Joseph's Cent

Suppose Joseph had invested a cent at a bank at the beginning of the year 1 of our calendar, at the birth of Christ, with an annual interest rate of 5%. Let's further assume that the bank and the interest rate have survived the times. How large would the wealth created by this be in the year 2012?

The reader may briefly consider and note an answer. One would probably rightly assume that if Joseph were to invest a cent at the bank at the beginning of the year 1 with an annual interest rate of 5%, he would indeed be a wealthy man today. However, the situation is much more dramatic than one intuitively assumes, because:

By the end of the year 2012, Joseph would have amassed a fortune of 4.29408 × 10 to the power of 40 €. At an exchange rate of 1 € = 1.3151 US$[16] this fortune would be equivalent to 5.64714 × 10 to the power of 40 US$. At a gold price of 53,231.99 US$ per kg of gold[17] Joseph could buy 1.06085 × 10 to the power of 36 kg of gold for his money. With an earth mass of 5974 × 10 to the power of 24 kg, this corresponds to 1.77579 × 10 to the power of 8 earths made of gold. With a moon mass of 7349 × 10 to the power of 22 kg, the gold that Joseph could buy corresponds

[16] As of: 19.03.2012, 14.34 hrs.

[17] As of: 19.03.2012, 14.33 hrs.

to 1.44354 × 10 to the power of 10 moons, so: In the year 2012, the one cent would have become 14,435,297,320.00 moon masses of gold.

Amasing, isn't it?[18] ◀

Dörner notes on this:

> The intuitive handling of nonlinear growth processes is quite difficult for all of us, and we are well advised in such cases not to rely on intuition, but rather on mathematics and the computer (Dörner, 2007, p. 167).

All of this shows us that intuition is not a good guide, especially in complex situations. None of the other strategies presented apparently help us to successfully master complex challenges. The fundamental problem was described by Herbert *Simon* through his principle of 'bounded rationality' as follows:

> The capacity of the human mind for formulating and solving complex problems is very small compared with the size of the problems whose solution is required for objectively rational behaviour in the real world—or even for a reasonable approximation to such objective rationality (Simon, 1957, p. 198).

So if even in simple systems humans can systematically fall into a multitude of traps, how problematic can action in complex systems be. We have gained a first impression of this. There remains the hope that a horizon of solutions will open up in the scientific examination of complexity. We therefore want to devote ourselves more intensively to the scientific analysis of the problem in the following and clarify above all why one—and especially economics—is so oriented towards traditional explanatory patterns, what the historical backgrounds for this are, how the findings around the topic of complexity have developed and how one can approach the scientific concept of complexity. Complexity is a dazzling, difficult to access term. At first, it is as if we were looking at a blank, white *canvas,* which will gradually fill with colours, contours and patterns until we see the picture.

References

Akerlof, G. A., & Shiller, R. J. (2009). *Animal Spirits: Wie Wirtschaft wirklich funktioniert.* Campus.

Aries, P. (2011). *Geschichte der Kindheit.* dtv Sachbuch.

Attneave, F. (1971). Multistability in perception. *Scientific American, 225*(6), 62–71.

[18] By the way, this compound interest effect shows that a good and simple strategy for private retirement provision is: Start early! And: Unfortunately, one has to admit that this example is rather a bad example for the scientific concept of complexity, as we will recognise later; it seems complicated, but it is not complex.

Beck, U. (1986). *Risikogesellschaft*. Springer.

Beck, H. (2012). *Denkfehler, die uns Geld kosten (34) – Auf die Verlierer kommt es an*. Frankfurter Allgemeine Zeitung.

Beck, U., & Beck-Gernsheim, E. (1990). *Das ganz normale Chaos der Liebe*. Suhrkamp.

Beck, U., & Beck-Gernsheim, E. (1994). *Riskante Freiheiten*. Suhrkamp.

Blankart, C. B. (2008). *Öffentliche Finanzen in der Demokratie*. Vahlen.

Brost, M., & Rohwetter, M. (2004). *Das große Unvermögen*. Wiley-VCH.

Capra, F. (1988). *Wendezeit*. Knaur.

Dahrendorf, R. (2003). *Die Krisen der Demokratie – Ein Gespräch*. Beck.

Dörner, D. (2007). *Die Logik des Misslingens – Strategisches Denken in komplexen Situationen*. Rowohlt.

Dummer, N., & Salz, J. (2016). Matthias Schranner über Monsanto-Übernahme: „Das Risiko für Bayer ist groß".

Festinger, L., Irle, M., & Möntmann, V. (1978). *Theorie der kognitiven Dissonanz*. Huber.

Garber, P. M. (2000). *Famous first bubbles: The fundamentals of early manias*. MIT.

Gigerenzer, G. (2008). *Bauchentscheidungen – Die Intelligenz des Unbewussten und die Macht der Intuition*. Goldmann.

Goldberg, J., & Nitsch, R von. (2000). *Behavioral finance*. Finanzbuch.

Halford, G. S., Baker, R., McCredden, J. E., & Bain, J. D. (2005). How many variables can humans process? *Psychological Science, 16*(1), 70–76.

Hochman, D. (2016). The tiny start-up challenging the big FedEx machine.

Jonas, H. (1984). *Prinzip Verantwortung*. Suhrkamp Taschenbuch.

Kempe, C. (2011). Die größten Unternehmen im Wandel der Zeit. *Portfolio Institutionell, 1*, 14–16.

Kluger, J. (2007). *Simplexity – The dimple rules of a complex world*. Murray.

Kruse, P. (2010). *Next Practice: Erfolgreiches Management von Instabilität* (5th edn.). GABAL.

Küstenmacher, W. T., & Seiwert, L. J. (2006). *Simplify your life* (15th edn.). Campus.

Liening, A. (2009). Complexonomics – Über den Zusammenbruch des Laplaceschen Weltbildes und die Anmaßung des Wissens in der Ökonomie. In J. Weyer & I. Schulz-Schaeffer (Eds.), *Management komplexer Systeme – Konzepte für die Bewältigung von Intransparenz, Unsicherheit und Chaos* (pp. 91–118). Oldenbourg.

Liening, A., & Mittelstädt, E. (2010). *Verhaltensökonomische Theorie der Börse. Behavioral Business Gaming*. Institut für Verbundstudien NRW.

Lotter, W. (2014). Wird schon schief gehen. *brandeins. Wirtschaftsmagazin, 11*, 35–44.

Mazanek, L. (2006). *Der Einfluss von Emotionen auf das individuelle Entscheidungsverhalten privater Anleger*. Dissertation, Düsseldorf.

McCracken, H. (2018). How Shyp sunk: The rise and fall of an on-demand startup.

Merath, M. (2006). *Verhaltensanomalien des Managements in der Unternehmenskrise*. GRIN.

Metzger, G. (2018). KfW-Gründungsmonitor 2018.

O. V. (2021a). NACA-Profile.

O. V. (2021b). Brute-Force-Methode.

Patel, N. (2015). 90% of startups fail: Here's what you need to know about the 10%.

Pierce, D. (2017). Inside the downfall of doppler labs.

Pressman, M. (2018). Betting On Elon Musk Means Betting On Rapid Trial & Error – Volkswagen Wanted In. https://cleantechnica.com/2018/09/06/betting-on-elon-musk-means-betting-on-rapid-trial-error-volkswagen-wanted-in/.

Pruckner, M. (2005). *Die Komplexitätsfalle*. Books on Demand.

Riesman, D. (2001). *The lonely crowd*. Yale University Press.

Rosenbaum, H. (1982). *Formen der Familie*. Suhrkamp.

Sartre, J.-P. (1989). *Drei Essays*. Ullstein.

Schopenhauer, A. (1980). *Aphorismen zur Lebensweisheit* (3rd edn.). Goldmann (Ersteveröffentlichung 1851).

Schweinfurth, R. (2022). *Energiechaos in Deutschland: Die Schlafmützenrepublik.* BSZ. Verlag Bayerische Staatszeitung.

Shiller, R. J. (2000). *Irrational exuberance*. Princeton University Press.

Simon, H. A. (1955). A behavioral model of rational choice. *Quaterly Jounal of Economics, 69*, 99–118.

Simon, H. A. (1957). *Models of man, social and rational: Mathematical essays on rational human behavior in a social setting*. Wiley.

Smith, A. (1776). *An inquiry into the nature and causes of the wealth of nations*. The Modern Library.

Strunk, G. (2009). Die Komplexitätshypothese der Karriereforschung. In A. Liening (Ed.), *Komplexe Systeme und Ökonomie* (Vol. 2). Lang.

Thaler, R. H., & Sunstein, C. R. (2012). *Nudge – Wie man kluge Entscheidungen anstößt* (2nd edn.). Ullstein.

Volkmann, C. K., & Tokarski, K. O. (2006). *Entrepreneurship: Gründung und Wachstum von jungen Unternehmen*. UTB.

Weber, M. (2007). *Genial einfach investieren*. Campus.

Canvas—From the Mechanistic to the Complex View of the World

3

Before I was enlightened, rivers were rivers and mountains were mountains. When I started on the path of enlightenment, rivers were no longer rivers and mountains were no longer mountains. Now that I am enlightened, rivers are rivers again and mountains are mountains again.

(a ZEN master, quoted n. Fromm et al., 2011, *p. 151)*

Contents

3.1 A Brief Look into History—About Newtonian Physics and Analogies in Economics 71
3.1.1 A Brief Look into the History of Economics and the Worldview at the Beginning of the Modern Era. 71
3.1.1.1 Physiocracy and the Mechanical Man 71
3.1.1.2 The Classical National Economy 76
3.1.1.3 The Neoclassicism and its Image of Man. 77
3.1.1.4 The Historical Human Image of Economics: Controversial Receptions of the Entrepreneur. 80
3.1.2 About Classical Mechanics and Newtonian Physics—'natura non facit saltus' ... 82
3.1.2.1 From the Principle of Mimesis to the Modern Understanding of Science (Liening, 1996) 83
3.1.2.2 The "Laplacian Demon" as a Symbol of Determinism 86
3.1.2.3 "Everything is reversible"—Reversibility 87
3.1.2.4 "From a follows b"—(strong) Causality. 88
3.1.2.5 Systems are Decomposable—Summativity 88
3.1.3 Analogy between Classical Mechanics and Economics 89
3.1.3.1 The Influence of Classical Mechanics on Economics. 89
3.1.3.2 An Illustrative Linear, Static Supply-Demand Model: Multicopter Engineers Wanted for a Startup. 91

A. Liening, *Complexity and Entrepreneurship*,
https://doi.org/10.1007/978-3-658-44032-9_3

3.1.3.3 The Cobweb Model—Dynamisation of a Linear Supply-Demand Model: "Multicopter engineers wanted for a startup" 95
3.1.3.4 Background Information: Mathematical Considerations on a Linear Cobweb Model 100
3.1.3.5 Philosophical Consideration of the Analogy Formation between Classical Mechanics and Economics—The Danger of Knowledge in the Essential Spell of Technology 103
3.2 The Collapse of the Laplacian Worldview 107
3.2.1 First Doubts 107
3.2.2 The Weather Forecast and the Butterfly Effect 110
3.3 A Paradigm Shift is Announced—Characteristics of the New Approach 113
3.3.1 Paradigm Shift in Economics 113
3.3.2 Describing the World with Systems and Models—What is a System, What is a Model? 115
3.3.2.1 Historical 115
3.3.2.2 The Concept of System 119
3.3.2.3 Basic Characteristics of Systems 122
3.3.2.4 What are Models? 140
3.4 Modeling and Simulation of Complex Systems 141
3.4.1 Systems Dynamics—The 'new' Language 141
3.4.2 Simulations with Counterintuitive System Behaviour 143
3.4.2.1 Positive Feedback Loops 144
3.4.2.2 Negative Feedback Loops 148
3.4.2.3 Double Feedback Loops 154
3.4.3 System Archetypes—Dealing with Complexity 156
3.4.3.1 Equilibrium Process with Delay 157
3.4.3.2 Limits of Growth 158
3.4.3.3 Problem Shifting 159
3.4.3.4 Eroding Goals 162
3.4.3.5 Escalation 164
3.4.3.6 Success to the Successful 166
3.4.3.7 Tragedy of the Commons 167
3.4.3.8 Error Corrections 169
3.4.3.9 Growth and Underinvestment 171
3.4.4 Why are Simulations so Important? 174
3.4.5 Simulation of a 'Complex System' Using the Example of a Supply-demand Model—"Multicopter Engineers Wanted for a StartUp" 177
3.4.6 First Steps to Understanding Complexity 182
3.4.6.1 On the Irreversibility of Time and Catallaxy 182
3.4.6.2 What does Complexity Mean?—The End of Reductionism? 187
3.4.7 Consequences for the Example of the Supply-Demand Model 194
3.5 First Conclusion—Summary of Important Aspects and a Brief Plea for a (Free) Market Economy and the Consideration of Entrepreneurship as a Complex Phenomenon 197
3.5.1 Complexity and Behavioural Economics 197
3.5.2 Complexity, the Laplacian Demon, and Economics 197
3.5.3 Complexity and (Free) Market Economy 198
3.5.4 Complexity and Entrepreneurship 199
3.5.5 Outlook 200
References 200

3.1 A Brief Look into History—About Newtonian Physics and Analogies in Economics

3.1.1 A Brief Look into the History of Economics and the Worldview at the Beginning of the Modern Era

3.1.1.1 Physiocracy and the Mechanical Man

The question of the significance of the natural sciences, especially the findings of classical mechanics, in the development of economics is of great relevance for understanding economics. For the influence of mechanistic thinking on economics extends to the present day, where it must and is being critically questioned (Liening, 1998).[1]

To better understand the influence of classical mechanics, ultimately the *Newtonian* physics, on economics, a historical review is first given.

If one looks into the history of economics, one finds that a multitude of economic schools of thought have developed over time, which were or are granted a more or less important position in the discussion about the development of the economic discipline. Figure 3.1 provides an overview of the most important economic schools of thought from a model-theoretical perspective.

In the middle of the eighteenth century, *Quesnay,* one of the precursors of the classical economic school, developed his 'Tableau économique', which graphically illustrated the entire national economy. It was initially assumed that *Quesnay*[2] was inspired by the circulatory system in the construction of his 'Tableau'. Later research, however, showed that "it was rather a mechanistic analogy" (Schmidt, 1994, p. 52), as *Quesnay* intended to transfer physical findings of *Descartes* to the level of political economy (Schmidt, 1994, p. 52). In comments on his Tableau, *Quesnay* himself emphasised the mechanical and mathematical character of his presentation, as he wanted to prove that the economy works like a machine (Denis, 1985, p. 140).

In general, with the spread of classical mechanics, it had become popular to develop explanatory models based on a machine metaphor. Life itself was not excluded. Already around the middle of the sixteenth century, the oldest surviving automaton figure in

---

[1] Some parts of this chapter were written over twenty years ago and first published in Liening (1998). They have not lost their relevance and validity to this day, so it does not seem sensible to express them again in different words. Nevertheless, selected passages have been clarified, deepened and supplemented. In the context of this book, they give a more rounded picture overall than in their first publication, which is particularly due to the completely new subchapters on systems, models and simulations, including the system archetypes. Furthermore, the older aspects in particular motivate and justify the newly developed entrepreneurship concept presented in Chap. 7.

[2] *Quesnay* was certainly a famous doctor; after all, he was the personal physician of Madame *de Pompadour* at the court of Louis XV. *Schmidt* emphasises that *Quesnay* was a physician, but that he imagined the living body as a machine (Schmidt, 1994, p. 52).

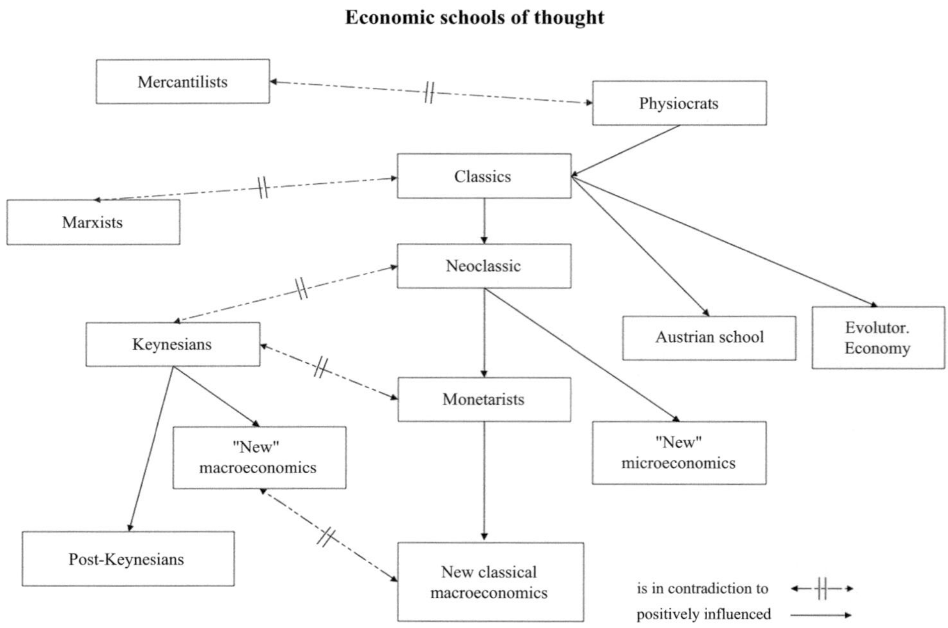

Fig. 3.1 Economic Schools of Thought. (It should be noted that the diagram with its links between the listed economic schools of thought represents only a *rough* simplification. It includes significant model-theoretical schools of thought that are essentially in an 'institutional vacuum'. This means that, for example, directions of thought of the New Political Economy, the New Institutional Economics etc. are not listed. Since this does not further hinder the argumentation, this simplification is justified.)

human form, a lute player, was created. The French mathematician and philosopher René *Descartes* saw the bodies of animals as complex machines.

Automaton figures, like the android 'the Writer' by Pierre Jaquet *Droz* (see Fig. 3.2), who was capable of writing a letter in beautiful handwriting, fueled the idea that life was ultimately mechanical and that it was only a matter of time before vivification could be made possible. The 'mob', however, did not share this view, and so *Jaquet-Droz* narrowly escaped death by hanging at the hands of the enraged crowd, as hardly anyone believed that his automatons were mechanical art. Instead, they suspected a devil-driven magic (Gerwin, 1964).

The 'Writer', as *Wittig* describes this mechanical human, who externally resembled a three-year-old boy, "dips his quill into an inkwell, shakes off excess ink over the glass, and then begins to write a text of about forty letters on a sheet of paper, pausing twice to replenish the ink supply of his pen." (Wittig, 1997, p. 54).

Johann N. *Mälzel,* who is still known today as the inventor of the metronome and studied mechanics, also invented automatons. He became famous in his time with a mechanical trumpeter and with a 'Chess Turk' he acquired and improved from the estate of Wolfgang von *Kempelen* (Schulz, 2012; Breidenstein, 2012).

Fig. 3.2 The Writer by Pierre Jaques-Droz (1773)

With his music automaton and the 'Chess Automaton', as shown in Fig. 3.3, *Mälzel* traveled the country and caused quite a stir, especially in the USA. The *Duke of Saxony-Weimar-Eisenach* described the automaton as follows during a trip to America:

> The automaton represents a Turk sitting behind a table, who has a chessboard in front of him. Opposite, a table with another chessboard is placed, at which someone from the company starts a game of chess with the automaton. When the automaton has to make a move, one hears a gear mechanism moving inside the table; and at the same time, the Turk raises his left hand, which is resting on a cushion, opens his fingers, grabs the piece, makes the move, closes his hand and puts it back on the cushion. If the opponent makes a wrong move, the Turk taps impatiently on this table with his right hand, which is lying next to the chessboard on the table, shakes his head and utters a sound of displeasure (Luden, 1828, p. 254 f.).

In every city that *Mälzel* visited at the beginning of the nineteenth century, he had the best chess players compete against his 'Chess Turk' (see Fig. 3.3) and they almost always lost to the supposed automaton. Some of the spectators believed in a trick, but many considered the 'Chess Turk' a mechanistic creation of intelligence, today one would say, a chess computer. However, the fact was that a very good chess player was hidden inside the 'automaton', who was a master of his craft. Edgar Allen *Poe,* who wanted to expose the authenticity of the 'Chess Turk' as an automaton as false, reports in his essay "Maelzel's Chess Player" that a gentleman named *Schlumberger Mälzel*

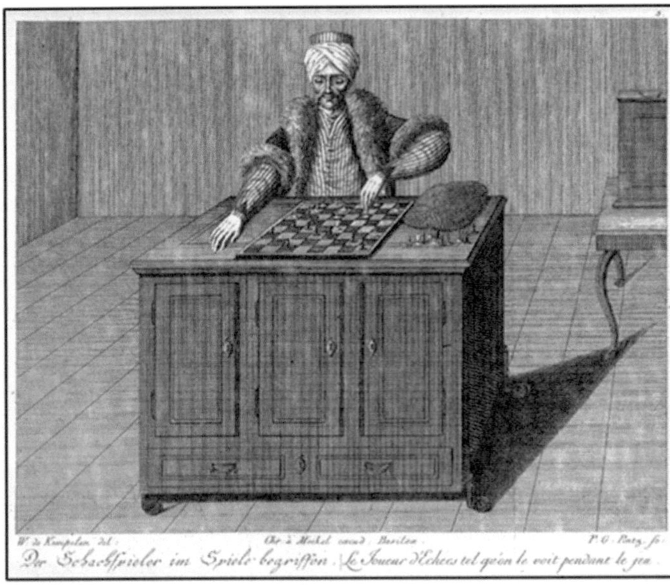

Fig. 3.3 The 'Chess Automaton' by Kempelen, copper engraving by Windisch. (Note: The images shown here are in the public domain, as their copyright protection period has expired.)

followed him everywhere, but was never seen during the chess games, but often immediately before and after the games. And when *Schlumberger* fell ill once, the chess automaton did not appear either (Poe, 1836).

Whether it is really true that *Schlumberger,* who was indeed a close companion of *Mälzel,* was seen coming out of the 'box', is not really proven, but *Poe* was right with his attempt at unmasking and people were too easily seduced by the magic of a mechanical intelligence (Wimsatt, 1993, p. 82).

Julien Offroy de La *Mettrie* already dismissed the soul, which in his view was not provable and probably only added out of fear of theologians, from *Descartes*' approach in the middle of the eighteenth century and postulated the animal as a machine and the human organism as the perfect form of the animal machine (Strunk & Schiepek, 2006, p. 14 f.). La *Mettrie* wrote:

> The human body is a machine that winds its own springs, a living embodiment of eternal motion. The food supplied ensures that it keeps running. Without food, the soul gradually loses strength until it briefly rallies and then dies of exhaustion (Mettrie, 1985, p. 26).

This machine metaphor and the associated transfer of the insights of classical mechanics to areas other than physics, now also made its way into economics: *Mainzer* notes that the school of *Quesnay* represented the economic process, as shown in Fig. 3.4, as a scientifically founded spherical course in the fixed grooves of a clockwork, as was in use at the time (Mainzer, 1995, p. 116).

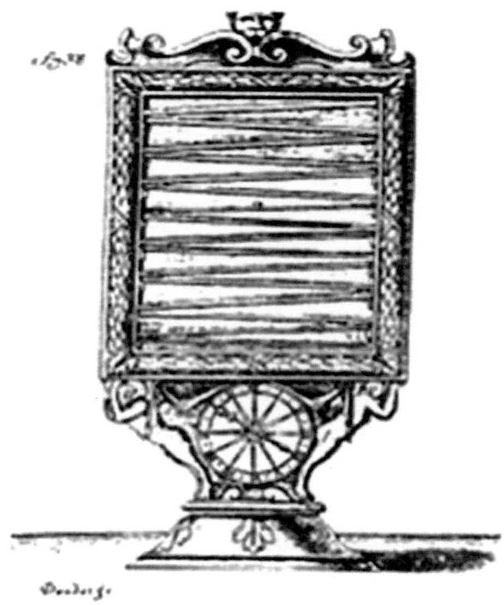

Fig. 3.4 Tableau Economique. *Source* Schmidt (1994, p. 53)

Quesnay was thus one of the first economists to transfer scientific thinking to economics and to advocate self-regulation of the market in analogy with the findings there (Stavenhagen, 1969, p. 42). The motto of the Physiocrats 'laissez faire, laissez passer' has become world-famous.

Interestingly, the theories of Francois *Quesnay* (1694–1774) contain a structured description of the term entrepreneur, which was published in 1758. His theories emphasised the importance of the organisational and innovation-related abilities of an entrepreneur. In the context of entrepreneurship, it should be noted that Richard *Cantillon* (1680–1734) previously described the entrepreneur, the entrepreneur as an "adventurer" who invests in the purchase of goods and materials to sell them in the future, without knowing what price he can take. With *Cantillon*, the concept of risk in connection with economics and also the concept of entrepreneurs is discussed for the first time (Editorial Team, 2014).

If the Physiocrats have created an analogy between scientific findings and economics, then due to the significance of this fact, the concept of analogy must be discussed in more detail:

An analogy is a special kind of comparison. Thus, *Quesnay* compares economics with mechanics.

The elements of a machine are linearly related to each other, when one wheel turns, the wheel connected to it moves, etc. This is also how the economy of a country can be understood, in which all elements interlock and are linearly related to each other. According to this view, economics and machine have something in common without being identical. The reason for the comparability must be worked out in a separate act of reflection, in this example the interlocking of the individual elements is meant.

An analogy consists of three parts:

- from the base (What is known as a successful concept? Here: mechanics)
- from the Interrogatum (What is compared with the base? Here: economics)
- from the Tertium Comparationis (Why compare? Here: To understand the interlocking of the individual elements) (Liening, 1998, p. 11)

3.1.1.2 The Classical National Economy

The classical economics that emerged in the 1770s with Adam *Smith,*John Stuart *Mill* and others displaced Physiocracy. Although *Smith* also advocated for market self-regulation, he differed in some aspects from his predecessors (Lentz, 1993, p. 26), especially since he did not support unrestricted 'laissez faire'.[3] His work, in which the physiocratic motto was developed into a coherent economic concept, can be seen as an application of *Newtonian* physics according to *Bürgin* (Schmidt, 1994, p. 52), although there was at least some hesitation on the part of *Smith* to simply adopt a mechanistic view.[4] But similar to how *Newton's* theory of gravitation provides for distant forces, according to which freely floating celestial bodies enter a state of equilibrium in their interactions, according to *Smith* an 'invisible hand' (Smith, 1776, p. 485), an 'invisible hand' should coordinate millions of individual plans in such a way that a balance of supply and demand is achieved. He states:

> By preferring the support of domestic to that of foreign industry he (the individual person, the author) intends only his own security; and by directing that industry in such a manner as its produce may be of the greatest value, he intends only his own gain, and he is in this, as in many other cases, led by an *invisible hand* (emphasis, the author) to promote an end which was no part of his intention (…). By pursuing his own interest he frequently promotes that of the society more effectually than when he really intends to promote it (Smith, 1776, Book IV, Chap. II, p. 485).

In 1776, entrepreneurs faced their first criticism in the scientific literature. In his work "The Wealth of Nations", Adam *Smith* (1723–1790) completely ignored the entrepreneurial aspect of human behaviour. He described its absence as a natural characteristic of human behaviour and gave priority to diligence.

---

[3] In areas where the market fails from *Smith's* perspective, such as the provision of public goods and the tendency towards monopoly formation, he sees government intervention as entirely justified. From the regulation of banking to the levying of taxes to reduce alcohol consumption, the moral philosopher Smith sees many possibilities for state intervention. However, *Smith* was able to demonstrate for the first time in history that *only* through individual economic freedoms can "the maximum possible economic growth and level of prosperity be achieved under given conditions" (Tilly, 1993, p. 34). See also: Smith (1776).

[4] The reasons for this hesitation are outlined in *Smith's* theory of moral sentiments. See Smith (1994). See also the explanations by Denis (1985).

The classicist Jean Baptiste *Say* (1776–1832) corrected this previous devaluation: in 1803, his work included the famous phrase "Supply creates its own demand" and deepened it, as *Say* explained the importance of entrepreneurs for the economy. He justified the importance of E. for the functioning and growth of all industrial sectors with their organisational skills, which they use to satisfy consumer demand. Other important qualities that *Say* attributes to entrepreneurs are: foresight, risk-taking, and analytical skills. Further endorsement for entrepreneurs was found in John Stuart *Mill's* (1806–1873) "Principles of Political Economy", which he published in 1848.

In terms of the image of man, *Smith* does not see the individual, but the division of labour of many as the source of wealth. This assumes an individual driven by self-interest. This assumed self-interest of the individual works to the advantage of the general public. *Schlösser* points out that the economic image of man appears "pessimistic and meager". Apparently, the Homo Oeconomicus is guided only by self-interest and is driven by financial incentives (Schlösser, 2006, pp. 113–127, passim).

A position that emphasises the free development of personality and other aspects apparently leads to higher self-expectations. The Homo Oeconomicus, on the other hand, is seen as a petty trader in the eyes of his detractors. He suffers from a lack of vision. He lacks grandeur, heroism, as *Sombart* also writes (Sombart, 1915). However, one must consider: Who calculates, is calculable! So writes *Schlösser:*

> The calculating actor, focussed on his material advantage, may not rise to the status of a moral beacon, but his path is paved with fewer collateral damages than that of the natural man. Even the breach of law seems more bearable when pure financial greed directs the procedure: Lucky are the women who fell into the hands of such pirates who were only after money (Hirschman, 1980)[5]. And when the economic calculus takes hold of the military leaders, battles tend to become bloodless and the actors lean towards negotiation solutions (Schlösser, 2006, p. 115).

3.1.1.3 The Neoclassicism and its Image of Man

While the Physiocrats and later the Classics limited themselves to forming analogies between mechanics and economics, the Neoclassics, initiated in the mid-nineteenth century by Alfred *Marshall* and Leon *Walras* and continued in this century by Kenneth *Arrow,*Gérard *Debreu* and Frank *Hahn*, carried out the concrete formalisation of these thoughts (Arrow & Hahn, 1971). With *Walras*' main work "Elements d'économie politique pure: ou théorie de la richesse sociale (1874)", mathematics entered economics, its application having a lasting influence on economics to this day (Walras, 2010). Furthermore, starting with the *Newtonian* doctrine in the seventeenth century, mathematicians such as *Leibniz,* the *Bernoulli* family, and in the eighteenth and nineteenth centuries through *Euler, Lagrange, Laplace, Fourier, Gauss, Cauchy* and numerous other

---

[5] This formulation, which is questionable from today's perspective, must naturally be viewed within the historical context in which it arose.

great mathematicians[6] developed a new mathematical symbolism and a multitude of new mathematical insights and began early to apply these insights to natural phenomena. This proximity to the 'world' in mathematics was not uncontroversial. The thesis is: Mathematics is at best an auxiliary science, something that should serve to support other 'real' sciences. It only makes sense if it can contribute to solving concrete problems in practice. The antithesis is: Mathematics is *the* science par excellence. It does not require any legitimation outside of itself. It is thus an end in itself.[7] Even in the nineteenth century, we find in the writings of famous mathematicians hints of this dispute. For example, the German mathematician Carl Gustav *Jacobi* from Königsberg and the French mathematician Jean Baptiste *Fourier* had exactly this dispute. *Jacobi* writes in a letter to the mathematician *Legendre* in 1830:

> Il est vrai que M. Fourier avait l'opinion que le but principal des mathématiques était l'utilité publique et l'explication des phénomènes naturels: mais un philosophe comme lui aurait dû savoir que le but unique de la science, c'est l'honneur de l'esprit humain…[8]

So obviously, *Fourier* was among the advocates who saw the main goal of mathematics in public utility and the explanation of natural phenomena, whereas *Jacobi*, full of incomprehension towards this position, very impressively formulated the main goal of mathematics: The honour of the human spirit.

Walras and other economists apparently took the position of *Fourier*. They introduced mathematics and with it the mechanistic, the *Newtonian* thinking, into economics. Thus, mechanics took on more than just the basis in an analogy to economics, whose tertium comparationis was the mechanistic functioning of the physical world. Rather, in the Neoclassics, economics came under the regulation of mechanics, or, as *Söllner* writes with reference to *Mirowski*, there was an upgrading of economics to the "physics of the social sciences" (Söllner, 1993, p. 442).

The neoclassical school turned the Homo Oeconomicus into a permanent calculator, who maximises a target function under constraints (Buchanan, 2001, p. 27). The "Homo Oeconomicus" makes decisions in such a way that he achieves a given goal with the least

---

[6] The list could be continued indefinitely. Especially in the nineteenth century, we find an enormous productivity among German mathematicians. Names like *Jacobi, Weierstrass, Kronecker, Riemann, Dedekind, Lipschitz, Schwarz, Cantor* and *Klein* are just some of the names whose insights are still of great importance today.

[7] The dispute about the above thesis and antithesis is not new. Already *Euclid,* who was born around 330 BC, like *Pythagoras* who lived two hundred years earlier, believed that the central concern of mathematics was the search for truth for its own sake, and the question of practical use was secondary. There is an anecdote that once a student asked *Euclid* during a lecture what the practical use of the mathematics he had to deal with here would be. At the end of the lecture, *Euclid* is said to have called out to his slave: "Give the student a coin, since he wants to draw a benefit from everything he learns." The student was then no longer taught by *Euclid* (Liening, 2005, p. 4).

[8] *Jacobi* to *Legendre* on 02.07.1830, in: Jacobi (1881, p. 454 f.).

possible use of resources or, with given resources, with the highest possible degree of goal achievement. This is also referred to as the economic principle or the principle of efficiency.

Classical mechanics and "the constructivist form of rationality that founded it," according to *Röpke,* "understands the living world as consisting of rationally determined beings, controllable by a superior reason from the outside, beings without an 'inner principle of action' *(Kant),* only capable of continuing a movement once received from the outside (in *Descartes* from the Creator God). This mechanistic-constructivist basic trait of early enlightenment has solidified paradigmatically in a part of modern economics" (Röpke, 1977, p. 19 f.). Thus, *Röpke* sees this mechanistic basic principle in three areas of economic theory:

a) Firstly, on the *individual level*, the mechanistically influenced theory type is reflected in the image of man in economics. The neoclassical 'Homo Oeconomicus' with its implicitly used psychology is rather to be assigned to the field of behaviourism, which is based on the stimulus-response-reinforcement principle.[9] The 'Homo Oeconomicus' systematically reacts to the constraints imposed on him and their changes. His preferences (desires, goals, motives) are set constant. Thus, the actions of the 'Homo Oeconomicus' are viewed as a reaction determined by the environment or directed from the outside, not as a spontaneous, self-organising activity.[10]
b) Secondly, on the *level of companies*, one finds the 'machine-command organisation' (Luhmann, 1968) or the 'mechanistic organisation' (Burns & Stalker, 1966). The internal life of companies, their internal organisation, production, and contract problems are not of interest. Rather, their members are able "to reproduce optimal adaptation reactions according to the respective environmental constellation" (Röpke, 1977, p. 20).
c) And finally, on the *level of the market*, one encounters "clearly delineated, assumed as historically given, market structures assigning certain behaviours to individual market participants; their change and evolution remain unnoticed; their respective overall economic efficiency and optimality (with regard to the allocation of scarce resources or other supra-individual goals) can be theoretically demonstrated and at least tendentially also realised in social technology" (Röpke, 1977, p. 20).

Starting from the principle of efficiency, with the neoclassical assumptions, an optimal environmental constellation can thus be realised or assumed to exist on the level of the individual, the companies, and the market. Overall, one can agree with *Schlösser*, who consistently notes that a "theory of spontaneous social orders (...) is not feasible with the neoclassical fiction" (Schlösser, 2006, p. 69).

---

[9] For more on behaviourism, see: Watson (1984), or: Skinner (1974).

[10] For a detailed presentation of the neoclassical image of man, see the critical analysis in: Schlösser (1992).

It is interesting in this context that some representatives of neoclassicism had a technical-scientific or mathematical education.[11] For example, Vilfredo *Pareto* was a trained engineer (Graß, 1994, p. 70); Alfred *Marshall* was a mathematician (Oltmanns, 1994, p. 76) and Stanley *Jevons* was a trained scientist (Lentz, 1993, p. 26), who wrote in his main work: "My theory is, however, of a purely mathematical character" (Jevons, 1924, p. 3). But this educational background of the representatives of neoclassicism cannot alone be the reason for a formalised adoption of the thought material used in mechanics into neoclassicism. To answer the question of the reasons, some remarks on classical mechanics and its philosophy are made.

3.1.1.4 The Historical Human Image of Economics: Controversial Receptions of the Entrepreneur

If one focusses on the development of the human image in economics with regard to the person of the entrepreneur, interesting developments also emerge, some of which are referred to here:

Within **physiocratic** approaches, Richard *Cantillon* (1680–1734) has already dealt with the entrepreneur and described him as an "adventurer". He is an adventurer because he invests in the purchase of goods and materials to sell them in the future, without knowing what price he can take for them. With *Cantillon*, the concept of risk in connection with economics and also the concept of the entrepreneur is discussed for the first time (Cantillon, 1755). This implies that he anticipates future needs and aligns his actions accordingly. As a risk taker and speculator, he receives profit as compensation for the risk taken, because otherwise there would be no incentive to take on such uncertain business (Berghoff, 2016, p. 29). It is also interesting that in the theories of François *Quesnay* (1694–1774) a structured description of the term entrepreneur is found, which was published in 1758. The Physiocracy emphasises the importance of the organisational as well as the innovation-related abilities of an entrepreneur (E.T., 2014). *Berghoff* emphasises that the physiocrats with their first macroeconomic cycle models moved away from "vague terms like 'adventurer', 'project maker' or simply 'merchants' (Berghoff, 2016, p. 29)

In the school of **classical political economy**, Jean-Baptiste *Say* (1767–1832) is to be mentioned in this context. In 1821, his famous *Say's* Law "L'offre crée sa propre demande (La loi de Say)"—"Supply creates its own demand" (Say, 2013) was included and deepened in his work. Although according to *Say* there is always enough purchasing power to prevent a general overproduction, the entrepreneur ultimately coordinates the use of the factors of production, so the function of the entrepreneur lies in the importance of his organisational abilities, which he uses for the functioning and growth of all industrial sectors to satisfy consumer demand (Berghoff, 2016, p. 30). Other important

[11] Even *Lentz* points out that a "number of the most prominent representatives previously underwent a technical-scientific education" (Lentz, 1993, p. 26).

characteristics that *Say* attributes to entrepreneurs are: foresight, risk-taking and analytical abilities (Say, 2013). A comparable attribution that entrepreneurs received in the course of classical political economy was found in John Stuart *Mill* (1806–1873) "Principles of Political Economy", which he published in 1848. *Mill* sought a justification for "profits" and saw it in the function of the entrepreneur as a risk taker (E.T., 2014; Mill, 2015; Berghoff, 2016, p. 29).

With the advent of **neoclassicism**, a fundamental paradigm shift occurred, which was particularly evident in the subjective value theory and the associated focus on microeconomic issues of price formation. The subjective evaluation of goods by the consumer moved to the centre of considerations, thus shifting the focus away from the supply side and therefore the entrepreneur (Berghoff, 2016, p. 28). Frank *Knight* (1885–1972) modified, among other things, his concept of the entrepreneur's *Cantillon* definition by explaining the concepts of risk and profit factors in his work "Risk, Uncertainty and Profit" (Knight, 1921). The distinction between risk and "true" uncertainty is of great importance. Risk is divided into two categories by *Knight*: on the one hand, he sees theory-guided risks and on the other hand, empirically recorded risks. The former are a priori logically derived probabilities (e.g., using certain probability distributions), the latter are empirically determined probabilities (see 1.4). He refers to "true uncertainty" as estimated or intuitive probability, where neither potential realisations nor probabilities of occurrence are known.[12] This constitutes a significant distinction from the concept of risk, as *Neinhaus* rightly points out: "Risks can therefore be objectively and quantitatively determined. Uncertain situations cannot, because they occur unexpectedly and are usually unique." (Neinhaus, 2013) Interestingly, *Knight* does not see the unpredictability hidden in this uncertainty as something negative per se. Rather, he says that if changes were predictable, there would be no opportunity for profit. For the person of the entrepreneur, this results in the challenge of remaining capable of action in the face of non-knowledge—probably also why the *Knightian* concept still enjoys great attention within entrepreneurship research today.

However, it must be emphasised once again that *Knight* could not have known the current state of complexity research, and therefore his concept of uncertainty, which Sarasvathy incidentally refers to as "*Knightian* uncertainty" (Sarasvathy, 2009), must be considered scientifically outdated (Strunk, 2019: 79).

In the major economic schools of the last century, as in **neoclassicism**, the theoretical debate with the entrepreneur remained rather low in **Keynesianism** as well, since with *Keynes* the macroeconomic level in the sense of global demand control, in which the state should act counter-cyclically, was in the foreground (Keynes, 1936). *Berghoff* writes that the "entrepreneur (…) reappears only as a responder who picks up the signals of the now centrally manipulated market." (Berghoff, 2016, p. 28) None other than

[12] In German usage, different terms such as "uncertainty" or "insecurity" have been established for "true uncertainty".

Schumpeter (1883–1950) was the one who confronted the homo oeconomicus optimising under given constraints in his theory of economic development with the "active entrepreneur or homo innovativus who tears down these conditions" (Kurz, 2020, p. 562). The term "creative destruction" of markets, which goes back to him, is based on the consideration that a novel combination of production factors can lead to a shift, even to the dissolution of existing market equilibriums—for example, when demand for existing offers collapses due to innovations (Schumpeter, 1912). Major industrial revolutions, such as the introduction of steam power or currently digitisation, can not only serve as examples, but also highlight the actions of companies and individual entrepreneurs. *Schumpeter* assigns them the role of the innovator, whose actions have far-reaching consequences beyond his own person. In this way, *Schumpeter* bridges the gap between the innovative actions of individual people on the one hand and macroeconomic changes such as growth and decline on the other hand (Schumpeter, 1912).

Thus, he was one of the first to question the "perfection of markets" and ultimately also the mechanistic thinking of overall economic development. "Parallel to this, the mechanistic theory of general economic equilibrium originally highly praised by Schumpeter Léon Walras' increasingly recedes into the background" (Kurz, 2020, p. 562 f.).

Sombart hits the nail on the head when he argues that capitalism would not have prevailed without the entrepreneur (Sombart, 1915). However, the reliance on the mechanistic worldview has often overlooked the entrepreneur as a creative mind who creates new things and questions and tears down the old. The mechanistic worldview and the Homo Oeconomicus as a permanent calculator, dominant with the mathematisation in neoclassicism, do not fit with the type of the homo innovativus as a specific form of homo oeconomicus. *Berghoff* therefore rightly quotes *Sombart,* when he writes: *"In the beginning was the creative act (…) of a daring entrepreneurial man who courageously decides [!sic] to step out of the tracks of conventional economic management" (Berghoff,* 2016, *p. 31).* It is therefore not surprising that the *Schumpeter* entrepreneur as creator and designer is assigned a rather subordinate role in theories shaped by the mechanistic worldview, as he stands diametrically opposed to the mechanistic homo oeconomicus.

3.1.2 About Classical Mechanics and Newtonian Physics—'natura non facit saltus'

Through the 'Philosophiae Naturalis Principia Mathematica' of *Newton*[13] (Newton, 1686) and the principle of continuity of *Leibniz*[14] (1700), which can be paraphrased by

[13] *Hawking* considers *Newton's* contributions to be the "probably (…) most important physical work written by an individual" (Hawking, 1988, p. 17).

[14] *Kant* referred to *Leibniz* as a mechanic. See Weischedel (1983).

the famous saying 'natura non facit saltus', the most important principles of mechanics were established.[15] These principles to be described in the following are:

- the determinism
- the reversibility
- the (strong) causality

as well as the assumption

- of summation (that the whole consists of the sum of its parts)

and

- that the complex is composed of a large number of simple components.

Let's take a closer look at the individual principles:

With the help of the *Newtonian laws*, relationships between quantities such as speed, acceleration, force, and mass can be established. Thus, for example, it can be calculated how long an apple falling from a tree takes to hit the ground. But these laws can also describe the orbits of the planets around the sun or the path of a space shuttle into orbit.

The examples given show, among other things, that classical mechanics can particularly illustrate the time development of physical systems. *Newton* was the first to master this art. From him we know that if the initial state of a system is known, any other state at any other time can be derived. This results in a completely deterministic worldview. The mathematician *Poincaré* formulates this as follows:

> Every phenomenon, no matter how insignificant, has its causes, and an infinitely comprehensive mind, infinitely well informed about the laws of nature, could have foreseen it since the beginning of the world (Poincaré, 1914, p. 53).

3.1.2.1 From the Principle of Mimesis to the Modern Understanding of Science (Liening, 1996)

The concept of determinism, that everything is predetermined or calculable, has a long tradition:

Already in antiquity, the imitation principle of *Aristotle* (384–322 BC) stands out, which is based on a double determination, according to which man can imitate nature on the one hand and on the other hand can complete what nature cannot finish. The principle of mimesis of *Aristotle* goes back to *Plato's*myth of the Demiurge in the *Timaeus*, according to which the Demiurge realises the original images given from the world of

---

[15] It is well known that *Leibniz* and *Newton* were not exactly friends, and that *Newton's* realism is in conflict with *Leibniz's* realism. Nevertheless, the outstanding importance of both for physics and also mathematics (just think of the infinitesimal calculus) is undeniable.

ideas according to the principle of optimal effect. Thus, the Demiurge fully exploits the potential of the ideas and does not allow man to be creative at all due to the completeness of the cosmos with regard to the ideal model. Thus, everything that exists goes back to what already exists. This is also how *Aristotle's* words are understood when he says that 'the one who builds a house does exactly what nature would do if it grew houses'.[16] The insights do not give the world's givens a new order, but fit into a predetermined order (Plato, 1994).

Only after *Augustine* (354–430 AD) does this idea change. The thought comes into play that the finitely conceived cosmos does not exhaust the infinity of possibilities of being. But this creates a scope for human creativity beyond what is given by nature.

Although, for example, *Aristarch(us)* (310–230 BC) had already claimed against everyday observation that the earth orbits the sun, it was only Johannes *Müller* (1457) who considered this in the West. With Nicolaus *Copernicus* (1473–1543), the departure from the then prevailing Ptolemaic worldview, according to which the earth is at the centre of the universe, was initiated. He supported the heliocentric worldview, in which the planets orbit the sun on a circular path, the earth rotates around its own axis and the moon around the earth. However, Copernicus was apparently not fully convinced of his own theses for a long time, and so his views were only published in the year of his death (Kinnebrock, 2002, p. 6 ff.).

Johannes *Kepler* (1571–1630) worked on improving the Copernican worldview (elliptical instead of circular orbits, laws regarding orbit time, speed and path), which led to the still recognised *Kepler's* laws. Ultimately, however, he had no solid arguments for his views. On the contrary: there were numerous 'counter-proofs' that could not be refuted. For example, Tycho *Brahe,* who did not recognise the Copernican system, argued that the angles from which the fixed stars can be seen in summer are exactly the same as in winter, which is why the earth cannot possibly orbit the sun.[17]

Galileo *Galilei* (1564–1642) was an advocate of the Copernican worldview. *Kinnebrock* writes that he was "not entirely innocent in his overzealousness that the doctrine was banned by the Pope in 1614" (Kinnebrock, 2002, p. 7). In 1633, he was put on trial because he would not deviate from his teachings and claimed: 'And yet it moves' (Kinnebrock, 2002, p. 7).

Finally, in the thinking of René *Descartes* (1596–1650), the concept of freedom becomes decisive: Just as God chose a world from the possible, so too does man have the ability to shape the world according to his will. *Descartes'* search for truth leads him to

[16] In this context, it is also interesting that *Plato* elsewhere in a dialogue between *Menon* and *Socrates* has the latter say that knowledge is ultimately nothing more than recollection (Anamnesis). (Cf. Plato).

[17] *Brahe's* experiments, however, presuppose that the fixed stars are so close to the earth that their parallax movement would actually be measurable with his instruments, which was not the case in the least.

sobering conclusions. In the end, he finds a kind of counter-truth to every truth; nothing seems absolutely provable. Amid all the pessimism and contestability, the only incontrovertible fact that cannot be refuted is that one who seeks knowledge exists: 'cogito, ergo sum' (Kinnebrock, 2002, p. 9).

No less than Sir Isaac *Newton* (1642–1727) succeeded in what *Kepler* had sought in vain: The justification for the *Kepler's* Laws: The law of gravitation, from which *Newtonian* mechanics ultimately emerged. *Newton* is also credited with the invention of calculus, which allows for the precise analysis of mathematical functions.

Independently of him, Gottfried Wilhelm *Leibniz* (1646–1716) also invented calculus. For *Leibniz,* who wanted to preserve freedom and at the same time refer back to the divine, "the phenomena of the physical world do indeed occur for certain reasons, but they are not absolutely necessary" (Pépin, 2014, p. 7).

Pierre-Simon *Laplace* (1794–1824) appeared stricter in this respect, as we will see shortly, regarding the relationship between freedom and causality. He spread the *Newtonian* Mechanics further and was considered an atheist. When *Napoleon Bonaparte* once asked him where God was in his system, he is said to have replied: 'Sire, I did not need this hypothesis'.

The prediction of the appearance of the *Halley's* Comet confirmed *Laplace's* assumption of the correctness of the *Newtonian* mechanical worldview: The world functioned like a clockwork and everything followed the same simple laws; everything was, starting from certain initial conditions, predetermined and calculable with mathematical functions.

Blumenberg notes a crucial difference to the development from *Aristotle's* idea of imitating nature as the only way to shape the world, towards the modern science of *Newton, Laplace* and others. For him, it is clear that man now no longer looks at nature to read his rank in being, but at the world of things, which has arisen 'sola humana arte' (Blumenberg, 1957, p. 268).

However, this also develops science into a progress in knowledge, "which tends to subject everything given (...) to human domination and arbitrariness" (Benner, 1989b, p. 46). Modern science, in its self-understanding, does not simply imitate nature, but constructs hypothetical laws that "explain and make available the diversity of the given, without being able to justify the validity and meaning of our knowledge and our rule" (Benner, 1989b, p. 46). Modern science is not based in an order of the world presupposed to cognition. The hypothetically thought laws by which we order the world are "by no means the laws of nature itself, but laws that we give to nature, in order to explain nature, abstracting from its possible purposiveness, and to subject it to our rule" (Benner, 1989a, p. 50).

Despite the criticism, which notes a fundamental change compared to the Greek philosophy of *Aristotle*, there is a common, deterministic approach underlying from *Aristotle* to *Copernicus, Galilei, Kepler* and *Descartes*, which found its perfect, because mathematically exactly calculable, manifestation in the classical mechanics of *Newton.*

3.1.2.2 The "Laplacian Demon" as a Symbol of Determinism

As a symbol for the **determinism** of classical mechanics, the (fictitious) *Laplacian* demon (Worg, 1993, p. 15 f.) is considered. The *Laplacian* demon is that institution that has all the data of the universe, so that it could predict future movements up to any point in time or calculate those of the past back to the earliest times. *Pépin* emphasises that the *Laplacian* approach "necessarily relies on a theoretical fiction, that is, on an idea of what the world could be like" (Pépin, 2014, p. 9). Thus, writes *Laplace:*

> Une intelligence qui, pour un instant donné, connaîtrait toutes les forces dont la nature est animée, et la situation respective des êtres qui la composent, si d'ailleurs elle était assez vaste pour soumettre ces données à l'analyse, embrasserrait dans la même formule, les mouvemens des plus grands corps de l'univers et ceux du plus léger atome: rien ne serait incertain pour elle, et l'avenir comme le passé, serait présent à ses yeux (Laplace, 1814, p. 3 f.).[18]

"The higher intelligence," says *Pépin,* "that Laplace has in mind, is not a pedagogical trick, but allows him to approach a strict, universally valid model. (…) The complete world system of Laplace requires discovering unchangeable mathematical relationships with exact and stable dependence between variables" (Pépin, 2014, p. 9).

The enthusiasm for classical mechanics with its deterministic basic concept and its lasting acceptance, especially in the nineteenth century, is not surprising. *Kinnebrock* rightly emphasises:

> Had not all the newly built machines like steam engines, electric motors, pumps and all the other devices changed and facilitated life in an enormous and never experienced way and did these machines not work deterministically (Kinnebrock, 2002, p. 19)?

And he continues, following the then enthusiasm for classical mechanics:

> If such admired objects as these machines run according to deterministic rules, then presumably also the rest of the world (Kinnebrock, 2002, p. 19).

In the extreme sense, we find these approaches in economic terms in the planned economy, but also Keynesianism with its countercyclical fiscal policy ultimately relies on deterministic-mechanistic approaches. For *Kinnebrock*, under the premises of Determinism, it is "quite logical and inevitable that economic processes follow causal templates that are manipulable and planable" (Kinnebrock, 2002, p. 18).

[18] *Ruelle* translates this crucial passage in *Laplace* as follows: "An intelligence that, at a given moment, knew all the forces by which nature is animated, and the respective position of all the parts that compose it, and was broad enough to subject all these data to analysis, would embrace in the same formula the movements of the largest body in the universe and those of the smallest atom. Nothing would be uncertain for it, and the future as well as the past would be present to its eyes" (Ruelle, 1993, p. 27).

By asking how the idea of free will behaves, determinism was sometimes pushed to the extreme. Or as *Kant* formulated in the conflict of the transcendental antinomies:

> There is no freedom, but everything in the world happens only according to the laws of nature (Kant, 1995, p. 391).[19]

If one thinks this thesis to the end in the sense of *Newtonian* mechanics, humans ultimately act like machines. One could then ask: Can humans be held accountable? Can criminals, for example, be held accountable under this condition? How far does the responsibility of the individual extend if everything is determined? "Murderers and criminals are consequently victims of inheritance and environment. This radical form (of the *Laplacean* demon, which absolutised its effects, the author.) was referred to as the 'specter of determinism'" (Kinnebrock, 2002, p. 19).

3.1.2.3 "Everything is reversible"—Reversibility

In classical mechanics, not only determinism prevails, but also **reversibility** or time reversibility.

A system can be considered reversible if it could just as well run backwards. For example, the first *Newtonian* Law, the law of inertia, is reversible insofar as for the equation of a force-free motion at time t there also exists a solution at time $-t$. The time reversal is expressed by a change of sign in the direction of motion. Since mechanistic processes are identically reproducible, time is only the duration of an event that passes between the beginning and end of the mechanical processes, i.e., until the new equilibrium.

This can be most easily illustrated using a video film. If, for example, you let a pendulum swing in a vacuum, gravity-free room and record this with a video camera, you will not be able to detect any difference in the sequence of motion, regardless of whether the film is running forwards or backwards. Reversibility can also be formulated differently and say that it means the possibility of (exact) repetition of an initial state: processes can run back and forth infinitely often with always the same results.

---

[19] To this antithesis, *Kant* opposes a thesis, according to which "it is necessary to assume a causality through freedom to explain the same" (Kant, 1995, p. 390), where he defines freedom as the ability to "start a state by oneself, whose causality therefore does not stand under another cause according to the law of nature, which determined it in time." He sees here only an apparent antinomy, which he resolves in his work, whereby the distinction between appearances (phaenomena) and things in themselves (noumena) becomes important, as *Helm* emphasises: "Kant tried (...) to resolve the contradiction between the necessity of free will and the contemporary thinking in chains of causality, and for this he considered man from a double perspective and sees man as a 'thing'. Thus, man is subject to the laws of nature—the cause-effect principle—and is controlled as a 'thing' by feelings, passion, drives and instincts. Kant believed that man as a rational being is also a "thing in itself" and thus also belongs to the 'realm of freedom'. From this, Immanuel Kant concluded that man would thus have the possibility to resist mechanical causality and orient himself towards moral principles" (Helm, 2006).

3.1.2.4 "From a follows b"—(strong) Causality

In the context of the discussion of determinism, we have also discussed the question of **causality** with reference to *Kant*. While *Hume* still held the view that man and nature were subject to the same causalities, *Kant* tried to expose the contradiction as an apparent antinomy between the necessity of free will and thinking in chains of causality.

The special thing in classical mechanics is now that not only a law of causality is assumed, according to which equal causes have equal effects and thus causality is invariant. Such a law is also referred to as the weak law of causality. A much stronger assumption, and therefore also referred to as the strong law of causality, is that similar initial states always lead to similar results.[20]

3.1.2.5 Systems are Decomposable—Summativity

Descartes, who certainly would not have accepted every aspect of the later *Newtonian mechanics*,[21] is nevertheless considered one of the most important representatives of this mechanistic way of thinking. It is not an exaggeration to say that the basic conception of classical mechanics can be traced back to him. *Descartes* was particularly interested in the methods that allowed for secure, scientific knowledge. For this, he drew on logic and chose from the multitude of rules that can determine logic, four that, in his opinion, constitute logic. The second rule is of particular importance in this context. *Descartes* writes in 1637:

> The second, to divide each of the difficulties that I would examine, into as many parts as possible, and as would be required to better resolve them (Descartes, 1637/1990, p. 30).

In other words: If a problem is too complex to be solved all at once, then break it down into as many sub-problems, which are then correspondingly so small that each can be solved on its own. With this analytical view, it is implicitly assumed that the whole consists of the sum of its parts. This is also referred to as **'summativity'.**

Descartes' third rule states that scientific thinking is about "always arranging all my thoughts in a certain order when exploring the truth: starting with the simplest and most comprehensible, to gradually, as it were step by step, arrive at the knowledge of the more difficult and complicated, and also to arrange things that do not naturally stand in such

[20] Especially an empirical science that relies on causality needs such a law, since no situation can be exactly the same. One can only examine similar situations for the purpose of the investigation and then hope that the strong law of causality applies.

[21] Example: From *Newton* we know that the gravitational force of two celestial bodies is inversely proportional to the square of the distance between the two bodies. This concept of 'action-at-a-distance forces' would have been suspect to *Descartes*. "He would have wanted a mechanistic explanation that allows contact forces, like those that act from one gear to another, but no distant forces" (Ruelle, 1993, p. 27).

a sequence, yet in a certain order" (Descartes, 1983, p. 35)[22]. Here too, it becomes clear that Descartes fundamentally believes it is possible to break down complex things into a multitude of simple elements and reassemble them. In principle, since *Democritus* and *Aristotle*, scientists have believed that behind the complexity of the world lies a multitude of simple objects and forces (Briggs & Peat, 1993, p. 220).

The entire worldview of classical mechanics is characterised by the focus on closed, simple and often linear systems (Lentz, 1993, p. 32), which include exactly the characteristics of determinacy, reversibility, (strict) causality, the assumption that the whole consists of the sum of its parts, and that the complex is composed of a **large number of simple elements**.

3.1.3 Analogy between Classical Mechanics and Economics

3.1.3.1 The Influence of Classical Mechanics on Economics

To get to the reasons for an analogy between classical mechanics and economics, the following should be noted: Economics is often said to be not an exact or certain science.[23] It is not a certain science insofar as economic findings do not have objective validity. This made the lack of certain knowledge in economics a problem, especially since economics was then part of the humanities, which was not always viewed with the respect it deserved from the perspective of natural science.

On the other hand, there was mechanics, which had spread quickly due to its practical use. The fascinating thing about classical mechanics is that everything is exactly describable, mathematically derivable and predictable, provided all initial parameters are known. No wonder, then, that the optimism it spread also spilled over to other disciplines and to economics as well. Classical mechanics could thus successfully support the efforts of economists to make economics an 'exact' science.

Three fundamental assumptions of classical mechanics have, according to *Dopfer*, found their way into economics:

- A mechanical whole can be broken down into its components. These components can be analysed individually and reassembled into the whole.
- The causalities are invariant, and the relationships between the elements can be described by linear functions.

[22] It should be noted here that *Descartes* resisted the term 'treatise' and insisted on the original title 'Discours' or 'exposition', as he did not want to teach the method, but only to talk about it.

[23] Thomas *Carlyle,* a historian and philosopher of the nineteenth century, once referred to economics as a "dismal science"—"dismal science" (Carlyle, 1849). However, he referred this to the pessimistic view in the predictions of the economist Robert *Malthus* and not to the scientific nature of economics.

- Similar or identical conditions lead to similar or identical dynamic paths of a system (Dopfer, 1988, p. 689).

As mentioned, the classics had already established analogies between economics and mechanics. For example, John Stuart *Mill* impressively writes in reference to the first assumption:

> The order of nature, as perceived at first glance, presents at every instant a chaos followed by another chaos. We must decompose each chaos into single facts. We must learn to see in the chaotic antecedent a multiple of distinct antecedents, in the chaotic consequent a multitude of distinct consequents (Mill, 2002, p. 322).

Beyond this analogy, the neoclassical school that emerged from the 'marginalist revolution' has transferred the ideas of mechanics into mathematical-economic models. This borrowing enabled the emergence of neoclassical equilibrium theory.

A typical example of the adoption of thoughts from mechanics is Marshall's partial analysis*Marshall's*. To better analyse complex reality, the economist relies on the examination of partial aspects of economic events. This corresponds to the first fundamental assumption of classical mechanics, according to which the whole can be broken down into its components and analysed individually to obtain an image of the whole. This idea is also reflected in *Marshall's* Ceteris-Paribus rule, which allows changing a variable under the assumption of constant conditions and examining the effect of the change in the model.

Marshall's successor *Pareto,* after whom the well-known *Pareto* optimum[24] is named, has heavily relied on mathematics in his economic models. His thoughts also show a great affinity for mechanics, as the following quote shows:

> As far as immediate utility is concerned, for example, the study of exchange in pure economics corresponds to the study of free fall of bodies in physics textbooks. A feather falling in the air follows the laws of fall no more than certain exchange transactions follow the laws of exchange (Graß, 1994, p. 73).

And *Jevons* also highlights the parallels to mechanics by attributing something like potential energy to the individual utility function, and so he writes: "The concept of

---

[24]According to *Pareto*, goods and services in an economy are optimally distributed when someone can only improve their situation by taking something away from someone else. However, it is still doubtful to this day whether this is actually a positive state, as the optimum can be achieved regardless of how goods are distributed between the rich and the poor: distribution justice versus efficiency! See also Graß (1994, p. 72).

Although economics, in the sense of Max *Weber's* claim, aspires to be value-free, it is not without values: *Pareto* efficiency, for example, is a high value in economics. Even if it is often argued that this criterion says nothing about justice in distributions, it should be noted that anything that is not efficient is wasteful!

value in our science corresponds to the concept of energy in mechanics". (quoted from Mirowski, 1989, p. 219)

Dopfer goes even further—possibly a bit too far—when he quotes Frank *Knight* as saying that economics is a 'sister science' of classical mechanics (Dopfer, 1992, p. 102).

Overall, however, one can agree with *Dopfer* when he states that the neoclassicists "have missed few opportunities in their work to emphasise the role model character of mechanics for economics" (Dopfer, 1992, p. 100).

3.1.3.2 An Illustrative Linear, Static Supply-Demand Model: Multicopter Engineers Wanted for a Startup

To understand the functioning of market processes in the traditional way of thinking, it is initially useful to illustrate a supply and demand situation using a simple, linear example.

Let's assume an innovative project idea that is described by the following example:

Example: "Multicopter engineers wanted for a startup"

Let's assume that we are in the 'Multicopter' market. Numerous entrepreneurs are trying here to start 'StartUps' with innovative ideas for multicopters, which could revolutionise the possibilities and thus the market, for example, in terms of range, payload, automation of flights, particularly precise flight control, etc. The challenge is that experienced engineers are needed in the short term to implement the idea, who can further develop the respective product ideas to market maturity within the framework of a project, so that inventions become innovations. So, let's assume that we are in a labour market where, on the one hand, HR managers of young companies are looking for project staff for initially one year and, on the other hand, potential employees are looking for attractive jobs in this field. This labour market differs from a regular labour market in that there are no collective wages, no minimum wages, no restrictions in the design of wages, no market access or market exit restrictions; in short: there are no restrictions, and the free forces of the market can fully unfold. In other words: We are dealing here with a market that economics would describe as 'perfect':

First, let's explain the **supply side** (i.e., that of potential employees) of this example:

It is known that no potential qualified employee (supplier) is willing to offer his labour for €10,000 or less per year for such a project on the market. However, for €20,000 per year, there are ten potential employees. Eight suppliers want an annual salary of €28,000. Twelve suppliers are willing to work for an annual salary of €40,000. For €50,000 per year, 10 more suppliers are willing to participate in the market. €60,000 annual salary is the expectation of another 10 potential employees. With an annual salary of €75,000 per year, fifteen more interested parties are added. Both for €85,000 and for €95,000, 10 more employees each offer their labour. And finally, five people are willing to take on the responsible task of further developing the innovative product idea to market maturity for €100,000. In total, there are thus 90 potential employees or 90 suppliers on this labour market.

Table 3.1 Cumulative supply of 'Multicopter' engineers

No.	Salary (in 100,000 €)	Number of providers	Cumulative supply (number of providers)
1	0.10	0	0
2	0.20	10	10
3	0.28	8	18
4	0.40	12	30
5	0.50	10	40
6	0.60	10	50
7	0.75	15	65
8	0.85	10	75
9	0.95	10	85
10	1.00	5	90

Since each of the 10 providers who would work for €20,000 a year would also be willing to work for €28,000, a total of 18 people, including the 8 providers who have indicated they would work for €28,000, are willing to work for a salary of €28,000. This consideration continues with increasing wage expectations. The data (number of providers) must therefore be accumulated to derive the aggregated supply curve (see Table 3.1).

The supply curve can thus be illustrated as in Fig. 3.5.

Obviously, the curve is linear. If the variable *A* represents the suppliers and *P* represents the salary (or the price of labour), the following equation results from the graph:

$$P = 0.1 + 0.01 \cdot A \text{ or } A = -10 + 100 \cdot P$$

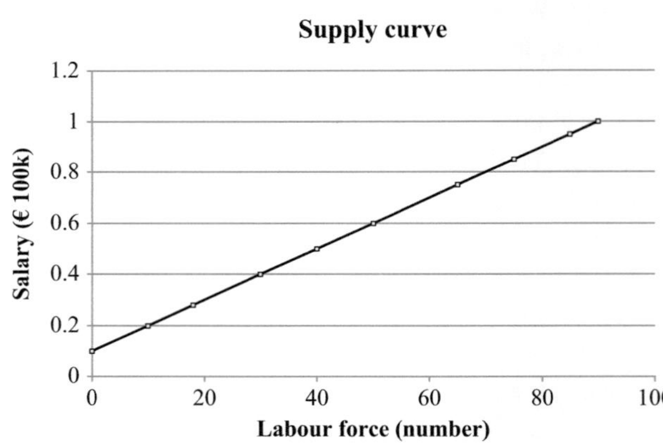

Fig. 3.5 Linear supply curve

So, the supply curve is generally formulated as follows:

$$A = -a + b \cdot P, \text{ with a, b} > 0.$$

The **demand side** is characterised in this example as follows:

At a salary of 100,000 €, only one HR manager is willing to hire a person. At an even higher salary, there is no company that would employ someone for the project. For 95,000 €, a total of 5 people are demanded in the market. At a salary of 80,000 €, they are willing to hire 15 employees. At a salary of 75,000 €, there are 5 job positions offered by the companies. If the salary is 55,000 €, then 20 people are demanded at this salary. 20 employees are sought in the market, provided the salary is 55,000 € per year. At 45,000 €, there are 10 employees demanded. 25 employees are sought at a salary of 20,000 €. Finally, at a salary expectation of 11,000 €, HR managers have advertised 9 employee positions. In total, 90 employees are demanded in the market.

Now, it is the case that for €11,000 per year, certainly all other HR managers who would be willing to pay a higher salary would employ their desired employees. Thus, the cumulative demand at €11,000 is a total of 90 employees. At a salary of €20,000, almost all HR managers in the market are willing to hire employees for the project. The only exceptions are those who are only willing to pay a maximum of €11,000. Therefore, for €20,000, a total of 81 employees are demanded etc. This results in the demand situation in Table 3.2.

Figure 3.6 illustrates the situation of the demanders for project employees.

This curve is also linear, and it obviously results in the following equation for the demand side y:

$$P = 1.01 - 0.01 \cdot N \text{ or } N = 101 - 100 \cdot P$$

In general terms, the supply curve is therefore:

$$N = c - d \cdot P, \text{ with c, d} > 0.$$

When both equations are now combined, i.e. suppliers and demanders meet, it becomes apparent that a balance situation arises at a salary of €55,500 and around 46 workers.

Not every demander and every supplier gets a chance. The situation, as illustrated in Fig. 3.7, shows that a market equilibrium does not result in the satisfaction of all suppliers and demanders.

There are companies that are not willing to hire someone at this salary or workers who are not willing to sign a corresponding employment contract at this salary. We learn nothing about the reasons for this from the equations. Companies may not hire anyone because the equilibrium wage seems too high to them for the corresponding activity or because they may not be financially able to pay higher wages. Potential workers who do not get a chance have too high wage expectations because they may overestimate themselves and their qualifications etc. ◀

Table 3.2 Cumulative demand for 'Multicopter' engineers

No.	Salary (in 100 thousand €)	Number of demanders	Cumulative demand (number of demanders)
1	0.11	9	90
2	0.20	25	81
5	0.45	10	56
6	0.55	20	46
7	0.75	5	26
8	0.80	15	21
9	0.95	5	6
10	1.00	1	1

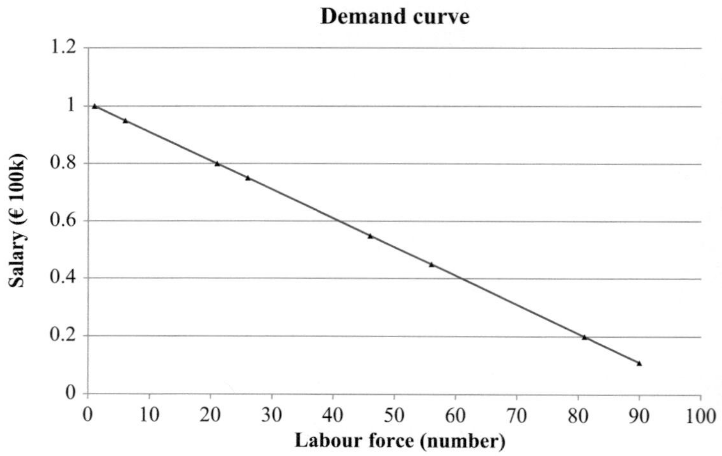

Fig. 3.6 Linear demand curve

The example shows a balance situation, which also clearly shows that this situation only reflects a momentary state. Whether and how the situation on the market will possibly change over time is not decided by this. However, since many influencing factors play a role in reality, the conditions that lead to the constitution of supply and demand constellations change. It is therefore sensible to carry out statically comparative analyses in a further step. This refers to the comparison of two equilibrium situations that can be described by different supply and demand curves. However, how the exact adjustment process towards an equilibrium situation occurs is the task of dynamic analysis, which will be considered in the next step.

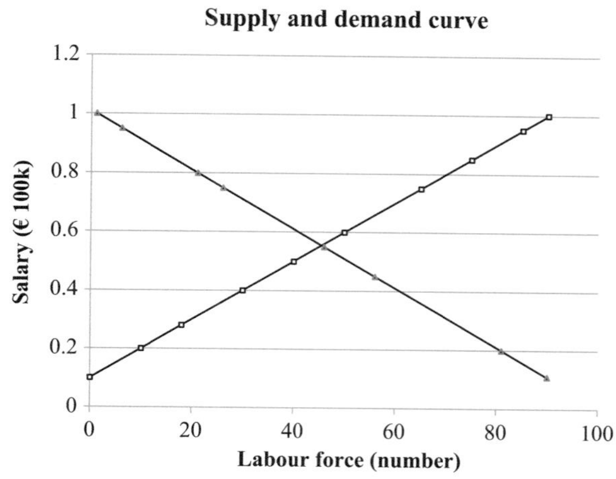

Fig. 3.7 Linear supply and demand curve

3.1.3.3 The Cobweb Model—Dynamisation of a Linear Supply-Demand Model: "Multicopter engineers wanted for a startup"

As an example, the static model considered so far should be dynamised, whereby we could, for example, vary the parameters (a to d). This results in the well-known Cobweb model, which is based here on linear difference equations. It shows the market economic adjustment path of prices and quantities over many periods, i.e. the reactions of market participants, i.e. suppliers and demanders, to market results. Here we consider salaries as prices and the number of workers as quantities.

The supply situation in the above example was reflected by the following general equation: $A = -a + b \cdot P$, with $a, b > 0$, where A should represent the offered quantity (number of job providers) and P the price of work (salary).

To dynamise the model, we introduce a variable t (= time) that is supposed to symbolise the individual periods to be considered. This gives us the following (linear!) supply function, which reflects the workers' ideas about the desired salary over several periods:

$$A(t) = -a + b \cdot P(t-1), \text{ with } a, b > 0 \text{ and the Period } t > 1.$$

Since the suppliers ('Multicopter' engineers) determine their offer in response to price development (salary), there is a certain time delay (time-lag), which can be described as follows: The higher the price (salary) of the past period (t − 1), the higher the offered quantity (number of workers) and vice versa.

The demand function, in turn, is based on the 'law of demand' and generally shows the households' purchase wishes over some time periods as a constant relationship. In the context of a labour market, the function reflects the wishes of employers or their demand for workers at certain salary expectations. The demand function of our previous model was of the form, where N should represent the demanded quantity (number of

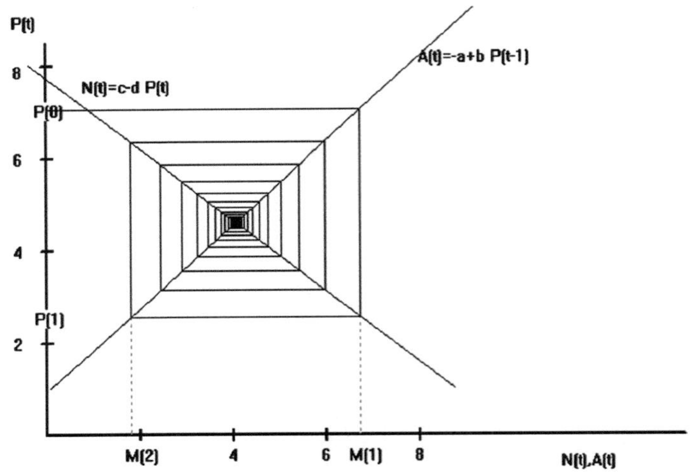

Fig. 3.8 Converging Cobweb Model. *Source* Liening (2012)

demanded employees) and P the price of work (salary). If you dynamise this equation as well, you get:

$$N(t) = c - d \cdot P(t), \text{ with } c, d > 0 \text{ and the Period } t > 1$$

Now to our concrete model:

Example: Continuation "Multicopter Engineers Wanted for a StartUp"

Figure 3.8 shows the well-known Cobweb model based on the two equations above. In this example, the individual parameters of the model are: a = 1, b = 1.1, c = 10.0, d = 1.3, so that the demand and supply equations have the following form:

$$N(t) = 10.0 - 1.3 \cdot P(t),\ A(t) = -1.0 + 1.1 \cdot P(t-1), \text{ with } t > 1.$$

In the case of the supply in period $t = 0$, a price (salary) of $P(0)$ results from the demand curve. In period $t = 1$, due to the high price (salary), M(1) suppliers from the previous period are willing to offer their labour. A surplus supply forms, which is only demanded at a much lower price (salary) of $P(1)$ on the market. In the following period, the suppliers take this price as the basis for their next supply decision. According to their supply parameters, only M(2) workers offer themselves at this low price (salary).

However, the demand for labour is considerably higher from the personnel managers at this low price (salary). So there is an excess demand, which leads to rising prices (salaries).

In principle, one is now back in the initial situation, but the current price $P(2)$ is a little lower than $P(0)$. The cycle starts again, and one can observe how the equilibrium price slowly but steadily settles. ◀

Krafft points out that the Cobweb model is empirically confirmed and price and quantity fluctuations occur especially where there are time-lags between production decisions and actual supply. *Krafft* describes the most famous example of this: the Pig Cycle, where the breeding and supply of or demand for pigs can lead to the described adjustment process (Krafft, 1982, p. 47 f.).

Now, we want to deviate from the usual representation, in which normally the supply function and the demand function are graphically depicted and the change in prices as well as the associated changes in the supply of and demand for 'goods' are illustrated.

Instead, only the price function should be considered here and the quantity process should be ignored. In fact, it doesn't matter whether the supply and demand quantity are considered at a certain price or whether two different prices are considered for a certain quantity. It is therefore sufficient if A and N are equated and the price mechanism is studied:

$$A(t) = N(t)$$

This applies to the price function:

$$P(t+1) = \frac{a+c}{d} - \frac{b}{d} \cdot P(t), \text{ with a, b, c, d} > 0, \text{ t} > 1$$

With slight mathematical transformations, we get:

$$P(t) = \lambda + \gamma, \text{ with}$$
$$\lambda = \left(P(0) + P^G\right) \cdot \left(-\frac{b}{d}\right)^t \text{ and } \gamma = \mathrm{P}^G$$

where P^G is the equilibrium price, with: $P^G = \frac{a+c}{b+d}$.

Only the left term λ depends on t and can therefore vary with changes in t.

Since by definition $b > 0$, $d > 0$, the quotient is always positive. Let's consider three possible cases:

First: Let $\frac{b}{d} < 1$, then the term λ becomes smaller with increasing t and the system obviously converges towards λ, the equilibrium price. Figure 3.9 illustrates this relationship.

In Fig. 3.9 you can see the price function (or the salary function), which runs from top left to bottom right. The slope is negative, as by definition: $-\frac{b}{d} < 0$. Furthermore, in this diagram, the 45° line, the diagonal, is drawn. The simulation starts with an arbitrary price $P(0)$. As in the traditional scheme, a new, but higher price $P(1)$ is also obtained here. In order for this to become the starting value for the new calculation again, it is plotted on the diagonal. From $P(1)$ then follows $P(2)$. This value is lower than $P(1)$, but higher than $P(0)$. $P(2)$ is again used as the starting value for the calculation of $P(3)$ and is therefore plotted on the diagonal again, etc. You can see that the prices develop exactly as they were represented in the traditional scheme.

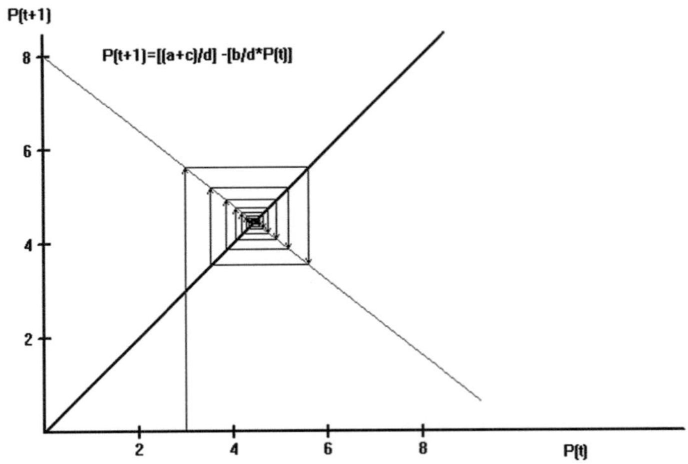

Fig. 3.9 Convergent price model. *Source* Liening (2012)

Second: Now let $\frac{b}{d} = 1$, this leads to the fact that there is no approach to a single equilibrium price. You get a harmonic pendulum movement that swings back and forth between two equilibria, as Fig. 3.10 illustrates.

Thirdly: The last case is fulfilled for $\frac{b}{d} < 1$. So if the slope of the price function (in absolute terms) is greater than that of the diagonal, then λ grows with increasing t and there is no compensation.

This is therefore a diverging system, as illustrated in Fig. 3.11.

The above explanation given for the example of the price function can be generalised to all difference equations and all linear differential equations. It can be concluded that in such modeled economic systems, a regular, recurring, and periodic behaviour is present.

In order to describe irregularities using linear equations, a system must be 'disturbed' exogenously, i.e., from the outside. None of the known patterns of dynamic-linear systems can form such behaviour on their own (Loistl & Betz, 1993, p. 2). Because if you look at linear models, there are only three ways a system can develop: A linear dynamic system can

- converge towards a fixed point
- exhibit a cyclical movement, i.e., 'circle' at the same distance around a fixed point and thus have two accumulation points

and

- diverge, i.e., move away from a fixed point (Liening, 1998, p. 28 ff.).

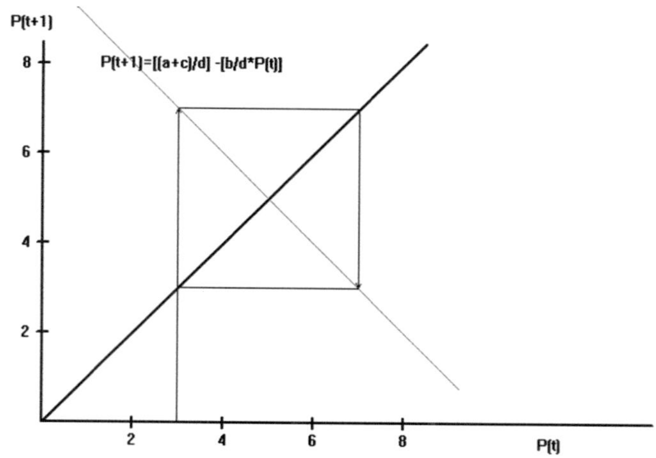

Fig. 3.10 Cyclic price model. *Source* Liening (2012)

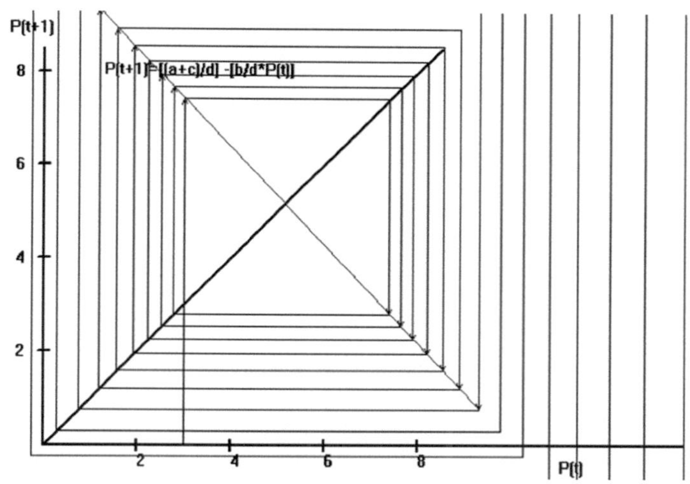

Fig. 3.11 Divergent price model. *Source* Liening (2012)

However, this makes it clear that in linear systems, in principle, nothing unpredictable, new, or surprising is possible. The economic events remain, historically considered, timeless. *Röpke* emphasises this fact when he says:

> The closed models of equilibrium economics can therefore—even if they are 'dynamised'—have no explanatory relevance beyond deterministically mechanical processes (Röpke, 1977, p. 21).

3.1.3.4 Background Information: Mathematical Considerations on a Linear Cobweb Model

The market supply describes the relationship between price and the quantity of a good offered. Normally, there is a positive correlation, which can be described by the following supply function:

$$S(t) = -a + b \cdot P(t-1), \text{ with } a, b > 0 \tag{3.1}$$

The demand function, which assumes a negative correlation between price and the quantity of a good demanded, looks as follows:

$$D(t) = c - d \cdot P(t), \text{ with } c, d > 0 \tag{3.2}$$

To consider the price mechanism, one sets:

$$S(t) = D(t)$$

For $S(t)$ and $D(t)$ we now substitute the equations and let it be without loss of generality $t := t - 1$. This gives us:

$$-a + b \cdot P(t) = c - d \cdot P(t+1)$$

If we solve the equation for $P(t+1)$, we get:

$$P(t+1) = \frac{a+c}{d} - \frac{b}{d} \cdot P(t) \tag{3.3}$$

When equilibrium is established, the price of the current period is equal to that of the next. Therefore, $P(t+1) = P(t)$ must apply. That is, for the equilibrium price P^* obviously applies:

$$P^*(t) = \frac{a+c}{b+d}$$

How can the price of any period t be determined from a given initial price? From Eq. 3.3 it can be seen that the price of the next period directly depends on that of the past. This makes it clear that knowing the price of the 1st period allows the price of the 2nd period to be determined. If you now know the price of the 2nd period, the price of the 3rd period can also be calculated, etc. That is, this is a so-called recursive model. To illustrate the recursive development more simply, a substitution is performed:

$$A = -\frac{b}{d} \text{ and } B = \frac{a+c}{d}$$

With this, Eq. 3.3 now has the following form:

$$P(t+1) = A \cdot P(t) + B$$

Starting from $P(0)$ we can now, for example, calculate $P(2)$:

$$P(2) = A \cdot P(1) + B$$

If we now also replace $P(1)$, we get:

$$P(2) = A(A(P(0) + B)) + B = A^2P(0) + AB + B = A^2P(0) + B(1 + A)$$

For $P(3)$ the following applies:

$$P(3) = P(0)A^3 + B(1 + A + A^2)$$

or generally formulated:

$$P(t) = P(0)A^t + B(1 + A^2 + A^3 + A^4 + \cdots + A^{t-1}) = P(0)A^t + B\sum_{n=0}^{t-1} A^n$$

Excursion: Sum formula for geometric series
Claim:

$$\text{For all } x \neq 1 \text{ applies: } \sum_{\mathrm{n}=0}^{\mathrm{t}} x^n = \frac{1 - x^{t+1}}{1 - x}$$

Proof (by complete induction):

1. Induction start: $t = 0$

$$\sum_{\mathrm{n}=0}^{0} x^n = 1 = \frac{1 - x^{0+1}}{1 - x}$$

2. Induction step: $t \to t + 1$
   Assumption:
   Let $\sum_{n=0}^{t} x^n = \frac{1-x^{t+1}}{1-x}$ true for an arbitrary but fixed t.
   To prove:

$$\sum_{\mathrm{n}=0}^{\mathrm{t}+1} x^n = \sum_{\mathrm{n}=0}^{\mathrm{t}} x^n + x^{t+1} = \frac{1 - x^{t+1}}{1 - x} + x^{t+1}$$

$$= \frac{1 - x^{t+1} + (x^{t+1} - x^{(t+1)+1})}{1 - x} = \frac{1 - x^{(t+1)+1}}{1 - x}$$

   Then it follows: $\sum_{n=0}^{t+1} x^n = \frac{1-x^{t+2}}{1-x}$

   q. e. d.[25]

[25] To show that our proof is actually complete and the following sentences have nothing to do with the line of argument, we write, for example, q. e. d. This abbreviation, which goes back to *Euclid*, stands for "quod erat demonstrandum", and thus means '**w**hat **w**as **t**o **b**e **p**roven'. Therefore, at the end of a successful proof, one sometimes also writes w. t. b. p.

Following the sum formula for geometric series, we now get[26]:

$$P(t) = P(0)A^t + B\frac{1 - A^t}{1 - A}$$

If we now substitute A and B back with the original values, we get:

$$P(t) = P(0)\left(-\frac{b}{d}\right)^t + \left(\frac{a + c}{d}\right)\frac{1 - \left(-\frac{b}{d}\right)^t}{1 + \frac{b}{d}}$$

This results in after simple transformation:

$$P(t) = P(0)\left(-\frac{b}{d}\right)^t + \left(1 - \left(-\frac{b}{d}\right)^t\right)\frac{a + c}{b + d}$$

And further:

$$P(t) = \left(P(0) - \frac{a + c}{b + d}\right)\left(-\frac{b}{d}\right)^t + \frac{a + c}{b + d}$$

As we have already determined, the equilibrium price is:

$$P^* = \frac{a + c}{b + d}$$

From this[27] follows: $P(t) = (P(0) - P^*) \cdot \left(-\frac{b}{d}\right)^t + P^*$

Now set: $\alpha = (P(0) - P^*) \cdot \left(-\frac{b}{d}\right)^t$ and $\beta = P^*$

Then it follows: $P(t) = \alpha + \beta$

Only the left term α depends on t and can therefore vary with changes in t.

Since by definition b, d > 0, the quotient is always positive. If first

$$\frac{b}{d} < 1,$$

then the term α becomes smaller as t increases and the system obviously converges towards β, the equilibrium price. It follows:

$$\lim_{t\to\infty} P(t) = \lim_{t\to\infty}\left((P(0) - P^*) \cdot \left(-\frac{b}{d}\right)^t + P^*\right) = P^*$$

If, on the other hand, secondly

---

[26] Note: Since $A = -\frac{b}{d}$ and $b, d > 0$. Thus, $A \neq 1$ applies and the formula can be used.

[27] *Lentz* comes to the same conclusion in a comparable example. However, he cannot convincingly derive the result. Instead, he refers to a general formula, which he does not explain further, but merely asserts. See Lentz (1993, p. 91).

$$\frac{b}{d} = 1,$$

then there is no approach to the equilibrium price, i.e. the sequence also diverges. However, a harmonic pendulum motion is obtained. The sign is positive when t is even, and negative when t is odd. There are two accumulation points:[28]

$$+(P(0) - P^*) + P^* = P(0)$$

and

$$-(P(0) - P^*) + P^* = 2 \cdot P^* - P(0)$$

If thirdly

$$\frac{b}{d} > 1,$$

then α grows with increasing t, the system diverges and there is no balance. The sequence grows alternately beyond all limits.

3.1.3.5 Philosophical Consideration of the Analogy Formation between Classical Mechanics and Economics—The Danger of Knowledge in the Essential Spell of Technology

As already noted, only three types of motion sequences can be simulated using a linear, discrete, and dynamic difference equation.

And yet, numerous economists still adhere to neoclassical, mechanistic ways of thinking, without being able to provide answers to the numerous challenges in our complex economic world characterised by numerous crises and opportunities.

Often, old ideas even prevent the emergence of new thoughts. We find this assumption already in *Keynes,* who points out in the preface of his fundamental work 'The general theory of employment, interest, and money' how difficult it often is to free oneself from old ideas that have permeated every corner of our minds and prevent the way to new ways of thinking. And so he says:

> The difficulty lies, not in the new ideas, but in escaping from the old ones, which ramify, for those brought up as most of us have been, into every corner of our minds (Keynes, 1936, p. xii).

If one transfers *Keynes'* remarks to the current situation of economics, one must state that it is largely still under the influence of the mechanistic 'mainstream' shown, which hinders the emergence or rather the unfolding of new ideas.[29] As early as 1977, *Röpke*

[28] Although the convergence or divergence of the sequences is intuitively understandable, the interested reader is referred to the (comparable) simple proofs in: Forster (2004, p. 27 ff.).

[29] See also the various essays by leading economists that explain this circumstance, in: Hanusch and Recktenwald (1992).

stated that there were "clear signs of widespread dissatisfaction with the current state of national economics" (Röpke, 1977, p. 1). He referred this opinion to the—as he formulated it—"so-called neoclassical economics perceived as 'dominant'" (Röpke, 1977, p. 1). The equilibrium-analytical approaches of this economic direction reveal from his perspective in many respects a 'nomological helplessness'. *Röpke* notes:

> If one strives for competing considerations, one is astonished to find that outside the neoclassical paradigm [...] approaches beyond an equilibrium-mechanical grasp of economic reality are available. However, these are not interpretable within the prevailing doctrine and they have not been further developed since then (Röpke, 1977, p. 1).

Although more than thirty years have passed since this writing, these words have only partially lost their relevance. The neoclassical worldview still has a lasting influence on the thinking of numerous economists. Economic processes are still represented and explained in very specific, namely linear or lineal-causal relationships. The term *lineal* is deliberately used here to add an even more general principle to linearity.

Example: Lineality—Who is to blame for the downfall of the kingdom?

In lineal systems, for example, the culprit is quickly identified, as the following lineal causal chain—taken from an old folk wisdom—shows:

The blacksmith forgot to put a nail in the hoof of the horse when attaching a new horseshoe. Because a nail was missing, the horseshoe was lost. Because the horseshoe was missing, the horse was lost. Because a horse was missing, an important rider was lost. Because an important rider was missing, a battle was lost. Because a battle was lost, the kingdom was lost. And all this because a nail was missing on the horseshoe. So, the blacksmith was clearly to blame for the downfall of the kingdom.[30] ◄

Strunk describes his illustration (see Fig. 3.12) of the lineal relationships as follows.

> An event A is followed by an event B and so on. The event chain has a lineal structure, so it does not take into account feedback processes. The system structure is similar to the gear mechanism of a clock (Strunk, 2009, p. 155).

On the other hand, economic reality has changed. *Weyer* mentions, for example, two aspects that could be supplemented arbitrarily:

[30] The example shows the naivety inherent in lineal chains. In reality, we will find circular causal chains, especially and unfortunately also in conflicts, so the question of who is to blame is often difficult to answer. And who is to blame then? If A follows B and B follows A, this cannot be seen on the chain. And if the conflict lasts a very long time, no one knows anymore who really started, A or B? However, there is also a solution here: A political scientist would probably say: The solution is that the more powerful one in this causal cycle defines who is to blame, i.e., the one who wins the war, who dominates the conflict, etc.

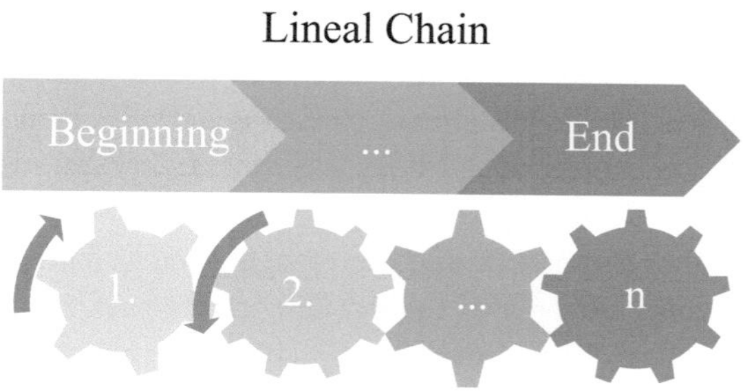

Fig. 3.12 Lineal cause-effect chain

- "the increasing networking of a globalised economy, which is reflected in the increased demands on supply chain management, which is expected to integrate heterogeneous actors, processes and structures,
- the interdependence of financial markets, where events in one area can have avalanche-like consequences in other areas, thus strengthening the perception that despite increased scope for action by the actors, control of the overall situation is hardly possible" (Weyer, 2009, p. 3).

At this point, we want to introduce a philosophical consideration associated with the name Martin *Heidegger*, who in his memorable essay "The Question Concerning Technology" highlights the dangers of the mechanistic worldview (Heidegger, 1962). In our context, one could say that for *Heidegger*, mechanistic thinking, *Newtonian* mechanics, indeed, technology as a whole, is closely related to the concept of 'unconcealment'. He defines unconcealment as a bringing forth of what is hidden, towards the unconcealed.

This makes *Newtonian* mechanics a "mode of 'aletheuein', unconcealment" (Heidegger, 1962, p. 12), as one can extract coal from the ground with its help. The once earth-resting, hidden from humans coal comes forth through unconcealment and becomes visible. The ground unconceals, reveals itself through the application of mechanistic thinking as a coal field.

But this unconcealment is for the philosopher much more than just a challenging in our current understanding. It prevails in every kind of mechanistic application, ultimately, one could add, also in the analogy formation to economics. And even more: For *Heidegger*, the bringing forth of the hidden towards the unconcealed means that one recognises whatever one unconceals, that the reality of what is unconcealed comes to light. The appearance of the real is the truth.

Thus, the realm of unconcealment is the realm of knowledge, the realm of truth. And thus, mechanics as a mode of unconcealment is far more than just something instrumental, far more than just a means, because "technology resides in the realm (...), where truth happens" (Heidegger, 1962, p. 13), where for *Heidegger* truth is the concealing and unconcealing being as the source of all beings.

If one follows *Heidegger's* thoughts, then *Newtonian* mechanics is ultimately a way of being, a possibility of bringing truth to light, a possibility of understanding the world.

This possibility has, according to *Heidegger*, through its challenging character, namely to view everything only in terms of technical availability, developed into the dominant mode of unconcealment, beside which all other possibilities are suppressed. The diversity in all perceived objects is lost. Everything is only viewed as it fits into the framework of modern technology.

For example, a tree is no longer seen as a tree in itself with its many properties and its beauty, but only as timber. Only one aspect, namely that of the timber, still plays a role. Everything becomes 'stock'[31], as *Heidegger* says.

Even man, he suspects, becomes part of the stock. Man himself becomes a disposable mass in the age of modern technology. "The circulating talk of human material, of patient material in a clinic speaks for this" (Heidegger, 1962, p. 17). Man is no longer viewed as a whole through a mechanistic view, but only under a partial aspect. This view culminates in statements like the following by *Skinner,* which catapults our representations of the mechanical man as an artifact of the late Middle Ages into modern times[32]:

> Man **is** a machine, albeit an incredibly complex one (Skinner, 1974, p. 244).

Goethe, who doubted *Newton's* ideas, particularly in the field of optics, accuses *Newton* of separating natural research from humans, which would ultimately lead to a disastrous self-sufficiency of technology.[33] Polemically, *Goethe* writes:

> This is the so-called experimentum crucis, where the researcher tortures nature to force it to confess what he had already determined. But nature is like a steadfast and noble person who remains true even under all torments. If the protocol says otherwise, the inquisitor has misheard, the scribe has written down incorrectly (Goethe, 1810, p. 423).

Elsewhere, *Goethe* writes accusingly:[34]

> The phenomena must once and for all be brought out of the gloomy empirical-mechanical-dogmatic torture chamber before the jury of common sense (Goethe, 2014, p. 48).

If one follows *Heidegger's* line of argument, technology, as he would say, 'the essence of being', reduces the possibilities of access to truth. Anyone who perceives the world through mechanistic views only sees a section of the whole and therefore gains a false impression. This impression is not only limited to humans, but to any thing-world.

---

[31] Even the concept of stock goes beyond the ordinary understanding of this word in *Heidegger's* definition. For him, everything that comes into 'unconcealment' through modern technology, in order to then again "be available for further ordering"—as it is called in *Heidegger's* language—belongs to the stock (Heidegger, 1962).

[32] See Sect. 3.1.1.1 for the discussion of the mechanical man.

[33] The resulting problems are very eloquently expressed in *Heidegger's* philosophy, as we will see in more detail later. See Heidegger (1962) for this.

[34] An interesting evaluation of *Goethe's* dispute with *Newton* can be found in ZEIT: Thadden (2010).

Economics, on the one hand, deals with humans and their behaviour in the world and, on the other hand, applies the mechanistic thought not only to the image of humans, but also to any other object—think of our simple Cobweb model—of economic perspectives. If we transfer *Heidegger's* philosophical considerations to this, it inevitably leads to the conclusion: The formalisation of *Newtonian* concepts and the mechanistic approaches in the context of economics reduces it to a mechanistic-linear, at least a mechanistic-lineal perspective, and thus prevents a comprehensive, complex understanding of the world.

3.2 The Collapse of the Laplacian Worldview

As became clear in the previous chapter, there was a not insignificant influence of classical mechanics on economics, which first found concrete formalisation in neoclassical economics. Many of the economic approaches are based either on comparative statics—which allows the comparison of equilibrium situations, e.g., based on different constellations of demand and supply curves—or often on lineal-dynamic systems, which allow a processual analysis.

3.2.1 First Doubts…

However, the mechanistic worldview began to falter at the end of the nineteenth and the beginning of the twentieth centuries. The Swedish King *Oskar II* had offered a prize of 2500 crowns in 1887 to answer the question of whether the solar system was stable; a question that had been asked repeatedly before, but could not be precisely answered even by mathematicians like *Lagrange* or *Poisson*. Thus, *Königsberger* writes:

> Lagrange and Laplace gave apparent proofs for stability; in fact, they only dealt with approximate problems (Königsberger, 2004, p. 163).

The problem with *Newtonian* mechanics or specifically the *Keplerian* laws is that while they provide exact calculations, these only apply to two bodies, for example, describing the relationship between the Sun and the Earth; the fact that the other planets attract each other and influence their orbits could not be exactly taken into account. The French mathematician Henri *Poincaré* now took on this challenge and confronted the physical worldview that had been valid until then with completely new insights, which essentially boil down to the fact that it is not possible to calculate the orbits of three or more interrelated bodies using *Newtonian* equations. The Sun attracts the Earth; however, the Earth's orbit is influenced, for example, by Saturn, and Saturn's orbit around the Sun is also influenced, for example, by the Earth. And so there are infinitely many feedback loops that make it impossible to solve the so-called three-body problem using *Newtonian* differential equations. Poincaré could not solve the three-body problem either, but he was the first to prove that there is no exact solution (Chen, 2011, p. 23).

The only way out, after a solution using (infinite) power series diverged, was to resolve into difference equations and then find an approximate solution. The crucial problem that arose was that these equations, even with only minor changes in the initial conditions, sometimes produced very irregular, chaotic trajectories. *Poincaré* wrote:

> One is appalled by the complexity of the figure of the trajectories, which I do not even attempt to sketch (quoted n. Leiber, 1996, p. 383).

In relation to the solar system, this means that when considering more than two planets, even minimal deviations in the initial conditions could destabilise a previously completely stable system through completely eccentric orbits that question the stability of the solar system.[35] In the course of his considerations, *Poincaré* showed that systems that have been stable for a long time can become unstable even without external influences. This introduced the concept of disorder, of chaos, triggered by an arbitrarily weak disturbance. To illustrate the problem associated with *Poincaré's* approach, let's consider two examples:

Example: Three-body problem

Svante Elis *Strömgren* (1870–1947) calculated a solution to the three-body problem using the method proposed by *Poincaré* 35 years after *Poincaré's* work: Allegedly, 56 employees worked under his direction for fifteen years (Kriz, 1998, p. 17). Consequently, *Kriz* points out: "It will now probably be understandable why further calculations for similar—or even more real and thus even more networked—development processes were not to be expected before the dawn of the computer age." (Kriz, 1998, p. 17). ◀

This example alone shows that in principle, high-performance computers are required to solve such tasks. However, this presents another problem: To calculate approximate solutions with the necessary accuracy, for example, for weather forecasting, even the fastest conceivable computers would take so much time that the weather would develop faster than the forecast (Kinnebrock, 2002, p. 118).

Example: Idealised billiards game

James P. *Crutchfield* (*1955) made the following thought experiment with idealised billiard balls and an idealised (i.e., perfect) player: "In an idealised game of billiards, the balls are supposed to roll across the table without loss of energy and collide. With a single stroke, the player sends the balls into a longer sequence of collisions; he wants to estimate the effect of his stroke. For what period could a player with perfect

[35] This is not the place to explain all the details of *Poincaré's* results. For the interested reader, therefore, reference is made to: Poincaré (1899).

control over the stroke predict the path of the cue ball?" The calculations of *Crutchfield* and his team reveal something astonishing: "If only one effect is neglected, whose strength corresponds to the gravitational attraction of an electron at the edge of the Milky Way, the prediction would already be wrong after one minute." (Crutchfield et al., 1987, p. 11). ◀

Until then, chaos had been considered a kind of infection that could afflict a system from the outside. But now it was shown that a closed system, which could be described with a few mathematical equations, could exhibit unpredictable, chaotic behaviour (Briggs & Peat, 1993, p. 56). This seemed to call determinism into question. Seemingly so, because *Poincaré* reconciles chance and determinism through long-term unpredictability. He writes:

> A very small cause, which remains unnoticed by us, produces a considerable effect (…), and then we say that this effect depends on chance (Poincaré, 1914, p. 56).

But hardly any scientist at that time suspected the significance of his research results, because many economists either ignored his results or did not know them at all.[36] Despite some further important findings, such as those by *Birkhoff* (USA)[37] in the twenties and thirties or those by *Cartwright*and *Littlewood* (UK)[38] at the end of the thirties,

---

[36] Carl *Chiarella* notes that even most early authors on dynamic, time-dependent business cycle theory did not know the work of *Poincaré*. See Chiarella (1992, p. 75).

[37] The American mathematician John David *Birkhoff* already proved in 1913 a question posed by *Poincaré* that remained unsolved in the context of the three-body problem of celestial mechanics. In the field of aesthetics, *Birkhoff* was also able to generate interesting insights that clearly show that complexity and chaos reduce the aesthetic measure, while order increases it (Birkhoff, 1931; Ebeling & Schweitzer, 2002).

[38] Mary *Cartwright* and her doctoral advisor John *Littlewood* succeeded in 1938 in showing that the "Van der Pol equation" named after the head of the Philips Research Laboratory Balthasar *van der Pol* (Van der Pol, 1927) can exhibit chaotic solutions as soon as the system is confronted with the smallest disturbances. This did not solve the problem that non-linear distortions occur in radios or their amplifiers under certain settings, which lead to unpleasant auditory perceptions, but it explained the cause. The crucial component of an amplifier at that time was a vacuum tube with three electrodes (triode), as can still be found today in audiophile tube amplifiers. The behaviour of the current in a circuit containing this triode can be described by the Van der Pol equation. The Royal Air Force was confronted with the associated problem during the Second World War, as it was unable to operate radar systems above a certain power limit, as the amplifiers equipped with triodes exhibited unpredictable behaviour. Around 1942, *Cartwright* and *Littlewood* were able to show that the Van der Pol equation can exhibit exactly this behaviour with a sinusoidal input signal. If the power is low, the output signal has the same period as the input signal. If this is amplified, the output signal doubles. With further power increase, it quadruples etc., until the signal becomes aperiodic, i.e. chaotic, from a certain power level (Cartwright, 1945; Letellier, 2014, p. 24).

beginning of the forties of the twentieth century, who provided mathematical work in the field of dynamic systems, *Poincaré's* insight rested for many decades.[39]

3.2.2 The Weather Forecast and the Butterfly Effect

In the early sixties, the meteorologist Edward *Lorenz* made an interesting discovery, which can be considered a practical consequence of *Poincaré's* findings:[40]

To predict the weather, measurements are taken at numerous stations, for example, the temperature, wind speed, and humidity. *Lorenz* used his computer to solve non-linear equations in analogy to model convection currents within a layer of viscous fluid heated from below. The convection currents in the experimental setup show great similarities to the convection currents in the atmosphere, i.e., to the air currents caused by temperature differences in the atmosphere.

Previously, he had reduced the differential equations, consisting of complex *Fourier* equations etc., for the heat conduction processes of *Saltzman* (Saltzman, 1962) to three simple equations, which he now solved numerically:

$$\frac{\delta X}{\delta t} = -\sigma \cdot X + \sigma \cdot Y, \ \frac{\delta Y}{\delta t} = -X \cdot Z + r \cdot X - Y, \ \frac{\delta Z}{\delta t} = X \cdot Y - b \cdot Z$$

(Lorenz, 1963, p. 135), where *X*(*t*) represents the flow velocity within one of the hexagonal convection cells[41], that form, *Y*(*t*) the temperature difference between rising and falling current and *Z*(*t*) the deviation of the change in temperature depending on the height. The parameters $\sigma, r, b \in \mathbb{R}^+$ are also clearly defined. The values set by *Lorenz* were, following *Saltzman*, for $\sigma = 10$ und für $b = \frac{8}{3}$ (Lorenz, 1963, p. 136). Furthermore, he chose "the slightly supercritical value $r = 28$" (Lorenz, 1963, p. 136). So here we have a deterministic system in which chance plays no role. This is, of course, only an analogy to the atmosphere ("whether analogues" Lorenz, 1963, p. 141). *Peitgen* et al. write about this:

---

[39] See, for example, Medio (1992, p. 7).

[40] In addition to Edward *Lorenz*, scientists such as Andrei Nikolaievitsch *Kolmogorov* with his colleagues and Stephen *Smale* should also be mentioned, who also successfully researched in the field of non-linear dynamics in the sixties or already in the fifties. The interested reader is referred to, for example: Kolmogorov (1958). Or perhaps: Smale (1967).

[41] Convection means the carrying along by a current. Convection cells represent the honeycomb-like cloud structures sometimes visible in practice on satellite images, updraft regions, which show up, for example, as cumulus clouds. Examples of convection cells are "cylindrical structures and so-called *Bénard cells,* whose structure from above resembles honeycombs. In these hexagonal cells, warmed fluid rises in the middle, cools down further up and sinks back down at the edge of the cells" (Peitgen et al., 1992, p. 264). The *Lorenz* system is more similar to the cylindrical type of motion (Peitgen et al., 1992, p. 264).

> However, we are not far from the truth. The Lorenz model is indeed a model for thermal convection, which not only describes the movement of viscous fluids, but also the distribution of heat, the driving force of thermal convection (Peitgen et al., 1992, p. 264).

To check the result of the final phase in one of his calculations, *Lorenz* had the computer perform the calculations again from a certain intermediate step; ultimately, it was about saving time.

However, the result after an hour was a completely different "weather situation" than before.

The analysis revealed that it was not, as one might have suspected, a computer or computer programme error. The cause lay elsewhere: The computer calculated with 6 decimal places after the comma, but only output three. Therefore, the input data for the second calculation were based on the values with the three output decimal places. However, the re-entered values differed minimally from the first calculation, as they did not take into account the digits from the fourth place onwards. And so the input values deviated minimally from the first calculation run. For example, the temperature only deviated by $\frac{5}{10.000}^{\circ}$ from the original temperature. That is, the initial conditions for the calculation from the intermediate step were only minimally different in the test calculation, but the result differed fundamentally from the first result! *Lorenz* wrote about this:

> I immediately concluded that it would be impossible to make long-term and detailed weather forecasts if the real equations governing the atmosphere behaved exactly like this model (*Lorenz* quoted n. Kinnebrock, 2002, p. 117).

The following Fig. 3.13 shows the *Lorenz* system, in which the parameters used lead to the following path or trajectory, which is implemented here as a simulation for a time period *t*. The resulting structure, later more precisely referred to as attractor, visually resembles the two wings of a butterfly.

The current system state can indeed linger in a circle on one of the two wings for a while during the simulation. However, when the path reaches the threshold to the other wing, minimal differences in the initial situation can cause the path to shift to the other wing, or not.

Thus, *Lorenz* found that non-linear dynamic systems like the weather can be incredibly sensitive to very minimal changes and can thus become unstable. This confirmed *Poincaré's* assumptions. *Lorenz* stated:

> Our principal results concern the instability of nonperiodic solutions (Lorenz, 1963, p. 140).

This insight, which has become known as the '*butterfly effect*', is often formulated as follows:

> It is said that the flap of a butterfly's wings in Hong Kong could trigger a tornado in New York.

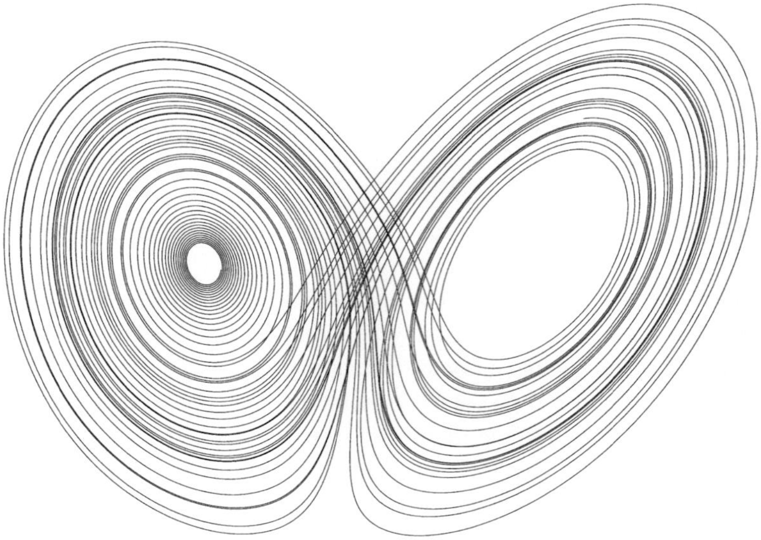

Fig. 3.13 The Lorenz Attractor

And indeed: Since the Earth's atmosphere, in which convections play an important role, behaves far more complicated than the three equations of *Lorenz* could even suggest, it is obvious that a long-term weather forecast is only possible to a limited extent. It remains open what "long-term" means. *Lorenz* was still very cautious about this:

> …conceivably it could be a few days or a few centuries (Lorenz, 1963, p. 145).

Georg Christoph *Lichtenberg* (1742–1799) had already described a similar effect two hundred years ago:

> If I had not written this book, today over 1000 years in the evening between 6 and 7 o'clock in many a city in Germany, completely different things would have been talked about than will actually be talked about. If I had thrown a cherry stone into the sea at Vardöhus, the drop of seawater that wipes Myn Heer's nose at the Cape would not have sat exactly in the same place. (Lichtenberg, 1998, p. 239).

The 'butterfly effect' should not be confused with the statement: "Small causes have big effects." This would only be a kind of compound interest effect, which is based on an enormous self-reinforcement and which we want to explain more precisely as a 'positive feedback process' later on.

Lorenz's studies make it clear that the lack of predictability in dynamic systems is not due to the fact that not all details are known. Even the knowledge of so many details does not necessarily allow for an accurate prediction in dynamic systems, especially since—metaphorically speaking—the butterfly can never know what its wing beat in

Hong Kong will later cause in New York. Nor would any computer, no matter how powerful, be able to calculate when the butterfly's wing beat would prevent the hurricane in New York and where exactly it would have to move its wings with which frequency.

If this is true, then the *Laplace's* Demon, that fictional figure who can predict the future in principle if it only knows all initial conditions exactly, is an absurd figure and the mechanistic worldview must be denied or at least relativised.

The loss of the *Laplace's Demon* has an interesting side effect here, as it will free some from Fatalism ("everything is predetermined, what can I do") and others from megalomania ("everything is determined and calculable and thus I can control everything"), depending on how the respective character is pronounced. However, we also all know those Hysteresis effects, which lead to the fact that even with knowledge of such relationships, no changes in behaviour will occur.

3.3 A Paradigm Shift is Announced—Characteristics of the New Approach

> *The true journey of discovery is not about*
> *looking for new landscapes,*
> *but about seeing with new eyes.*
> (Marcel Proust)

3.3.1 Paradigm Shift in Economics

Schefold points out that new economic ideas often turn out to be old ones that recur periodically:

> Keynesianism contains a mercantilist interest theory, the monetary nominalism of antiquity returns in this century—not for the first time—in the rejection of metallism (Schefold, 1992, p. 360).

For *Schmalensee* too, most scientists work on existing theories and methods, develop them further and apply them.

> "Only rarely," writes *Schmalensee,* "are there abrupt changes when seemingly insoluble anomalies or other problems are overcome by 'scientific revolutions'. Such revolutions are accompanied by a development that Thomas Kuhn has called a 'paradigm shift',—fundamental changes in worldview that radically reorganise both the entire discipline and its research agenda" (Schmalensee, 1992, p. 361 f.).

Such paradigm shifts have occurred more frequently in the history of economics. One thinks here of the methodological triumph of mathematical analysis or the subjective value theory of the neoclassicists, which radically changed the objective perspective.

Economists today, like *Schmalensee* twenty years ago, lament that "much of today's economic research is merely concerned with revising and refining concepts, such as rational behaviour and competitive markets, that were already familiar to *Marshall* or even *Smith*." (Schmalensee, 1992, p. 362)

The analogy between the *Newtonian Mechanics* and the (classical) economics and the even further integration of the mechanistic model by the neoclassicists has significantly shaped many areas of economics and is reflected in the static, static-comparative or linear-dynamic model considerations, not only of the neoclassicists. It has also prepared the ground for the economic approaches running counter to the neoclassicists: For example, the Keynesian, mechanistic total model suggests that the state can positively influence the economic process of an entire national economy through countercyclical fiscal policy and global control. However, the stagflation problems in the nineteen seventies already showed that these mechanistic concepts do not work or, if they do, only in the short term. The failure of the mechanistic control approach is even more drastic in the former Eastern Bloc countries, whose centrally controlled economic systems collapsed in the nineties of the twentieth century. The theoretically justified collapse of the *Laplace's* worldview and the empirical findings in economics therefore also question the mathematical-mechanistic ways of thinking in economics.

The shift in perspective depends on how quickly economic development occurs in highly industrialised countries, thereby favouring constant change. Static theories based on linear resp. lineal systems are a good approximation for an economy with a constant structure. However, they cannot explain evolutionary, non-linear dynamic phenomena.[42]

Some economists therefore advocate a departure from mathematics in economics.[43] However, this is neither necessary nor sensible[44], because:

> But where danger grows, the saving power also grows (Hölderlin, 2001, Patoms 1st verse),

writes the poet *Hölderlin,* and so it is precisely the mathematically influenced 'complexity sciences' that initiate a rethink in economics.[45]

---

[42] See, for example, the explanations by Lentz (1993, p. 31).

[43] For example, *von Hayek* developed a theory of complex phenomena entirely without recourse to mathematical concepts. See Hayek (1996, p. 281 ff.).

[44] Who would want to deny that scientifically valid explanations could do without precise mathematical empirical and model-theoretical analysis methods.

[45] Static modeling goes back to *Marshall* as a supply-demand scheme. It shows that there is a tendency towards equilibrium in a functioning competition. In static comparative considerations, for example, changes in demand or supply would be realised by shifting the curves in the graphical representation.

Initial indications of a paradigm shift emerge from the now numerous publications that present a conscious departure from traditional economic models towards a 'Complexonomics'.

In business administration, for example, deterministic, market-oriented growth models are designed to explain irregular corporate developments. In the theory of corporate development, for example, there are non-mechanistic approaches to explain why many processes are not predictable in the long term. From the organisational and process structure in companies, through personnel development, marketing, knowledge management, to strategic management, and especially 'change management' and the broad field of entrepreneurship, the new concepts are found.[46]

For example, recent works even in a rather 'soft' discipline such as personnel development, and especially in career research, show a departure from traditional linear-mechanistic views with numerous new empirical findings due to innovative empirical methods beyond traditional statistical procedures (Strunk, 2009).

Since startups or young growth companies in particular are confronted with rapid change and dynamism and have to plan their business activities with chaos, uncertainty, instability, non-linearity and imbalance, the consideration of complexity science findings is increasingly important for entrepreneurship research. One area is the exploration of entrepreneurship -characteristic order-creation processes (McKelvey, 2004).

Interesting research that advocates a departure from the mechanistic model can also be found in economics, for example in the field of business cycle and growth models, especially in endogenous growth theory, consumption choice models and overlapping generations models. Other economic topics that indicate a paradigm shift include studies and model formations in areas dealing with exchange rate fluctuations, stock price trends, gross national product developments and associated time series analyses.[47]

3.3.2 Describing the World with Systems and Models—What is a System, What is a Model?

3.3.2.1 Historical

The terms 'system' and 'model' have often and rather casually been used in the previous considerations. So far, a closer specification of these terms was not necessary. However,

---

[46] See, for example, in relation to organisational and process structures Warnecke (1996), in relation to marketing Gerken (1994), for knowledge management see, for example, Liening and Mittelstädt (2008), for change management see, for example, Glazinski (2007), for entrepreneurship see, for example, McKelvey (2004), Kompf (2012) and Faschingbauer (2013).

[47] In recent years, numerous interesting publications on the topic of chaos theory and economics have appeared. The following monographs are cited as examples: Puu (2003), Trosky (2006), Mandelbrot and Hudson (2007), or also: Beinhocker (2007).

if systems and models are to be subjected to a thorough analysis in the following discussions, an exact definition of these formulations is required (Page, 1991, p. 2 ff.).

The term 'system' has played an important role in research since the beginning of the twentieth century, although the term was already in use in the seventeenth century, for example, by *Galileo* (Baecker, 2005, p. 146).

Terms such as 'system' or 'model' can be defined on the basis of systems theory, which can be described as a general theory of the relationship between structures and behaviour of systems. The concepts of system and model can then be used as a basis for a unified approach.

In the previous considerations, sections of reality have usually been referred to as a system. Implicitly, criteria were applied by which the described observations were evaluated and ordered.

This makes it clear that there is a great deal of freedom in the analysis of systems, as the systems are described depending on specific, goal-oriented questions, while other characteristics of reality are considered less important and thus excluded a priori (Neumann, 2009).

Systems theory is by no means a self-contained theory. Rather, it is interpreted differently when viewed from various disciplines.

It is therefore not surprising that there are authors who believe that there is no general systems theory (François, 1997, p. 155). Others, on the other hand, believe that systems theory is *the* crucial basis of complexity theories or sciences (Gell-Mann, 1997).[48] *Zeeuw* points out that observations such as the permanent decline in the members of the Dutch 'systems group'[49] since the seventies of the twentieth century suggests otherwise (Zeeuw, 2005, p. 147).

[48] See also the popular science contribution by the Nobel laureate in physics, which is nevertheless recommended: Gell-Mann (1996).

[49] There are a multitude of scientific societies dealing with systems theory, such as the *'International Society of Systems Studies'*, which emerged in 1988 from the *'Society for General Systems Research'* and the *'United Kingdom Systems Society'*, the *'International Federation for Systems Research'*, the *'World Organisation for Systems and Cybernetics'* or the German *'Society for System Dynamics'*, which underline the vitality of this approach.

Arthur *Koestler*[50], Talcott *Parsons*[51], Humberto *Maturana* and Francisco J. *Varela*[52], William Ross *Ashby*[53], Wolfgang *Tschacher,*Jürgen *Kriz* and Günter *Schiepek*[54], as well as Ludwig *von Bertalanffy*[55] are names that are partly associated with the development of systems-theoretical thinking or also with its application in different disciplines. They come from various fields such as biology, psychology, sociology, etc. *Parsons*, for example, is considered the founder of sociological systems theory and had a significant influence on the ideas of Niklas *Luhmann,* whose concept of system we want to discuss later.

From the multitude of literature on system theory, particularly in the context of complexity and economics, Jamshid *Gharajedaghi* stands out with his book: "Systems thinking—Managing Chaos and Complexity: A Platform for Designing Business Architecture", who has approached the topic from the perspective of systemic thinking and should be the significant basis of the following section (Gharajedaghi, 2005). *Gharajedaghi* states:

---

[50]A. *Koestler* coined the term *'Holon',* which is simultaneously a whole and a part. See: Koestler (1990). He is concerned with a systems-theoretical model of a self-regulating open order, "which he seems to derive mainly from *Bertalanffy's* 'The Biological Worldview' (...)" (Benedikt).

[51]T. *Parsons* (*13.12.1902, died 08.05.1979) is considered the founder of sociological systems theory, which had a significant influence on Niklas *Luhmann's* ideas. See, for example, the commemorative publication: Schluchter (1980).

[52]H. *Maturana* (*14.09.1928) and F. *Varela* (*07.09.1946) are considered the founders of the biological concept of *'Autopoiesis',* a concept that attempts to describe living beings or living systems with the term of systems theory. They influenced, for example, N. *Luhmann,* in whose work the concept of autopoiesis is crucial for the examination of social systems. See Maturana and Varela (1987), or also: Zeleny (1981). *Maturana* uses the cell as a standard example of an autopoietic system: "A cell," says *Maturana,* "is a network of chemical reactions that produce molecules in such a way that they 1. generate exactly the network of reactions through their interactions or recursively participate in it, which they themselves generated, and 2. realise the cell as a material unit" (Maturana, 1985, p. 158).

[53]W. R. *Ashby* (*06.09.1903, died 15.11.1972) is considered an influential figure in the field of systems sciences. Even though he may not be as well-known as, for example, *von Bertalanffy, 'Ashby's Law'* is nevertheless considered one of the foundations of self-organisation. See www.Rossashby.info/biography.html.

[54]Scientists like W. *Tschacher* (*1958), J. *Kriz* (*1944) or also G. *Schiepek* (*1958) are significant for the inclusion of systems theory in psychology. See, for example, Tschacher (1997) as well as, for example, Kriz (1998) and for instance Schiepek (1991).

[55]L. *von Bertalanffy* (*1901, died 1972) was an Austrian biologist who founded a 'General System Theory' (General System Theory), which he—like later also *Maturana*—considered as a theory of the living. He distinguished himself from N. *Wiener's* cybernetics, but could not prevent a convergence of these two approaches, which are very similar in terms of their formal claim of 'universality'. See Bertalanffy (1956), or for an introduction also: Zeeuw (2005, pp. 145–173).

> Natural science has discovered 'chaos'. Social science has encountered 'complexity'. But chaos and complexity are not characteristics of our new reality; they are features of our perceptions and understanding. We see the world as increasingly more complex and chaotic because we use inadequate concepts to explain it. When we understand something, we no longer see it chaotic or complex (Gharajedaghi, 2005, p. 25).

Apparently, he believes that the researched chaos and complexity are not characteristics of our new reality, but rather features of our perception and understanding. We perceive the world as increasingly chaotic and complex because we have inadequate concepts for explanation.

From the perspective of 'complexity sciences', one might need to specify that many processes in the world are described as complex or even chaotic, which are actually only complicated, but not necessarily complex in the complexity scientific sense. A clarification of the terminology is obviously urgently needed. This will be worked out in the course of this treatise.

Perhaps the first solution to the problem is to use a new language, the language of 'systems thinking'. Over time, *Gharajedaghi* says, people have always used different types of languages to grasp the world. First, we told our history in myths. We sang them, danced them, and expressed them in rituals. This gave us security in an uncertain environment. As our skills increased over the millennia, so did our learning and creativity abilities. We began to speak and write in the language of poetry, mathematics, philosophy, and science (Gharajedaghi, 2005, p. 25).

In the last century, we specialised in a particular language, the language of analytical science and as *Gharajedaghi* emphasises:

> As we emphasised one language to the exclusion of all others, we became unidimensional—and boringly predictable (Gharajedaghi, 2005, p. 25).

Today, the analytical language has permeated our entire thinking, indeed our entire way of life: Our systems of production, organisation, interaction, and communication. Our entire life seems to be affected by it. So *Gharajedaghi* points out:

> (…) our choice of recreation, sport, and foods—is done in terms of the assumptions and applications of analytical tools (Gharajedaghi, 2005, p. 26).

And he gives a warning hint, which points in a similar, albeit not directly comparable direction, as we have already learned from the explanations of *Heidegger's* knowledge danger in the context of *Newtonian* mechanics or the corresponding remarks of *Goethe*:

> History, unfortunately, has not been too kind to those who have capitalised so extensively on a single winning strategy (Gharajedaghi, 2005, p. 26).

Relying solely on a single winning strategy can be dangerous in the long run. What we lack is a holistic view of things. This does not mean that as an economist one should abandon the economic perspective in favour of a multiperspective, which could also include other perspectives such as the sociological one. Rather, it means freeing the economic perspective from the purely mechanistic, neoclassical mainstream to expand it with a holistic view. This should not lead to abandoning the economic perspective, but to making it future-proof. Such a view requires a language that allows us to understand and design systems, that ultimately allows us to see through the chaos and understand and master complexity. “Increasingly, we are confronted in all areas (…) with the problem of organised complexity, which apparently requires new thinking tools” (Bertalanffy, 1972, p. 20), says Ludwig *von Bertalanffy*, referring to system theory.

3.3.2.2 The Concept of System

“Once you start looking for systems, they appear everywhere—in physics, in economics, in psychology, and in history.” (Bertalanffy, 1972, p. 3). For *von Bertalanffy*, the universe, a dog, a cell, and an atom represent “real systems” (Bertalanffy, 1972, p. 21), which he defines as “a set of elements between which there are interrelationships” (Bertalanffy, 1972, p. 38).

If one follows Niklas *Luhmann,* then the concept of system can be defined according to the ontological tradition of thought as follows:

> A system consists in units being connected as parts to a whole through relationships. The system is the interdependence of the parts within a whole. The way in which the parts are arranged into a whole constitutes the structure of the system (Luhmann, 1976, p. 23).

At this point, it can be noted that this definition usually defines a *closed system*; a system that is isolated from its environment. Such a system does not draw any information or the like from its environment, nor does it give anything away. Therefore, a closed system only uses the information that is initially provided about the individual parts.

If one isolates a system, then it quickly comes to rest “due to the effect of internal frictions, disintegrates, decays” (Röpke, 1977, p. 15). Physically speaking, such a system tends to increase its *entropy* until equilibrium is reached. Under entropy, one can simply understand the degree of disorder of the individual elements of the system that arises when energy is consumed.[56] Equilibrium is the state of greatest probability on the one hand and greatest disorder on the other, as no relationships exist between the elements of the system in the equilibrium state.

---

[56] Rudolf *Clausius* introduced the term *entropy* in the sixties of the nineteenth century to describe the spontaneous increase of heat in closed systems as an irreversible process. This neologism is composed of the Greek word for energy ‘ergon’ and the Greek word for transformation ‘tropos’ (Mainzer, 1995, p. 75). In information theory, entropy represents the expected value over the information density of a source as a measure, as we will see in more detail in the empirical part (Shannon, 2001, p. 3).

Open systems[57], which underlie the new way of thinking, are characterised by the exchange of, for example, information. In contrast to closed systems, the path to equilibrium can be stabilised at a certain level of order in them. They can even strive for states of higher order by integrating energy from the system's environment. In contrast, closed systems cannot evolve and thus cannot achieve a higher degree of complexity. *Röpke* points out that there are "no great difficulties" (Röpke, 1977, p. 15). in accommodating the neoclassically oriented economic theory in a dichotomy of open and closed systems. He emphasises that late classical formalism interprets the economic world as a closed system that examines the conditions for the existence of equilibria. Thus, in economic equilibrium analysis, the cause of a disturbance is considered an exogenous variable outside the explanatory context, so that, for example, feedback processes of the system with its environment are ignored (Röpke, 1977, p. 15).

It must be considered that, in contrast to closed systems, the existence of the system in a changing environment is constantly problematic in open systems. In the above definition, which *Luhmann* presents, it is not taken into account that the system needs an internal order to remain unchanged in a changing environment and to enable system preservation. For example, such problem areas are considered in functional analysis. Thus, the system is defined "by relative invariance of its boundaries against an environment" (Luhmann, 1976, p. 23).

In relation to this viewpoint, one can therefore call everything a system on which, on the one hand, the distinction between inside and outside can be applied. This means that there must be an internal and external difference. So there must be an order that does not expand arbitrarily, but is limited due to its internal structure. Because of this structure, the system behaves relatively invariant to any change in a different environment. Nevertheless, open systems can evolve into elements of other systems (Zeeuw, 2005, p. 151). On the other hand, a system fulfils a certain function, i.e., a system purpose can be defined, which we as observers recognise.

And finally, a system ceases to exist when it loses its system integrity, which can happen by removing certain, namely systemic or system-relevant elements and their relationships with each other. In this respect, a system is not divisible, as it would otherwise lose its coherent structure.

Definition *(Open System)*

An open system can therefore generally be defined as a set of interrelated elements that interact for a common purpose, and that maintains its coherent structure in exchange with its environment. Furthermore, an open system can evolve in such a way that the elements of the system coordinate the use and distribution of resources themselves and regulate them.

The following definition describes the individual components of a system, which are illustrated in Fig. 3.14.

[57] *Von Bertalanffy* introduced the term 'open system' as early as 1932. Cf. Bertalanffy (1932).

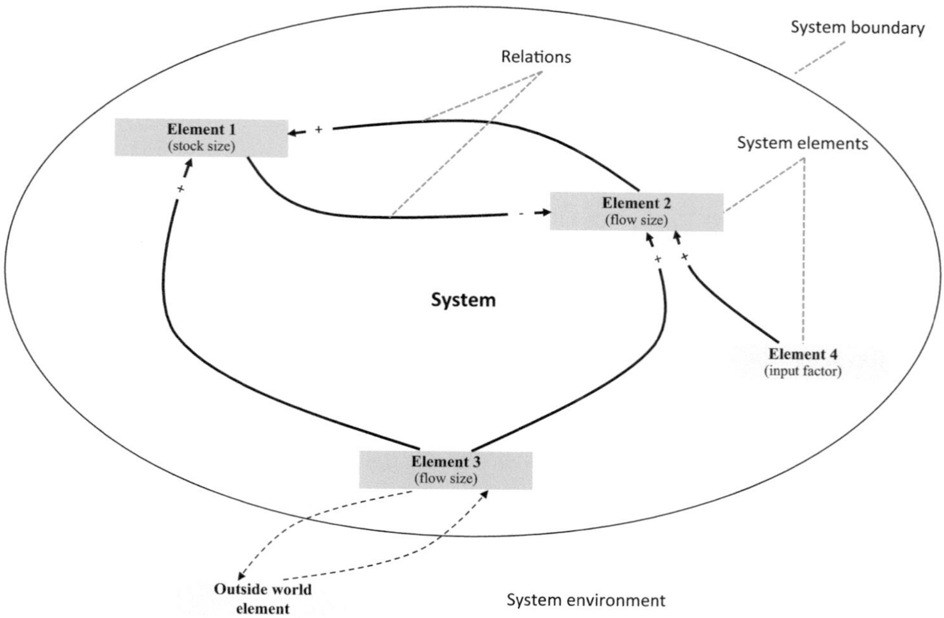

Fig. 3.14 Representation of a system

Definition *(Element, Attributes and Methods, Subsystems and Relations of an Open System)*

- An *element* or a *factor*[58] is an object of a system or a subsystem that is not further divisible or is thought of as not further divisible.
- Parts of a system can be combined into a *subsystem*. Each subsystem itself can be considered a system. This creates a hierarchy of systems within a system.
- Elements or factors can be assigned *properties*. Properties that do not change are referred to as *attributes,* changeable ones as *methods*, each of which has at least one manifestation (e.g., value).
- *Relations* are the relationships between elements. They can be positive (+) or negative (−).

[58] In the language of 'System Dynamics', we speak of factors. This language is important for quantitative analysis. For qualitative analysis, the terms mentioned above are sufficient. However, since we want to use this language for quantitative analysis in simulation models at a later stage, the terms for this are already mentioned here: Thus, factors can be *stock variables* whose initial value can change over time due to inflows and outflows. But they can also be *flow variables* that change the stock variables through inflows and outflows. Furthermore, there are *information* and *inputfactors,* which can be described by value series or functions.

Example: Open-Source versus Closed Source—Godzilla Teaches Fear

Computer science students Dave *Sander* and Steve *Gaig* have had enough: Their browser is constantly crashing. However, the access to the Internet via browser is dominated by the large software corporations. Even with existing know-how, improvements for users are impossible to make, as the programme code of the browsers is not disclosed by the corporations. In this respect, the companies act as closed systems regarding their browsers. The IT-savvy friends decide to develop their own browser. After months of tinkering, it's finally done, "Godzilla" is ready. From now on, the browser is available to all Internet users free of charge. The special feature and at the same time the difference to existing browser programmes is the open-source concept of Godzilla. Everyone can actively further develop this browser. It is therefore an open system. Dave *Sander* and Steve *Gaig* are proud: "Finally a programme where the users can participate!". After a short time, a 'community' has grown worldwide, which further develops the browser and generates a huge competitive advantage over some traditional providers, especially because this approach, supported by developers worldwide, places the browser much more sustainably in the market than if it were only supported by one company.[59] ◄

3.3.2.3 Basic Characteristics of Systems

In order to intervene in a Complex System, the question that *Dörner* raises ultimately always arises:

> Does our thinking meet the requirements of a 'thinking in systems' (Dörner, 2007, p. 14)?

In the above definitions of a system and the terminology used, some hints were already given in advance as to what basic characteristics make up a system. These aspects are so crucial that we want to examine them more closely in order to finally be able to answer *Dörner's* question constructively. The points that were addressed individually are:

i) Openness versus Closedness
ii) System Purpose—Purposefulness
iii) System Boundaries—System Environment and
iv) System Integrity—Systemic Elements

[59] As a concrete practical example, compare the open-source online learning platform Moodle with comparable commercial products. Especially state or semi-state institutions rely on commercial solutions, which are very expensive, but from which they expect a more lasting service and higher seriousness (e.g., in terms of data security) than from a "suspect" open-source project. In fact, some commercial companies have already disappeared from the e-learning market. The e-learning platform Moodle, on the other hand, is prospering and is becoming increasingly popular in universities, for example.

Gharajedaghi, who speaks of emergent properties (emergent property) instead of systemic elements (Gharajedaghi, 2005, p. 45), goes even further and adds two more principles to his consideration, which in his view are important for a dynamic, open system and which we want to formulate here following him (Gharajedaghi, 2005, pp. 29–55):

v) Multidimensionality

and

vi) Counterintuition[60]

i. The characteristic of 'Openness'

At its core, the principle of 'openness' is first and foremost about emphasising that one can distinguish between open and closed systems. For example, living systems, such as a market economy, are open systems. These can ultimately only be understood in the context of their environment, with which they are in exchange. It is trivial that in such systems everything is connected to everything and everything depends on everything. What is interesting is which of these dependencies are random, which cannot be changed, and which allow a choice. One could initially divide the dependencies into two categories: those that can be influenced and those that cannot be influenced.

While people used to believe, and to some extent still do today, that they could control complex systems, the idea is increasingly gaining ground that we cannot control very much, but we can influence a lot (Gharajedaghi, 2005, p. 30 ff.).

According to the first law of thermodynamics, which simplifies to say that energy remains constant in closed systems, such a system tends towards its most probable state: the equilibrium state.

Example: Pendulum

A pendulum consists of a weight, which is suspended on a string or rod so that it can swing. This is a closed system, whose entropy increases: Once set in motion and left to itself, it swings under the influence of gravity until it comes to rest or stops. In the state of highest entropy, the pendulum points downwards in the direction of gravity and is there at the lowest point it can occupy. This is the most probable state. Of course, it would also be possible for the pendulum to point to the side, but that is quite unlikely (but not impossible). ◀

---

[60] The principles i) ii) and iv)–vi) are integral parts of the 'Systems-View' of the third generation according to *Gharajedaghi*. The first generation of systemic thinking (Operations Research) is to be seen in the context of mechanistic thinking. It deals with complexities of interdependent variables as opposed to approaches that see the whole as the sum of independent variables. The second generation (Cybernetics) deals with the behaviour of self-organising open systems and the potential of feedback loops and control mechanisms. These principles mentioned here are now integral parts of the 'Systems-View' of the third generation, according to Gharajedaghi (2005, p. 29).

This is very reminiscent of the traditional mechanistic view of economics, which indeed starts from the *Walrasian*equilibrium hypothesis, according to which an economic system (under ideal conditions) always tends towards equilibrium (Walras, 2010). There is therefore much to suggest that *Walras,* speaking in the language of system theory, assumed a *closed system*. The associated idea of a system always tending towards equilibrium is in line with the first law of thermodynamics.

However, there is the problem that *Walras* and Co. did not know or could not have known the second law of thermodynamics at that time, especially since its significance was only recognised in the late nineteenth or twentieth century. It ultimately states that entropy in a (closed) system always increases and thus any order turns into disorder. Therefore, order is not created on the way to equilibrium. On the contrary, disorder increases.

Example: Sand pile versus sand castle

A sand castle built on the beach with great effort and joy by children quickly disintegrates into a pile of sand; the pile of sand is the most probable state of the sand, not the sand castle. Here, entropy is at its highest, the sand system is in equilibrium. ◀

Moreover, the growing entropy is what allows us to distinguish between past, present, and future. It gives time a direction! *Panta rhei*—'everything flows' as *Heraclitus* already said, pointing to the dynamic nature of all being (Russell, 1950, p. 66 ff.). In a closed system, all freely moving molecules distribute evenly in space. The energy released in the process is converted into heat. It is also colloquially said: The world will ultimately die the heat death. In this final state, the system is in equilibrium. It is the most probable state, which can be described by uniformity and disorder. It is the state of simple complexity or chaotic simplicity. The entropy increases permanently on the way to the final state. The final state of a closed system is always predictable:

An equilibrium state with maximum entropy is the death of the system. Therefore, an equilibrium state may not be so desirable after all.

Reality often appears to us differently than the equilibrium thesis suggests. Identical goods are rarely traded at the same prices on the markets (even disregarding transaction costs etc.). And this is not referring to the price differentiation known in economic literature, where the same goods are offered to different customers at different prices.[61] Sometimes there are bargain prices in one shop, a few meters away we find exorbitant prices for the same product in another shop, even though the conditions for a perfect market seem to be given. Of course, economics often assumes a high vantage point on the markets; the term 'macro'-economics already shows this. But price differences of

[61] According to economic theory, price differentiations can only exist in imperfect markets. In perfect markets, there is only a single price (Mankiw, 2004, p. 359).

50% etc. cannot be explained by this. Or the conditions are not met upon closer inspection, then the perfect market with its equilibrium would be nothing more than a pure utopia in many cases.

The *Walrasian* equilibrium hypothesis seems to be incorrect in many cases. However, the question could also be whether the correct analogy is being used in the context of mechanistic analogy formation? The collapse of the *Laplacian* worldview has shown that something fundamentally different seems to underlie this.

Let's consider *open systems.* Unlike closed systems, they can have negative entropy. In other words. They can resist chaos and produce (temporary) order.

Example: Pendulum clock

The pendulum of a (pendulum) clock, on the other hand, is an open system. It constantly receives energy from the weights, i.e., from the outside, so that it can maintain its system integrity. It swings back and forth evenly, provided it receives the appropriate energy from the outside. When the weights have completely released their energy, the pendulum stops, as heat is generated by the friction at the pendulum's suspension etc. and without further energy supply, the entropy increases. It strives for the equilibrium point. The external energy is therefore necessary to create order in the clock system. However, the energy does not dictate the movement of the pendulum, it does not determine what happens in the system, but it is necessary for maintaining the dynamics of the system. ◀

While closed systems always tend towards equilibrium with absolute reliability, open systems have an energy and material exchange with the environment, which repeatedly stops the growing entropy, creating order patterns. However, they are not predictable, they can form complex, unforeseen patterns and structures.

The question is therefore whether an economy ultimately does not represent an open system. The answer would have to be 'yes' contrary to the neoclassical dictum. If the economy were a closed equilibrium system, then according to the second law, less and less order and more and more chaos would have to set in, there would be no self-organisation that creates new structures, everything would inevitably tend towards equilibrium—and die.

Every economic activity is an attempt to curb the growing entropy, to create order, to bring about something new. However, this only works in open systems.

Every economy needs energy in material form from natural gas, oil, coal, uranium, sun, wind, food, etc., or in immaterial form like money and especially ideas from brave, but also inventive personalities: inventors and entrepreneurs. Only the supply of energy into the economic system makes it possible to shape the economy and form order patterns, without—as in the example of the pendulum clock—the type of energy in any way determining the activities in advance. On the other hand, every economy releases entropy in the form of CO_2 emissions, heat, etc. into the environment. If you turn off the energy supply, by stopping the food supply or turning off the oil or gas tap, boycotting the uranium or coal deliveries, entropy increases and the system comes to a standstill. If this analogy should apply, the economy cannot be a closed equilibrium system. It must rather represent an open system, in which other (physical) laws apply, than *Walras* and Cie. have assumed or could assume.

On the one hand, you don't have to be a physicist to advance economics. On the other hand, you certainly need a high degree of mathematics to be able to create meaningful economic theories and models at all. But the mathematics used should shape economics in such a way that they do not contradict the physical laws that also claim validity for the economy, namely seeing the economy as an open system.

ii. The characteristic of 'purposefulness'

Systems have a purpose by definition. To answer the question of the purpose of a system, we need information, knowledge, and ultimately we need to understand all of this.

But what is 'information', what is 'knowledge', what does 'understand' mean? While information initially only represents unrelated facts, knowledge means that this information is put into context, that it is networked. However, this does not yet say anything about their significance, which includes the level of understanding. While we ask "What" is with information, we ask "How" with knowledge. Understanding focusses on the question of "Why".

In earlier times, one could be successful in business if one had, for example, information about the (potential) customers. That was a competitive advantage. Today this is no longer the case. To achieve a competitive advantage, a higher level must be climbed, the level of knowledge: One must learn *how* the customers do this or that, think etc. To then be an effective player, one sometimes has to go even higher in fast, fiercely contested markets and reach the level of understanding and learn *why* the customers do what they do.

The why question is ultimately the question of purpose.

Example: The Company as a System

a) To represent the system of a company, one could ask what the main purpose of the company is. Many would answer: "Success". So, starting from the purpose of success, one would model the company to capture the system. Starting from the term success, one could ask what influences success directly in the present, both positively and negatively. One could capture all factors, such as costs, services, employee motivation, quality, marketing, etc., and represent and analysse the relations in a system or model.

   But is the purpose of a company success? One could argue quite differently and say that the reason for a company arises from its fundamental existence. So we could ask: Why do companies exist at all?

b) To model the system of a company, one could therefore start from the question of why companies exist, why they grow or dissolve, for example? The classic transaction cost analysis (Coase, 1937) attributes the emergence of firms to a consequent reduction of costs. The question of whether a company carries out this or that transaction under its own direction (i.e., the question of whether a company emerges, grows, or dissolves at all) or arises through price-finding mechanisms of the market is a question of the balance of costs. Thus, Ronald *Coase:* writes:

> The question always is, will it pay to bring an extra exchange transaction under the organising authority? At the margin, the costs of organising within the firm will be equal either to the costs of organising in another firm or to the costs involved in leaving the transaction to be 'organised' by the price mechanism. Business men will be constantly experimenting, controlling more or less, and in this way, equilibrium will be maintained (Coase, 1937, p. 404).

If one views the company as an organisation, then from another perspective, James *March* and Herbert *Simon* see the resulting difference between the highly coordinated and ordered structure of organisations as opposed to the unordered environment. They write:

> The high specificity of structure and coordination within organisations—as contrasted with the diffuse and variable relations among organisations and among unorganised individuals—marks off the individual organisation as a sociological unit comparable in significance to the individual organism in biology (March & Simon, 1958, p. 4).

Referring to basic principles of cybernetics (Wiener, 1948), Chester *Barnard* (Barnard, 1968, p. 6) points out that the survival of an organisation depends on how well it maintains equilibrium in a constantly fluctuating environment. Uncertainties arise from the environment or from internal processes, and these must be met with a minimum of order and structure (Daft & Lengel, 1984, p. 192). A key characteristic of an organisation is therefore its order and active distinction from the environment, so here too the system purpose "enterprise" can be sought. ◀

What purpose the system company has or should have is ultimately a decision. The observer defines the purpose depending on a question that is important to him. Whether we decide for variant a) or b) in the above example cannot be answered universally. We have to choose. The *why* question, ultimately the question of purpose, is the question of choice. And the choice is, according to man *Gharajedaghi,* the result of interactions between three dimensions:

- Rationality
- Emotionality
- Culture (Gharajedaghi, 2005, p. 33 ff.)[62]

Purpose-driven systems are ultimately value-driven systems. It is values that purpose-driven actors strive to achieve. Often they are an implicit part of the culture, and the decision-maker does not even know that he has a choice.

Finally, the idea of purposefulness according to *Gharajedaghi* can only be understood if one takes into account the three types of system behaviour according to *Ackoff*: reaction, response, and action (Ackoff, 1973). A reaction is a system behaviour for which an event in the environment is necessary and sufficient at the same time. This reaction is an event that deterministically presupposes another event and follows it. A response is a system behaviour for which an event in the environment is necessary but not sufficient. A response is an event in which the system itself is a co-producer. An action is a system behaviour for which the change in the environment is neither necessary nor sufficient. It is a self-determined event or represents autonomous behaviour. *Gharajedaghi* states:

> Choice has three aspects: rational (self-interest), emotional (excitement), and cultural (default). While rational choice is risk averse, emotional choice is not (Gharajedaghi, 2005, p. 38).

And he further states:

---

[62] – *Rational-Choice*, rational action is first and foremost meaningful action.

It is the realm of self-interest or the realm of decision-makers, not that of observers, says *Gharajedaghi:* "The world is not run by those who are right; it is run by those who can convince others they are right." (Gharajedaghi, 2005, p. 34)

– *Emotional-Choice* is the realm of beauty and attraction or excitement, says *Gharajedaghi:*

Much of what we do, we do because it attracts us or more precisely, because things challenge us. If you constantly win at a game like Monopoly, the attraction to challenge your fellow players one more time is rather low. It is more likely that you would want to play with a group that challenges you, that demands you. These fellow players are ironically just those who have strategic skills in Monopoly that could lead to them beating you (Gharajedaghi, 2005, p. 35). If the attraction of a good challenge were not part of our decision criteria, our life would be boring. Setting and seeking achievable goals is, as *Gharajedaghi* writes, an everyday occurrence: "This may come as a surprise to many 'human resource managers', but for sure it explains the boredom and meaninglessness associated with huge segments of corporate life." (Gharajedaghi, 2005, p. 35) While 'rational choice' refers to extrinsic, instrumental values, 'emotional choice' deals with stylistic, intrinsic, values. It is the joy and satisfaction derived from the emotional level. Risk-taking is an important attribute of challenge and excitement.

– *Cultural-Choice* according to *Gharajedaghi* defines the ethical norms of the collective, of which the decision-maker is a member. The ethical values are the limiting elements of the decision-making process.

> Choice is a matter of competence; it implies power-to-do. Liberty without competence is an empty proposition (Gharajedaghi, 2005, p. 38).

Only when we have recognised or named the purpose of a system can we attempt to understand the system. This requires a specific competence. This is ultimately necessary to understand complex systems and to be able to act within them.

iii. The characteristic of 'system boundaries'

If we can observe a multitude of systems in our environment, this presupposes that systems have a system environment. So there are elements and relationships that belong to the system and others that do not belong to the system. In other words, there must be a system boundary that separates the system from its environment. While closed systems still relatively easily reveal the system boundary (after all, they are defined by the fact that they do not exchange with the environment), it becomes more difficult with open systems. Nevertheless, it is relatively easy for us to say where the open system automobile has its boundaries and where, for example, the human being as an open system begins and ends. Hartmut *Bossel* proposes three criteria, which apply individually or in combination, which we adopt in a similar form here:

The system boundary is to be drawn where

a) the relationships to the environment are much weaker than within the system
b) existing relationships to environmental elements do not shape the system structure
c) on the one hand, environmental impacts are not determined by the system itself or, on the other hand, the environment cannot be influenced by feedback from system effects (Bossel, 1994, p. 37 ff.)

iv. The characteristic of 'system integrity'—Systemic elements

To understand the concept of systemic elements, we want to adopt here the idea of 'emergent properties' following *Gharajedaghi*. Properties can be measured. They have an extension or a colour, they make noises or have a taste. In short: properties can often be grasped with one of the five senses. But how is it, so asks *Gharajedaghi,* with a property like love (Gharajedaghi, 2005, p. 45 f.)?

When one loves, then the whole person loves, not just a part of him. Also, love cannot be assigned to one of the five senses. It has no colour, makes no noise and has no aroma; you can neither touch it nor taste it.

So how do you measure love? The consequences of love can certainly be measured: "If you love me, why don't you call me?", someone could ask.

But something is not right here. The concept of love does not fit into the classic description of a property. Yet it is not alone in its peculiarity. Comparable phenomena such as success, failure or happiness have similar characteristics.

These types of properties *Gharajedaghi* calls ***'emergent properties'*** (Gharajedaghi, 2005, p. 46 f.).

Emergent properties are thus properties of the *whole* system. They can neither be properties of an element of the system, nor can they be derived from properties of the elements. They are properties of a structure that its elements do not have. Emergence therefore does not mean the emergence of something that is hidden in the parts of a system, but it can only arise from the interaction of the system elements and become visible in the whole.

Thus, emergent properties are a product of interactions and not a sum of the actions of the parts. They cannot be measured directly. If you want to measure them, then only through their manifestations. They cannot naturally be analysed. And they do not follow causal explanations. Behind the already extensively discussed sentence "The whole is more than the sum of its parts", which, as we have seen, contradicts the traditional mechanistic way of thinking, ultimately hides the idea of emergent properties.

Example Sandcastle

When we look at a sandcastle, this sandcastle system consists of many grains of sand. But in none of these grains of sand, which we can look at on a micro level, is the idea of the castle. On the macro level we see the whole, here the sandcastle, and it is much more than just the sum of grains of sand. So there is also here an emergent property, which defines the sandcastle system from the micro level to the macro level. ◀

It is therefore not possible to explain emergent properties solely by the factors involved, as those who follow the paradigm of classical mechanics try to do. Rather, these properties spontaneously emerge when elements of the system are assembled or disassembled, which qualitatively differ from the emergent properties. So *Anderson* states:

> At each stage, the world we perceive emerges through 'emergence'. That is, through the process by which considerable aggregations of matter can spontaneously develop properties that have no meaning for the simpler units from which they consist.—A cell is not yet a tiger. Nor is a single gold atom yellow and shiny (Anderson, 2000, p. 178).

Example: Success of a Young Company

What is meant by the term 'success' of a young company? Regardless of the specific definition, 'success' could initially serve as an example of an emergent property, which clearly shows that it is not about independent variables, but rather dependent variables. Or as *Gharajedaghi* says: "The all-star team is not necessarily the best team in the league." (Gharajedaghi, 2005, p. 46)

The all-star team is not necessarily the best in the league, it can even lose to an absolutely average team. The decisive factor is not only the quality of the actors (independent variables), but also the quality of their interactions (dependent variables). So, not only very good entrepreneurs are needed, but also the quality of their interaction matters. How, for example, can the property 'success' be measured in a startup?

"Two turkeys will not make an eagle" (Gharajedaghi, 2005, p. 48), says *Gharajedaghi*. Growth could be a measurable manifestation of the success of a young venture, as a successful venture usually grows. However, and this is what *Gharajedaghi* implies, not every venture that grows is necessarily successful: "One can easily grow by 'faking', or making lousy acquisitions." (Gharajedaghi, 2005, p. 107) ◀

So, in order not to draw false conclusions, one must measure at least several manifestations. Thus, the EVA concept[63] may be better suited to measure success than pure growth figures. The reliability may be higher here, for example, than with growth.

Example: Wealth of a Nation

For Adam *Smith*, everyone at the micro level only pursues their own interests. Nevertheless, this individual behaviour at the macro level forms the wealth of a nation, although this was not intended in the individual interest. The individual thus acts selfishly, and this self-interest benefits the community. *Smith* notes in this context:

> By preferring the support of domestic to that of foreign industry he (the individual person, the author) intends only his own security; and by directing that industry in such a manner as its produce may be of the greatest value, he intends only his own gain, and he is in this, as in many other cases, led by an *invisible hand* (emphasis, the author) to promote an end which was no part of his intention... By pursuing his own interest he frequently promotes that of the society more effectually than when he really intends to promote it (Smith, 1776, Book IV, Chap. II, p. 485). ◀

With that 'invisible hand', *Smith* describes what we refer to in our context as emergence.

The manifestation of an emergent property in its entirety can only be grasped by projecting future development into current behaviour.

While emergent properties are attributed to the overall system, whose integrity depends on the maintenance of these properties, there will always be elements within the system that are indispensable for system integrity. Such elements can be referred to as systemic elements.

Examples: About Tables, Piles of Sand, Automobiles, and Economic Systems

a) For instance, a *table* represents a closed system. Initially, two important prerequisites for a system are met, as a table consists of elements, such as a tabletop and at

[63] EVA stands for 'Economic Value Added'. It is more than just a key figure. It takes into account both the demands of management and shareholders, as not only performance but also market value is calculated. The EVA results from the NOPAT (Net Operating Profit after Tax, i.e., profit after taxes) minus the capital required to generate the profit multiplied by the cost of capital.

least three legs, which are interrelated. Since the maintenance of its structure does not depend on external factors, the table is a closed system. However, if one or two specific elements, e.g., two table legs, were removed, the system integrity would be destroyed, and the original system purpose would no longer be given.

b) But is, for example, a *pile of sand* also a system? A pile of sand consists of grains of sand, which could be referred to as elements. One could certainly also assign a purpose to a pile of sand, perhaps it serves as a play area for children within a sandbox. However, if one were to shovel away half of the pile of sand, its function would still be preserved. Therefore, it cannot be said that the grains of sand as elements are systemic and essential for the coherent structure of the pile of sand. Only when all grains are removed, the pile of sand disappears. But there are no systemic elements. In this respect, the pile of sand does not represent a system on the one hand. On the other hand, this is the typical end state of a closed dynamic system. No more order can be found in the system. It is in disorder, i.e., the grains of sand no longer form a recognisable structure, but lie evenly distributed on top of each other. The entropy is at its highest, there is equilibrium.

c) An *automobile* is an example of an open system. It consists of elements (body, engine, seats, etc.), many of which can be described as systemic. Without an engine, the system integrity of the car is destroyed, as *autonomous* movement would no longer be possible. All elements are interrelated. Furthermore, a car only drives if it receives oxygen and fuel from the outside and if it can emit exhaust gases to the outside. It also requires a driver (originating from outside). Therefore, a car is an open system, especially since it would not move without exchanging with its 'environment'.

d) The *economic system* of the Eurozone consists of a multitude of elements, such as companies, households, banks, etc. While the removal of one or another company through insolvency from the system would not endanger its integrity, the insolvency of significant banks leads to the collapse of the system, so these elements can be described as systemic. ◀

v. The characteristic of 'Multidimensionality' (Gharajedaghi, 2005, p. 38 ff.)

> Fundamentally, we all divide the world into true and false, good and bad, black and white. Hence comes the indignant rejection of the seemingly soulless idea that a relationship is more and differently constituted than the sum of the properties of the two relationship partners (Paul *Watzlawick*).

Multidimensionality is the ability to see complementary to opposing relationships and to design functioning wholes (feasible wholes) from parts that cannot function on their own (unfeasible parts).

Example: Profit maximisation as a central business objective?

Often in business administration, it is argued very one-dimensionally that profit maximisation is the central goal of a company. The profit maximisation hypothesis is then justified as follows:

- In a market economy, competitors are in a constant struggle, in which the non-performers must drop out.
- Profits facilitate technological progress and thus lead to an increase in performance.
- The higher the profit, the greater the chances for performance improvement and survival in competition.
- If one of the competitors refrains from achieving the highest possible profits, he thereby diminishes his own future prospects and will not survive.
- In this way, the objective of 'profit maximisation' is enforced by competition.

However, it is assumed that the buyer always chooses the cheapest offer, that competition forces the providers to 'tight calculation', and that the owners of the company manage it themselves.

If one follows, for example, *Katona,* one finds numerous objections to this one-dimensional view. He writes: "(…) It is usually not possible for the entrepreneur to rationally weigh all occurring alternatives against each other and then decide which of them will yield the highest profit." (Katona, 1960, p. 242 f.)

Furthermore, he says:
"It is generally considered bad business policy to antagonisse customers, suppliers, competitors, employees, or public opinion in general, even if this should lead to higher profits." (Katona, 1960, p. 242 f.)

In addition, he believes:
"Unusually high profits could, in the opinion of some entrepreneurs, lead to the introduction of new taxes or government control and supervision. They could also provoke wage demands from the workforce or attract new enterprises. Therefore, the targeted profits may be below those that one considers to be the highest possible." (Katona, 1960, p. 242 f.).

And finally, he comes to the conclusion:
"Where do these questions lead us? If entrepreneurs want to make profits, but not maximum profits, what then is their clear intention? It is conceivable that they aim for 'satisfactory' profits (…) Striving for satisfactory profits primarily means avoiding a decline in profits as much as possible." (Katona, 1960, p. 242 f.) And these questions mean that there are indeed multi-dimensional goals that a company pursues if it wants to be successful. ◀

Multidimensionality is required, one-sidedness should be avoided. Nevertheless, multidimensional goals can indeed contradict each other. Goals do not always go hand in hand harmoniously, but often lead to goal conflicts, as the next example shows:

Example: Magic Square

In 1 of the German federal Stability Act, four dimensions of macroeconomic goals are mentioned, for the realisation of which the state is responsible. These four dimensions are often described with a *Magic Square*[64] and also referred to as such (see Fig. 3.15). It is called 'Square' because it contains four dimensions that are linked by target relationships: These goals are: 'Steady and appropriate economic growth', 'Price level stability', 'High level of employment' and 'External economic balance'. It is called 'Magic' Square because it has not yet been possible to realisse all four dimensions simultaneously. The target relationships are responsible for this. If, for example, one tries to achieve price level stability in the short term through restrictive monetary policy, this quickly comes at the expense of jobs. The level of employment decreases (Philips Curve). Even if this trade-off is only demonstrable in the short term and there is even a target harmony in the long term, it is often difficult for current politics to convey long-term positive effects, which is why people often shy away from short-term painful decisions. ◀

Nevertheless, *Gharajedaghi* believes that for the majority of cultures it is a fallacy to see opposing tendencies only in the duality of a zero-sum game. Everything comes in a pair of opposites: security/freedom, order/complexity, order/chaos, collectivity/individuality, modernity/tradition, art/science etc.

In the context of a zero-sum game, opposing tendencies come in two types:

First: Opposing tendencies can be understood in the form of a dichotomy: X or not-X. If X is correct, not-X must be wrong.

This represents an 'either/or relationship', a winner/loser struggle with the moral obligation to win.

Second: Opposing tendencies can also be formulated in such a way that they are represented by a continuum, rather than a dichotomy. Between black and white, there are any number of shades of grey. Thus, a compromise is conceivable. However, such a compromise is unstable, as the compromise position will change again if the balance of power changes. *Watzlawick* says that the one who can say at the end which position is right or wrong is the one who has the greater power (Watzlawick, 2001, p. 186 ff.).

[64] In addition to these economic policy goals, there is also a demand to explicitly include issues of education and distribution of income and wealth in the catalogue of objectives. This results in a *magic pentagon*. A further extension to the *magic hexagon* could be achieved by including *environmental protection*.

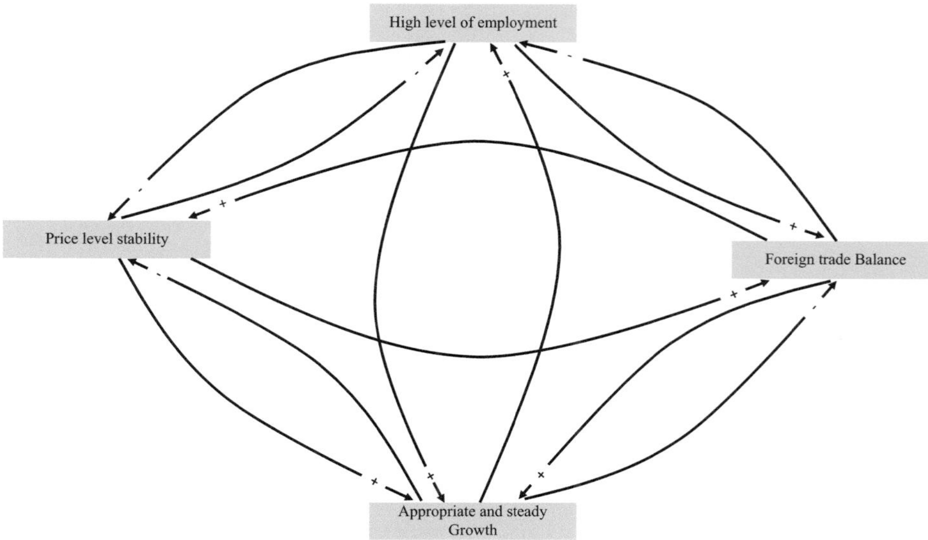

Fig. 3.15 Stability Act: Interactions of individual goals

Churchman's concept of environmental fallacies (1979)[65], *Boulding's* rejection of suboptimisation (1985)[66] and *Ackoff's* concept "separately infeasible parts making feasible whole" (1987)[67] are reflections of the same object.

It seems as if we live in a time of paradoxes. Even values like freedom and security are not exempt from this. *Boulding* described the dilemma in 1953 that some fear freedom because they always see anarchy lurking behind it. Others, on the other hand, are frightened because of security, as they always suspect the danger of tyranny behind it. When one considers the relationship between freedom and security, it becomes clear

[65] An environmental fallacy arises when people conjure up a crisis and, due to a limited perception of the problem situation, see inadequate solution options and even overlook far more significant ones. For *Churchman*, one of the typical examples of this is "the failure to recognise history as part of our environment (…) we tend to regard every current crisis as essentially a novel one, and show little interest in its historical roots." (Churchman, 1979, p. 29).

[66] Herbert *Simon* notes that if we optimise at all, we always do so in the sense of suboptimisation (cf. Simon 1962, p. 467 ff.). *Gibson* et. al. write about this: "By suboptimisation, Boulding meant the optimisation of one small, accessible element of a complex problem to the neglect of the overall context." (Gibson et al., 2007, p. 146) *Boulding* opposes this approach. He says: "I have discovered the real name of the Devil. It isn't Lucifer. It is suboptimisation." (Boulding, 1968)

[67] Russel *Ackoff,* who already laid the foundations of OR together with Charles W. *Churchman* in the 1950s, is considered one of the pioneers of systems thinking. As early as 1973, he wrote: "A system is more than the sum of its parts; it is an *indivisible whole.* It loses its essential properties when it is taken apart. The elements of a system may themselves be systems, and every system may be part of a larger system." (Ackoff, 1973, p. 663) See also: Ackoff (1987).

Fig. 3.16 Complementary relationships. (Based on: Gharajedaghi, 2005, p. 40)

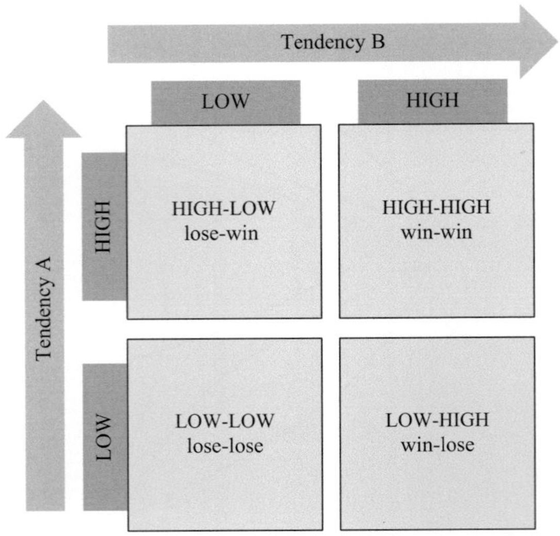

that one cannot be free if there is not also security. Conversely, no one can feel safe if they are not also free. For *Gharajedaghi*, it may be that security, freedom, and justice are three aspects of the same thing. At least their isolated consideration has caused many problems (Gharajedaghi, 2005, p. 39).

And so for him, the mutual dependencies of opposing tendencies are characterised by an 'and' relationship, not an 'either-or' relationship.

This means that each tendency can be characterised by its own dimension, which flows into a multidimensional scheme in which low/low, high/high, and the combinations low/high and high/low are conceivable. This is a non-zero-sum game, in which one may lose, but not necessarily the other wins, as can be derived from Fig. 3.16.

The distinction between 'low' and 'high' does not have to be fluid. Rather, it can involve a qualitative break:

Example: Eating habits and income

If you imagine that you have an income that allows you to spend 10 € per week on food, then you might eat a currywurst once a week, with 20 € you might eat two, with 30 € maybe three currywursts, perhaps each enriched with a portion of chips. However, if you have, let's say, 1000 € per week for food, you will not eat 100 currywursts with chips, but possibly avoid fast food altogether. The quantitative change in income thus possibly leads to a qualitative change in lifestyle habits. ◀

The various combinations of (low or high) will evoke different behaviours. Each type represents a new system.

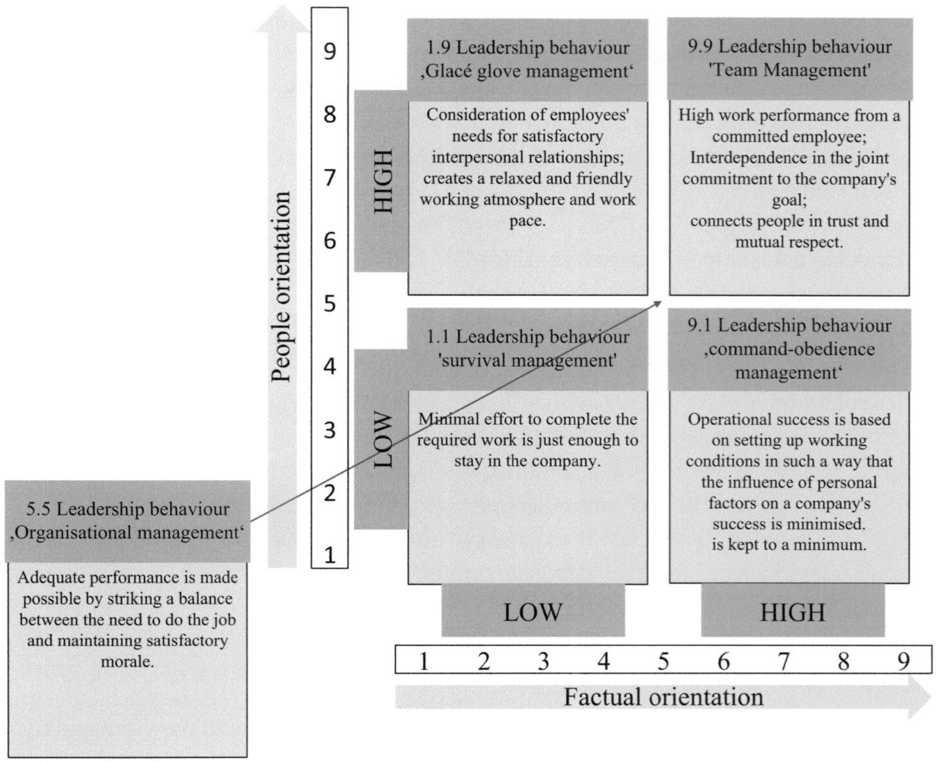

Fig. 3.17 Leadership typologies. (Adapted from: Cope, 2003, p. 354)

Example: Leadership Typologies in Companies

In the discussion about leadership typologies, the typology of *Blake* and *Mouton* emphasises the same aspect.

An essential part of this approach is the integration of task orientation or relationship orientation within the leadership situation. This results in two dimensions, the dimensions of relationship orientation and task orientation. *Blake* and *Mouton* refer to these as the dimension of 'emphasis on people' and 'emphasis on the task', as shown in Fig. 3.17.

Although 1.9 and 9.9 both represent a high emphasis on people in the context of leadership style, these emphases manifest in different ways in both cases:

1.9 describes the populist leadership personality: There is a high emphasis on people, but a low emphasis on the task. Interpersonal relationships are highly valued, and there is a friendly and pleasant working atmosphere without performance pressure. This is also referred to as 'kid glove' or 'Country Club' management. 9.9: Here, the leadership personality is the motivator who respects the abilities of the employees and their individuality. High performance motivation or striving for achievement is combined with a pleasant working atmosphere among each other, referred to as 'Team Management' (Hungenberg & Wulf, 2006, p. 354). ◀

In a multidimensional schema, quantifiable differences in degrees are qualitative differences in kind.

vi. The characteristic of 'counterintuition'[68]

> From Thomas More in 1515 to Pogo in the mid twentieth century it has long been acknowledged that people seeking to solve a problem often make it worse (John D. Sterman).

Under counterintuitive events, *Gharajedaghi* understands events that contradict the intuitions (presumptive grasping) underlying everyday experiences. The idea that the earth is not a disc, but a sphere, is not intuitively comprehensible. Similarly, the fact that the earth revolves around the sun contradicts everyday intuitive knowledge.

For him, counterintuitive behaviour means "that actions intended to produce a desired outcome may, in fact, generate opposite results" (Gharajedaghi, 2005, p. 49). Here are three examples:

Example: Milk Shortage in England

During World War II in England, there was a milk shortage due to the German blockade, which particularly affected the poorer population. It is hardly surprising that the Labour Party demanded, in essence: "We want milk for the children of the poor and no milk for the cats of the rich…" (see Samuelson, 2007, p. 69) And indeed, a maximum price for milk was set to achieve the targeted goal. But what happened was the exact opposite. Numerous farmers in England saw no sufficient profit in producing more milk and focussed on other, more lucrative agricultural activities. The result was that milk became even scarcer. ◀

In this case, non-intervention might have achieved the desired effect. High milk prices attract more farmers to take up or expand milk production. Due to the increasing supply, the price drops and milk becomes affordable for the poor again.

Example: Problems with Cattle Breeding in Kenya

A similar example (well-intentioned, but achieving the opposite) occurred in Kenya, where the 'Kenya Meat Commission (KMC)' believed it was undemocratic that beef prices had become unaffordable for ordinary citizens. So, they decided to freeze the

[68] Jay *Forrester* first introduced this term in this context. See Forrester (1971).

prices. Six months later, the 'managing commissioner' of the KMC gave the following statements in a press interview, clearly showing that exactly the opposite of what was intended had happened:

a) "Cattle are scarce in the country, but I do not know why."
b) "People are eating too much beef, and unless they diversify their eating habits and eat other foodstuffs, the shortage of beef will continue." (Lipsey & Courant, 1996, p. 127). ◀

Here we have the same effect as in the first example and the obvious admission of the Commission President that he cannot explain the development.

Finally, another example from the series of counterintuitive behaviours:

Example: Problems in the housing market

To provide better protection for tenants, the state decides to cap rental prices (maximum prices). This initially reduces the price of rental flats. However, this may deter potential landlords, causing them to build fewer houses and renovate existing ones less frequently. In the medium term, this makes housing more scarce. This state intervention of introducing maximum prices will ultimately fail to achieve the goal of creating sufficient affordable housing. On the contrary, the housing shortage will increase. ◀

The series of such examples could be continued indefinitely and, for example, applied to 'minimum wages for workers', 'maximum wages for top managers', 'interest rate caps for the euro area', etc.

The cause of the intuitive misinterpretation of events lies in a lack of understanding of simple economic market processes.

Finally, one last aspect:

It is said that a frog thrown into boiling water will immediately jump out of the pot. But if you put it in warm water and heat it slowly, it will stay in the pot without resistance until it is cooked. This is also referred to as the 'Pan Am Syndrome'[69], when one slowly and continuously, little and a little too late, adapts to a barely noticeable change in the system. And so *Gharajedaghi* states:

> Passive adaptation to a deteriorating environment is a road to disaster (Gharajedaghi, 2005, p. 49).

---

[69]The airline Pan Am, founded in 1927, experienced exactly what is described above and had to declare bankruptcy at the end of a long period in 1991. Five years later, it was reestablished by former employees, only to cease operations shortly thereafter. See "Pan Am—the history of a legendary airline". http://www.austrianwings.info/2011/12/pan-am-die-geschichte-einer-legendaeren-airline/.

3.3.2.4 What are Models?

Models are also systems, but they have emerged from other systems. In this book, the definition of *Niemeyer* is used. He defines models as follows:

Definition: Model

> Models are material or immaterial systems that represent other systems in such a way that an experimental manipulation of the depicted structures and states becomes possible (Niemeyer, 1977, p. 57).

Model building usually results in a simplification compared to the original. Since the results from the consideration of the models are to be transferred to the original system, an as exact as possible representation is necessary. However, this means that the important, central properties of the system must be found in the model. What is understood by 'important' or 'central', however, depends on the questions or the objective of the planned investigation. Thus, neoclassical economics works with closed models, with problems of simple relationships that tend towards equilibrium and can only be disturbed by exogenous shocks. In this book, however, the focus is on models that do not rely on exogenous stimuli and can explain evolutionary diverse equilibrium and disequilibrium processes as endogenous developments.

This brings model building close to the idea of theory building. Theories also want to simplify reality, make it 'graspable'. If one were to depict reality 1:1, one would no longer have a theory and the construct would be useless.[70]

Example of a pointless theory

One can compare a theory, for example, with a city map of Dortmund. The most complete and comprehensive city map would have a scale of 1:1. This map would therefore be able to capture all the details of Dortmund, but it would also be exactly as large as the area of Dortmund itself and therefore pointless. Only a different scale,

[70] Lewis *Carroll* writes in one of his works about such a map: "We actually made a map of the country on the scale of a mile to the mile." It was not often used because the potential users protested against unfolding it: "'It has never been spreadout, yet', said Mein Herr: 'The farmers objected: they said it would cover the whole country, and shut out the sunlight! So we now use the country itself, as its own map, and I assure you it dows nearly as well'," it says in a consistent manner at one point. See Carroll (1893).

In his treatise 'On the Rigor of Science' *Borges* tells a similar story. In this story, ever larger maps are produced, until the map of a province took up the size of a city, the size of the map of the empire the size of a province. But all the maps were not accurate enough, so a map was created that exactly matched the size of the empire. The strict science, however, which had completely captured the empire, sinks into insignificance along with the map, since the empire already exists and does not need an exact copy. The map thus falls apart over the years into pieces and all that remains are ruins of the map, "inhabited by animals"… (Borges, 2005).

e.g. 1:5000, allows you to get a good overview of the city centre with its main streets, squares and buildings in a handy form. The fact that not every rubbish can and every ATM is listed here is the result of reducing the scale and focussing on certain questions, such as: What streets are there in the city centre? Where can I find the train station? Where is the pedestrian zone? etc. We must metaphorically apply *Ockham's* Razor (Mole, 2010) to finally represent the necessary, but no more.

Only these questions enable the focus on the essentials and the design of a city map. Ultimately, it is a reduction of reality under certain questions with the result of getting an answer to these questions that satisfies me as the questioner. In the case of the city map, for example, a visitor to the city can quickly find the theatre without wandering around the city for hours. ◀

So if we have so far referred to our models as systems, this was quite correct in the sense of the above definition. With the help of models, we can try to depict real systems. The model as a system is supposed to help us better understand the real systems.

In the following, the basic features of the new approach will be presented and discussed with introductory simulations.

3.4 Modeling and Simulation of Complex Systems

3.4.1 Systems Dynamics—The 'new' Language

In order to qualitatively and quantitatively investigate the behaviour of complex systems using small simulation models, methodologies should be used that are mastered by a variety of simulation tools. These tools include software programmes such as 'AnyLogic'[71], 'Consideo Modeler'[72], 'Gamma'[73], 'Heraklit'[74], 'iThink'[75],

[71] In addition to 'Systems Dynamics', AnyLogic is also based on Process centric (Discrete Events) (1960s) and 'Agent Based-Modeling' (1990s). See http://www.xjtek.com/anylogic/approaches/.

[72] The company *Consideo* GmbH has developed the *Modeler* software, which allows both qualitative and quantitative analyses. Since 2012, the *iModeler* has also been available as a web tool that shows the interrelationships on a three-dimensional football that can be rotated as desired, thus allowing flexible perspectives. See http://www.consideo-modeler.de/index.html.

[73] The company *TopSim* from Tübingen pursues a purely qualitative approach with its software *'Gamma'* and is therefore also suitable for users who are not mathematically versed; which does not mean that the other mentioned products can only be used if you have studied mathematics! Especially since there, for example, only qualitative solutions can be simulated. See http://www.topsim.com/de/vernetztes_denken/gamma/.

[74] The *Heraklit* software is a tool that ranges from simple effect networks to authoring systems for business games. See http://www.vernetzt-denken.de/index.htm.

[75] The software from the company *isee systems* received the Forrester Prize in 1987 as the first corresponding Systems-Dynamics software.

'mystrategy'[76] 'Powersim'[77], 'Simulistics'[78], 'True World'[79] and e.g. 'vensim'[80], are used: *Systems Dynamics.*

In the qualitative analysis, interrelationships are shown that illustrate the behaviour of the system in different scenarios in the short or long term as well as the behaviour and influence of individual factors. These can be described, for example, with terms of *Systems Thinking*. For the purpose of quantitative analysis, however, one often resorts to the (stricter) terminologies of Systems Dynamics. This methodology was developed by Jay Wright *Forrester* in the 1960s to be able to quantitatively simulate the dynamic behaviour of control loops in cybernetics on computers (Forrester, 1972). Ultimately, with the help of the Systems Dynamics approach, complex, dynamic problems can be investigated in order to develop forecasts, for example, by entering specific numerical values. However, one also finds different notations in the literature that mean the same thing in content (Strohecker & Fischer, 2008). The notations necessary here have been mentioned in the context of the system concept.

Even in the historical consideration of the concept of systems, it became clear that there are large degrees of freedom in the analysis of systems, as the systems are described depending on certain, goal-oriented questions. This is an important aspect in modeling. Ultimately, 'modeling' is only successful if not everything is linked with everything, but rather, starting from a concrete question, the model is created with a focus on the essential aspects. Thus, one could proceed according to the *Know-Why-Method* and ask after identifying the target factor, which measures are specifically needed to achieve the factor considered important. In doing so, one could include both the present and the future in detail and ask: What helps the factor to be achieved, what endangers the achievement, what will be needed in the future for the achievement and what could happen in the future (Neumann, 2009, p. 33 ff.)? This method assumes that a system is successful if it moves on the dynamic wave between integration and innovation. Figure 3.18 shows the associated questioning technique for model building once again in an overview:

---

[76] *'mystrategy'* offers itself as an alternative to traditional work with tables (calculations); the developers speak of a 'powerful approach to strategy and business management'. The director Kim Warren received the Forrester Prize in 2005 for his contribution to Strategy and System Dynamics. http://www.strategydynamics.com/.

[77] The Norwegian company *Powersim* Software AS has created a product with its strategic simulation software *Powersim* that was specifically designed for business simulations and sees itself as a leader in the field of BI (Business Intelligence). See http://www.powersim.com/.

[78] *'Simulistics'* is based on Systems Dynamics and also allows object-oriented modeling and simulation. See http://www.simulistics.com/index.htm.

[79] The French company *'True World'* develops Systems Dynamics software and offers, among other mathematical subtleties, e.g. '4D virtual Prototyping', with the help of which plastic 3D scenarios can be designed and animated. See http://www.true-world.com/index.html.

[80] *Vesim* is an American product of *Ventana Systems,* Inc from Harvard. See http://www.vensim.com/index.html.

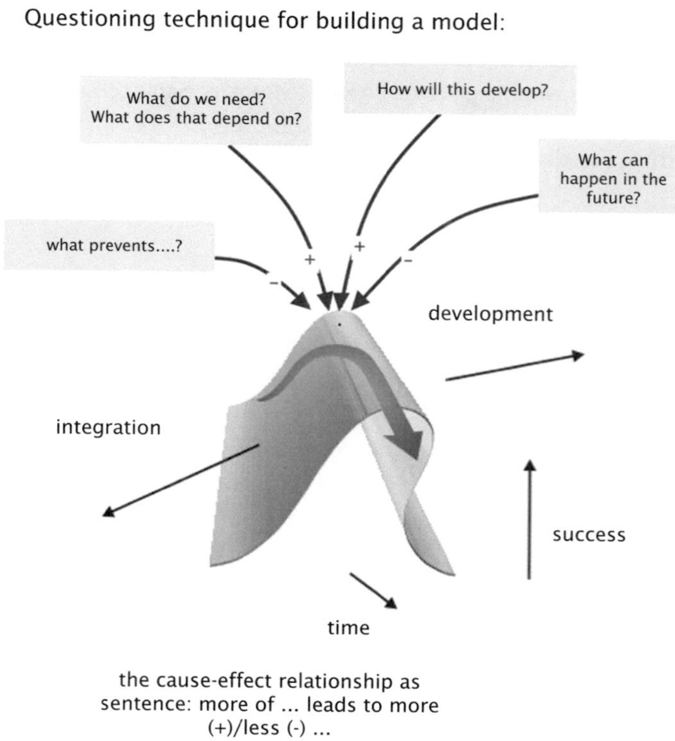

Fig. 3.18 Questioning technique for model building. *Source* Figure provided by Consideo. www.consideo.de

3.4.2 Simulations with Counterintuitive System Behaviour

In this section, we want to examine feedback loops. Initially, the problem is that we colloquially evaluate the term feedback differently than it is done here. For example, if someone receives "feedback" from their supervisor during an employee interview, one wonders whether this feedback is positive or negative, i.e., whether the work performed was good or bad from the supervisor's perspective. In the context of systems, however, it is not about such evaluations as 'praising' or 'criticising', as we will see shortly. Rather, positive feedback loops are about self-reinforcing and negative feedback loops are about self-correcting processes.[81] Such feedbacks have been known since classical antiquity and were initially described as contradictions. *Strunk* and *Schiepek* therefore rightly point out that, for example, in the original designation "vicious circle", which refers to permanently reinforcing feedbacks, *Aristotle* (384 to 322 BC) "did not mean system

[81] See also Sterman (2000, p. 14).

dynamics, but a logical fallacy (he meant, the author), in which what is to be proven is already assumed as a premise. Only later did the logical vicious circle become a system structure and dynamics with positive feedback" (Strunk & Schiepek, 2014, p. 22).

3.4.2.1 Positive Feedback Loops

Example: Saving—Part 1

Franz *Simple* turns twenty years old and wants to do something for his retirement provision. He has saved 10,000 € and wants to invest it profitably for old age. His goal is to have the money available at the age of sixty. He deposits the money in the bank, which guarantees him 5% interest per year until the end of his sixtieth year of life. After one year, he has thus earned 10,500 €. He takes down the 500 € interest and hides it under his pillow. After another year at 5% interest, he receives another 500 €. After forty years, he has thus (ceteris paribus) saved a total of 29,500 €, almost tripling his initial stock. ◀

Figure 3.19 shows the relationship outlined in the example in the language of Systems Dynamics. We have a stock size (the account balance) and a flow size (the interest). Furthermore, we have a relationship from the interest towards the account balance. This relationship is positive (symbolised by the plus sign). That is, if the interest rises, the account balance also rises.

Example: Saving—Part 2

Anna *Complex* also saves 10,000 € and takes it to the bank. She also receives 5% interest. After one year, she has thus also earned 10,500 €. However, she leaves the interest at the bank. Thus, in the second year, she receives 525 € interest for the 10,500 € at 5% interest. So in total, she has 11,025 € after the second year. After 40 years, she has thus saved 70,399.89 €, seven times her initial amount. ◀

Figure 3.20 shows the change compared to the first case. While in the first case we only had a positive arrow from the interest to the account balance, now a positive arrow goes back to the interest. So we have a feedback process that leads to the extreme growth of the account balance compared to the first case.

Figures 3.21 and 3.22 vividly show the linear growth of the account balance in the first example and the exponential growth of the account balance in the second example.

Fig. 3.19 Lineal relationship

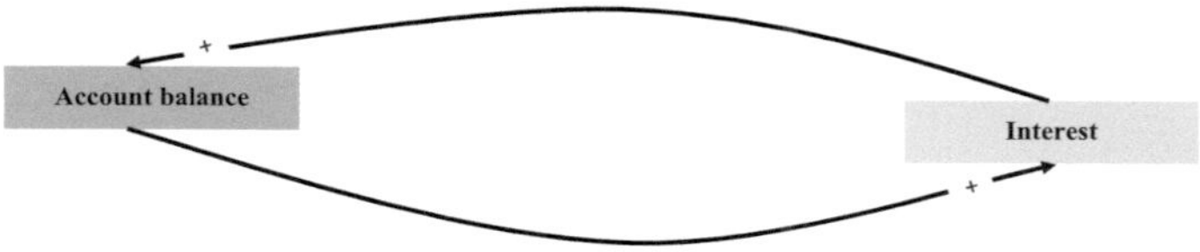

Fig. 3.20 Positive Feedback

Fig. 3.21 Linear Growth

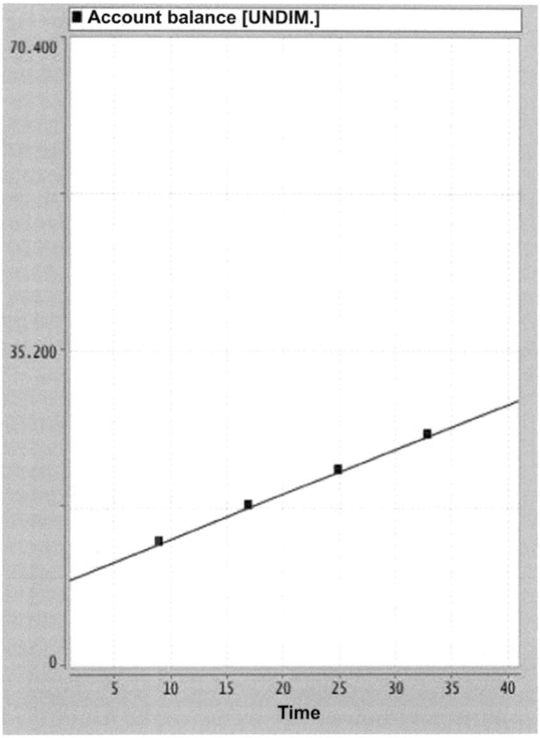

Positive feedback loops are therefore self-reinforcing. The more interest, the more in the account, the higher the account balance, the more interest. If this loop is the only one influencing the account balance, then the account balance grows exponentially and is at most limited by the finite time limit.

But downward spirals also belong to positive feedback, even if those affected may not find anything positive about it, as the following example shows:

Example: positive feedback—economic downturn

Due to a country's debt, its interest rates rise. The high interest rates lead to a decrease in the demand for investment goods, as loans become too expensive. As a result, the supply of investment goods also decreases. This leads to a decrease in

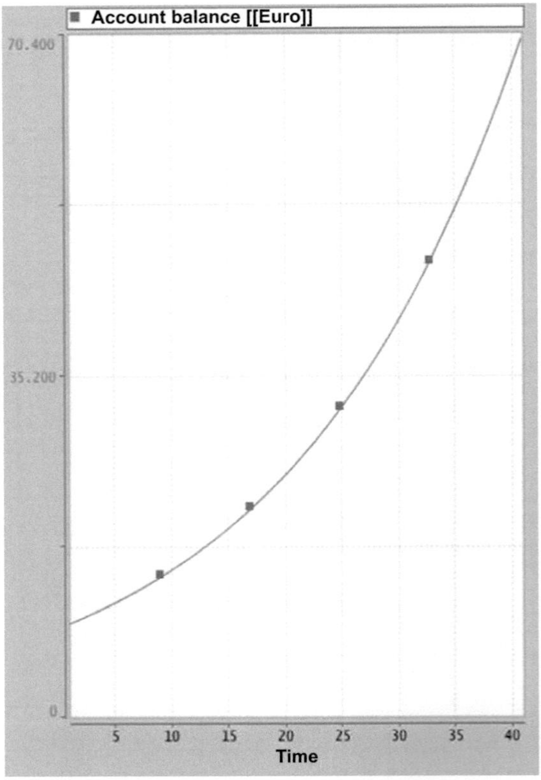

Fig. 3.22 Exponential Growth

employment or an increase in unemployment, and thus to a decrease in national income. This leads to a decrease in the demand for consumer goods. As a result, the supply of consumer goods decreases. Employment continues to decrease or unemployment continues to increase, and national income continues to decrease. This leads to a further decrease in the demand for consumer goods etc. ◀

But growth scenarios can also reach their limits. The overshoot and collapse scenario shows the cases where a growth strategy has a negative impact on the performance limits of a system. This phenomenon explains, for example, the collapse of dotcoms, the Enron debacle, and the fate of many companies that pursue a short-sighted growth strategy without considering capacity limits and/or their environment.

Examples: Limits of Growth

a) The more young people find it 'cool' to wear 'lifestyle brands' from America, the more desirable they become. But: Today's fashion trend can quickly become tomorrow's fashion sin.

b) The more a stock is bought, the more people want to acquire it. But: Speculative bubbles can burst quickly. ◀

Each of us knows that—even if the interest rates are high—our account balance rarely grows indefinitely. So there must be limits to growth[82]. These limits are created by negative feedback loops.

When we incorporate the influence of performance limits, capacity limits into our simple positive feedback loop, we create a system that generates an oscillating curve.

Example: Saving with a Goal

Anna *Komplex* saves 10,000 € and takes it to the bank. She receives 5% interest annually and wants to have the money available after 40 years. Unlike her previous plan, she does not need more than 50,000 €. To achieve this goal, she checks every year whether she has already reached the 50,000 €. If this is the case, she withdraws an amount x from the account. She calculates this by determining the discrepancy between her goal and the account balance, multiplying this difference by three, and subtracting it from the account balance. She could also choose a different amount for correction, but Anna is satisfied with her choice.

Figure 3.23 shows the positive loop system with integrated target-actual comparison (discrepancy).

The result is a curve that initially grows exponentially due to self-reinforcing processes. However, from a certain point in time, when the target-actual comparison takes effect, it begins to oscillate. Figure 3.24 shows the exact course of the curve, the development of the account balance over 40 years. ◀

The exponential growth resulting from a positive feedback loop assumes unlimited resources. In reality, these are rarely unlimited, so positive feedback loops are slowed down and begin to oscillate as performance limits are reached.

Here is a final example from the startup scene:

Example: 'Air Bed and Breakfast' (positive feedback loop)

The Expo in Hanover is a popular event for business people. All of Hanover is booked out! Whether it's a hotel, inn, or small youth hostel. All beds are occupied. The prices for the last available rooms in the exhibition city are skyrocketing. On a whim, Theo *Lienzo* and Yvonne *Holzmacher* offer their guest room to two businessmen from Jordan. They not only accept gratefully, but also send a request for more rooms to the

[82] The term 'limits to growth' reminds of the study of the same name ('Limits to Growth') by the Club of Rome in 1972. And indeed, none other than Jay W. *Forrester's* 'Institute for System Dynamics' was involved in the creation of this study, by Donella and Dennis *Meadows* and their colleagues creating a world model using Systems Dynamics (Meadows et al., 1972).

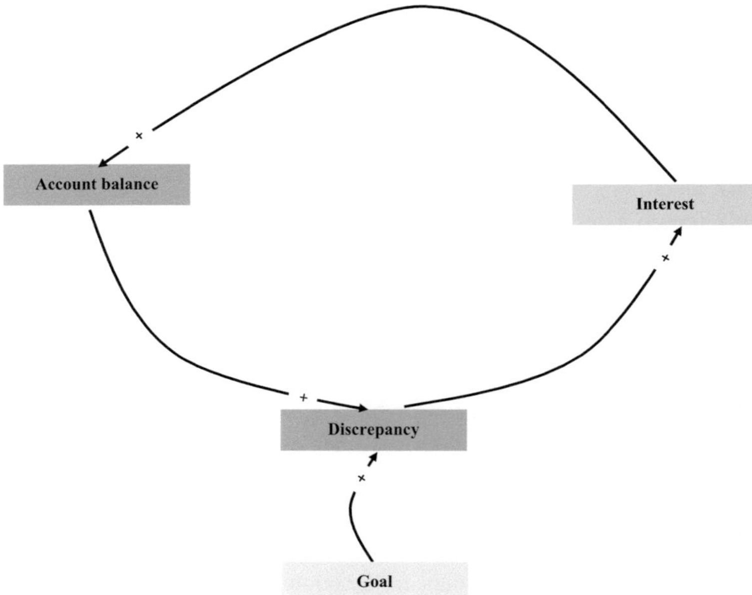

Fig. 3.23 Positive feedback with target-actual comparison or control variable (discrepancy)

two hospitable landlords. Their business partners from Berlin are also facing the problem of finding accommodation. Mr. *Lienzo* and Ms. *Holzmacher* did not expect this high demand! They 'spin' the idea further: "Why not develop a business model out of it?!", thinks Mr. *Lienzo*. "Where a scarce supply of accommodations meets high demand, private providers could make good revenues." "But it would have to run professionally via an internet platform," replies Yvonne *Holzmacher*. Said and done! Just a year later at the IAA, the site they call "Air Bed and Breakfast" is live. It is a self-reinforcing system: The more travellers demand the offered private flats, the more providers join. But it could also be formulated the other way around: The more providers there are, the more people book the private flats. ◀

3.4.2.2 Negative Feedback Loops

Example: Consumption and Saving

Franz *Simpel* still has 10,000 €, which he deposits in his bank. By standing order, he now transfers 1000 € annually. The account balance grows and grows. The higher the account balance grows, the more Franz's needs to spend the money also grow. The desire to buy increases. We could assume, ceteris paribus, that Franz's wish is to always spend 5% of the saved sum per year. Assuming that the influence of Franz's purchasing desires is the only feedback loop that affects the account balance, then the

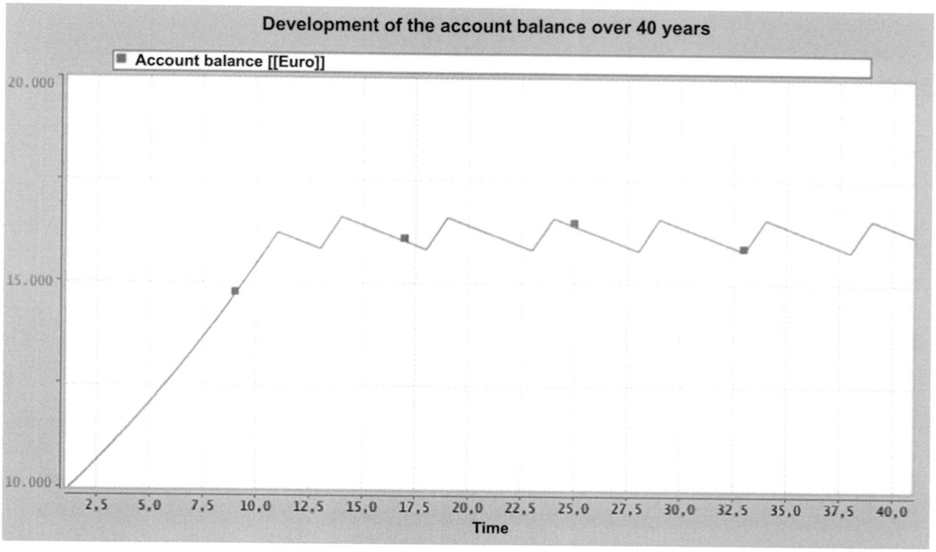

Fig. 3.24 Positive feedback with delay

increase caused by saving is reduced by the negative impact on the account balance, as Fig. 3.25 shows, so that the account balance eventually aims for a fixed amount.

We assume that Franz initially has 10,000 € in his current account. At the end of the year, he takes 5%, or 500 €, off the account. 1000 € are automatically deposited on 01.01. of the following year. Thus, since there are no interest rates, there are still 10,500 € in the account on 01.01. So we have a net increase of 500 €. In the second year, Franz thus takes 525 €, etc. The process should not last longer than 40 years. We see that the money in the account actually increases, but the increase decreases (diminishing marginal returns). After 20 years, the annual increase is only 200 €, after 40 years just 70 €, and he has about 18,647 € in the account at the end of the term.

Figure 3.26 shows the negative feedback loop. We see that the loop leading from the desire to consume to the account balance is marked with a minus sign, indicating the negative feedback. ◀

Example: Diminishing Marginal Utility

The economic example for the above curve progression is the law of marginal utility, which concerns the demand side. Jeremy *Bentham's* approach of Utilitarianism ("the greatest happiness of the greatest number"—"The greatest happiness of the greatest number" (Bentham, 1822, p. 20). motivates collective utility maximisation. The law of marginal utility states that initially the marginal utility of consuming a good increases disproportionately, but then the marginal utility decreases until eventually the consumption of another unit of the good generates no additional utility and

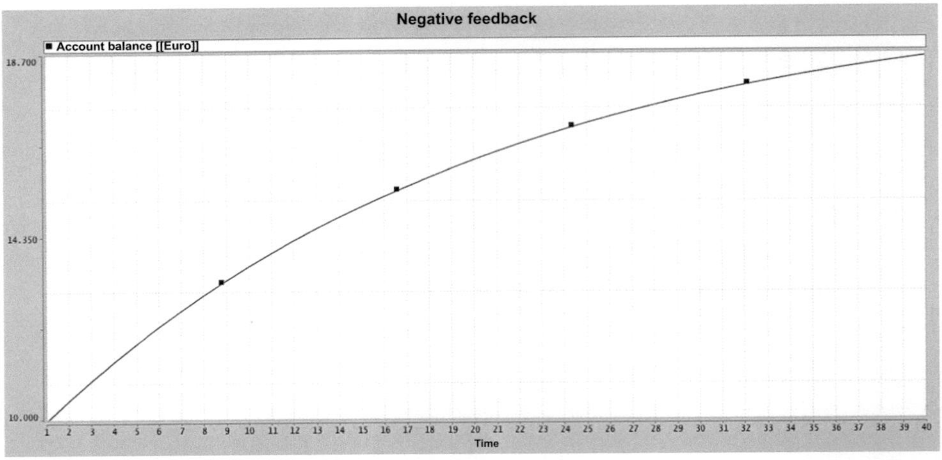

Fig. 3.25 Negative Feedback

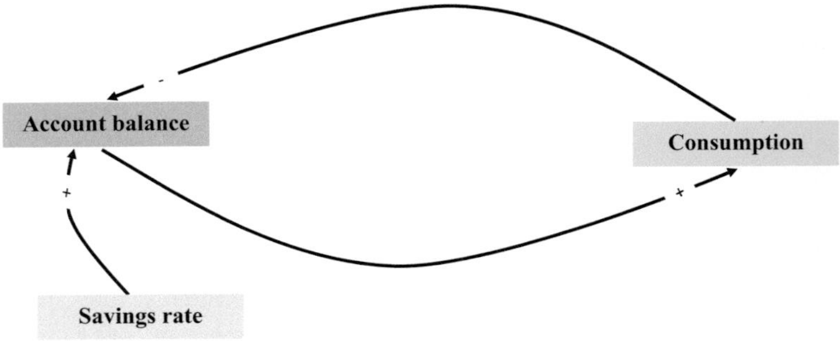

Fig. 3.26 Negative Feedback

thus the demand for this good does not further increase.[83] *Gossen's*[84] first law, the law of diminishing marginal utility on the demand side, and the law of returns with its diminishing marginal returns on the production side, contribute to the equilibrium of the above-described supply-demand model through the price. ◀

---

[83] By the way, marginal utility and marginal returns can also become negative.

[84] Hermann Heinrich *Gossen* derived the law of diminishing marginal utility from *Bentham's* utilitarian philosophy. *Gossen* himself describes his law as follows: "The size of one and the same pleasure decreases continuously if we continue to prepare the pleasure without interruption, until saturation occurs" (Gossen, 1854, p. 4 f.). In addition to this first law, we find a second law in *Gossen* that states that the total utility in a household is greatest when the marginal utility caused by the (last) purchased goods is equal. Together, these are referred to as the *Gossen* Laws.

If we integrate a target here, e.g. build capacity limits into our simple positive feedback loop, we create a system that generates an oscillating curve.

Example: Saving and Consuming with a Goal

Anna *Complex* saves 10,000 € and takes it to the bank. She consumes 5% annually. Unlike Franz *Simple*'s plan, she actually doesn't need more than 800 € per year. To achieve this goal, she checks every year if she has already reached the 800 € at 5% consumption. If this is not yet the case, she takes the 5% from the account. Otherwise, she tries to approach the desired consumption through a correction factor. Figure 3.27 shows the negative loop system with integrated target-actual comparison (discrepancy).

The result in the account balance is a curve that initially has decreasing marginal returns like a negative feedback. Only at the moment when consumption is above the desired maximum amount, the correction factor comes into play, which due to the time delay leads to an oscillating curve. Figure 3.28 shows the exact course of the non-linear curve. ◀

The longer the time delays last, the more difficult the control process of systems becomes.

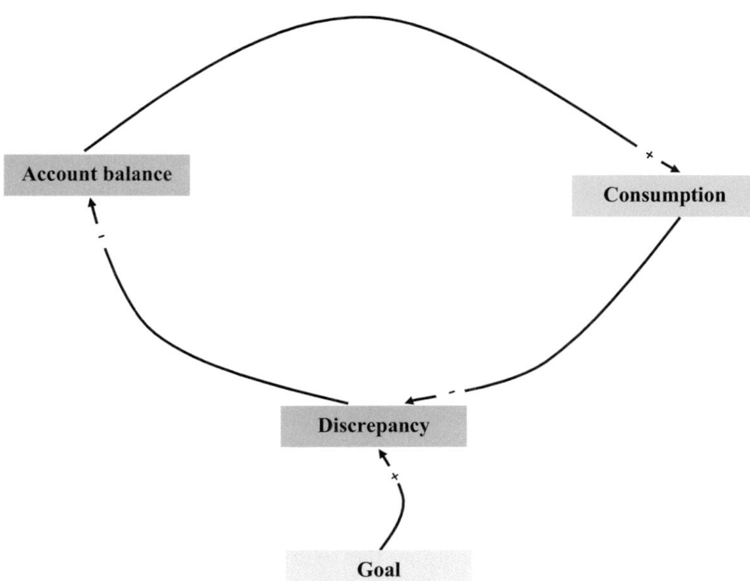

Fig. 3.27 Negative feedback with target-actual comparison or control variable (discrepancy)

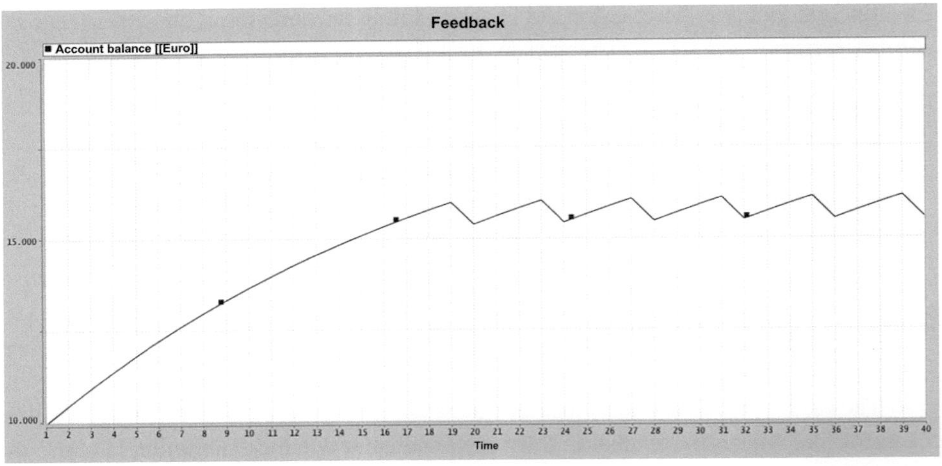

Fig. 3.28 Negative feedback with delay

Example: Showering with Warm Water

Everyone knows this situation. You are a guest in a hotel and decide to use the shower to freshen up before the evening. You want to shower with pleasantly warm water and find a mixer tap in the shower, which, depending on the deflection, adds warm or cold water. Since you have no experience with the shower in the hotel, you first open the tap in the presumably correct position. If only cold water comes, you turn the tap more towards 'warm'. With a bit of bad luck, it suddenly becomes boiling hot and you turn the tap towards 'cold'. The water suddenly becomes ice cold. And so it takes quite a while until you have found out which position of the mixer tap produces the ideal water temperature. The problem of finding the right water temperature is related to the small time delays between turning on and changing the temperature. And the longer the time delay lasts, the more difficult it is to adjust the temperature correctly. ◀

Let's look at a pure negative feedback loop without delays:

Example: Thermostat (Negative Feedback Loop)

In this example, we have a typical negative feedback procedure. The heating warms up the room. The heating temperature, which is determined by a warming factor, i.e., the output of the heating, serves as input for the thermostat, which measures the room temperature. The rule is: the higher the heating temperature, the higher the room temperature. The thermostat tells the heating how warm the room is and gradually regulates the heating down: the higher the room temperature, the lower the heating temperature. The relationship between heating (heating temperature) and thermostat (room temperature) represents a negative feedback loop.

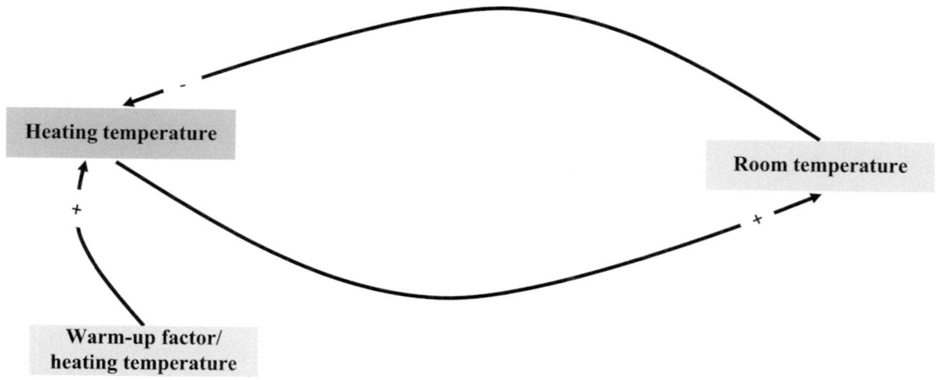

Fig. 3.29 Negative feedback using the example of a heating system (thermostat)

Figure 3.29 illustrates the idea of 'negative feedback' using the example of a heating system.

The result in Fig. 3.30 shows a room heating that slowly approaches the desired room temperature. ◀

Finally, let's look at an example on the topic of founding:

Example: The History of Mini-Looms

Gregor *Saal* watched his daughters Lilly and Laura with fascination. The two were weaving spectacular bracelets out of colourful rubber bands. They spent hours trying out new creations. The engineer was impressed by the skill of his offspring, but at the same time, he thought: "There must be a better solution!" True to the often

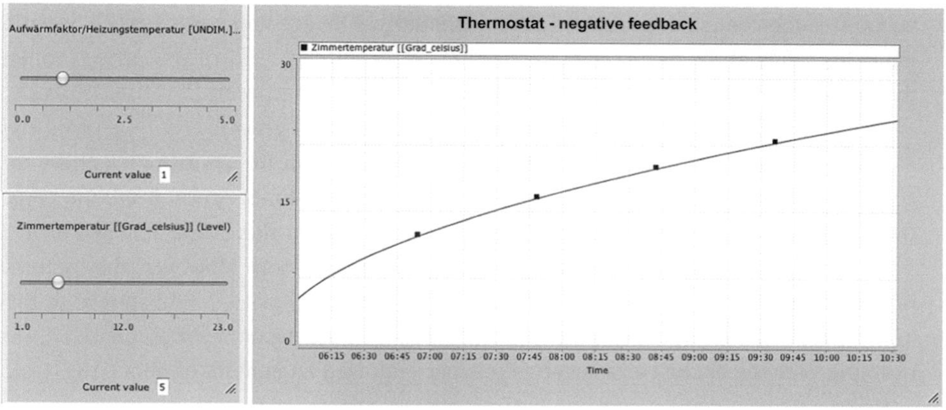

Fig. 3.30 Simulation of room temperature—negative feedback

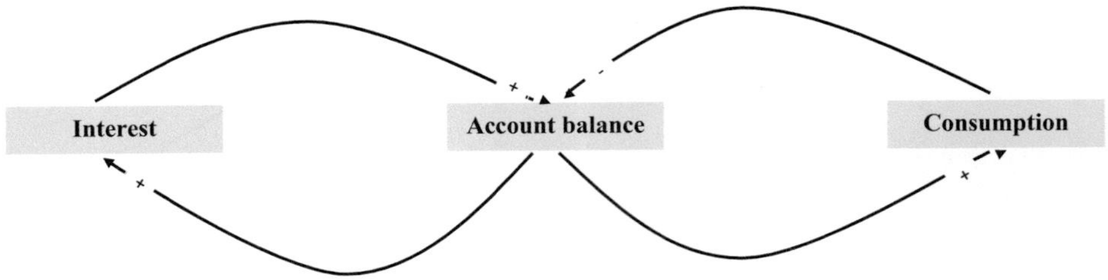

Fig. 3.31 Double feedback loop

humorously formulated motto of his profession "nothing is too hard for an engineer", he set to work developing a mini-loom. The goal was to make the manual work easier with the help of the machine and, not least, to impress his daughters. Mr. *Saal's* daughters tested the prototype and confirmed that making the bracelets was now much easier. "Think big!", he thought and went into mass production with a friend from Beijing. The mini-looms were a hit! No girl in the schoolyard was without a mini-loom. Even stars and celebrities were thrilled by the innovation. Everyone loved these bands—and everyone wore them! But if everyone had it, where was the appeal? People simply got tired of the bands, the trend was over. Mr. *Saal's* sales figures rose more and more slowly, but they stabilised at a level that he still considered good, but that also made it clear that the turnover was not "skyrocketing". ◀

3.4.2.3 Double Feedback Loops

Positive and negative feedback loops can naturally also be coupled together, as illustrated in Fig. 3.31.

Example: Saving—Consuming

Anna Komplex has decided to put the 10,000 € she has saved into a savings account and add a constant savings rate of 1000 € annually. The account earns her 1% interest annually. Once at the end of the year, she wants to withdraw 5% of the savings to use the money for Christmas shopping, i.e., for consumption purposes.

How does the account balance develop over the next 40 years?

Well, due to the fact that the interest rate is lower than the consumption rate, the account balance will probably increase less and less over time. And indeed, the negative feedback loop overlays the positive feedback loop to the extent that we have a similar effect as with the exclusively negative feedback loop. However, the increase in the amount of money does not decrease quite as quickly as Fig. 3.32 shows, so that at the end of the 40 years she has about 21,947 € in the account. In comparison, the example with the exclusively negative feedback showed an amount of about 18,647 €.

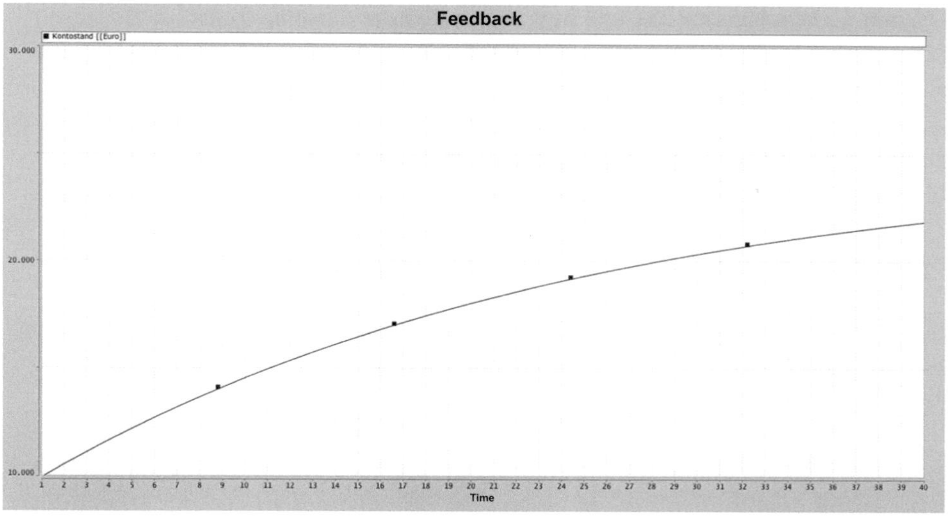

Fig. 3.32 Decreasing marginal returns: "Feedback"

If Anna *Komplex* were to receive 8% interest each year instead of just 1%, then the positive feedback loop would clearly dominate, leading to exponential growth and she would have the enormous sum of about 103,904 € in her account at the end of the 40 years, as Fig. 3.33 shows. ◀

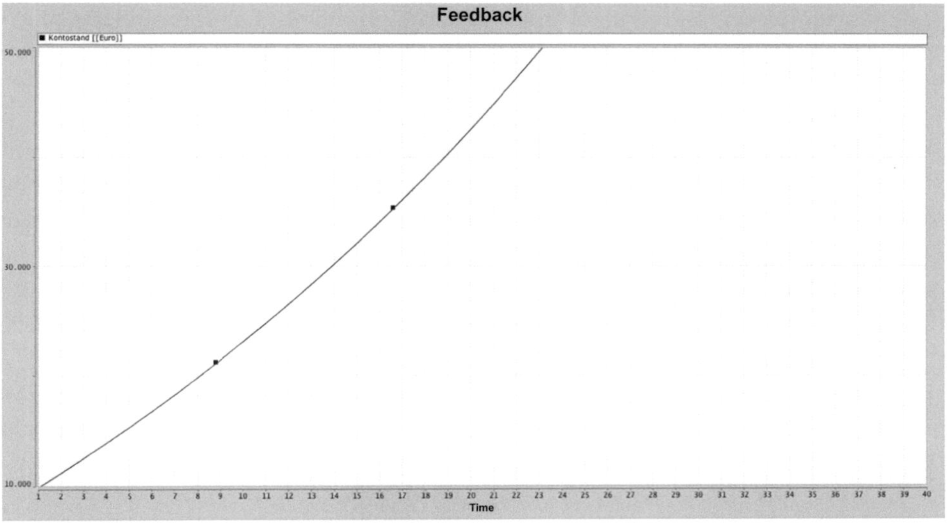

Fig. 3.33 Increasing marginal returns: "Feedback"

Overall, we can thus consider four important aspects of dynamic feedback:

a) **Positive feedback:**
   Positive feedback loops amplify and accelerate processes, regardless of whether the amplification processes are upward or downward spirals.
b) **Negative feedback:**
   Negative feedback loops have a weakening effect. Changes are slowed down and oscillations are dampened, so that a balance point is eventually reached.
c) **Double feedback:**
   The coupling of negative and positive feedback loops leads, depending on the strength of one or the other feedback, to different behaviours of the system.
d) **Time delays:**
   Time delays make the feedback processes independent and lead to oscillating movements within the feedback loops.

3.4.3 System Archetypes—Dealing with Complexity

At the beginning of our explanations, we saw that even the behaviour in relatively simple systems can sometimes cause difficulties and that there are a multitude of systematic errors that we can make in simple systems. It also became clear that there are four typical strategies, 'trial and error', 'fading out', 'simplify' and 'rational behaviour—reduction', which can be observed in the context of complex situations. We further claimed that none of the listed strategies will help to master complex situations.

In the previous discussions, it became clear how significant dynamic feedback is for understanding systems. Peter *Senge* points out that, from a system standpoint, delays and feedback loops are usually oriented towards long-term developments and can often be ignored from a short-term perspective. But they "take their revenge in the long run" (Senge, 2011, p. 112), he says. Based on the first studies, for example, of the Club of Rome, which are based on the 'System Dynamics' approach, *Strunk* and *Schiepek* point out that *Senge* refers to the fact that "similarities in problem situations and system dynamics would have repeatedly arisen in the consultation of companies based on the system approach" (Strunk & Schiepek, 2014, p. 35). *Senge* refers to these in his book 'The Fifth Discipline' as system archetypes, whose building blocks are the feedback loops and delays (Senge, 2011, p. 112).

Based on our new insights, we therefore want to now examine typical behaviours in systems by working out these system archetypes. However, one must pay attention to *Strunk* and *Schiepek* when they say:

> These archetypes exemplify how one can describe the basic dynamics of at least simpler or moderately complicated systems quite vividly with simple means (Strunk & Schiepek, 2014, p. 35).

In other words: They apparently do not describe truly complex systems either. Nevertheless, *Strunk* and *Schiepek* encourage us when they say:

> Even if the world is indeed more complex, these models are a first step into the application of the instruments of system thinking (Strunk & Schiepek, 2014, p. 35).

3.4.3.1 Equilibrium Process with Delay

The archetype in Figs. 3.34 and 3.35 describes a feedback within a system that is associated with a delay.

To illustrate this type using simulation, we take the following example:

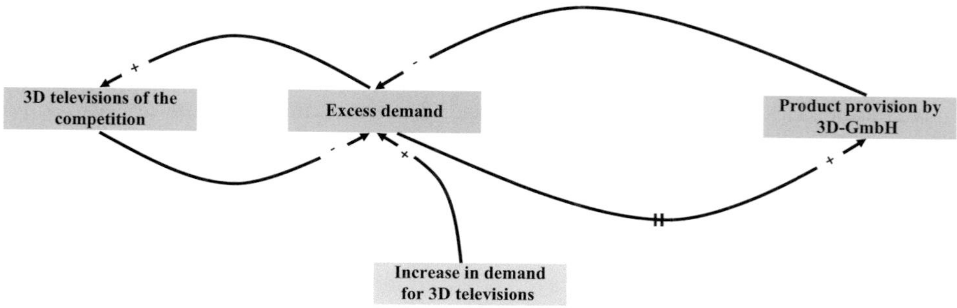

Fig. 3.34 Archetype 1—Model—Equilibrium process with delay

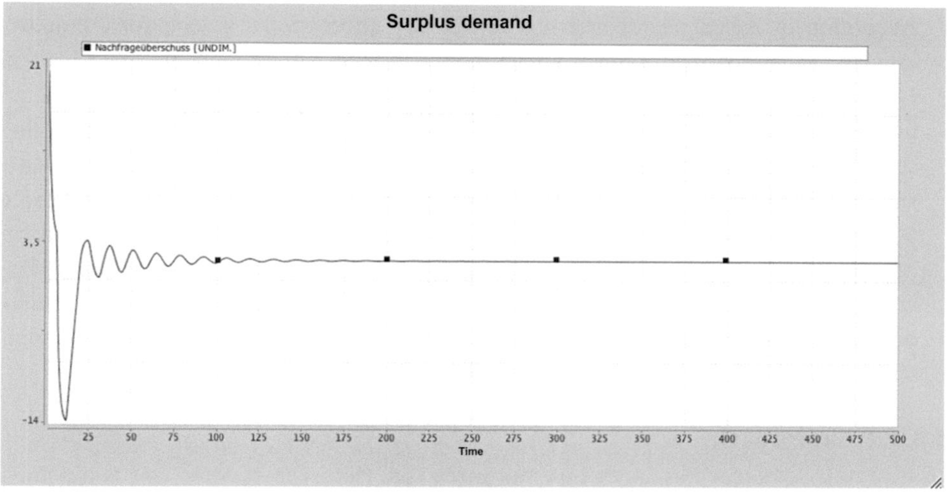

Fig. 3.35 Archetype 1—Simulation—Equilibrium process with delay: "Surplus demand"

Constructed Example: Market Reaction

The young growth company '3D-GmbH' responds to an observed excess demand with a corrective measure (product manufacturing), which, however, is delayed (based on market conditions) and thus is no longer aligned with the current market condition. The modeling shows how initially more corrective measures are taken than necessary, until finally an equilibrium is established with a delay. ◀

Example of Modeling: Expansion of Production or Production Stop at '3D-GmbH'?

"The current market research results show that the demand for 3-D televisions is not yet fully met. We can expand production further!" With these words, Mr. *Ermel,* an entrepreneur and managing director of '3D-GmbH', sets the production strategy and looks forward to the expected profits. But after the products are finished, disillusionment sets in. "We find fewer buyers than expected. The competition was faster in the meantime. The market seems to be saturated for now. I order a temporary production stop," Mr. *Ermel* records at the next company meeting, only to find a few weeks later that this measure also failed and was too drastic. "The market is damn tricky. Now there is suddenly an excess demand again and we could have continued production," grumbles Mr. *Ermel* and is annoyed with himself for not considering in his first decisions that the measures have a delayed effect. If he takes this into account, production will be better aligned with future market conditions and will not be subject to further extreme strategy changes. ◀

Real Example: Demand for Engineers

According to a Spiegel report from 06.09.2011, professional associations, employers and the Minister of Economics dramatise the lack of technicians (engineers) in Germany. In June 2011, 76,400 engineering positions could not be filled, despite an unemployment rate of 20,400 engineers. The result is that the number of engineering students is drastically increasing. In the last decade, they increased by almost 100,000 students. This increases the concern about triggering a pig cycle. For example, about 9000 positions for mechanical engineers become available each year. The number of graduates, with 22,000 students, is significantly above the demand numbers! The actual reason for the unfilled positions is not necessarily a lack of engineers, but a gap between supply and demand for specific disciplines (e.g., electrical, mechanical engineers, etc.) (Ilg & Kaufmann, 2011). ◀

3.4.3.2 Limits of Growth

Growth processes reach limits that are not perceived: Here, for example, one could think of economic crises. Let's choose the following example:

Constructed Example: Market Saturation

A process (here: produced and sold quantity in a market) initially reinforces itself and leads to a phase of growth acceleration. A balancing process (here: the approach to market capacity) leads to a slowdown of the action, until the growth eventually comes to a standstill. ◀

Example for Modeling: The Beetles are Dying Out

When one thinks of "beetles", one not only thinks of small crawling creatures, but also of the famous car that populated German roads for many years. While the beetles multiplied rapidly from the sixties to the eighties and significantly influenced the streetscape of Germany, they are now threatened with extinction. New technology, new models, and new developments put clear limits on the number of beetles (see Figs. 3.36 and 3.37). ◀

Here is another real example:

Real Example: Computer Toy—'Boom and Bust' of an Innovation

At the end of the nineties of the twentieth century, an engineer from Japan invented the 'Tamagotchi', a computer toy that needs to be 'cared for'. It became a hit as many children got the feeling of owning a pet. The product spread rapidly all over the world. But after a year, the market was already saturated and the product was "out" (Schindelbeck, 2009). ◀

3.4.3.3 Problem Shifting

Short-term solutions are applied that promise immediate improvement, but in the long term often apparently turn into their opposite.

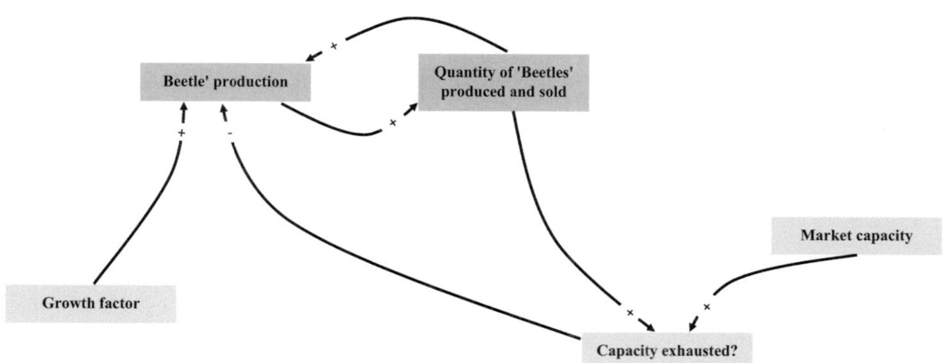

Fig. 3.36 Archetype 2—Model—Limits of Growth

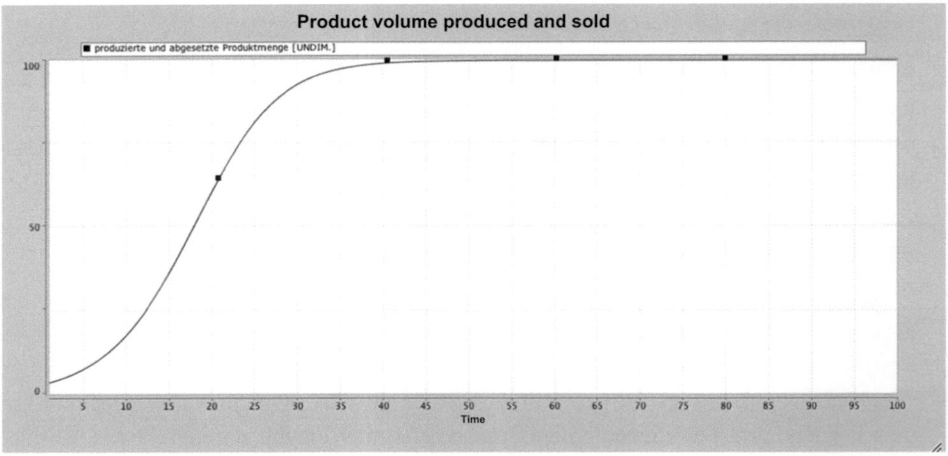

Fig. 3.37 Archetype 2—Simulation—Limits of Growth: "Product volume produced and sold"

Constructed Example: Stress Problems

Regarding the problem (here: stress problems), instead of relying on a fundamental/long-term corrective measure (here: reduction of work), a short-term solution (here: alcohol & nicotine consumption) is resorted to. This short-term solution apparently brings about an immediate improvement in the situation, but has side effects (here: illness) that initially make the fundamental problem solution (here: due to the illness, more work piles up) more difficult and increasingly prevent it, so that the problem intensifies. ◀

Example for Modeling: Alcohol is also not a Solution

Eliana *Zumsiek*, a mathematics student, has had enough. In addition to her job in the cafeteria and housework, there is also a difficult exam in linear algebra. "Studying and working—that can't be all there is," thinks Ms. *Zumsiek* and picks up the phone to plan the evening with her best friend: A cocktail party is supposed to provide relief and distract her. The morning after and several cocktails later, all that's left of the hoped-for distraction is a hangover, which to make matters worse, prevents concentration on the study material for that day. "Tomorrow, double the work awaits me," groans Eliana *Zumsiek*. Alcohol is indeed not a solution. The modeling is illustrated in Figs. 3.38 and 3.39. ◀

Real Example: Debt Trap of Young People

Between 1999 and 2002, the number of 20- to 24-year-olds registered with the debtor register Schufa due to personal bankruptcy increased by almost a third to around 174,000.

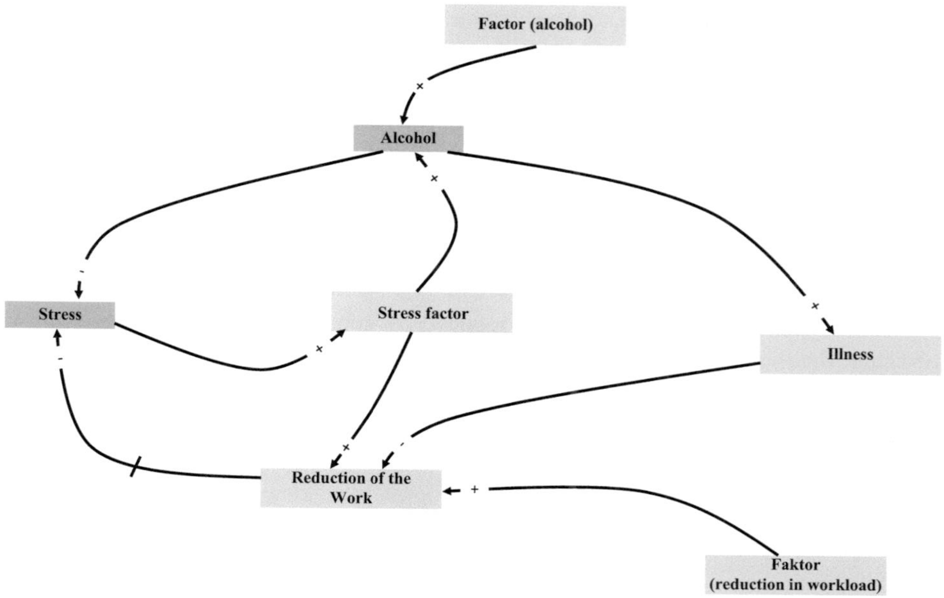

Fig. 3.38 Archetype 3—Model—Problem Shifting

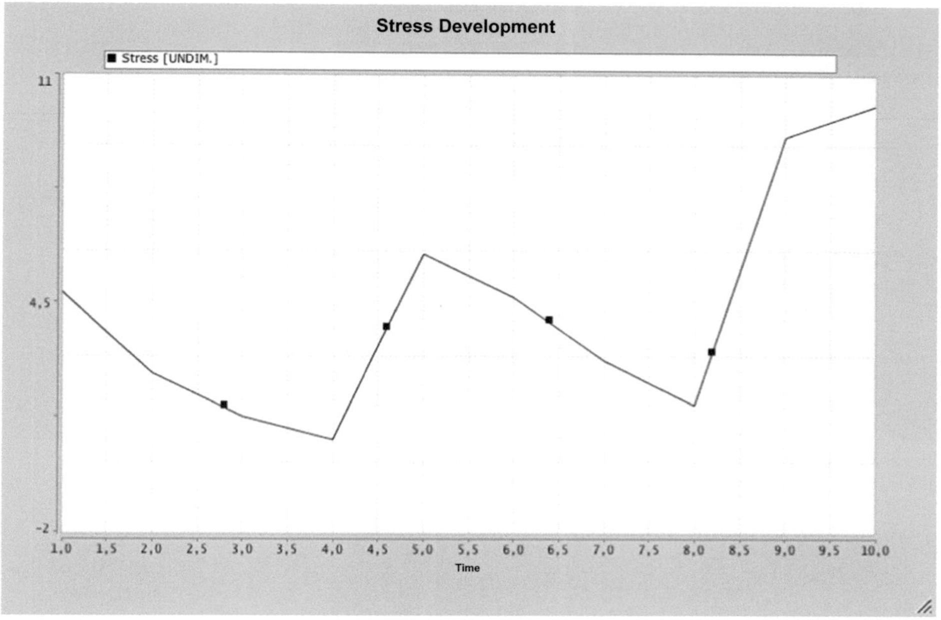

Fig. 3.39 Archetype 3—Simulation—Problem Shifting: "Stress Development"

Many young adults want to wear current fashion, use the latest mobile phone, and preferably own a modern car, despite lacking financial means. For this, more and more of them are taking out loans and solving their "money problem" in the short term, instead of working on a long-term solution, such as finding a part-time job or spending less.

Thus, they slide further and further into the debt trap and make a fundamental solution to the problem impossible (Pletter, 2003). ◀

3.4.3.4 Eroding Goals

In a situation of "eroding goals," there exists a gap between a target goal and the actual situation. This target-actual gap can be reduced by appropriate measures that improve the actual situation (medium-term) or by lowering the target level (short-term). However, this could potentially jeopardise the fundamental goals in the long term, as shown in Figs. 3.40 and 3.41.

Constructed Example: Goal Adjustment of a Shipping Company

A shipping company identifies a discrepancy between the desired and actual customer satisfaction.

- *Target goal:* 90 out of 100 customers claim to be "completely satisfied."
- *Actual state:* Only 80 out of 100 customers are actually completely satisfied.
- *Target-Actual-Gap:* 10

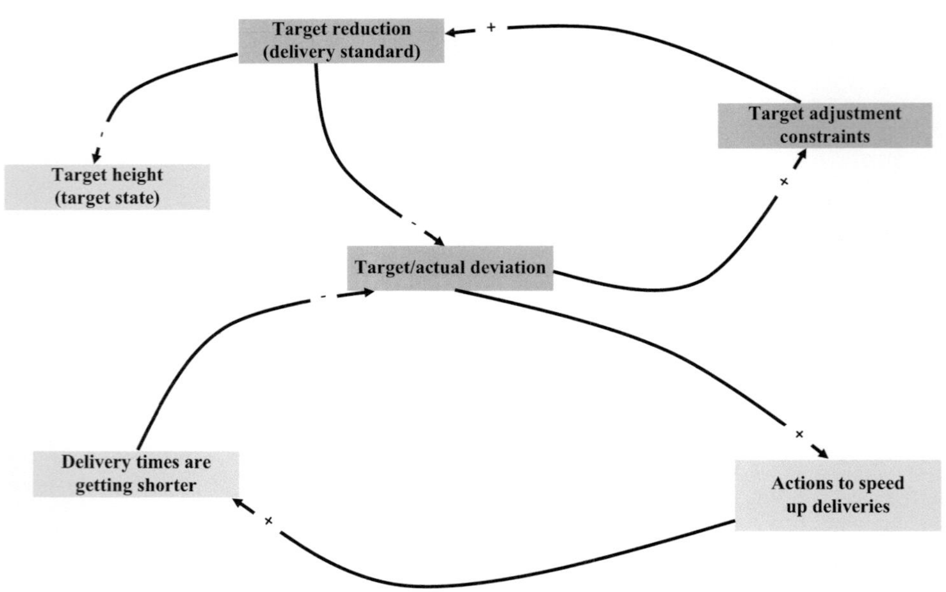

Fig. 3.40 Archetype 4—Model—Eroding Goals

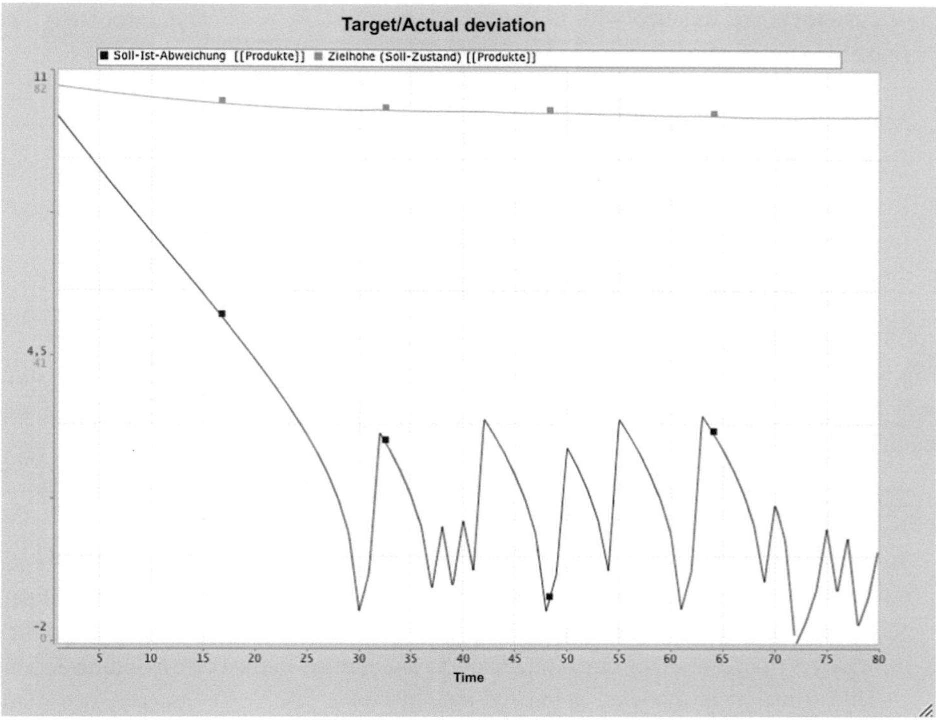

Fig. 3.41 Archetype 4—Simulation—Eroding Goals: "Target/actual deviation"

Medium-term actions for customer satisfaction are opposed to a short-term goal reduction. The short-term solution (goal adjustment) downgrades the company's fundamental goal. ◀

Modeling Example: The Customer is King?

The customer is king, and so the shipping company 'Mississippi' has committed itself to customer satisfaction. "More than 9 out of 10 customers are completely satisfied—Mississippi makes people happy," is therefore a slogan on the company's online presence. However, the currently incoming numbers show that the claim of 90% completely satisfied customers is outdated—according to the latest survey, it's just 80%. "We need to create and implement new concepts for customer satisfaction, otherwise the slogan cannot remain as it is!" notes Marketing Director *Schmitz* at the next board meeting. However, there is a veto—after all, it's just a slogan that can be easily renamed, and 80% customer satisfaction is still a good value. From now on, Mississippi advertises with the new slogan "Majority of customers completely satisfied—Mississippi makes people happy." "At least the slogan can remain until less than 50%

of customers are satisfied with us," notes Marketing Director *Schmitz* ironically and shakes his head. ◀

Real Example: Pollutants in Toys

Instead of following Germany's stricter regulations regarding pollutants in toys, the EU Commission plans to increase the limits for lead, mercury, and arsenic. However, for an optimal solution, one should go the other way and reduce the limits, because the health of children is our highest good after all (Westen, 2012). ◀

3.4.3.5 Escalation

This is about the fact that often there is mutual escalation, instead of looking for solutions that allow both parties to win. Figures 3.42 and 3.43 illustrate the archetype "Escalation".

Constructed Example: Price War

Two parties believe that their well-being depends on gaining an advantage over the other side. If Party A gains an advantage over Party B through an action, this is perceived by Party B as a threat and Party B responds with a countermeasure, which increases A's perception of threat and leads to an increase in the corresponding action.

This situation is modeled using the example of a price war between two companies, who try to gain a market share over the competitor by an "escalating" price reduction. ◀

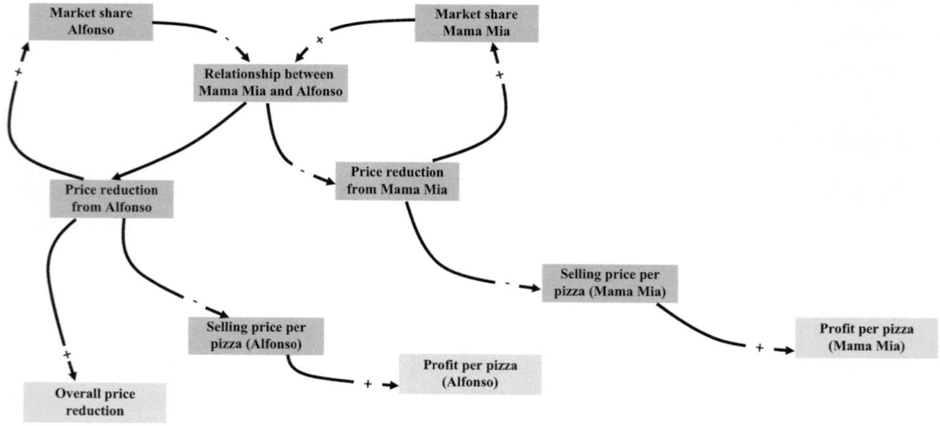

Fig. 3.42 Archetype 5—Model—Escalation

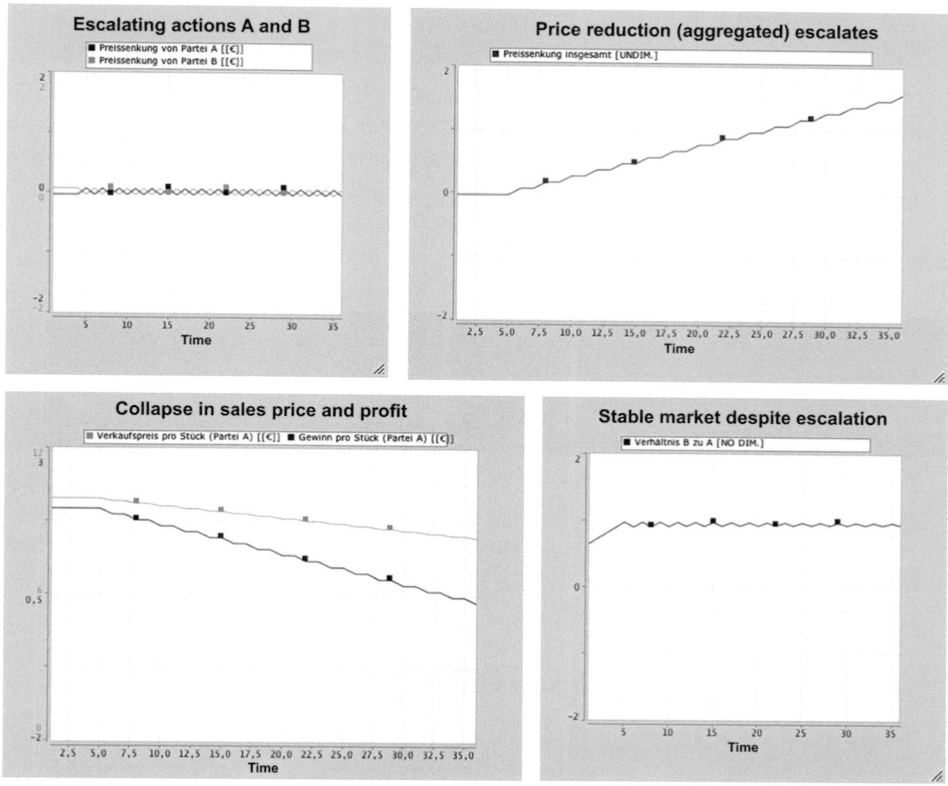

Fig. 3.43 Archetype 5—Simulation—Escalation: "Price reduction escalates"

Modeling Example: Giving Away Pizza

The pizzeria 'Alfonso' has got competition in the neighbourhood, because the pizzeria 'Mama Mia' is now also attracting customers—and thus away from 'Alfonso'. But they already have an idea how to win back the customers: No matter what price is charged at 'Mama Mia' for a pizza, at 'Alfonso' it will be offered for 10 cents cheaper. However, this strategy did not take into account that the owners of 'Mama Mia' have the same idea…

The result: 'Alfonso' and 'Mama Mia' successively undercut each other in the price of pizza, without being able to change the number of customers, and the people in the neighbourhood are asking: "When will the day come when the pizza is given to us?" ◀

Real Example: Discount War

In the price war of food discounters for customer acquisition, Aldi reacted to the strong price reductions of competitor Lidl and drastically reduced the prices for over

120 products at the beginning of 2009. With this price reduction, both Lidl and the entire food trade are now under pressure to also make price reductions again. The two leading food discounters thus accept losses in product margins in order to expand and strengthen their market leadership. The price war is expected to intensify due to the serious pursuers Penny and Netto and will also affect the earnings of the suppliers (Weber, 2009). ◀

3.4.3.6 Success to the Successful

The more successful one is, the more successful one becomes, even if the solution may be suboptimal (see Figs. 3.44 and 3.45).

Constructed Example: Financial Resources

Two activities compete for limited support or resources. The more successful one of these activities becomes, the more it receives and the more is taken away from the other.

This is exemplified by modeling two products A and B, which require the same resources for their production. The allocation of the (scarce) resources is based on the success (market share of the products) of the two products. ◀

Concrete Example for Modeling: The Trend is Blue

Yellow polo shirts are piling up in the fashion boutique "Trendy", while the sales shelves of the blue polo shirts are empty—they are sold out; until the next delivery arrives! Boutique owner Julie *Beau* is not entirely happy with this situation: Customers repeatedly leave the shop empty-handed because they only want to buy the polo shirt in blue. The yellow polo shirt, on the other hand, does not meet the taste of the

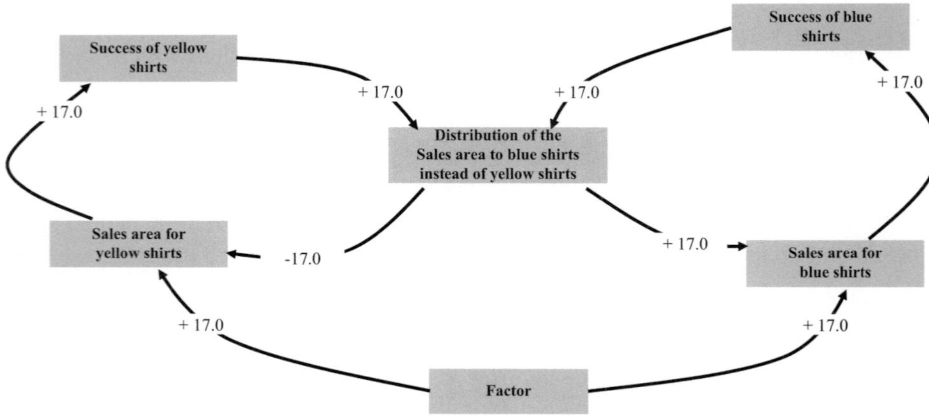

Fig. 3.44 Archetype 6—Model—Success to the Successful

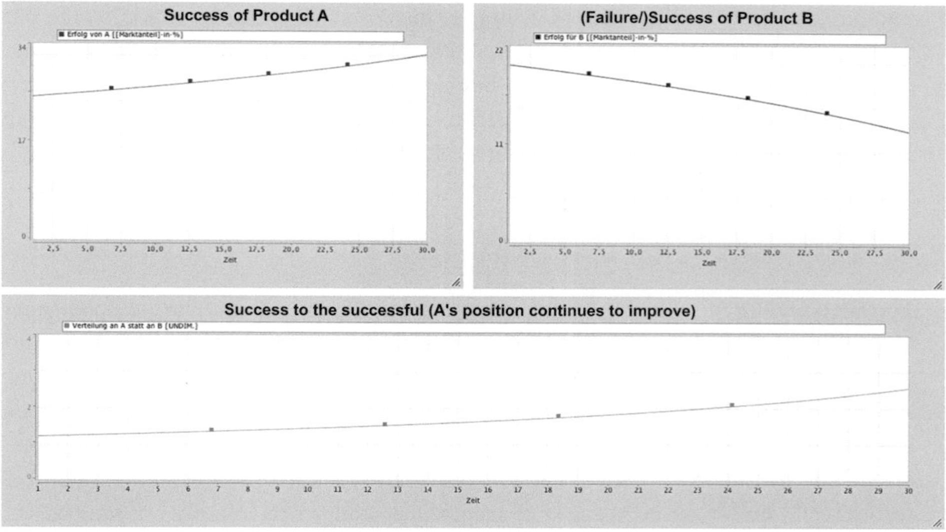

Fig. 3.45 Archetype 6—Simulation—Success of Product A – Failure of Product B – Success to the Successful

majority of customers. Mrs. *Beau* has already reacted to this when reordering: The yellow shirt is to gradually disappear from the shelves and the blue shirt is to get more space in the sales room. The colour "blue" promises profits, and Julie *Beau* is happy to follow this trend. ◀

Real Example: School Paths

On average, every 20th student attends a special school. Children who are "pushed" there because of their learning disability have already lost their future, as statistics show that about 80% will remain without a school leaving certificate. This makes the chances of a qualified job poor. A full-time school is rarely funded by the government. These children are neglected. They would especially need stronger support.

On the other hand, for example, high school students get significantly better chances. They enjoy an excellent school education, can then study and enter the job market as qualified professionals (Taffertshofer, 2007). ◀

3.4.3.7 Tragedy of the Commons

So far it was enough for everyone, now it's getting less, so I have to make an extra effort…

Constructed Example: Fishing Quotas

Individual parties (here: Party A and Party B) jointly use a resource accessible to all but limited (here: fish stock) and orient themselves according to their own interests (maximisation of benefits, here: catching as many fish as possible). Initially, the parties are rewarded for their use/individual effort (here: the amount of fish caught per trip by each party initially increases)—but in the long run, the overall situation deteriorates (here: fish stocks decrease, individual amount of fish caught per trip decreases) and this even despite additional efforts, until the resource becomes increasingly scarce. ◀

Example for Modelling: Fish, where are you?

The successful years for the fishing boats around the largest lake in the country are over: While the fishing nets were long well filled, the boats now increasingly return with empty nets—and this, although the boats stay longer at sea. The fish are gone, and the fisheries themselves are to blame. For years, the boats tried to catch as many fish as possible on their trips. After all, they wanted to sell more fish than the competition. The fact that the fish population decreased to such an extent that the fish offspring could no longer be ensured in sufficient quantity was initially not noticed and fishing continued as usual—the consequences are all the more evident today in the empty fishing nets. Figs. 3.46 and 3.47 illustrate the model and the simulation of this archetype. ◀

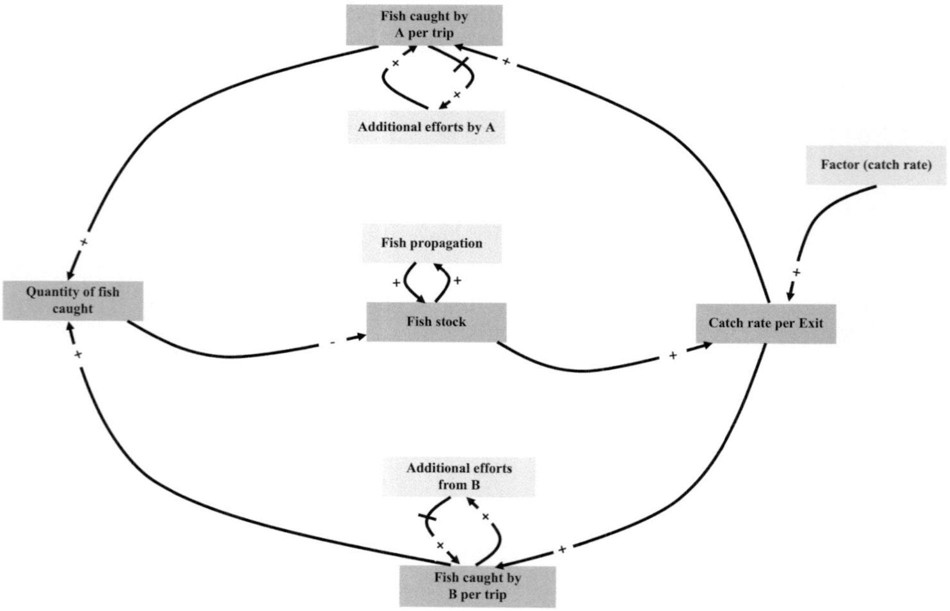

Fig. 3.46 Archetype 7—Model—Tragedy of the Commons

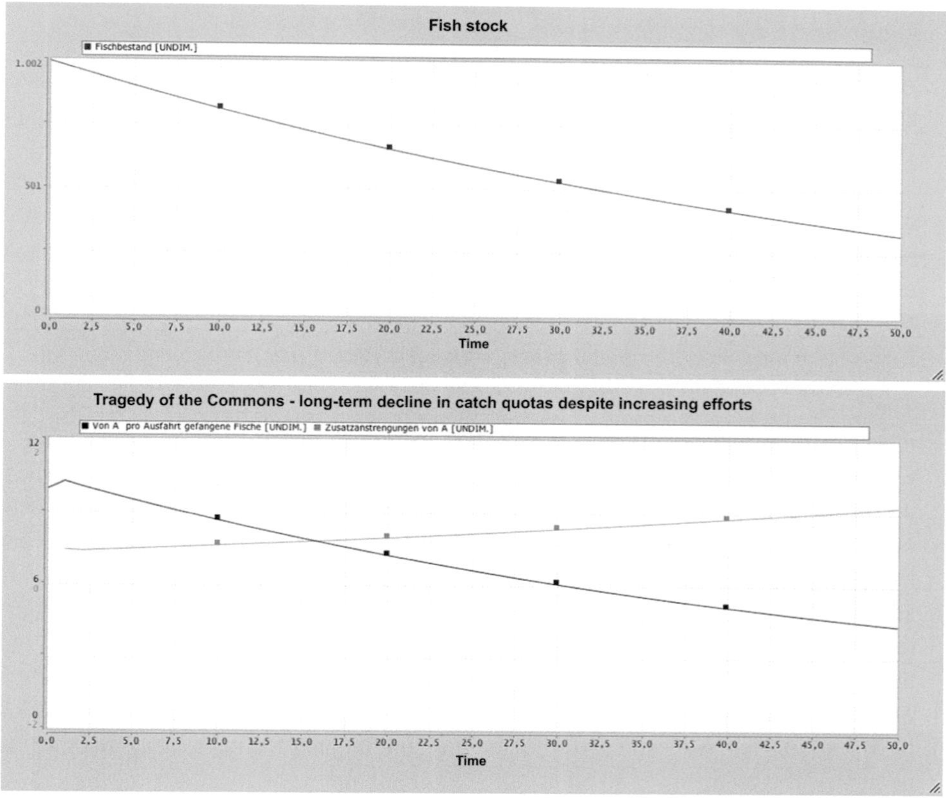

Fig. 3.47 Archetype 7—Simulation—Tragedy of the Commons: "Fish stock" – Long-term decline in catch quotas despite increasing efforts

---

Real Example: Oil Extraction

Oil is a limited common good and is consumed all over the world. However, many states have already reached their maximum extraction. Since 1980, despite better search methods, more oil has been extracted worldwide than discovered, and when huge oil sources are discovered, they are difficult to reach, such as off the coast of Brazil. Here, one would first have to penetrate 5000 m of water and then 3000 m of ground to reach the newly found oil. Even in Saudi Arabia, which supplies 13.5% of global oil, water is already being pumped under the desert floors to extract the last of it. In 100 years, oil will presumably only be offered in 'pharmacies'. A new energy age is dawning for mankind. However, it is questionable whether this will happen without conflicts (Illinger, 2009). ◀

3.4.3.8 Error Corrections

It used to always work, but now it doesn't, why?

Constructed Example: Liquidity Shortage

A problem symptom calls for a solution. The applied (short-term) solution reduces the problem, but has unintended consequences. These require corrections of the same kind, and in the long run, this worsens the problem symptom.

This is exemplified by a company plagued by a liquidity shortage. Short-term borrowing reduces this problem, but has long-term, unintended consequences in that the payment obligations associated with the borrowing increase the liquidity shortage, necessitating further borrowing. ◀

Example for Modeling: The 'Bankruptcy Vultures LLC' lives up to its company name

The 'Bankruptcy Vultures LLC'—specialist for business liquidations—calls a board meeting: Loan payments are due that can no longer be serviced and a solution is sought. The first solution proposal comes promptly from Mr. *F.*, head of the 'Finance' department: "No reason to worry. I have already negotiated a favourable loan with our house bank, which provides us with the necessary funds and also allows further investments." While board member Mr. *K.* frowns and raises concerns, the proposal is accepted by majority. Just a few weeks later, Mr. *K.* feels vindicated when he learns that the company is having trouble meeting the repayment and interest payments of the borrowed loan and is considering taking out another loan to meet the payment obligations. Worried, he writes a letter to his board colleagues, the message of which is: By taking on more and more loans, the 'Bankruptcy Vultures LLC' lives up to its name. The company is steering itself into bankruptcy, as illustrated by Figs. 3.48 and 3.49. ◀

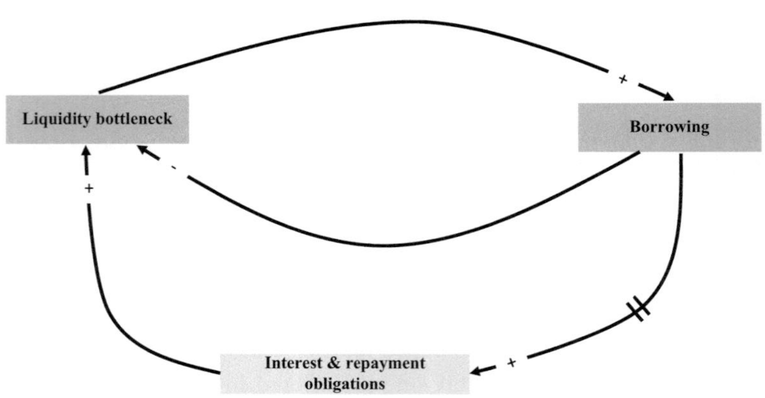

Fig. 3.48 Archetype 8—Model—Error Corrections

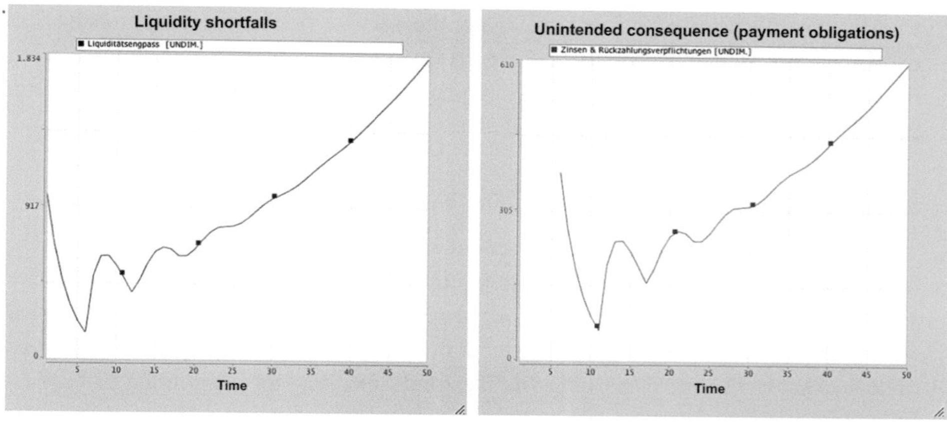

Fig. 3.49 Archetype 8—Simulation—Error Corrections: "Liquidity shortfalls"

Real Example: The Path into the Debt Trap

Debt in Germany is continuously increasing. Even in times of economic upturns and enormous state revenues, the debt is further increased instead of being reduced. Thus, the state's tax revenues increased by 10.2% compared to the previous year in 2011 (Herzog, 2012). At the same time, new debt of around 32 billion € was planned for the federal budget 2012. And even without the ESM-Euro rescue umbrella, over 26 billion € new debt had already been calculated (Handelsblatt, 2012). Instead of working on long-term solutions, repayment expenses that are due are refinanced by taking out new loans. The same is true for the growing compound interest to be covered (total debt at the end of 2012: approx. 2.114 trillion €). The mountain of debt continues to rise. This in turn incurs higher compound interest. A vicious cycle is created (Meyer, 2011). ◀

3.4.3.9 Growth and Underinvestment

We are growing well, so let's save on investments for now…

Constructed Example: Airline

The last example is intended to include the archetype description by *Senge*: Growth hits a limit that can be removed or postponed if the company invests in additional "capacity". However, if the investment is delayed, this underinvestment leads to growth stagnating or coming to a halt. Therefore, early investment is advisable.

This is therefore an exemplary model of *Senge's* own example of an airline (Senge, 2011, p. 146). To respond to the rising or exploding demand, the necessary service capacity would need to be expanded. As the service performance approaches the capacity limit, demand decreases. An early investment in service capacity is therefore advantageous for the company, while underinvestment (delayed investment) more severely restricts demand. ◀

Example of Modeling: Queues as a Warning Signal

The following phenomenon can be observed at the counter of the new airline 'SkyFly': The queues of travellers wanting to check in are getting longer week by week! The reason is quickly found: More and more travellers choose 'SkyFly', which the airline of course notices with approval. But what the service staff at the check-in counters also notice: Discontent due to the long waiting times and it is not uncommon to hear the following sentence from the passengers: "Of course, SkyFly is so cheap—they probably save on service". And so it is not surprising that the "queue problem" is on the agenda at the next management meeting. After all, dissatisfied customers do not look good for 'SkyFly', and long queues certainly do not attract new customers, so a decision should be made to invest in additional check-in counters and service staff—satisfied and especially more new customers should be won in this way. Figures 3.50, 3.51 and 3.52 illustrate the problems that can arise from growth and underinvestment. ◀

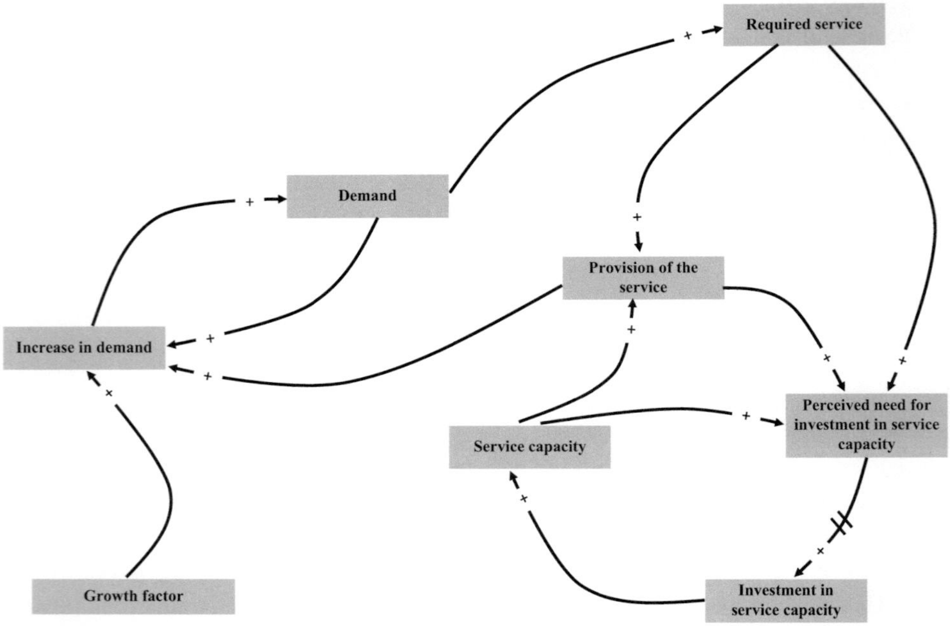

Fig. 3.50 Archetype 9—Model—Growth and Underinvestment

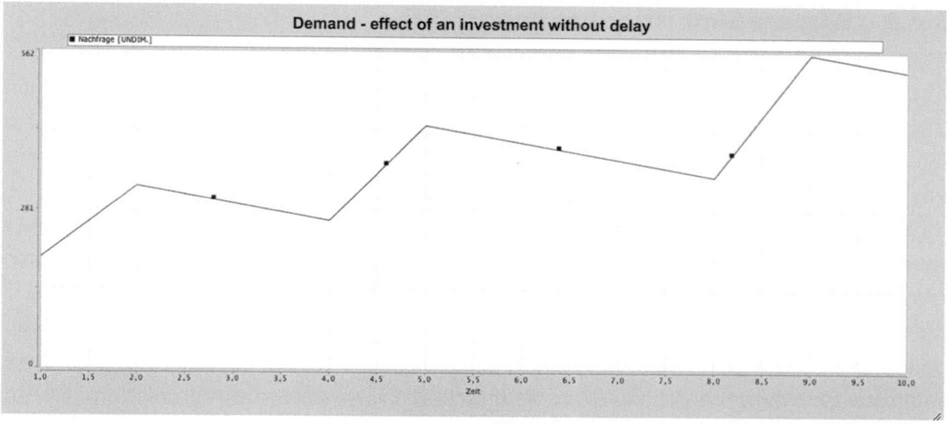

Fig. 3.51 Archetype 9—Simulation a)—Effect of an investment without delay

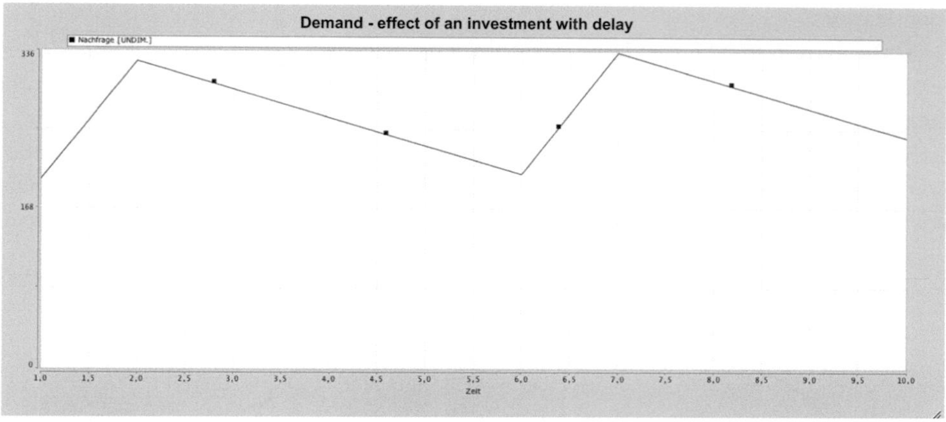

Fig. 3.52 Archetype 9—Simulation b)—Effect of an investment with delay

Real Example: Luxury Watches

The demand for luxury watches from A. Lange & Söhne is booming. Due to this excess demand, the company is to be further internationalised in order to continue to grow in the future. They start capacity expansions in time and do not make the mistake of scaling back their goals (Stölzel, 2011). ◀

3.4.4 Why are Simulations so Important?

The reason why we ultimately study systems is because we want to better understand the world, because we want to learn, so that mistakes or even crises can be avoided in the future, to recognise opportunities and to shape the future. Simulations contribute to arranging such learning processes effectively and efficiently.

With the distinction between 'single-loop-' and 'double-loop-learning', Argyris*Argyris* and Schön emphasise the preserving and stabilising aspect of learning processes (Argyris & Schön, 1978). Thus, for an unhindered maintenance of the status quo, it is most effective to first respond to errors with a single-loop. Single-loop-learning is based on the basic assumptions and beliefs that have been successfully used in the past. Here, solutions for emerging problems are sought first. Only when these corrections are not sufficient, a double-loop-learning is initiated, in which important basic assumptions and beliefs that one has had so far are generated and changed if necessary. Questioning proven basic assumptions involves a threat to central pillars of the existing, so such learning processes are often carried out reluctantly. Figure 3.53 illustrates the 'double-loop-learning'.

This dualism, in which a 'lower-level-learning' is distinguished from a 'higher-level-learning' (Fiol & Lyles, 1985; Cope, 2003), is found in a similar form, but with different names, in various theoretical approaches (Cope, 2003; Easterby-Smith et al., 2004).

Jean Piaget*Piaget* (Piaget, 1977) also represents a similar dualism with the distinction between assimilation and accommodation. Neisser (Neisser, 1976) concretises this schema-theoretical view by referring to the insoluble problem of distinguishing between

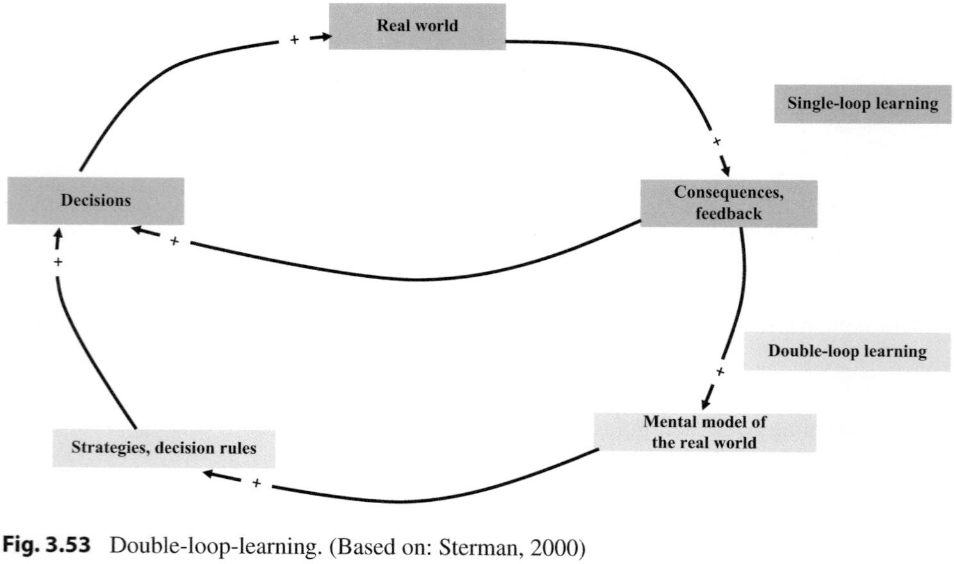

Fig. 3.53 Double-loop-learning. (Based on: Sterman, 2000)

reality and construction (see also Piaget, 1972). It is the imagination and the schemas that guide the exploration of the world and thus essentially provide such predictable information. Only when expectation and 'reality' diverge too much, the schemas are adjusted.

The distinction between single- and double-loop-learning clearly shows how processes of self-organisation can lead to misjudgements in sudden crisis situations. For the 'lower-level-learning' corresponds to 'business as usual' and is preferred. The 'higher-level-learning' requires comprehensive changes that question previously successful beliefs. So there is something like resistance to this higher form of learning, as it would be associated with major upheavals. The more a crisis situation contradicts what has been known so far, the more difficult and delayed the handling of it will be.

First, there are already obstacles in perceiving that a crisis exists at all (see the perception cycle of Neisser, 1976). Previously helpful perception schemas look for possible problems where they have always occurred and are therefore not able to see problems in the 'blind spot' or 'blind spot'. So the perception of the problem situation will only occur delayed and will particularly surprise the well-established organisations. If the crisis is indeed comprehensive (such as oil crises or financial crises), it will also require a rethinking of the organisation's central beliefs (double-loop-learning) *Double-loop-learning*. This will only be used hesitantly, experienced as a threat and thus leads to a further delay.

In summary, it can be assumed that serious events are perceived hesitantly and processed even more hesitantly in terms of a comprehensive learning process. This delay is sometimes also referred to as hysteresis (see e.g. Haken, 1990, p. 183; Stadler & Kruse, 1990; Stadler et al., 1991). In such events, such as crisis situations, those who show little tendency towards hysteresis should be able to act more successfully.

Why are simulations of systems so important in this context?Simulation

Already *Papert* pointed out the advantages of microworlds in the analysis of the real world in the early 1980s (Papert, 1980).[85] Microworlds or virtual worlds, as *Schön* calls them (Schön, 1983), are ultimately nothing more than models of systems that are observed in the real world. To investigate these models, simulations are suitable, i.e., one looks at the models over time and changes, depending on the focus of the study, e.g., initial conditions of the model.

One can follow *Sterman*, who clearly shows the advantages of virtual worlds (see also Fig. 3.54) compared to real worlds: Sterman (2000, p. 35 ff.).

Virtual worlds …

- firstly represent laboratories:
  - Space and time can be compressed or expanded.
  - Actions can be repeated under the same conditions.

[85] *Papert's* book "Mindstorms" remains a significant work to this day, especially when it comes to integrating computers into learning processes. See already: Liening (1992).

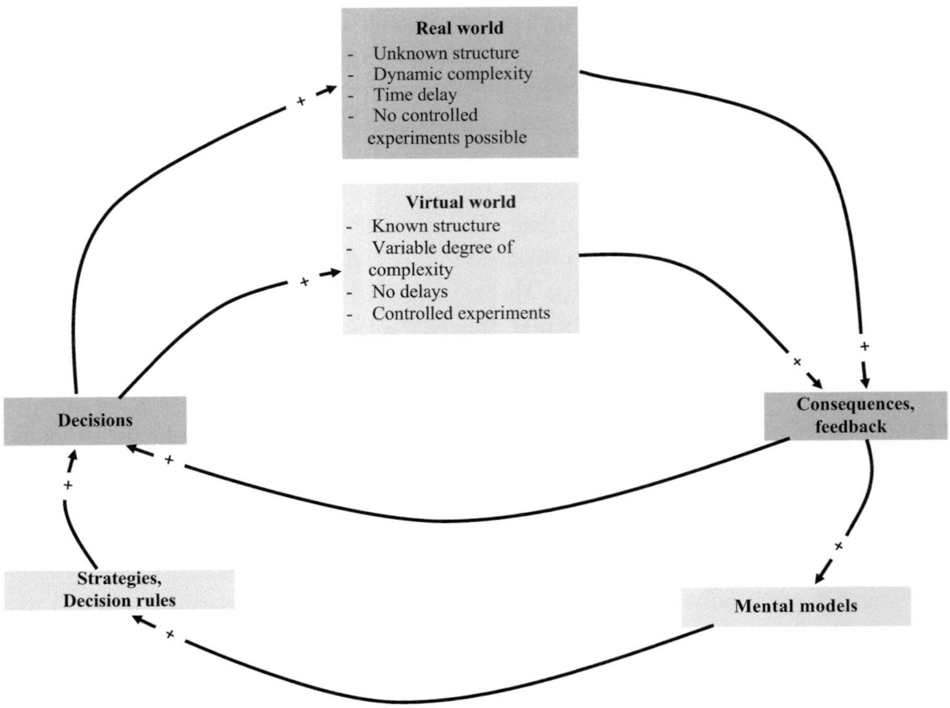

Fig. 3.54 Idealised learning process involving virtual worlds. (Based on: Sterman, 2000)

- Actions can be stopped for reflection.
- Decisions that are considered dangerous, unfeasible, or unethical in the real system can be carried out in the virtual world.
- Controlled experiments become possible.
- Time delays in the learning loop (Learning Loop), caused by the real world, are dramatically shortened.
- In the virtual world, strategies and dynamics that are likely to lead to poor performance or even to (simulated) disasters can be tried out—there is no opportunity for such experiments in the real world.

- secondly provide high-quality feedback:
  - The degree of random deviations can be controlled in the virtual world.
  - Virtual worlds give the learner greater control over the strategy, lead to more consistent decision-making, prevent the implementation of errors and frivolities.
  - Unlike in the real world, which—like a *Black Box*—is not very transparent, virtual worlds can be described as *White Boxes*, whose assumptions are known and can even be modified by the learner.

If one follows *Sterman,* formalising and testing qualitative and quantitative models via simulation often leads to radical changes in the way reality is understood (Sterman, 2000, p. 38). Simulations strengthen and accelerate the Learning Feedback. Discrepancies between formal and mental models simulate improvements, changes in basic assumptions such as system or model boundaries, time horizon, and dynamic hypotheses included. "Without the discipline and constraint imposed by the rigorous testing enabled by simulation, it becomes all too easy for mental models to be driven by ideology or unconscious bias" (Sterman, 2000, p. 37).

Sterman rightly points out that some may not believe that human behaviour can be developed, as there are no laws for human behaviour. However, this view overestimates our understanding of nature and underestimates the regularities of human decision-making.

If experiments in the real system are unfeasible, simulations are the only way to find out for oneself how complex systems work. The alternative is receptive learning *(rote learning),* which is based on the authority of the teacher and the material (Sterman, 2000, p. 38).

3.4.5 Simulation of a 'Complex System' Using the Example of a Supply-demand Model—"Multicopter Engineers Wanted for a StartUp"

Let's assume that we find ourselves once again in the 'multicopter' market, which we have already described in Chapter A. Numerous entrepreneurs are still trying to establish 'start-ups' with innovative ideas for multicopters that could revolutionise the market. The challenge remains that experienced engineers are needed in the short term to develop the respective product ideas to market maturity within the framework of a project. In this way, inventions can become innovations. So, let's assume we are in such a highly dynamic labour market, where on the one hand, the HR managers of young companies are looking for project staff for initially one year, and on the other hand, potential employees are looking for attractive jobs in this field. This labour market differs from an ordinary labour market in that there are no collective wages, no minimum wages, and thus no restrictions in the design of wages, no market entry or exit restrictions; in short: there are no restrictions and the free forces of the market can fully unfold. In other words: We are dealing here with a market that economics would describe as 'perfect'. Unlike Chapter A, however, this market can now be described as highly dynamic non-linear.

The following supply-demand model, whose equations result in a non-linear price function and which was implemented as a computer simulation (Liening, 2012) in the form of an object-oriented software concept, is intended to illustrate that even very simple non-linear equations can exhibit irregular behaviour.

The following price function is considered: $P(t+1) = \lambda \cdot P(t) - \lambda \cdot P(t)^2$

Or in other words: $P(t+1) = \lambda \cdot P(t) \cdot (1 - P(t))$

This function is also referred to as the logistic function and is a fundamental discrete function in the 'complexity sciences'.

This function is a recursive function, i.e., the respective price depends on the preceding price, as the model in Fig. 3.55 shows.

This dependency is quadratic here, i.e., non-linear. The market calculations in the simulation are done by iteration, i.e., the calculated value is reinserted into the same equation as the starting value, and this process can be repeated as often as desired. For the considered market model, a number of framework conditions apply: There is a high number of demanders and suppliers who behave rationally as quantity adjusters and can freely enter and leave the market. None of the actors is so significant that they could individually influence the price. Furthermore, there are no transaction costs, no taxes, and only one homogeneous good. This economic model essentially corresponds to that of 'perfect competition'.

It is assumed that the market described in this way is again a labour market, where demanders for work (entrepreneurs) and suppliers of work (potential employees) meet. The price is the salary that can be achieved on the market, and the homogeneous good is the labour force that is offered or demanded.

At a price or annual salary of 0.00 €, no supplier would be willing to offer his labour. At an annual salary of 100,000 € and higher, on the other hand, there would be no demand for labour (prohibitive price), so the market price is between 0.00 € and 100,000 €.

The value λ in this model reflects the position of the price or salary curve in the coordinate system between salary and number of workers.

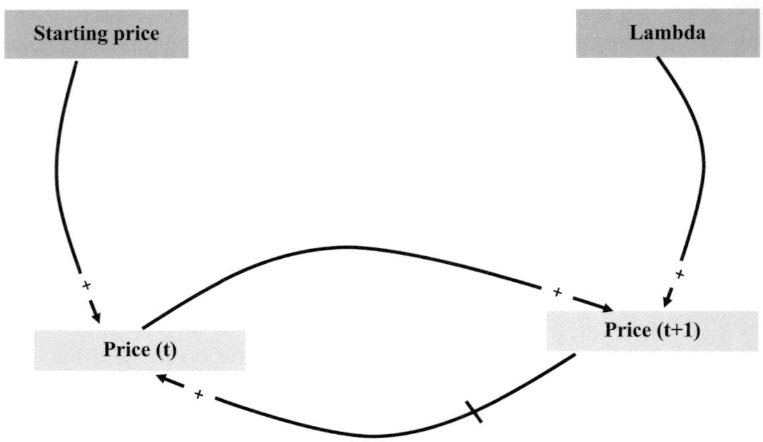

Fig. 3.55 Systemic Model—Logistic Equation

We start a first simulation initially with a value $\lambda = 2.75$. With any starting price, here 0.03 €, one gets a converging development of the system with a fixed point, as Figs. 3.56 and 3.57 illustrate.

The price P, which is relatively arbitrarily set very low in the initial situation, is still relatively far away from the actual higher equilibrium price at the beginning. Already in the fifth period, the price has climbed to a peak and numerous suppliers are willing to offer their labour at this high price, with new suppliers being pushed into the market by high salary expectations. However, the price has risen so much that the demanders now react more cautiously and overall demand decreases. As a result, prices also fall because the suppliers are apparently no longer able to offer the desired amount of labour at the high prices. The prices fall, but not as low as they were in the fourth period, as this price was obviously too low. However, the decrease in prices increases the interest of demanders in labour. The increase in demand leads to rising salaries, especially since the suppliers cannot immediately satisfy the increased demand. The scarcer the supply, the higher the price. This time, however, the suppliers increase the salaries (prices) more cautiously in order not to scare off the demanders, as happened with the last increase.

Nevertheless, after the salary demands, some demanders withdraw again. The decrease in demand with a constant supply leads to lower salary expectations. The salary fluctuations thus become smaller each time and a balance salary is established relatively quickly. This corresponds to the traditional pig cycle or cobweb model.

If we now increase the value λ to, for example, $\lambda = 3.2$, the system seems to diverge, but then stabilises after some time. A single equilibrium salary, as in the first situation, is not achieved. However, one obtains two fixed or accumulation points, as Fig. 3.58 shows.

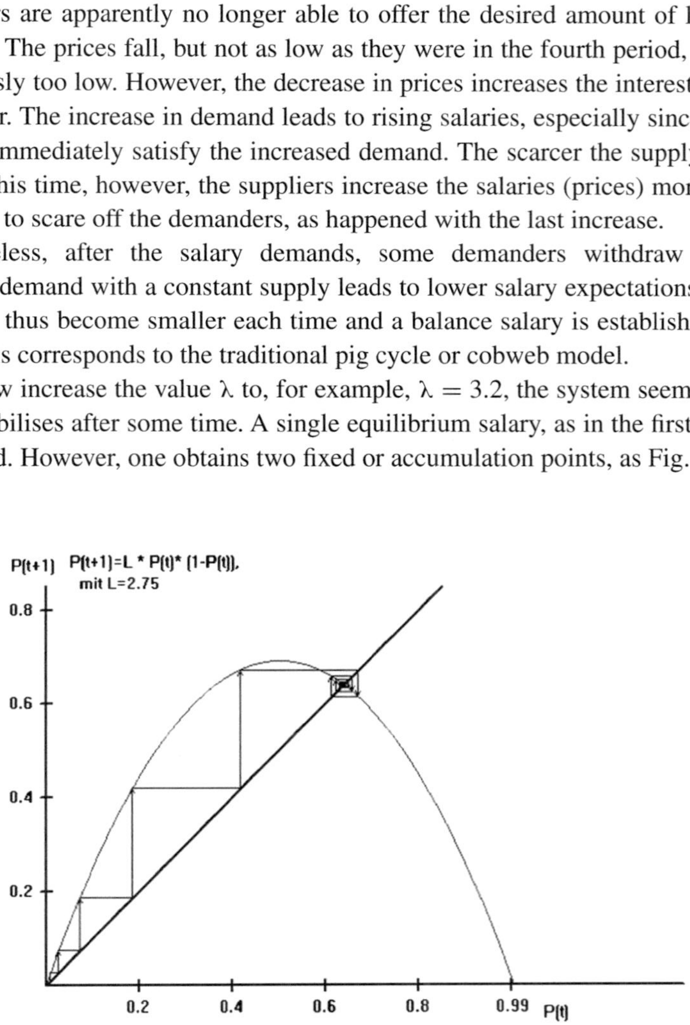

Fig. 3.56 Fixed point attractor in the price system. *Source* Liening (2012)

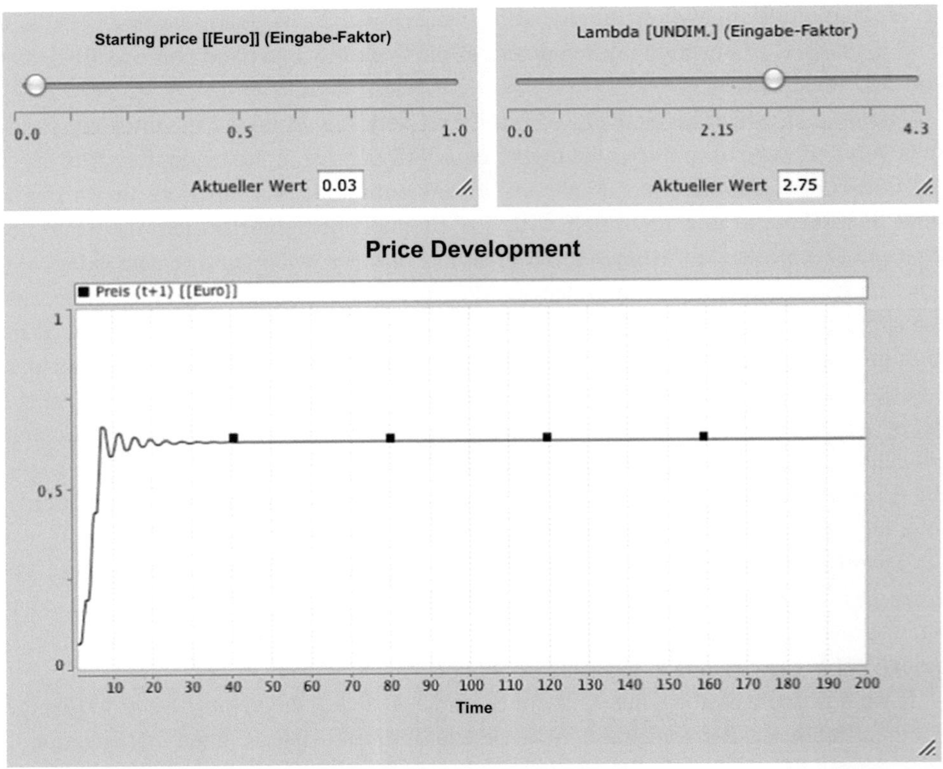

Fig. 3.57 Fixed point attractor in the price system—Simulation – (starting price, lambda, price development)

In this case, the salary thus fluctuates back and forth between two values. At a higher salary, the suppliers will be inclined to offer more labour. However, many demanders perceive the salary as too high, and thus the demand is no longer willing to accept the entire number of labour offered. The salary falls. However, with the falling salary, demand increases again. The increased demand cannot be fully satisfied by the suppliers, which is why the prices (salaries) climb. The workers ultimately demand too high salaries again, so that the demand from the entrepreneurs falls again and consequently the salaries. Thus, the salaries ultimately oscillate back and forth, without achieving a constant equilibrium value, as Fig. 3.59 shows.

If one changes the system in such a way that, for example, $\lambda = 4.0$ is chosen, then something unexpected happens: The system suddenly goes completely haywire, so that both suppliers and demanders can no longer oversee the market. There are irregular fluctuations, as illustrated in Fig. 3.60.

On the one hand, too high salaries lead to a decrease in demand and an increase in supply, on the other hand, falling salaries lead to an increase in demand and a decrease

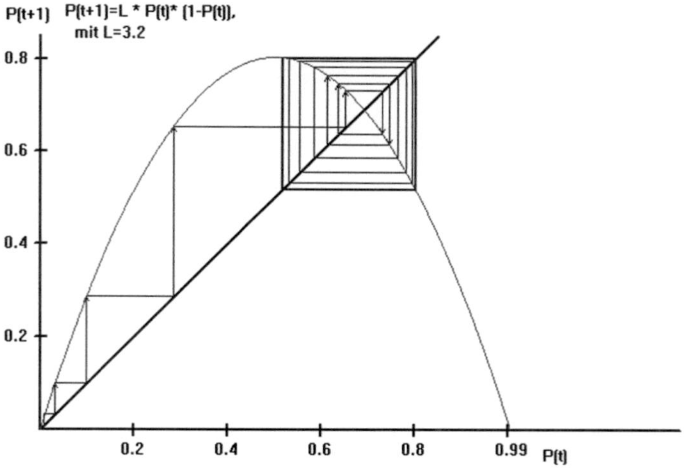

Fig. 3.58 Two-cycle attractor in the price system. *Source* Liening (2012)

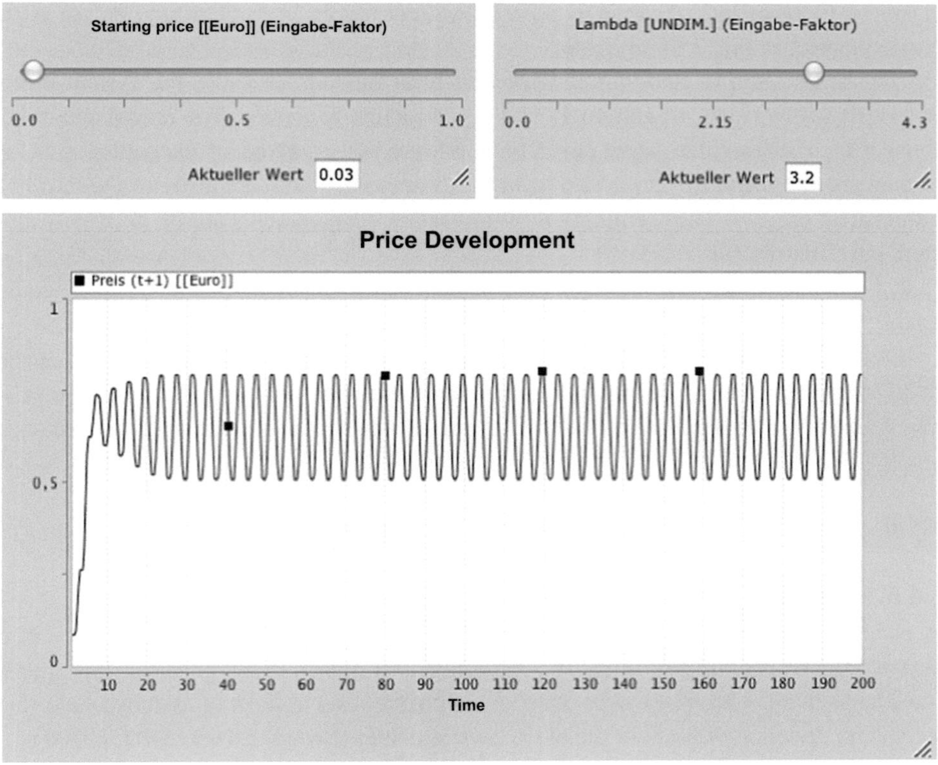

Fig. 3.59 Two-cycle in the price system—Simulation – (starting price, lambda, price development)

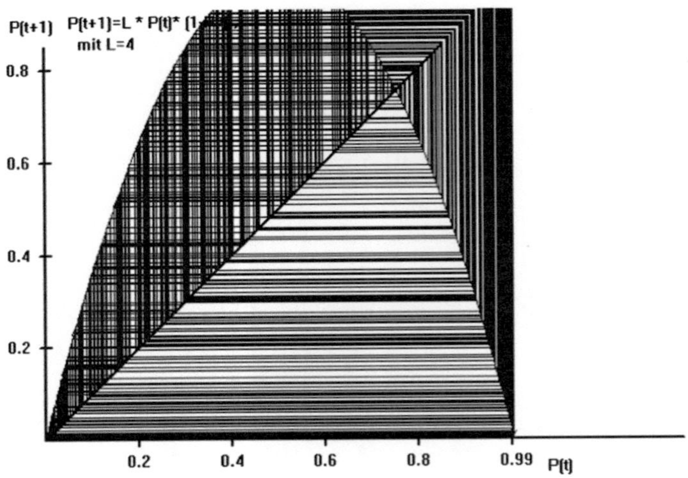

Fig. 3.60 Chaos in the price system. *Source* Liening (2012)

in supply. Nevertheless, the salaries do not develop towards an equilibrium point or settle into any cycle, as Fig. 3.61 suggests.

The values seem to jump around completely at random. In short, the system reacts chaotically. As a result, an extremely complex structure is created. The remarkable thing about it is: The irregular salary developments were not triggered by exogenous shocks, so they are endogenously explained from the system itself, and are also not the result of a stochastic process. The seemingly arbitrary salary developments are by no means random, but deterministic.

If, for example, the state wanted to regulate this seemingly chaotic market, what could it do?

If one were of the opinion that salaries are much too low, this could be seen as a scandal calling for intervention. Conversely, the situation could arise where one perceives the salaries as absurdly high and unfair to other workers. So how could the state steer this market?

3.4.6 First Steps to Understanding Complexity

3.4.6.1 On the Irreversibility of Time and Catallaxy

In presenting important aspects of classical mechanics, we have already found that it assumes the reversibility of time. This certainly also applies to the physical phenomena considered there. The *Newtonian* equations are time-reversible. It is assumed here that there is no direction of time for the basic laws of matter (Briggs & Peat, 1993, p. 198).

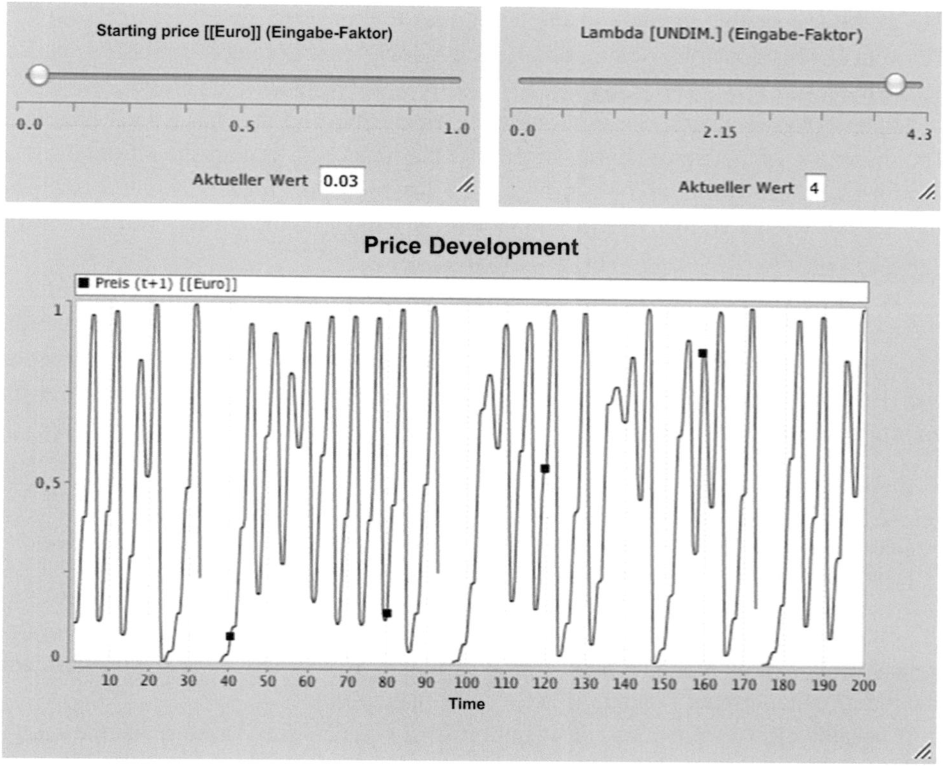

Fig. 3.61 Chaos in the price system—Simulation - (starting price, lambda, price development)

However, the economic world is much more complex. If one adheres to the concept of reversibility, one will quickly be disappointed in this direction:

Raw materials, such as coal and natural gas, are irreversibly consumed. Machines become obsolete, cars rust, and the economic structure of a country never remains constant. In short: The economic world is irreversible.

Certainly, one can find partial aspects for which the economic world is also reversible. However, viewed globally, there is a one-sided historically directed development. Reversible processes can thus be contained as a limit case in the irreversible ones, but the reverse does not apply.

For example, *Ruelle* notes, "(…) that history systematically produces unpredictable events with important long-term consequences" (Ruelle, 1993, p. 94).

However, irreversible events cannot be modeled with linear systems. The models preferred in classical mechanics implicitly assume the reversibility of time. While physicists in earlier times assumed that time was reversible, leading physicists today believe that due to the irreversible increase in the entropy of the universe, time is not reversible.[86] These new considerations cannot simply be ignored when developing physical or economic models.

Modern physics clearly shows that time is irreversible and thus has a clear direction. The discovery of the irreversibility of time in the nineteenth century manifests itself in two forms, an optimistic and a pessimistic one. The optimistic form is evolution, the pessimistic form is the entropy already explained. Nevertheless, the concept of the irreversibility of time did not prevail until much later.

For a long time, physicists believed that "at the deepest foundation of matter, time is reversible" (Briggs & Peat, 1993, p. 217).[87] Thus, *Einstein* is said to have referred to the distinction between past, future, and present as a kind of illusion, albeit a very persistent one (Briggs & Peat, 1993, p. 200). To this, *Prigogine* counters that reversibility at the microscopic level is an illusion:

> With a dynamic system made up of atomic particles, you can never conduct an experiment in which past and future are the same. If we start with particles of the same speed and then let collisions happen, the thing will end with random speeds. But we can't do the reverse experiment at all. There are no reversible experiments (quoted n. Briggs & Peat, 1993, p. 219).

It is interesting now that irreversibility manifests itself on the one hand as entropy, i.e., as heat death, but on the other hand also as evolution. It thus also has a creative function and therefore represents a prerequisite for self-organisation.

It became clear in previous considerations that classical mechanics made the *Laplacian* demon conceivable, who—if he only knew all initial conditions—could predict the future exactly. One might now suspect that irreversibility creeps into a system due to approximation methods and thus is based on our ignorance of the exact initial states. *Prigogine* raises a serious counter-argument to this.

> The investigations, far away from equilibrium states, led me to the conviction that this cannot be the right point of view. Irreversibility plays a constructive role. It creates shape. It brings forth human beings. How could our ignorance of the initial conditions be the reason for this? Our ignorance cannot justify our existence (quoted n. Briggs & Peat, 1993, p. 218 f.).

---

[86] *Boltzmann,* a physicist who co-founded statistical mechanics, bases his approach on thermodynamics, the theory that deals with entropy and irreversibility. His explanation for the irreversibility of time is simple and subtle at the same time. It is a probabilistic explanation: It can be shown that the initial state of a system with low entropy is very unlikely. The time development leads to high entropy, which corresponds to a very likely state. Over a very long period of time, the system will return to its unlikely initial state. One can say: The number of particles in a system tend towards infinity and thus also the time of return. In this limit consideration, true irreversibility is shown. See Ruelle (1993, p. 119).

[87] The concept of reversibility presented here is based on the time reversibility of the linear equations that describe the motion of atoms etc.

Poincaré points out that it can be claimed, "the future (is, d. Verf.) determined by the past (…), but not the past by the future" (Poincaré, 1914, p. 59). In other words: If you know the present, you may be able to predict the future, but not derive the past.

Dynamic systems take time into account, and the respective system state is causally dependent on previous states. Dynamic systems thus have a history that influences both the current and future behaviour.

When studying dynamic systems, not only the identification of equilibrium points and the state far from equilibrium is of interest; the temporal course of changes in state variables and the speed of changes is also of great importance.

There are two concepts for capturing time: discrete and continuous time recording. Which of these two concepts should be preferred?

To answer this question, let's take an example from business economics: The balance sheet of a company is recorded on a specific date. Payments such as material, interest, and wage payments are made at a specific point in time. Even period variables such as expenses and revenues are recorded at a specific date.

Also, data on the national economy are recorded and published at regularly recurring points in time.

Lentz points out that there are no fixed time spans, no universally valid time grid in economics. For example, cost accounting in a company can be done monthly, quarterly, etc., and each company will choose a different time. Furthermore, discrete data collection does not mean that the data are discretely generated; *Leibniz* says: 'Natura non facit saltus'. In this context, *Lentz* logically advocates a continuous system, as "a continuous time concept can in many cases more adequately represent the economic reality (is capable, d. Verf)" (Lentz, 1993, p. 50). But here, mechanistic thinking creeps into *Lentz's* line of argument. Too easily, as the historian and *Newton* expert *Wagner* notes, one adopts "the model of a uniform and continuous movement, according to which all time sequences are regulated, from the findings of mechanics. In this sense, we then also want to see all events of the entire history as so many points of a single, undifferentiated continuous flow, which would be the course of time itself" (Wagner, 1976, p. 179).

But it has already become apparent that nature indeed makes leaps and is therefore by no means as continuous as, for example, *Leibniz* claims. Sudden irregularities, abrupt jumps, and turbulences etc. are by no means rare in nature. The same can be observed in economics: Just think of unpredictable stock market crashes and stock price fluctuations or the major financial crises.

Thus, in a mathematical economic model, one would at least have to work with nonlinear, discontinuous functions.

Another critical moment regarding the thesis, 'a continuous time concept often better represents economic reality', lies in the observation of the measurement of this reality itself:

If an exact measurement is to be made, one must work with real numbers. One may come to the conclusion that, for example, the development of economic growth in two past periods does not differ. Perhaps one gets the same result from both periods and this result is possibly even accurate to five places after the decimal point. But one cannot necessarily determine whether the solutions also match after twenty places after the decimal point. And if so, what if one were to consider twenty-five places? One may never find an exact result, as only finitely many places can be measured. In other words:

> The mathematical continuum (…) is not *empirically* accessible to us (Eisenhardt et al., 1995, p. 105).

Already the mathematician *Cantor* had asked whether the individual points of a continuum can be assigned to natural numbers. The answer is: No! The set of all real numbers is not countable, but uncountable.[88]

Therefore, the continuous perspective should be viewed with caution. One must always be aware of the inadequacy of this method when using it. Just remember the butterfly effect that *Lorenz* discovered by changing the calculation accuracy.

Taking these concerns into account, it makes sense from an economic point of view to choose a discrete representation.

However, for the sake of completeness, it should be pointed out that from a purely mathematical-model-theoretical perspective, both cases can be applied in complexity sciences.[89] In this context, it should be emphasised that using various methods, such as the *Poincaré* section, discrete mappings can be generated from continuous mappings.[90]

Also, *Ebeling* ties his considerations on irreversibility to everyday experiences. He states.

> The coal in our stove combines with atmospheric oxygen to form carbon dioxide and ash, the sand mountain in front of our house melts away, our tools and machines wear out (Ebeling, 1994, p. 31).

The irreversibility expressed in these examples is the prerequisite for self-organisation. As *Ebeling* notes:

> Self-organisation is, so to speak, the counterpart to the generally observed tendency towards the spontaneous 'dissipation of sand mountains'. But it is in any case—like the latter—an irreversible process; albeit a very special one (…). Just as irreversibility is a consequence of the 'creative character' of mechanical movements, namely their tendency to diverge, to diversity, to variety, so self-organisation forms a new form of the creative potentials of matter (Ebeling, 1994, p. 35).

---

[88] For proof see Forster (2004, p. 83).

[89] In the continuous case, one can examine first-order n-dimensional differential equation systems. Such a rewritten dynamic system generates a flow mapping. In the discrete case, one considers a sequence of points generated by iteration.

[90] It is easy to see that the system becomes one dimension lower through such a section. If the continuous system is, for example, of dimension three, then after the section the discrete system is of dimension two. For the *Poincaré* section see, for example: Tu (1994, p. 183 ff.).

The principle of self-organisation states that order patterns do not arise from a determination from 'outside', but from within the system itself.[91] It is a process of emergence that leads to self-reproducing dynamic structures.

Self-organisation is therefore understood as processes that, starting far from equilibrium, lead to more complex order structures through system-immanent forces (Ebeling, 1994, p. 36). Self-organisation is thus an attribute of systems, specifically of non-linear complex systems, which comes into play under certain conditions. But it is not just a mere 'sur-plus' of those systems, but an inseparable property. Self-organisation is *one,* or as *Ebeling* even says, "perhaps even the decisive component of the evolution of complexity" (Ebeling, 1994, p. 36).

Irreversibility and self-organisation thus represent two important characteristics of the new approach.

3.4.6.2 What does Complexity Mean?—The End of Reductionism?

> *Economics (…) offers itself to mathematisation (…) and celebrates in the avoidance of the great cyclical crises and in 'tailor-made' economic policy triumphs, that remind of the triumphs of natural science Yet its subject, viewed with the eye of the natural scientist, remains almost hopelessly complex.*
> (Weizsäcker, 1974, p. 31)

This statement of the physicist *von Weizsäcker* will certainly also find approval among many economists. The analysis of economic systems can indeed find its limits where it is confronted with increasing structural diversity. In such a case, the 'complexity argument' is often used. This argument makes complexity appear like a veil. Because it gives the impression that the continuation of the analysis is merely opposed by "the phenomenon of the 'large number'" (Blaseio, 1986, p. 13), as *Blaseio* puts it. Thus, it is assumed that it is merely a question of quantitative effort to cope with complexity using traditional analysis tools.

> The goal of science has always been to reduce the complexity of the world to simple rules (Briggs & Peat, 1993, p. 151).

With this statement, *Briggs* and *Peat* highlight a central aspect of the scientific approach, namely the application of reductionism. The basis of scientific reduction is to break down complex structures into simple, concrete entities with exactly measurable magnitudes (Wesson, 1995, p. 15).

---

[91] See also the explanations of *Pasche:* Pasche (1994, p. 75 ff.).

Reductionism corresponds to the view of a watchmaker: A mechanical watch can be disassembled and take apart into its components, wheels, levers, and springs. The watch can also be reassembled from these parts. In principle, reductionists believe that complex systems are composed of simple elements that are linked together by relatively simple rules. According to this view, a system can be better understood if the individual elements are examined *ceteris paribus*.

But what is actually a complex system, what should one understand by complexity? First, the general first definition of the system concept should be briefly revisited:

▶ **Definition (System)** A **system** is a set of elements with attributes that are related to each other, whereby while maintaining coherence, a system can be part of a more comprehensive system.[92]

Complexity is often viewed as the opposite of simplicity. A system can then be described as simple if it consists of one or a few elements.[93] But what distinguishes complex systems from simple ones?

At first, one might think that a complex system consists of a high number of elements. But a system is certainly not complex solely due to the *number of elements*.

In addition, the *number of connections* and the type of connections, which determine the complexity of a system, must be considered.[94] For this reason, a hierarchically structured system is seen as simple and a networked system as complex (Lentz, 1993, p. 33). The concept of complexity can thus be interpreted through the *linked diversity*, or more clearly, through the "multilayered, intricate connection" (Blaseio, 1986, p. 20). This type of interpretation of the concept of diversity can also be found in *von Hayek* (Hayek, 1996, p. 281 ff.) or in *Ashby* (1974, p. 186 ff.). *Porr* rightly points out that there must also be a minimum amount of diversity for each system that must not be further reduced. "The fatal thing would be," says *Porr,* "that the system could no longer react to disturbances at a certain point in its self-reduction" (Porr, 2002, p. 12). This idea is also reflected in *Ashby's* concept of required diversity (*Ashby,*1974, p. 293).

In everyday life, it can certainly happen that something appears very complex to one person, while it appears simple to another.

---

[92] Cf. the definition of system at the beginning of Sect. 3.3.2.2 or the definition of a system by Bernd *Schiemenz:* Cybernetics and system theory as aids to solving complex problems. In: Schiemenz (1994, p. 9). In this context, the epistemological question is often discussed whether reality is a system or whether a system is a certain view of reality. The author tends to the second statement. Cf. some critical remarks on the danger of one-sided knowledge: Liening (1992, p. 49 ff.).

[93] *Cohen* and *Stewart* point out that the question of simplicity often lacks in science and is by no means as trivial as one might think. However, for our purposes, the above-mentioned idea of simplicity is sufficient. For a more detailed discussion of the problem of simplicity, see Cohen (1994).

[94] This concept of complexity is represented, for example, by *Luhmann*. See Luhmann (1980, col. 1064 f.).

Example

Take the skier who is skiing down a small mogul slope for the first time: He has to pay attention to his body posture, the position of his poles and skis, as well as carefully observe and analyse the terrain in relation to his skiing goal. A very complex undertaking. On the other hand, the experienced skier: He skis down this mogul slope with confidence and routine. For him, it is a simple undertaking. Both skiers, as observers of their environment and their actions, perceive the situation they are in differently. ◀

This reveals another criterion: Obviously, the complexity of a system also depends on its observer. Thus, *Ashby* points out that a system is described by the observer as "very extensive" when "in some way it triumphs over him through its complexity and intricacy" (Ashby, 1974, p. 98). Therefore, complexity is not only an objective property, but depends on a *subjective relation. Blaseio* also shares this view when he says that the "predicate 'complex' (…) is to a large extent always also self-predication, i.e., self-description of the observer" (Blaseio, 1986, p. 25). An extreme variant of this view has been known to us since the development of quantum theory. The atomic physicist *Capra* writes about this:

> The decisive characteristic of quantum theory is that the observer is not only necessary to observe the properties of an atomic event, but even necessary to bring about these properties. My conscious decision, for example, how I want to observe an electron, will to a certain extent determine the properties of the electron. (…) The electron *possesses* no properties independent of my consciousness (Capra, 1988, p. 91).

The complexity of a system therefore always depends on the observing subject, which attributes a certain structure to the system. *Lentz* points out that the observer imposes a structure on reality for better understanding, without it being clear whether reality actually corresponds to this structure (Lentz, 1993, p. 39). However, this objection is irrelevant, because *Kant* states that all knowledge begins with experience. But knowledge does not follow the objects, but the objects follow knowledge. According to *Kant*, science only deals with appearances (Phaenomena) and not with things in themselves (Noumena). The world is recognised as one sees it, more precisely, as one *can* see it. Because: Universal laws can be discovered, since all humans have the same (a priori) forms of intuition and forms of thinking or ordering (Kant, 1995, p. 49 and 262 ff.).

Therefore, it must be taken into account that a description of the concept of complexity with linked diversity corresponds to a capture of the static moment of complexity. The dynamic aspect is not necessarily addressed with this.

First, the difference between static and dynamic systems should be considered again to clarify this issue:

We speak of static systems when they do not or apparently do not change over time. In static systems, all forces acting on the system are balanced and the system is in equilibrium (Lentz, 1993, p. 44). The question of whether a system is static or dynamic is often a matter of the time horizon.

As an example, let's take the distinction between fixed and variable costs in business economics. While variable costs change with the alteration of production outputs, fixed costs, such as rent, interest, or wage costs, remain constant, as the term suggests. However, in the long term, fixed costs can also change due to restructuring, innovation, inflation, etc. It is always a matter of the time horizon and the relation. In contrast to the goods market, the money market can be considered always in equilibrium, and thus static, considering that it reacts much faster than the goods market. As *Dornbusch* and *Fischer* state:

> We assume (…) that the money market is cleared quickly and continuously, while the output adjusts slowly (Dornbusch & Fischer, 1992, p. 156).

But it is a matter of the time horizon whether one agrees with this view or not.

Due to the dynamics of a system, states can occur that are far removed from any static equilibrium point. The study of simple dynamic systems in the previous section has illustrated the variety of possible developments. Complexity therefore arises not only from the variety of links, but also from the variety of development possibilities, i.e., through *dynamics*.[95] The two simple market models have shown that these possibilities increase not only quantitatively but also qualitatively when one adopts a non-linear rather than a linear perspective. Because the possible erratic behaviour of non-linear systems cannot be easily grasped with the terms convergence and divergence, as is the case with linear systems. *Non-linearity* is therefore another criterion of complexity.

Thus, various criteria have emerged that describe *complexity* (provisionally!) through:

- the number of elements of a system
- the number of links between these elements
- the diversity and complexity of intertwined links

and

- the non-linear dynamics of a system.[96]

---

[95] *Willke* also attempts a very general and far-reaching definition of complexity. He also includes temporal development in his consideration, speaking of *consequence load*. Literally, he says: "Complexity denotes the degree of multilayeredness, networking and consequence load of a decision field" (Willke, 1991, p. 16).

[96] It should be noted at this point that besides this definition, which is meaningful for economics and social sciences, there are other definitions that are of little relevance for our considerations. For example, complexity is often equated with computational effort: "The complexity of an algorithm is the required computational effort in a concrete realisation of the algorithm within the calculation

It should be noted that the complexity of a system can be described both by these objective criteria and by a subjective relation.

> We only know a few drops from the vast sea of facts and navigation in this ocean seems to far exceed human capabilities (Wesson, 1995, p. 13).

With these words, *Wesson* describes the desire for simplified theories, the intention to dissect things and reduce the complex to its individual components. In this way, one can examine the interaction of individual parts to understand deeper processes. This form of reductionism is based on the idea that complexity builds up from an unmanageable multitude of simple forms. *Tietz* goes even further and claims:

> In order to arrive at presentable theories, the scientist *must* (emphasis, the author) simplify the complexity of the real world (Tietz, 1994, p. 270).

Since there is always a difference between the complexity of a model and the complexity of the corresponding system, the complexity of the model must have been limited or reduced. For *Luhmann*, complexity practically means compulsion to select. For him, selection is a reduction of complexity, which can be measured in the decrease of diversity (Habermas & Luhmann, 1971, p. 33). *Lentz* points out that this reduction of complexity usually occurs through aggregation or elimination. For example, *Boulding* proposed a reduction of complexity through aggregation as early as 1956 (Boulding, 1968, p. 40).

For example, economics at the lowest level considers the individual who appears as a producer or consumer.

The national economy consists of a multitude of such individuals. To describe and analyse the national economy of a country, it is not possible to consider each individual separately. Therefore, homogeneous groups are formed, which can, for example, result in a rough division into demand and supply side.[97]

Aggregation reduces the number of elements and links according to a certain ordering or hierarchy principle, thus making reality more manageable. It is implicitly assumed that "the respective aggregate behaves in principle like the sum of its individuals or a representative individual or company is constructed from the aggregate" (Lentz, 1993, p. 41).

Aggregation and the often associated abstraction have brought about decisive advances in economics.

---

model. The complexity of a function is the complexity of the best possible algorithm from the set of *all* algorithms that calculate the function. (…) Instead of talking about the complexity of a function, one often also speaks of the complexity of the problem that is solved by the function" (Claus et al., p. 342).

[97] For this, see, for example, the derivation of the aggregated demand and supply curve in: Dornbusch and Fischer (1992, pp. 229–238) or Dornbusch and Fischer (1992, pp. 501–507).

For example, neoclassical economics succeeded in reducing the diversity of human behaviour patterns to simple and applicable assumptions with the creation of the 'Homo Oeconomicus'. This is linked to the idea that all people behave like 'Homo Oecomomicus'. If the fiction of the 'Homo Oeconomicus' is to make sense, it can at least be expected that there are stable and statically recordable relationships between individual and aggregated behaviours. Otherwise, the economic image of man in the form of the 'Homo Oecomomicus' would be irrelevant for macro or microeconomic analysis. The problem of economics, however, is on the one hand that there are a multitude of individuals whose individual behaviour cannot be captured. On the other hand, human behaviour is subject to change. Through creative engagement with the environment in learning, thinking, and communicating with others, humans are constantly evolving, and the statically defined 'Homo-Oeconomicus' of neoclassical economics cannot do justice to this change in any way. *Schlösser* therefore rightly emphasises that the "recent developments in consumption theory (…) have undoubtedly led to a subtle modeling of human behaviour", but that with the "restrictive homo-oeconomicus fiction of traditional neoclassical economics (…) no 'state' can be made anymore" (Schlösser, 1992, p. 161)[98].

This also makes *Tietz's* view correct, according to which the process of simplification implies the risk that "decisions are based on a rudimentary image of the world, which is faulty precisely in the important relationships that are relevant for the current question. Such an incomplete theory is then little suited for explicative and prescriptive purposes in unusual and new situations" (Tietz, 1994, p. 270). It should therefore be noted:

> Reductionism, which intends to break down complex systems into simpler basic components for the purpose of better understanding, is always of limited value and can also lead to misinterpretations.

Many people seem to have an intuitive understanding of complexity, which could be described as 'conservation of complexity':

Complicated effects must have complicated causes and simple effects simple causes.

In this sense, one might think that inflation is a simple, albeit fatal effect. The general price level rises. Therefore, inflation must have a simple cause, and there must also be simple methods to combat it.[99]

If this form of conservation of complexity were true, then there is only one way for complex structures to emerge from simple elements: It requires a very large number of interconnected simple elements. This characteristic was also assumed in the preliminary description of complexity given here (Cohen, 1994, p. 67).

---

[98] Note *Schlösser's* words that he draws a sharp distinction between fiction and hypothesis. While the hypothesis is a result of thinking, for him the fiction is a mere tool, "a scaffold, which can even be discarded again when 'thinking' throws away its crutches over time" (Schlösser, 1992, p. 37).

[99] This trivially illuminating example to explain the intuitive understanding of complexity is pointed out by *Cohen* and *Stewart* (Cohen, 1994, pp. 32 f.).

And if this assumption is correct, then one must consider that the underlying order can be obscured if one is not quantitatively able to capture each of these elements. Thus, the phenomenon of large numbers appears again.

But this view is very problematic. Recall the (simple!) modified non-linear cobweb model. It consists of a few parameters and can lead to incredibly complex results with the appropriate parameter constellation.

This model reveals another problem in our preliminary description of complexity. It has been assumed so far that complex phenomena are based on a large number of links. So here again, the argument of large numbers came into play.

However, the elements in the model were connected by a simple non-linear equation: $P(t+1) = \lambda \cdot P(t) \cdot (1 - P(t))$

Therefore, the complexity can only have arisen through the feedback of the system, through iteration. It is formed by reinserting the calculated value as the initial value into the same equation. This process can be repeated as often as desired.

The relationship hinted at here becomes clear when looking at geometrically entangled objects, so-called fractals, which indeed are based on simple rules.[100]

Cohen and *Stewart* point out that the reverse process, that complex causes can produce simple effects, can also occur (Cohen, 1994, p. 33). Thus, complexity can not only be generated, but also lost.

Complex systems require higher-level explanations and reveal laws that cannot be derived from a large number of simple components or a large number of links. Complex systems are made up of subsystems, but the type of links that become visible through the dynamisation of the system seems to be crucial:

But if complex systems arise through the feedback and iteration of dynamics, then they are not reducible to individual components. For these components only generate complexity through the permanent feedback on themselves—through recursion.

Therefore, it can be stated that the complexity of a system is not determined by the number of elements and the number of links between these elements, but rather by the nature of the links. Due to this fact, a reductive decomposition of the system for the purpose of understanding does not help. We therefore define:

▶ The **complexity** of a system is determined by

- the recursive nature of the links

and

- the non-linear dynamics of the system

where complexity can not only be generated, but also lost (Liening, 1998, p. 62).

---

[100] In Sect. 4.1.2 in the second part of the book, the phenomenon of fractals is explicitly addressed.

If complexity arises as described above, then understanding it does not require the abolition of reductionism, but rather a new way in which the complex and the simple are closely intertwined, where simple iterations release the complexity hidden in the seemingly simple and—as *Briggs* and *Peat* put it—"access to creative potential" (Briggs & Peat, 1993, p. 151) is created. Thus, the equations and their parameters do not form the blueprint, but merely the starting point for the evolution of a shape, which—as a kind of 'creatio ex nihilo'—gradually emerges in itself through the feedback of the equations (Briggs & Peat, 1993, p. 151).

In conclusion, it can be stated at this point that the whole in complex systems can indeed be more or at least something different than the sum of its parts, which has made the old reductionist view questionable. Thus, reductionism is not at an end, but must be provided with a new perspective, as described above. Then reductionism serves the understanding of complexity and recognises that complexity does not have to arise from a multitude of simple objects and links.

3.4.7 Consequences for the Example of the Supply-Demand Model

What consequences arise for our example of the labour market for 'multicopter' engineers?

Is state intervention conceivable in this highly complex, chaotic situation to regulate the market?

Example: Salaries are considered excessively high—Maximum wages

It is conceivable that salaries are seen as significantly excessive and thus unfair. The state could go ahead and set maximum prices for wages. What would happen? The maximum price would have to be set below the market equilibrium in order to be effective. This would lead to a decrease in the number of suppliers (i.e., potential employees) and an increase in the number of demanders (i.e., companies or jobs) under rational behaviour. Numerous positions would thus remain vacant, resulting in a surplus of supply (see Fig. 3.62). ◀

Example: Salaries are considered too low—Minimum wages

Similarly, it is conceivable that salaries are seen as too low and thus also considered unfair. In this case, the state could, for example, introduce a minimum wage. What would happen now? The minimum price would have to be set above the equilibrium price to be effective. This would decrease the demand for workers and increase the supply of potential workers, resulting in a surplus of demand (see Fig. 3.62). This would result in unemployment, which—from a strictly liberal perspective—equates to a prohibition of work for numerous employees. ◀

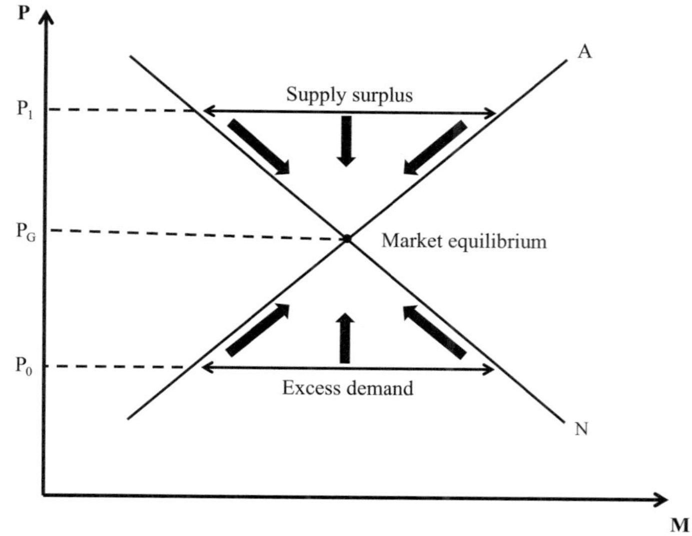

Fig. 3.62 Maximum and minimum prices

The economic perspective thus shows clear reservations about state interventions. It seeks market-based solutions that are incentive-compatible, with the state playing the role of setting the framework conditions.

One does not have to agree with this view, and there are a multitude of other scientific explanations and solution options that do not lose their significance due to the economic perspective presented here. Therefore, one should be aware that the economic perspective is just one of many. Nevertheless, it seems worthwhile for managers in the healthcare sector to also consider this perspective in order to make sensible strategic decisions.

In any case, in our example, a direct intervention by setting minimum or maximum wages[101] would be of little help, as this would only lead to the 'price mechanism' coming to a standstill. This would further diminish the important signaling function of prices

[101] Even if the market wanted to show a convergent cyclical movement and the state had come to the conclusion that the equilibrium price that was settling in was too high (e.g., rents for student flats), an intervention by setting maximum prices (here: maximum rents) would be economically problematic. For the maximum price to have an effect, it would have to be significantly below the equilibrium price. However, this would result in a decrease in supply (using the example of the student housing market: the supply of student flats) and would end up being significantly lower than the demand (here the demand for student flats), which would rather increase due to the lower maximum price. This excess demand induced by the maximum price would be the result of the state intervention (in the case of maximum prices for student flats, the number of missing flats would therefore increase significantly).

(here salaries) on which a market can function at all. And it is highly likely that further interventions would have to be made to counteract the unwanted consequences of the intervention, with the risk of the described oil spot theorem occurring.

The only sensible possibility of state intervention would consist in establishing the conditions for the functioning of the market (in the sense of periodic salary cycles); and in our model, this means first recognising what the position of the supply and demand curves must be in order for a cyclical salary development to emerge from the chaos of salary developments and then promoting this accordingly. To recognise how large the value λ must be in order for the salaries to stabilise, one would traditionally tend to decompose or reduce the system for the purpose of analysis. However, due to the butterfly effect, a reductive decomposition of the system for the purpose of understanding does not help. Many systems, including economic ones, cannot be simplified and decomposed without significant problems. In particular, complex systems cannot be disassembled and reassembled like a mechanical clock. If one wants to stick with the clock analogy, one can see that economic processes in particular probably function more like a quartz clock, whose connections between the individual parts are not mechanical, and which is irreversibly destroyed when disassembled. Thus, one must agree with *Wesson* when he says that the world of simplicity only exists in the imagination. It is, according to *Wesson,* "a nirvana in which science, just like a wish, ends" (Wesson, 1995, p. 40). Therefore, methods other than the traditional ones are needed to explore complex systems.[102]

The complexity can ultimately only have arisen through the feedback of the system, through iteration. But if complex systems arise through the feedback and iteration of the dynamics, then they are not reducible to individual components. Because these components only generate complexity through the permanent feedback on themselves—through the recursion. The whole is more and something different than the sum of its parts!

The model described above shows that even with a mathematically simple, non-linear recursive function, a much wider spectrum of possible system developments can be represented than is the case with linear functions. Due to the non-linear feedback of the system, the irreversibility of the system is expressed, in which it is no longer irrelevant

[102] In the following chapters, we will go into more detail about these methods. In addition to the method of bifurcation analysis, for example, the methods of chaos research include the calculation of *Lyapunov* exponents, the *Li/Yorke* theorem, or dimension calculation (e.g., box dimension, Hausdorff dimension, etc.). A detailed presentation, explanation, and application can be found, for example, in: Liening (1998, p. 64 ff.). Especially in the context of empirical studies, it has always been difficult to prove chaos solely on the basis of, for example, the calculation of *Lyapunov* exponents. It is suspected that in particular the noise in the data, caused by random influences and exogenous shocks, makes the proof difficult (Liening, 1998: ibid). Nevertheless, other methods, which in some cases must be considered in combination, offer the possibility of compensating for this deficit. These include methods that can be described with the keywords *Grammar Complexity, Recurrence Plots, Kolmogorov-Sinai-Entropy* or *Permutation Entropy*. See, for example, Strunk et al. (2004, p. 481 ff.).

whether one looks at it in time forward or backward. This irreversibility is the prerequisite for self-organisation.

Irreversibility and self-organisation, in addition to non-linearity and recursive linkage of system elements, are thus two further important characteristics of complex systems.

3.5 First Conclusion—Summary of Important Aspects and a Brief Plea for a (Free) Market Economy and the Consideration of Entrepreneurship as a Complex Phenomenon

3.5.1 Complexity and Behavioural Economics

The behavioural economic analyses in Chap. 1 have clearly shown how even in simple systems people tend to make systematic errors. From the perception of information, its processing, the evaluation of information to control behaviour—pitfalls lurk everywhere that we can stumble over.

We have referred to these systems as "simple" from a complexity science perspective. "Simple" here does not mean that the situations, processes or structures in which one moves cannot be perceived as difficult or complicated. Rather, "simple" means that they are perceived as causally lineal and that they can be considered "simple" after a successful solution has been worked out. The advantage of the behavioural economic analysis is now that we have recognised a series of wrong decisions as systematic and deterministic. Such misjudgements can be avoided, however, once the causes are understood. Nevertheless, we are still talking about "simple" systems here, while we can only guess what dangers we can encounter in "complex" systems.

One reason for the widespread belief that we just need to have enough detailed knowledge, deal intensively enough with a problem, so that we can solve it, lies in the fact that this *Laplacian* demon, that symbol for the omnipotence fantasy just described (the overconfidence bias sends its regards), is firmly anchored in us. This is of course also due to the experience that this *Laplacian* demon has its justification, as it is valid in lineal and little networked systems, and the associated problem-solving strategies can indeed be successful there. Only in modern times, when networking, whether through the globalisation of the economy, networking in the information sector via the Internet etc., has explosively changed the world, do the traditional approaches not necessarily work anymore.

3.5.2 Complexity, the Laplacian Demon, and Economics

Before this above-described conception of mechanistic-deterministic thinking, economics is apparently not immune. On the contrary: the historical review in Sect. 3.1 has shown that it was only through the adoption of mechanistic-causal thinking that economics achieved "fame and honour". From physiocracy through classical political economy to mathematically sophisticated neoclassicism, we find the *Laplacian* demon everywhere.

The explanations in Sect. 3.2 have also illustrated how this worldview began to falter, the *Laplacian* demon was called into question. For example, it became clear that systems cannot simply be disassembled and analysed. Especially with complex systems, a systemic view of the whole is needed. To scientifically clarify the associated questions of complex systems, it was therefore useful to deal extensively with the concept of the system. In the simplest case, a system is understood as a set of elements that can be considered as units in themselves and that are related to each other in such a way that a clear system boundary becomes recognisable. The discussion in Sect. 3.3 has shown that, for example, *Gharajedaghi* has identified a wealth of interesting features that are helpful for the detailed analysis of systems. For this purpose, however, one must engage in model building and distinguish models of systems. The explanations in Sect. 3.4 have allowed, through model building and simulation, to gather a multitude of insights about systems, such as the discussed archetypes of *Senge*,.

3.5.3 Complexity and (Free) Market Economy

Complex systems, when viewed in summary, reveal laws that cannot be derived from a high number of simple components or a large number of connections. Complex systems can also be composed of subsystems, but the type of connections that become visible through the dynamisation of the system seems to be decisive. Therefore, it can be stated that the complexity of a system is not determined by the number of elements of a system alone and the number of connections between these elements, but rather by

- the recursive nature of the connections

and

- the non-linear dynamics of the system

which generate themselves in a self-organising and irreversible manner. If complexity arises as described in the above explanations, then a new way of viewing is needed to understand this complexity. We must make other, new demands on our thinking, as we have already speculated in the first chapter. In this new way of thinking, the complex and the simple are closely intertwined. The complexity hidden in the seemingly simple is released here through simple iterations, and thus—as *Briggs* and *Peat* formulate it—"access to creative potential" (Briggs & Peat, 1993, p. 151) is created. Thus, the equations and their parameters of a model do not form the blueprint, but merely the starting point for the evolution of a shape, which—as a kind of 'creatio ex nihilo'—"gradually emerges" in itself through the feedback of the equations (Briggs & Peat, 1993, p. 151).

For these reasons and the demonstrated butterfly effect, it is hardly possible to generally control a complex system such as the "economy" of a country, because every minimal intervention can have unforeseeable consequences 'in the long run'. The failure of countercyclical fiscal policy in the seventies of the Federal Republic, or even more extreme: the failure of the planned economy in the Eastern European states, can be used as empirical evidence. Almost any kind of state intervention in the economic processes of a market, no matter how well-intentioned, must ultimately fail if it intends to do more than just provide the necessary framework conditions for the system to function.[103] Without *von Hayek* possibly being able to know the theoretical approaches presented here when writing his eponymous work, as the mathematical insights were only made possible in the nineties through the increased use of computers, he rightly speaks in the presented context of the presumption of knowledge (Hayek, 1996).[104]

And *van Suntum* asks, how "can a state planning authority know in the face of this complexity which goods are to be demanded when, in what quantity and at what location? How should it manage the concrete satisfaction of this diversity of demand? Only the decentralised knowledge of hundreds of thousands of companies, merchants and managers, all seeking their advantage, can solve this 'search problem'" (Suntum, 2005, p. 13). Or as *von Hayek* says, the great achievement of the market is to "make a far-reaching division of labour possible and to bring about a continuous adaptation of economic actions to millions of special facts and events, which in their entirety can be known by no one" (Hayek, 1996, p. 309).

3.5.4 Complexity and Entrepreneurship

When considering the field of Entrepreneurship in the context of a market economy as a Complex System, it can initially be stated that the stages and phases associated with the founding process function as subsystems in the complex market system and are thus exposed to and shaped by complexity. The usual distinctions are entrepreneurship in

[103] However, this does not exclude the possibility that in certain areas (provision of public goods, toll goods, common goods) market failure can occur due to "moral hazard" or "adverse selection" caused by information asymmetries, even without state intervention, and that state solutions may need to be considered. See, for example, the explanations on the topic "Market Failure and Public Policy" in: Ekelund and Tollison (1988, p. 440–460). Nevertheless, there are also economists who can imagine market-based solutions that include social goals. See, for example, in the health sector: Blankart (2008, p. 400 ff.).

[104] Friedrich August *von Hayek's* essay on the theory of complex phenomena contained therein was first published in 1967.

the founding process, Entrepreneurship within a growth process, and Entrepreneurship within an organisation, with entrepreneurship education playing a special role in the general as well as occupation-specific educational process. Regardless of the breadth of the field outlined, all stages and phases of Entrepreneurship and Entrepreneurship Education have one thing in common: complexity and uncertainty (Wiltbank et al., 2009; Alvarez & Barney, 2007; Sarasvathy, 2008).

Complexity and uncertainty even seem to be the decisive factors for entrepreneurship. Numerous authors emphasise that Entrepreneurship itself represents a non-linear and complex process (Sarasvathy, 2001; Swanson & Zhang, 2011), without the essence of complexity having been really described so far.

The initial insights from the 'complexity sciences' presented here therefore provide an important basis for the scientific view of Entrepreneurship.

3.5.5 Outlook

We have already indicated in the previous section that the central aspects associated with Entrepreneurship are characterised by complexity and uncertainty (Dew et al., 2009; Grichnik & Gassmann, 2013).

However, how exactly 'Complex Systems' play a role in relation to entrepreneurship-related questions, and how Entrepreneurs can recognise for themselves whether they are able to deal with dynamics and complexity, will be discussed in more detail later. Ultimately, entrepreneurs need methods that enable them to deal with complexity as an inherent characteristic of every entrepreneurship process. The initial findings of the previous chapters suggest that it may be worthwhile, especially with regard to dynamic, non-linear events, such as in the context of innovative company foundations, to learn more about the topic of complexity.

For this, it is essential that we take a more specific look at the theories behind the outlined concept of complexity. Since the field of entrepreneurship not only includes a theoretical but also an empirical canon of topics, especially when we pursue the question of suitable methods for Entrepreneurs, it is important in this context to also discuss the findings of complexity science that serve to generate empirical findings in the field of Entrepreneurship. In this context, newer possibilities and methods of empirical investigation of Complex Systems should also play a role.

References

Ackoff, R. L. (1973). Science in the systems age: Beyond IE, OR, and MS. *Operations Research, 21*(3), 661–671.

Ackoff, R. L. (1987). President's symposium: OR, a post mortem. *Operations Research, 35*(3), 471–474.

Alvarez, S. A., & Barney, J. B. (2007). Discovery and creation: Alternative theories of entrepreneurial action. *Strategic Entrepreneurship Journal, 1*(1–2), 11–26.

Anderson, P. W. (2000). In J. Brockman (Ed.), *Die wichtigsten Erfindungen der letzten 2000 Jahre* (p. 178). Ullstein.

Argyris, C., & Schön, D. (1978). *Organizational learning: A theory of action perspective*. Addison-Wesley.

Arrow, K. J., & Hahn, F. H. (1971). *General competitive analysis*. Holden-Day.

Ashby, R. (1974). *Einführung in die Kybernetik*. Suhrkamp Taschenbuch.

Baecker, D. (Ed.). (2005). *Schlüsselwerke der Systemtheorie*. VS Verlag.

Barnard, C. I. (1968). *The functions of the executive (Thirteenth Anniversary Edition)*. Harvard University Press.

Beinhocker, E. (2007). *The origin of wealth: Evolution, complexity, and the radical remaking of economics*. Random House.

Benner, D. (1989a). Auf dem Weg zur Öffnung von Unterricht und Schule. Theoretische Grundlagen zur Weiterentwicklung der Schulpädagogik. *Die Grundschulzeitschrift, 27*, 46–55.

Benner, D. (1989b). Wissenschaft und Bildung. In FB Erziehungswissenschaft der WWU (Ed.), *Aufgaben der Erziehungswissenschaft in der Universität. Veranstaltung am dies academicus (13.6.1989) der WWU*. WWU.

Bentham, J. (1822). *An introduction to the principles of morals and legislation*. Blackwell.

Berghoff, H. (2016). *Moderne Unternehmensgeschichte: Eine themen- und theorieorientierte Einführung*. De Gruyter Oldenbourg.

Bertalanffy, L. von. (1932). *Theoretische Biologie*. Borntraeger.

Bertalanffy, L. von. (1956). General system theory. In L. von Bertalanffy & A. Rapoport (Eds.), *General systems yearbook I*. University of Michigan Press.

Bertalanffy, L. von. (1972). Zu einer allgemeinen Systemlehre. In K. Bleicher (Ed.), *Organisation als System*. Gabler.

Birkhoff, G. D. (1931). A mathematical approach to aesthetics. *Scientia, 25*(50), 133–146.

Blankart, C. B. (2008). *Öffentliche Finanzen in der Demokratie*. Vahlen.

Blaseio, H. (1986). *Das Kognos-Prinzip. Zur Dynamik sich-selbst-organisierender wirtschaftlicher und sozialer Systeme*. Duncker & Humblot.

Blumenberg, H. (1957). Nachahmung der Natur – Zur Vorgeschichte des schöpferischen Menschen. *Studium Generale, 10*(5), 266–283.

Borges, J. L. (2005). *Borges und ich (El hacedor): Kurzprosa und Gedichte 1960*. Fischer Taschenbuch.

Bossel, H. (1994). *Modellbildung und Simulation – Konzepte, Verfahren und Modelle zum Verhalten dynamischer Systeme* (2nd edn.). Springer.

Boulding, K. (1968). *Beyond economics: Essays on society, religion and ethics*. University of Michigan Press.

Breidenstein, H. (2012). Mälzels Mord an Mozart – Die untauglichen Versuche, musikalische Zeit zu messen (Dieser Aufsatz erschien zuerst in „Das Orchester" Mainz 2007/11, S. 8–15). http://www.mozarttempi.de/maelzel.html. Accessed 15 Aug 2012.

Briggs, J., & Peat, D. (1993). *Die Entdeckung des Chaos*. Deutscher Taschenbuch.

Buchanan, J. M. (2001). Game theory, mathematics and economics. *Journal of Economic Methodology, 8*(1), 27–32.

Burns, T., & Stalker, G. M. (1966). *The management of innovation*. Tavistock.

Cantillon, R (1755). Essai sur la Nature du Comerce en General. Entrepreneurship. M. Casson: 5–10

Capra, F. (1988). *Wendezeit*. Knaur.

Carlyle, T. (1849). Occasional discourse on the negro question. *Fraser's Magazine for Town and Country, 1,* 672–673.

Carroll, L. (1893). *Silvie and Bruno concluded – The man in the moon* (2nd edn.). Macmillan & Co.

Cartwright, M. L., & Littlewood, J. E. (1945). On the non-linear differential equation of the second order. *Journal of the London Mathematical Society, 20*(3), 180–189.

Chen, S. (2011). *Das Drei-Körper-Problem der Himmelsmechanik.* GRIN.

Chiarella, C. (1992). Entwicklungen der nicht-linearen, dynamischen ökonomischen Theorie: Vergangenheit, Gegenwart und Zukunft. In H. Hanusch & H. C. Recktenwald (Eds.), *Ökonomische Wissenschaft in der Zukunft – Ansichten führender Ökonomen* (pp. 74–91). Wirtschaft und Finanzen.

Churchman, C. W. (1979). *The systems approach and its enemies.* Basic Books.

Coase, R. H. (1937). The nature of the firm. *Economica, 4,* 386–405.

Cohen, J., & Stewart, I. (1994). *Chaos – Antichaos Ein Ausblick auf die Wissenschaft des 21. Jahrhunderts.* Byblos.

Cope, J. (2003). Entrepreneurial learning and critical reflection: Discontinuous events as triggers for ‚Higher-level' learning. *Management Learning, 34*(4), 429–450.

Crutchfield, J. P., Farmer, J. D., Packard, N. H., & Shaw, R. S. (1987). Chaos und Fraktale. *Spektrum der Wissenschaft, 2,* 78–90.

Daft, R. L., & Lengel, R. H. (1984). Information richness. A new approach to managerial behavior and organization design. *Research in Organizational Behavior, 6,* 191–233.

Denis, H. (1985). *Geschichte der Wirtschaftstheorien* (Vol. 1). Schäuble.

Der Westen. (2012). Schadstoffe im Spielzeug – Deutschland verklagt EU-Kommission. http://www.derwesten.de/gesundheit/schadstoffe-im-spielzeug-deutschland-verklagt-eu-kommission-id6646135.html. Accessed 23 Aug 2012.

Descartes, R. (1983). Abhandlung über die Methode. In A. Müller (Ed.), *Erkenntnis- und Wissenschaftstheorie* (pp. 33–46). Aschendorff.

Descartes, R. (1990). *Discours de la méthode.* Meiner (Erstveröffentlichung 1637).

Dew, N., Read, S., Sarasvathy, S. D., & Wiltbank, R. (2009). Effectual versus predictive logics in entrepreneurial decision-making: Differences between experts and novices. *Journal of Business Venturing, 24*(4), 287–309.

Dopfer, K. (1988). Classical mechanics with an ethical dimension: Professor Tinbergen's economics. *Journal of Economic Issues, 22*(3), 675–706.

Dopfer, K. (1992). Evolutionsökonomie in der Zukunft: Programmatik und Theorieentwicklungen. In H. Hanusch & H. C. Recktenwald (Eds.), *Ökonomische Wissenschaft in der Zukunft – Ansichten führender Ökonomen* (pp. 96–125). Wirtschaft und Finanzen.

Dornbusch, R., & Fischer, S. (1992). *Makroökonomik.* Oldenbourg.

Dörner, D. (2007). *Die Logik des Misslingens – Strategisches Denken in komplexen Situationen.* Rowohlt.

Easterby-Smith, M., Antonacopoulou, E., Simm, D., & Lyles, M. (2004). Constructing contributions to organizational learning: Argyris and the next generation. *Management Learning, 35*(4), 371–380.

Ebeling, W. (1994). Selbstorganisation und Entropie in ökologischen und ökonomischen Prozessen. In F. Beckenbach & H. Diefenbacher (Eds.), *Zwischen Entropie und Selbstorganisation – Perspektiven einer ökologischen Ökonomie* (pp. 29–45). Metropolis.

Ebeling, W., & Schweitzer, F. (2002). Zwischen Ordnung und Chaos. Komplexität und Ästhetik aus physikalischer Sicht. *Wissenschaft und Kunst, 2002*(Frühjahr), 46–49.

Editorial Team. (2014). What is an entrepreneur? Learn what defines an entrepreneur, what they do and what constitutes an entrepreneur in the modern era | Updated July 27, 2021 | Published

November 22, 2014 Entrepreneur Handbook. https://entrepreneurhandbook.co.uk/define-entrepreneur.
Eisenhardt, P., Kurth, D., & Stiehl, H. (1995). *Wie Neues entsteht. Die Wissenschaften des Komplexen und Fraktalen*. Rowohlt.
Ekelund, R. B., Jr., & Tollison, R. D. (1988). *Economics*. Little, Brown & Co.
Faschingbauer, M. (2013). *Effectuation – Wie erfolgreiche Unternehmer denken, entscheiden und handeln*. Schäffer-Poeschel.
Fiol, C. M., & Lyles, M. A. (1985). Organizational learning. *Academy of Management Review, 10*(4), 803–813.
Forrester, J. W. (1971). *World dynamics*. Wright-Allen.
Forrester, J. W. (1972). *Grundzüge einer Systemtheorie*. Gabler.
Forster, O. (2004). *Analysis 1*. Vieweg & Teubner.
François, C. (Ed.). (1997). *International encyclopedia of systems and cybernetics*. Saur.
Fromm, E., Martino, R. de, & Suzuki, D. T. (2011). *Zen-Buddhismus und Psychoanalyse*. Suhrkamp.
Gell-Mann, M. (1996). *Das Quark und der Jaguar. Vom Einfachen zum Komplexen. Die Suche nach einer neuen Erklärung der Welt*. Piper.
Gell-Mann, M. (1997). The simple and the complex. In D. S. Alberts & T. J. Czerwinski (Eds.), *Complexity, global politics and national security* (pp. 2–12). National Defense University.
Gerken, G. (1994). *Die fraktale Marke*. Econ.
Gerwin, R. (1964). *Intelligente Automaten – Die Technik der Kybernetik und Automation*. Belser.
Gharajedaghi, J. (2005). *System thinking: Managing chaos and complexity: A platform for designing business architecture*. Elsevier.
Gibson, J. E., Scherer, W. T., & Gibson, W. F. (2007). *How to do systems analysis*. Wiley-Interscience.
Glazinski, B. (2007). *Innovatives change management*. Wiley-VCH.
Goethe, J. W. von. (1810). *Zur Farbenlehre* (Vol. 1). http://www.deutschestextarchiv.de/goethe_farbenlehre01_1810. Accessed 22 Oct 2015.
Goethe, J. W. von. (2014). *Maximen und Reflexionen* (3rd edn.). Hofenberg.
Gossen, H. H. (1854). *Entwicklung der Gesetze des menschlichen Verkehrs, und der daraus fließenden Regeln für menschliches Handeln*. Vieweg.
Graß, R.-D. (1994). Vilfredo Pareto – Marx der Bourgeoisie. In N. Piper (Ed.), *Die großen Ökonomen* (pp. 69–74). Schäffer-Poeschel.
Grichnik, D., & Gassmann, O. (2013). *Das unternehmerische Unternehmen*. Springer.
Habermas, J., & Luhmann, N. (1971). *Theorie der Gesellschaft oder Sozialtechnologie – Was leistet die Systemforschung?* Suhrkamp.
Haken, H. (1990). Synergetics as a tool for the conceptualization and mathematization of cognition and behavior – How far can we go? In H. Haken & M. Stadler (Eds.), *Synergetics of cognition* (pp. 2–31). Springer.
Handelsblatt. (2012). Bundestag bewilligt höhere Neuverschuldung. http://www.handelsblatt.com/politik/deutschland/wegen-euro-rettung-bundestag-bewilligt-hoehere-neuverschuldung/6753412.html. Accessed 24 Aug 2012.
Hanusch, H., & Recktenwald, H. C. (Eds.). (1992). *Ökonomische Wissenschaft in der Zukunft – Ansichten führender Ökonomen*. Wirtschaft und Finanzen.
Hawking, S. (1988). *Eine kurze Geschichte der Zeit*. Rowohlt.
Hayek, F. A. von. (1996). *Die Anmaßung von Wissen*. Mohr Siebeck.
Heidegger, M. (1962). *Die Technik und die Kehre*. Klett-Cotta.
Helm, Daniel von der. (2006). Immanuel Kant. http://www.daniel-von-der-helm.com/kant/kant-philosophie.html. Accessed 21 Oct 2015.

Herzog, B. (2012). Positive Effekte von Steuersenkungen nicht unter den Tisch kehren! http://www.insm-oekonomenblog.de/6686-positive-effekte-von-steuersenkungen-nicht-unter-den-tisch-kehren/. Accessed 22 Dec 2015.

Hirschman, A. O. (1980). *Leidenschaften und Interessen. Politische Begründungen des Kapitalismus vor seinem Sieg*. Suhrkamp.

Hölderlin, F. (2001). *Sämtliche Gedichte und Hyperion*. Insel.

Hungenberg, H., & Wulf, T. (2006). *Grundlagen der Unternehmensführung*. Springer.

Ilg, P., & Kaufmann, M. (2011). Mit Karacho in den Schweinezyklus. http://www.spiegel.de/karriere/berufsstart/0,1518,784325,00.html. Accessed 23 Aug 2015.

Illinger, P. (2009). Erdöl wird knapp – Luxusgut Benzin. http://www.sueddeutsche.de/wissen/erdoel-wird-knapp-luxusgut-benzin-1.154334. Accessed 24 Aug 2012.

Jacobi, C. G. J. (1881). *Gesammelte Werke I*. Borchardt.

Jevons, S. W. (1924). *Die Theorie der politischen Ökonomie*. Fischer.

Kant, I. (1995). Kritik der reinen Vernunft. In I. Kant (Ed.), *Werke in sechs Bänden*. Könemann.

Katona, G. (1960). *Das Verhalten der Verbraucher und Unternehmen*. Mohr.

Keynes, J. M. (1936). *The general theory of employment, interest and money*. Prometheus Book.

Kinnebrock, W. (2002). *Bedeutende Theorien des 20. Jahrhunderts*. Oldenbourg.

Knight, F. (1921). *Risk, uncertainty and profit*. University of Chicago Press.

Koestler, A. (1990). *The ghost and the machine*. Penguin.

Kolmogorow, A. N. (1958). Über die Entropie der Zeit. Eins als metrische Invariante von Automorphismen. *Dokladyi Akademii Nauk (UDSSR), 119*, 861–864.

Kompf, M. (2012). *Entreplexity = Entrepreneurship + Complexity – The writing and thoughts of Gene Luczkiw*. Sense.

Königsberger, K. (2004). *Analysis 2*. Springer.

Krafft, D. (1982). *Märkte, Preise, Wettbewerb*.

Kriz, J. (1998). *Systemtheorie – Eine Einführung für Psychotherapeuten, Psychologen und Mediziner* (2nd edn.). facultas wuv universitätsverlag.

Kurz, H. D. (2020). Kapitalismus, Sozialismus und Demokratie: Schumpeters Entwurf einer histoire raisonnée der Moderne. *Wirtschaft und Gesellschaft, 46*(4), 559–607.

Laplace, P. S. (1814). *Essai philosophique sur les probabilités*. Courcier, Imprimeur-Libraire pour les Mathématique et la Marine.

Leiber, T. (1996). *Kosmos, Kausalität und Chaos*. Ergon.

Lentz, W. (1993). *Neuere Entwicklungen in der Theorie dynamischer Systeme und ihre Bedeutung für die Agrarökonomie*. Duncker & Humblot.

Letellier, C. (2014). Chaos unter Kontrolle. *Spektrum der Wissenschaft, 14*(1), 24–31.

Lichtenberg, G. C. (1998). *Schriften und Briefe* (Vol. I). Zweitausendeins.

Liening, A. (1992). *Intelligente Tutorielle Systeme (ITS) – Eine kritische Analyse unter besonderer Berücksichtigung ihrer Einsatzmöglichkeiten in der Wirtschaftsdidaktik*. LIT.

Liening, A. (1996). Moralische Erziehung im Wirtschaftsunterricht. In Bundesfachgruppe für ökonomische Bildung (Ed.), *Ethik und Ökonomische Bildung* (pp. 179–186). Springer.

Liening, A. (1998). *Komplexe Systeme zwischen Ordnung und Chaos*. LIT.

Liening, A. (2005). *Einführung in die Mathematik* (3rd edn.). Institut für Verbundstudien NRW.

Liening, A. (2012). *Komplexe Systeme – Eine Software zur Simulation und Analyse*. iLearning.

Liening, A., & Mittelstädt, E. (2008). Wissensbilanzierung im Bildungsmanagement für eine deregulierte Professionalität im Berufsfeld Ökonomischer Bildung. In G. Seeber (Ed.), *Forschungsfelder der Wirtschaftsdidaktik* (pp. 238–253). Wochenschau.

Lipsey, R. G., & Courant, P. N. (1996). *Economics*. Longman Higher Education.

Loistl, O., & Betz, I. (1993). *Chaostheorie. Zur Theorie nichtlinearer dynamischer Systeme*. Oldenbourg.

Lorenz, E. N. (1963). Deterministic nonperiodic flow. *Journal of the Atmospheric Sciences, 20*(2), 130–141.

Luden, H. (Ed.). (1828). *Reise Sr. Hoheit des Herzogs Bernhard zu Sachsen-Weimar-Eisenach durch Nordamerika in den Jahren 1825–1826*. Hoffmann.

Luhmann, N. (1968). *Zweckbegriff und Systemrationalität*. Mohr (Siebeck).

Luhmann, N. (1976). *Funktionen und Folgen formaler Organisation* (3rd edn.). Duncker & Humblot.

Luhmann, N. (1980). Komplexität. In E. Grochla (Ed.), *Handwörterbuch der Organisation* (2nd edn.). Poeschel.

Mainzer, K. (1995). *Zeit – Von der Urzeit zur Computerzeit*. Beck.

Mandelbrot, B. B., & Hudson, R. L. (2007). *Fraktale und Finanzen. Märkte zwischen Risiko, Rendite und Ruin*. Piper.

Mankiw, N. G. (2004). *Grundzüge der Volkswirtschaftslehre*. Schäffer-Poeschel.

March, J. G., & Simon, H. A. (1958). *Organizations*. Wiley.

Maturana, H. R. (1985). *Erkennen: Die Organisation und Verkörperung der Wirklichkeit* (2nd edn.). Vieweg.

Maturana, H. R., & Varela, F. J. (1987). *Der Baum der Erkenntnis. Die biologischen Wurzeln des Erkennens*. Scherz.

McKelvey, B. (2004). Towards a complexity science of entrepreneurship. *Journal of Business Venturing, 19*(3), 313–342.

Meadows, D. H., Meadows, D. L., Randers, J., & Behrens, W. W. (1972). *Limits to growth*. Universe Books.

Medio, A. (1992). *Chaotic dynamics/ theory and applications to economics*. Cambridge University Press.

Mettrie, J. O. de La. (1985). *Der Mensch als Maschine*. LSR.

Meyer, D. (2011). Staatsverschuldung – Ein Zinseszins-Teufelskreis. http://www.staatsverschuldung-online.de/. Accessed 23 Aug 2012.

Mill, J. S. (2002). *A system of logic: Ratiocinative and inductive*. University Press of the Pacific.

Mill, J. S. (2015). *Principles of political economy*. CreateSpace Independent Publishing Platform.

Mirowski, P. (1989). *More heat then light. Economics as social physics, physics as nature's economics*. Cambridge University Press.

Mole, P. (2010). Ockham's Razor cuts both ways: The uses and abuses of simplicity in Scientific theories. *Skeptic, 10*(1), 40–47.

Neinhaus, A. (2013) Der vergessene Vater der Risikoforschung. https://www.fuw.ch/article/der-vergessene-vater-der-risikoforschung/.

Neisser, U. (1976). *Cognition and reality. Principles and implications of cognitive psychology*. Freeman.

Neumann, K. (2009). *Know-Why – Management kapiert Komplexität*. Books on Demand.

Newton, I. (Ed.). (1686). *Philosophiae naturalis Principia Mathematica*. Kindle-Version.

Niemeyer, G. (1977). *Kybernetische System- und Modelltheorie: System Dynamics*. Vahlen.

Oltmanns, T. (1994). Alfred Marshall – Ökonomie gegen die Armut. In N. Piper (Ed.), *Die großen Ökonomen* (p. 76). Schäffer-Poeschel.

Page, B. (1991). *Diskrete Simulation*. Springer.

Papert, S. (1980). *Mindstorms. Childrens, computer and powerful ideas*. Basic Books.

Pasche, M. (1994). Ansätze einer evolutorischen Umweltökonomik. In F. Beckenbach & H. Diefenbacher (Eds.), *Zwischen Entropie und Selbstorganisation – Perspektiven einer ökologischen Ökonomie* (pp. 75–118). Metropolis.

Peitgen, H.-O., Jürgens, H., & Saupe, D. (1992). *Chaos – Bausteine der Ordnung*. Springer.

Pépin, F. (2014). Zufall und Determinismus. *Spektrum der Wissenschaft, 14*(1), 6–11.

Piaget, J. (1972). *To understand is to invent*. Viking.

Piaget, J. (1977). *The development of thought: Equilibration of cognitive structures (originally published in French, 1975)*. Viking.

Platon. (1994). *Sämtliche Werke – Timaios, Kritias, Minos, Nomoi* (4th edn.). Rowohlt.
Pletter, R. (2003). Dank Bankberater in die Schuldenfalle. http://www.spiegel.de/wirtschaft/jugendliche-dank-bankberater-in-die-schuldenfalle-a-262857.html. Accessed 23 Aug 2012.
Poe, E. A. (1836). Maelzel's chess-player. http://www.eapoe.org/works/essays/maelzel.htm. Accessed 21 Aug 2012.
Poincaré, H. (1899). *Les Méthodes Nouvelles de la Méchanique Céleste*. Gauthier-Villars.
Poincaré, H. (1914). *Wissenschaft und Methode*. Teubner.
Porr, B. (2002). *Systemtheorie und Naturwissenschaft – Eine interdisziplinäre Analyse von Niklas Luhmanns Werk*. Deutscher Universitäts-Verlag.
Puu, T. (2003). *Attractors, bifurcations, and chaos: Nonlinear phenomena in economics*. Springer.
Röpke, J. (1977). *Die Strategie der Innovation*. Mohr Siebeck.
Ruelle, D. (1993). *Zufall und Chaos*. Springer.
Russell, B. (1950). *Philosophie des Abendlandes. Ihr Zusammenhang mit der politischen und der sozialen Entwicklung*. Europa.
Saltzman, B. (1962). Finite amplitude free convection as an initial value problem. *Journal of the Atmospheric Sciences, 19*(4), 329–341.
Samuelson, P. A. (2007). *Volkswirtschaftslehre* (3rd edn.). Redline.
Sarasvathy, S. D. (2001). Causation and effectuation: Toward a theoretical shift from economic inevitability to entrepreneurial contingency. *Academy of Management Review, 26*(2), 243–263.
Sarasvathy, S. D. (2008). *Effectuation – Elements of entrepreneurial expertise*. Elgar.
Sarasvathy, S. D. (2009). *Effectuation – Elements of entrepreneurial expertise*. Elgar.
Say, J.-B. (2013). *A treatise on political economy, or, the production, distribution, and consumption of wealth*. CreateSpace Independent Publishing Platform.
Schefold, B. (1992). ‚Wenn Du den Halys überschreitest' – Gedanken zur Zukunft ökonomischer Wissenschaft. In H. Hanusch & H. C. Recktenfeld (Eds.), *Ökonomische Wissenschaft in der Zukunft – Ansichten führender Ökonomen* (pp. 346–361). Wirtschaft und Finanzen.
Schiemenz, B. (1994). Kybernetik und Systemtheorie als Hilfen zur Lösung komplexer Probleme. In B. Schiemenz (Ed.), *Interaktion – Modellierung, Kommunikation und Lenkung in komplexen Organisationen* (pp. 9–30). Duncker & Humblot.
Schiepek, G. (1991). *Systemtheorie der klinischen Psychologie*. Vieweg.
Schindelbeck, D. (2009). 1997: Es tanzte nur einen Sommer: Das Tamagotchi. http://dirk-schindelbeck.de/archives/2100. Accessed 23 Aug 2012.
Schlösser, H. J. (1992). *Das Menschenbild in der Ökonomie*. Wirtschaftsverlag Bachem.
Schlösser, H. J. (2006). Ausgewählte Menschenbilder der Wirtschaftswissenschaft. In H. Schmidinger & C. Sedmak (Eds.), *Der Mensch – Ein zoon politikon?* (pp. 113–127). WBG.
Schluchter, W. (Ed.). (1980). *Verhalten, Handeln und System. Talcott Parsons' Beitrag zur Entwicklung der Sozialwissenschaften*. Suhrkamp.
Schmalensee, R. (1992). Kontinuität und Wandel in der Wirtschaftswissenschaft. In H. Hanusch & H. C. Recktenfeld (Eds.), *Ökonomische Wissenschaft in der Zukunft – Ansichten führender Ökonomen* (pp. 361–370). Wirtschaft und Finanzen.
Schmidt, K. H. (1994). Merkantilismus, Kameralismus, Physiokratie. In O. Issing (Ed.), *Geschichte der Nationalökonomie* (pp. 37–62). Vahlen.
Schön, D. (1983). *The reflective practitioner – How professionals think in action*. Basic Books.
Schulz, A. (2012). Der Schachtürke – Der erste Schachcomputer war keiner. http://www.chessbase.de/spotlight/spotlight2.asp?id=11. Accessed 15 Aug 2012.
Schumpeter, J. (1912). *Theorie der wirtschaftlichen Entwicklung: Nachdruck der 1. Auflage in 2006*. Duncker & Humblot.
Senge, P. M. (2011). *Die fünfte Disziplin – Kunst und Praxis der lernenden Organisation*. Schäffer-Poeschel.

Shannon, C. E. (2001). A mathematical theory of communication. *ACM Mobile Computing and Communications Review, 5*(1), 3–55.

Simon, H. A. (1962). The architecture of complexity. *Proceedings of the American Philosopical Society, 106*(6), 467–482.

Skinner, B. F. (1974). *Die Funktion der Verstärkung in der Verhaltenswissenschaft*. Kindler.

Smale, S. (1967). Differentiable dynamical systems. *Bulletin of the American Mathematical Society, 73*(6), 747–817.

Smith, A. (1776). *An inquiry into the nature and causes of the wealth of nations*. The Modern Library.

Smith, A. (1994). *The theory of moral sentiments*. The Modern Library.

Söllner, F. (1993). Neoklassik und Umweltökonomie. *Zeitschrift für Umweltpolitik und Umweltrecht, 4*(93), 431–460.

Sombart, W. (1915). *Händler und Helden*. Duncker & Humblot.

Stadler, M., & Kruse, P. (1990). The self-organization perspective in cognition research: Historical remarks and new experimental approaches. In H. Haken & M. Stadler (Eds.), *Synergetics of cognition* (pp. 32–52). Springer.

Stadler, M., Richter, P. H., Pfaff, S., & Kruse, P. (1991). Attractors and perceptual field dynamics of homogeneous stimulus areas. *Psychological Research, 53*(2), 102–112.

Stavenhagen, G. (1969). *Geschichte der Wirtschaftstheorie*. Vandenhoeck & Ruprecht.

Sterman, J. D. (2000). *Business dynamics. Systems thinking and modeling for a complex world*. McGraw-Hill.

Stölzel, T. (2011). A. Lange & Söhne kann Nachfrage nicht bedienen. http://www.wiwo.de/unternehmen/luxusuhrenhersteller-a-lange-und-soehne-kann-nachfrage-nicht-bedienen/5241094.html. Accessed 24 Aug 2012.

Strohecker, J., & Fischer, M. M. (2008). Bestands- und Flussgrößen. In J. Strohecker & J. Sehnert (Eds.), *System Dynamics für die Finanzindustrie, Simulieren und Analysieren dynamisch-komplexer Probleme* (pp. 105–140). Frankfurt School.

Strunk, G. (2009). Die Komplexitätshypothese der Karriereforschung. In A. Liening (Ed.), *Komplexe Systeme und Ökonomie* (Vol. 2). Lang.

Strunk, G. (2019). Entrepreneurship als Management von Komplexität – Versuch einer begrifflichen Klärung mit praktischen Implikationen. In T. Bijedić, I. Ebbers, & B. Halbfas (Eds.), *Entrepreneurship education* (pp. 79–96). Springer.

Strunk, G., & Schiepek, G. (2006). *Systemische Psychologie – Eine Einführung in die komplexen Grundlagen menschlichen Verhaltens*. Elsevier – Spektrum Akademischer.

Strunk, G., & Schiepek, G. (2014). *Therapeutisches Chaos – Eine Einführung in die Welt der Chaostheorie und der Komplexitätswissenschaften*. Hogrefe.

Strunk, G., Schiffinger, M., & Mayrhofer, W. (2004). Lost in transition? Complexity in organisational behaviour – The contributions of systems theories. *Management Revue, 15*(4), 481–509.

Suntum, U van. (2005). *Die unsichtbare Hand*. Springer.

Swanson, L. A., & Zhang, D. D. (2011). Complexity theory and the social entrepreneurship zone. *Emergence: Complexity and Organization, 13*(3), 39–56.

Taffertshofer, B. (2007). Sonderschulen – Bei den Schwächsten wird gespart. http://www.sueddeutsche.de/karriere/sonderschulen-bei-den-schwaechsten-wird-gespart-1.788097. Accessed 23 Aug 2012.

Thadden, E. von. (2010). Goethes Farbenlehre – Schöner irren. http://www.zeit.de/2010/20/Farbenlehre. Accessed 23 Aug 2012.

Tietz, R. (1994). Vereinfachung und Komplexität. Das Dilemma der Wirtschaftstheorie. In B. Schiemenz (Ed.), *Interaktion – Modellierung, Kommunikation und Lenkung in komplexen Organisationen* (pp. 237–261). Duncker & Humblot.

Tilly, R. (Ed.). (1993). *Geschichte der Wirtschaftspolitik – Vom Merkantilismus zur sozialen Marktwirtschaft*. De Gruyter Oldenbourg.
Trosky, F. (2006). *Heterogene Erwartungen auf dem Geldmarkt*. Duncker & Humblot.
Tschacher, W. (1997). *Prozessgestalten. Die Anwendung der Selbstorganisationstheorie und der Theorie dynamischer Systeme auf Probleme der Psychologie*. Hogrefe.
Tu, P. N. V. (1994). *Dynamical systems. An introduction with applications in economics and biology*. Springer.
Van der Pol, B. (1927). Forced oscillations in a circuit with non-linear resistance. (Reception with a reactive triode). *Philosophical Magazine, 3*(13), 56–80.
Wagner, F. (1976). *Isaac Newton im Zwielicht zwischen Mythos und Forschung*. Alber.
Walras, L. (2010). Elements d'économie politique pure: Ou théorie de la richesse sociale (1874).
Warnecke, H.-J. (1996). *Die fraktale Fabrik: Revolution der Unternehmenskultur*. Rowohlt.
Watson, J. B. (1984). *Behaviorismus*. Fachbuchhandlung für Psychologie.
Watzlawick, P. (2001). *Die erfundene Wirklichkeit* (13th edn.). Piper.
Weber, S. (2009). Aldi im Preiskampf – Unter Zugzwang. http://www.sueddeutsche.de/wirtschaft/aldi-im-preiskampf-unter-zugzwang-1.405801. Accessed 23 Aug 2012.
Weischedel, W. (Ed.). (1983). *Immanuel Kant. Werke in sechs Bänden* (Vol. I). Wissenschaftliche Buchgesellschaft.
Weizsäcker, C. F. von. (1974). *Die Einheit der Natur*. dtv.
Wesson, R. (1995). *Chaos, Zufall und Auslese der Natur*. Leipzig Insel.
Weyer, J. (2009). Dimensionen der Komplexität und Perspektiven des Komplexitätsmanagements. In J. Weyer & I. Schulz-Schaeffer (Eds.), *Management komplexer Systeme – Konzepte für die Bewältigung von Intransparenz, Unsicherheit und Chaos* (pp. 3–28). Oldenbourg.
Wiener, N. (1948). *Cybernetics, or control and communication in the animal and the machine*. Wiley.
Willke, H. (1991). *Eine Einführung in die Grundprobleme der Theorie sozialer Systeme* (4th edn.). UTB.
Wiltbank, R., Read, S., Dew, N., & Sarasvathy, S. D. (2009). Prediction and control under uncertainty: Outcomes in angel investing. *Journal of Business Venturing, 24*(2), 116–133.
Wimsatt, W. K. (1993). Poe and the chess automaton. In L. J. Budd & E. H. Cady (Eds.), *On Poe: The best of „American Literature"* (pp. 78–91). Duke University Press.
Wittig, F. (1997). *Maschinenmenschen: zur Geschichte eines literarischen Motivs im Kontext von Philosophie, Naturwissenschaft und Technik*. Königshause & Neumann.
Worg, R. (1993). *Deterministisches Chaos – Wege in die nichtlineare Dynamik*. BI-Wiss.-Verl.
Zeeuw, G. de. (2005). Auf der Suche nach Wissen. In D. Baecker (Ed.), *Schlüsselwerke der Systemtheorie* (pp. 145–173). Springer.
Zeleny, M. (1981). *Autopoiesis. A theory of the living organizations*. Elsevier Science.

Part II

Theory and Empiricism—Recent Developments in Complexity Research

Theory—Theoretical Approaches to Complexity

4

Contents

4.1 (Strange) Attractors and Fractals 213
4.1.1 Attractors of All Kinds 213
4.1.1.1 What is a Phase Space? 213
4.1.1.2 What is Meant by an Attractor? 215
4.1.1.3 'Benign' Attractors 216
4.1.1.4 Background Information: The Ratio and the Recurrence—Rational Numbers 224
4.1.1.5 Background Information: Excursion to "Square Root of 2" (Liening, 2005, p. 40 ff.) 225
4.1.1.6 'Strange' or 'Chaotic' Attractors 229
4.1.2 Fractals for Describing Deterministic Chaos 231
4.1.2.1 Self-similarity or Scale Invariance as a Characteristic of a Fractal 231
4.1.2.2 The Tree as an Analogy to the Fractal 231
4.1.2.3 The 'Mandelbrot Set' or: About the Emergence of Self-Similar Structures 231
4.1.2.4 About the Length of a Fractal Edge—'How long is the Coast of Britain'?—Koch Curves and Similar Considerations 235
4.1.2.5 Background Information: Calculation of the Area of the Koch Island 237
4.1.2.6 The Oddity of Fractional Dimensions 240
4.1.2.7 Background Information: (Box-)Dimensions 242
4.2 Bifurcations 248
4.2.1 Bifurcations in Dynamic Systems 248
4.2.1.1 What are Bifurcations? 248
4.2.1.2 The Discovery of Bifurcations 249
4.2.1.3 Bifurcation Scenario Using the Example of the Logistic Function 249
4.2.1.4 Intermittency and Bifurcations 256
4.2.2 Evidence of Erratic Behaviour 257

A. Liening, *Complexity and Entrepreneurship*,
https://doi.org/10.1007/978-3-658-44032-9_4

4.2.2.1 The ***Li/Yorke*** Theorem ... 257
4.2.2.2 ***Lyapunov*** Exponents ... 259
4.2.2.3 Background Information: Basic Calculation of the ***Lyapunov*** Exponent ... 260
4.3 Catastrophe Theory ... 263
4.3.1 René ***Thom's*** Theory ... 263
4.3.1.1 'Catastrophes' from a Scientific Perspective ... 263
4.3.1.2 About Singularities, Manifolds and Catastrophe Sets ... 263
4.3.2 Hermann ***Haken's*** Criticism ... 266
4.4 Synergetics—The Theory of Self-Organisation ... 266
4.4.1 The Basic Idea of Synergetics ... 266
4.4.1.1 Explaining Self-Organisation Phenomena ... 266
4.4.1.2 About the Laser ... 267
4.4.1.3 Swarm Intelligence—The Migration of Birds (Liening & Mittelstädt, 2008, pp. 41–43) ... 270
4.4.2 Interpreting Companies and Innovations Synergistically ... 270
4.4.2.1 Partial and Total Systems in Synergetics ... 270
4.4.2.2 The Mathematical Trick: The 'Slaving Principle' ... 271
4.4.3 Critical Remark ... 272
4.5 Order and Chaos only in the Computer? About Definitions, Bolzano-Weierstraß and 'Controlling Complexity' ... 273
4.5.1 'Working definitions' ... 273
4.5.1.1 The Genesis of the Term 'Chaos'—Sharpening of the Complexity Concept ... 273
4.5.1.2 Preliminary Interpretation of the Concept of Chaos ... 277
4.5.1.3 Definitions of Chaos and Complexity ... 277
4.5.1.4 'Order' as a Counter-concept to 'Chaos'? ... 281
4.5.2 Does Chaos Only Exist in the Computer? ... 282
4.5.2.1 Ignis Fatuus?—Does the Computer Generate Chaos? ... 282
4.5.2.2 The First Argument: Increased Computational Accuracy in Complex Systems Does Not Lead to More Accurate Results ... 283
4.5.2.3 The Second Argument: The 'Shadow Lemma' ... 285
4.5.2.4 Third Argument: The 'L-Density Argument' ... 287
4.5.2.5 Background Information: The Proof of the Purely Algebraic "Butterfly Effect" in the Logistic Equation: The L-Density Argument ... 288
4.5.3 'Controlling Complexity'—Can Chaos be Controlled? ... 292
4.5.3.1 Chaotic Systems and Control—A Contradiction? ... 292
4.5.3.2 A Little Hope—Influence Possibilities in Chaotic Systems ... 293
4.5.3.3 An Alternative (synergetic) Approach: Complexity as an Opportunity ... 295
4.5.3.4 'Nudges' and the Emergence of ***Desired*** Order Parameters ... 300
4.5.3.5 Measuring Complexity to Determine the Placement of 'Nudges' ... 302
4.5.3.6 There is Even a Predictable Path in Chaos—At Least Theoretically (Theorem of ***Bolzano-Weierstraß***) ... 303
4.5.3.7 Background Information: There must be a Predictable Path in Chaos!—The Theorem of ***Bolzano-Weierstraß*** ... 304
4.6 Second Conclusion—Summary of Important Aspects and the (Heuristic) Value of a Science of Complex Systems for Economics in General and the Topic of Entrepreneurship in Particular ... 307

4.6.1 Brief Summary of Important Aspects ... 307
4.6.2 What can a Science of Complex Systems do for Economics?... 308
4.6.2.1 Complex versus Mechanistic Viewpoint... 308
4.6.2.2 Methods of the Science of Complex Systems as Heuristic Analysis Tools ... 309
4.6.2.3 Economic Significance from a Macroeconomic Perspective ... 309
4.6.2.4 Economic Significance from an Entrepreneurship Perspective ... 310
4.6.3 Outlook: Predictions—Even at the Company Level—Are not Trivial in Complex Situations, Processes or Structures, Empirical Studies are Nevertheless Useful and Necessary... 310
References... 311

4.1 (Strange) Attractors and Fractals

4.1.1 Attractors of All Kinds

4.1.1.1 What is a Phase Space?

> "Most complex systems," writes *Lewin,* "exhibit so-called attractors, a mathematical term for states in which the system eventually settles depending on its properties" (Lewin 1993, p. 34).[1]

These attractors exist in an abstract world, which is referred to as phase space. To navigate in such a phase space, one needs 'maps'.[2]

Maps allow the mind to focus on sections or specific aspects of reality. They are vivid images.

[1] Significant parts of the present theory chapter were written over twenty years ago and first published in Liening (1998). They have not lost their relevance to this day, but have been clarified, deepened, and supplemented here, so it does not seem sensible to express them again in different words. The following theory part forms the decisive basis for the newly presented empirical methods (Chap. 5). In the context of this book, the theory chapter gives a more rounded picture overall than in its first publication, as theory and practice are put more strongly into context and a methodological approach is shown. In recent years, synergetics as a theory of self-organisation has been particularly taken up and used in publications (Liening, 1998, 2006, 2007, 2009, 2013, 2015). In this book, the insights from over twenty years of research and publication activity lead to a synergetic overall concept, which is presented for the first time and with a content focus on the new topic of entrepreneurship in Chap. 7.

[2] The analogy between maps and phase spaces goes back to John *Briggs* and F. David *Peat* (Briggs & Peat, 1993, p. 41 ff.).

Thus, the image of a city can be depicted with a street map or, for example, with a underground map. Depending on which aspect of reality is projected onto this map, one gets a specific, usable idea of a city for different purposes. Street and underground maps have in common that they are maps of the plane. Only two dimensions (length and width) are represented. But one can also imagine maps that reflect three dimensions (length, width, and height). Think of topographic maps, in which, in addition to the area dimensions of the terrain, contour lines are drawn. With the help of a map, the dynamics of a system can also be illustrated. Consider as an example the motion change of a car in a roller coaster, which can be described by accelerating, braking, and stopping. A map of this motion change will now be created as follows: For each point in time, the location where the vehicle is can be specified. Instead of the location, one could also specify the acceleration or the speed for each point in time. Depending on which parameters are chosen to design the map, a fantasy space is created that has little in common with the traditional concept of space. This fantasy space is referred to as phase space, as already mentioned. A phase space now consists of as many parameters or dimensions as are necessary to describe the movements of the system.

As an example for illustration, a ride on a roller coaster should serve. Figure 4.1 represents the first phase of a roller coaster ride in a two-dimensional phase space, in which one dimension is characterised by the speed and the other by the height of the car on the track.

First, the car starts moving, the speed increases constantly until a certain speed is reached. The car is at point A. At constant speed, it is now pulled to the highest point B of the track. Now the car plunges into the depths and the speed increases rapidly until the first valley is reached (point C). Here the car accelerates once again before it goes uphill.

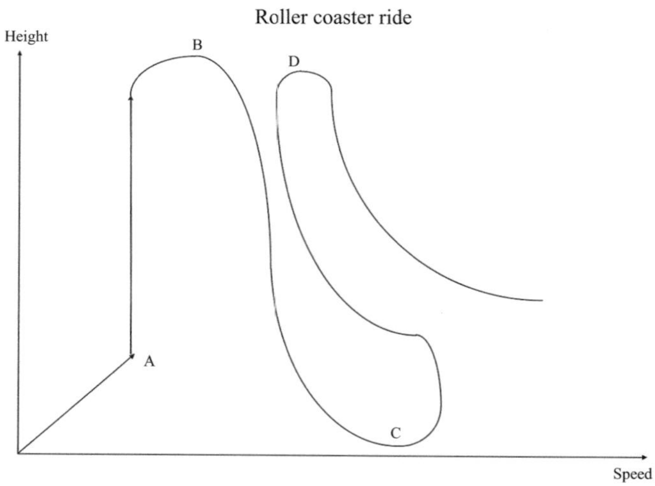

Fig. 4.1 Roller coaster ride

The higher it climbs, the slower the car becomes now, until it has reached the second peak (point D), to plunge from there again with increasing speed into the depths.

In the above representation, the speed was considered solely in relation to the height of the car on the roller coaster. If one were to take into account the three-dimensionality of space, one would have to consider the three spatial dimensions (height, width, depth) and a speed parameter for each of these dimensions. In this case, the phase space would be six-dimensional. Such a structure cannot be drawn due to the fact that the drawing plane is two-dimensional, but it can be represented algebraically, i.e., in the form of systems of equations or matrices.

Phase spaces are therefore maps that reflect aspects of reality, with the phase spaces potentially eluding perception depending on the number of parameters considered. However, they can always be captured mathematically.

4.1.1.2 What is Meant by an Attractor?

In phase spaces, depending on the system or its parameter selection, various system behaviours can be observed. It has already been explained that in linear dynamic systems, either convergence, divergence or harmonic oscillations can occur. Non-linear dynamic systems can represent a variety of developments, from harmonic to chaotic development lines, everything is conceivable. In connection with phase spaces, it should be noted that a distinction can be made between between conservative and dissipative systems. In conservative systems, unlike in dissipative systems, the associated state space is preserved over time. In two dimensions, this would be equivalent to maintaining the area. In a three-dimensional phase space, however, this would aim at the immutability of the volume. At most, a deformation occurs. Such conservative systems are closed to their environment, unlike dissipative systems. In such a system, cause and effect are clearly linked and can be calculated with any desired accuracy. In such a system, for example, a chaotic development is conceivable, but it does not lead to any convergence.

In economics, it can be assumed that such systems are irrelevant, as economic systems are open systems that exchange energy with other systems. Therefore, an economic dynamic system will have a different structure, it will consequently be of a dissipative nature. Transferred to the concept of phase space, this means that a volume element of a phase space will contract under the effect of the underlying mapping until the volume content reaches zero.[3] In such a transition, the system is on an attractor, "whose dimension is smaller than that of the phase space" (Loistl & Betz, 1993, p. 13). In complex interaction with the individual system elements, synergetic effects arise, which "in self-organisation processes ('phase transitions') strive for forms and shapes, but also chaos, as attractors" (Mainzer, 1995, p. 82). Therefore, only those system courses that are of a

[3]The volume element shrinks until it becomes zero when $t \to \infty$, i.e., when the time course is infinite, cf. Canty (1995, p. 93).

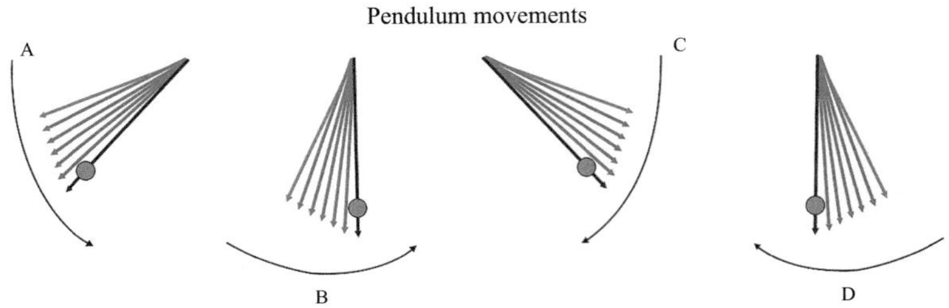

Fig. 4.2 Pendulum movements

dissipative nature will be discussed here. Thus, for example, chaotic courses that do not move on an attractor are excluded from further consideration in the analysis.

If one picks up *Lewin's* definition of an attractor again, then this is a mathematical term for a state in which the system eventually settles depending on its properties. There are a number of different attractors, which will be briefly discussed here. The different attractor structures will be examined using the familiar example of the movement of a pendulum (Loistl, 1993, p. 48 passim).

4.1.1.3 'Benign' Attractors

First, a system of periodic behaviour is considered, i.e., a system that always returns to the initial conditions. Thus, the path in the phase space also always returns to the same point, as the example of the pendulum in Fig. 4.2 shows.

At point A, the pendulum is at rest. Now the pendulum moves with increasing speed to the right, where it has the greatest momentum[4] at point B. Then it heads, slowing down, to the right point C, where it turns around and swings back with increasing acceleration. At point D, the pendulum has its greatest momentum again and it swings from there, slowing down, to the left top to point A.

In a force-free state, the pendulum would have to repeat this outlined movement permanently. If air resistance or gravity are present, the pendulum swings slower and slower until it remains at point B or D.

The pendulum is a very simple system. It only has *one* degree of freedom, as it can only swing back and forth in one direction. This swinging back and forth between two places A and C, or the change of location of the pendulum, can be illustrated on a time axis by a sine curve as shown in Fig. 4.3.

Assuming that the pendulum is, for example, continuously driven by a weight with constant energy, or is in a frictionless state, then the pendulum will permanently swing

[4] Momentum = mass · speed.

between two points A and C and always have the greatest momentum at two points, e.g. B and D, as Fig. 4.4 shows. The momentum (i.e. speed · mass) can be illustrated on a time axis by a cosine curve.

Now, as outlined in Fig. 4.5, a two-dimensional phase space is to be considered, which is spanned by a location and a momentum vector.

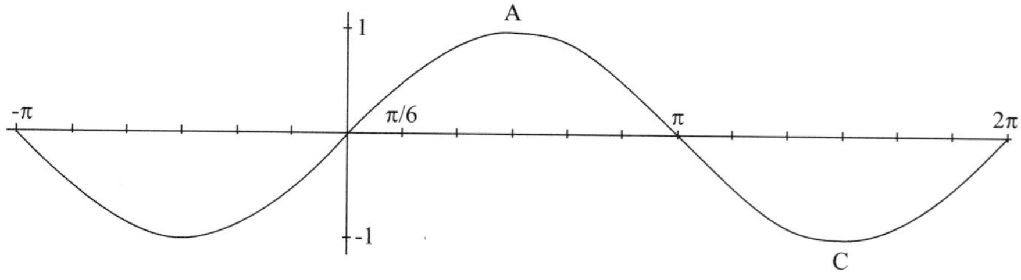

Fig. 4.3 Pendulum motion—sine curve

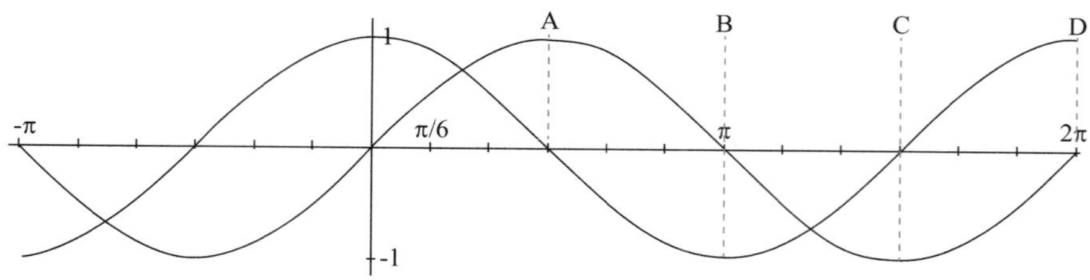

Fig. 4.4 Pendulum motion—location and momentum curve

Fig. 4.5 Two-dimensional phase space, part 1

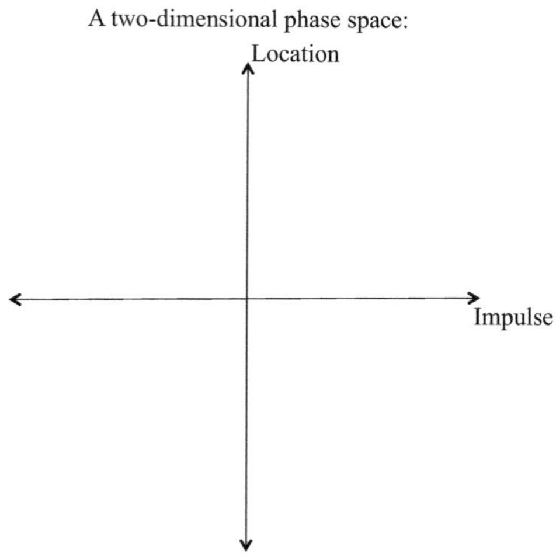

Now the four points A to D, already identified on the time axis, are drawn in, starting with A and C, as shown in Fig. 4.6.

At point A, the pendulum has the greatest deflection on the left side and the momentum is zero here. At the right, the highest point taken by the pendulum, point C, the momentum is also zero. If you set the intersection of the two lines equal to zero, then the two points must be on the location line. Exactly here, the momentum is zero everywhere.

The pendulum has the greatest momentum when it swings to the right at point B and when it swings to the left at point D. Then the pendulum is in the middle between the maximum left and the maximum right deflection. This is the intersection of the two lines. Thus, points D and B are exactly on the momentum line, as Fig. 4.7 shows. Now point

Fig. 4.6 Two-dimensional phase space, part 2

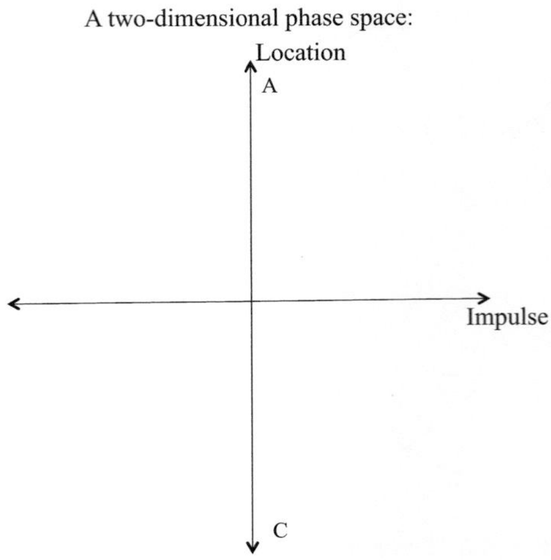

Fig. 4.7 Two-dimensional phase space, part 3

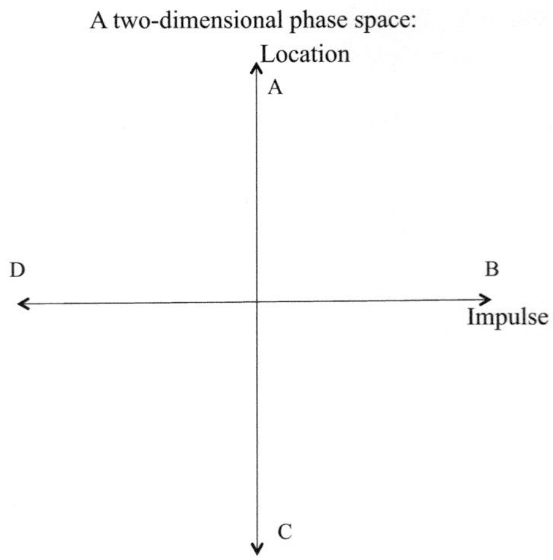

D is plotted on the left side of the momentum line and point B on the right side of the momentum line.

Now the path of the pendulum can be plotted in the phase space. Assuming that the pendulum is not subjected to any forces, then the pendulum will permanently swing between points A and C and always have the greatest momentum at points B and D, as Fig. 4.8 shows.

When the pendulum swings under 'normal' conditions, i.e., it is subject to friction due to air resistance, etc., the pendulum slowly swings out and comes to rest at a point, as sketched in Fig. 4.9. It is as if it is attracted to this point. This point of attraction is referred to as an attractor or more specifically as a point attractor. Even small external disturbances do not change the fact that the pendulum movement tends towards this attractor. A comparable situation was already represented in the Cobweb model. Here too, in the case of convergence, a point attractor is present, which reflects the equilibrium price.

Back to the pendulum. If the pendulum now experiences a recurring constant impulse from the outside, it swings back and forth, but the path is not drawn to a fixed point, but performs a cyclic movement. Such an attractor is called a limit cycle attractor. Think of the pendulum of a grandfather clock or, for example, the development of gasoline prices within a week, where they are regularly rather low at the beginning of the week and always higher towards the weekend.

The point attractor and the limit cycle attractor are stable, as Fig. 4.10 is intended to illustrate. Small disturbances from the outside will always lead the system back to the attractor. The lines outside the limit cycle attractor outlined above indicate possible disturbances.

It should be emphasised that Fig. 4.8, which shows the pendulum system in a force-free state, is otherwise without an attractor. Although a cyclic movement is also performed

Fig. 4.8 Two-dimensional phase space, part 4

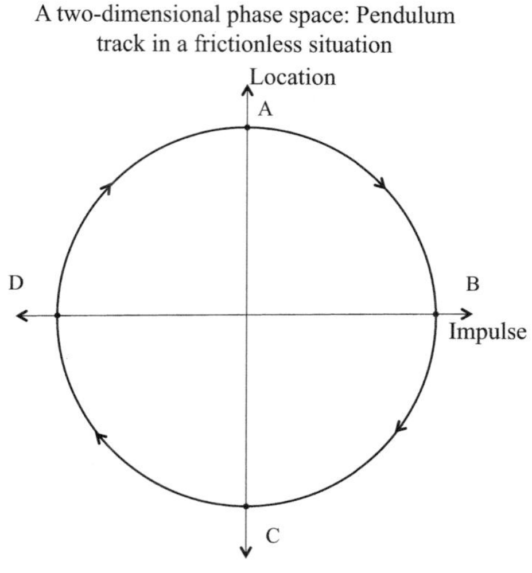

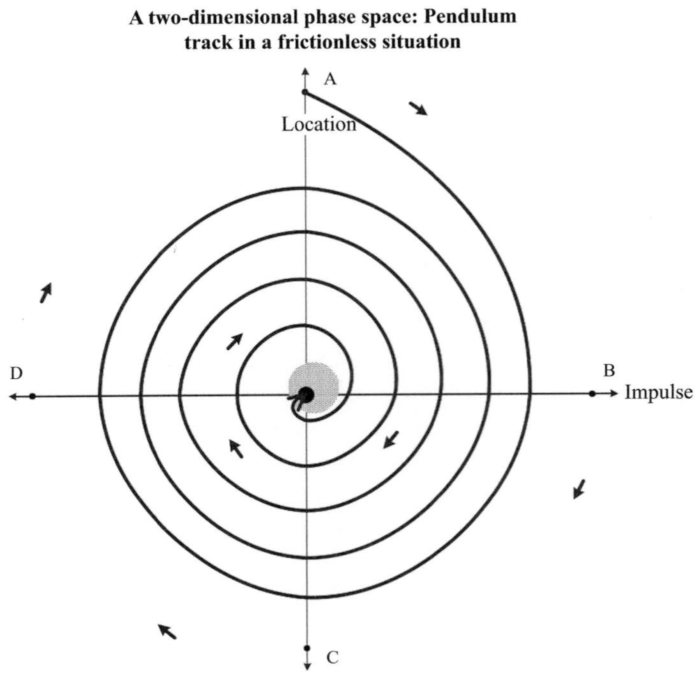

Fig. 4.9 Two-dimensional phase space with point attractor

here, the smallest disturbance can completely and permanently change the path. An attractor is only spoken of when there is a stable attraction situation.

All dynamic stable systems have limit cycles in their phase spaces. A typical example of this is the well-known 'predator-prey system', in which, for example, foxes and rabbits are considered. The foxes eat the rabbits. If there are many rabbits, the foxes multiply; the number of rabbits decreases. The food for the foxes becomes scarcer; their number decreases; this leads to the rabbits being able to reproduce better again, etc. The system is also stable if, for example, the number of foxes is reduced to a few or additional rabbits are released. The limit cycle also exists, for example, between rabbits and food. If the rabbits multiply, the food will eventually become scarce; the rabbit population decreases; the plants can recover; then there are more rabbits again, etc.

So far, a system with *two* parameters has been considered. But one can also imagine systems with more than two parameters. Then you get a higher-dimensional phase space.

For example, the fox-rabbit and the rabbit-food system can be transferred into an overall system. Here you find three state variables and a three-dimensional space.

For the fox-rabbit cycle, it can apply: You get a closed curve that, after e.g., three years, goes back into itself and starts again; the rabbit-food cycle could, for example, only last one year.

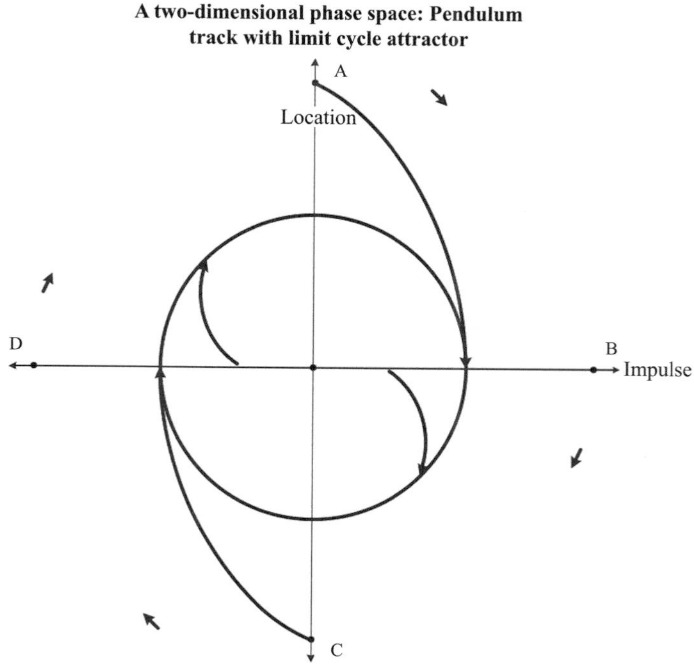

Fig. 4.10 Two-dimensional phase space with limit cycle attractor

If you plot the fox-rabbit cycle in a three-dimensional space and then plot the closed curves of the rabbit-food cycle around the points of this curve, you get a system on which a point in space drives around on an elliptical path and another point circles around this point at any time. This other point is the point of the total limit cycle and lies on a torus, as Fig. 4.11 shows. A torus-shaped attractor is a two-dimensional attractor in a three-dimensional phase space.

Suppose you had two pendulums driven by a uniform impulse. Each pendulum follows a limit cycle attractor. Both pendulums are movable in all directions, i.e., the system no longer has one, but many degrees of freedom. If both pendulums are now coupled, you get a three-dimensional phase space in which the two limit cycles are linked in such a way that one limit cycle pulls the other in a circle behind it.

The state of a simple pendulum system can be described by a point that moves in the plane on the limit cycle attractor or, in the event of a disturbance, always moves back towards it.

The state of a coupled pendulum system can be described, as with the coupled fox-rabbit-food system, by a point that moves on the surface of a three-dimensional ring-shaped structure, a so-called torus attractor Torus.

The shape of the curve on the torus depends on the frequencies of the involved subsystems. If one subsystem, for example, has twice the frequency of the other subsystem, then the curve travels twice around the torus and then returns to itself.

Fig. 4.11 Torus

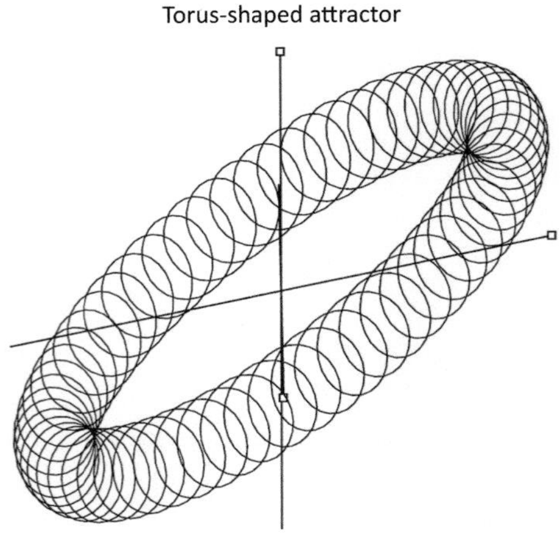

If the ratio of the oscillations to each other is in a rational ratio[5], then this is a strictly periodic system. This is exactly the case when the point moving on the surface of the torus is observed at a position x and hits exactly this position again after each round of the attractor. In other words: If the ratio is rational, i.e., a fraction, the curve always returns to itself after a finite number of rounds.

However, if the subsystems oscillate in a rational ratio to each other, this is not without problems. In the event of a (small) disturbance of the system, a resonance behaviour can occur that amplifies the oscillations (since the paths always return to themselves). The torus could thus inflate and ultimately burst. This is, for example, the reason why large groups of people (think of a company of soldiers) never march across a bridge in step. Another example is the heart rate. If the heart actually beat evenly (rational oscillation), one would suffer a heart attack. Market failure could also be explained in this way.

The system behaves differently when the ratio of the oscillations of coupled systems is irrational[6]. This means that the point moving on the surface of the torus never meets its path again. In such systems, whose ratio of the oscillations of the subsystems is irrational to each other, such as the square root of 2, the curve wanders forever on the torus

[5] By a rational ratio, we mean a fraction in which there is a whole number in both the numerator and the denominator. An examination of the ratio of the oscillations of a coupled system shows that, for example, the frequency or period of one system can be half as high as that of the other. So, the rational ratio 1:2 or 1/2 is present. Rational numbers can be represented either by a decimal number with a finite number of decimal places (2/4 = 0.5; 3/4 = 0.75 etc.) or with periodically, infinitely repeating decimal places (2/3 = 0.6666…; 1/7 = 0.142857142…;1/9 = 0.1111… etc.).

[6] By an irrational ratio, we mean numbers that cannot be represented by any fraction. For example, the circle number π is an irrational number. The approximate value of π is: 3.1415927. As mentioned, this is only an approximate value. The decimal places do not actually break off and there is no recurring pattern.

without ever returning to itself. Such cycles are called quasi-periodic. In this context, one also speaks of "asymptotic predictability" (Briggs & Peat, 1993, p. 57). The instantaneous position is unknown, but one can trust that the system is on the surface of the torus and does not wander arbitrarily in the phase space.

If the frequencies are (sufficiently) irrational, then the trajectories remain on their attractor even in the event of a disturbance, and the attractor is thus stable.

Systems whose behaviour does not undergo any qualitative change due to perturbations, i.e., the trajectory of the undisturbed and the disturbed system are topologically equivalent, are also called *structurally stable* (Argyris et al., 2010, p. 500).

Example: The Three-Body Problem and the *KAM*-Theorem—the Particle Accelerator at CERN

In the context of structurally stable systems, consider *Poincaré's* three-body problem and the associated investigation of the question of the stability of the solar system, which we have already discussed in more detail in Part I, Sect. 3.2.1. A possible answer to the question of whether the solar system is (structurally) stable or not could be: If the frequencies of the planetary orbits are irrational to each other, i.e., quasi-periodic solutions exist, then the system can be stable. Otherwise, there is a risk that the system will eventually disintegrate. However, a warning must be issued at this point that from a physical perspective—one could also say, from an empirical perspective—due to limited measurement accuracies, it is difficult to distinguish between rational and irrational numbers, so excessive euphoria would be misplaced here.

As another example closely related to *Poincaré's* investigations, one can mention the *KAM* theorem (***K**olmogorov*, ***A**rnold*, ***M**oser*), which makes a statement about the stability of so-called *Hamiltonian* systems.[7] It becomes clear that the *KAM* theorem only provides sufficient conditions for the existence of invariant tori with minimal changes in the initial conditions, i.e., slight disturbances, which thus guarantee the existence of quasi-periodic solutions. However, it can be suspected that the tori disintegrate in the vicinity of rational frequency ratios (Argyris et al., 2010, p. 168).

[7] A nice introduction to the *KAM* theorem can be found in: Ott (1994, p. 224 ff.). The *KAM* theory makes a statement about the stability of so-called *Hamiltonian* systems. *Argyris, Faus* et al. note that historically, the realisation that "the determination of a single function, namely the Hamilton function H, is sufficient to set up the equations of motion and thus describe a deterministic motion, was in accordance with the laws of reason (and therefore one spoke of rational mechanics)" (Argyris et al., 2010, p. 143). *Poincaré* ultimately thwarted the efforts of nineteenth-century mathematicians and physicists to find a *Hamilton* function that proves the integrability of systems by investigating his three-body problem. *Argyris* et al. point out that with the establishment of the *Bohr* atomic model, the *Hamiltonian* formalism experienced "a new bloom" and that classical dynamics is by no means a closed field, as the insights of *Kolmogorov, Arnold, Moser* etc. show (Argyris et al., 2010, p. 143 f.).

From a physical point of view, there is, for example, an important practical application of the *KAM* theorem, namely the particle accelerator at CERN in Geneva. In this particle accelerator, electrons or protons are accelerated in a circular tube until they reach almost the speed of light. In the so-called storage rings, about 10^{10} to 10^{11} orbits are necessary to reach the highest possible speed. *Argyris* et al. therefore point out that the "question of the stability of the orbits (…) is of fundamental importance for the construction of such accelerators" (Argyris et al., 2010, p. 168). If chaotic movements were to occur, then the particles would hit the wall of the tube and thus uncontrollably lose a large part of their energy.

Through the *KAM* theorem, so *Argyris, Faus* et al., "the stability of most orbits is now ensured" (Argyris et al., 2010, p. 168). Furthermore, they argue that if one equated one orbit of the protons in the storage ring with one year in astronomical problems, the number of 10^{10} to 10^{11} orbits would correspond to a time that far exceeded the age of our planets, which brings us back to *Poincaré's* question. *Argyris, Faus* et al. emphasise in this context that this "justifies the initially unrealistic-seeming question of stability for infinite periods of time" (Argyris et al., 2010, p. 168) ◄

With such 'benign' attractors, for example, all converging linear-dynamic system developments known from classical mechanics can be described in principle. If the current position of a system is known, it can be precisely predicted where and when the system will be in the future. Or at least asymptotic predictability is given, which allows the observer a high degree of predictability.

4.1.1.4 Background Information: The Ratio and the Recurrence—Rational Numbers

To understand developments and draw conclusions from them, we must examine them qualitatively or quantitatively.

Any quantitative analysis of empirical data relies on numerical material. The art lies in capturing, analysing, interpreting, and evaluating these numbers.

Such a series of numbers could, for example, consist of the decimal places of a rational or real number like $\frac{1}{9}$: 0909090909…

Rational numbers are fractions whose numerator and denominator consist of whole numbers, with the denominator always being different from zero, and which, when converted to a decimal number, have a finite or infinite number of decimal places. It is conceivable that fractions not only have an infinite number of decimal places, but also a pattern in the sequence of these places is evident, as with $\frac{1}{3} = 0.333333\ldots = 0.\overline{3}$ For example, two cycles are conceivable as with: $\frac{1}{11} = 0.090909090909\ldots$. We already know this from the consideration of point and cycle attractors. Fractions with several different decimal places are also conceivable, such as: $\frac{1}{7} = 0.1428571\ldots$

But all rational numbers have one thing in common: There is a predictable pattern:

$\frac{1}{7} = 0.142857\underline{1428571\ldots}$

Sometimes you have to calculate for a very long time until you recognise a pattern like with:

$\frac{1}{49} = 0.020408163265306122448979591836734693877551020408163265306122448\ldots$

However, you can be sure that at some point after the calculation of many decimal places, a pattern will become visible, even if you have to calculate more than 40 decimal places like with $\frac{1}{49}$ before a pattern becomes recognisable.

Rational numbers are deterministic in this respect, i.e., you can predict the further digits (decimal places) from the previous ones. It can be formulated even more clearly:

The decimal places of a rational number always show a pattern!

This recurrence of digits, which occurs after the calculation of a sufficient number of decimal places, is a characteristic of rationality, which corresponds to thinking in the context of the Laplace's demon. You can predict the future using reason, the ratio,, from past values, if you have enough information (here: have calculated enough decimal places)!

Dynamic development lines of systems can, for example, run recursively. This means in relation to "rational" development lines that they meet again at some point and thus the path taken is retraced. Such development lines, also called trajectories, would not be described as complex, at most as complicated.

In addition to infinitely many rational numbers, there are also infinitely many irrational numbers, which, for example, lead to quasi-periodic trajectory courses in the context of dynamic systems, which could also be referred to as recurrence (Recurrence), although the paths never meet exactly again.

4.1.1.5 Background Information: Excursion to "Square Root of 2" (Liening, 2005, p. 40 ff.)

$\sqrt{2}$ is nearly 7/5! Quasiperiodicity in the sense that the ratio of orbits of two subsystems to each other is irrational is anything but intuitive, because the concept of the existence of irrational numbers is not immediately obvious.

The Pythagoreans probably already discovered the irrational numbers, but the mere concept of their existence was so repugnant to *Pythagoras* that he probably denied them. His statement "Everything is number" referred to whole numbers and fractions, with which he believed he could describe and explain all natural phenomena in an aesthetically pleasing way. Allegedly, he even sentenced his student *Hippasus* to death by drowning because he was convinced of the irrationality of the number $\sqrt{2}$ (Liening, 2005, p. 51).

The difficulty in accepting irrational numbers is also related to the fact that one can determine that the set of fractions, i.e., the rational numbers, on the number line (from minus to plus infinity) is *dense*. What does this mean? Let's choose an arbitrary rational number on the number line (Fig. 4.12), for example, $7/5 = 1.4$.

Furthermore, we construct a sequence of numbers, also called a *number sequence*, which is described by the development law $x_n = 7/5 + 1/n \cdot (-1)^n$. This means that the

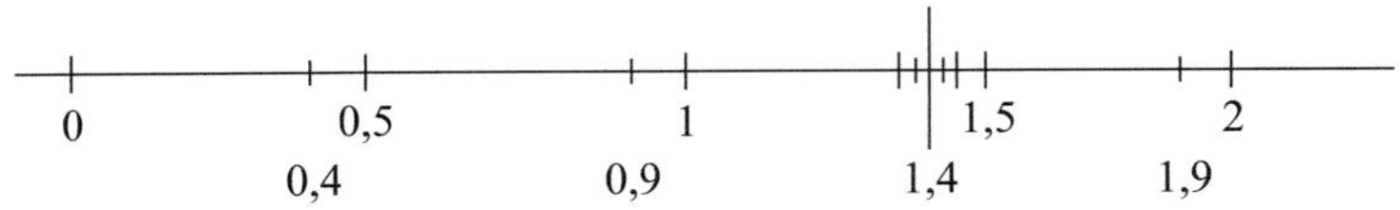

Fig. 4.12 Number line

nth member of the sequence is created by adding or subtracting the fraction *1/n* to the rational number 7/5. The expression $(-1)^n$ causes the change of sign: If n is even, then $(-1)^n = 1$ and *1/n* is added, if n is odd, then $(-1)^n = -1$ and 1/n is subtracted.

The first members of the sequence are therefore:

$$x_1 = 7/5 - 1, \quad x_2 = 7/5 + 1/2, \quad x_3 7/5 - 1/3, \quad x_4 = 7/5 + 1/4.$$
$$\text{Also}: \quad x_1 = 0.4, \quad \mathrm{x}_2 = 1.9, \quad x_3 = 1.0667, \quad x_4 = 1.65,$$

Furthermore, it is

$$\begin{aligned} x_5 &= 1.2, \quad x_6 = 1.5667, \\ x_{10} &= 1.5, \quad x_{20} = 1.45, \\ x_{100} &= 1.41, \quad x_{1001} = 1.399, \ldots \end{aligned}$$

Already from these first sequence members x_n one can see that apparently one can get arbitrarily close to 7/5 = 1.4 with fractions. And indeed, it can be mathematically proven that the sequence defined above *converges* towards 7/5[8] $\lim_{x\to\infty} \frac{1}{n} = 0$, i.e., it approaches 7/5 more and more closely with increasing *n*, without ever reaching 7/5. We write $\lim_{x\to\infty} x_n = \frac{7}{5}$ and read: Limes for n towards infinity—x of n—equals 7/5.

And just as one can get arbitrarily close to the fraction 7/5 with fractions, one can also get arbitrarily close to any other fraction with fractions. In other words, if we choose any section, i.e., a subset of the number line (where the boundaries of the subset are not supposed to count as part of the subset, i.e., it is open), then we always find rational elements in it, no matter how small the subset may be.

Although the concept of the number line is mathematically imprecise, we want to venture at least an illustrative definition:

[8] Many quantities cannot be calculated exactly with a finite number of calculation steps, but can only be approximated with arbitrary accuracy. This is also referred to as convergence. A sequence of numbers $(x_n)_{n\in\mathbb{N}}$ converges if the members of the sequence, the x_n with increasing index n, approach a limit (Limes). For example, the sequence $x_n = 1/n$ approaches the value 0 as n increases. The first sequence members of this sequence are: 1, 1/2, 1/3, 1/4, We write: and speak: Limes for n towards infinity—from (the sequence) 1 through n—equals 0.

▶ **Illustrative Definition** A set is dense on a 'number line' if any arbitrary open subset of the 'number line' contains elements from the set.

This specifically means for our above considerations: The rational numbers are dense.[9]

It seems unimaginable that there could be more numbers between the densely packed fractions. But nevertheless: Although the rational numbers are dense, they are still not gapless! This astonishing fact brings us to a new set of numbers, the real numbers.

With the help of the theorem of *Pythagoras* we know: $1^2+1^2= D^2$, where D is the length of the hypotenuse of a right-angled triangle with cathetus length 1. So:

$2 = D^2$ or $\sqrt{2} = D$ (pronounced: root two). But what number is hidden behind $\sqrt{2}$ and can this number also be grasped as a rational number?

The first assertion is now: $\sqrt{2} = 1.4142136\ldots$

And the second assertion is: $\sqrt{2}$ is not a rational number at all. This root is not a fraction. Or to put it another way: The number $\sqrt{2}$ is irrational!

Let's first consider the first assertion that $\sqrt{2} = 1.4142136\ldots$: For this, we want to discuss a method that the *Babylonians* knew in a similar form. It works through recursion, which means the repeated application of a formula: Starting from any initial value, a first intermediate result is calculated using a formula. This intermediate result is then reinserted into the formula and another intermediate result is calculated, etc. With sufficient repetition of this process, the final result is obtained approximately. By the way, the following recursive method works exceptionally fast and is well suited as an exercise for creating a computer programme.

So what does the method for determining $\sqrt{2}$ look like? The following sentence shows the way:

▶ **Theorem**

Let the sequence $(x_n)_{n \in N}$ be recursively defined by $x_{n+1} = \frac{1}{2} \cdot (x_n + \frac{2}{x_n})$.

Then the sequence defined in this way converges to $\sqrt{2}$.

It is easy to get an idea of why the sequence actually converges to $\sqrt{2}$:

If x is the root of 2, thus satisfying the equation $x^2 = 2$, then $x = 2/x$ applies, otherwise: $x \neq 2/x$. The mean, the arithmetic mean $x' = 1/2 \cdot (x + 2/x)$ is then already

[9] In principle, with the idea that the rational numbers are dense, we are drawing on the realisation that there is a comprehensive set of numbers. Because we have to ask ourselves: In which set of numbers are the rational numbers dense? The correct answer should be: The rational numbers are dense in the real numbers, which makes it clear that any real number can be approximated arbitrarily accurately by rational numbers. However, since the term 'real numbers' has not yet been further motivated, we are simplifying here by speaking of a number line on which all conceivable numbers line up and on which the rational numbers are dense.

a better approximation for the root. This suggests that by repeating this process, a sequence of numbers is created that converges to $\sqrt{2}$.

Ultimately, one proves the above theorem by considering the following four steps:

Proof

a) As one can easily see by complete induction, $x_n > 0 \ \forall n \in \mathbb{N}$

b) $x_n^2 \geq 2$, da $x_n^2 - 2 = \frac{1}{4} \cdot (x_{n-1} + \frac{2}{x_{n-1}})^2 - 2 = \frac{1}{4} \cdot (x_{n-1}^2 + 4 + \frac{4}{x_{n-1}^2}) - 2 = \frac{1}{4} \cdot (x_{n-1} - \frac{2}{x_{n-1}})^2 - \geq 0.$

c) $x_{n+1} \leq x_n$, da $x_n - x_{n+1} = x_n - \frac{1}{2} \cdot (x_n + \frac{2}{x_n}) = \frac{1}{2} \cdot x_n - \frac{1}{x_n} = \frac{1}{2x_n} \cdot (x_n^2 - 2) \geq 0.$

d) Due to c), $(x_n)_{n \in \mathbb{N}}$ is a strictly monotonically decreasing sequence and is bounded below. Such sequences converge, as can be easily shown.
And with
$\lim_{n \to \infty} x_{n+1} = \lim_{n \to \infty} x_n = x$ folgt: $\lim_{n \to \infty} (2x_{n+1} x_n) = \lim_{n \to \infty} (x_n^2 + 2) \Leftrightarrow 2x^2 = x^2 + 2 \Leftrightarrow x^2 = 2$
Thus, the sequence $(x_n)_{n \in \mathbb{N}}$ converges and it holds: $\lim_{n \to \infty} x_n = \sqrt{2}$ **q. e. d.**

If one now applies the above formula, one obtains the following first sequence members, starting with any sequence member x_0:

Let $x_0 := 2$. Then

$$\begin{aligned}
x_1 &= 1/2(2 + 2/2) = & 1.5 \\
x_2 &= 1/2(1.5 + 2/1.5) = & 1.4166667\ldots \\
x_3 &= & 1.4142157\ldots \\
x_4 &= & 1.4142136\ldots \\
x_5 &= & 1.4142136\ldots \\
x_6 &= & 1.4142136\ldots
\end{aligned}$$

The first sequence elements suggest that this method obviously converges quickly to the number 1.4142136…[10] So $\sqrt{2}$ is indeed approximately 7/5 or $\sqrt{2} = 1.4142136\ldots$

A bit more illustratively, *Heron of Alexandria* already formulated this in the second half of the first century with the method named after him, the *Heron*-method. Sometimes it is also referred to as "Babylonian root extraction", as—as already mentioned—the method probably originally goes back to the Babylonians (1700 BC).

Let $D = \sqrt{2}$ Furthermore, let the rational number D_0 be the first approximation for D. Then there are two possibilities. Either D is greater or smaller than D_0. If $D > D_0$, then due to $D = \sqrt{2}$ resp. $D^2 = 2$ it is obviously $2 > {D_0}^2$ and thus $\frac{2}{{D_0}^2} > 1$ and extended by 2 to $\frac{2}{{D_0}^2} \cdot 2 > 2$. If $D < D_0$, then analogously $2 < D_0^2$ and thus $\frac{2}{{D_0}^2} \cdot 2 < 2$.

[10] Of course, this is not a mathematical proof, which we want to owe at this point. Moreover, by replacing the number 2 with any real number a, any root of a can be calculated.

It follows that $\frac{2}{D_0{}^2} \cdot 2 > 2$ or $\frac{2}{D_0^2} \cdot 2 < 2$ is. Therefore, it follows that $\frac{2}{D_0^2} \cdot 2 < 2 < D_0{}^2$ or $D_0{}^2 < 2 < \frac{2}{D_0^2} \cdot 2$ is, resp. that $\left(\frac{2}{D_0}\right)^2 < 2 < D_0{}^2$ or $D_0{}^2 < 2 < \left(\frac{2}{D_0}\right)^2$ is.

Since $D^2 = 2$, it follows from the root extraction of the inequalities that $\frac{2}{D_0} < D < D_0$ or $D_0 < D < \frac{2}{D_0}$ is. In any case, D is thus between $\frac{2}{D_0}$ and D_0. If one now wants to find an approximation for D that is better than D_0, that is, whose distance to D is smaller than the distance between D_0 and D, then this is fulfilled by the arithmetic mean of $\frac{2}{D_0}$ and D_0. It follows that $D_1 = \frac{1}{2}\left(D_0 + \frac{2}{D_0}\right)$ and again it holds that $\frac{2}{D_1} < D < D_1$ or $D_1 < D < \frac{2}{D_1}$ is. The second approximation D_2 is then the arithmetic mean of $\frac{2}{D_1}$ and D_1 etc.

In general, this results in the already known recursive sequence:

$$(D_n)_{n \in \mathbb{N}} \cdot D_{n+1} = \frac{1}{2}\left(D_n + \frac{2}{D_n}\right) \forall n \in \mathbb{N}$$

And yet: √2 is not a fraction! The second question remains to be clarified: Why is the number $\sqrt{2}$ not a rational number, why is it irrational? The associated claim can be proven relatively easily. The following proof is conducted indirectly. The indirect proof is a powerful and daring proof method at the same time.

You put everything on one card by assuming the opposite of what you want to prove and try to discover a contradiction by logical transformations of this assumption. If this succeeds, the assumption is false and thus the opposite, i.e. the actual claim, is true. Therefore, instead of indirect proof, one also speaks of the "reductio ad absurdum", the proof by derivation of a contradiction.

Claim$\sqrt{2}$ is irrational, i.e. $\sqrt{2} \neq$ p/q

Proof (indirect): Assume: $\sqrt{2}$ is rational, i.e. $\sqrt{2}$ = p/q with p and q being coprime, whole numbers (this means the fraction is reduced to its simplest form: instead of, for example, 4/6 we write 2/3). So: $\sqrt{2}$ = p/q => p = $\sqrt{2}$q => $p^2 = 2q^2$ (1) => p^2 is divisible by 2 => p^2 is even. => p is even. This remains to be proven! (Proof by Contradiction: Claim: p^2 is even => p is even. Assumption: p is odd => p = 2m + 1 => $p^2 = 4m^2 + 4m + 1 = 2(2m^2 + 2m) + 1$, Let: k := $2m^2 + 2m$ => $p^2 = 2k + 1$ => p^2 is odd. Contradiction; thus, p is even!) So, we have: p = 2k => $p^2 = 4k^2 = 2q^2$ (compare with 1) => $q^2 = 2k^2$ => $q^2$is divisible by two (i.e., q^2 is even) => q is even.

However, if p and q are even, then p and q cannot be coprime. This is a contradiction. Therefore, $\sqrt{2}$ is not rational, or in other words: $\sqrt{2}$ is irrational!

q. e. d.

4.1.1.6 'Strange' or 'Chaotic' Attractors

In addition to the above-described 'benign' attractors, which can describe all converging linear-dynamic system developments known from classical mechanics in principle and allow at least a large degree of predictable behaviour, there are also attractors of a completely different nature. In these so-called 'strange' or 'chaotic attractors', the system's movement is fragmented over a larger area of the phase space, but remains confined to a ring-shaped environment of the attractor. Such a shattered attractor can also be described with the term the *turbulence*, making it clear that strange attractors are not something new.

Turbulences are known in economics. Think of economic crises that gain catastrophic proportions, sudden stock market crashes, erratic developments in the stock market, irregular company developments that can lead to the collapse of the company, etc.

Strange attractors also remind us of cyclical developments that have long been observed in economics; recurring events that have a lasting impact on a country's prosperity, on its citizens' provision with financial and material resources, with work and leisure. In this context, economic cycles of relatively short duration (approx. 3-5 or 7-11 years) can be distinguished from those of long-term duration (approx. 30-50 years).[11]

While parallels can be found between the individual cycles, they are by no means completely identical: History never repeats itself in exactly the same way.

The assumption is close that the historical development of the economy moves along a strange attractor. The moving point of a dynamic system that creates a strange attractor is inevitably attracted by it. It orbits the attractor without returning to the starting point with each orbit. A system can also have several of these strange attractors, e.g. a small attractor around which the moving point of the system often and quickly orbits before it is drawn into the spell of the large attractor: business and *Kondratieff* cycles!

However, to actually prove a strange attractor, another important condition must be met: With strange attractors, a change in certain initial parameters can lead to completely different results. However, this is difficult to prove in practice.

If the trajectory of a system is drawn into a strange attractor, then the position of the moving system point cannot be predicted. Two arbitrarily close points can diverge arbitrarily far from each other over time. This is also referred to as chaotic behaviour. A fundamental property of strange attractors is the exponential divergence of neighbouring orbits. With the help of so-called *Lyapunov* exponents, one can measure the 'distance' between two neighbouring points after a period of time.[12] The reason for this behaviour lies in the recursive non-linear structure of complex systems. Two neighbouring points are separated from each other due to the inherent non-linearity and amplified by the repetition process, the recursion, so much that the points drift apart exponentially.

Interestingly, this chaotic, unpredictable behaviour is due to fixed initial conditions. Therefore, this chaotic behaviour can also be referred to as deterministic chaos. If the system previously exhibited 'benign' attractors, it can tip into deterministic chaos with the slightest changes in the initial parameters. A strange attractor can therefore be characterised by saying:

A*Strange Attractor* is an attractor with a sensitive dependence on initial conditions.[13]

---

[11] 2-4 year cycles, whose existence is not entirely undisputed, are called *Kitchin* cycles. Cycles that can last 5 to 11 years are called *Juglar* cycles. Such Juglar cycles are generally referred to as business cycles. The long-term cycles of about 50 years are triggered by technological innovations and are named after *Kondratieff*. Cf. Liening (1995, p. 246 f.).

[12] See Sect. 4.2.2.2 for reference.

[13] This definition of strange attractors is based on *Jetschke:* See Jetschke (1989, p. 143). If at least one *Lyapunov* exponent is positive, there is sensitive dependence, i.e. a strange attractor, see also Sect. 4.5.

Despite the irregularities, however, structures can be recognised in the chaos, as the next section will show in more detail.

4.1.2 Fractals for Describing Deterministic Chaos

4.1.2.1 Self-similarity or Scale Invariance as a Characteristic of a Fractal

To better recognise structures in chaos, reference is made to the concept of the fractal, which has a close relationship with chaos. Fractals are patterns that repeat themselves permanently and produce unpredictable variations. One of the best-known simple fractal patterns is the mathematician *Mandelbrot* set named after *Mandelbrot*. This is a graphic that, when viewed from a distance, has the shape of an apple equipped with a kind of head and two 'arms'. The *Mandelbrot* set is therefore also known as the ' Apple man'. If you look at a section of the picture, you will notice that the initially seen apple man has countless other apple men at its edges. An edge enlargement shows that these apple men in turn—albeit smaller—have apple men. This process of section enlargement can be continued indefinitely, the result is always the same. This is a classic case of self-similarity. The existing self-similarity can also be interpreted as scale invariance. Scale invariance means that when the scale changes, the graphic shape of the structure being viewed is ultimately preserved, or the basic form can be rediscovered in changed scale ranges.

4.1.2.2 The Tree as an Analogy to the Fractal

Self-similarity is known from nature. If you look at a tree, as in Fig. 4.13, it can serve as a good example of an analogy to a fractal.

If you now look at a section of this tree, like the upper tree crown in Fig. 4.14, you will find branches that, apart from their size, look very similar to the whole tree.

If you look at further branches from this tree crown, they look very similar to the whole tree and the initially considered tree crown when appropriately enlarged, as Fig. 4.15 shows.

This process can be repeated until the structures are too small to be further decomposed.[14] In the mathematical idealisation, as becomes clear with the Mandelbrot set, the regression can be carried out infinitely often.

4.1.2.3 The 'Mandelbrot Set' or: About the Emergence of Self-Similar Structures

How does a self-similar structure arise in a dynamic system? To answer this question, the *Mandelbrot*-set should be examined more closely. First, you need an equation of the

[14] Such and similar examples of self-similarity are described in great detail in: Peitgen et al. (1994, p. 82 ff.).

Fig. 4.13 Tree—Fractal

Fig. 4.14 Tree crown—Fractal

simple non-linear form $z^2 + c$, where z and c are complex numbers[15] are. For simplicity's sake, under z and c initially also real numbers, i.e., whole numbers, fractions, or irrational numbers like the circle number π can be imagined.

[15] A complex number z can be defined as follows: $z = x + i \cdot y$, with x and y as real numbers (i.e., whole numbers, fractions, or irrational numbers like the circle number π etc.) and with the 'imaginary' number i, for which: $i^2 = -1$.

Fig. 4.15 Branches—Fractal

Furthermore, you need a (finite) iteration, i.e., that the result of the first calculation of this equation with certain initial values is used as the basis for the following calculation. The result achieved from this serves as the starting value for the next calculation and so on.

In these considerations, you can also remember the initial example of the Cobweb model, where the possible equilibrium price also came about through repeated calculations, i.e., iterations, or through recursion.

For any but fixed value of c, a sequence of numbers is created by iteration:

$$z \to z^2 + c \to \left(z^2 + c\right)^2 + c \to \left(\left(z^2 + c\right)^2 + c\right)^2 + c \ldots$$

This sequence must have one of two properties: Either the sequence is unbounded or it is bounded.

The set of points that lead to the first behaviour is called escape set, the other is called prisoner set for c. Both sets are not empty. For example, one can easily find a z for a given c, for which (z^2 + c) is greater than z. Thus, the results grow beyond all limits when iterating. If z is chosen such that for a given c (z^2 + c) is less than z, one obviously obtains a non-empty prisoner set, as the sequence then tends towards zero. If, on the other hand, z is chosen such that for a given c (z^2 + 1) equals z, the iteration stands still, but a prisoner set is still obtained, this time consisting of z-points.[16]

This iteration sequence can now be calculated and visualised using a computer by plotting the results in the complex plane. This plane is spanned by two vectors, a purely complex (i) and a purely real (r) one. As many points c in the complex plane are used for the calculation as are necessary to create a 'comprehensive' image.[17] The division

[16] See the explanations by: Peitgen et al. (1994, p. 149 f.).

[17] 'Comprehensive' here means: Comprehensive to the human eye.

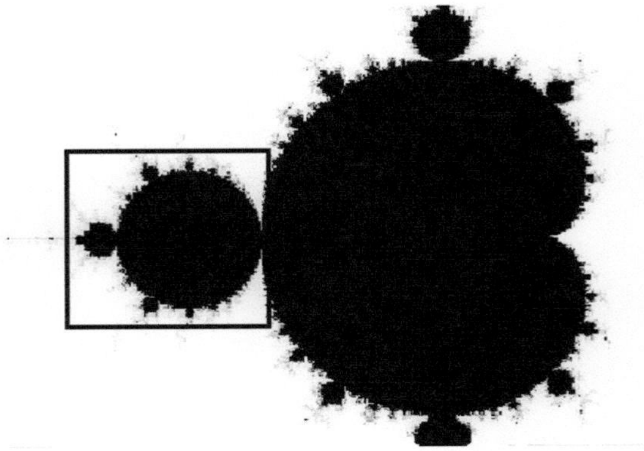

Fig. 4.16 The *Mandelbrot* set ('apple man')

of the computer screen into individual pixels is used for this purpose. Each pixel, i.e., each point on the screen, is to represent a number c of the complex plane. For each of these numbers, the iteration of the function $z^2 + c$ is now performed. If the sequence for the respective number c does not rise beyond all limits after a finite number of iteration steps, then it belongs to the prisoner set, otherwise to the escape set.[18]

The prisoner set, which forms the interior of the figure here, is coloured white. The escape set is marked with a different colour shading depending on the speed of divergence. The transitions between individual colour shadings can be regarded as 'contour lines'.

The arbitrarily irregular edge of the white inner surface is the boundary between the two possibilities of a point c.

The result of the calculations is the apple man described above, as Fig. 4.16 clearly shows.

If you look at the edge of the apple man more closely, you can see further smaller apple men at this point. When enlarging a section, it becomes apparent that this self-similarity extends down to the smallest areas of the edge. Figure 4.17 shows an enlargement of the area framed in black in Fig. 4.16:

The result of the calculations is a fractal filigree, the complexity of which is limited only by the resolution of the screen (and the printer). The phenomenon corresponds to

[18] The increase of the sequence value 'beyond all limits' cannot of course be followed to infinity on the computer. However, it is sufficient to take, for example, the number 100 as a limit and to allow a maximum of 20 iteration steps. If the limit is exceeded before the maximum number of iteration steps has been reached, then there is indeed no return for the sequence, and it is ensured that it diverges for the chosen c, i.e., that this c thus belongs to the escape set. If the limit is not exceeded after the maximum number of iterations, c belongs to the prisoner set.

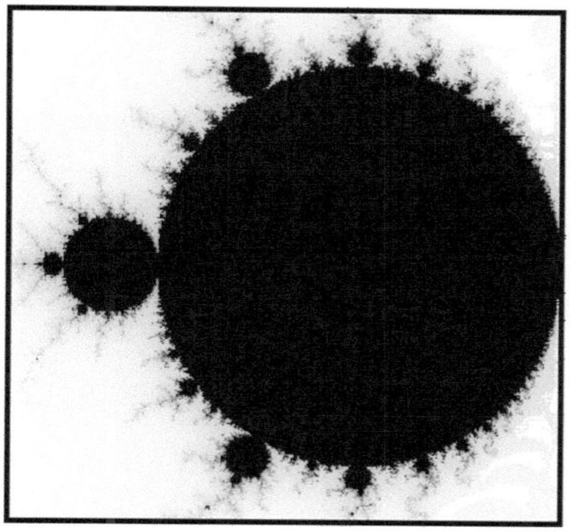

Fig. 4.17 The *Mandelbrot* set—enlargement of a section ('apple man')

the observed chaos: An arbitrarily subdivided, unpredictable disorder, which, as *Wesson* emphasises, "is simultaneously deterministic and repeated within a basic pattern in infinite variety" (Wesson, 1995, p. 53). As with the strange attractor, the infinite variations of a fractal remain within certain limits.

4.1.2.4 About the Length of a Fractal Edge—'How long is the Coast of Britain'?—Koch Curves and Similar Considerations

Fractals, however, are not only recognised by their self-similar structure. If the structure of the fractal leads to similar patterns emerging at any arbitrary magnification, the question arises as to how long the edge of a fractal is. And indeed, with this question, one encounters another criterion by which a fractal can be analysed and recognised.

Mandelbrot posed this question against the backdrop of examining country borders and, in particular, the coastline of Great Britain. In his 1967 essay "How long is the coast of Britain?" he tells the story of two different measurements for the length of the border between Portugal and Spain. In a Spanish lexicon, this was given as 991 km and in a Portuguese one as 1220 km. If one considers the length of the coast of Great Britain, values between 7200 and 8000 km emerge. One might believe that the differences in the calculation of the respective lengths are due to a lack of precision in the calculations. With the introduction of satellite surveying and laser technology, the results should undoubtedly improve. *Mandelbrot* asserts, however, that this is not the case. It makes a difference whether one draws a figure on a sheet of paper or looks at a coastline. The concept of the length of such a figure has little in common with the length of a coastline (Mandelbrot, 1967).

One can imagine that the coast of Great Britain is measured by first looking at a conventional satellite photo. This shows comparatively few details. A measurement of the

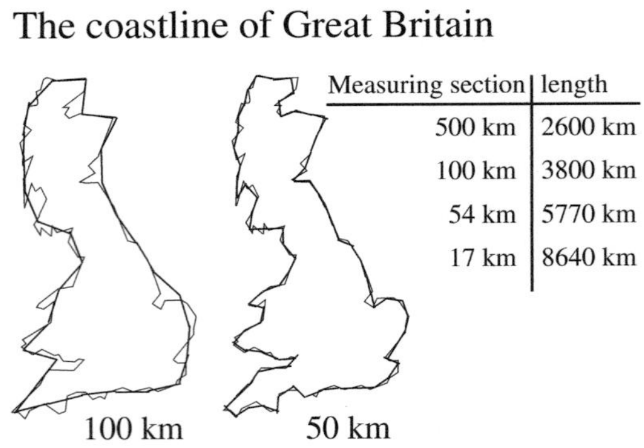

Fig. 4.18 Coastline length of Great Britain. *Source* Peitgen et al. (1994, p. 233)

coastline based on such a photo would leave smaller peninsulas and bays unconsidered. Using a pair of compasses, whose compass width is adjusted to the resolution of the photo, the length of the coast can be measured. The coastline is thus approximated by a polygonal line. The sides of this polygon are of equal length, and the coastline winds around the polygonal line.

Suppose, in a second attempt, the accuracy of the satellite image could be doubled. Then the survey would require a smaller compass width for calculation. If one now moved the compass along the coastline, there would undoubtedly be a longer line than in the first attempt, as the number of bays and peninsulas that can be taken into account has now increased. If there were the possibility to double the resolution of the photo again and further reduce the compass width, one would again obtain a different length of the coastline, as Fig. 4.18 suggests.

Based on such an experiment, one might think that with ever higher resolution of the satellite photo and a corresponding reduction of the compass width, an increasingly precise length and ultimately a well-defined limit for the length of the coast of Great Britain would emerge. This assumption is quite legitimate, as it is confirmed, for example, in the calculation of a circle's circumference.[19] However, this assumption does not hold true when calculating the coastline. Rather, the length will increase the more precisely the

[19] The idea of calculating the circumference of a circle goes back to *Archimedes*. He used inscribed and circumscribed regular polygons to calculate π (circumference$=2\pi$ r, r=radius). One starts, for example, with two polygons, each consisting of six sides. The two polygons approach each other as their side lengths are halved. By appropriate transformations of the side lengths, one thus obtains an upper and a lower bound for π, which becomes increasingly exact as the halving of the side lengths increases.

measurement is carried out, or the higher the resolution of the satellite photo and the smaller the width chosen for the compass.

If it were not for the physical limit imposed by the nature of the compass and the satellite system, the process of reduction and measurement could be carried out infinitely often without obtaining an exact value for the length of the coast. This thesis is explained by a simple example:

The example refers to the Swedish mathematician Helge von *Koch* who described the curve named after him in 1904. The *Koch* curve resembles a natural coastline, consisting of bays and peninsulas with even smaller bays and peninsulas etc. The construction of the *Koch* curve follows a simple rule:

- The creation of the curve begins with a line of length L.
- Then this line is divided into thirds, the middle part is removed and replaced by an equilateral triangle, with its base removed. This results in four segments.
- This operation is repeated on each of these segments. The result consists of sixteen segments.
- The new segments are again processed with the basic operation (dividing into thirds and inserting the equilateral triangle) and so on …

Figure 4.19 shows the first six steps (orders) to create a *Koch* curve:

In the initial situation, the length of the curve is L. The length of the segment after dividing by thirds is $L/3$. The total length of the curve after the first step is $4 \cdot L/3$. The length of the segment in the second step is $(L/3)/3$. The total length of the curve at this stage is $4 \cdot 4 \cdot (L/3^2)$. In general, it follows that the length of the *Koch* curve after the k-th iteration step is $L \cdot (4/3)^k$. Since 4/3 is greater than 1, the length obviously increases with increasing k. In other words, the length of the *Koch* curve tends towards infinity for increasing k!

$$\lim_{k \to \infty} L \cdot ({}^4\!/_3)^k = \infty$$

This *Koch* curve now makes up one third of the edge of the *Koch* island, as seen in Fig. 4.20.

It has just been proven that the length of the *Koch* curve tends towards infinity. Therefore, the length of the edge of the *Koch* island also tends towards infinity. In contrast to the edge length, however, the area is finite.

4.1.2.5 Background Information: Calculation of the Area of the Koch Island

In the initial situation, the *Koch* Island consists of an equilateral triangle with side length L and height H. From the theorem of *Pythagoras* we know: $\left(\frac{L}{2}\right)^2 + H^2 = L^2$. From this it follows that $H = \frac{\sqrt{3}}{2} \cdot L^2$. For the area of the triangle, this results in:

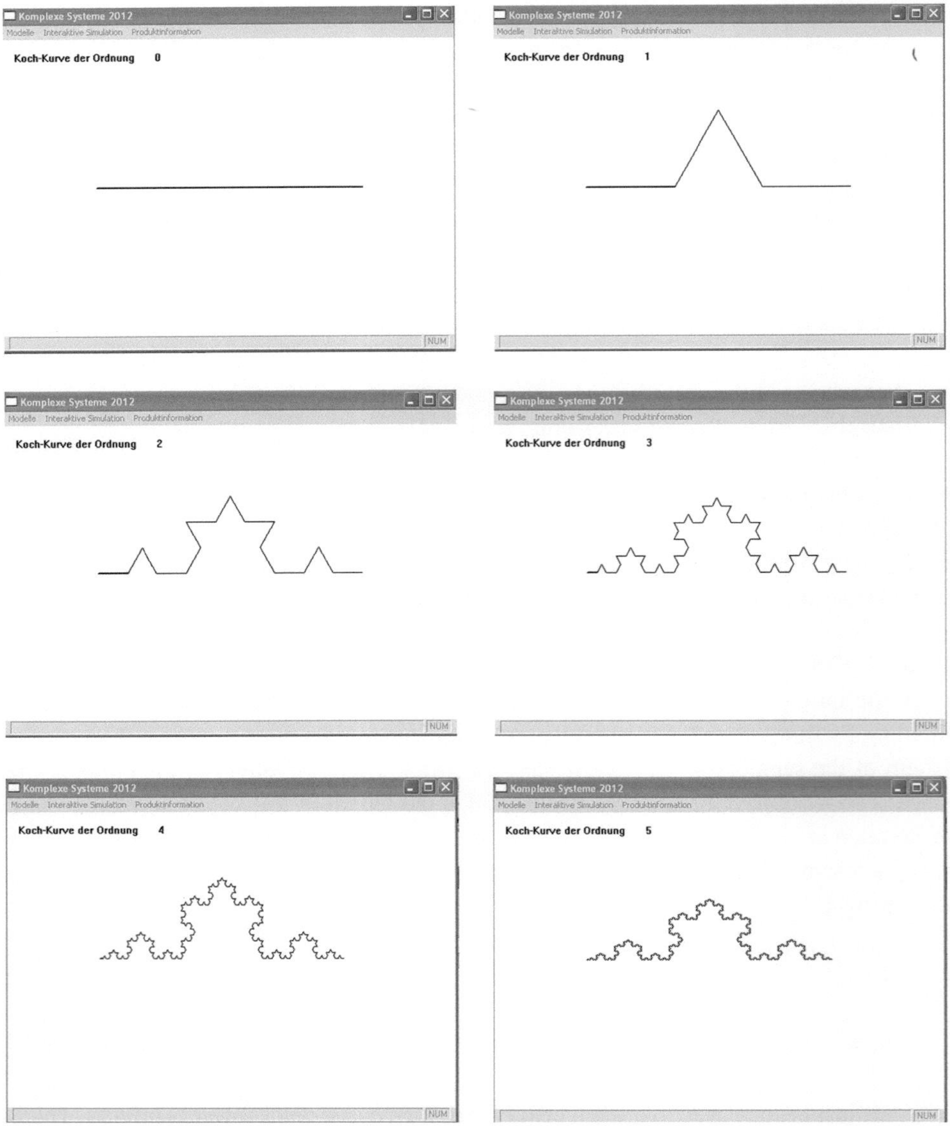

Fig. 4.19 Development of the *Koch*-curve of order 1-5

$$F_0 = \frac{1}{2} H \cdot L = \frac{\sqrt{3}}{4} \cdot L^2.$$

At the k-th step, n_k equilateral triangles with side length l_k are added. $n_k = 3 \cdot 4^{k-1}$.
l_k results from reducing the triangles by a third: $l_k = \left(\frac{1}{3}\right)^k \cdot L$.

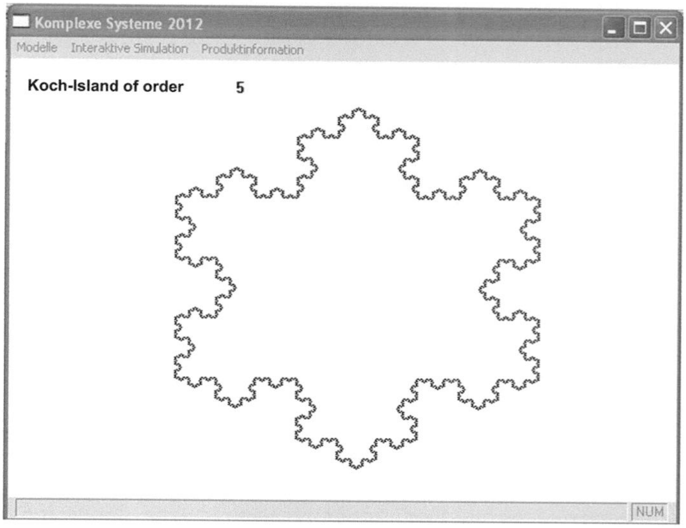

Fig. 4.20 *Koch*-Island

$$
\begin{aligned}
F_{k+1} &= F_k + n_k \cdot \frac{\sqrt{3}}{4} \cdot l_k^2 \\
&= F_k + 3 \cdot 4^{k-1} \frac{\sqrt{3}}{4} \left(\frac{1}{3}\right)^{2k} L^2 \\
&= F_k + \frac{\sqrt{3}}{12} \cdot \left(\frac{4}{9}\right)^{k-1} L^2 \\
F_{k+1} &= F_0 + \frac{\sqrt{3}}{12} \left(1 + \frac{4}{9} + \left(\frac{4}{9}\right)^2 + \ldots + \left(\frac{4}{9}\right)^{k-1}\right) L^2.
\end{aligned}
$$

For the calculation of the area, one now lets k tend towards infinity. Since the expression in brackets obviously corresponds to the geometric series, the result is:

$$\sum_{k=0}^{\infty} \left(\frac{4}{9}\right)^k = \frac{1}{1 - \frac{4}{9}} = \frac{9}{5}$$

Therefore, the following applies:
$F = F_0 + \frac{\sqrt{3}}{12}\left(\frac{9}{5}\right)L^2$. Since $F_0 = \frac{\sqrt{3}}{4}L^2$ applies:

The area of the Koch curve is finite and exactly: $F = \frac{2}{5}\sqrt{3}L^2$

A central characteristic of a fractal is thus to have a finite area and an infinite length of the edge.

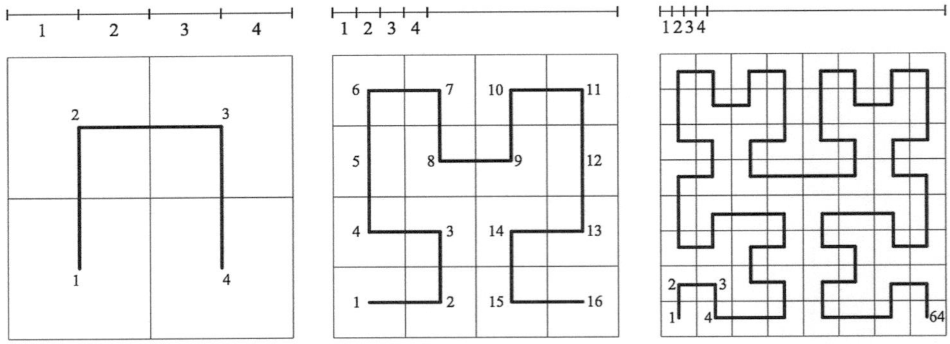

Fig. 4.21 *Hilbert* curves

4.1.2.6 The Oddity of Fractional Dimensions

Fractals are characterised by another important attribute, the dimension,. In everyday understanding, we can distinguish three or four dimensions: A point has no extent and therefore has dimension 0, a line has dimension 1, a surface has dimension 2, and a body has dimension 3. One can also (purely algebraically considered) imagine four- or five-dimensional bodies, etc.[20]

However, there are, for example, lines whose dimension is not equal to 1. A simple example of this is the *Peano* and *Hilbert* curves (see Fig. 4.21). The mathematicians *Peano* and *Hilbert* discussed curves in 1899 and 1891, respectively, whose dimensions have little in common with our everyday understanding. Through a clever algorithm, a line can be so*densely* drawn into a surface that it is completely filled. About these curves, *Hilbert* writes:

> A point can move continuously in such a way that it hits all points of a surface piece during a finite time (Hilbert, 1891, p. 459).

On the one hand, the curve is a one-dimensional line, on the other hand, it completely fills a two-dimensional surface. This curve is therefore neither properly one- nor properly two-dimensional. Rather, its dimension is *fractal.*[21] It is a fractional rational num-

[20] In mathematics, especially linear algebra, dimensions of any order are known. Generally, a vector space is called n-dimensional if it can be spanned by n linearly independent vectors, i.e., if none of the vectors can be represented by the others (combined together). For example, a two-dimensional space (surface) can be spanned by two perpendicular vectors, a three-dimensional space by three perpendicular vectors, a four-dimensional space by four 'perpendicular' vectors, etc.

[21] In mathematics, there are a variety of dimension concepts, such as the *Hausdorff* dimension, the *Euclidean* dimension, box dimension, etc. The term *fractal dimension* goes back to *Mandelbrot*. The word "fractal" comes from the Latin 'frangere', which means 'to break'.

ber between one and two. The trace left by such a curve is a strange attractor. *Hilbert* describes the procedure for the continuous mapping of the points of a line onto a surface:

> The line to be mapped—say a straight line of length 1—we first divide into 4 equal parts 1,2,3,4 and the surface piece, which we assume in the shape of a square with side length 1, we divide by two perpendicular lines into four equal squares 1,2,3,4. Secondly, we divide each of the parts 1,2,3,4 again into 4 equal parts, so that we get the 16 parts 1,2,3, … 16 on the line; at the same time, each of the 4 squares 1,2,3,4 is divided into 4 equal squares and the numbers 1,2, … 16 are then written into the resulting 16 squares, however, the order of the squares is to be chosen so that each following square adjoins one side to the previous one. If we continue this procedure (…) it is easy to see how one can assign a single specific point of the square to any given point of the line (Hilbert 1891, p. 459 f.).

With this curve, one actually obtains a mapping that is space-filling, i.e., the end product of the iteration is a self-similar curve that completely fills a square. What dimension does this curve now have? Normally, a curve is one-dimensional. On the other hand, the curve completely fills a surface. But a surface is two-dimensional. The answer to the question asked is therefore: The dimension is neither 1 nor 2, but is somewhere in between, it is a real, non-integer value!

The following once again takes up the example of the coastline of Great Britain:

Already in 1961, Lewis F. *Richardson* had calculated that the coastline of Great Britain is not rectifiable, i.e., not measurable in length. If one plots the length of the polygon sides and the length of the coast resulting from the number of polygon lines logarithmically against each other, one obtains a series of points through which one can draw a straight line (using the method of least squares) whose deviations from the found points are minimal. This line is of the form $y = a \cdot x + b$. *Richardson* had determined the value $a = -0.23$ for the slope of this line to describe the coastline of England. If the coastline itself were a straight line, then $a = 0$ would apply. But the dimension of a straight line is just $d = 1$. In accordance with this consideration, one sets $a := 1 - d$. Then for the coast of Great Britain: $-0.23 = 1 - d$, or in other words: The dimension of the coastline of Great Britain is: $d = 1.23$ (Zeitler, 1993, p. 152 f.)!

For dimension calculation, the so-called box dimension is often used. The idea of dimension calculation is as follows:

The curve to be examined consists of individual points upon closer analysis, so instead of the curve, one can also consider the set of points from which the curve is composed.

The question now is whether the points are arranged in such a way that they form, for example, a line (dimension 1), a surface (dimension 2), a space (dimension 3), or another dimensional structure. To do this, one covers the points of an m-dimensional phase space with m-dimensional boxes (edge length l).

So: A two-dimensional phase space is examined using squares; a three-dimensional phase space by boxes, etc. The covering does not exclude overlaps. However, the coverings should be minimal in the sense that the intersection of the boxes is as small as possible. If one divides the phase space into m-dimensional boxes of edge length l, it is possible to count how many boxes are necessary to completely cover the fractal or the attractor.

Let $N(l)$ be the minimum number of boxes required. Then the so-called 'covering dimension' or the so-called box dimension is given by $D_0 = \lim_{l \to 0} \frac{\log_2(N(l))}{\log_2(\frac{1}{l})}$.

A fractal is, negatively formulated, a structure that does not have the form of a Euclidean object (point, line, surface, etc.), regardless of how much one may enlarge a section of the object. The analyses have shown that a fractal rather represents a finite figure with an infinitely long, self-similar edge, whose dimension is fractional.

It turns out that 'strange attractors' in phase space often have a self-similar structure. Such self-similar structures are, however, fractals, whose edges are infinite and whose dimension is fractional! Another similarity between strange attractors and fractals arises from the fact that both originate from non-linear dynamic equations.

In other words: If the dimension of the attractor is fractional and the length of the edge of the attractor is infinite, a 'strange attractor may be present and we are dealing with a system that can be described as complex (with all its consequences (butterfly effect etc.)).

However, it should be noted that if, conversely, an attractor does not have a fractional dimension (see logistic equation), this does not mean that the attractor is not 'strange'. The condition is therefore at best sufficient, but not necessary![22]

Ultimately, there are at most four types of attractors in dynamic systems:

1. The simplest type of attractor is the point attractor.
2. The next type of attractor is the limit cycle attractor or the three- or higher-dimensional torus, whose frequencies are rational.
3. The third type of attractor is the multi-dimensional torus with irrational frequencies, which however lead to an almost periodic movement on the torus (quasi-periodic).
4. The fourth type of attractor is the 'strange' or 'chaotic' attractor, whose state of motion is neither periodic nor quasi-periodic (deterministic chaos).

4.1.2.7 Background Information: (Box-)Dimensions

▶ i. Box dimension

With $N(l)$ we denote the number of required n-dimensional 'boxes' to cover a structure (line, surface, cube, etc.). l is the edge length of the respective box.

The volume of the examined structure V is then calculated in the case of a line, a surface and a cube as follows:

---

[22] *Lorenz* critically notes about the criterion of dimension that the proof of a fractal dimension is neither necessary nor sufficient. Because there are attractors with fractal dimension that are not at all 'strange' and conversely there are strange attractors that are not fractal. See Lorenz (1988) or also: Grebogi (1984).

$$V_{Linie} = N(l) \cdot l, \; V_{Fläche} = N(l) \cdot l^2, \; V_{Würfel} = N(l) \cdot l^3$$

Generally speaking, it turns out that $V = N(l) \cdot l^D$, where D corresponds to the dimension of the measured structure. The edge length l of the considered boxes must be smaller than the dimensions of the observed structure.

If l is only small enough, the number of minimally required boxes $N(l)$ will be proportional to a power of l, which corresponds to the sought dimension.

$N(l) \approx \frac{1}{l^D}$ or considering the general volume of the structure: $N(l) = V \cdot \frac{1}{l^D}$. What does it mean in this context that l should be "only small enough"? If we consider, for example, any surface $V_{Fläche}$, then with ever decreasing l the number of coverings becomes ever larger. When l becomes arbitrarily small, almost 0, we also speak of a limit process. This means that the area can finally be calculated as a limit: $V_{Fläche} = \lim_{l \to 0} N(l) \cdot l^2$.

The logarithm is a fantastic function, not least because of the functional equation, which reveals a homomorphism between addition and multiplication. Thus, the product of two numbers is equal to the addition of the logarithms of the two numbers, up to homomorphism, i.e., up to the mapping of the logarithm of the product. Therefore, in general: $\log_a(x \cdot y) = \log_a(x) + \log_a(y)$, where here '$\log_a$' stands for the logarithm to the base a.[23]

If we now solve this equation $N(l) = V \cdot \frac{1}{l^D}$ for D using the logarithm, we get:

$$N(l) = V \cdot \frac{1}{l^D} \Leftrightarrow l^D = V \cdot \frac{1}{N(l)} \Leftrightarrow D \cdot \log_2(l) = \log_2(\frac{V}{N(l)}) = \log_2(V) - \log_2(N(l))$$

$$\Leftrightarrow D = \frac{\log_2(V) - \log_2(N(l))}{\log_2(l)} \Leftrightarrow D = \frac{\log_2(N(l)) - \log_2(V)}{-\log_2(l)} \Leftrightarrow D = \frac{\log_2(N(l)) - \log_2(V)}{\log_2(\frac{1}{l})}$$

For arbitrarily small l results from the above outlined limit process:

$D = \lim_{l \to 0} \frac{\log_2(N(l)) - \log_2(V)}{\log_2(\frac{1}{l})} = \lim_{l \to 0}(\frac{\log_2(N(l))}{\log_2(\frac{1}{l})} - \frac{\log_2(V)}{\log_2(\frac{1}{l})}) = \lim_{l \to 0} \frac{\log_2(N(l))}{\log_2(\frac{1}{l})}$, since the volume V is limited and $\lim_{l \to 0}(\frac{1}{l}) \approx \infty$ thus results in $\lim_{l \to 0}(\frac{\log_2(V)}{\log_2(\frac{1}{l})}) = 0$ (null sequence).

This dimension formula is also called box dimension or capacity dimension and is denoted by D_0. So for the calculation of the box dimension:

$$D_0 = \lim_{l \to 0} \frac{\log_2(N(l))}{\log_2(\frac{1}{l})}$$

This formula was already proposed by *Kolmogorov* in 1958.

[23] Let $p = \log_2(x)$ bzw. $x = 2^p, q = \log_2(y)$ bzw. $y = 2^q$. Then $x \cdot y = 2^p \cdot 2^q = 2^{p+q}$. thus $\log_2(x \cdot y) = \log_2(2^{p+q}) = p + q$ or $\log_2(x \cdot y) = \log_2(x) + \log_2(y)$. Because of this relationship, the dimension calculation also works to any other base a. Therefore, some authors also use the natural logarithm ln in the formulas. See Grassberger and Procaccia (1983) and Liening (1999).

ii. Information dimension

Comparable to the box dimension, the information dimension can be determined: $D_I = \lim_{l \to 0} \frac{I(l)}{\log_2(\frac{1}{l})}$

The information dimension is a measure of how fast the information I grows, which is needed to define a point on the attractor, when $l \to 0$ goes.

Argyris et al. point out that, if all boxes have the same probability, the average information per single measurement reaches the maximum value and in this case the information dimension coincides with the box dimension. However, they note: "Since the information gain is smaller for different probability distributions (...), generally: $D_I \leq D_c$" (Argyris et al., 2010, p. 263).

iii. General extension of the concept of dimension

First considerations Just as one can imagine a two-dimensional entity (surface) by spanning it with two perpendicular, i.e., linearly independent vectors, the fractal dimension of an attractor can be understood as follows:

The fractal dimension is to be understood as the number of pairwise independent state variables that characterise the movement on the attractor.

This extends the concept of dimension: not only curves are allowed, but any sets of points. Furthermore, these sets of points are now covered with m-dimensional cubes or spheres—generally boxes—of edge length l. Covering means that there can also be overlaps. However, the overlaps should be minimal in the sense that the intersection of the boxes is as small as possible.

If one divides the phase space into m-dimensional boxes of edge length l, it is possible to count how many of these boxes are necessary to completely cover the attractor. Let $N(l)$ be the minimum number of boxes needed for this. Then, by D_0 with

$$D_0 = \lim_{l \to 0} \frac{\log_2(N(l))}{\log_2\left(\frac{1}{l}\right)}$$

the so-called 'covering dimension' or the general box dimension is given.[24] For example, the number of squares needed to cover a point in the plane is equal to 1. From this it obviously follows for a point:

$$D_0 = 0.$$

Further canonical examples include the calculation of the dimension of a line, a surface, and a cube, as illustrated in Table 4.1.

[24]The dimension formula for D was already introduced in 1932 by *Pontrjagin* and *Schnieremann* as a covering formula and further developed by *Kolmogorov* in 1951.

Table 4.1 Dimension of a line, a surface, and a cube

The edge length is equal to l of the geometric figure:	Scaling of l:	Number of minimal boxes $N(l)$:	Dimension D_0 :[a]
Line	1/3	3	$\log_2(3)/\log_2(3) = 1$
Surface	1/3	9	$\log_2(9)/\log_2(3) = 2$
Cube	1/3	27	$\log_2(27)/\log_2(3) = 3$

[a]To simplify the calculation of dimensions, we here forgo the limit process, because: Example surface: Choose $l = 1/4$. Then $\log_2(16)/\log_2(4) = 2$, $l = 1/5$
Then $\log_2(25)/\log_2(5) = 2$ etc. The limit process can obviously be neglected in these canonical cases. The neglect of the limit process leads us to a simple form of the so-called *Hausdorff*-dimension. The number of minimal boxes $N(l)$ is obviously in a very specific ratio to the scaling factor. For the *Hausdorff*-dimension see: Hausdorff (1919)

In the following, the dimension of the *Koch*-curve is calculated by a renewed representation:

In the initial situation, let $l = 1$. Then $N(l) = 1$. In the first step, let $l = 1/3$. Then obviously $N(l) = 4$. In the second step, $l = 1/9$ and $N(l) = 16$. In general: From $l = \left(\frac{1}{3}\right)^k$ follows $N(l) = 4^k$, where $k \in \mathbb{N}$ represents the number of iteration steps.

This results in the dimension of the fractal *Koch* curve:

$$D_0 = \lim_{k\to\infty} \frac{\log_2\left(4^k\right)}{\log_2\left(\frac{1}{(1/3)^k}\right)} = \lim_{k\to\infty} \frac{k \log_2(4)}{k \log_2(3)} \approx 1.2618595.$$

Simplified calculation of the box dimension of the Koch curve In the *Koch* curve, the length of the line l changes with each step of the construction by 1/3 of the initial situation to 4/3 of the initial length.

In other words: The enlargement by a factor of 3 results in a fourfold increase in length.

This results in the dimension of the fractal *Koch*- curve:

$$\text{Mit}\, N(l) = \left({}^1/_l\right)^D,$$
$$\text{und}\, N(l) = 4\, \text{sowie}\, l = {}^1/_3\, \text{folgt:}$$
$$4 = 3^D,$$
$$\text{da}\, D = \frac{\log_2(N(l))}{\log_2({}^1/_l)} \Rightarrow D = \frac{\log_2(4)}{\log_2(3)} \approx 1.26$$

Information dimension In addition to the box dimension $D_0 = \lim_{l\to 0} \frac{\log_2(N(l))}{\log_2\left(\frac{1}{l}\right)}$ as already mentioned, there is the so-called Information dimension D_I with

$D_1 := \lim_{l \to 0} \frac{I(l)}{\log_2(\frac{1}{l})}$, wobei $I(l) := -\sum_{i=1}^{N(l)} p_i \cdot \log_2(\frac{1}{p_i})$ for determining the dimension of a fractal (Argyris et al., 2010, p. 263).

Correlation dimension Of particular interest is also the Correlation dimension D_k. Especially the D_2 is often very helpful for practical purposes of investigating strange attractors, as it allows to operate very well with time series, i.e., empirical data, as we will see. Floris *Takens* (Takens, 1981) was able to show that a single variable of a trajectory over time is sufficient to determine the dimension of the corresponding attractor.

A fractal structure in the $\mathbb{R}^n$, is considered, for example, a strange attractor.

After the trajectory, described by $X(t) := \{X_i(t)|, 1 \leq i \leq N\}$, is located in the attractor, one determines in a fixed short time interval Δt N points of the trajectory in the attractor: $\{X_i, 1 \leq i \leq N\}$ according to the formula $X_i := X(t + i \cdot \Delta t)$.

Due to the butterfly effect, most pairs of points $(X_i, X_j)_{i \neq j}$ will not correlate with each other, as can be shown using autocorrelation. Each point X_i in phase space consists of n components: $X_i := \begin{pmatrix} x_{i,j=1} \\ x_{i,j=2} \\ \cdots \\ x_{i,j=n} \end{pmatrix} \in \mathbb{R}^n$

For the determination of dimensions, however, only the spatially correlated pairs of points are of interest.

For this purpose, we subdivide the attractor with $N(l)$ -boxes of edge length l.

If we denote the number of points in the i-th box with N_i, then the probability that a randomly selected point is in the i-th box is obviously: $p_i = \frac{N_i}{N(l)}$. The probability that two points are in the same i-th box is therefore, due to the independence of the event: $p_i^2 = (\frac{N_i}{N(l)})^2$. If we consider all $N(l)$ boxes, the probability that two randomly selected points land in one of the boxes is: $\sum_{i=1}^{N(\varepsilon)} p_i^2$. However, this is obviously identical to two randomly selected points X_i and X_k having a distance $\leq l$, so that$|\mathrm{X}_i - X_k| \leq l$ gilt, wobei: $|\mathrm{X}_i - X_k| = \sqrt{\sum_{j=1}^{n} (x_{i,j} - x_{i,k})^2}$.

Here we are referring to the Euclidean distance, as we usually speak of Euclidean spaces when we have the concept of a, for example, three-dimensional space in mind.

Let's now denote this probability with $C(l)$, so:

$C(l) = \frac{1}{N(l)^2} \cdot \left\{ (\mathrm{X}_i, X_k)_{i \neq k} \middle| |\mathrm{X}_i - X_k| \leq l \right\}$.

The bracket can be formally described with the *Heaviside* function:

$$\left\{ (\mathrm{X}_i, X_k)_{i \neq k} \middle| |\mathrm{X}_i - X_k| \leq l \right\} = \sum_{k=1}^{N(l)} \sum_{i=1, k \neq i}^{N(l)} \Theta(l - |X_i - X_k|) = \sum_{i=1, k=1, k \neq i}^{N(l)} \Theta(l - |X_i - X_k|)$$

The Heaviside function is given by:

$$\Theta(x) := \begin{cases} 1, & \text{falls } \mathrm{x} \geq 0 \\ 0, & \text{sonst} \end{cases}.$$

This means that the expression marked with the *Heaviside* function $\Theta(l - |X_i - X_k|)$ thus only takes into account those distances that are actually smaller than l, as all other distances are weighted with 0. The considered distances each receive the value 1. This way, it can be determined how many and which distances actually lie in the l interval.

We thus obtain $C(l) = \frac{1}{N(l)^2} \cdot \sum_{i=1,k=1,k\neq i}^{N(l)} \Theta(l - |X_i - X_k|)$

The above formula is easier to imagine if you first consider the number of points N on an attractor that lie in a box with edge length l around the point X_0: $N_{absolut} := \sum_{i=1}^{N} \Theta(l - |X_i - X_0|)$, where Θ is the Heaviside function.

$C(X_0, l) := \frac{1}{N} \sum_{i=1}^{N} \Theta(l - |X_i - X_0|)$ is then the relative frequency of the number of points in the box measured by the total number of points in the attractor.

If you now not only consider the point X_0, but go over all points $\{X_k, 1 \leq k \leq N\}$, it obviously results:

$$C(l) := \frac{1}{N} \sum_{k=1}^{N} \frac{1}{N} \sum_{\substack{i=1 \\ (i\neq k)}}^{N} \Theta(l - |X_i - X_k|) = \frac{1}{N^2} \sum_{k=1}^{N} \sum_{\substack{i=1 \\ (i\neq k)}}^{N} \Theta(l - |X_i - X_k|)$$

or $C(l) := \lim_{N\to\infty} \left(\frac{1}{N^2} \sum_{i,k=1,(i\neq k)}^{N} \Theta(l - |X_i - X_k|) \right)$ (Grassberger & Procaccia, 1983, p. 346)

If the number of points N is sufficiently large, the following results for arbitrarily small values l: $C(l) \approx l^{D_2}$, from which the so-called correlation dimension D_2 can be easily determined by logarithmising:

$$C(l) \approx l^{D_2} \Rightarrow \log_2(C(l)) \approx D_2 \log_2(l) \Rightarrow D_2 \approx \frac{\log_2(C(l))}{\log_2(l)}.$$

The limit is obtained by:

$D_2 = \lim_{l\to 0} \frac{\log_2(C(l))}{\log_2(l)}$.

Grassberger and *Procaccia* have shown that the correlation dimension represents the lower bound for both the information and the box dimension: $D_2 \leq D_1 \leq D_0$ (Grassberger & Procaccia, 1983).

The algorithm for D_2 can be generalised and one obtains

$C(l) \approx l^{(q-1)D_q} \Rightarrow \log_2(C(l)) \approx (q-1) \cdot D_q \cdot \log_2(l) \Rightarrow D_q \approx \frac{\log_2(C(l))}{(q-1)\cdot\log_2(l)}$

Dimension calculations D_q, where by forming limits $D_q = \lim_{l\to 0} \frac{\log_2(C(q,l))}{(q-1)\cdot\log_2(l)}$ with $C(q,l) = \frac{1}{N} \sum_{k=1}^{N(l)} \left(\frac{1}{N-1} \sum_{i=1}^{N(l)} \Theta(l - |X_i - X_k|) \right)^{q-1}$ applies.

To minimise computation time in practice, one should try to use only such pairs of points that have sufficiently small distances from each other. For example, *Theiler* and

Grassberger have proposed an effective algorithm for finding the points and for calculation (Theiler, 1987; Grassberger, 1990).

Thus, the D_2 by *Theiler* based on these considerations is calculated as follows for an n-dimensional phase space, in order to drastically reduce the computation time: $C_n(w, N, l) := \left(\frac{2}{(N+1-w)(N-w)} \sum_{k=w}^{N-1} \sum_{i=0}^{N-1-k} \Theta(l - |X_i - X_{i+k}|) \right)$ (Theiler, 1989, p. 1070), where thus

- n is the dimension of the phase space in which the attractor is embedded,
- l denotes the maximum distance between two points,
- N is the number of data points considered in the attractor,
- Θ is the Heaviside function,
- $|X_i - X_{i+k}|$ describes the (Euclidean) distance between two points,
- w is the so-called 'Theiler Window', with w > 0, which ensures the 'exclusion' of neighbouring points to prevent spurious correlations.

Essentially, the above formula is given by the considered correlation integral of *Grassberger* and *Procaccia*:

$C(l) := \lim_{N \to \infty} \left(\frac{1}{N^2} \sum_{i,k=1,(i \neq k)}^{N} \Theta(l - |X_i - X_k|) \right)$ (Grassberger & Procaccia, 1983, p. 346)

All distances between all points on the attractor are determined, but each distance is actually measured only once. Points that follow directly in time are skipped. The number of skipped points indicates the *Theiler* Window.

4.2 Bifurcations

4.2.1 Bifurcations in Dynamic Systems

4.2.1.1 What are Bifurcations?

In Sect. 4.1 of this book, various types of attractors have been introduced. Starting from fixed point attractors to limit cycle attractors to torus attractors, a number of 'benign' attractors have been worked out, which have a relatively simple structure and in whose vicinity a system moves on simply designed paths. Only with the torus can there be more complicated, quasi-periodic path sequences. However, these attractors have in common that the solutions of two arbitrarily close starting paths do not diverge from each other over time. In short: trajectories do not diverge in these cases. But attractors were also introduced on which non-periodic movements take place with sensitive dependence on the initial conditions. Such attractors were referred to as '*Strange*' or '*Chaotic* Attractors'.

Now the behaviour of dynamic systems usually depends on a multitude of parameters. Changes in parameters can lead to enormous changes in the behaviour of the system and thus also to qualitative changes in the attractors. With a small change in parameters, the topological structure of attractors usually changes only slightly. However, if a certain critical value is exceeded, the structure of the attractor changes abruptly. For example, a point attractor can become a two-cycle. This sudden change in the structure of the attractor is called a bifurcation.[25]

4.2.1.2 The Discovery of Bifurcations

Historically, in 1948, Eberhard *Hopf* was the first scientist to describe bifurcations using a mathematical model. It is one of the most famous bifurcation scenarios (Loistl, 1993, p. 22 f.). In this model, when a critical value is exceeded, the transition from a point attractor to a limit cycle attractor occurs first. The critical point is now called *Hopf* instability. *Hopf* went further and proposed a multitude of other instabilities. The first consists of a jump from the point attractor to the limit cycle attractor. The next jump occurs when a limit cycle attractor transitions into the surface of a torus. Subsequently, a jump to a four-dimensional torus attractor is supposed to occur, followed by a jump with five dimensions, and so on.

In 1982, it was proven that turbulence sets in much earlier than *Hopf* had suspected. This instability was named *Bénard* instability. *Ruelle* and *Takens* developed a new theory of faster transition, according to which the jump to turbulence, to chaos, sets in much earlier.[26] Instead of transitioning from a torus attractor into a four-dimensional torus, the torus itself begins to break into pieces, with the surface entering the space of broken, i.e., *fractal* dimension. The surface moves between plane and body.

Bifurcations and finally turbulence, i.e., chaos, arise because all elements of a system are related to each other and because the feedback between the parts of the system constantly produces new parts. The decay of order into a Strange Attractor is essentially an indication of the internal coherence of the system. Or as *Briggs* and *Peat* put it, this decay of the system into irregularity and chaos is “a sign of its wholeness” (Briggs & Peat, 1993, p. 73).

4.2.1.3 Bifurcation Scenario Using the Example of the Logistic Function

There is a relatively simple function that can clearly visualise these different bifurcations.

In the first part of the book, an example of this, namely a non-linear price function, was already introduced in Sect. 3.4.5:

$$P(t+1) = \lambda \cdot P(t) \cdot (1 - P(t))$$

---

[25] The term is borrowed from Latin, in which the word *‘furca’* exists, which denotes a two-pronged fork.

[26] Both *Ruelle* and *Takens* and later *Newhouse* have provided this proof that a Strange Attractor appears after just two instabilities. See Ruelle (1971, p. 178 ff.) and Newhouse (1980, p. 35 ff.).

This function is the simple mapping generally referred to as the logistic function, which can be used to vividly illustrate bifurcation scenarios.

For the investigation, the parameter λ was changed several times. It was found, for example, that at $\lambda = 0.7$ and an arbitrary initial value, a converging development of the system with a fixed point occurs.

Figure 4.22 shows the p(t) values, plotted on the time axis t. Next, we see again the well-known figure from Sect. 3.4.5 of the first part of the book (see Fig. 4.23).

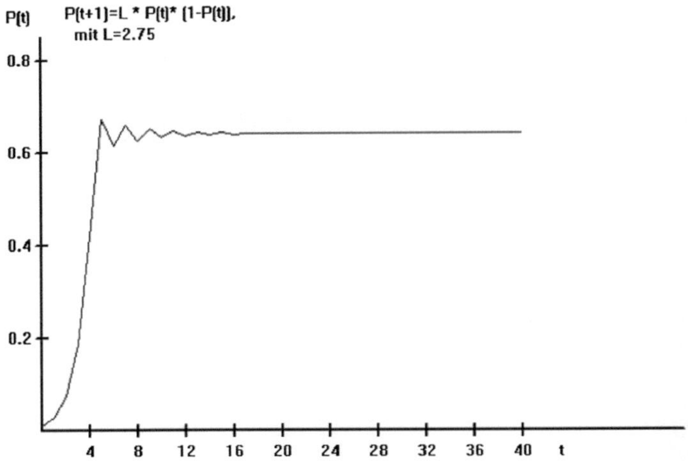

Fig. 4.22 Point attractor

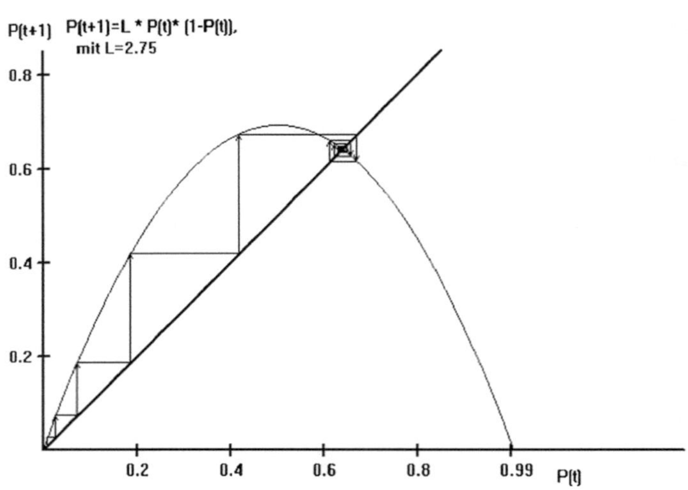

Fig. 4.23 Point attractor

After the previous considerations on the topic of attractors, it can now be stated at this point that the orbit of the system is moving towards a fixed point attractor.

If you set L = 3.2, then the system also converges, as illustrated by Figs. 4.24 and 4.25. However, you get two fixed points. In other words, there is a limit cycle attractor. If you reach the value 3.2, for example, by changing the parameter λ, then a period doubling occurs. This is an example of a bifurcation.

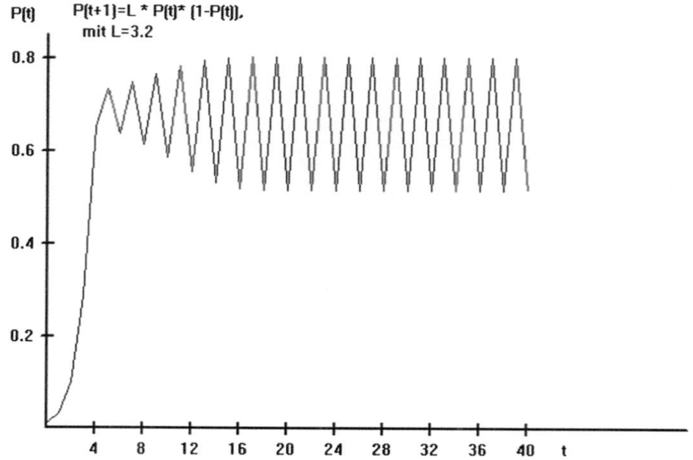

Fig. 4.24 Limit cycle attractor on the time axis

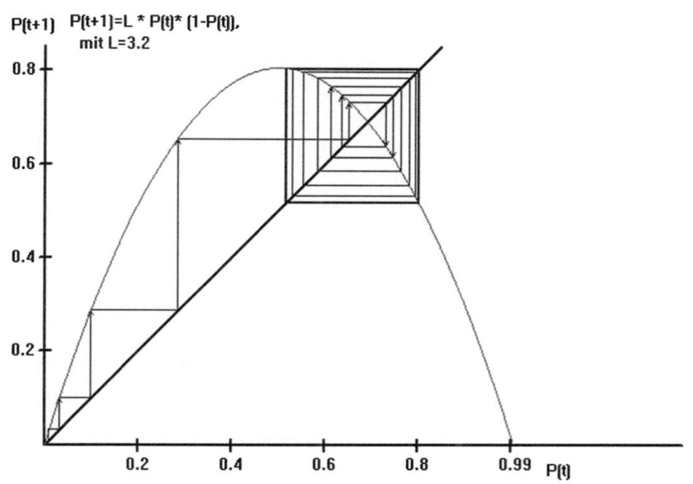

Fig. 4.25 Limit cycle attractor

With a further minor change of λ with $\lambda = 3.5$, the two fixed points lose their stability and a new limit cycle emerges, with the system now having four fixed points. At this λ value, which generates a cycle of period four, there is again a period-doubling bifurcation. Figures 4.26 and 4.27 show this four-cycle.

If one chooses, for example, $\lambda = 4.00$, then the behaviour of the system changes dramatically. One obtains a chaotic motion sequence with infinitely many non-periodic cycles, as shown in Figs. 4.28 and 4.29—each from a different perspective.

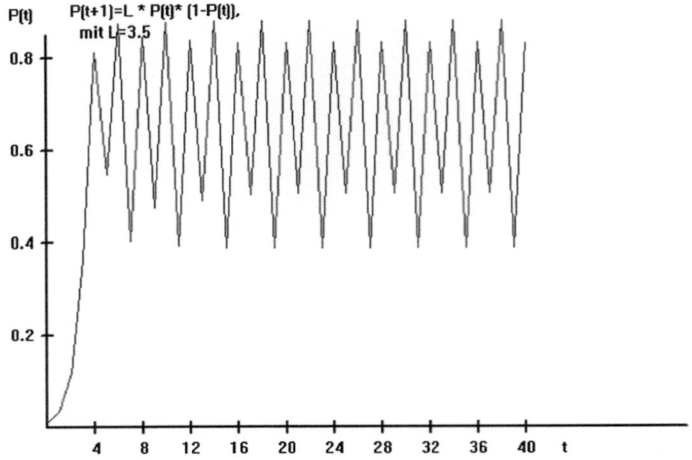

Fig. 4.26 Four-cycle on the time axis

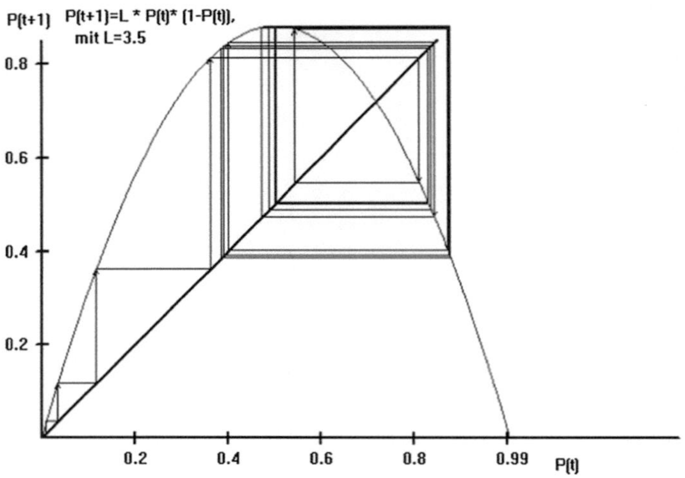

Fig. 4.27 Four-cycle

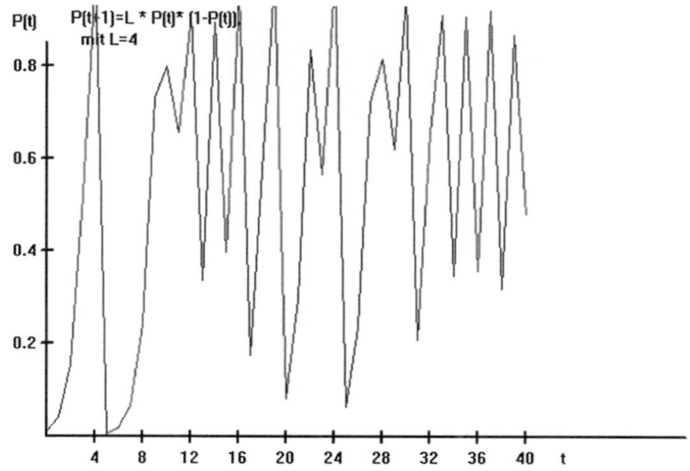

Fig. 4.28 Chaotic or strange attractor on the time axis

So far, three λ values have been examined. Each of these three values represents a different bifurcation situation. The exact points at which a bifurcation occurs can be illustrated using a graph. The results of the iteration, i.e., the P-values, are plotted against the parameter λ. In the graphical representation, a total of 2500 iterations per λ value are performed, with the first 1500 iterations over P being disregarded so that the bifurcation behaviour of the function becomes clearly apparent.[27] Fig. 4.30 shows the result of the bifurcation diagram.

A vertical cut through the bifurcation diagram shows the corresponding attractor for each λ value. A detailed analysis of the diagram confirms the previous diagrams: If λ is less than 3.0, the system is based on a single fixed point attractor. At this point, a series of so-called period-doubling bifurcations begins. Thus, λ values between 3.0 and 3.45 lead to a two-cycle. At $\lambda = 3.45$, the two-cycle changes into a four-cycle. If λ reaches the value 3.54, then the four-cycle four-cycle becomes an eight-cycle, and so on. If λ is greater than or equal to 3.57, then a cycle is created that is no longer recognisable as such, but rather consists of infinitely many points and at the same time does not have a continuous structure.[28]

---

[27] The previous graphs show that the system always needs a more or less long settling phase before it is drawn into an attractor. To eliminate these settling phases in the bifurcation graph, the first 1500 iterations in the graph are cautiously neglected. The high number of iterations, a total of 2500, ensures that the impression of the system's final state can actually be represented.

[28] The continued division in the figure illustrates why the Latin word furca—two-pronged fork—was used here.

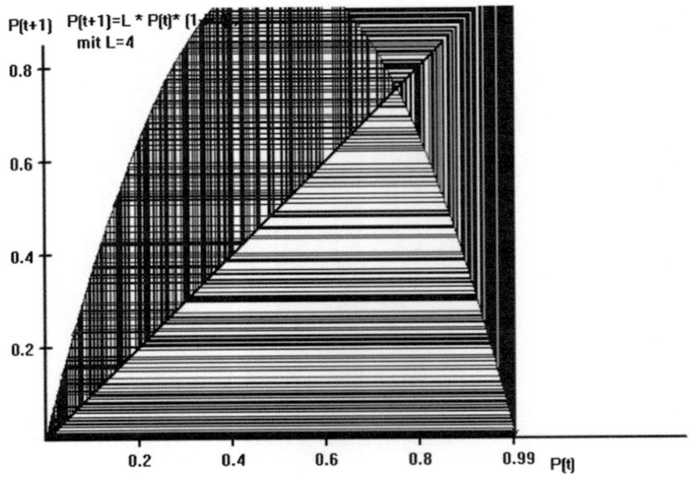

Fig. 4.29 Chaotic or strange attractor

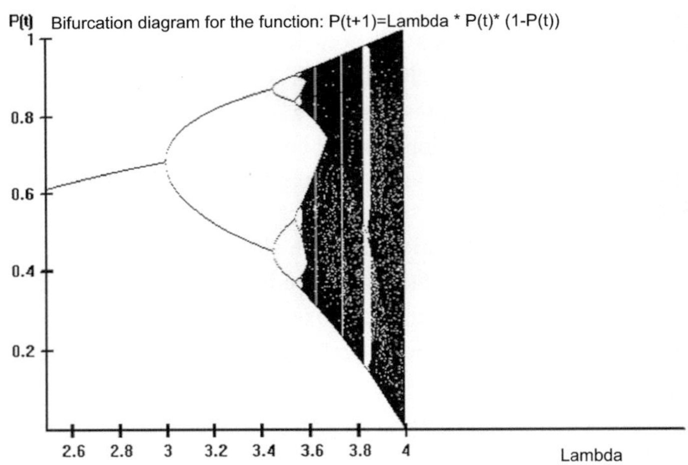

Fig. 4.30 Bifurcation diagram

There are interesting relationships between the individual bifurcation points:

The following will examine the first seven bifurcation points λ_i, $0 < i < 7$ is considered, where the accuracy is increased to six places after the decimal point.[29] The difference d_i

[29] A list of the first seven bifurcation points can be found, for example, in Peitgen et al. (1992b, p. 105).

Table 4.2 Calculation of the Feigenbaum constant

$\lambda_1 = 3.000000$		
$\lambda_2 = 3.449490$	$d_1 = \lambda_2 - \lambda_1 = 0.449490$	
$\lambda_3 = 3.544090$	$d_2 = \lambda_3 - \lambda_2 = 0.094600$	$q_1 = d_1/d_2 = 4.75148$
$\lambda_4 = 3.564407$	$d_3 = \lambda_4 - \lambda_3 = 0.020317$	$q_2 = d_2/d_3 = 4.65620$
$\lambda_5 = 3.568759$	$d_4 = \lambda_5 - \lambda_4 = 0.004352$	$q_3 = d_3/d_4 = 4.66843$
$\lambda_6 = 3.569692$	$d_5 = \lambda_6 - \lambda_5 = 0.000933$	$q_4 = d_4/d_5 = 4.66452$
$\lambda_7 = 3.569891$	$d_6 = \lambda_7 - \lambda_6 = 0.000199$	$q_5 = d_5/d_6 = 4.68844$

is formed from every two adjacent bifurcation values. Subsequently, the quotients q_i of these successive differences are calculated (see Table 4.2).

Firstly, it is observed that the bifurcations occur at increasingly shorter intervals with increasing λ. The intervals are described here by the respective difference d_i. A more detailed analysis reveals that each interval is smaller by a constant factor δ than the previous one. This factor is related to the quotients q_i. Upon closer examination of these quotients, it is found that they are not exactly identical, but approach a certain value with increasing i. This value is the constant factor δ, which was first described by the physicists Siegfried *Großmann* and Stefan *Thomae*. They showed that:

$$\delta = \lim_{i \to \infty} \frac{d_i}{d_{i+1}} \approx 4.669201609103$$

At first glance, this number merely describes the behaviour of our specific dynamic system. Mitchel*Feigenbaum*, however, was able to prove that δ is of universal nature. Thus, the constant δ also occurs in a dynamic system that can be described using a trigonometric function like

$$f(x) = \lambda \cdot x^2 \cdot \sin(\pi \cdot x)$$

. In all mappings that, like the logistic equation, have a parabolic maximum, the analysis of the bifurcation points always leads to the constant δ, which is also called the also *Feigenbaum*-constant.[30] The mapping is referred to as the *Feigenbaum*-diagram in this context (Feigenbaum, 1978).

The following will examine the area beyond $\lambda = 3.57$ in more detail. For this purpose, a magnification of the previous diagram is considered in Fig. 4.31.

In this diagram, the black areas that indicate a continuous structure for certain λ are initially noticeable. For other λ, however, cycles occur again, the length of which seem to

[30] Studies show that the Feigenbaum constant apparently also applies to all families of mappings that are twice continuously differentiable and exhibit a period-doubling bifurcation. See Steeb and Kunik (1989, p. 19).

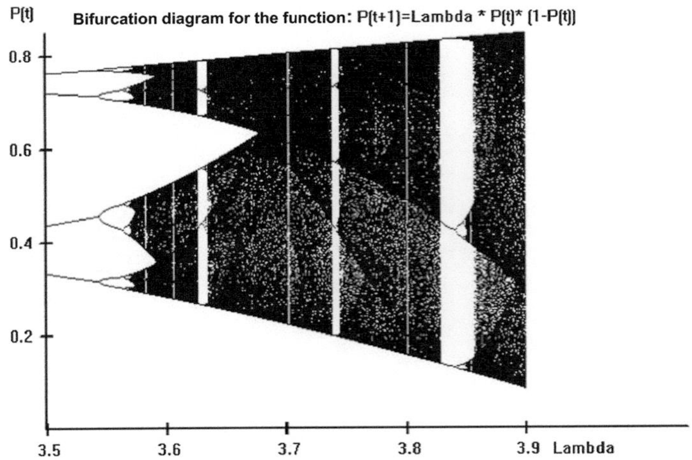

Fig. 4.31 Bifurcation diagram

halve at increasing intervals, as two adjacent black areas merge into each other. A closer analysis of the *P(t)* values shows that they cyclically switch back and forth between the black stripes according to a fixed pattern. However, their position within the black stripes varies completely irregularly. White spots appear in the black areas, which upon closer investigation reveal triple cycles, quadruple cycles, etc. These cycles continue to double until they merge into continuous black areas. The white stripes suggest that irregular areas alternate with regular ones.

This reveals a whole series of regularities that can be used to describe the chaotic areas of the system under investigation:

For example, there are period doublings between $\lambda = 2.5$ and about $\lambda = 3.57$. However, the information about *P(t)* becomes less the more inaccurately the initial value is determined and the further one progresses in time *t*. On the other hand, it can be observed that *P(t)* can only be in a very specific sub-range between 0 and 1 from a sufficiently large number *t*, and thus it can be ruled out that *P(t)* takes a value outside this sub-range.

Overall, there is a mix of order and chaos from the value $\lambda = 3.57$, about which lawful statements can be made.

4.2.1.4 Intermittency and Bifurcations

The previous section made it clear that areas of order alternate with chaotic areas, that order creates chaos and that conversely chaos can also produce order. In other words: There are something like 'islands' in the chaos (or in the order) (Seiler, 1994, p. 567). This is also referred to as intermittency intermittency.

Intermittency can therefore mean that irregular motion sequences are temporarily interrupted by regular motion sequences (Loistl, 1993, p. 23).

Table 4.3 Dynamic behaviour at selected bifurcation points

Dynamic Behaviour	λ-values and bifurcation points
Stable Point Attractor	$0.00 < \lambda < 3.00$
• Monotone Convergence	$0.00 < \lambda < 2.00$
• Oscillation	$2.00 \leq \lambda < 3.00$
Stable Cycle Attractors of Period 2^n	$3.00 \leq \lambda < 3.57$
• 2-periodic cycles	$3.00 \leq \lambda < 3.45$
• 4-periodic cycles	$3.45 \leq \lambda < 3.54$
• 8-periodic cycles	$3.54 \leq \lambda < 3.56$
• 16, 32, 64, 128, 256 etc.	$3.56 \leq \lambda < 3.57$
Irregular, Chaotic Behaviour	$3.57 \leq \lambda \leq 4.00$
• First aperiodic cycle	$\lambda = 3.68$
• 3-periodic cycle (Intermittency)	$\lambda = 3.83$

This phenomenon was graphically illustrated in the above section. The graphics show how areas of order with regular, recurring movements and areas with complex, erratic movements can exist in the same system, with both extremes alternating.

Intermittency is a kind of memory in non-linear systems, a memory of non-chaotic attractors. Intermittency is by no means a rarity in non-linear dynamic systems and suggests that both order and disorder are characteristics of the same process in a complex system.[31]

Table 4.3 provides an overview of the dynamic behaviour at certain bifurcation points.

4.2.2 Evidence of Erratic Behaviour

4.2.2.1 The *Li/Yorke* Theorem

The dynamic behaviour of a system can, in a specific case, be analysed using the theorem by *Li/Yorke*.

Li and *Yorke* describe in their article "Period three implies Chaos" (Li & Yorke, 1975) a system as chaotic if it essentially fulfils the following properties:

- A dynamic system of the form $z(t+1)=f(z(t))$ possesses periodic solutions of arbitrarily high order.
- Every non-periodic solution approaches another arbitrarily closely.
- Regardless of how closely non-periodic solutions approach each other, they will separate again.

---

[31] An interesting representation of intermittency can be found, for example, in the chapter "The intermittency transition to a chaotic attractor." in: Ott (1994, p. 272).

- Regardless of the degree of approximation of a non-periodic solution to a cycle, it will not converge to the cycle but will diverge. Thus, there are no non-periodic solutions that converge to all other solutions.

Li and *Yorke* were able to prove that the following conditions are sufficient for this:

There must be a value $z \in J$, where J is an interval that is mapped onto itself by the system-describing function f, so that:

$$f^3(z) \leq z < f(z) < f^2(z)$$

where f^n represents the n-fold composition of f with itself.

So, if you start with a starting value z at time t, i.e., $z(t)$, and insert this value into the system-describing function f, it turns out that first, the calculated value $f(z(t))$ is greater than $z(t)$ and second, inserting the value $f(z(t))$ into the function yields a result that is again greater than the previous one. A final calculation shows thirdly that the repeated application of the function to the previous result leads to the finally calculated value being less than or equal to the starting value. In this case, a chaotic area exists.

In other words: If at least one solution of period three can be proven, a chaotic area exists. Furthermore, of course, any mapping that has a three-period cycle also has a chaotic area.[32]

However, there are two criticisms that must be made regarding the *Li/Yorke* theorem:

- With the help of the *Li/Yorke* theorem, only evidence can be provided that unstable, irregular cycles exist. Due to the theorem, it is not possible to determine how frequently these cycles occur and where they can be found. Thus, in a specific case, the *Li/Yorke* theorem can provide evidence of chaotic cycles, but these may be very difficult to find.
- Another problem is the initial sensitivity of a system. In the systems considered so far, initial sensitivity has always played a major role in the assessment of a dynamic system. However, this sensitivity does not have to be given in the proof of the *Li/Yorke* theorem.

Pinkwart has precisely summarised the criticism of this theorem:

> Although the theorem proves the existence of a chaotic area, it does not exclude the possibility that there is a stable cycle for period 3 or an unstable periodic cycle of any period. Furthermore, it is possible that for a given input value, the movement may possibly converge to this cycle (Pinkwart, 1992, p. 51).

Therefore, it makes sense to add another analysis tool for the study of complex systems: The *Lyapunov* exponents.

---

[32] For the proof of this formula, refer to the article by Thien-Yien *Li* and James A. *Yorke*: Li and Yorke (1975, p. 986 ff.).

4.2.2.2 *Lyapunov* Exponents

The behaviour of a dynamic system can be analysed using the so-called *Lyapunov* exponents. The *Lyapunov* methods are named after the mathematician of the same name, Alexander M. *Lyapunov,* who provided these and many other contributions to theoretical mechanics and mathematics . The question is whether the system exhibits initial sensitivity or not.[33] To do this, two arbitrary neighbouring starting points of the dynamic development are considered and these points are tracked over time. If the points are still close together after a very long period of time, the strong law of causality applies. According to this law, similar causes lead to similar effects. Since the test result must apply to any points, no irregular behaviour would be proven in this case. However, if the points diverge strongly, i.e., exponentially far, from each other after some time, then there is an initial sensitivity of the system, which is an important, necessary criterion for irregular, chaotic system behaviour. The strong law of causality is suspended in such a case.[34]

Let z_0 and z_1 be two neighbouring points at the starting time $t = 0$. Then $\Delta z = |z_0 - z_1|$ denotes the distance between the two points. After a time t has elapsed, the points have either moved very far apart from each other or they remain close together, i.e., it holds: $|\Delta z(t)| = |\Delta z(0)| \cdot e^{L \cdot t}$.

If L takes the value 0, then $|\Delta z(t)| = |\Delta z(0)|$, i.e., the two points are still as close together after time t as they were at time 0. If $L < 0$, then $e^{L \cdot t}$ is a number between 0 and 1. This means that in this case, after a time t has elapsed, the two points are even closer together.

However, if L is greater than 0, then the two points are exponentially further apart at time t than at time 0. This value L is called *Lyapunov* exponent, named after a Russian mathematician. If you now calculate the *Lyapunov* exponent for the logistic function for other λ values, then an image like in Fig. 4.32 results.

If you follow the *Lyapunov* values in the above figure, you will find that the *Lyapunov* exponent is negative up to about $\lambda = 3.00$. This suggests that points arbitrarily close to each other still remain close to each other even after a long time and have even moved a little closer together.

---

[33] At this point, reference should again be made to the *KAM* theorem, *Kolmogorov*, Arnold and *Moser* established and proved in the sixties, according to which the movement in the phase space of classical mechanics is neither completely regular nor completely irregular, but the trajectory is sensitive to the initial conditions.

[34] Positive *Lyapunov* exponents are generally considered in the literature as a necessary, but not sufficient, criterion for the presence of chaotic system behaviour. However, there are—albeit rarely—non-chaotic cases in which the *Lyapunov* exponent is also positive, so that the criterion is not even a necessary one: $z' = z$ is a linear differential equation that is certainly not chaotic. On the other hand, obviously: $|\Delta z(t)| = |\Delta z(0)| \cdot e^{Lt}$, $(L = 1)$, since the derivative of the exponential function is again the exponential function. This means that the system completely drifts apart and is extremely dependent on the initial situation. In chaotic systems, therefore, the phase space must also be limited if one wants to prove chaos using the *Lyapunov* criterion.

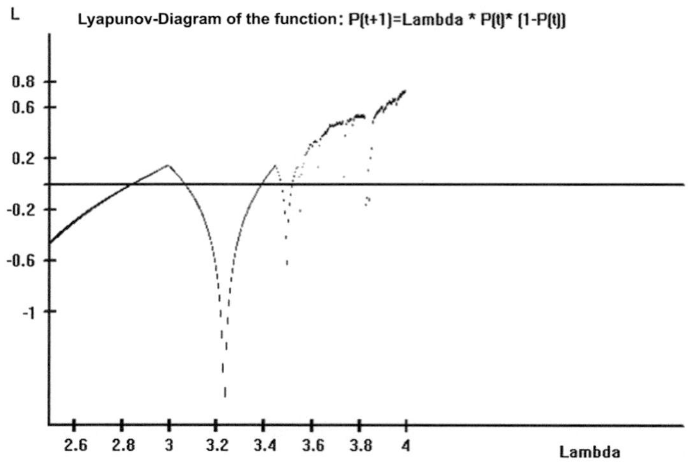

Fig. 4.32 *Lyapunov* Diagram

After this phase, the *Lyapunov* exponent reaches the value 0. This means that two points close to each other remain just as close to each other after a (finite) time course as they were at the start.

Subsequently, there is another negative phase, which is interrupted at about $\lambda = 3.449$ by a *Lyapunov* exponent with the value 0. From about $\lambda = 3.57$, positive *Lyapunov* exponents occur, indicating a chaotic behaviour of the system, as there is an initial sensitivity of the parameters in this area. From this λ value, some negative *Lyapunov* exponents are occasionally observed. They indicate areas of intermittency.

Figure 4.33 illustrates the relationship between the bifurcations and the *Lyapunov* exponents. The vertical lines refer to some bifurcation points where the *Lyapunov* exponent reaches the value zero.

4.2.2.3 Background Information: Basic Calculation of the *Lyapunov* Exponent[35]

In a system's attractor, we find numerous points of the system that are on common, but also different trajectories. The question here is whether two neighbouring starting points

[35] It should be noted that only one-dimensional systems, i.e., systems with one variable, are examined here. As a result, there is only one *Lyapunov* exponent. In multi-dimensional systems, the number of *Lyapunov* exponents is correspondingly higher. If the behaviour of a multi-dimensional system is stable and it has a point attractor, then all *Lyapunov* exponents are negative. If there is periodic behaviour with a limit cycle attractor, all but one *Lyapunov* exponents are negative. One *Lyapunov* exponent is equal to zero. In quasi-periodic systems, which have a stable n-torus, *n Lya-*

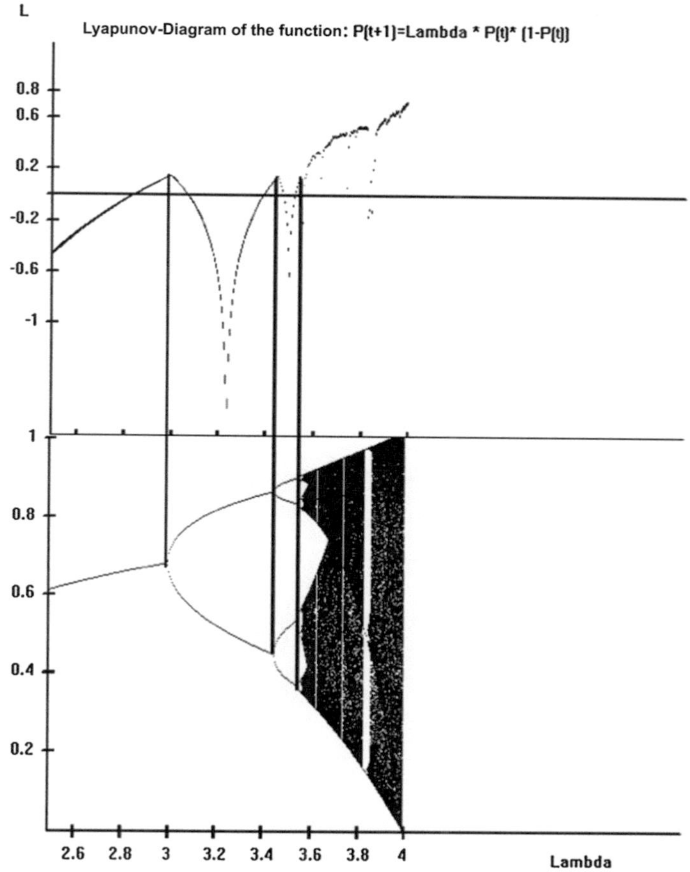

Fig. 4.33 *Lyapunov* and Bifurcation Diagram

of two trajectories are still close together after a very long period of time or diverge very strongly, i.e., exponentially far, from each other. If the latter is the case, then there is an initial sensitivity of the system, which is an important, necessary criterion for irregular, chaotic system behaviour.

Therefore, two neighbouring points $x_0(0)$ und $x_1(0)$ of a system at time $t = 0$ are considered, which should be described by the mapping f. We assume that the phase space in

punov exponents are equal to 0, the others are negative. In the case of irregular behaviour and a strange attractor, there is one positive *Lyapunov* exponent in a multi-dimensional system. Another *Lyapunov* exponent is equal to zero and the remaining exponents are negative (Loistl, 1993, p. 63).

which the trajectory is located is already constructed.[36] The points should be very close together, i.e.:

$x_1(0) = x_0(0) + h$, with $0 < h << 1$, i.e. $h \in \mathbb{R}$ is very small. So, for the distance between both points from each other:

$$\Delta x(0) = |x_0(0) - x_1(0)| \ll 1.$$

The two points are considered after two iterations and a function g is defined:

(i) $x_0(2) = f(x_0(1)) = f(f(x_0(0))) := g(x_0(0)).$
$x_1(2) = f(x_1(1)) = f(f(x_1(0))) := g(x_1(0)).$

The two points are now around

(ii) $\Delta x(2) = |x_0(2) - x_1(2)|$ apart from each other.

The Taylor series expansion[37] of the function g around the point $x_1(0)$ yields:

$$g(x_1(0)) = g(x_0(0)) + g'(x_0(0)) \cdot (x_1(0) - x_0(0)) + \ldots$$

with $g'(x_0(0)) = \left[\frac{\delta g(x_0)}{\delta t}\right]_{x_0 = x_0(0)}$

From (i) and (ii) follows:

(iii) $|x_0(2)| = |g(x_1(0)) - g(x_0(0))| = |g'(x_0(0))| \cdot |\Delta x(0)|$

Using the chain rule for derivatives results in:

$\left|\Delta x(2) / \Delta x(0)\right| = \left|g'(x_0(0))\right| = \left|f'(x_0(1))\right| \cdot \left|f'(x_0(0))\right|$

Using (iii) results in:

(iv) $g'(x_0(0)) = f'(f(x_0(0))) \cdot f'(x_0(0)) = f'(x_0(1)) \cdot f'(x_0(0))$

It is now assumed that the distance between two points in a dynamic non-linear system grows or shrinks exponentially:

$|\Delta x(t)| = |\Delta x(0)| \cdot e^{L \cdot t}$, L is called *Lyapunov* exponent, t is a discrete time variable.

Now consider the case $t := 2$:

Then the following applies:

$$|\Delta x(2)| = |\Delta x(0)| \cdot e^{L \cdot 2}$$

From this equation, using (iv) and taking the logarithm, follows:

$$\begin{aligned} \ln\left(\left|\Delta x(t) / \Delta x(0)\right|\right) &= 2 \cdot L = \ln\left(\left|f'(x_0(1)) \cdot f'(x_0(0))\right|\right) \\ &= \ln\left(\left|f'(x_0(1))\right|\right) + \ln\left(\left|f'(x_0(0))\right|\right) \end{aligned}$$

[36] The construction of the phase space is anything but trivial, especially when dealing with empirical time series from which the attractor with the associated phase space is to be constructed. This will be discussed in detail in the empirical part of this book.

[37] In general, for the Taylor series expansion of a function f around the point a: $f(x) = \sum_{k=0}^{\infty} \frac{f^{(k)}(a)}{k!} \cdot (x - a)^k$.

A slight transformation results in the following formula for the calculation of the *Lyapunov* exponent for $t = 2$:

$$L = \frac{1}{2} \cdot \left(\ln\left(\left|f'(x_0(1))\right|\right) + \ln\left(\left|f'(x_0(0))\right|\right)\right)$$

$$\Leftrightarrow L = \frac{1}{2} \cdot \sum_{k=0}^{1} \ln\left|f'(x(k))\right|$$

In general, the calculation of the *Lyapunov* exponent L results in:

$$L = \lim_{t\to\infty} \frac{1}{t} \cdot \sum_{k=0}^{t-1} \ln\left|f'(x(k))\right|$$

There are also a number of other analysis methods, such as considering the metric or topological entropy.

For our purposes, however, the considered analysis methods for determining the dimension, especially the Hausdorff *Hausdorff* dimension, the theorem of *Li/Yorke*, as well as the calculation method for determining the *Lyapunov* exponents are sufficient, as they provide a good overview of the existing possibilities for analysing dynamic systems.

4.3 Catastrophe Theory

4.3.1 René *Thom's* Theory

4.3.1.1 'Catastrophes' from a Scientific Perspective

A specific theoretical component, which is also discussed here under the heading 'Complexity Sciences' or 'Science of Complex Systems' due to its great affinity to the previous considerations, is the so-called Catastrophe Theory.[38] It goes back to the French mathematician René *Thom* and deals with Complex Systems, whose dynamics suddenly and unexpectedly change due to external forces. For this reason, *Thom's* theory can be understood as an analysis of morphogenesis, i.e., the emergence of new forms (Thom, 1975).

Cramer notes that the term catastrophe has become established in the underlying mathematics and probably dramatises the event too much (Cramer, 1988, p. 160).

4.3.1.2 About Singularities, Manifolds and Catastrophe Sets

In complex systems, as has become clear in the previous sections, breakpoints can occur that cause the system to become destabilised and jump from one stable state to another. In the language of catastrophe theory, such breakpoints are referred to as singularities *singularities.*

[38] A brief mathematical introduction to this topic can be found in: Zhang (1991).

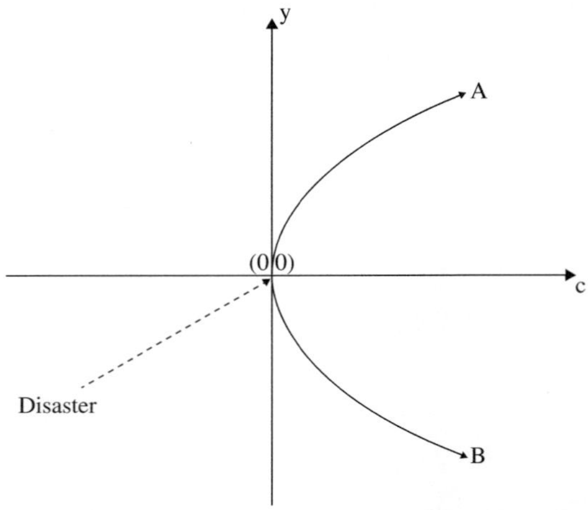

Fig. 4.34 Bifurcation

The simple Fig. 4.34, which reflects the solution set of a differential equation of the form $c - y^2 = 0$, illustrates this scenario, where $c = c_1, c_2, \ldots, c_n$ represent the external parameters of the system and $y = y_1, y_2, \ldots, y_n$ are the internal variables. The external parameters are also referred to as control variables.

The system *S* to be examined is thought of as a as *manifold*. Simplified, a manifold is understood as metric sections of a of a *topological space*. Normally, a space is measurable with a metre measure. This is also referred to as metric spaces. This measurability does not apply to a topological space. However, a topological space can be constructed from a point like a metric space. This construction, however, is not done by measurable vectors, but rather by (open) environments of the point.[39]

For catastrophe theory, only those mappings from a topological space to another space that exhibit a singularity are of interest. Usually, functions that have at least cubic powers are considered in this context. However, to maintain the connection to the previous considerations, a parabola, i.e., a function with a square power, is examined here

[39] Definition of a topological space: Let X be a set. A system of subsets T of X is called a topology on X if the following applies:

i. The empty set and X are subsets of T.
ii. If U and V are subsets of T, then their intersection is also a subset of T.
iii. If I is an arbitrary index set and U_i for all i from I is a subset of T, then the union of all U_i is also a subset of T.

If you follow this definition of topology, then a topological space is understood as a pair (X,T), which consists of a set X and a topology T on X. See Forster (1981, p. 8).

as an exception. The singularity therefore corresponds to a bifurcation. The bifurcation point is located at the intersection of the coordinate system in the example $c - y^2 = 0$.

Driven by the external parameters c_i, the system traverses the abscissa. The parameters or control variables are dependent on the internal variables y_i. At the point (0,0), a qualitative change occurs: The control variables bring the system out of balance. If $c < 0$, there is no solution. If, on the other hand, $c > 0$, there are two possible solutions. The system is called *degenerate* when it runs into an unstable area. The degenerate part of the system is called called *catastrophe set.*

Now consider the mapping from the original system to a control system. The behaviour of the system is captured by a vector that moves across the manifold. The number of control variables is smaller than the number of internal variables. If the number of control variables is at most four, then according to *Thom* there are exactly seven types of catastrophes, from the fold, the cusp, the swallowtail to the so-called parabolic mist. The disturbed function must look significantly different from the undisturbed one. An exception is the parabola, which is why it is of lesser interest for catastrophe theory. However, if the function is disturbed—the simplest case is the so-called fold—then the system S is projected onto a control parameter space K in such a way that the catastrophe set is obtained. To achieve this, the extreme values of the function are projected onto the parameter level, as illustrated in Fig. 4.35.

The points, lines, surfaces of the fold edges that are projected are called called *singularity set,* those that are located on the parameter level are referred to as *catastrophe-* or

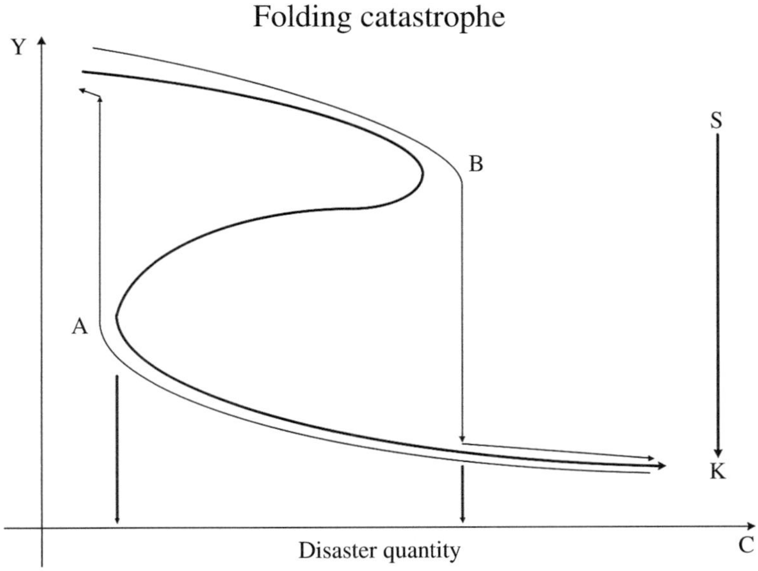

Fig. 4.35 Fold catastrophe

bifurcation set. The underlying mathematics of the catastrophe set is differential topology, i.e., the theory of differentiable manifolds.

4.3.2 Hermann *Haken's* Criticism

If one follows Hermann *Haken*, then the possibility of a topological version of instability and emergence is only given under very limited conditions, namely exactly when the system is subject to a potential, i.e. is attracted by a force that always originates from the same point, regardless of the path the system chooses.[40]

In contrast, *Haken's* theory, the *Synergetics*, is tailored to emergent self-organisation. Self-organising systems often do not follow a potential. They create their own target points. This is particularly important for socio-economic systems. Despite his criticism, *Haken* considers it possible to integrate catastrophe theory, as he says, "even into the conceptual structure of synergetics," since *Thom* "refers to the qualitative changes ('catastrophes') of (in our words) order parameters, which satisfy potential equations, as they often occur in synergetics" (Haken, 2014, p. 41). What order parameters should be, among other things, we will see in the following chapter, in which the concept of *Synergetics* is explained.

4.4 Synergetics—The Theory of Self-Organisation

4.4.1 The Basic Idea of Synergetics

4.4.1.1 Explaining Self-Organisation Phenomena

The so-called also finds its place in the science of complex systems, as it, like catastrophe theory, has great affinities to the chaotic theoretical considerations of the first sections of this chapter.[41]

Synergetics is an interdisciplinary approach that allows the self-organisation of complex systems to be investigated.[42] *Eckert*, *Schiepek* et al. state:

[40] The problem of classifying static instabilities is explained by *Haken* in: Haken (1981, p. 145 ff.).

[41] *Ehrensberger* points out that there are a multitude of term variants and synonyms for the term 'synergetics'. He counts synergy effect, synergy potential, synergetic potential, synergisms, and synergy effect among the term variants, with the synonymous use of synergy and synergy effect having a tradition in the literature. *Ehrensberger* cautions that the discussion of the topic of synergetics is complicated by the inconsistent and inconsistent use of the term. Cf. Ehrensberger (1993, p. 13 ff.).

[42] The author first dealt with this in detail in his habilitation thesis (Liening, 1999).

> From the field of self-organisation theories, the *synergetics* of Stuttgart physicist Hermann Haken is the most elaborate (Eckert et al., 2006, p. 31).

In this context, emergence, the emergence of a new property through interactions[43] of the individual components of the system can be spoken of, whereby the newly emerged quality of the emergent structure cannot be reduced to its original components.[44]

Synergetics was founded in 1969 by physicist Hermann *Haken*. He was the first to show that laser light can only be explained by self-organisation phenomena.

▶ **Synergetics** The *synergetics* describes self-organised order formation in systems through the behaviour of the system components. It refers to systems that are characterised by openness, dynamics, and complexity (Schiepek et al., 1997, p. 122).

Haken himself writes:

> The basic idea that synergetics has borrowed from nature is easy to explain. To imprint a structure on an object or to equip it with certain functions, we usually use the thought model of the sculptor who chisels out the individual parts of the marble block in the finest detail, for example to create a head. In a similar way, we systematically determine the conductor tracks and the arrangement of its individual elements in a chip so that it can perform predetermined computing operations or logical links. In a company, each employee is precisely told what to do.
>
> All these steps require a high level of planning and control effort. In contrast to this planned organisation and detailed control of a system, synergetics, following nature, presents another principle, namely that of self-organisation, in which only certain framework conditions are given to the system, which generally consists of many parts, and then the system finds its structure and especially function by itself (Haken, 2006b, p. 17)

4.4.1.2 About the Laser[45]

Every laser system essentially consists of three components: two mirrors and a laser medium, which can be designed differently depending on the type of laser.[46] In the case of a gas discharge lamp, the laser arrangement consists of a tube at the ends of which are the two mirrors, one of which is partially transparent. In between is a gas mixture.

---

[43] The term synergetics is borrowed from the Greek word 'συνηεργειη', which means 'working together'.

[44] It should be noted, however, that not every emergent process must already be a process of self-organisation.

[45] Laser is an acronym, the letters of which stand for: "**L**ight **A**mplification by **S**timulated **E**mission of **R**adiation". The term thus literally describes a light amplification by a stimulated radiation emission.

[46] There are different types of lasers such as solid-state lasers (ruby lasers), liquid lasers, free-electron lasers or the gas laser described here. Cf. Kurnaz and Willemsen (2004).

In the consideration of systems, synergetics initially starts from an initial structure. In synergetics, a distinction is made between a macro and a micro level (Haken, 2006a).

The actual system is located at the *micro level*. It is characterised by a high number of elements and usually has a multitude of degrees of freedom. On this micro level, in the case of lasers (example of a gas discharge lamp), countless atoms or molecules in the gas mixture are continuously energetically excited by electricity. This current serves as an external parameter or *control parameter* (Haken, 2006a, p. 21).

Below a critical value, the corresponding experimental setup functions like a normal lamp: The atoms or molecules emit random, incoherent, chaotic light waves or, depending on the perspective, photons (light particles).[47] When these photons hit other atoms, they release additional photons. The experimental setup reflects the photons at the ends of the tube, thus greatly amplifying the entire process. This system can be described by non-linear evolution equations that include internal variables, so-called *modes*, (Haken, 2006a, p. 21).

However, above the critical current strength, this specific value, which is specifically referred to as 'laser threshold' or more generally as *phase transition*, the property of the light changes dramatically in a *self-organising* way. Self-organisation at this level now means the reduction of degrees of freedom. The system becomes unstable due to the change in the control parameter, with a large number of stable variables now being expressed by a small selection, possibly even by just one unstable internal variable: This variable, this emergent laser light wave, is referred to as the *order parameter*. It determines the emission actions of all other atoms or molecules, so that the bundled laser light is created by all atoms oscillating almost in unison or emitting light of almost only one wavelength, which escapes from the partially transparent mirror. *Haken* speaks in this context of 'enslavement'. The unstable modes thus enslave the stable modes (Haken, 2006a, p. 22).

In the process of self-organisation, a few elements crystallise out of the multitude of elements, influencing the enslavement of the system. This *enslavement principle* thus creates a new structure. These few parameters, the order parameters, can be observed on a macro level. On this macro level, the dynamic patterns or order structures of the system become visible. While the initial system has a homogeneous structure, the symmetry is broken in the emerged end system.[48]

---

[47] Here, photon and wave are somewhat sloppily equated. This is based on the generally accepted idea that light has both particle and wave characteristics. The physicist among the readers may forgive the author for the layman's description of the physical processes in the laser.

[48] *Haken* points out in a lecture explaining the symmetry break that we also find broken symmetries in language: "…for example, when we say the word 'castle', it can mean a door lock, but also a manor. Or the word 'cock' can mean faucet or rooster. Obviously, the symmetry must be broken here by additional information" (Haken, 1979). The word 'castle' thus contains mirror-symmetrically two lines of development, two interpretations. This development would normally be illustrated in the form of a so-called bifurcation diagram. The fact that only one of the two interpretations applies in the concrete case breaks the symmetry of the word system. At this point, reference should be made to the fundamental work on synergetics (Haken, 1981).

Now, this theory of laser light is by no means just a theory of physics. It is a general theory that can serve to describe and explain self-organisation processes in biology, medicine, sociology, psychology, but also in economics.

The theory of self-organisation is a powerful alternative to the typical traditional, mechanistic views, which, as elaborated in the first part of the book, are still partly found in economics.

Figure 4.36 illustrates the concept of synergetics.

A prerequisite for the self-organisation process is that the system is operationally closed, but thermodynamically or energetically considered an open system, i.e., consuming energy or dissipative. Because a system can only exist in a self-organising way if energy is supplied and consumed from the outside, as the example of the laser shows; just like a pendulum can only swing permanently if it is continuously supplied with energy. The energy does not determine the specific behaviour of the system, the type of movement—in the case of the pendulum, the pendulum movement—but without it, the movement, the dynamics of the system, would come to a standstill.

In short: Only open systems can produce self-organised evolutionary structures, all others die, chemically speaking, the heat death (Prigogine & Nicolis, 1987). In this context, we speak of control parameters, which, however, at best symbolise unspecific control by the environment (Tschacher & Brunner, 1997, p. 102). Ultimately, these do not dictate the order structure, but they do enable it on the one hand by influencing the micro level through the control of energy supply. On the other hand, there is also an interplay between order parameters and control parameters due to mutual influence. Once such

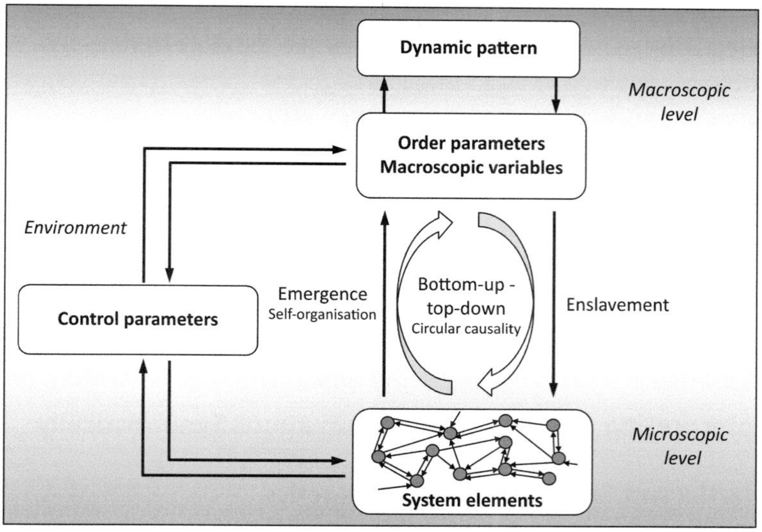

Fig. 4.36 The Synergetic Concept. (Based on: Strunk and Schiepek 1994, p. 27, see also: Strunk and Schiepek 2006, p. 81)

patterns have emerged, they can destabilise again, which can lead to new order parameters. Which of the possible behaviours ultimately manifest as order parameters can often only be predicted with difficulty, as even the smallest change in the initial conditions can lead to completely different order parameters, which would have been unlikely without this change (butterfly effect).

4.4.1.3 Swarm Intelligence—The Migration of Birds (Liening & Mittelstädt, 2008, pp. 41–43)

The migration of birds to their winter quarters can serve as an example of synergetics. Self-organisation refers to the reduction of degrees of freedom at the micro level, i.e., each bird could indeed choose and follow a flight route completely independently, but this does not happen. In the process of self-organissation of migratory birds, flocks of birds form. From the multitude of parameters that could influence the system of the bird swarm, a few crystallise out that influence the self-organisation of the system. These few parameters are called order parameters and can be observed at a macro level. In the case of the bird swarm, this is, for example, the wing shape or the size of the birds. From these parameters, the distance between the birds and thus the reaction behaviour as well as the energetic effect of the wind shadow are derived. At the macro level, this results in the formation of the system, which the system components (here: the birds) adhere to. Not the observation of individual birds, but of the swarm, makes the patterns or the order structures of the system recognisable. The swarm intelligence described here is a very simple form of self-organisation, which is based on only three rules that the individual bird follows (Otto et al., 2007, p. 155):

- Cohesion: Try to move towards the centre of the swarm.
- Separation: Move outward as soon as someone gets too close to you.
- Alignment: Move like your direct neighbour.

As a result, the group acts without central command, as each is autonomous, and the swarm does not need central supervision, but acts dynamically and self-organised (synergetics). Moreover, swarms are very flexible, they show a high adaptability to different conditions (mountains, houses, lakes). Swarms are very robust against the failure of individuals. Overall, the order is in the swarm, not in the individual bird (Liening & Mittelstädt, 2008, pp. 41–43).

4.4.2 Interpreting Companies and Innovations Synergistically

4.4.2.1 Partial and Total Systems in Synergetics

In the following, two systems S_1 and S_2 are considered as examples. The system S_1 is a company without innovations and system S_2 are innovations. The state of the systems can be characterised by a multitude of modes. For example, the system S_1 can be described by a variety of key figures such as sales, profit, ROI, liquidity, debt ratio, number of employees, labour productivity, return on sales, capital turnover, etc., and the system S_2 can be described by the degree of novelty (first, uniqueness), uncertainty, degree of complexity, conflict content, etc.

Furthermore, it is assumed that the system S_2 can act on the system S_1 through certain 'forces': For example, in system S_2, an innovation could demand a restructuring of the organisation because the innovation initiates an entrepreneurship process within the company, which is associated with a completely new production process that greatly increases labour productivity. The innovation would then cause a change in state in S_1. However, it could be that the innovation leads to (unwanted) layoffs of employees in S_1, as the specific innovation is also associated with rationalisation measures. If S_2 no longer intervenes to the same extent by changing its parameters in S_1, for example by turning the original radical innovation into an incremental innovation by significantly reducing the scope of change, then S_1 moves back towards its initial state, i.e., the wave of layoffs triggered by the innovation in this example would be significantly mitigated. In the language of synergetics, it is said that the system S_2 *organises* the system S_1.

It was again noted that synergetics is tailored to self-organisation. Therefore, it is a very insightful step to now consider all forces acting on the system S_1 as parts of a total system (Haken, 1981, p. 211 ff.). For this purpose, the total system $S = S_1S_2$ is considered, i.e., a company system with innovations. Then it can be said that S organises itself, so that the effects of the subsystem S_2 on the subsystem S_1 represent internal forces. *Haken* states:

> The remarkable process in self-organising systems (…) is the following: Although energy is supplied to the system in a completely irregular manner, it forms itself in a precisely defined macroscopic mode (Haken, 1981, p. 15).

4.4.2.2 The Mathematical Trick: The 'Slaving Principle'

However, there is a problem when describing self-organising systems: Such complex systems can usually only be described by many variables and thus often only by a comprehensive system of equations. For this reason, a mathematical trick is used, which consists of describing the stable variables directly by unstable order parameters. It turns out that in general, many stable and few unstable variables occur. Therefore, part S_1 of a system immediately follows part S_2. It is said that system S_2 has *enslaved* system S_1 (slaving principle). This reduces the number of degrees of freedom and thus the complexity and establishes a new state that is expressed by a few order parameters.

In synergetics, the enslavement principle is meant completely value-neutral. It does not represent a coercive measure triggered by certain actors. *Erdmann* states from an economic perspective:

> Rather, enslavement occurs in decision-making situations when the economic subjects involved—in pursuit of their own benefit and the resulting actual or perceived constraints—make their behaviour dependent on the existing order (e.g., price system, legal order), an

> explicit or implicit norm, or a prevailing fashion. With their behaviour, the actors simultaneously and spontaneously create the order to which they submit in their decisions (Erdmann 1993, p. 33).

Haken compares the results obtained from a direct computer calculation with the calculated results based on the enslavement principle using the example of a specific system of equations[49]. It turns out that for a certain time interval a very accurate match can be demonstrated, but suddenly a discrepancy occurs that "remains for all later times" (Haken, 1981, p. 351). Thus, *Haken* shows that—when the enslavement principle fails and the previously stable solution is destabilised by changing a control parameter—irregular, chaotic movements occur, so that chaos in systems is closely related to the failure of the enslavement principle.

Instead of enslavement, one could also speak of consensualisation or synchronisation (Eckert et al., 2006, p. 34). While the self-organisation arrow in the scheme emphasises that a new order parameter, that something new emerges from the micro level—we could also speak of emergence here—the enslavement arrow indicates that this new order parameter is stabilised, and only then receives its ordering character, by permanent feedback with the micro level, a synchronisation of an unstable situation there occurs.

When viewing systems synergistically, as described in the above explanations, a new kind of view is needed to understand them, which makes clear that it is generally hardly possible to comprehensively control a complex system such as an innovative growth company, because the consequences of even the smallest intervention can be unpredictable (butterfly effect).

4.4.3 Critical Remark

Overall, synergetics is a theory of self-organisation in which there is no global stability criterion. According to Haken , all internal variables can even be expressed by order parameters. All stable modes are thereby eliminated. Thus, only the unstable modes, the order parameters, are of importance. Modes are therefore presupposed. Through the enslavement, new system properties emerge. However, the question of how these properties come about at the bifurcation point, that point at which the system state changes, and in what relation the old state stands to the new one, is not answered. In synergetics, the old structure is not mapped into the new one. In this respect, a topological variant is missing. Despite this point of criticism, overall, synergetics provides a suitable approach to profitably describe and analyse self-organising systems, and especially economic systems, which are based on free, market-economic principles.

[49] *Haken* considers the so-called Lorenz system, which exhibits a strange attractor. See Haken (1981, p. 342 ff.).

Synergetics shows that at the micro level of a system, there is not a finished blueprint, but merely the starting point for the evolution of a form, whose shaping energy is added from the outside through control parameters and which—as already outlined in Chap. 3 of the first part of the book, as a kind of 'creatio ex nihilo'—gradually emerges on the macro level through feedback loops as a dynamic structure using order parameters.

The exciting thing about the synergetic interpretation of the economy becomes clear in that it shows that complex systems like economies can only generate themselves in a self-organising *manner.*

For these reasons, and also because of the above-mentioned butterfly effect, it is generally hardly possible to comprehensively control a complex system like, for example, the economy of a country, because even the smallest intervention can have unforeseeable consequences in the long run.

The initial insights from synergetics presented here can also help us to open our eyes to profitably utilise the self-organising forces of freedom inherent in the market economy.

Both chaos theory, catastrophe theory, and synergetics have in common that they study non-linear complex systems. If we subsume these three comparable approaches under the term 'science of complex systems' or 'complexity sciences', it is of central importance to assign a special status to the terms 'order' and 'chaos'. In the following, an exact definition for these terms will be developed. Furthermore, important questions and points of criticism will be addressed and critically discussed in this context.

4.5 Order and Chaos only in the Computer? About Definitions, Bolzano-Weierstraß and 'Controlling Complexity'

4.5.1 'Working definitions'

4.5.1.1 The Genesis of the Term 'Chaos'—Sharpening of the Complexity Concept

In the preceding sections, it has become clear that a wide variety of developments can occur when considering non-linear systems. Linear or more generally lineal systems, on the other hand, represent rather a primitive idealisation of dynamic processes, as they can only reflect a small number of behaviours. For example, the instability of equilibria does not necessarily mean that the system must 'explode', as would be the case with linear systems.

There are much more complicated and multifaceted behaviours that can only be modeled using non-linear systems. For example, possible irregular behaviour that occurs with the smallest changes in initial conditions is one of the central events that distinguish non-linear from linear systems.

This irregular behaviour is often described as complex behaviour, as *complexity,*.

Depending on the respective discipline, time, and perspective, there are quite different views on the concept of complexity. The computer scientist and physicist Seth *Lloyd* has a collection of more than 45 definitions of the concept of complexity (Backlund, 2002; Horgan, 1995).

Overall, however, two main currents can be distinguished, which point in a phenomenological and an empirical-mathematical direction.

In the phenomenological direction, the focus is on implications of complex system behaviour. This means that a system is considered complex here if it exceeds the cognitive performance of humans (Langefors, 1995).

This raises questions about technical aids as well as individual and temporal context dependencies.

On the other hand, if one considers the empirical-mathematical approaches, these are based on calculation methods of empirical system measurement, such as the calculation of *Lyapunov* exponents. Such approaches examine the sensitivity of the system (butterfly effect) or search for patterns in time series (e.g., fractal geometry). They claim to provide universal measurement methods for objective complexity assessment.

The dynamics of a system, in the sense of the empirical-mathematical direction, is the functional progression between trivial and random behaviour, as shown vividly in Fig. 4.37 by Guido *Strunk*.

The illustration specifically suggests a measure of complexity that allows the distinction between simple, complicated, complex, and finally, systems based on randomness. The simpler the dynamics, the lower the complexity, and vice versa. It is noticeable in the diagram that complexity, starting from simple order, continues to grow with increasing dynamisation, but the moment it reaches randomness, it abruptly drops to zero. This is intended to show that the supposedly maximum complexity, randomness, should be

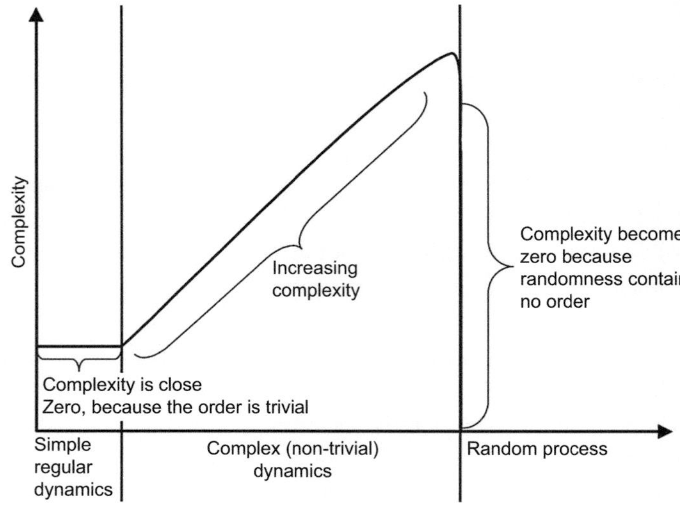

Fig. 4.37 Dynamics and complexity. *Source* Strunk and Schiepek (2014, p. 79)

separated from actual complexity. This makes sense, as complex systems contain an order, even if it is difficult to recognise. When we say that an economic problem is very complex, we do not mean that it is subject to a random process. Therefore, it makes sense not to refer to randomness as complexity due to the absence of order.

Traditionally, one observes order patterns and attributes deviations from them to statistical measurement errors or a random process. In complexity research, this perspective is reversed by first filtering out the trivial order from the supposedly ordered systems. And what remains, i.e., the supposed measurement error or the supposed random process, is then examined more closely. And often, more can be learned about the structure of the system from this seemingly random noise than by observing the obvious order (Strunk & Schiepek, 2014, p. 79).

Complexity in this context means a dynamic that behaves deterministically chaotic: deterministic in the sense that the behaviour of the system arises from its properties and chaotic in the sense that the system imitates randomness through its sensitivity and is only predictable in the very short term.

The reduction of complex system behaviour to deterministic-chaotic processes may seem abstract at first glance, but in fact, such systems are the subject of numerous research fields, such as chemistry (Belousov, 1959; Prigogine, 1955, 1987, 1995; Prigogine & Stengers, 1984, 1986, 1993; Zhabotinsky, 1964), astronomy (Buchler et al., 1995a, b; Contopoulos, 2002; Hasan & Norman, 1990; Wisdom, 1987a, b), biology (May, 1974, 1975; Olsen et al., 1988; Petrovskii & Malchow, 2001), psychology (Strunk & Schiepek, 1994; Guastello, 2001; Haken & Schiepek, 2010; Strunk & Schiepek, 2006; Tschacher, 1997), sociology (Willke, 1989; Young, 1991; Gregersen & Sailer, 1993; Urry, 2005) or electrical engineering (Cuomo & Oppenheim, 1993; Feely, 1997; Lynch & Steele, 2011; Mork & Stuehm, 1994). Numerous complexity science works are also located in economics (Baumol & Benhabib, 1989; Day, 1992, 1994; Gouel, 2012; Liening, 1998; Mullineux et al., 1993; Strunk, 2012). In the *Journal of Economic Behaviour and Organisation*, more than 50 articles dealt with chaotic market dynamics alone between the years 1990 and 2011 (Strunk, 2012, p. 67).

Often, the two terms complexity and chaos were used synonymously in this work. The diverse aspects of non-linear systems that have been addressed in the previous sections now allow for a precise definition of complexity. While we always spoke of complexity in the initial situation, we now want to sharpen the language by actually speaking of chaos, in order to finally generate a scientifically meaningful definition of complexity.

If one initially places the term chaos in a pre-critical observation space, then this word does not represent a scientific term. Because the scientist suspects a law behind what is colloquially referred to as chaotic, which is just not accessible to the layman. However, the previous explanations have shown that chaos is indeed scientifically describable and analysable.

This raises the question, what exactly is meant by the scientific term chaos?

In answering this question, an etymological approach is first attempted. Although the etymology of a term does not always decide its current use, the origin of the word 'chaos' points to some central aspects that are still important today:

The term comes from Greek, $\chi\alpha\iota\nu\omega$, where it was originally interpreted as 'the gaping', 'open', as 'the formless primordial mass' or referred to as 'the emptiness of space'.

References to the term can be found in ancient cosmogonies, such as those of the pre-Socratic philosophers. Many creation myths of peoples begin with chaos. In the Theogony, the 'birth of the gods' *of Hesiod*,[50] chaos is described as the boundless, yawning void[51] of space filled with unformed primal matter, from which the well-ordered cosmos forms. 'Etoi men prostista chaos genet'—'First of all, truly, chaos arose'. With these words begins the myth of the creation of the world in *Hesiod's* narrative. By placing chaos at the beginning, it is contrasted with the world, it becomes the opposite of the (ordered) world. Due to the fact that chaos is also included in the genealogy, it becomes part of the world. *Ebach* notes:

> The terror of chaos is both defused and intensified. For as an attack on every order, this abyss intrudes into the order. Ever new achievements of order must be mobilised against chaos. And every act of banishment creates new chaos. But the greatest chaos arises from the attempt to completely banish chaos, as nothing creates such great uncertainty as the attempt to establish total security (Ebach, 1995, p. 17 f.).

Paslack interprets *Hesiod's* myth in such a way that he considers the beginning of the world in *Hesiod* to be a multiple and, in structural terms, extremely complicated process. He notes that chaos contributes to the constitution of the world.

> (Chaos, the author.) does not disappear from the world, but remains 'underground': it forever forms the 'dark' side of reality, although—in a strange inversion of polarities—the bright 'ether' and the 'daylight' also originate from it (Paslack 1996, p. 31 f.).

A comparable[52] reference of chaos and (ordered) world can be found in the Genesis of the Bible, where the desert and emptiness is the primal ground of all becoming (Tohuwabohu), from which the ordered structure of the cosmos emerges (Genesis). 'Tohuwabohu' "is an alliterative word combination, where bohu, which does not exist alone, serves as an intensification of tohu. Tohu—that is not nothing, but the nullifying,

---

[50] It should be noted that scholars do not agree on whether the Theogony can actually be attributed to *Hesiod*. See: Sitzler (1984, p. 61 ff.).

[51] The word chaos is related to the term 'chasko' (yawn).

[52] The term 'similar' is used deliberately here, as a more precise etymological description of the term 'chaos' actually requires a specification corresponding to the respective mythological context. Thus, *Hesiod's* definition of chaos is specifically Greek. However, since the above explanations are only intended to provide a basic historical interpretation of the concept of chaos, the chosen description of the historical interpretation patterns is sufficient.

annihilating. It is this null state of the world before creation that God transforms into a world enabling life. This transformation is creation, not the creation of something from nothing" (Ebach, 1995, p. 22).

If one follows modern physics, one cannot fully agree with this kind of embedding of chaos in the world. Some physicists, including *Hawking*, rather reverse the just presented relationship of chaos and order. They assume that at the beginning of the creation of the cosmos, it was in a state of highest order and thus lowest entropy. This entropy has been increasing ever since, causing the *arrow of time*, the irreversibility (Hawking, 1993).

But regardless of whether one follows the modern physicists or the ancient myths, the concept of chaos is closely linked to the concept of order, and one cannot be thought of without the other.

The references to the ancient myths show that chaos is conceived as a state of beginning from which order arises.

Modern physics, on the other hand, shows that chaos can also be seen as the decay of order.

If one leaves this global perspective, then it can happen, when viewed as a whole, in dynamic (local) processes that seemingly stable situations at certain critical points tip over into chaotic ones, which can then stabilise into new orders.

4.5.1.2 Preliminary Interpretation of the Concept of Chaos

Nowadays, the term 'chaos' is often seen as negative. This is because it is often associated with confusion, unrest, destruction, and fear. We speak of traffic chaos, chaotic discussions, days of chaos, chaos, etc. Thus, Harold *Bloom*, for example, labels our era from a literary perspective as the 'chaotic age'.[53]

The term 'order', on the other hand, is colloquially rather positively connoted, "because", as *Lentz,* says, "it is directly associated with structure, clarity, determinacy, and trust" (Lentz, 1993, p. 9).

The term chaos can also be defined positively if it is associated with 'creativity, surprise, and entertainment'.

Similarly, the concept of order can have a negative side, which is associated with "sterility, rigidity, and boredom" (Lentz, 1993, p. 9).

4.5.1.3 Definitions of Chaos and Complexity

Cramer notes that chaos "in our current language usage is a rather worn-out word" (Cramer, 1988, p. 158). If we consider the everyday notions of chaos presented above, it

[53] *Bloom* formulates a literary canon for the 'aristocratic', the 'democratic' and the 'chaotic age', including authors such as Franz *Kafka,* Marcel *Proust,* Sigmund *Freud* or James *Joyce* in the latter (Bloom, 1994). *Bloom* does not justify the new age scientifically or historically, but, as *Zils* writes, with "the obvious. Although our century claims to continue the democratic age, the examination of the leading, thus typical authors (...) suggests the characterisation as 'chaotic'" (Zils, 2009, p. 116).

becomes clear that the new approach reveals a general principle that can be rather misleadingly described with the term chaos.[54]

Therefore, a scientific term should be introduced in the following, which should be called complexity, but which includes those notions of chaos that we have already hinted at. A clear definition is not quite as simple as *Devaney* has rightly noted:

> There are many possible definitions of chaos in a dynamical system, some stronger and some weaker … (Devaney, 1989, p. 50)

Also, *Loistl* and *Betz* point out that it is not clearly defined in the scientific literature what is to be understood by chaotic or complex behaviour. They discuss a multitude of chaos definitions, from which two are briefly selected, and then a third aspect is added:[55]

In connection with the analysis of erratic behaviour, the theorem of *Li* and *Yorke* has already been explained. Indeed, this criterion represents the first definition of complexity. Therefore, it should be summarised again.

▶ **Complexity according to *Li/Yorke*** A system is called chaotic or complex if it essentially fulfils the following properties:

- A dynamic system of the form $x(t+1) = f(x(t))$ has periodic solutions of arbitrarily high order.
- Any non-periodic solution approaches another arbitrarily closely.
- Regardless of how closely non-periodic solutions approach each other, they will diverge again.
- Regardless of the degree of approximation of a non-periodic solution to a cycle, it will not converge to the cycle, but diverge. Thus, there are no non-periodic solutions that converge to all other solutions (Li & Yorke, 1975).

Li and *Yorke* were able to prove that it is sufficient if a cycle of period three is present.

This definition offers a relatively simple way to prove complex functions. If there is a cycle of period three in a one-dimensional, discrete system, then the system goes through periodic cycles of arbitrarily high order as well as aperiodic cycles, thus exhibiting chaos.

As already explained, however, this definition does not make it clear whether a certain dynamic behaviour is independent of its initial values. The example of a simple non-linear

[54] This opinion is also shared by *Wesson*. Cf. Wesson (1995, p. 50).

[55] *Loistl* and *Betz* analyse the definition of chaos according to *Li/Yorke,* according to *Devaney, Marotto* and according to *Diamond.* We leave out the definition of *Marotto* and *Diamond* in our consideration, because the explanation of their strictly mathematical definitions would go too far at this point. Cf. Loistl (1993, pp. 37–49 passim).

function has shown that the slightest changes in the initial conditions can lead to drastically different system behaviours. *Loistl* and *Betz* point out that the definition of *Li/Yorke* also allows solutions that do not have a sensitive dependence on the initial conditions, which is necessary for chaos or complexity in the modern sense.

Secondly, we look at the definition of *Devaney*.

▶ **Complexity (according to *Devaney*)** A mapping *f*: from a set V to itself is called complex if the following characteristics apply:

- *f* is sensitively dependent on initial conditions, making the solution paths unpredictable,
- *f* is topologically transitive, so the overall system cannot be broken down into subsystems, and
- there exist periodic points that are dense in V, representing an element of regularity amidst the seemingly random solution behaviour (Devaney, 1989, p. 50).

In the section on attractors and fractals (Sect. 4.1), it became clear that a key characteristic of dissipative chaotic systems is the presence of Strange Attractors.

▶ **Complexity (in reference to *Mandelbrot*)** A system is called complex if it exhibits a Strange Attractor. In contrast to other attractors, they are characterised by self-similarity and fractal dimension.

The paraphrased definitions reflect much of what has been established so far in this work:

Dynamic systems can have both periodic and non-periodic solutions. Such a system cannot be simply broken down into its components and reassembled. Moreover, irregular developments are characterised by unpredictability. Important in this context is also the system's sensitivity to initial conditions, which can be investigated using *Lyapunov* exponents.

Therefore, it can be concluded that the following points are essentially sufficient to define chaos or complexity:

▶ **Complexity**

- The dynamic system is non-linear (Non-linearity).
- The dynamics of the system are deterministic (Determinism).
- The system arises through iteration or feedback (Recursion/Non-lineality).
- The system does not have any external disturbances added (Endogeneity).
- The behaviour of observed trajectories is sensitive to arbitrarily small changes in the initial conditions (Positive *Lyapunov* exponent).
- The underlying attractor is 'strange', i.e., its structure is self-similar, has an infinitely long boundary, and exhibits a fractal dimension (Strange attractor).

- In the systems considered or the above definitions of complexity, a certain openness is always assumed, so that energy can flow through (dissipativity).[56]
- Finally, continuous systems can only exhibit complex behaviour if at least three system variables are present.[57]
- The system exhibits a three-period cycle (Three-cycle).
- There is an element of regularity amidst the apparently random solution behaviour (or vice versa) (Intermittency).

The first four aspects can be described as necessary prerequisites for the emergence of chaos in dynamic systems. The fifth and sixth aspect is important for proving chaos in a dissipative, dynamic system. The last two aspects can be used as alternative criteria for proving chaos.

In short, concise terms, Chaos or Complexity can be defined in a three-step process:

▶ **Complexity** The complexity of a dissipative system can be described by the following three criteria:

i. In a dynamic, dissipative, mathematically describable system, complexity *can* arise when the following conditions are met:
   - *Non-linearity*
   - *Recursion/Non-lineality*
   - *Three system variables (in the continuous case)*
ii. Complexity occurs in a dissipative system *when* the following aspects are met:
   - *Initial sensitivity (positive Lyapunov exponent)*[58]
   - *(possibly) Strange attractor (fractional dimension)*[59]

---

[56] For a system to generate complex behaviour patterns, it must be open to energies or energy flow. For example, if the control parameter in the logistic equation cannot be externally changed, the dynamics cannot become chaotic unless the system is chaotic from the start. It is also important to remember that without external energy, the 2nd law of thermodynamics would apply, which we have already discussed.

[57] The necessity of three system variables for generating complexity can be illustrated, for example, by the *Lorenz* system, with the basics of this necessity already made clear by *Poincaré* when considering three-body systems. Three system variables are necessary in the continuous case for mixed feedback to occur. With two variables influencing each other, you would either have a control loop (one variable has a positive effect, one negative), or a devil's/angel's circle (the variables reinforce themselves). However, in fact, in discrete models/systems, fewer system elements can be present, as the example of the logistic equation (*Verhulst* system) shows.

[58] In the empirical part of the book, it will be necessary to clarify whether there are alternative measures to the *Lyapunov* exponent that meet the challenges in practice more adequately.

[59] This aspect of the fractional dimension naturally only applies in the theoretical case. In practice, due to the calculation method, one will almost always determine fractional dimensions, regardless of their degree of complexity.

iii. Sometimes the following can be observed:
- *Three-cycle (Li/Yorke theorem)*
- *Intermittency.*[60]

This clearly outlines the concept of complexity to be used here. The associated chaos is therefore a kind of uncertainty relation of the macroscopic world, a tendency in the concrete system course towards irregularity and unpredictability within the regularity of the global structure of the system and its determinism.

It is a tendency of non-linear systems with positive feedback towards a behaviour that is deterministic, but unpredictable.

4.5.1.4 'Order' as a Counter-concept to 'Chaos'?

In the following, the concept of order is considered. Complex systems can be characterised using new concepts of order, which are closely related to self-organisation, self-similarity, and spontaneity. Thus, the term 'spontaneous order' does not denote a state, but rather describes a process of how order arises. Spontaneous ordering is closely related to self-organisation. One can agree with *Roth's* formulation, who describes self-organissing processes as those processes that "within a more or less wide range of initial and boundary conditions assume a very specific ordered state or a sequence of ordered states (limit cycle). Such a state or sequence of states can be understood as an attractor in the mathematical sense. The achievement of the specific state of order is not or not significantly imposed from the outside, but results from the specific properties of the components involved in the process. The state of order is achieved 'spontaneously' (Roth, quoted after Schmidtchen, 1990, p. 78). This means that order in this sense is neither "the goal of a plan of one of the elements involved in the process, nor the result of a plan of a 'master mind'" (Schmidtchen, 1990, p. 81).

Furthermore, it can be shown that the most diverse non-linear systems behave *similarly* when transitioning from ordered structures into chaos. Moreover, order structures can be identified within chaos itself, which have been described as 'strange attractors'. This leads to a certain ambivalence when considering that long-term behaviour in complex systems is actually unpredictable: On the one hand, the predictability of long-term behaviour is questioned when chaotic developments occur. On the other hand, a closer knowledge of the laws leading to chaos and prevailing in chaos itself allows to anticipate or at least better estimate the occurrence or development of initially completely random processes for the near future (Pinkwart, 1992, p. 28 ff.).

This makes it clear that chaos and order are not only a pair of concepts, but, as *Cramer* says, "are in a dialectical or functional relationship to each other (stand, d. Verf.)" (Cramer, 1988, p. 159).

---

[60] The iii. criterion is a sufficient, but by no means necessary criterion: Thus, the title of *Li/Yorke's* fundamental essay is 'Period three implies chaos', and not 'Chaos implies period three'! (Li and Yorke 1975).

4.5.2 Does Chaos Only Exist in the Computer?

4.5.2.1 Ignis Fatuus?—Does the Computer Generate Chaos?

Now that the complexity between chaos and order and their inseparable relationship to each other have been clarified, a fundamental question arises: Is this chaos, which has been observed and analysed so far, system inherent, i.e., actually present, or is it merely a fiction in the sense that it only exists in the computer?

Opponents of the chaos theoretical considerations, which were discussed and analysed in the previous chapters, often argue that the whole theory is null and void, as the observed chaos is exclusively computer-generated and due to the insufficient computational accuracy of computers. Thus, a minimal error that occurs at the beginning of the iteration process, for example due to a rounding error, would multiply over the course of the calculations and trigger the butterfly effect, i.e., the chaos. For example, *Brügge* claims:

> The tool, without which it was impossible to trace deterministic chaos, generates the sought-after itself! (Brügge 1993a, p. 164).

The computer distorts the results and this leads to the observed chaos:

> Because a digital computer can't handle the actually necessary differential equations. In addition, the rapid exponentiation of rounded numbers uncontrollably and powerfully distorted the results (Brügge, 1993a, p. 164).

Furthermore, he accuses the proponents of the chaos theory of using 'incompatibly' large time steps in their experiments, which grossly distort the results and contribute to the chaos being generated from the nature of the computer itself. Consequently, it would be impossible to make reliable statements about the areas that want to demonstrate chaos (Brügge, 1993a, p. 164).

Even though *Brügge* criticises mathematical methods in an impermissible way, as he neither explains them in detail nor names them, such objections must still be taken seriously. Because the question of whether chaos in non-linear dynamic systems is actually only computer-generated is by no means a trivial question. This problem can indeed be seen in general, even with the discussed fractals. A typical critical question in connection with visualised fractals is therefore:

> Is the figure real, or is it merely an artifact of chaos-amplified computer round-off? (Ott 1994, p. 18).

These critical remarks are often countered by the argument that the same effect that can be observed on personal computers also occurs on mainframes, albeit a few iterations later. According to other arguments, the problem lies in the fact that all data important for the calculation are real numbers, which have an infinitely long decimal fraction development. Even if one could calculate to ten thousand places exactly, only a finite number of places would be considered and an infinite number would be neglected. So far, the problem is formulated correctly. However, it is erroneously concluded from this that the chaos does not lie in practical inadequacies, such as computational accuracy, but is an integral part of the theoretical considerations (Thoma, 1996, pp. 4 f.).

Although this work also supports the thesis that chaos is an integral part of theoretical considerations, the above line of argument must nevertheless be rejected as insufficient, even tautological. Because one cannot argue that all computers calculate inaccurately and then conclude from this that the chaos is not based on these inadequacies.

4.5.2.2 The First Argument: Increased Computational Accuracy in Complex Systems Does Not Lead to More Accurate Results

To prove the thesis nonetheless, it is sufficient to find an equation where the chaos is system inherent and not computer dependent. For this purpose, the simple logistic equation is considered. Two arguments should be in the foreground:

It is correct, for example, that the irregular fluctuations and the initial sensitivity in this model decrease when the step sizes, i.e., the time intervals t, are reduced.[61] This is because an infinitesimal process is initiated as the distances become ever smaller, so that the difference equation successively turns into a differential equation. However, for the dynamics of a differential equation system that is at most two-dimensional (here: one-dimensional), it is impossible to exhibit chaotic behaviour, as two trajectories obviously can never intersect.

But what about computational accuracy? Certainly, the result will be completely different with an accuracy of one digit compared to an accuracy of two digits. This exactness will again deviate from an iteration that calculates with three digits of accuracy, and so on. This is undisputed. However, if the computational inaccuracy is the cause of the chaos, then the chaos should disappear with an infinitely accurate—impossible for a computer—calculation. But this also means that the calculation would become more and more correct with an increasing number of decimal places. In other words, if you form a sequence of results that result from increasing computational accuracy, the sequence should converge. However, Fig. 4.38 shows for the first seventeen values of this sequence that it does not converge at all.[62]

---

[61] This fact is used by *Brügge* as an occasion to criticise the results of *Peitgen* regarding his results of the 'Three-Body Problem' (see the explanations on *Poincaré* in Sect. 3.2.1 of the first part of the work). He refers to a method of the University of Karlsruhe, in which one body orbits the other two with beautiful regularity, in contrast to the calculations of *Peitgen*. However, the Karlsruhe team chose a completely different time interval than *Peitgen*. But which time interval is the 'right' one cannot be determined by the Karlsruhe method either. See Brügge (1993b, p. 238).

[62] Since the computing platform and the software used affect the specific results, it should be noted here that the calculations were carried out with a specially developed 32-bit software, written in C++ by Borland and used on an Intel-Core-i7 chip under the operating system Windows-XP.

x(t) after 2000 iterations of the function x(t)=4x(t) (1-x(t)), starting value x(0)=0.01

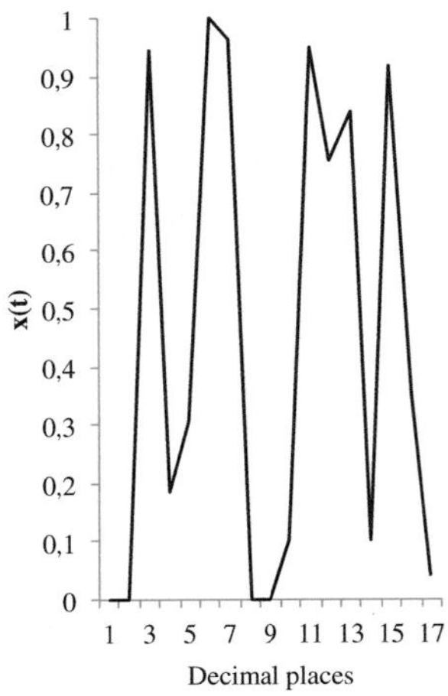

1-digit accuracy	: 0
2-digit "	: 0
3-digit "	: 0,944
4-digit "	: 0,1856
5-digit "	: 0,30696
6-digit "	: 0,999808
7-digit "	: 0,9636204
8-digit "	: 0,00104164
9-digit "	: 0,00040546
10-digit "	: 0,1004746712
11-digit "	: 0,94870139888
12-digit "	: 0,754034021072
13-digit "	: 0,8388628946272
14-digit "	: 0,10401692878844
15-digit "	: 0,918142940528752
16-digit "	: 0,35428960735115
17-digit "	: 0,0416820694296092

Fig. 4.38 Higher computational accuracy does not yield better results (17 decimal places)

The results do not get better or more correct if the number of digits with which the iteration is calculated is increased. For example, the result obtained with an accuracy of thirteen digits after the decimal point is smaller than the result with an accuracy of fourteen digits. But the result with an accuracy of fifteen digits is closer to the first result.

If you look at the first members of the sequence, you can only diagnose a highly irregular behaviour, but no convergence. Unfortunately, this is undoubtedly not a proof, because you are only looking at the first seventeen members of the sequence and neglecting infinitely many. Theoretically, of course, it could be that the sequence begins to converge against all expectations from the eighteenth member onwards. This is unlikely, but possible.

To substantiate our assumption, another Fig. 4.39 is created, which shows the same sequence, but this time calculated with a different programme and to a hundred decimal places.[63]

Also, the result in Fig. 4.39 is not a mathematically exact proof that computational accuracy is not the cause of the chaos. Nevertheless, it is at least an important indication that opponents of chaotic theoretical considerations cannot simply ignore. The irregular, chaotic trend is not to be overlooked! On the other hand, if one considers a (benign) mapping, such as the numerical calculation of the root function (with root of a)

[63] The calculations to a hundred decimal places are carried out with an Intel-Core-i7 chip and the mathematical system MAPLE 15. This software offers integrated symbolic, numerical and graphical facilities.

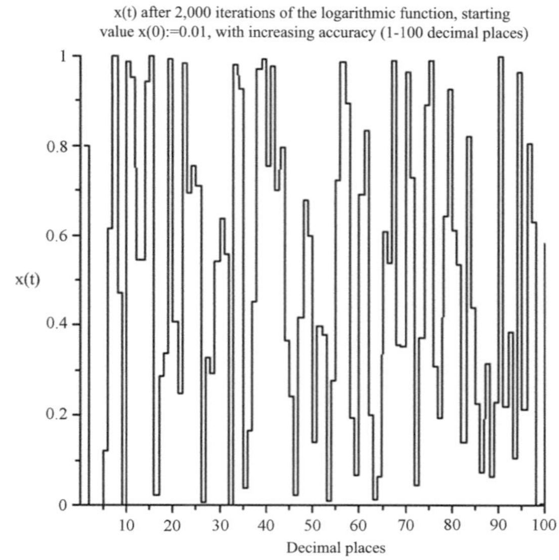

Fig. 4.39 Higher computational accuracy does not yield better results (100 decimal places)

$$x(t+1) = {}^{1}\!/_{2} \cdot \left(x(t) - {}^{a}\!/_{x(t)}\right), \text{ mit } a > 0$$

, one obtains a very good result after just a few places, as the example $a = 2.00$, i.e. (root of 2), and $x(0) = 1.00$ in Fig. 4.40 shows.[64]

As soon as the number of places is increased, the sequence of results converges very quickly approximately[65] to the value 1.414.

In fact, this recursively defined sequence generally converges to the square root of a.[66] From an accuracy of four places, the computer actually displays this result.

4.5.2.3 The Second Argument: The 'Shadow Lemma'

Another argument against the thesis that chaos only exists in the computer can be found in mathematical proofs of the ' shadowing property' (Hammel, 1987). Here, the term

---

[64] By the way, the exact value of the logistic equation for $\lambda = 4$ is calculated as follows: $x(t) = \frac{1}{2} - \frac{1}{2} \cdot \cos(2^t \cdot \cos^{-1}(1 - 2 \cdot x(0)))$. For $x(0) = 0.01$, this results in $t = 2.00$: $x(t) = 0.6371765141$. The logistic equation, by the way, is only exactly solvable in the case of $\lambda = 4.00$. See also: Steeb and Kunik (1989, p. 21).

[65] Approximately means that the root function as an irrational function has infinitely many decimal places, the next place of which can be calculated, but not predicted. Thus, the value of root of 2 at 100 decimal places is approximately: 1.414213562373095048801688724209698078569671875376948073176679737990732478462107038850387534327641573.

[66] See also the proof by Otto *Forster*: Forster (2004, p. 54f.).

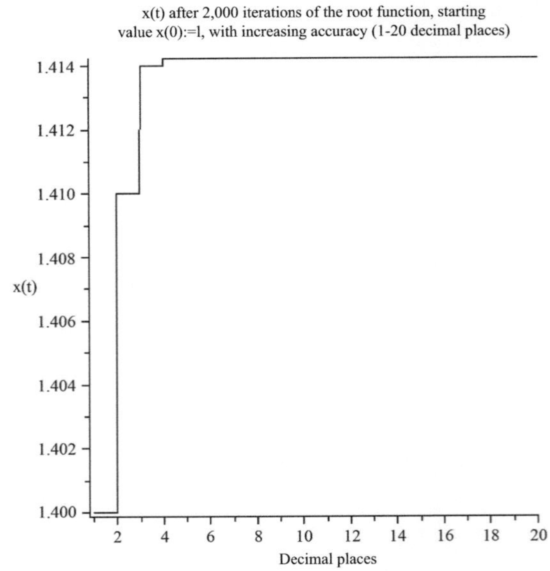

Fig. 4.40 Higher accuracy provides more accurate results for root of 2

designation Shadow Lemma is introduced. This lemma applies to certain chaotic systems:

A numerically calculated non-linear system has rounding errors. These are amplified with each calculation step, so that after a time t, the trajectory thus created deviates exponentially from the 'true' trajectory with the same initial conditions. *Hammel, Yorke* and *Grebogi* must therefore be agreed with when they state the following:

> It is therefore of crucial importance to understand how much of what we see in computer-generated pictures of chaotic attractors are artifacts due to chaos-amplified roundoff error, and how much is real (Hammel 1987, p. 137).

The Shadow Lemma now states that a 'true', i.e., error-free, trajectory with minimally different initial conditions can always be found that almost matches the numerically calculated trajectory, so to speak, lies in its shadow.

Figure 4.41 illustrates the Shadow Lemma. Thus, there exists an initial value that leads to a trajectory without rounding errors, which closely resembles the trajectory of the (erroneous) computer iteration. *Peitgen, Jürgens* et al. state the following:

> This is a very astonishing fact, especially when you consider that the exact size of the allowed errors in the path does not matter at all, as long as it remains limited everywhere (Peitgen et al., 1992a, p. 124).

Thus, the trajectories trajectories calculated by the computer due to rounding errors are also part of the system without calculation errors. So even though the trajectory generated by the computer is wrong, it is equally correct, as it approximates a 'true' trajectory

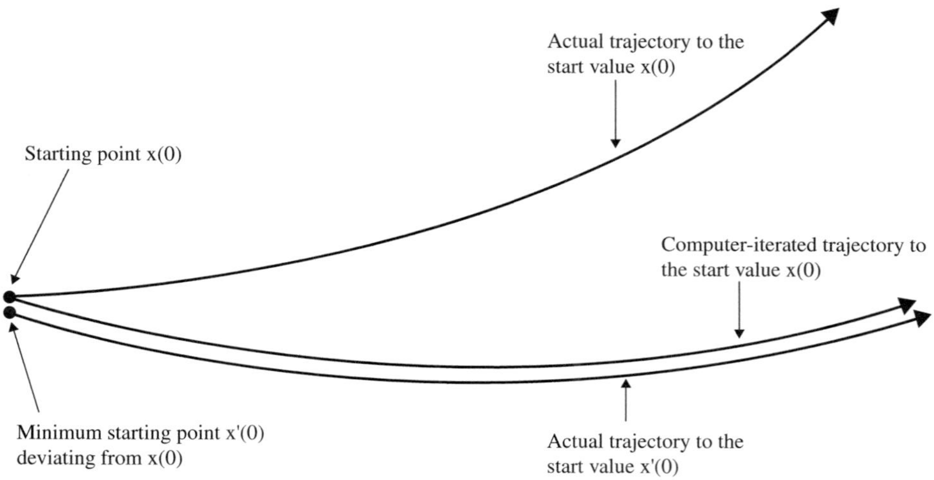

Fig. 4.41 The Shadow Lemma

of the same system remarkably well. The chaos can therefore by no means be computer-generated, but is actually based in the theoretical construction.

The Shadow Lemma shows that one cannot calculate the trajectories using computers that belong to the respective initial conditions, but one has the certainty that the result corresponds to an exact trajectory.[67]

4.5.2.4 Third Argument: The 'L-Density Argument'

A third and final argument against the thesis that chaos only exists in the computer can be easily found in the mathematical properties of the logistic function itself: It can be shown that the initial sensitivity does not only occur in computer calculations, but is of a purely algebraic nature! The statement required for this, in relation to the logistic function, is to be called the *L-Density Argument*[68]. Using the logistic function as an example, the argument developed here states that the zeros for large t are almost dense in the basic interval [0,1]. Due to the fact that the values between two zeros are mapped twice bijectively onto the unit interval, minimal deviations in the initial values lead to arbitrary differences in the final values.

---

[67] The Shadow Lemma can be proven, for example, by analysing the sawtooth function, where $x(t+1) = Frac(2\ x(t))$ is. Frac is a function that calculates the non-integer remainder of a number. Such an illustrative proof can be found in: Peitgen, Jürgens et al. (1994, p. 122 ff.). The shadow property for tent functions (e.g. $x(t+1) = 2x(t)$ for $0<x(t)<0.5$ and $x(t+1) = 1\text{-}2\ x(t)$ for $0.5 \leq x(t) < 1.0$) is explained in detail in: Coven et al. (1988).

[68] The letter *L* here refers to the author.

It can be shown that the so-called butterfly effect, that minimal deviations in the starting values lead to large differences in the temporal course of the trajectories, also occurs purely algebraically in the logistic equation and is thus independent of inaccurate computer calculations. This is called the **L-Density Argument** by the author.

4.5.2.5 Background Information: The Proof of the Purely Algebraic "Butterfly Effect" in the Logistic Equation: The L-Density Argument

Claim

The so-called butterfly effect, that minimal deviations in the starting values lead to large differences in the temporal course of the trajectories, also occurs purely algebraically in the logistic equation and is thus independent of inaccurate computer calculations.

To do this, set $f(x) = 4x \cdot (1-x)$, and $f^{(t)}(x) = f \circ f \circ \ldots \circ f(x)$ is the t-fold composition of f with itself. Then let $x(t) := f^{(t)}(x(0))$. To better distinguish multiplications with bracket expressions from the composition rule in the following, instead of $x(t)$ the notation $x^{(t)}$ is chosen.

Figure 4.42 shows the function graphs of $f^{(t)}$ with t = 1, 2, 3 and 4, where for example:

$$f^{(3)} = 64 \cdot \mathrm{x} \cdot (1-x) \cdot (1-4 \cdot x \cdot (1-x)) \cdot (1-16 \cdot x \cdot (1-x) \cdot (1-4 \cdot x \cdot (1-x))).$$

First, some important properties of $f^{(t)}$ are considered. By complete induction, it can be shown that the following statements are true:

i) $f^{(t)}$ has $2^{t-1}+1$ zeros
ii) $f^{(t)}$ has $2^{t-1}-1$ points of contact with the x-axis.
iii) $f^{(t)}$ has 2^{t-1} maxima with the value 1.
iv) $f^{(t)}$ has $2 \cdot \left(2^{t-1}-1\right)+2 = 2^t$ zeros with multiplicity.
v) $f^{(t)}$ is a polynomial of degree 2^t and thus completely decomposes into $\mathbb{R}$.

The proof of the most important of these statements will be briefly outlined here.

Proof Sketch

To i) Zeros of $f^{(t)}$

1. *Base case (t = 1):*
$f^{(1)}\left(x^{(0)}\right) = f\left(x^{(0)}\right) = 4 \cdot x^{(0)} \cdot \left(1-x^{(0)}\right) = 0 \Leftrightarrow x^{(0)} = 0$ or $x^{(0)} = 1$, d.h.$f^{(1)}$ has $2^{1-1}+1 = 2$ roots.
2. *Inductive step* ($t \rightarrow t+1$):
Assume that $f^{(t)}\ 2^{t-1}-1$ has roots, where obviously $f^{(t)} = 0$ or $f^{(t)} = 1$.
Since $f^{(t+1)} = f \circ f^{t}$, it follows for $f^{(t+1)}$ therefore: $f^{(t+1)}$ has $2^{t-1}+2^{t-1}+1 = 2^t+1$ roots, q. e. d.

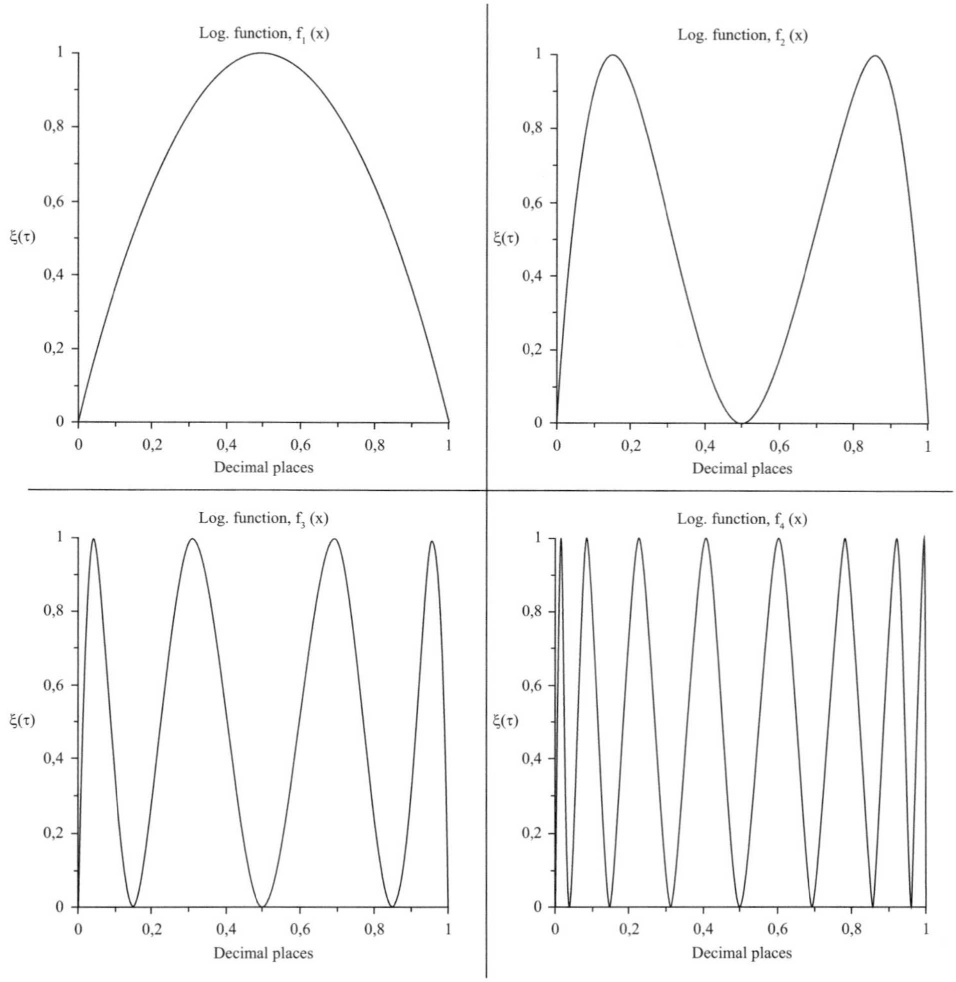

Fig. 4.42 Logistic function after different iteration stages

To ii) Points of contact of $f^{(t)}$:
Since $f^{(t)} \geq 0$, these roots, except for the values 0 and 1, are points of contact. Thus, for $f^{(t)}$ there are $2^{t-1} + 1 - 2 = 2^{t-1} - 1$ points of contact, q. e. d.

Regarding iii) Maxima of $f^{(t)}$:
Between two zeros of $f^{(t)}$ there is a maximum, which takes the value 1. The polynomial of degree 2^t has at most $2^t - 1$ extrema. According to the induction assumption, there are $2^{t-1} - 1$ minima (here: zeros), so there are at most 2^t maxima remaining.

According to the *Intermediate Value Theorem* (Forster, 2004, p. 102 f.) there are at least two values between two zeros where $f^{(t)}(x)$ takes the value $\frac{1}{2}$, so $f^{(t+1)}(x) = 1$ is at this point.

From these last two considerations it follows: There are exactly $f^{(t)}\, 2 \cdot 2^{t-1} = 2^t$ maxima with the value 1, q. e. d.

Further Considerations If we consider the function $f^{(t)}$, it can be said based on the previous considerations that there is a maximum with the value 1 between two zeros. Each subinterval between a zero and a maximum is obviously mapped bijectively onto the interval [0, 1]. That is, the interval [0, 1] is covered exactly twice between two zeros.

There are $2^{t-1} + 1$ zeros, and there are two intervals between two zeros. Taking into account that the first and the last zero must each be counted only once, it follows that there are $2 \cdot \left(2^{t-1} + 1\right) - 2 = 2^t$ subintervals. In total, the function $f^{(t)}$ divides the interval [0, 1] into 2^t subintervals $\left[\varepsilon_i,\, \varepsilon_{i+1}\right]$, so that $f^{(t)}\left(\left[\varepsilon_i, \varepsilon_{i+1}\right]\right) = [0, 1]$.
The 'average'[69] interval length is therefore $\frac{1}{2^t}$.

Obviously, with a minimal difference of $x(0)$ and $x'(0)$ for example in a range of 10^{-10} and at $t \geq 50$ a completely arbitrary result can be obtained by applying $f^{(t)}$.

The problem here is that the zeros do not necessarily have to be evenly distributed. It could be that the zeros, for example, accumulate towards the outside.

Therefore, the interval length should be further restricted next. To do this, the conditions that must apply to the interval boundaries ε_i must first be considered:

For motivation, we now consider the interval boundaries given by zeros for t+1, t, t−1, t−3, and t−4. Then it is obvious:

$$f^{(t+1)}(x) = 0;\; f^{(t)}(x) = 0,\, 1;\; f^{(t-1)}(x) = 0,\, 1/2,\, 1$$
$$f^{(t-2)}(x) = 0,\, 1/2 - 1\Big/\left(2\sqrt{2}\right),\, 1/2,\, 1/2 + 1/2\sqrt{2},\, 1$$
$$f \circ f^{(t-3)}(x) = a_i;\; f^{(t-3)}(x) = b_{1/2};\; f\left(b_{1/2}\right) = a_i;$$

i.e. $4b(1-b) = a$, with $b_{1/2} = b$ and $a = a_i$

$$b - b^2 = a/4 \Leftrightarrow b^2 - b + 1/4 = 1/4 - a/4$$
$$\Leftrightarrow (b - 1/2)^2 = (1-a)/4 \Leftrightarrow b = 1/2 \pm \sqrt{1-a}/2$$

Let it now be

$$f^{(t-2)}(x) = a_i^{(t-2)} \text{und}$$
$$f^{(t-3)}(x) = a_k^{(t-3)} \text{mit} f\left(a_k^{(t-3)}\right) = a_i^{(t-2)}$$

[69] The term 'average' is put in quotation marks here because it is not immediately obvious that there is actually a uniform distribution.

Then for the length of an interval in the case of t−3, expressed by the values in the case of t−2:

$$\left|a_k^{(t-3)} - a_k^{(t-3)}\right| = \left|\left(\frac{1}{2} \pm \frac{\sqrt{1 - a_i^{(t-2)}}}{2}\right) - \left(\frac{1}{2} \pm \frac{\sqrt{1 - a_j^{(t-2)}}}{2}\right)\right|$$
$$= \frac{1}{2}\left|\sqrt{1 - a_i^{(t-2)}} \pm \sqrt{1 - a_j^{(t-2)}}\right|$$

In the following, the minimum length δ of a corresponding interval for t−2 is studied.

Let it be

$$\min_{i<j}\left|a_i^{(t-2)} - a_j^{(t-2)}\right| = \delta$$

Also consider the function $F(x) = \sqrt{1 - x}$.

Then for the length of the associated interval at t−3, it is at least $\delta / 4$:

$$\left|a_k^{(t-3)} - a_{k'}^{(t-3)}\right| \geq \frac{1}{2}\left|\sqrt{1 - a_i^{(t-2)}} - \sqrt{1 - a_j^{(t-2)}}\right| \geq \frac{1}{2}\left|1 - \sqrt{1 - \delta}\right| \geq \frac{1}{2} \cdot \frac{\delta}{2} = \frac{\delta}{4}, \text{ da } F'(0) = -\frac{1}{2}.$$

This inequality is easily understood when considering the following:

$$\left|\sqrt{1 - a_i^{(t-2)}} - \sqrt{1 - a_j^{(t-2)}}\right| \cdot \left|\sqrt{1 - a_i^{(t-2)}} + \sqrt{1 - a_j^{(t-2)}}\right| = \left|1 - a_i^{(t-2)} - \left(1 - a_j^{(t-2)}\right)\right| = \left|a_i^{(t-2)} - a_j^{(t-2)}\right| \geq \delta$$

with which it follows:

$$\left|\sqrt{1 - a_i^{(t-2)}} - \sqrt{1 - a_j^{(t-2)}}\right| \geq \frac{\delta}{\left|\sqrt{1 - a_i^{(t-2)}} + \sqrt{1 - a_j^{(t-2)}}\right|} \geq \frac{\delta}{2}.$$

By complete induction, it follows for the interval length of the interval $\left[\varepsilon_i, e_{i+1}\right]$:

$$(\varepsilon_{i+1} - \varepsilon_i) \geq \left(\frac{1}{4}\right)^t$$

Similarly, it can be shown that the interval can also be estimated from above.

The sequence of zeros is bounded on the interval [0, 1]. Therefore, the sequence has at least one accumulation point, as according to the theorem of *Bolzano-Weierstraß*[70] every bounded sequence has an accumulation point. Due to the above estimation, the distance

[70] The detailed proof of the theorem of *Bolzano-Weierstraß* can be found in Sect. 4.5.3.7.

between two zeros is at least $\left(\frac{1}{4}\right)^t$ and also bounded from above. Therefore, there must be infinitely many accumulation points.

Thus, the zeros can accumulate in the interval [0, 1], but for example, they cannot accumulate at the edges, but are somewhat evenly distributed. That is, for sufficiently large t, the zeros are almost dense. Between two zeros there is always a maximum, so that each interval from the zero to the maximum (here: 1) and from the maximum to the zero is bijectively mapped onto the entire interval [0, 1] by the function. It is therefore clear that minimal deviations in the initial conditions are sufficient to produce arbitrary differences in the results.

For λ- values less than four, this density statement does not apply in the strictness formulated above. However, it would be sufficient to show that the minima and maxima do not converge to each other and are approximately equally distributed. The density argument outlined above would then essentially apply. The proof of this, however, will not be provided here, as it had to be demonstrated with an example (here: the logistic function with $\lambda = 4.00$) that chaos exists in non-linear systems independently of their calculations using computers.

Thus, overall, computer mappings do have a connection to 'reality', contrary to critical objections. Chaos can be proven algebraically in non-linear systems, so it is inherently present, or in other words:

> Chaotic developments in non-linear complex systems do not only exist in the computer. They are not a will-o'-the-wisp, not an ignis fatuus, which only the fool follows, but a scientifically serious insight!

4.5.3 'Controlling Complexity'—Can Chaos be Controlled?

4.5.3.1 Chaotic Systems and Control—A Contradiction?

For many years, it has been almost dogmatically accepted that a chaotic, or rather complex system, due to its characteristic that minimal changes in initial conditions can escalate into significant differences in system behaviour, is uncontrollable. The sensitive dependence on the initial conditions of a complex system, that insight referred to as the 'butterfly effect', makes any intervention doubtful: How can a butterfly in Hong Kong know if it triggers a devastating storm in New York just by flapping its wings a little? Conversely, it seems at least equally impossible to deliberately let a butterfly fly in Hong Kong to prevent a storm in New York. And so one reads sentences like these:

> No computer in the world, even if it took into account the wing beats of all the butterfly's colleagues and all other breezes in the world, could tell the butterfly the moment at which its wing beat would avert the hurricane (Pöppe, 2008, p. 49).

Nevertheless, the exploration of possibilities for controlling a system in areas of chaotic developments is a tempting endeavour. For example, Edward *Ott* states:

> (...) one can imagine that it will often be the case that it is desired that chaos be avoided and/or that the system dynamics be changed in some way so that improved performance is obtained (Ott 1994, p. 145).

And indeed, in recent years, scientists have engaged with this topic and developed methods that are supposed to enable complex or chaotic developments to be transformed into ordered states.[71]

4.5.3.2 A Little Hope—Influence Possibilities in Chaotic Systems

When a Strange Attractor is present, one might be inclined to make large changes in the system to achieve the desired goal, system stability.

Here, the possibility of gaining influence on system development through comprehensive changes will be considered once again using the logistic function:

$$x(t+1) = \lambda \cdot x(t) \cdot (1 - x(t))$$

Using this function as an example, the project could mean changing the parameter λ from the value 4.00—which is known to lead to chaotic system progressions—to a value below 3.57.[72]

However, such a modifying approach, which radically changes the system properties, is often not possible or too costly for realistic situations. For example, in a company, you cannot simply dismiss all employees and replace them with new ones if the existing ones are apparently not yet willing to change their negative attitude towards necessary change measures. Although the 'exchange' of all employees would represent one of the most dramatic (and at the same time absurd) radical changes in a company, there are countless other measures that are also difficult to implement due to their high costs, in order to bring about a radical change in system properties.

Therefore, this option of radically changing the system properties is initially discarded as a sensible possibility. Instead, the case should be considered where there is a cost-effective access to some parameters of the system, which, however, can only be changed relatively weakly. In this context, *Ott* critically asks:

> Can we achieve what we want in this type of circumstances? (Ott, 1994, p. 145).

He fundamentally affirms this question and describes the project to control the chaos in a three-step process as follows:

---

[71] An overview of various scientists and works that have already researched the field of 'controlling chaos' in the nineteen nineties can be found in: Ott (1994, p. 148).

[72] For more details, see the specific explanations of the logistic function in Sect. 3.4.5 in the first part of the book.

> The key point is that chaotic attractors typically have embedded within them a dense set of unstable periodic orbits. Because we can make only small changes, we cannot create new orbits with very different properties from the existing ones. Thus the approach is to determine first some of the low-period unstable periodic orbits embedded in the chaotic attractor. Then we examine these orbits and choose one which yields improved system performance. Finally we attempt to programme our small parameter adjustments so as to stabilise this unstable periodic orbit (Ott, 1994, p. 145).

Consider, for example, a discrete mapping *G(x,p)*, where *p* represents a system parameter. It is assumed that at $p = \bar{p}$ there is a strange attractor that includes an unstable fixed point $x_F(\bar{p})$. The goal now is to transition the chaotic movement of the trajectory into a stable orbit $x = x_F(\bar{p})$ by making small changes to the parameter *p*.[73]

Kopel explains a comparable method using the example of the logistic function (Kopel 1996). He assumes that the system is in the initial state with $X(0) = 0.8$ and $\lambda = 4,0$. It is known that in the interval between 0 and 1, periodic points of any period exist. For example, there is a fixed point *X'* = 0.75 (Kopel 1996, p. 490).

A way is now sought to reach one of these points by making suitable minimal changes to λ. The radical form of changes to the parameter λ out of the chaotic area is not allowed, as already justified above. Rather, the λ variation should move within a small range, for example between 3.9 and 4.0. Furthermore, the variation should only occur in the first period, as it is not to be assumed that interventions are feasible in every period in reality. Once the fixed point is reached, the stabilisation of the system is successful, as each period then takes on the reached value.

It is easy to calculate that by changing the parameter λ in the interval [3.9;4] in the first period for *X(1)* values from the range [0.624;0.64] are obtained. If you then reset λ back to the original value of 4.0, the following bandwidths of system development are obtained for the next periods (Table 4.4).

These initial results clearly show the sensitive dependence on the initial conditions, as the range of the interval at the beginning of the system's course is still 0.016, whereas already in the fifth period the interval width has increased to approximately 0.24, thus almost fifteen times. Since the calculated fixed point $X' = 0.75$ is within the interval range of the realisable values of *X*(4), there is the possibility of reaching this value already in the fourth period. Therefore, there exists a value λ^* in the interval [3.9;4] for the period 0, so that in the period 4 a value $X^* = X(4)$ can be calculated, with $X^* = X'$. The correction value only needs to be applied once at the beginning of the system start (period 0). In the other periods, the original control parameter $\lambda = 4$ is used. The value λ^* can be easily calculated from the logistic equation and one obtains: $\lambda^* \approx 3.92582$. *Kopel* notes on this:

[73] A detailed description of the mathematical procedure sufficient for stabilisation can be found in the chapter 'Controlling Chaos' by Ott (1994, p. 145–149). *Ott* describes the procedure for a mapping of dimension two and considers an unstable fixed point. He points out that the transfer of considerations to higher periodic cases would be 'straightforward'.

Table 4.4 Logistic function with minimal changes in initial conditions

Calculation of the bandwidth of possible X-values of the logistic function when changing the parameter λ in the first period ($t = 1$) within the interval [3.9;4]		
Let it be: $X(0)=0.8$, $X(t+1)= \lambda X(t) (1-X(t))$, $\lambda = 4$ for all $t > 1$		
$X(t)$, with the period $t>0$, from:	Interval with the interval width:	
$X(1)$ from:	[0.624	0.64]
$X(2)$ from:	[0.9216	0.938496]
$X(3)$ from:	[0.230885	0.289014]
$X(4)$ from:	[0.710309	0.821939]
$X(5)$ from:	[0.585421	0.823081]

> With this small change of the control parameter, we have achieved a dramatic change in the dynamic behaviour of the system: While the system behaved chaotically without intervention, it now follows an equilibrium path (Kopel 1996, p. 491).

Even with a restriction of the interval for λ e.g. to [3.94;4], where λ^* obviously lies outside the interval, it is possible to reach the described equilibrium point. For this, with a suitable choice of λ^*, either more than four periods are needed or more than one correction must be made. *Kopel* further shows that points of a two-cycle in the considered system can be aimed for in the same way.

The problem with this method is that λ^* is only an approximate value. Under certain circumstances, the system only gets close to the desired equilibrium state. However, it can be shown that it is possible to maintain the system state even in this case through repeated interventions. *Kopel* points out that this method proves to be very robust even with stochastic overlays:

> By repeatedly applying the algorithm, the system can be controlled even when overlaid with stochastic disturbances (Kopel, 1996, p. 492).

This method, presented by *Kopel* and taken up in this work, is often referred to as 'targeting' in the literature, as a stable cycle is targeted (target) through variations in control parameters (Shinbrot et al., 1993).

The above explanations show that by small but targeted modifications of a control parameter, the dynamics of a system that is on chaotic development paths can be successfully and permanently stabilised.

4.5.3.3 An Alternative (synergetic) Approach: Complexity as an Opportunity

So far, complex systems and their potentially complex or chaotic behaviour have been perceived more as a threat than as an opportunity. At this point, it should be illustrated that complexity primarily represents an opportunity to fundamentally change things, if one has the 'right' methods available. However, the option to radically change system properties has so far been discarded as a too costly and practically unimplementable possibility. Here we pick up this option and even go one step further by consciously creating complexity.

Let's consider the following example:

Example: Initiating change processes—Hysteresis effects in the stable attractor

Let's assume that the conditions in a market have radically changed. The top management of a company significant in this market wants to fundamentally change the company strategy, as it has recognised that without fundamental changes in the new market situation, the company could be permanently at risk. But how do you achieve the willingness among employees to accept the necessary change processes and also to help shape them? For years, the company has been on the same track. There is a stable order structure in place, which every employee has sufficiently adapted to, so initially the willingness to change is low. Announcements from the management are therefore met with skepticism. Perhaps an external intervention is needed? One approach could therefore be to involve an external management consultancy, which could, for example, conduct appropriate training with the employees.

Let's now look at the employees of the company who need to be trained. Their current stable attitudes can be represented by a ball in a valley, as shown in Fig. 4.43.

This is meant to describe that the employees' attitude towards their work can be described as stable, albeit wrongly stable in relation to the new challenges. This high degree of stability in attitudes means that other opinions do not quickly lead to reconsidering one's own ideas. Hence the attempt with the external management consultants.

If one now wanted to change the state of the ball, one would have to move the ball out of the stable valley with a lot of energy, as Fig. 4.44 suggests. This could be

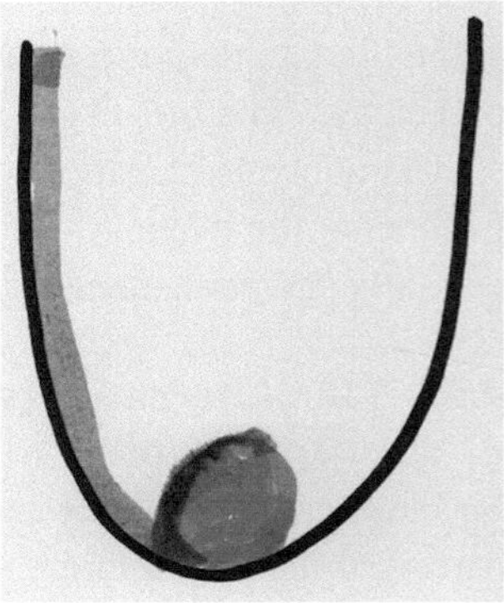

Fig. 4.43 Stable situation—'Ball in the valley'

Fig. 4.44 Change—'Pushing the ball out of the valley'

done by having experienced management consultants conduct the training, who are well versed in such problem cases. But as soon as this energy is removed, i.e. the experienced management consultant has left the company and can therefore no longer constantly push for the acceptance of the necessary changes, the ball could, as shown in Fig. 4.45, inevitably roll back. ◀

This 'holding on too long' to certain attitudes towards the company, the work, etc., can also be described with the term *hysteresis*. This is a physical system inertia that we also find in pattern formation in our brains ('cognitive set'). The behavioural economist would speak here of 'status quo bias'. We recognise that a stable attractor is not always a desirable state and that change processes in particular have a hard time dealing with such attractors.

Explicitly newly founded companies or young growth companies in innovative dynamic markets need a permanent willingness to change, which can appear more than endangered by stable attractors. A complex system (here the market) apparently requires a complex structure of the part and their subsystems acting in it (Here: The company, the department, the employees etc.).

Fig. 4.45 'Rolling back the ball'—Hysteresis effects in the stable attractor

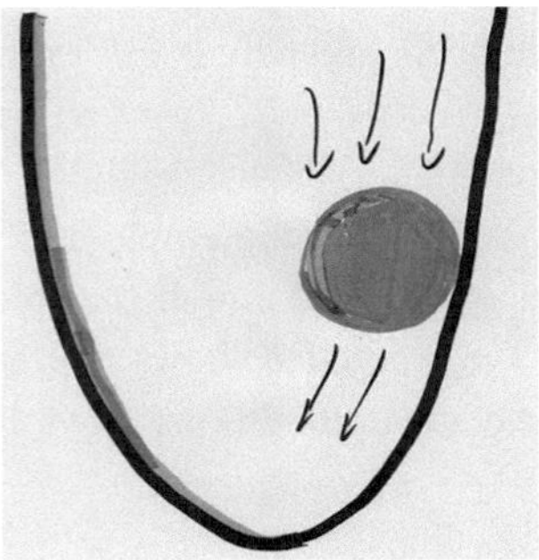

Fig. 4.46 Tilt image—'Frog—Horse'

In a self-experiment, one can easily understand the behavioural anomaly "status quo bias" described in the above example using so-called 'tilt images'.[74] When viewing a tilt image, a viewer sees a specific image, e.g., a frog. If you turn or tilt the image, you no longer see a frog, but instead, for example, a horse's head. Depending on the viewing angle, you see the frog or the horse, the more difficult it is to recognise the other pattern (frog or horse) in the image. What you don't see are both interpretations of the image at the same time. When you leave the perception of one pattern in the image, this does not happen successively, but abruptly and you suddenly recognise, for example, the horse instead of the frog. It then becomes difficult to recognise the initially recognised pattern again. The inclined reader may understand these phase transitions associated with hysteresis effects in the context of a self-experiment using Fig. 4.46.

So how can the ball described in the above example be moved without having to continuously add energy from the outside? One answer is to leave the stable attractor, generate complexity, and thus cause a new stable attractor. But how is this supposed to happen, and why is this even a solution approach?

At this point, we can refer back to synergetics and the importance of the control parameter and ask again:

How can the employees' wrong attitude from a management perspective be sustainably changed into the desired attitude from a synergetic perspective?

Synergetics shows that not the direct change of the ball, but rather the change of the incentive conditions plays the central role. The economist would say: The preferences

[74] In the first part of the book, we had already addressed this issue and considered the example of a tilt image (old woman—young woman).

of people are assumed to be constant. But you can change the framework conditions, the incentives in such a way that people's behaviour changes given preferences. This is where the control parameter comes into play in the context of synergetics. The control parameter changes the environment of the ball as an external incentive by transforming the stable situation into an unstable one, by causing a phase transition that could stimulate a new order pattern from an existing order pattern. However, the control parameter does not move the ball itself.

Continuation of the example: Initiating change processes—Hysteresis effects in the stable attractor

So instead of temporarily moving the ball upwards from the outside—which, as soon as the energy lifting the ball upwards is withdrawn, is highly likely to roll back—the company management should think about changing the permanent incentive situation for the employees.

Through the external incentives, the position of the ball can become unstable, i.e., the previous settings can appear questionable. In other words: The stability of the previous behaviour pattern gradually decreases. At the same time, external influences become more important. The system loses its old stability and becomes more and more a plaything of its environment. This behaviour can be demonstrated by an increase in complexity and is referred to as *critical fluctuation*. At some point, the valley turns into a mountain and the ball is faced with the choice of rolling down in some direction. Figure 4.47 outlines this phase transition. The direction in which the ball now rolls can be triggered by a minimal disturbance. The flap of a butterfly's wings, one could say with reference to the 'butterfly effect' in complex systems, may be enough to let the ball roll in one direction or another. Once the ball has rolled down, it takes up a stable position in the next valley, which, with the right choice of incentives, leads to the desired acceptance and willingness to participate in the necessary change processes. ◀

The above example makes the following clear: A system whose trajectories move in a stable attractor cannot be permanently changed by adding energy, unless the system

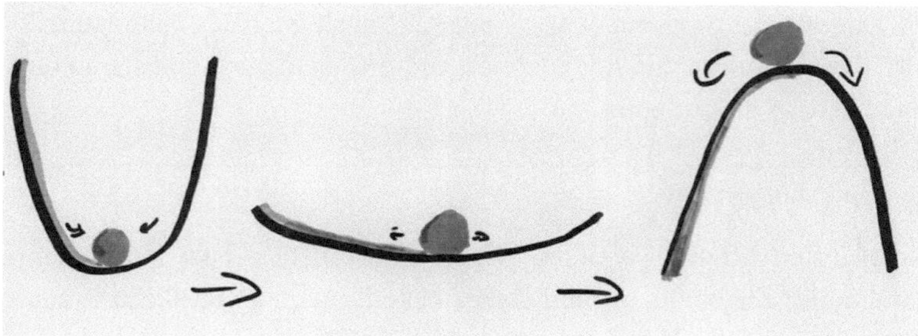

Fig. 4.47 Phase transition

environment is changed in such a way that a phase transition becomes possible. Then a small energy boost in the right direction is enough to bring about a stable new situation.

In our example, this means: Through training that is based on mediation or appeals, the 'ball' of attitudes and also of pre-judgements (if one wants to add the aspect of attitude here) is indeed moved to another position, namely the one desired by the teacher or the company management. However, this does not have a lasting effect. As soon as the measure is ended, and the energy supply is thus withdrawn, the ball rolls back to the initial situation. Here, the 'status quo bias' comes into play.

However, if the incentive conditions in the company are modified in the sense of a synergetic control parameter, a situation is created that finds the 'ball' on a mountain again. Where the ball rolls, however, is not really clear. Through the self-organisation process described in synergetics, an attitude emerges among the employees in relation to the above example, which pushes aside all other previous attitudes. This *one* attitude *'enslaves'* in the synergetic sense the others and thus becomes the order parameter.

Whether the order parameter that arises accordingly, however, is the one desired by the company management, depends very much on how the control parameter possibly reacts to change processes and how it is possibly readjusted. Synergetics sees no need for additional intervention here, as it merely describes how self-organisation processes lead to the formation of order. It can therefore be described as value-free. Whether the resulting order parameter 'attitude' is the one aimed for by the top managers of the company is therefore not decided by the fact that a new 'attitude' has manifested itself as an order parameter. One could also say: The formation of order in synergetics is blind to specific goals.

4.5.3.4 'Nudges' and the Emergence of *Desired* Order Parameters

In the context of a strategic repositioning of a company as in our above example, the blindness described above cannot be accepted. If no other assistance than a rational argument as a control parameter seems possible, the company management should trigger the butterfly effect, which happens one way or another, through their commitment. In an unstable state, a small nudge, a 'Nudge', is indeed enough to point in the right direction, as Fig. 4.48 suggests.

What is meant by these 'Nudges' will be examined in detail in the following examples:

The term is closely associated with the concept of *'libertarian paternalism'* as used by Richard *Thaler,* Cass *Sunstein* et al. (Thaler & Sunstein, 2012; Neumann, 2013). They explain why these 'Nudges' are not coercion and give some examples, one of which will be mentioned here as an example.

Example: Open Enrollment

Companies often offer a so-called 'Open Enrollment'. This allows employees to check and adjust the status of their salary benefits such as health insurance or retirement provision online. There are some who do not log in to make a decision, for example, within the designated period at the end of the year. One could now set the

Fig. 4.48 Phase transition—'Nudges'—Butterfly effect

payments of everyone who does not actively log in to zero (he seems to have no interest in further payment and it is avoided that amounts continue to be debited although the customer has not expressly requested this) or one keeps the same amount. The decision is completely free. For the benefit of the employees, the latter variant would certainly be the better one. It does not determine the amount of payment and leaves the free decision to each individual. However, the arrangement of the online procedure contains a 'Nudge' in the direction that would generally be considered good (Thaler & Sunstein, 2012, p. 23 f.). ◀

The obvious problem with the concept is that from an economic point of view, there is no real qualitative difference between paternalism (i.e., state coercion) and libertarian paternalism, as we are led to believe by *Thaler* and *Sunstein*. Ultimately, both those who favour paternalism and those who act as representatives of libertarian paternalism only manipulate prices by, for example, changing the transaction costs. These increase, for example, when, as in the above example, health insurance has to be deliberately cancelled instead of simply expiring at the end of the year. This changes the behaviour of the actors given their preferences.

If the state were to ban cigarette consumption for the benefit of public health (this would probably be strict paternalism), transaction costs and thus prices would increase enormously, as demanders would have to switch to a black market or this would have to be established first, but would indeed be established. In any case, even with paternalism, there are alternatives, only the cost and thus price changes are possibly much higher compared to "libertarian paternalism".

The actual difference between paternalism and libertarian paternalism is therefore quantitative, not qualitative in nature. Therefore, it is difficult to draw a clear distinction between paternalism and libertarian paternalism, i.e., between coercion (here: exercised by the company management) and slightly nudged self-determined decisions, as suggested by the libertarian paternalism. One could, for example, take a look at the transaction costs to find the boundary between libertarian and non-libertarian paternalism: Whenever the transaction costs of all alternatives change relatively, but remain constant in absolute terms, libertarian paternalism would be present. But whenever the intervention changes the *absolute* transaction costs of all possible decisions (and thus their prices), the undesirable paternalism is present, which appears all the more questionable, the more the transaction costs change absolutely, i.e., in total, through the intervention. But this measurement remains hypothetical for the time being, as it seems difficult to implement from analysis to evaluation.

To bring about the desired changes in attitude through gentle nudges, the question arises as to how one knows when to intervene. This is where complexity research and its empirical measurement methods are needed.

4.5.3.5 Measuring Complexity to Determine the Placement of 'Nudges'

Indeed, in the above example, a problem for the leadership of the company is to recognise whether the employees are on the verge of a phase transition or not. Only then does it make sense to intervene with a 'nudge'. The problem, of course, is not only in our example, but is rather generally the challenge when one wants to consciously bring about a phase transition using a synergetic concept, which then also ends in the 'right' direction.

By now, there are a number of empirical methods that allow measuring complexity. Because complexity is greatest when the ball is at the top of the mountain and least when the ball is in the valley (order). Order and complexity are thus two antipodes that can be measured using certain methods.

In addition to the method of bifurcation analysis, the most important traditional methods of complexity science include the calculation of *Lyapunov* exponents, the *Li/Yorke* theorem, or dimension calculation (e.g., box dimension, *Hausdorff* dimension, etc.), which we have already considered in an introductory manner.

Especially in the context of empirical studies, it has always been difficult to prove complexity solely on the basis of, for example, the calculation of *Lyapunov* exponents, as we will see later. Nevertheless, other methods, which partly need to be considered in combination, offer the possibility to compensate for this deficit. These include methods that can be described with the keywords *Grammar Complexity, Recurrence Plots, Kolmogorov-Sinai entropy* or *Permutation entropy* (Strunk & Schiepek, 1994, p. 481 ff.). We will go into this in more detail in the next chapter.

However, the phase transitions to be measured can only be detected via time series data, which—and this is the difficulty—first need to be collected. The explanations have, however, illustrated that change processes can succeed more easily and sustainably with the support of complexity than when the situation is in a stable state of order.

Table 4.5 Accuracy—logistic function: Assumed result

Accuracy	Assumed result for x_n
1 place after the decimal point	0.2
2 places after the decimal point	0.22
3 places after the decimal point	0.223
4 places after the decimal point	0.2229
5 places after the decimal point	0.22287
...	

4.5.3.6 There is Even a Predictable Path in Chaos—At Least Theoretically (Theorem of *Bolzano-Weierstraß*)

In the previous section, we heard how one can profitably use the complexity of systems to achieve certain new states of order: First destabilise the ordered system, bring about a phase transition, and at the point of greatest critical fluctuation, achieve the new state of order with a slight 'nudge'.

But not always is the complexity, as we find it, desired, because actually people do not want chaos, they want order! But how can chaos be controlled?

To consider this, let's look again at the logistic function or equation:

$x_{n+1} = \lambda \cdot x_n(1 - x_n)$, where n corresponds to the number of iterations or the accuracy of determining the value x. To achieve high accuracy, we want to iterate the equation 1000 times.

In a naive (i.e., pre-complexity science) view, it seems likely that with more precise information, or more exact calculation, the result becomes better and 'more correct'. Let $\lambda = 4,0$. Calculated to one place after the decimal point, the value for x_n is 0.2. One would therefore now assume that with more precise calculation, for example, Table 4.5 could result.

In fact, something completely different happens, as we have already seen, with the values fluctuating between 0 and 1, so that the logistic function or the recursively generated sequence of numbers is thus limited (see Table 4.6).

The table shows: No matter how precisely we calculate, we will not be able to achieve a result that we could call correct.[75] Where are we in the system after 1000 iterations? Depending on the initial condition and the accuracy of the calculation, nothing seems to be predictable if the respective trajectory of the system moves in a chaotic attractor.

And yet: There is a predictable path, a predictable trajectory within the strange attractor!

At least this is suggested by the following consideration of the logistic equation. First of all, we can mathematically consider this equation as a recursively defined sequence $(x_n)_{n \in \mathbb{N}}$, whose sequence members are determined by $x_{n+1} = \lambda \cdot x_n(1 - x_n)$.

[75] This relationship between calculation accuracy and chaotic systems was extensively justified in Sect. 4.5.2.

Table 4.6 Accuracy—logistic function: Actual result

Accuracy	Actual result, limited to two decimal places, for x_n
1 place after the decimal point	0.20
2 places after the decimal point	0.80
3 places after the decimal point	0.30
4 places after the decimal point	0.60
5 places after the decimal point	0.35
...	

It can be shown that this sequence is bounded. For bounded sequences, according to the mathematical theorem of '*Bolzano-Weierstraß*', there must be at least one convergent subsequence. That is, there must be a path that corresponds to the first approach—thus the 'becoming more exact'. Therefore, there must be a predictable path in chaos!

4.5.3.7 Background Information: There must be a Predictable Path in Chaos!—The Theorem of *Bolzano-Weierstraß*

Assertion Within a strange attractor, there is a predictable path, a predictable trajectory within the strange attractor.

The following consideration of the logistic equation suggests this. First of all, we can consider this equation as a recursively defined sequence $(x_n)_{n \in \mathbb{N}}$, whose sequence members are determined by $x_{n+1} = \lambda \cdot x_n(1 - x_n)$.

It can be shown that this sequence is bounded. For bounded sequences, according to the theorem of '*Bolzano-Weierstraß*', there must be at least one convergent subsequence. That is, there must be a path that corresponds to the first approach—thus the 'becoming more exact'. Therefore, there must be a predictable path in chaos! To substantiate the above thesis, we first show the boundedness of the logistic equation.

Subthesis 1: The logistic equation is bounded The logistic equation

(1) $x_{n+1} = \lambda \cdot x_n(1 - x_n)$

is bounded with respect to the variable x_n and also with respect to the factor λ:

(2) $0 \leq \mathrm{x}_n \leq 1$

and

(3) $0 \leq \lambda \leq 4$

To (2): x_n indicates the population size. In nature, the growth of a population is limited by density limiting factors, which prevent exceeding the natural threshold value (= environmental capacity/upper limit).

If the maximum population size is at $100\,\% = 1$, then x_n can only take values between $0\,\% = 0$ (extinction of the population) and $100\,\% = 1$ (largest possible population):

(4) $x_n \in [0; 1]$

To (3): First, it must be determined at which values of x_n the logistic equation reaches its maximum: For which x_n is the first derivative of the logistic function equal to zero?

$$\begin{aligned} &\frac{\delta x_{n+1}}{\delta x_n} = \lambda - 2 \cdot \lambda \cdot x_n \stackrel{!}{=} 0 \\ &\Leftrightarrow \lambda = 2 \cdot \lambda \cdot x_n \\ &\Leftrightarrow 1 = 2 \cdot x_n \\ &\Leftrightarrow \frac{1}{2} = x_n. \text{Da} \ \frac{\delta x_{n+1}}{\delta \delta x_n} = -2\lambda < 0 \end{aligned}$$

At the point $x_n = 0.5$ there is a maximum of the logistic equation. Since x_n can only take values between 0 and 1, it must be:

$$\begin{aligned} &x_{n+1} \geq 0 && \wedge \quad x_{n+1} \leq 1 \\ &\Rightarrow \lambda \cdot (1 - x_n) \cdot x_n \geq 0 \wedge && \lambda \cdot (1 - x_n) \cdot x_n \leq 1 \end{aligned}$$

If you insert the x_n value for the local maximum into the inequalities, the restrictions for λ result:

$$\begin{aligned} &\Rightarrow \lambda \cdot (1 - 0.5) \cdot 0.5 \geq 0 && \wedge \ \lambda \cdot (1 - 0.5) \cdot 0.5 \leq 1.0 \\ &\Leftrightarrow 0.25 \cdot \lambda \geq 0 && \wedge \ 0.25 \cdot \lambda \leq 1.0 \\ &\Leftrightarrow \lambda \geq 0 && \wedge \ \lambda \leq 4.0 \end{aligned}$$

$\Rightarrow \lambda$ is limited to the interval $\lambda \in [0.0; 4.0]$! For λ values > 4.0, the population already takes on negative values after a few iterations and moves away exponentially from the permissible interval.

Subthesis 2: The logistic equation has a convergent subsequence as a result of real numbers The second subthesis results directly from the *Bolzano-Weierstrass theorem*. To prove this, we first need the concept of a *Cauchy* sequence.

A *Cauchy* sequence is, somewhat loosely formulated, a sequence $(a_n)_{n \in \mathbb{N}}$, whose sequence members differ arbitrarily little from each other, if n is large enough. It can be proven that every convergent sequence of real numbers is a *Cauchy* sequence. Conversely, the definition of the sequence only refers to the members themselves and does not guarantee a limit. This is axiomatically[76] defined.

[76] Axioms are assumptions that cannot be questioned. They are immediately evident (usually anyway). The entire structure of mathematical theorems stands on the foundation of axioms. Typical examples are the *Peano* axioms. Here, for example, we know the following formulations: "0 is not the successor of a natural number." Or: "Natural numbers with the same successor are equal."

▶ **Cauchy Sequence** A sequence $(a_n)_{n\in N}$ of real numbers is called a *Cauchy* sequence, if:

$$\forall\varepsilon \in \mathbb{R}^{+}\exists N \in \mathbb{N} : |a_n - a_m| < \varepsilon \; \forall n,\, m \geq N$$

▶ **Theorem** Every convergent sequence of real numbers is a *Cauchy* sequence.

Proof The sequence $(a_n)_{n\in N}$ converges to a. Then there is for a given

$$\varepsilon > 0 \,\text{ein}\, N \in \mathbb{N} : |a_n - a| < \frac{\varepsilon}{2} \; \forall n \geq N.$$
$$\forall n, m \geq N : |a_n - a_m| = |a_n - a + a - a_m| = |(a_n - a) + (a - a_m)|$$
$$\leq |a_n - a| + |a_m - a| < \frac{\varepsilon}{2} + \frac{\varepsilon}{2} = \varepsilon.$$

q. e. d.
The reversal of the theorem is formulated as an AXIOM:

▶ **Completeness Axiom** In $\mathbb{R}$ every *Cauchy* sequence converges.

▶ **Definition (Subsequence)** If $(n_k)_{k\in\mathbb{N}}$ is a strictly monotonically increasing sequence of natural numbers, then the sequence $\left(a_{n_k}\right)_{k\in\mathbb{N}}$ is called a subsequence of the sequence $(a_n)_{n\in\mathbb{N}}$.

▶ **Definition (Accumulation Point)** a is called an accumulation point of the sequence $(a_n)_{n\in\mathbb{N}}$ if: $\forall\varepsilon \in \mathbb{R}^{+} \quad \exists \mathrm{N} \in \mathbb{N} : \quad \forall n_k \geq N : \left|a_{n_k} - a\right| < \varepsilon.$

Let's now move on to the interesting theorem of *Bolzano-Weierstraß* (see Forster 2013, p. 57):

▶ Theorem (Bolzano-Weierstraß Theorem) Every bounded sequence $(a_n)_{n\in\mathbb{N}}$ has at least one accumulation point.
(⇔ Every bounded sequence has at least one convergent subsequence.)

Proof

a) The sequence is bounded according to the assumption.
This means: $\exists a, b \in \mathbb{R}$ so dass $\forall \mathrm{n} \in \mathbb{N}$ gilt $a \leq a_n \leq b$.
The entire sequence thus lies within the interval $[a, b] = \{\mathrm{x} \in \mathrm{R} : \mathrm{a} \leq \mathrm{x} \leq \mathrm{b}\}$
Now we construct by complete induction a sequence of closed intervals $I_k \in \mathbb{R}, k \in \mathbb{N}$ with the following properties:
i) In I_k there are infinitely many members of the sequence $(a_n)_{n\in\mathbb{N}}$.
ii) $I_k \subset I_{k-1} \, \forall k \geq 2$.
iii) $\|I_k\| = 2^{-k}\|I_1\|$,where the double bars represent the length.
1. *Induction start*: $I_1 := [a, b]$

2. *Induction step*: $k \rightarrow k + 1$
Induction assumption:
Let the interval $I_k := [a_k, b_k]$ with properties i), ii) and iii) already be constructed.
Let $M := \frac{(a_k+b_k)}{2}$ be the middle of the interval I_k.
Since in I_k there are infinitely many members of the sequence, at least one of the subintervals $[a_k, M]$ oder $[M, b_k]$ must contain infinitely many sequence members.
We set $I_{k+1} = [M, b_k]$, if there are infinitely many sequence members in this interval, otherwise: $I_{k+1} := [a_k, M]$.
Obviously, I_{k+1} has the properties i), ii) and iii) again.

b) We now define inductively the subsequence $\left(\mathrm{a}_{\mathrm{n}_k}\right)_{k\in\mathbb{N}}$ mit $\mathrm{a}_{\mathrm{n}_k} \in I_k \, \forall k \in N$.
1. *Induction start*: Let now $n_1 := 1$, d. h. $a_{n_1} = a_1$
2. *Induction step*: $k \rightarrow k + 1$
Since in the interval I_{k+1} infinitely many sequence members of the sequence $(\mathrm{a}_\mathrm{n})_{n\in N}$ lie, there is a $n_{k+1} > n_k$ mit $a_{n_{k+1}} \in I_{k+1}$.

c) We now prove that the subsequence $\left(\mathrm{a}_{n_k}\right)_{k\in N}$ converges by showing that it is a *Cauchy*-sequence.
Let $\varepsilon < 0$ and furthermore N be chosen so large that $\|\mathrm{I}_\mathrm{N}\| < \varepsilon$.
then it follows: $\forall k, j \geq N : a_{n_k} \in I_k \subset I_N$ und $a_{n_j} \in I_j \subset I_N$.
Thus, $\left|a_{n_k} - a_{n_j}\right| \leq I_N < \varepsilon$.
q. e. d.

It should be noted that it is generally very difficult to control higher-dimensional systems. An alternative approach to the methods presented so far is to reduce the dimension of a system before applying one of the methods for controlling chaotic system developments (Auerbach, 1992).

With these remarks, the *general* considerations on the topic of complex systems are concluded here, in which a conclusion is ventured with regard to the significance of the previous explanations for economics.

4.6 Second Conclusion—Summary of Important Aspects and the (Heuristic) Value of a Science of Complex Systems for Economics in General and the Topic of Entrepreneurship in Particular

4.6.1 Brief Summary of Important Aspects

Section 4.1 illustrated the importance of attractors for the study of complex systems and particularly emphasised the concept of the strange attractor. From the theory of fractal geometry, interesting properties of fractals were then presented and related to attractors. In particular, the calculation of the dimension of fractals was introduced.

Section 4.2 showed the discovery of bifurcations and in particular the chaos-theoretical analysis of complex systems using the determination of *Lyapunov* exponents. These findings are of enormous importance for the calculation and handling of so-called phase transitions, i.e., order-order or disorder-order or order-disorder transitions, which can occur abruptly in complex systems.

In addition to the consideration of fractal geometry and chaos theory, the catastrophe theory of *Thom* was also presented in Sect. 4.3, which is significant in the discussion about crises. However, a particularly noteworthy theory is the theory of synergetics by *Haken,* presented in Sect. 4.4, which helps to explain and analyse self-organisation processes in complex systems, as they occur in market economies and in founding processes.

The explanations in Sect. 4.5 made clear how, scientifically viewed, chaos and complexity can be precisely defined on the basis of the theories presented. In this context, initial possibilities of 'controlling chaos' were pointed out.

4.6.2 What can a Science of Complex Systems do for Economics?

4.6.2.1 Complex versus Mechanistic Viewpoint

In previous sections, it became clear that there is an analogy between economics and classical mechanics. In both disciplines, linear systems play an important role in representing real-world conditions. However, one can go even further and even speak of a dominance of mechanistic ideas in economics: Thus, *Walras* and other significant economists formulated their theories in the spirit of classical mechanics.

Why was the mechanistic worldview so successful? Certainly not only because many economists had a scientific education. It was the successes of classical mechanics, being able to perform calculations with exact precision, that influenced its application in economics. Because it was an important concern of economists to make economics an exact science.

Nevertheless, one must state that economics can often be compared more with meteorology than with classical mechanics. Weather forecasting and economic development predictions are fraught with reservations due to their frequency of errors.[77] In both disciplines, attempts are made to model and predict a complex, macroscopic system with many interactively interconnected elements (Ginter, 1991, p. 87).

Not least in this realisation lies the view that the use of linear systems in modeling economic phenomena and developments is inadequate.

---

[77] For example, *Goodwin* asks in the introduction of his book 'Chaotic Economic Dynamics' the question: "Why is economic like the weather" and immediately answers it with the words: "because both are highly irregular if not chaotic, thus making prediction unreliable or even impossible" (Goodwin, 1992, p. 1).

Into this vacuum of economic explanatory deficits, the Science of Complex Systems is now flowing, the most important theories of which were revisited in the previous section. A new paradigm shift could thus be on the horizon. Unlike with the help of linear systems, non-linear systems can represent a very wide range of economic behaviours and explanatory patterns. Non-linearity, irreversibility, self-organisation and complexity or chaos are central keywords of this new approach.

For complex behaviour, non-lineality and non-linearity are of particular importance. Linear or more generally lineal models represent a very questionable idealisation of the dynamics of real systems, because their morphology is very limited, i.e., they can only represent a small number of possible behaviours.

If one asks about the significance for economics, one can see on the one hand that the equilibrium situations often considered in economics represent a strong simplification of reality. This is often much more intricate and complex than can be represented by linear systems.

On the other hand, for example, instability of equilibria does not necessarily mean 'explosion' of the system, as linear systems would suggest. There are much more complicated and interesting behaviours that can be modeled using non-linear systems. For example, self-organising processes far from equilibrium cannot be explained using linear systems.

4.6.2.2 Methods of the Science of Complex Systems as Heuristic Analysis Tools

In answering the question of the significance of the Science of Complex Systems for economics, it cannot of course be about the direct, uncritical transfer of insights from the Science of Complex Systems. This would essentially commit the error that was made in the uncritical adoption of mechanistic ideas into economics, as suggested by the neoclassical paradigm. Socio-economic systems cannot be treated like physical systems. And even if this only became implicitly clear: The scientific-theoretical background of the Science of Complex Systems is closely linked to modern physical thought structures. Aware of the possible dangers of transferring to economics, the methods of the Science of Complex Systems can be incorporated into economics and especially into the field of entrepreneurship as heuristic analysis tools, as we will see in more detail in the third part of the book.

4.6.2.3 Economic Significance from a Macroeconomic Perspective

The new approach is not only relevant for economics itself, but possibly also of economic policy significance. Economic textbooks largely deal with equilibrium situations between economic mechanisms that are capable of perfect prediction of the future. One gets the impression that it is the government's task to find and implement the most favourable equilibrium. However, the science of complex systems shows that certain dynamic situations can result in irregular, unpredictable developments, not equilibriums. It shows that self-organising processes without the attraction of a fixed point attractor prevail in the economy, which have little in common with the linear simplifications of the neoclassical paradigm.

For example, in the context of economic policy, the government must consider the possibility that its decisions can lead to unpredictable fluctuations with potentially negative effects, but that it may also be able to find ways out of chaotic developments through minimal interventions.[78]

4.6.2.4 Economic Significance from an Entrepreneurship Perspective

But not only on a macroeconomic level, but especially on a business level and particularly on the Entrepreneurship level, the insights we have gained so far have consequences. They show that situations, processes or structures that are perceived as complicated can in fact be permeated by complexity, which requires a different response than the traditional business methods designed for lineal challenges. The methods that seem suitable for business start-ups in lineal development processes may no longer apply in complex development processes, if they are recognised. The same applies to initial growth phases after the foundation. Methods that helped a company out of a crisis a few years ago may no longer work today, due to the fact that history does not repeat itself and therefore at least minimal changes in the new conditions are given. On the contrary, unforeseen turbulences could arise from intervening with supposedly proven, helpful, traditional methods, which rather exacerbate the problems than solve them.

However, if one recognises the situation as 'chaotic' or complex from a complexity science perspective, it could be significantly improved with slight nudges, so-called 'nudges'. But for this, one would first need to know whether the situation is complex, random or simple. The distinction between chance and complexity is particularly difficult, as complexity and chance are hardly distinguishable without the application of a complexity science theory. If the situation one is in is largely complex, one would also need to know at what point in the development one is. Is a phase transition imminent or is it still far away or has it already taken place? Answering these questions only enables an appropriate response, for which, however, the corresponding empirical methods are needed. Only immediately before or during the phase transition can one act successfully with 'nudges'.

4.6.3 Outlook: Predictions—Even at the Company Level—Are not Trivial in Complex Situations, Processes or Structures, Empirical Studies are Nevertheless Useful and Necessary

In the previous sections, the openness of non-linear systems to different behaviours was repeatedly highlighted as a major advantage over linear systems. This fact is considered

[78] See also the statements by David *Ruelle*: Ruelle (1993, p. 88).

very important in this book, especially with regard to the question of the significance of complex systems for the Entrepreneurship area.

Also *Arrow* addresses the many possible behavioural variants that can be represented in the same non-linear system. His judgement about economics as a superior science is unusually harsh, although his result coincides with the one presented here:

> The multiplicity of solutions is itself an embarrassment, since it suggests that economic theory, even if accurate, does not yield a unique pattern of dynamic behaviour an hence its predictions are far from sharp (Arrow, 1988, p. 277).

The question of the relationship between the theories presented in the previous sections and empirical practice, especially with regard to the Entrepreneurship area, is the central guiding question for the next chapter. Whether one wants to examine situations, processes or structures, like networks etc., as soon as Complexity plays a significant role, one needs an alternative 'tool-box' to the traditional approach. The basic understanding of concepts such as attractors, fractal dimension, *Lyapunov* exponents etc. as well as the systematic application of analytical and numerical methods like 'Controlling Chaos' procedures on dynamic models and time series represents a central link in the chain of scientific progress, which leaves the studies of lineal systems far behind.

References

Argyris, J., Faus, G., Haase, M., & Friedrich, R. (2010). *Die Erforschung des Chaos – Eine Einführung in die Theorie nicht-linearer dynamischer Systeme* (2nd ed.). Springer.

Arrow, K. J. (1988). Workshop on the economy as an evolving complex system. In P. W. Anderson (Ed.), *The economy as an evolving complex system* (p. 317). Addison Wesley.

Auerbach, D., Ott, E., Grebogi, C., & Yorke, J. A. (1992). Controlling chaos in high dimensional systems. *Physical Review Letters, 69*, 3479–3482.

Backlund, A. (2002). The concept of complexity in organisations and information systems. *Kybernetes, 31*(1), 30–43.

Baumol, W. J., & Benhabib, J. (1989). Chaos: Significance, mechanism, and economic applications. *Journal of Economic Perspectives, 3*(1), 77–105.

Belousov, B. P. (1959). Periodically acting reaction and its mechanism. *Collection of Abstracts on Radiation Medicine, 147*(145), 1.

Bloom, H. (1994). *The Western canon: The books and school of the ages*. New York: Riverhead Books.

Briggs, J., & Peat, F. D. (1993). *Die Entdeckung des Chaos. Eine Reise durch die Chaos-Theorie*. Deutscher Taschenbuch Verlag.

Brügge, P. (1993a). Mythos aus dem Computer, Teil 1. *SPIEGEL, 39*, 156–164.

Brügge, P. (1993b). Mythos aus dem Computer, Teil 2. *SPIEGEL, 40*, 232–241.

Buchler, J. R., Kollath, Z., & Mattei, J. (1995a). A choatic pulsating star: The case of R Scuti. *Physical Review Letters, 74*(6), 842–845.

Buchler, J. R., Kollath, Z., & Serre, T. (1995b). Chaos in Observational Variable Star Data: Irregularity from the Nonlinear Interaction of Standing Waves? *Waves in Astrophysics, Annals of the New York Academy of Sciences, 773*, 1–13.

Canty, M. J. (1995). *Chaos und Systeme*. Springer.

Contopoulos, G. (2002). *Order and chaos in dynamical astronomy*. Springer.

Coven, E. M., Kan, I., & Yorke, J. A. (1988). Pseudo-orbit shadowing in the family of tent maps. *Transactions of the American Mathematical Society, 308*(1), 227–241.

Cramer, F. (1988). *Chaos und Ordnung. Die komplexe Struktur des Lebendigen*. Deutsche Verlags-Anstalt.

Cuomo, K. M., & Oppenheim, A. V. (1993). Circuit implementation of synchronized chaos with applications to communication. *Physical Review Letters, 71*(1), 65–68.

Day, R. H. (1992). Complex economic dynamics: Obvious in history, generic in theory, elusive in data. *Journal of Applied Econometrics, 7*, 9–23.

Day, R. H. (1994). *Complex economic dynamics: An introduction to dynamical systems and market mechanisms*. The MIT Press.

Devaney, R. L. (1989). *An introduction to chaotic dynamical systems*. Addison Wesley.

Ebach, J. (1995). Gott und Chaos: Die Schöpfung im Werden. In V. Gorgé & R. Moser (Eds.), *Begegnungen mit dem Chaos*. Mohr.

Eckert, H., Schiepeck, G., & Herse, R. (2006). Management Synergetischer Prozesse: Grundlagen und Ansatzpunkte für ein evidenzbasiertes Management von Veränderungsprozessen. *Zeitschrift für Systemdenken und Entscheidungsfindung im Management, 5*(2), 25–50.

Ehrensberger, S. (1993). *Synergieorientierte Unternehmensintegration*. Deutscher Universitätsverlag.

Erdmann, G. (1993). *Elemente einer evolutorischen Innovationstheorie*. J.C.B. Mohr.

Feely, O. (1997). A tutorial introduction to non-linear dynamics and chaos and their application to sigma-delta modulators. *International Journal of Circuit Theory and Application, 25*, 347–367.

Feigenbaum, M. J. (1978). Quantitative universality for a class of nonlinear transformations. *Journal of statistical physics, 19*(1), 25–52.

Forster, O. (1981). *Analysis II* (4th edn.). Springer Vieweg.

Forster, O. (2004). *Analysis I* (7th edn.). Vieweg+Teubner Verlag.

Forster, O. (2013). *Analysis I* (11th edn.). Springer Spektrum.

Ginter, M. (1991). *Neue Aspekte der Finanzanalyse. Eine chaostheoretische Betrachtung von Aktienkursverläufen*. Institut für Sozialforschung der Universität.

Goodwin, R. M. (1992). *Chaotic economic dynamics*. Oxford University Press.

Gouel, C. (2012). Agricultural price instability: A survey of competing explanations and remedies. *Journal of Economic Surveys, 26*(1), 129–156.

Grassberger, P. (1990). An optimized box assisted algorithm for fractal dimensions. *Physical Review A, 148*(1–2), 63–68.

Grassberger, P., & Procaccia, I. (1983). Characterization of strange attractors. *Physical Review Letters, 50*(5), 346–349.

Grebogi, C. (1984). Strange attractors that are not chaotic. *Physica D: Nonlinear Phenomena, 13*(1–2), 261–268.

Gregersen, H., & Sailer, L. (1993). Chaos theory and its implications for social science research. *Human Relations, 46*(7), 777–802.

Guastello, S. J. (2001). Nonlinear dynamics in psychology. *Discrete Dynamics in Nature and Society, 6*(1), 11–29.

Haken, H. (1979). Zeigt die Synergetik Lösungswege für die Rechnerkopplung? – Die Selbstorganisation in Computernetzen. http://www.computerwoche.de/heftarchiv/1979/4/1191602/. Accessed 28. Aug. 2012.

Haken, H. (1981). *Synergetik*. Springer.

Haken, H. (2006a). Can synergetics be of use to management theory? In E. Brunner & T. Meynhardt (Eds.), *Selbstorganisation Managen. Beiträge zur Synergetik der Organisation* (pp. 19–30). Waxman.

Haken, H. (2006b). Die Rolle der Synergetik in der Managementtheorie: 20 Jahre später. In E. Brunner & T. Meynhardt (Eds.), *Selbstorganisation Managen. Beiträge zur Synergetik der Organisation* (pp. 17–18). Waxman.

Haken, H. (2014). *Entwicklungslinien der Synergetik. Wolfgang Tschacher. Forschungsberichte der Abteilung für Psychotherapie.* Universität Bern. 14.

Haken, H., & Schiepek, G. (2010). *Synergetik in der Psychologie: Selbstorganisation verstehen und gestalten* (2nd edn.). Hogrefe.

Hammel, S. M., Yorke, J. A., & Grebogi, C (1987). Do numerical orbits of chaotic dynamical processes represent true orbits? *Journal complexity, 3*(2), 136–145.

Hasan, H., & Norman, C. (1990). Chaotic orbits in barred galaxies with central mass concentrations. *Astrophysical Journal, 361*(1), 69–77.

Hausdorff, F. (1919). Dimension und äußeres Maß. *Mathematische Annalen, 79*(1), 157–179.

Hawking, S. (1993). Why Past Is Past. Newsweek.

Hilbert, D. (1891). Über die stetige Abbildung einer Linie auf ein Flächenstück. *Mathematische Annalen, 38*(3), 459–460.

Horgan, J. (1995). From complexity to perplexity. *Scientific American, 272*(6), 104–110.

Jetschke, G. (1989). *Mathematik der Selbstorganisation*. Vieweg+Teubner Verlag.

Kopel, M. (1996). Kontrolliertes Chaos: Ein Ausweg aus der Unternehmenskrise. *Zeitschrift für Betriebswirtschaft (ZfB), 4*, 487–503.

Kurnaz, T., & Willemsen, B. (2004). Laser – Funktionsweise und Anwendungen. http://www.rz.rwth-aachen.de/global/show_document.asp?id=aaaaaaaaaaavhvn. Accessed 28. Aug. 2012.

Langefors, B. (1995). *Essays on Infology*. Studienliteratur.

Lentz, W. (1993). *Neuere Entwicklungen in der Theorie dynamischer Systeme und ihre Bedeutung für die Agrarökonomie*. Duncker & Humblot.

Lewin, R. (1993). *Die Komplexitätstheorie: Wissenschaft nach der Chaosforschung*. Hoffmann u. Campe.

Li, T.-Y., & Yorke, J. A. (1975). Period three implies chaos. *The American Mathematical Monthly, 82*(10), 985–992.

Liening, A. (1998). *Komplexe Systeme zwischen Ordnung und Chaos*. LIT.

Liening, A. (1999). *Komplexe Systeme zwischen Ordnung und Chaos. Neuere Entwicklungen in der Theorie nicht linearer Systeme und ihre Bedeutung für die Wirtschaftswissenschaft und ihre Didaktik*. LIT.

Liening, A. (2005). *Einführung in die Mathematik* (3rd edn.). Institut für Verbundstudien NRW.

Liening, A. (2006). iLearning – Ein synergetischer Ansatz zum selbstorganisierten Lernen im Rahmen ökonomischer Bildung. In E. Brunner & T. Meynhardt (Eds.), *Selbstorganisation Managen. Beiträge zur Synergetik der Organisation* (pp. 179–205). Waxmann.

Liening, A. (2007). Ökonomische Chaostheorie. In H. May (Ed.), *Lexikon der Ökonomischen Bildung*. Oldenbourg.

Liening, A. (2009). Complexonomics – Über den Zusammenbruch des Laplaceschen Weltbildes und die Anmaßung des Wissens in der Ökonomie. In J. Weyer & I. Schulz-Schaeffer (Hrsg), *Management komplexer Systeme – Konzepte für die Bewältigung von Intransparenz, Unsicherheit und Chaos* (pp. 91–118). Oldenbourg.

Liening, A. (2013). Econoplexity: About the breakdown of Laplace's world view and the pretence of knowledge in economics. *Modern Economy, 4*(4), 305–319.

Liening A. (2015). *Ökonomische Bildung – Grundlagen und neue synergetische Ansätze*. Springer-Gabler.

Liening, A., & Krafft, K. (1995). *Elementare Wirtschaftslehre*. Kieser.

Liening, A., & Mittelstädt, E. (2008). *Wissensmanagement*. BARMER Akademie.

Loistl, O., & Betz, I. (1993). *Chaostheorie. Zur Theorie nichtlinearer dynamischer Systeme*. Oldenbourg.

Lorenz, H.-W. (1988). Neuere Entwicklungen in der Theorie dynamischer Systeme. *Jahrbuch für Nationalökonomie und Statistik, 204*(4), 295–315.

Lynch, S., & Steele, A. L. (2011). *Nonlinear optical fibre resonators with applications in Electrical Engineering and Computing. Applications of chaos and nonlinear dynamics in Engineering* (pp. 65–84). Springer.

Mainzer, K. (1995). *Zeit – Von der Urzeit zur Computerzeit*. Beck.

Mandelbrot, B. (1967). How long is the coast of Britain? Statistical self-similarity and fractional dimension. *Science, 155*(3775), 636–638.

May, R. M. (1974). Biological populations with nonoverlapping generations: stable points, stable cycles and chaos. *Science, 186*(4164), 645–647.

May, R. M. (1975). Patterns of species abundance and diversity. *Ecology and evolution of communities,* 81–120.

Mork, B. A., & Stuehm, D. L. (1994). Application of nonlinear dynamics and chaos to ferroresonance in distribution systems. *IEEE Transactions on Power Delivery, 9*(2), 1009–1017.

Mullineux, A. W., Dickinson, D., & Peng, W. (1993). *Business cycles: Theory and evidence*. Blackwell.

Neumann, R. (2013). *Libertärer Paternalismus: Theorie und Empirie staatlicher Entscheidungsarchitektur*. Mohr Siebeck.

Newhouse, S. E. (1980). Lectures on dynamical systems. In: J. Guckenheimer et al. (Eds.), *Dynamical Systems*. Boston.

Olsen, L. F., Truty, G. L., & Schaffer, W. M. (1988). Oscillations and chaos in epidemics: A nonlinear dynamic study of six childhood diseases in Copenhagen, Denmark. *Theoretical population biology, 33*(3), 344–370.

Ott, E. (1994). *Chaos in dynamical systems*. Press Syndicate of the University of Cambridge.

Otto, K.-S., Nolting, U., & Bässler, C. (2007). *Evolutionsmanagement – Von der Natur lernen: Unternehmen entwickeln und langfristig steuern*. Hanser Wirtschaftsbücher.

Paslack, R. (1996). Vom Mythos zum Logos: Chaos und Selbstorganisation bei den Griechen. In G. Küppers (Ed.), *Chaos und Ordnung* (pp. 28–43). Beck.

Peitgen, H.-O., Jürgens, H., & Saupe, D. (1992a). *Chaos – Bausteine der Ordnung*. Springer.

Peitgen, H.-O., Jürgens, H., & Saupe, D. (1992b). *Chaos: Iteration, Sensitivität, Mandelbrot-Menge*. Springer.

Peitgen, H.-O., Jürgens, H., & Saupe, D. (1994). *Bausteine des Chaos – Fraktale*. Springer.

Petrovskii, S., & Malchow, H. (2001). Wave of chaos: New mechanism of pattern formation in spatio-temporal population dynamics. *Theoretical population biology, 59*(2), 157–174.

Pinkwart, A. (1992). *Chaos und Unternehmenskrise*. Springer.

Pöppe, C. (2008). Der Dämon und der Schmetterling. *Spektrum der Wissenschaft, 8*, 47–49.

Prigogine, I. (1955). *Introduction to thermodynamics of irreversible processes*. Charles C. Thomas Publishers.

Prigogine, I. (1987). The behavior of matter under nonequilibrium conditions: Fundamental aspects and applications in energy-oriented problems. Progress Report for Period 1984 Novem-

ber 1987. Department of Physics at the University of Texas-Austin United States Department of Energy
Prigogine, I. (1995). *Die Gesetze des Chaos*. Campus.
Prigogine, I., & Nicolis, G. (1987). *Die Erforschung des Komplexen*. Piper.
Prigogine, I. & Stengers, I. (1984). *Order Out of Chaos*. Bantam.
Prigogine, I., & Stengers, I. (1986). *Dialog mit der Natur. Neue Wege naturwissenschaftlichen Denkens*. Piper.
Prigogine, I., & Stengers, I. (1993). *Das Paradox der Zeit: Zeit, Chaos und Quanten*. Piper.
Ruelle, D. (1993). *Zufall oder Chaos*. Springer.
Ruelle, D., & Takens, F. (1971). On the nature of turbulence. *Communications in mathematical physics, 20*(3), 167–192.
Schiepek, G., Manteufel, A., Strunk, G., & Reicherts, M. (1997). Kooperationsdynamik in Systemspielen. In W. Langthaler & G. Schiepek (Eds.), *Selbstorganisation und Dynamik in Gruppen* (pp. 123–160). LIT.
Schmidtchen, D. (1990). Preise und spontane Ordnung – Prinzipien einer Theorie ökonomischer Evolution. In U. Witt (Ed.), *Studien zur Evolutorischen Ökonomik I*. Duncker & Humblot.
Seiler, W. (1994). Was ist und was soll die Chaostheorie? *WiST, 11*, 563–569.
Shinbrot, T., Ott, E., Grebogi, C., & Yorke, J. A. (1993). Using small perturbations to control chaos. *Nature, 363*, 411–417.
Sitzler, J. (1984). *Griechische Literaturgeschichte*. Magnus.
Steeb, W.-H., & Kunik, A. (1989). *Chaos in dynamischen Systemen* (2nd edn.). BI-Wissenschaftsverlag.
Strunk, G. (2012). *Die Messung von Komplexität in der Wirtschaftswissenschaft*. Grundlagen, Methoden, Software und Beispiele. Dortmund.
Strunk, G., & Schiepek, G. (1994). *Dynamische Systeme - Grundlagen und Analysemethoden für Psychologen und Psychiater*. Asanger.
Strunk, G., & Schiepek, G. (2006). *Systemische Psychologie – Eine Einführung in die komplexen Grundlagen menschlichen Verhaltens*. Elsevier – Spektrum Akademischer Verlag.
Strunk, G., & Schiepek, G. (2014). *Therapeutisches Chaos: Eine Einführung in die Welt der Chaostheorie und der Komplexitätswissenschaften*. Hogrefe Verlag.
Takens, F. (1981). Detecting strange attractors in turbulence. In D. A. Rand & L. S. Young (Eds.), *Dynamicals systems and turbulence – Lecture notes in mathematics* (pp. 366–381). Springer.
Thaler, R. H., & Sunstein, C. R. (2012). *Nudge – Wie man kluge Entscheidungen anstößt* (2nd edn.). Ullstein Taschenbuchverlag.
Theiler, J. (1987). Efficient algorithm for estimating the correlation dimension form a set of discrete points. *Physical Review A, 36*(9), 4456–4462.
Theiler, J. (1989). Estimating fractal dimension. *Journal of the Optical Society of America, 7*(6), 1055–1073.
Thom, R. (1975). *Structural stability and morphogenesis*. Reading.
Thoma, B. (1996). *Chaostheorie, Wirtschaft und Börse*. Oldenbourg Wissenschaftsverlag.
Tschacher, W. (1997a). *Prozessgestalten. Die Anwendung der Selbstorganisationstheorie und der Theorie dynamischer Systeme auf Probleme der Psychologie*. Hogrefe.
Tschacher, W. & Brunner, E. J. (1997). Die Dynamik psychosozialer Systeme. In W. Langthaler & G. Schiepek (Eds.), *Selbstorganisation und Dynamik in Gruppen*(pp. 104–122). LIT.
Urry, J. (2005). The complexities of the global. *Theory, Culture and Society, 22*(5), 235–254.
Wesson, R. (1995). *Chaos, Zufall und Auslese der Natur*. Insel Verlag.
Willke, H. (1989). *Systemtheorie entwickelter Gesellschaften*. Juventa-Verl.
Wisdom, J. (1987a). Chaotic behaviour in the solar system. *Proceedings of the Royal Society of London. Series A, Mathematical and Physical Sciences, 413*, 109–129.

Wisdom, J. (1987b). Urey prize lecture: Chaotic dynamics in the solar system. *Icarus, 72*(2), 241–275.

Young, T. R. (1991). Chaos theory and symbolic interaction theory: Poetics for the postmodern sociologist. *Symbolic Interaction, 14*(3), 321–334.

Zeitler, H., & Neidhardt, W. (1993). *Fraktale und Chaos*. Wissenschaftliche Buchgesellschaft.

Zhabotinsky, A. M. (1964). Periodic liquid phase reactions. *Proceedings of the USSR Academy of Sciences, 157*, 392–395.

Zhang, W.-B. (1991). *Synergetic economics. Time and change in nonlinear economics*. Springer.

Zils, H. (2009). *Autonomie und Tradition – Innovativer Konservartismus bei Rudolf Borchardt, Harold Bloom und Botho Strauß*. Königshausen und Neumann.

Empiricism—Empirical Methods of Complexity Measurement

5

Contents

5.1 Complexity Measures in Discourse—Are ***Lyapunov*** Exponents and Fractal Dimensions Suitable? 319
5.1.1 On the Relationship Between Theory and Practice 319
5.1.1.1 The Inductive Perspective 319
5.1.1.2 The Deductive Perspective 320
5.1.1.3 Science as a Social Process 321
5.1.1.4 Sophisticated Falsification 322
5.1.1.5 Allowing Contradictory Theories 323
5.1.1.6 The Importance of Methods 324
5.1.2 Time Series in Empirical Analysis 325
5.1.2.1 Time Series as a Result of Non-linear Dynamic Processes 325
5.1.2.2 Preparation of Time Series for Complexity Science Investigations 329
5.1.3 Fractal Dimension, ***Lyapunov*** Exponents and other 'classic' Methods 335
5.1.3.1 An Initial Overview of Determining Complexity in Time Series 335
5.1.3.2 Reconstruction of a System's Phase Space 339
5.1.3.3 Special Features in the Reconstruction of Phase Spaces—The Determination of Time-Lag 347
5.1.3.4 Background Information: Correlation Coefficient—Autocorrelation 350
5.1.3.5 Background Information: Expected Value of a Random Variable & 'Mutual Information' 352
5.1.3.6 Special Features in the Reconstruction of Phase Spaces—The Determination of the Attractor Dimension: $\boldsymbol{D_2}$ 356
5.1.3.7 Special Features in the Reconstruction of Phase Spaces—Non-Overlap and Orthogonality 358
5.1.3.8 Special Features in the Reconstruction of Phase Spaces—Surrogate Test 360

A. Liening, *Complexity and Entrepreneurship*,
https://doi.org/10.1007/978-3-658-44032-9_5

5.1.3.9 About the Use of ***Lyapunov*** Exponents for Empirical Research: D_2, PD_2, ***Wolf***-, ***Briggs***-, ***Kantz***- and other Algorithms . . . 361
5.1.3.10 Background Information: Complexity Measurement . . . 364
5.1.4 Examples of the Application of 'Classical' Methods in the Context of Empirical Studies . . . 372
5.1.4.1 Macroeconomic Time Series, Such as GDP Time Series . . . 372
5.1.4.2 Price Developments . . . 373
5.1.4.3 Exchange Rate Fluctuations . . . 373
5.1.4.4 Stock Price Fluctuations . . . 373
5.1.5 Critical Examination of the 'Classical' Methods . . . 376
5.1.5.1 Reconstruction of the Phase Space . . . 376
5.1.5.2 Fractals and Reality . . . 377
5.1.5.3 Lyapunov Exponents Under Criticism . . . 378
5.2 Algorithmic Encodings as Alternative Complexity Measures?—Entropy Encodings and Other Measures . . . 379
5.2.1 Resignation or Opportunity? . . . 379
5.2.1.1 Sorting Algorithms: From 'Bubble' to 'Quick' Sort . . . 379
5.2.1.2 Compression Algorithms—Much Better . . . 381
5.2.2 Entropy as a Measure of Complexity . . . 384
5.2.3 Entropy in Information Theory—'Information Entropy' . . . 386
5.2.3.1 Introduction to ***Shannon*** Entropy . . . 386
5.2.3.2 'Variable Length Coding' (VLC) and the ***Shannon*** Entropy . . . 389
5.2.3.3 Huffman Encoding for Generating Optimal Variable Length Codes . . . 392
5.2.3.4 Entropy Encoding and Complexity . . . 399
5.2.4 'Permutation entropy' Versus 'Information Entropy' . . . 400
5.2.5 'Grammar Complexity' as an Inverse Alternative to 'Permutation Entropy' . . . 403
5.2.6 'Recurrence Plots'—Return Diagrams . . . 404
5.3 JPEG as a Solution?—Transformation Encodings . . . 416
5.3.1 ***LZW***-Compression Algorithm (Lempel, ***Ziv, Welch***) . . . 416
5.3.2 Transformation Encodings . . . 417
5.3.2.1 (Discrete) ***Fourier*** Transformation (FT and DFT) . . . 417
5.3.2.2 Discrete Cosine Transformation (DCT) . . . 421
5.3.2.3 The JPEG Compression Algorithm . . . 422
5.3.2.4 Audio Compression . . . 423
5.3.2.5 Background Information: Transformation Encoding . . . 425
5.3.3 Complexity Studies . . . 438
5.3.3.1 Application of Image Compression Methods . . . 438
5.3.3.2 Application of Audio Compression Methods . . . 438
5.3.3.3 Application of Text Document Compression Methods . . . 439
5.4 Third Conclusion—Numerous Methods for Determining Complexity . . . 439
5.5 Outlook . . . 441
References . . . 441

5.1 Complexity Measures in Discourse—Are *Lyapunov* Exponents and Fractal Dimensions Suitable?

5.1.1 On the Relationship Between Theory and Practice

You can't bargain with the truth.
(Yusuf Islam in 'An Other Cup')

It is undeniable that economic theories only possess a high degree of explanatory power when they are not only coherent in themselves, as is demanded for mathematical theories, but also when they have a convincing reference to economic reality.

5.1.1.1 The Inductive Perspective

The relationship between theory and practice is anything but trivial. Some advocate an *inductive*perspective: Here, one tries to infer generalisations in the form of a theory from observed individual cases. For example, Francis *Bacon* is an important early representative of this approach, which he recorded in his work "Novum organum scientiarum" in 1620[1]. Thus, *Bacon* demands that science should start from experience. He distinguishes the wrong approach in his view, the "anticipation of the mind", the 'anticipatio mentis', from the supposedly correct approach, the "interpretation of nature", the 'interpretatio naturae'. While in the first approach one "flies up from the senses and the individual to the most general propositions" (Bacon, 2014, p. 111), in the second approach one stays longer with the observation and only "gradually" (Bacon, 2014, p. 112) moves to generalisation, with verification playing a crucial role in the context of this approach. *Bacon* advocated the inductive approach with such euphoria that empirical sciences are also referred to as "inductive sciences" due to his influence on the discussion.

For example, David *Hume* did not agree with *Bacon's* justifications. For *Hume*, concepts without real meaning are useless, which is why he also considers it necessary to constantly ask what experience lies behind a concept. For *Hume*, experience therefore becomes a key concept, or as John *Locke* formulated:

> Nihil est in intellectu, quod non fuerit in sensu (Locke, 2012, p. 13)

Nothing is in the mind that was not previously in the senses. In his "Enquiry Concerning Human Understanding"[2] , which first appeared in 1748, *Hume* reverses the chain of

[1] Compare the German translation: (Bacon, 2014; Argyris et al., 2010, p. 307).

[2] Compare the German translation: Hume (2012).

argument: It is not the universally valid theories that are verified by individual examples of practice, thus justifying the theory-practice relationship; rather, it is the sensory experiences, i.e., the examples from practice, that suggest a meaningful theory (Hume, 2012, p. 48).

Hume points out that an absolute necessity in experiences, i.e., a causal relationship, cannot be proven, but can always only be assumed in the sense of a habit. From this it can be concluded that the inductive method does not allow the justification of an *objective* science (Hume, 2012, p. 7, 75).

The inductive process thus remains problematic (Fig. 5.1), because—starting from a few or many practical examples—one wants to infer general laws. Much later than *Hume,* namely in the twentieth century, but all the more clearly, Karl *Popper's* criticism is pronounced: According to him, there can be no induction, since "general theories cannot be derived from singular propositions" (Popper, 2010, p. 118). Sic!

5.1.1.2 The Deductive Perspective

Other researchers therefore advocate a *deductive* perspective (see Fig. 5.2). First, they formulate a theory that is then empirically tested. So, something general is formulated first and from there conclusions are drawn about the particular. The attempts to justify the deductive method, for example by Ludwig *Wittgenstein* in the 'Tractatus logico-philosophicus' (Wittgenstein, 1963), are also based on a similarly questionable approach, as ultimately only a subsequent interpretation of use is in the foreground. This is also how *Lenk* sees it (Lenk, 1968, p. 619).

According to *Popper,* in the end only falsification remains, the possibility of refuting a theory. If one follows *Popper* and the critical rationalism associated with him, theories ultimately cannot be justified, let alone objectively and universally verified. But they can be criticised, and one can accept those theories (provisionally!) that best withstand criticism and have the greatest explanatory power (Popper, 1995, p. 277). So says *Popper:*

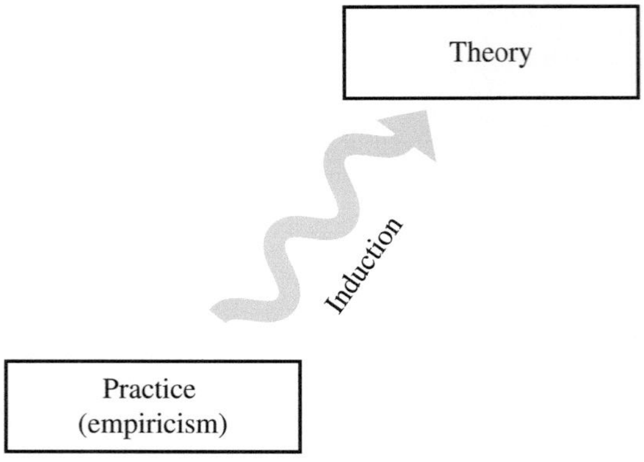

Fig. 5.1 (problematic) Induction

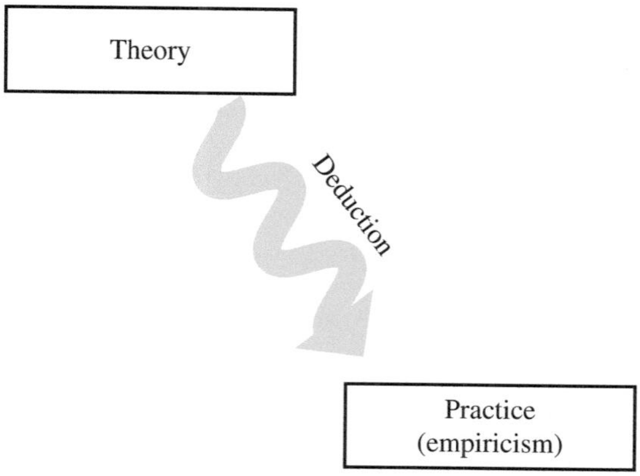

Fig. 5.2 (problematic) Deduction

> Science is a critical activity. We critically test our hypotheses. We criticise them to find errors; and in the hope of eliminating the errors and thus getting closer to the truth (Popper, 2004, p. 51).

Following this approach, one must design a theory in such a way that it not only makes sense in itself, but also faces the possibility of refutation, especially empirical refutation. A verification is therefore considered hopeless, but a provisional acceptance of the theory is thus guaranteed.

Let's assume that a counterexample is found in practice that casts doubt on the supposedly good theory: Is the whole theory then meaningless and wrong if it has perhaps proven itself in many other practical examples? It may still apply to almost all cases known. So when is a theory questioned? When two or three counterexamples have been found? What significance must a counterexample have to bring down a theory? Doesn't falsification imply a *finite* set of 'wrong' theories, as this intended exclusion procedure implicitly assumes that in the end the 'right' theories remain? Therefore, is the number of false theories actually finite? Thomas *Kuhn* concludes from the discussion not entirely unjustifiably with the following words:

> No process uncovered so far by the historical study of scientific development bears any resemblance to the methodological template of falsification by direct comparison with nature (Kuhn, 1996, p. 90).

5.1.1.3 Science as a Social Process

In addition to all these questions, one must also consider that science is always a social process. For example, who, as a young scientist whose career still seems uncertain, would completely question a theory if it has so far been highly regarded as a paradigm? Who likes to go against the mainstream when they have just taken the first steps in the 'Scientific Community'? *Strunk* raises the question of whether, in the end, it might even be a matter of societal and social power structures that decide whether a theory is accepted or not? In this context, he points to works by Karin *Knorr-Cetina* that, in his view, tend in a similar direction (Knorr-Cetina, 2002). Thus, *Strunk* writes about *Knorr-Cetina:*

> In her analysis of interaction processes in scientific working groups, she concludes that science is a social process that does not differ from other social processes. Power structures, communication patterns, and interaction dynamics determine the findings, not so much the 'objective' facts of the investigated 'reality' (Strunk, 2016, p. 26).

Lakatos succinctly says about the thesis of science as a social process: "Truth would then lie in power" (Lakatos, 1974, p. 91). A "truth" defined by power can never be seen as legitimate. But even a democratically brought about "truth" lacks legitimacy. Just because a majority considers a certain theory to be true, it does not necessarily have to be valid. One could postulate that truth can neither be dictated nor can one vote on it.

All in all, all the questions raised are at least difficult questions that can hardly be objectively assessed, if at all. What remains is a high degree of uncertainty regarding the theory-practice relationship. In the end, one is faced with the dilemma of having to "either deal with every charlatan or risk putting some serious researchers in a strait-jacket" (Brandes, 1985, p. 128).

Apparently, there is currently no scientifically secured way, neither from theory to practice nor vice versa. At least it seems that even the line drawn by *Popper* between science and non-science has become "fragile" (Brandes, 1985, p. 130).

5.1.1.4 Sophisticated Falsification

In the end, there is hardly anything left but *Popper's* minimal requirement for the possibility of falsification. Because this variant seems to be the most rationally defensible way to build a bridge between theory and practice, if one wants to adhere to the postulate of rationality, which forms the basis of all science and especially economics. One could perhaps save *Popper's* approach through *Lakatos'* proposal of a *sophisticated* falsification, who thereby admittedly attempts to save rationality. According to this, a theory is only eliminated by falsification when a) in a new theory to be tested there is an empirical surplus of content compared to the predecessors, b) part of the empirical surplus of content can be verified and c) the new theory contains the previous success of the existing theory, i.e. the part of the existing theory that could not be falsified (Lakatos et al., 1982, p. 114).

Here it becomes apparent that *Lakatos* is eroding one of *Popper's* foundations, namely logical falsification: A theory against which no empirical facts speak and therefore should be considered temporarily *true* in the sense of *Popper,* could still be falsified in the sense of *Lakatos* if a new theory emerges that contains an empirical surplus of content. On the other hand, a theory that would be shaken by counterexamples in the

Popperian sense could persist as long as there is no better theory. "There is no falsification before the emergence of a better theory," proposes *Lakatos*, although his search for the "most trustworthy" and "most reliable" theories is also rather vague at many points (Lakatos, 1974, p. 117). Nevertheless, one does not have to go as far as Paul *Feyerabend*, who advocates an 'anything goes' in rejection of a methodological compulsion, when he claims:

> Successful research does not obey general rules—it relies on one standard or another, and the moves that promote it often become clear to the researcher only after the research is completed (Feyerabend, 1986, p. 376).

Furthermore, *Feyerabend* states that there is "no general theory of science, there is only the process of research and rules of thumb that help us to continue it, but which must constantly be checked for their usefulness" (Feyerabend, 1986, p. 380).

It would therefore already be a great achievement if one were to critically but rationally look beyond the horizon of the prevailing paradigms from time to time and finally not consider any of the proposed methods for clarifying the relationship between theory and practice as the ultimate wisdom.

5.1.1.5 Allowing Contradictory Theories

"Normal research," claims *Andersson,* "is not critical, but tradition- and paradigm-driven. It does not attempt to falsify a fundamental and paradigmatic theory" (Andersson, 1988, p. 44). Despite the above example of the young researcher who, knowing better, does not dare to stand against the mainstream, one does not have to follow this thesis. This is especially true when looking at economics. There, in particular, there is already—one might almost be tempted to say—a tradition of allowing and appreciating contradictory theories of (renowned) researchers. Consider, for example, the theories of Friedrich August von *Hayek* and John Maynard *Keynes*, which could hardly be more contradictory in most issues. While one ultimately advocates for the state to stay out of private economic activities to promote economic growth, the other calls for permanent state intervention to counter the supposedly persistent demand pessimism in the economy.[3]

Could it therefore not also be that a theory is falsely falsified, not because its hypotheses are wrong, but because the possibly multitude of framework conditions and temporal

[3] *Keynes'* theory may never have been logically consistent, but it worked in practice, if one thinks, for example, of the economic policy *Keynesianism* of the Federal Republic in the late nineteen sixties and early seventies. Hardly any politician could be found at that time who did not claim: I am a *Keynesian!* One can indeed stand on one leg. But since the stagflation from the mid-seventies, the empirical support for *Keynes'* approaches has disappeared strikingly.

as well as dynamic factors, under which a theory only applies, cannot be correctly captured in the end? Whether, for example, in the IS-LM system one curve lies horizontally or even vertically, determines which theory is to be preferred. The position of these curves, however, must be empirically determined. And this is, for example, very dependent on the temporal dimension and a multitude of other conditions that need to be correctly captured and analysed.

Is it not rather due to the methods we use in empirical research that we find this theory-practice relationship so difficult?

Hayek and *Keynes* have received great recognition for their diametrically opposed theories. *Hayek* even received the Nobel Prize in Economics in 1974, which surprised many, as the world had sworn by *Keynes'* theories well into the seventies. The Nobel Prize Committee is apparently aware of the problems of the theory-practice relationship. *Strunk* recalls the 2012 Nobel Prize and the fact that Eugene *Fama* and Robert *Shiller* even two economists received the Nobel Prize, whose theories could hardly be more contradictory. *Strunk* writes:

> Eugene Fama understands the market as a system driven by rational interests, which, using the mathematical laws of the random walk or at least a martingale model, knows how to escape manipulation and external control as well as crises. And Robert Shiller claims the opposite in all points: no rationality, no random walk, no optimism regarding the healthy self-organising forces of the market (Strunk, 2016, p. 18).

Insights from economics, viewed in this way, can therefore have no claim to timeless universality or, more clearly stated, to 'truth'. They are also constantly subject to change and compete with each other.

5.1.1.6 The Importance of Methods

It very much depends on the exact empirical determination of the conditions under which a theory temporarily holds validity, the (measurement) accuracy, and the type of methods with which we conduct empirical research. The empirical *methods* probably represent the central key to the theory-practice relationship.

As a real science, economics is based on two pillars: a coherent theory and corresponding empirical content. However, neither can we apparently conclude securely from theory to practice nor vice versa, and even the statement that a theory is valid until it is refuted allows for doubt.

However: On the one hand, an economic theory without any empirical content appears questionable. This is especially true in relation to the theoretical models presented, what *Sterman* critically notes for the non-linear decision models he considered:

> Worse, without empirical tests of the decision rules, the verisimilitude of the models was open to doubt. In the absence of empirical data the relevance of nonlinear phenomena remained questionable (Sterman, 1989, p. 173).

On the other hand, a theory that has so far received no empirical attention can certainly stimulate viewing empirical observations from a new perspective. In this respect, theory can positively influence practice as well as empirical research.

The theoretical engagement with complex systems indeed implies seeing empirically observable economic time series in a different light. This particularly affects especially time series, whose course can be described as irregular. Examples of this include can exchange rate fluctuations, stock price trends, or gross domestic product developments.

The new insights into complex behaviour of systems lead to the question of whether the observable irregular behaviour—as previously believed—is solely due to stochastic or exogenous influences, or whether the time series are the result of non-linear deterministic systems?

Answering this question is a difficult undertaking, especially since the simple or usual statistical methods in econometrics, such as the use of linear regression analysis tools, do not always lead further in the context of complexity.[4] Therefore, there is a need for additional methods that contribute to illuminating the theory-practice relationship in a meaningful way and generating helpful insights that further develop the theories and also benefit a 'better' practice.

5.1.2 Time Series in Empirical Analysis

5.1.2.1 Time Series as a Result of Non-linear Dynamic Processes

To illustrate the problem of traditional statistics, let's consider a simple example in which we visualise three number series. But first, let's clarify what we mean by a time series:

Definition (Time Series (Discrete))

A sequence of numbers is called a (discrete) time series if it represents a sequence of real numbers with $(a_t)_{t \in \mathbb{N}} \in \mathbb{R}$, with t = time unit (e.g., years, days, hours, seconds).

A time series can follow a pattern, i.e., be reproducible, or not. In the first case, the process that generates the time series is deterministic, in the second case stochastic.

If t does not represent a unit of time, then any type of number sequence could be meant here. Let's consider three number sequences, as shown in Figs. 5.3, 5.4 and 5.5.

[4]Traditional methods often do not allow for the reconstruction of non-linear dynamic processes and the investigation of emerging strange attractors and emergence processes. For traditional econometrics see Heil (2000).

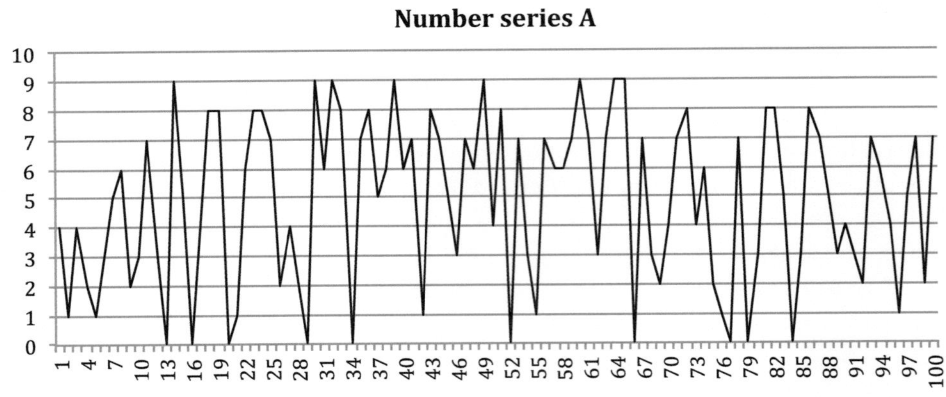

Fig. 5.3 Number sequence A

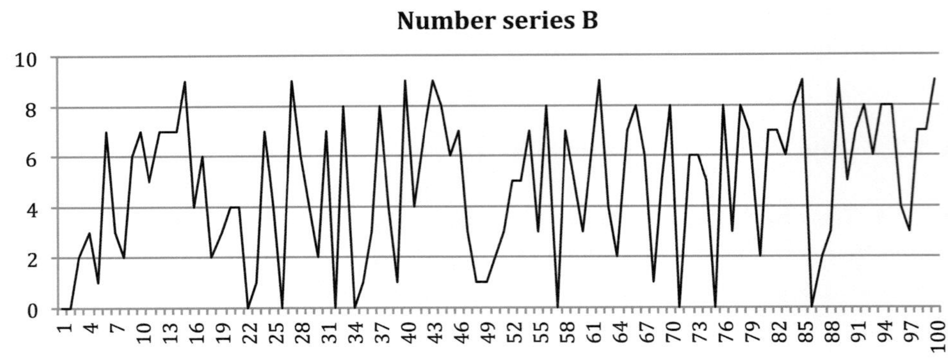

Fig. 5.4 Number sequence B

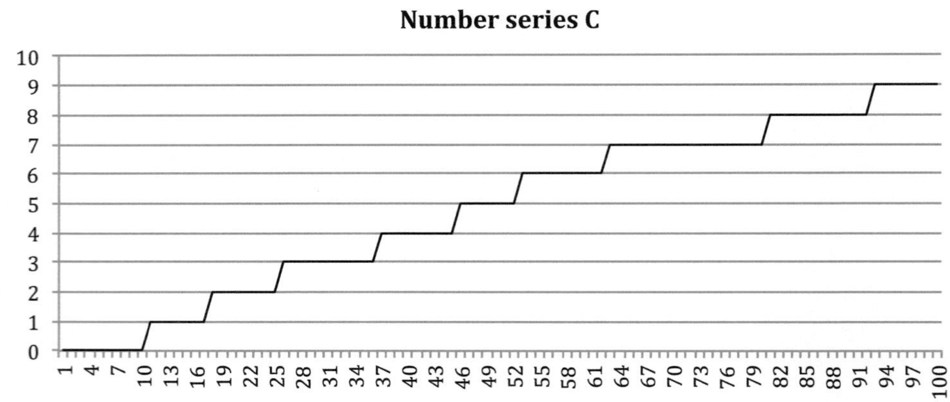

Fig. 5.5 Number sequence C

At a simple optical analysis, the first two number sequences A and B appear random, whereas the number sequence C appears ordered.

If we now examine the three number sequences with simple statistical methods, the following picture emerges (see Table 5.1).

Obviously, no differences between the data series can be identified from the above static studies. All three number sequences are statistically considered equal, although a first visual analysis already reveals differences between the third sequence C and the other two sequences A and B.

If we now consider how the number sequences were created, the problem becomes clear.

A first closer analysis shows that the same digits appear in all three number sequences and that the decisive difference between the three sequences lies in the respective different order of the digits.

In the first **number sequence A**, the sequence is derived from the first 100 decimal places of $\sqrt{2}$. The 'square root of two' can be calculated from a simple recursive equation: $x(t+1) = \frac{1}{2} \cdot \left(x(t) + \frac{2}{x(t)}\right)$, $x(0) > 0$.

So here we have a simple deterministic system that already shows the above values as a result after a few iterations. Since the square root of two is irrational, this means that the number cannot be represented by any fraction (i.e., no rational number) and thus the decimal places not only represent an infinite number, but are also non-periodic. That is, no digit window can be found that repeats itself after a finite time. So we have here a complex system, albeit a very simple one.

The second **number series B** is also complex, but even maximally complex, as here the same digits were arranged using a random generator. So there is a **random** order. The arrangement of the individual digits is stochastically independent.

For the third **number series C**, the following digit is always greater than or equal to the preceding one. By connecting the individual digits, an **ordered** system is therefore present.

We can see, therefore, that with the statistical measures used, the specific dynamics of the system play no role and the order of the digits is also irrelevant.

An initial indication of how significant the dynamics are is shown in the following example of the well-known **logistic function:** $x(t+1) = \lambda \cdot x(t) \cdot (1 - x(t))$. With an arbitrary starting value of e.g. $x(0) = 0{,}01$, the time series as shown in Fig. 5.6 results from 100 iterations and $\lambda = 4{,}0$.

Table 5.1 Number sequences

Number sequence	Sum	Average	Median	Standard deviation	Variance
A	481	4.81	5.00	2.83	8.09
B	481	4.81	5.00	2.83	8.09
C	481	4.81	5.00	2.83	8.09

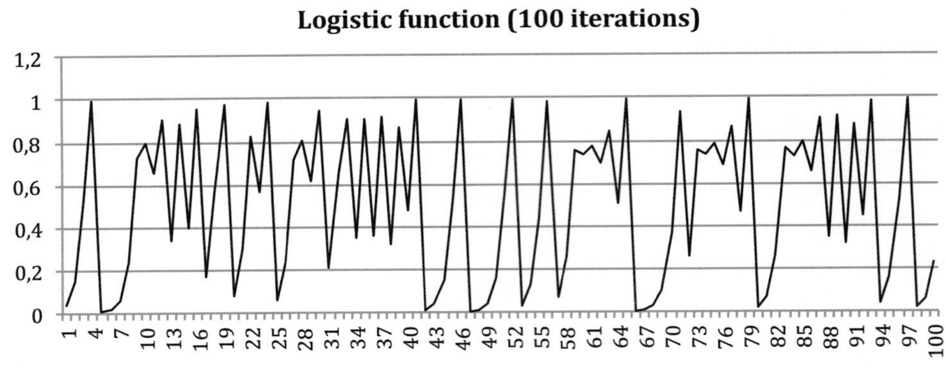

Fig. 5.6 Logistic Function

An obvious order pattern is not recognisable at first glance. The values seem to jump around wildly.

In the case of randomness: If, for example, you had rolled a 6 with a *(Laplace-)*die[5] 99 times, it cannot be concluded that you will probably roll a 6 the 100th time. The desired further 6 is just as likely, whether I had previously rolled a 1 99 times. The probability (unless the die was manipulated) for a 6 is always 1/6, regardless of the previous dice results.

In this time series, which is generated by the logistic function, there seem to be extreme turbulences, but a random development of the time series can be ruled out due to the underlying deterministic development law. So the whole thing must be more complex and therefore also of a deterministic nature.

Determinism on the other hand, in contrast to chance, means that the next value in some way results from the previous values, i.e., a connection between the values can be demonstrated. In the case of very low complexity, the simplest possible thesis could be: the next value directly depends on the previous value. If this were the case, one would have to recognise a pattern at the moment when the respective value $x(t)$ is plotted against the value $x(t + 1)$. Indeed, in this example, we then obtain the already known pattern, which can be interpreted as the Strange Attractor of the dynamic system based on the logistic function, as shown in Fig. 5.7.

[5]A *Laplace* experiment is a random experiment in which all possibilities of the experimental outcome have the same probability. In this case, this means that the probability of rolling a 1 is the same as that of rolling any other number on the die.

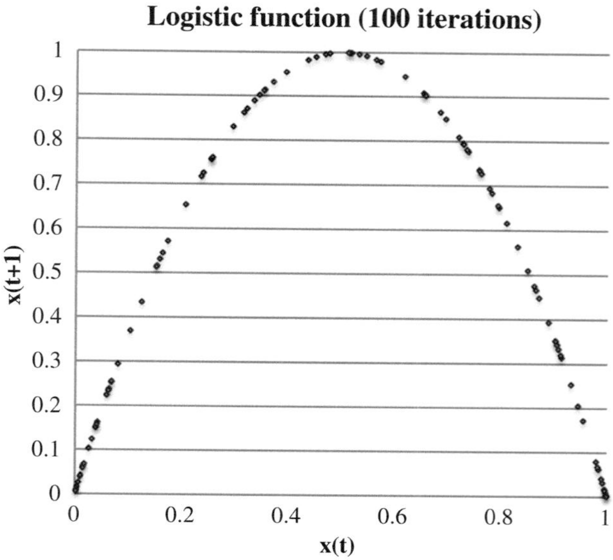

Fig. 5.7 Attractor based on the logistic function

Now, the dynamics of the logistic function are very simple. Complex systems with a multitude of dimensions and underlying time series taken from practice will not easily reveal their attractor, if it exists at all.

However, there are a number of methods that can be used to examine complex systems for exactly this; methods that allow the differences discussed in such systems (ordered, random, complex) to be captured within the framework of model-theoretical but also empirical studies.

5.1.2.2 Preparation of Time Series for Complexity Science Investigations

From financial mathematics, we have learned that it makes sense not to look at the absolute values of a time series, but rather the changes between the values. Let's consider the following time series, see Fig. 5.8:

On the x-axis, 100 time points are plotted (e.g., days). On the y-axis are values from 11 to 110 (e.g., the price of a stock). This could describe the development of a stock's price as it could evolve over 100 days. At first glance, it looks as if everything is going steeply upwards and an investment in this stock appears lucrative. And indeed, mathematically, the curve can be described by a simple linear function like $f(x)=x+10$. Thus, the starting value of the price development is $f(1)=1+10=11$ and $f(100)=100+10=110$. The slope can be easily determined: $f'(x)=1$. This means that the absolute change

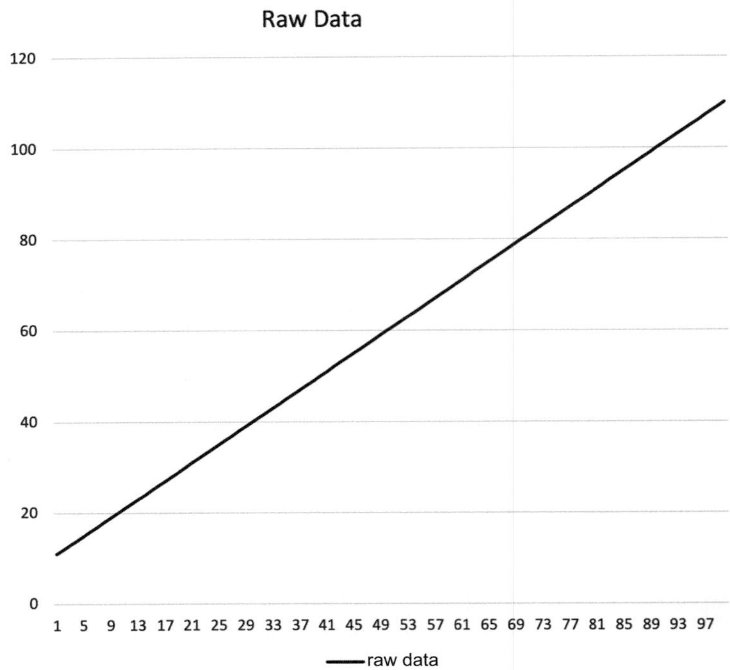

Fig. 5.8 Raw data

from price to price, i.e., the price gain, or the "Return" is exactly 1 (Fig. 5.9) with $r_{abs}(x_t) = x_t - x_{t-1}$.

However, the interpretation of the result changes instantly when, instead of the absolute "Returns", relative "Returns" (Fig. 5.10) are considered, i.e., when the respective "Return" x_t -x_{t-1} is related to the previous price x_{t-1},

with $r_{rel}(x_t) = \frac{x_t - x_{t-1}}{x_{t-1}}$

or expressed in percent:$r_{rel}(x_t) = \frac{x_t - x_{t-1}}{x_{t-1}} \cdot 100$

One can see that the "return" in relation to the previous course value, for example at a course of 20 with 5.25%, is significantly larger than for example at a course of 90, where the "return" is only 1.12%. Thus, an investment in this share does not seem to be as rewarding as it initially appeared. Therefore, it makes sense to consider the relative "returns" for further analysis.

Considering "relative returns" has advantages over "absolute returns". However, they too can lead to misleading results, at least at a superficial glance. How can this be?

Suppose the price of our share is 50 and it rises to 100 in the first period and then falls back to 50. If you calculate relative returns, then the share price has increased by 100% in the first period: $r_{\mathrm{rel}}\,(100) = \frac{100-50}{50} \cdot 100 = 100\,\%$

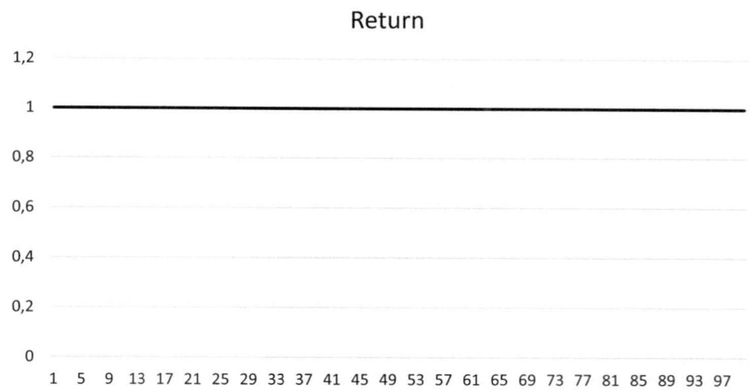

Fig. 5.9 Return

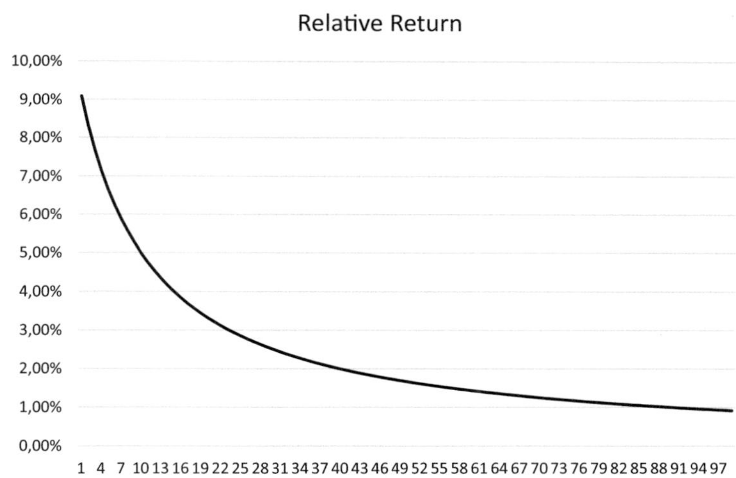

Fig. 5.10 Relative Return

In the second period, it fell by 50%: $r_{\text{rel}}\,(50) = \frac{50-100}{100} \cdot 100 = -50\,\%$

If you simply added the "relative returns", you would find that you would have earned a total return of 100% – 50% = 50%, even though the price has not actually changed and is still at 50 as it was at the beginning. "Relative returns" are not additive. The *arithmetic mean* would also be wrong here: $\frac{100\,\%-50\,\%}{2} = 25\%$ is not the average increase.

To determine, for example, the average growth rate ($D{=}d{-}1$), we must calculate as follows:

$50 + 50 \cdot 1.0 = 50 \cdot (1 + 1.0) = 100$ and $100 + 100 \cdot -0.5 = 100 \cdot (1 - 0.5) = 50$, so in summary:

$50 \cdot (1 + 1.0) \cdot (1 - 0.5) = 50 \cdot 2.0 \cdot 0.5 = 50.$

In other words, $d^2 = 2{,}0 \cdot 0{,}5$ so: $d = \sqrt{2 \cdot 0{,}5} = 1$, so d=1+0.0, so D=0.0 or 0%. That is, no "return" was earned overall. What we have calculated here and need to calculate is nothing other than the *geometric mean*:

$$D = \sqrt[n]{x_1 \cdot \ldots \cdot x_n}$$

The "relative return" is therefore incorrect in terms of additivity (whether calculated absolutely or as an arithmetic mean). Therefore, "relative returns" are completely unsuitable for investment decisions at a simple glance, unless we consider geometric means in the analysis.

To address these and other minor challenges that arise, for example, with large changes, the literature often suggests another calculation, the so-called logarithmic change:

"Log Return". To calculate this, one computes the logarithms to the base of Euler's number *e* (the inverse function of the logarithm is the exponential, or *e*-function), the so-called "natural logarithm" of the two consecutive values and forms the difference, as with the simple returns, thus: $r_{\log}(x_t) = \ln(x_t) - \ln(x_{t-1})$

This formula can be simplified with a mathematical transformation and one obtains: $r_{\log}(x_t) = \ln\left(\frac{x_t}{x_{t-1}}\right)$.[6]

"Log-Returns" are additive, unlike "relative Returns".

Assuming, the price of our stock is again 50 and it rises in the first period again to 100 and then falls back to 50. If we compare the "relative Returns" with the "Log-Returns", we can easily see the additivity of the "Log-Returns" (Table 5.2):

By the way, one can see from the next table that the "Log Returns" correspond almost exactly to the "relative Returns" with slight fluctuations (Table 5.3):

The deviations between the "relative returns" and the "logarithmic returns" only become apparent during strong fluctuations, i.e., turbulence (Table 5.4):

However, the "logarithmic return" becomes problematic with values close to zero (Table 5.5):

[6] This follows directly from the **functional equation** that establishes a **homomorphism** between multiplication and addition, since the multiplication of two numbers *a* and *b* is actually structurally the same as the addition of the logarithms of these two numbers, i.e., *ln(a)*+ln*(b); "the same"*, except for homomorphism. And the homomorphism is the logarithm, thus: *ln(a·b)=ln(a)·ln(b)*. From this it follows easily: *ln(a/b)=ln(a)-ln(b)*.

Table 5.2 Various Returns—Price is at 50, rises by 50, falls by 5

Data	Rel. Return (%)	Log. Return (%)	Abs. Return
50			
100	100.00	69.31	50
50	−50.00	−69.31	−50
Total:	50	0	0

Table 5.3 Various Returns—Slight Price Fluctuations

Data	Rel. Return (%)	Log. Return (%)	Abs. Return
119	−0.83	−0.84	−1
118	−0.84	−0.84	−1
117	−0.85	−0.85	−1
118	0.85	0.85	1
119	0.847	0.844	1
120	0.840	0.837	1

Table 5.4 relative, logarithmic, and absolute returns

Data	Rel. Return (%)	Log. Return (%)	Abs. Return
120	20.00	18.23	20
140	16.67	15.42	20
160	14.29	13.35	20
160	0.00	0.00	0
140	−12.50	−13.35	–20
120	−14.286	−15.415	–20
100	−16.667	−18.232	–20
100	0.000	0.000	0

Table 5.5 Various returns—data close to zero

Data	Rel. Return	Log. Return	Abs. Return
100			
0.00001	−100.000%	−1611.810%	−99.99999

The values of the "logarithmic return" can be explained by the course of the logarithmic curve (Fig. 5.11):

One can see from the curve that at the point 1 on the x-axis, the logarithm takes the value zero. The slope at the point 1 is exactly: $\ln'(x) = \frac{1}{x} \Rightarrow \ln'(1) = 1$. This means that

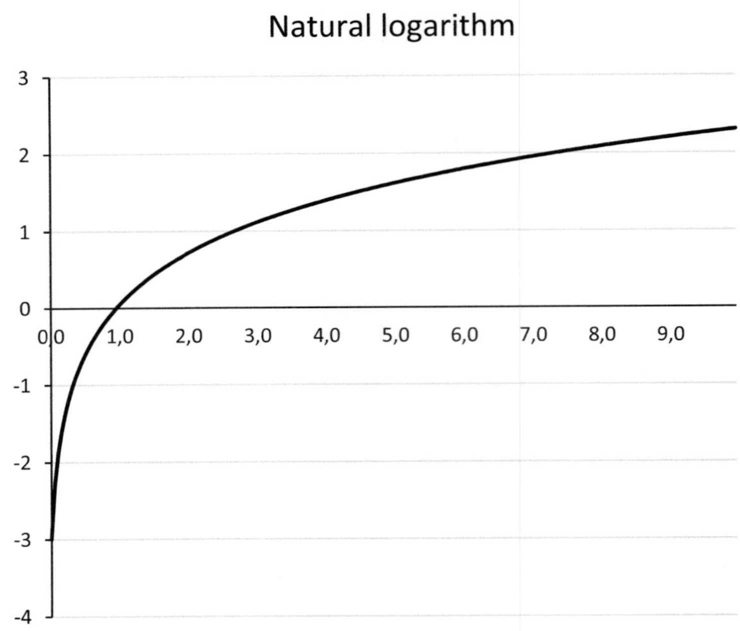

Fig. 5.11 Natural logarithm

here the curve almost has the shape of the bisector, i.e., the effects upwards and downwards are almost identical, as long as the values are close to 1. This explains why small deviations both downwards and upwards show almost the same values. Since the function diverges towards "minus infinity" in the direction of the zero point on the x-axis, it is clear why values close to zero become immensely large, far larger than corresponds to the "relative returns". Also, values less than zero are not allowed, as the logarithm is only defined for positive values.

For our data set, this results in the following "Log Return" curve (Fig. 5.12):

The differences to the "relative returns" are negligible in this case. The average of the deviations is 0.0004. In total, we have thus learned four ways, including the raw data, with which we can work to perform a complexity analysis.

1. **Raw Data** (n raw data, i.e., absolute values)
   $x_t, t \in \{1, \ldots, n\}$
2. **Abs. Return** (the absolute changes between the values, discrete)
   $r_{abs}(x_t) = x_t - x_{t-1}$

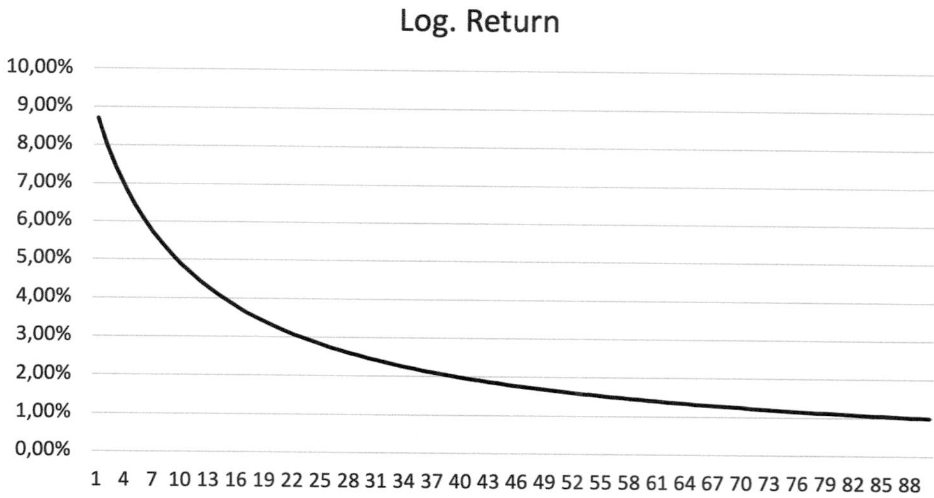

Fig. 5.12 Logarithmic Return—LogReturn

3. **Rel. Return** (the relative changes between the values, discrete)
   $r_{rel}(x_t) = \frac{x_t - x_{t-1}}{x_{t-1}}$
4. **Log. Return** (the logarithmic changes between the values, continuous[7]

5.1.3 Fractal Dimension, *Lyapunov* Exponents and other 'classic' Methods

5.1.3.1 An Initial Overview of Determining Complexity in Time Series

In Sect. 4.2.2 we discussed the basic calculation of *Lyapunov* exponents and fractal dimensions in a system for determining the complexity of a system. In empirical quantitative research, for example, we analyse time series. From a complexity science perspective, the question arises whether the time series to be examined is random, complex or ordered, i.e., how it is to be classified in the tension field of chance, chaos and order? Is there a mathematically describable equation behind the measured data, is there an

[7]The logarithmic return is the non-discrete version of the change measurement, i.e., continuous.) In general, we often use "Log Returns" in empirical studies to calculate complexity measures due to the mentioned arguments.

$r_{\log}(x_t) = \ln\left(\frac{x_t}{x_{t-1}}\right)$

ordered structure, even if the data appear random, or is everything just chance in the end? One faces the special challenge in such questions that one rarely has all the necessary variables (time series) available to adequately reflect a system. The question therefore arises first of all whether one can reconstruct the associated phase space from the available time series at all? Is a (one-dimensional) time series sufficient to span a possibly multi-dimensional phase space, and what criteria must the underlying time series meet, for example in terms of their length, so that suitable statements can be made here?

In order to be able to investigate systems in this way, a number of methods have been developed that can now be described as 'classic'. Some of these methods will be briefly mentioned below to give an idea of the range of possibilities. There is no claim to completeness. Subsequently, some of these methods will be explained in more detail, highlighting their respective advantages and disadvantages.

▶ i. Phase portrait and time course: Reconstruction of the phase space

A fundamental difficulty is that in econometric studies the potentially generating process of the system to be observed is not known.

First of all, the above formulation alone shows that one assumes a priori that a system exists at all. To gain clarity about the process underlying a dynamic system, a phase portrait should first be created. This requires the reconstruction of the associated phase space. Although a simple time course diagram already reveals a lot, the overall context of the system is only captured by considering sufficiently many dimensions. If the system is deterministic, the development lines, the trajectories of the system that are observed, may move towards an attractor,[8] so that the reconstruction of the phase space can produce such an attractor. The structure of the attractor already provides a more detailed understanding of the dynamics of the system: If, for example, a limit cycle attractor is found, this indicates periodic oscillatory behaviour of the system.

If, on the other hand, a stochastic process underlies the dynamic development, the development lines would have to fill the phase space, resulting in a very diffuse image, also known as white noise[9] , which contradicts the idea of a deterministic attractor. In complex processes, a strange attractor can be found, which, despite its fractal struc-

[8] It should be pointed out again at this point that in economics only dissipative systems are of interest. Conservative systems, whose phase space volume is preserved, are not considered. Therefore, the presence of an attractor can always be assumed.

[9] Noise can be generated by adding a random number to a dynamic variable at each individual measurement or time point. If this noise is Gaussian with a certain width, also called noise strength, it is also referred to as broadband or white noise. The term is analogous to white light, which contains all spectra or frequencies of visible light with equal strength or intensity. Filtered white noise, where there is a damping of higher frequencies, where, for example, the noise decreases with increasing frequency (so-called $1/f$ noise or $1/f^2$ noise), is also called coloured noise. Here, obviously, the random data are correlated with each other as opposed to white noise (Müller, 1990).

ture, appears more ordered than the result of a stochastic system behaviour. Ultimately, the structure of the attractor can be qualified using *Lyapunov* exponents and dimension determinations. In the next chapters, we will thoroughly consider the peculiarities to be aware of when reconstructing the phase space.

ii. Spectral Analysis—Creating a Power Spectrum

The is often used as a classic tool to distinguish between periodic and chaotic behaviours. With the help of spectral analysis, the time series can be broken down into harmonic series of different amplitudes or wavelengths. The observed trajectories are transformed into the frequency space. This allows the frequencies underlying the dynamic system to be read. *Schwager* says:

> The result of the spectral analysis is a power spectrum that shows a value for each frequency within the frequency range (Schwager, 2005, p. 617).

For periodic and quasi-periodic movements, the corresponding graphical representation of the spectral analysis, e.g., as a , results in "sharply pronounced peaks" (Argyris et al., 2010, p. 29). In contrast, chaotic or complex as well as stochastic behaviour is characterised by the fact that no dominant frequencies can be recognised and therefore continuous or noisy courses become visible. However, this method does not allow to distinguish between stochastic and chaotic behaviour (Lorenz, 1993, p. 202 ff.). Therefore, spectral analysis cannot be used as the sole method for determining complexity. In the context of transformation encodings (Sect. 5.3.2), we will deal more exhaustively with the background of this analysis method, which is based on the *Fourier* transformation.

iii. Representing Autocorrelations

In Sect. 5.1.3.3, we will deal more intensively with the in the context of phase space reconstruction. However, it should be noted here that autocorrelation can generate information about the development process of a system, so that autocorrelation can not only be part of a certain procedure, but also has a unique value. The autocorrelation determines the correlation, i.e., the relationship, between a function f at a time t and itself at a time $t + \tau$. It can be represented in a diagram in which the correlation $\alpha(\tau)$ is plotted against τ.

Argyris et al. point out that autocorrelation and are essentially comparable representations of the same development process (Argyris et al., 2010, p. 85). They crucially add:

> However, both forms of description highlight very different properties of the original signal: The autocorrelation reflects memory capacity and internal connections of the system, while the power spectrum provides information about dominant fundamental frequencies (Argyris et al., 2010, p. 85).

iv. Calculating Lyapunov Exponents

With another method, in which two neighbouring trajectories are observed in their temporal course, averaging over a multitude of trajectories, for example, *Lyapunov* exponents can be determined, which in turn provide information about the dynamics of the system. Positive *Lyapunov* exponents indicate initial sensitivity and thus complexity or chaos. Negative or zero values, on the other hand, indicate a continuous behaviour of the system trajectories. However, this method requires a phase space that may first have to be (re-)constructed. In a multidimensional phase space, a different *Lyapunov* exponent can occur in each direction, where one naturally considers the largest *Lyapunov* exponent. This is also referred to as the LLE, the '*Largest Lyapunov Exponent*'.

Let us briefly refer here to the *KAM* theorem mentioned,which *Kolmogorov, Arnold* and *Moser* established and proved in the sixties, according to which the movement in the phase space of classical mechanics is neither completely regular nor completely irregular, but the trajectory is sensitive to the initial conditions.[10]

From the variety of possible algorithms[11] for calculating *Lyapunov* exponents, the *Wolf*-,the*Briggs*- and especially the *Rosenstein*- and *Kantz*-algorithm stand out (Wolf et al., 1985; Briggs, 1990; Rosenstein et al., 1993; Kantz, 1994).

Some of these methods, which have different advantages and disadvantages depending on the approach, will be discussed in more detail later.

▶ v. Determining (Fractal) Dimension

One of the first developed methods for determining the fractal dimension of a strange attractor from given empirical data is the so-called *Grassberger/Procaccia*-method.If the dimension of the attractor does not continue to grow with increasing dimension of the phase space, but converges towards a fixed value, this is considered an indication that a deterministic structure is present. If the calculated dimension is also fractional, i.e. not an integer[12] , theoretically, the reconstructed attractor is a strange attractor, which means that non-linear laws and chaotic system behaviour underlie the observed empirical results. The method is based on this consideration.

▶ vi. Analysing the ***BDS*** Test

The so-called *BDS* Test, which is based on *Brock, Dechert* and *Scheinkman*, serves to examine the empirical data for the underlying dynamics and can be seen as a further development of the classic , which we will consider in more detail at the end of this

[10] See the explanations on the *KAM* theorem in Sect. 4.1.1

[11] There are indeed other algorithms in this context. For example, the algorithm of *Benettin*, which was developed in reference to the method of *Shinada* and *Nagashima*, the *Kurths-Herzel* and the *Ruelle* algorithm can be distinguished (Loistl & Betz, 1993, p. 70 ff.). Also, the algorithms proposed by *Brown* et al. and by *Holzfuß* et al. should be mentioned here (Loistl & Betz, 1993, p. 79).

[12] However, it must be critically noted that empirical data can probably hardly be measured with such precision that the method allows for an integer dimension to be achieved.

chapter (Brock et al., 1996). More precisely, the test allows to verify the null hypothesis that a variable is identically and independently distributed. Thus, it tests for a random process, or as *Strunk* specifies:

> The BDS Test is a direct test for white noise and provides a normally distributed Z-value, which is considered significant (and thus indicates a difference from white noise) as soon as it exceeds the critical value of 1.96 (Strunk, 2009, p. 340).

A rejection of the null hypothesis then allows the conclusion that the dynamics underlying the empirical data could be based on deterministic . However, this conclusion is not mandatory. The dynamics could just as well be non-linear stochastic movements. By adjusting linear and non-linear models to the observed data, this possibility can be ruled out. Therefore, the *BDS* Test seems more suitable for distinguishing between stochastic and chaotic processes than the (Kugler & Lenz, 1990, p. 114 ff.).

▶ vii. Calculating Kolmogorov-Sinai Entropy (KS-Entropy)

The concept of *Kolmogorov-Sinai* entropy, referred to as $h(\mu)$, goes back to the two Russian mathematicians Andrei Nikolajewitsch *Kolmogorov* and Jakow Grigorjewitsch *Sinai*. In the context of the general theory description in Part II of the book and the determination of the box dimension, reference was made in Sect. 4.1.2.7 to the D_I, which is based on the information gain from a single measurement. While a *static* quantity is measured there, which results from a kind of 'snapshot' of the system, the *Kolmogorov-Sinai* Entropy takes into account the *dynamics* by observing, as *Argyris* et al. emphasise, "a 'film' about the system" (Argyris et al., 2010, p. 296). If the dynamics of the system are based on deterministic laws, then correlations between individual points of the observed trajectory must be detectable at least for short time phases, so that the probability of a value occurring depends on a previous value. The *KS* entropy thus answers the question, "how much information can be gained about the initial state through a sequence of n consecutive measurements, or conversely, how much uncertainty about the future state remains when n previous states are known" (Argyris et al., 2010, p. 300). It can be shown that there is a connection between the positive *Lyapunov* exponent, which measures the exponential divergence of neighbouring trajectories, and the *KS* entropy (Argyris et al., 2010, p. 303 ff.).

Figure 5.13 shows (except for the BDS Test) the briefly introduced methods using the example of different attractors. The graphical results are presented using the example of a point, a cycle, a torus, and a strange attractor (here: using the example of the Lorenz system).

5.1.3.2 Reconstruction of a System's Phase Space

As we have seen, there are a number of classic methods for determining complexity in a system. In each case, a well-approximated reconstruction of the phase spaceallows the determination of the *Lyapunov* exponents as well as, for example, the determination of the dimension of the observed attractor, and can answer a multitude of questions: For

Basis Attractor type	**Phase portrait**	**Time course**	**Range of services**	**Auto-correlation**	***Lyapunov* exponents**	**Dimension** (e. g. D_c)	**KS-Entropy**
Fixed-point tractor	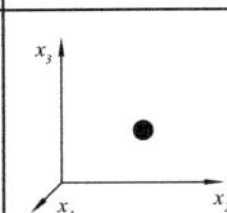	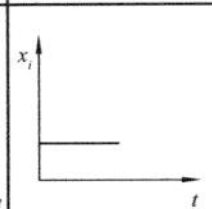	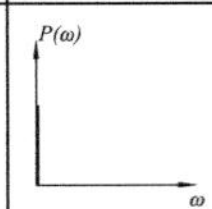	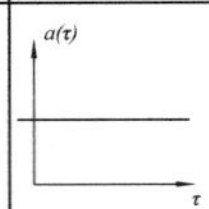	- - -	**0**	**0**
Periodic Limit cycle	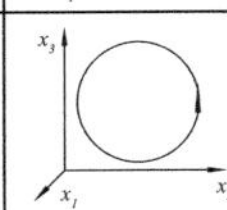	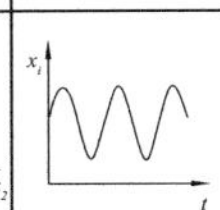	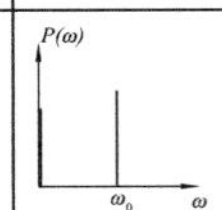	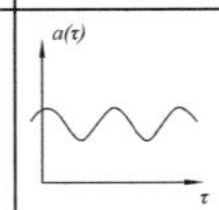	0 - -	**1**	**0**
Stable *m*-torus-Attractor Quasiperiodicity	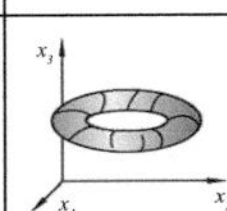	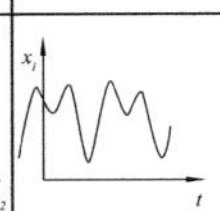	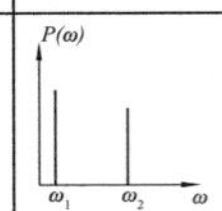	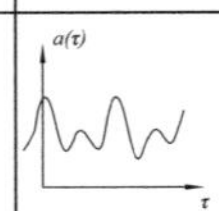	0 0 -	**2**	**0**
Stranger Attractor Complex behaviour	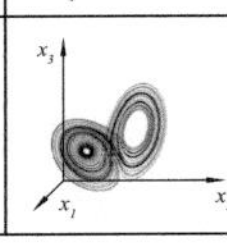	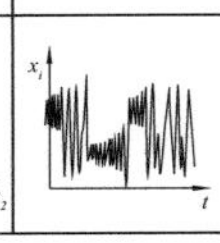	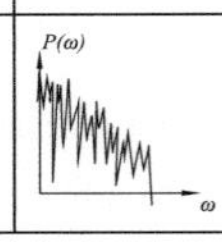	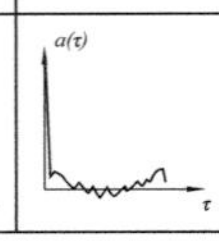	+ 0 -	$2<D_c<3$	*h(Œ)>0*

Fig. 5.13 Characterisation of various attractor types in three-dimensional phase space. *Source:* Argyris et al., 2010, p. 307

example, are there positive *Lyapunov* exponents, is the dimension of the attractor an integer or perhaps fractional?

i. Individual variables of the system contain information about the dynamics of the overall system

The initially surprising thing is that apparently information about other variables involved in the dynamics of the system (or time series) can be generated solely from the temporal development of one variable. For example, if one had a variable that provided information about the temporal development of a company, e.g., the 'Return On Investment' of the company, or the ROI, then further variables could be calculated from this existing one in such a way that one would get a valid approximation to the system behaviour of the entire company without having concrete empirical data about further variables.[13]

[13] One must consider that the ROI, for example, consists of the aggregation of a multitude of information about the company. Thus, the ROI can be represented as the product of capital turnover and turnover profitability. These key figures, in turn, depend on the capital stock, sales, and turnover. Here again, there is a direct connection to the goods produced, inventory levels, employees, etc. Behind this are ultimately management decisions and specific process sequences etc. If one considers this, it becomes apparent that a wealth of information already flows into a seemingly simple size like the ROI. In other words: The ROI is already a key figure that consists of a sum of

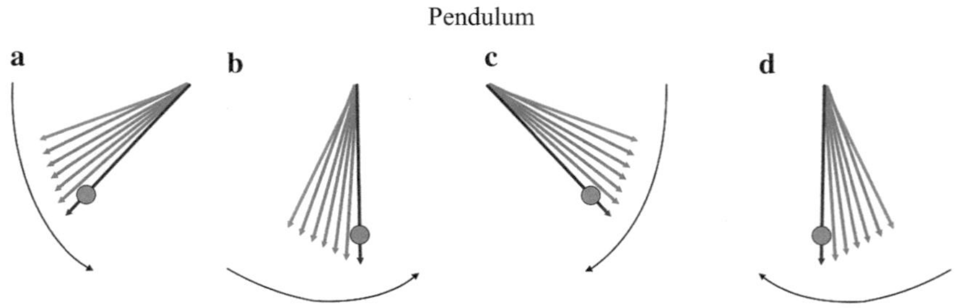

Fig. 5.14 Pendulum movements

Ultimately, the reason for this seemingly incredible possibility lies hidden in the complex dynamics of the time series themselves. Due to the dynamic character of the system, whose variables (or time series) are characterised by feedback and non-linearities, entanglements with other variables of the system, etc., this fundamental complexity causes each individual variable to already contain information about the dynamics of the overall system. The disadvantage of the impossibility of analysing a complex system in the sense of a decomposition of the overall system (the whole is indeed more than the sum of the individual parts) thus conversely contains an advantage: Due to the closely coupled, non-linear entanglement across all dimensions, few variables, possibly even only one variable, are sufficient to reconstruct the overall system. The basis for this approach results from the theorem established by Norman *Packard* and Floris *Takens* (Packard et al., 1980; Takens 1981).

The basic idea will be explained using a simple example that has already been used to explain the concept of phase space: The pendulum

ii. Reconstruction of a phase space and representation of an attractor using the example of the dynamics of a pendulum

In Sect. 4.1.1 of this book, we have learned about the example of the pendulum for the representation of a phase space:

For a pendulum in a frictionless vacuum, the following applies: If, for example, the pendulum is set in motion at a starting angle of 90°, it swings from left to right, i.e., in Fig. 5.14 from A to C always uniformly back and forth.

We have already explained that the situation of frictionlessness is not suitable for our purposes, as it has a serious disadvantage: In such a system, there is no attractor.[14] We

individual information of the company, which can usually only be disclosed by a comprehensive key figure system, in the simplest case, for example, a DuPont key figure system. It only becomes difficult when the information is also non-linearly intertwined, as it then cannot be analysed with such a simple key figure system. But the above ideas help here.

[14] See the explanations on attractors in the theory Sect. 4.1.1.2.

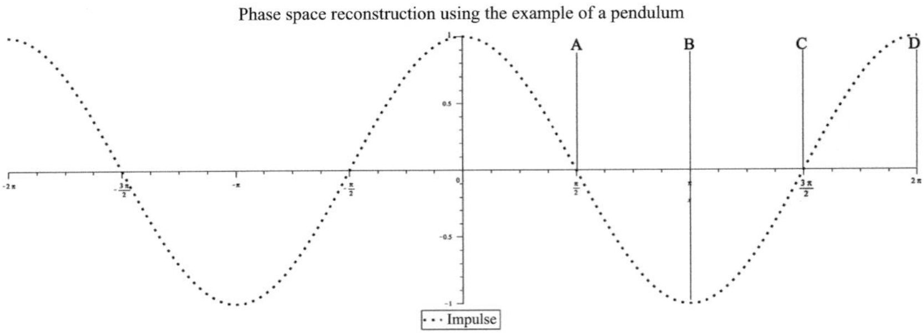

Fig. 5.15 Pendulum—(discrete) impulse curve. (The points A, B, C and D have already been explained in the context of the pendulum.)

therefore need a pendulum that, for example, receives the necessary energy for permanent swinging through a weight.

On the far left (at point A), the momentum is 0. It increases as the pendulum approaches the vertical (point B). There, the momentum reaches its maximum and then decreases until it becomes 0 again at the top right (at point C). Then the momentum reverses, and the pendulum swings in the opposite direction (D).

Now let's measure the specific momentum *X(t)*[15] , which results from the product of the velocity and the mass of the pendulum, we will obtain a data series over a certain time interval as expected, which we can normalise, i.e., the highest value is assigned 1 and the lowest value is assigned -1. All other values are assigned the corresponding numbers between 1 and -1, for example equidistantly. Of course, it is assumed that the measurements were also taken equidistantly. Initially, a time series *X(t)*, consisting of e.g. 100 data points $x(t_k) := x(t_1 + (k-1) \cdot \delta t)$, mit $1 \leq k \leq 100$, is recorded. The data points, which represent the momentum, are then (w.l.o.g.) measured at t_1 starting after a fixed time interval, let's say $\delta t := 0{,}1$, so $X(t) := \{x(t_k) | x(t_k) := x(t_1 + (k-1) \cdot \delta t), \text{mit } 1 \leq k \leq 100\}$. The data points indicate the size of the momentum with which the pendulum is being driven at the time $t_1 + (k-1) \cdot 0{,}1$, mit $1 \leq k \leq 100$.

Such a data series can then be illustrated using a cosine curve (see Fig. 5.15). In the depicted Cartesian coordinate system[16] , the time is plotted on the horizontal (abscissa) axis and the momentum on the vertical (ordinate) axis.

[15] X is a vector, because: $\vec{X} = m \cdot \vec{v}$, where m is the mass and $\vec{v}$ represents the velocity. We will omit the usual arrow symbol here.

[16] The Cartesian coordinate system is named after René *Descartes* (hence the name). The two axes of the coordinate system are orthogonal to each other. The horizontal axis is referred to as the abscissa or x-axis, and the vertical axis as the ordinate or y-axis.

To predict the exact behaviour of the pendulum from this curve, it is essentially sufficient to observe the development of a similar state of the pendulum system. It is easy to see that similar initial conditions lead to similar predictions, i.e., the strong law of causality applies. Therefore, you actually only need this one as accurately as possible measured time series to match all further states in the future with it.

However, there is still the problem that besides this one variable (momentum), other variables (e.g., the location where the pendulum is located) are actually necessary to describe the exact movement of the pendulum. However, there may be no further time series of other variables. But if one knew how large the momentum is, for example, one time step after a certain measurement point, then one could deduce from these two values due to the strong law of causality in which direction the pendulum will move in the near future. So at a time t besides the value $x(t)$ one will also consider a value $x(t+\tau)$, where τ should include as small time steps as possible (time delay—'time delay''). Instead of 'time delay', τ is sometimes referred to as 'delay-rate'.

By plotting the $x(t)$ values against the $x(t+\tau)$ values, a so-called embedding is created.

Definition (Embedding)
Embedding is understood as the topologically equivalent assignment of the unknown attractor to the unknown phase space from a one-dimensional time series.
In the resulting Fig. 5.16, one recognises the similarity to the trajectory of the phase space of a pendulum, which we have already learned about in Sect. 4.1.1.3. Such a system is predictable, i.e., it can be inferred from past values to future ones. The prediction is made by finding the next point $v^{(2)}(t_1)$, defined as $v^{(2)}(t_1) := (x(t_1), x(t_1+\tau))$, from a point $v^{(2)}(t_2) = (x(t_2), x(t_2+\tau))$ and ultimately infer the development of $v^{(2)}(t_k) = (x(t_k), x(t_k+\tau))$ from the development of this point.

The resulting ellipse is topologically equivalent to the actual trajectory, thus fulfilling the 'embedding' criterion, but the result is unsatisfactory, as we would have expected a circular path for the pendulum. The choice of time delay τ therefore cannot obviously be arbitrary. Rather, it must be a) very small, but then b) large enough to determine the 'true' trajectory. The idea is simple: Since $x(t)$ and $x(t+\tau)$ represent the coordinates of

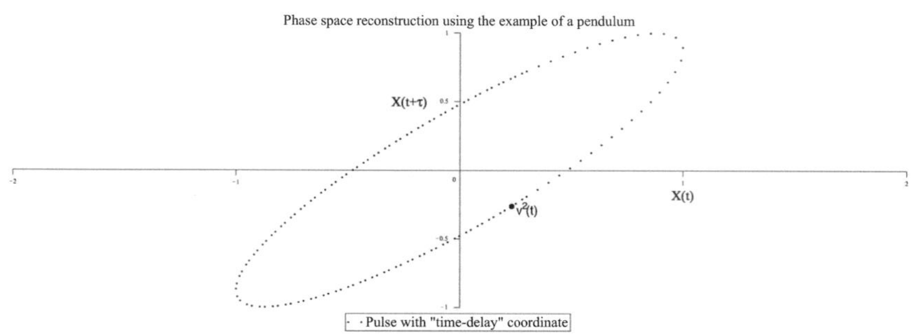

Fig. 5.16 Pendulum: 'time-delay' coordinates with $\tau = 1$

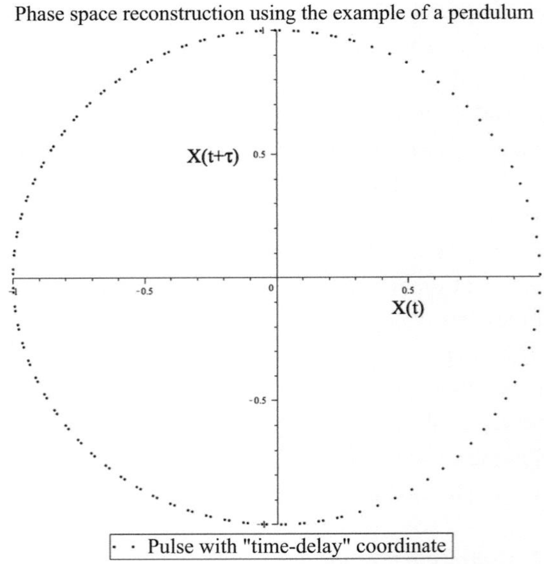

Fig. 5.17 Pendulum: 'time-delay' coordinates with τ = π/2

the system, the points should be independent of each other and perpendicular to each other, i.e., orthogonal to each other. Therefore, if we choose $\tau = {}^{\pi}/_{2}$ in this example, we get perpendicular coordinates and the expected Fig. 5.17.

So we shift the cosine function to the right using τ until the new time series (considered as a vector[17]) is orthogonal to the original. With a shift by $\tau = {}^{\pi}/_{2}$, the new function is perpendicular to the cosine function, resulting exactly in the sine function.

In a slightly different notation, each point on the circular path is represented by the vector: $v^{(2)}(t_k) = \begin{pmatrix} x(t_k) \\ x(t_k + \tau) \end{pmatrix}$ with $k \in \{1{,}2\ldots,100\}$.

If we imagine Fig. 5.17 as a mathematically complex plane[18] is present, with the x-axis as the real axis $\mathbb{R}$ and the y-axis as the imaginary axis $i\mathbb{R}$ (with $i^2 \;=\!-1$) and a

[17] Note: A time series described as a mathematical function can be represented as an element of a vector space of functions, for example from -π to π over a field e.g. $(\mathbb{R}, +, \cdot)$ (Liening, 2006a, p. 26 f.).

[18] The term 'mathematically complex' initially has nothing in common with our concept of complexity, especially since it was formed in the nineteenth century. The term was introduced by Carl Friedrich *Gauss*, who significantly expanded the known sets of numbers by embedding the number line into a plane, which is spanned by the previously known real axis and the new imaginary axis. The so-called imaginary numbers arise from the complex number *i*. This is, by definition, the root of -1. It should be remembered that negative roots do not exist in the real numbers. Each such conceived mathematically complex number is thus of the form: $z = x + i \cdot y$, with $i^2 = -1$.

Overall, this results in the set of numbers $\mathbb{C}$.

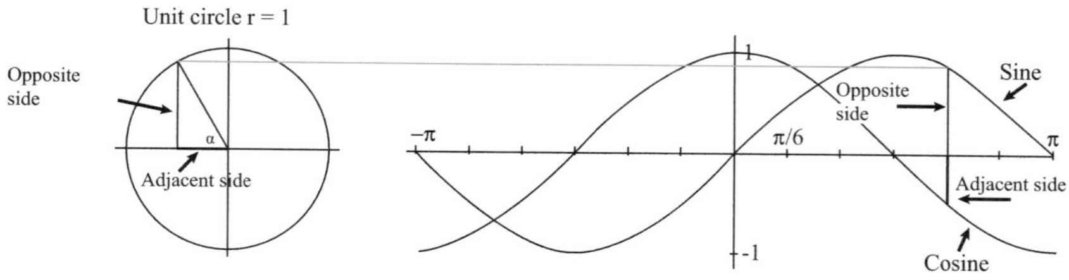

Fig. 5.18 Sine and cosine in the unit circle.

diameter of the circle with length 1, then one can visualise the relationship described above, as there in the unit circle[19] sine and cosine are perpendicular to each other, as Fig. 5.18 shows. The graphs of the sine and cosine functions are now formed by considering the unit circle (r = 1), by assigning the function values corresponding to the angles α to the angles plotted in radian measure on the x-axis.

In general, the example for empirical studies raises a number of questions that still need to be answered.

a) Depending on the dimension of the attractor determined in this way, it is obvious that the length of the existing time series plays a role. The higher the dimension of the attractor, the longer the time series must be in order to span the associated phase space at all. But how long does the time series actually have to be in order to obtain meaningful results?
b) In the case of the pendulum, we set the time delay $\tau = \pi/2$ in the reconstruction of the phase space. This ensured that the two-dimensional attractor is embedded in a space spanned by linearly independent vectors perpendicular to each other. But how do we know how τ must actually be chosen to span the space in such a way that it corresponds to the 'true' view?
c) In the case of the pendulum, it is known in advance that the result, i.e., the attractor on which the pendulum path moves, must be two-dimensional.

[19] In the unit circle, we have a right-angled triangle, as Fig. 5.18 shows. By definition, the following applies: $\sin(\alpha) = \frac{\text{Opposite}}{\text{Hypotenuse}}$ and $\cos(\alpha) = \frac{\text{Adjacent}}{\text{Hypotenuse}}$. The radius forms the hypotenuse in Fig. 5.13. α describes the angle between the radius, i.e., the hypotenuse, and the x-axis, on which the adjacent side lies. The adjacent side thus 'lies' at the angle α. The adjacent side thus corresponds to the cosine, since by construction of a unit circle the radius and thus the hypotenuse = 1. Opposite the angle α lies the opposite side, which by construction is perpendicular to the adjacent side. This corresponds to the sine due to the radius of 1. Sine and cosine are thus perpendicular to each other. Each point on the unit circle can be represented by e^{ix}, since $\left|e^{ix}\right| = 1$, $(\left|e^{ix^2}\right| = e^{ix}\overline{e^{ix}} = e^{ix}e^{-ix} = e^0 := 1)$. Overall, it apparently applies: $e^{ix} = \cos(x) + i \cdot \sin(x)$ (Liening, 2007, p. 30 ff.)

Let's assume we want to determine the development trajectory of a young growth company, with the only time series being the ROI data from recent years. How do we know that the trajectory, i.e., the entire company history, must be embedded in a two-dimensional attractor? How do we know, therefore, that it is sufficient to consider points like $v^{(2)}(t_1) = (x(t_1), x(t_1 + \tau))$, which are, for example, two-dimensional?

To a) Let's start answering the question by generalising the procedure first.

The vector v, which must first be constructed, can theoretically be finite-dimensional, let's say n-dimensional with $n \in \mathbb{N}$, i.e. $v^{(n)}(t_1) = (x(t_1), x(t_1 + \tau)), x(t_1 + 2 \cdot \tau), \ldots, x(t_1 + (n-1) \cdot \tau))$. As described above, in this method, which as already mentioned is based on *Packard*and *Takens*, each individual data point of the time series is plotted against itself in a coordinate system (Packard et al., 1980; Takens, 1981). Each data point of the time series initially forms the first dimension. For each individual data point, another data point is sought that has a small distance τ from the original point, where the necessary time delayτ must be chosen wisely. This additional point forms the next dimension. Then the process is repeated until n dimensions are formed, which allow a corresponding phase space embedding of the trajectory.[20] For a time series of length m, which thus contains m data points, one thus obtains $m - n \cdot \tau$ points of the n-dimensional trajectory, which is embedded in the thus reconstructed phase space:

$$v^{(n)}(t_k) = (x(t_k), x(t_k + \tau)), x(t_k + 2 \cdot \tau), \ldots, x(t_k + (n-1) \cdot \tau))$$
$$\text{mit}\, k \in \{1,2, \ldots, m - 1 - n \cdot \tau, m - n \cdot \tau\}$$

The number of data points of the trajectory becomes correspondingly shorter than the original data series depending on the choice of τ and the dimension. For each point $v(t_k)$ of the trajectory, the last selected data point of the time series $(n-1) \cdot \tau$ is removed from the first selected point. Thus, $v\left(t_{m+(n-1)\tau}\right)$ is the last data point of the trajectory that can still be determined. The time series is thus shortened by $(n-1) \cdot \tau$ data points.

For example, if there are $m = 5$ data points, the dimension $n = 2$ and $\tau = 1$ is, then four data points can be determined for the two-dimensional trajectory. If the dimension is, for example, $n = 3$, then there are only three trajectory points, etc. If τ increases to 2, for example, only one data point remains. It is therefore easy to imagine that depending on the dimension and choice of τ the time series must be relatively long in order to still be able to draw meaningful conclusions. *Strunk* points out that for "the reconstruction of a phase space depending on the dimensionality of the underlying system between one hundred and several thousand measurement points are necessary" (Strunk, 2009, p. 244), which, for example, in the application of complexity methods in the Entrepreneurship

[20] Alternatively, one could also work with successive derivatives, provided the corresponding derivable function exists, or the data series can be described by a function, which seems rather difficult in practice: $v_k^{(n)}\left(x(t_k), x(t_k)', x(t_k)'', \ldots, x(t_k)^{(n-1)}\right)$.

sector leads to a real problem, as particularly in newly founded companies such long data sets are usually not available.

To b) Various methods have been discussed in the literature to determine τ. The example with the pendulum has shown that only with a suitable choice of τ the reconstruction of the phase space is successful (Strunk & Schiepek, 1994; Takens, 1981; Fraser & Swinney, 1986).

In general, it should be noted that a too small choice of τ leads to $X(t_k)$ and $X(t_k + \tau)$ being almost identical due to measurement errors etc. and thus two vectors $v(t_k)$ and $v(t_{k+1})$ are almost linearly dependent. If τ is chosen too large, there is no causal connection between two vectors anymore, which leads to the structure of the attractor being lost in a "tangle of lines" (Argyris et al., 2010, p. 280).

Regarding c) As described above, the attractor is embedded in a sufficiently high-dimensional phase space. The calculation for the embedding space should be such that it at least corresponds to the actual dimensionality of the attractor.[21] To recognise the dimensionality of the attractor, it must be calculated using a method. For example, the D_2 is suitable. One way to calculate the D_2 using the function proposed by Peter *Grassberger*and *Procaccia* is possible through a limit formation (Grassberger & Procaccia, 1983, p. 346 ff.). We will deal more extensively with the calculation of the D_2 at a later point.

5.1.3.3 Special Features in the Reconstruction of Phase Spaces—The Determination of Time-Lag

In the above section, we have seen that the calculation of the *Time-Lag* presents a particular challenge. *Glushkov* et al. rightly emphasise:

> The choice of proper time lag is important for the subsequent reconstruction of phase space (Glushkov et al., 2014, p. 71).

Therefore, under this separate point, we will deal more extensively with the methods for determining the *Time-Lag* .

One method to determine meaningful *Time-Lags*, time delays τ and thus to reconstruct a phase space, whose individual coordinate axes or dimensions are perpendicular to each other and thus linearly independent of each other, is under certain conditions e.g., the so-called autocorrelation method.

[21] To ensure the correct embedding of the system, the dimension of the phase space should even be at least 2D+1, where D indicates the fractal dimension of the attractor. For noisy data, the use of time delay coordinates can even be suboptimal, so more complex methods for constructing the phase space would have to be used (e.g., Casdagli et al., 1991).

i. Autocorrelation Method

In this method, the time series is shifted point by point using the associated autocorrelation function corr(f, f) and the covariance is determined, which is normalised by the variance of the time series. The time delay or shift is carried out successively until the autocorrelation shows the value 0 for the first time. Then one has found τ, since at the τ, from which the correlation is 0, the independence of the points from each other is guaranteed (Strunk & Schiepek, 1994, p. 58 ff.).

The calculation is relatively simple, but there is a crucial disadvantage to this method: it only measures linear relationships and therefore seems to be unsuitable for non-linear relationships.[22]

ii. Heuristics and other approaches: 'Mutual Information', Singular Value Decomposition etc.

If the determination of a suitable τ by means of autocorrelation and the search for the first zero crossing does not work in the way described above, heuristics are often used

[22] In the context of interpretation, one must be careful not to mistakenly infer a causal relationship from a high correlation value. Correlation can indicate a causal relationship, but it does not have to, especially since the direction of causality, whether X actually follows Y or vice versa, cannot be derived from the correlation analysis.

The renowned statistician Walter *Krämer* describes an impressive example of the difficult relationship between causality and correlation: It was found on the New Hebrides that there is a high correlation between the number of lice and the health of the people. The pre-judgement that health could be promoted by having as many lice as possible persisted for a long time. But the cause-effect chain is exactly the other way around. "It's not the lice that drive away the disease, but the disease that drives away the lice" (Krämer, 2012, p. 174 f.).

On the other hand, one must beware of *spurious correlations*. For example, one could easily demonstrate a positive correlation between the ROI and the number of employees. But to conclude from this that the more people you hire, the greater the ROI will be, is an obvious fallacy, since at least a third highly correlated characteristic, such as the qualification of the employees, the organisation of production, etc., was overlooked in the observed characteristics.

Krämer lists a multitude of examples where in truth only spurious correlations exist and moreover there is no causal relationship, even though some believe this: "Starting with the storks, whose number is highly positively correlated with the births in Germany, over the number of unmarried aunts of a person and the calcium content of his skeleton (negative correlation), hay fever and wheat price (negative correlation), shoe size and readability of handwriting (positive correlation), education and income (positive correlation) to the proportion of foreigners and crime (positive correlation), a wide range of a misunderstood or intentionally misused correlation concept is spanned", adding that, according to *Krämer*, "the births and storks don't matter. Although they are indeed closely correlated in some areas, no one therefore believes that the stork brings the children. The positive correlation of the proportion of foreigners and crime in the municipalities of the Federal Republic is more dangerous; here the statistics may only support a popular but false prejudice, because large municipalities attract both foreigners and criminals" (Krämer, 2012, p. 172). If one looks at the last example, it becomes clear that the analysis lacks at least one crucial background variable, such as the 'municipality size', so that here too there is only a spurious correlation.

for the purpose of finding results. For example, one might choose the first relative minimum of the autocorrelation function to determine τ or one might set a previously defined limit, below which the autocorrelation value must be, such as 0.5 or 0.1, to stop the process when the limit is exceeded and output the associated τ value.

Or one calculates a so-called *Waver* product. It was introduced by *Liebert* et al. and can be derived directly from the *Taken*'s embedding theorem (Liebert et al., 1991). In this process, neighbourhood relations on the attractor are defined, from which the quality of the embedding as a topological mapping can then be read. In addition to the high effort, it must be noted that this method is only suitable for non-noisy data, which are rare in practice. Using another method, one tries to ensure, for example, that trajectories with different directions have a maximum distance from each other. However, this approach seems to work only for 'benign' attractors (Bräuer, 2002, p. 13 ff.). Another possibility, according to *Packard* et al., is to estimate τ in such a way that $\tau \ll \varepsilon/\Lambda$ is. Here, ε denotes the accuracy with which a state of a system can be specified and Λ is the sum of all positive *Lyapunov* exponents (Packard et al., 1980).

Mutual Information A promising approach for the choice of τ is the calculation of mutual information ('Mutual Information'). It indicates "how much information can on average be gained about a state at time $t + \tau$ based on the knowledge of the state at time t, and it offers a way to uncover nonlinear relationships" (Argyris et al., 2010, p. 280).

Circumventing the τ search: Singular Value Decomposition Another method that should be briefly mentioned here is, for example, the Singular Value Decomposition. It stands out from the mentioned methods because it deliberately circumvents the search for τ.

Here, vectors are again formed $v^{(n)}(t_i) = (x(t_i), x(t_i + \Delta t), x(t_i + 2 \cdot \Delta t), \ldots, x(t_i + (n-1) \cdot \Delta t))$, where τ here is the Δt *fixed* time interval of the original time series. If the vectors are considered as rows of a matrix, a (N x n)- trajectory matrix

$$X(t) = \begin{pmatrix} v^{(n)}(t_1) \\ v^{(n)}(t_2) \\ v^{(n)}(t_3) \\ \ldots \\ v^{(n)}(t_N) \end{pmatrix},$$

arises, where for a sufficiently large n the smallest sufficient embedding number coincides with the number k of linearly independent vectors.[23] matches the trajec-

[23] *Linear independence* is a set of vectors exactly when none of these vectors can be represented as a linear combination (i.e., through addition and scalar multiplication) of the others. In other words: n vectors $v_i \in V$ and $\lambda_i \in K$ with $1 \leq i \leq n$ are called linearly independent if: $\sum_{i=0}^{n} \lambda_i v_i = 0 \Leftrightarrow \lambda_1 = \lambda_2 = \ldots = \lambda_n = 0$ (Liening, 2006a, p. 31 ff.).

tory matrix. The number of linearly independent vectors k is obtained from the rank of the matrix.[24] To determine the rank k of the matrix, the aforementioned singularity or singular value decomposition is now used. This means that from X the $(n \times n)$ covariance matrix is formed, which also has the same rank as X and whose eigenvalues[25] $\lambda_1 \geq \lambda_2 \geq \ldots \geq \lambda_k \geq \lambda_{k+1} = \ldots = \lambda_n = 0$ as well as the corresponding eigenvectors are determined. However, noise and measurement inaccuracies in practice lead to a shift of the eigenvalues $\lambda_1 \geq \lambda_2 \geq \ldots \geq \lambda_k \gg \lambda_{k+1} \geq \ldots \geq \lambda_n > 0$.*Argyris* et al. point out that on the one hand, the "number k of significant eigenvalues above the noise level indicates a sufficiently large embedding dimension" (Argyris et al., 2010, p. 282). On the other hand, "a projection of the time series onto the space spanned by the corresponding eigenvectors can be considered as a noise-free reconstruction of the attractor" (Argyris et al., 2010, p. 282). They further note that one "advantage of the method over the time delay method is that it avoids the choice of a suitable time delay τ and can automatically determine a sufficient embedding dimension through the number of significant eigenvalues, while also incorporating a filter to reduce the noise component in the procedure" (Argyris et al., 2010, p. 282). We will discuss the problem of noise in the data in more detail later. As nice as the method appears at first glance, it also has some serious disadvantages, such as the fact that "only an optimal *linear* embedding can be found, as the covariance matrix only reflects linear, but not general dependencies" (Argyris et al., 2010, p. 283).

5.1.3.4 Background Information: Correlation Coefficient—Autocorrelation

For example, if the values for the observed characteristic X increase as the values for the characteristic Y also increase, a correlation between the values can be suspected. This assumption can be confirmed or refuted using the statistical measure of the empirical

---

For example, in the plane $V = \mathbb{R}^2$ the two unit vectors $e_1 = \begin{pmatrix} 1 \\ 0 \end{pmatrix}$ and $e_2 = \begin{pmatrix} 0 \\ 1 \end{pmatrix}$ are linearly independent. This is obvious, as the equation $\lambda_1 \begin{pmatrix} 1 \\ 0 \end{pmatrix} + \lambda_2 \begin{pmatrix} 0 \\ 1 \end{pmatrix} = \begin{pmatrix} 0 \\ 0 \end{pmatrix}$ only holds if $\lambda_1 = 0 \wedge \lambda_2 = 0$, because:

$$\lambda_1 \begin{pmatrix} 1 \\ 0 \end{pmatrix} + \lambda_2 \begin{pmatrix} 0 \\ 1 \end{pmatrix} = \begin{pmatrix} \lambda_1 \\ 0 \end{pmatrix} + \begin{pmatrix} 0 \\ \lambda_2 \end{pmatrix} = \begin{pmatrix} \lambda_1 \\ \lambda_2 \end{pmatrix} = \begin{pmatrix} 0 \\ 0 \end{pmatrix} \Leftrightarrow \lambda_1 = 0 \wedge \lambda_2 = 0.$$

[24] The (row) rank of a matrix is by definition identical to the maximum number of linearly independent (row) vectors of the matrix (Liening 2006b, p. 28f.).

[25] If $f: V \to V$ represents a linear mapping of a vector space V over a field K onto itself, this is also referred to as an endomorphism. By definition, a value $\lambda \in K$ is then an **eigenvalue** of f if there is a $v \in V$ with $v \neq 0$ and $f(v) = \lambda \bullet v$. Any non-zero vector $v \in V$ with $f(v) = \lambda \bullet v$ is then called an **eigenvector** of f (Liening, 2006c, p. 42f.).

correlation coefficient. The *Bravais-Pearson* correlation coefficient, which is frequently used in statistics, is defined as follows:

Definition (*Bravais-Pearson* Correlation Coefficient) Consider data $X = (x_1, x_2, \ldots x_n)$ and $Y = (y_1, y_2, \ldots y_n)$. Then, $r \frac{\sum_{t=1}^{n} (x_t - \bar{x}) \cdot (y_t - \bar{y})}{\sqrt{\sum_{t=1}^{n} (x_t - \bar{x})^2 \cdot \sum_{i=t}^{n} (y_t - \bar{y})^2}}$ is understood as the so-called *Bravais-Pearson* correlation coefficient with the averages $\bar{x}, \bar{y}$, where $-1 < r < 1$.

This means:

- $r > 0$: positive correlation, same direction linear relationship,
- $r < 0$: negative correlation, opposite direction linear relationship,
- $r = 0$: no correlation, no linear relationship (Fahrmeir et al., 2007, p. 135 ff.).

Upon closer examination, the so-called Covariance is in the numerator: $\bar{S}_{XY} = \frac{1}{n} \sum_{t=1}^{n} (x_t - \bar{x}) \cdot (y_t - \bar{y})$ and in the denominator, for normalisation, it is divided by the product of the standard deviations of the features X and Y: $\bar{S}_X = \sqrt{\frac{1}{n} \sum_{t=1}^{n} (x_t - \bar{x})^2}$ and $\bar{S}_Y = \sqrt{\frac{1}{n} \sum_{t=1}^{n} (y_t - \bar{y})^2}$. Since the standard deviations are always positive (squaring), the correlation coefficient r is positive if the numerator is positive, otherwise negative.

If one chose the point $(\bar{x}, \bar{y})$ as the centre of a coordinate system, one would get four quadrants in which the deviations $(X_t - \bar{X})$ and $(y_t - \bar{y})$ can be located, as Fig. 5.19 shows. If it holds that $(y_t - \bar{y}) \cdot (x_t - x) > 0$, since both partial deviations are greater than zero, the deviation point is in the 1st quadrant. If both partial deviations are negative, the deviation point is in the 3rd quadrant. With predominantly large X and Y values, the correlation coefficient is therefore positive. The relationship is direct.

If $(X_t - \bar{X} < 0)$ and $(y_t - \bar{y}) > 0$, then the deviation point is in the 2nd quadrant. In the opposite case, the point is in the 4th quadrant. Accordingly, the correlation coefficient is negative. Small x-values go hand in hand with large y-values and vice versa. The relationship is inverse.

This results in point clouds, which lead to a certain interpretation depending on their position. For example, in an extreme case, if all points lie on a straight line with a positive slope, then $r = 1$. This means that increasing x values are linearly matched by increasing y values, so the relationship is linearly direct. On the other hand, if all points lie on a straight line with a negative slope, then in this other extreme case $r = -1$. This means that for increasing x values, linearly decreasing y values and for decreasing x values, linearly increasing y values are present, so the relationship is linearly inverse.

The correlation coefficient thus measures the strength of the linear relationship. The more the points are on a straight line, the closer it is to 1 (positive slope) or -1 (negative slope). It is assumed that for values that are less than 0.5 in absolute value, the correlation

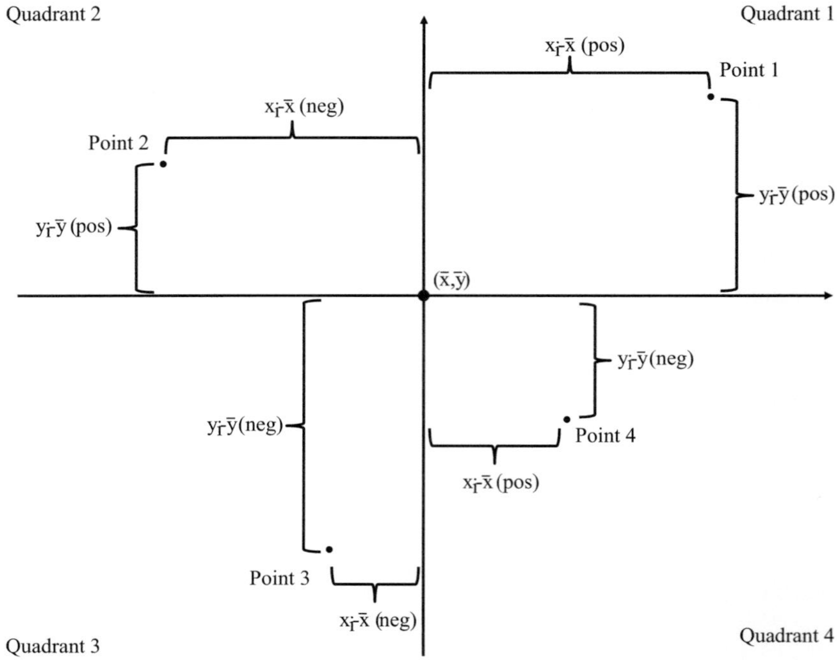

Fig. 5.19 Points in the coordinate system. *Source:* Fahrmeir et al., 2007, p. 137

is considered 'weak'. If the *r* value is greater than or equal to 0.5 in absolute value but still less than 0.8 in absolute value, one would speak of a 'medium correlation'. If the r-value is greater than or equal to 0.8 in absolute value, one would speak of a 'strong correlation'.

When *X* values are compared with themselves by shifting the *x* values by τ, one speaks of *autocorrelation.*

The autocorrelation can also be applied to functions corr(f,f), where the calculation of the function can be done by: $\text{corr}(f,f) = \int_{-\infty}^{\infty} f(\tau)f(t+\tau)dt$ (Argyris et al., 2010, p. 84). The autocorrelation function is often denoted by $a(\tau)$, so $\text{corr}(f,f) = a(\tau)$.

5.1.3.5 Background Information: Expected Value of a Random Variable & 'Mutual Information'

i. Excursion: Expected Value of a Random Variable

The 'Mutual Information', as already mentioned, is based on the *Shannon* entropy. This in turn is based on the idea of the expected value, which is why the concept of expected value should be explained here first.

The expected value is calculated in stochastics as the value of a random variable.

Definition (Random Variable) Let $(\Omega, \mathrm{A}, \mathrm{P})$ be a finite probability space.[26] A mapping Φ, which assigns a real number to each $\omega \in \Omega$, i.e., $\Phi : \omega \to \Phi(\omega) \in \mathbb{R}$, is called a random variable, if for each $x \in \mathbb{R}$ it holds that $\{\omega|\Phi(\omega) = x\} \in A$.

Example: Throwing an ideal coin, i.e., a Laplace coin, independently three times.

The outcome space is: $\Omega = \{KKK, KKZ, KZK, ZKK, KZZ, ZKZ, ZZK, ZZZ\}$, where K stands for head and Z stands for tail with the cardinality $|\Omega| = 8$. The mapping Ω is a random variable that is defined on Ω. Here, $\Phi(\omega) = 0$ means that the head appears 0 times, $\Phi(\omega) = 1$, that the head appears 1 time, etc. The associated decomposition is:

$$\{\omega|\Phi(\omega) = 0\} = \{ZZZ\}$$
$$\{\omega|\Phi(\omega) = 1\} = \{KZZ, ZKZ, ZKK\}$$
$$\{\omega|\Phi(\omega) = 2\} = \{KKZ, KZK, ZKK\}$$
$$\{\omega|\Phi(\omega) = 3\} = \{KKK\}$$

On Ω an event algebra $\mathbf{A}$ with a probability measure $P(\{\omega|\Phi(\omega) = x\})$ is defined. All events belong to the event algebra $\mathbf{A}$.

We thus obtain, overall, the following probability distribution of Φ :

x	$P(\{\omega\|\Phi(\omega) = x\}$
0	$^1/_8$
1	$^3/_8$
2	$^3/_8$
3	$^1/_8$

The expected value of a random variable is the value that emerges as the average of the results when the underlying experiment is repeated an arbitrary number of times.

[26] Here, Ω is the outcome space, i.e., the set of all possible outcomes of a random experiment; A is the event algebra, i.e., that non-empty set S of events from the outcome space, for which the following conditions apply:

$A \in S \Rightarrow \overline{A} \in S$ and $A \in S \wedge B \in S \Rightarrow A \cup B \in S$, where $\overline{A}$ is the event Not-A. P is the probability measure. This is a function that assigns a real number to each event from A and has the following axiomatic properties:

$$I : P(A) \geq 0, \text{II: } P(\Omega) = 1, \text{III: } A \cap \mathrm{B} = \{\} \Rightarrow P(A \cup B) = P(A) + P(B).$$

Definition (Expected Value) Let Φ be a random variable with the value set $W := \{x_1, x_2, \ldots, x_n\}$. Then $E(\Phi) := \sum_{i=1}^{n} x_i \cdot P(\Phi = x_i)$ is called the expected value of the random variable Φ.

Example: Expected Value in a Game of Chance with Two Dice

In a game with two dice, you receive the following winnings for a stake of 0.40 €:

- 1.00 € for the sum of eyes 10,
- 2.00 € for the sum of eyes 11,
- 3.00 € for the sum of eyes 12,
- otherwise no winnings.

What is the expected value of the net profit?

Φ let it be a random variable with the associated value set, here referred to as G:

$$G := \{x_1 = 0{,}60,\ x_2 = 1{,}60,\ x_3 = 2{,}60,\ x_4 = -0{,}40\},$$

G can therefore also be referred to as net profit, which can result if you subtract the stake from the possible winnings. For the associated probabilities P, it then obviously results:

$$P(\Phi = 0{,}6) = {}^{3}\!/_{36},\ P(\Phi = 1{,}6) = {}^{2}\!/_{36},\ P(\Phi = 2{,}6) = {}^{1}\!/_{36},\ P(\Phi = -0{,}4) = {}^{30}\!/_{36}$$

For the expected value **E** of the net profit, you therefore get:

$$E(\Phi) = \sum_{i=1}^{4} x_i \cdot P(\Phi = x_i) = 0{,}6 \cdot {}^{3}\!/_{36} + 1{,}6 \cdot {}^{2}\!/_{36} + 2{,}6 \cdot {}^{1}\!/_{36} + (-0{,}4) \cdot {}^{30}\!/_{36} = -0{,}122$$

So if you participate frequently in the game, you lose on average 12.2 cents per throw, so you *expect* a slight loss in this game. ◀

ii. 'Mutual Information'

'Mutual Information' is an information-theoretical approach. The question being answered is: How much information can be obtained from a measurement at time t about a result at time $t + \tau$? So, how strongly dependent are the values X($t + \tau$) on the values of X(t)? This can be calculated similarly to the Autocorrelation, the *Time-Lag*τ can be calculated, but the method does not distinguish between linear and non-linear dependencies, and therefore autocorrelation is always preferable as a method for determining the *Time-Lag*τ.

For the calculation, based on a suggestion by Guy *Jumarie*, the so-called *Shannon* - or information-*Entropy* is used, which is explained in more detail in Sect. 5.2, but essentially corresponds to the concept of the expected value explained above, with the special feature here being the information content $\log_2(P(\Phi = x_i))$ instead of x_i is included. The term Entropy is abbreviated with the Greek letter ***Eta*** $=H$:

$H(\Phi) := -\sum_{i=1}^{n} P(\Phi = x_i) \cdot \log_2(P(\Phi = x_i))$ is called *Shannon*-Entropy, where Φ represents a random variable with the set of values $W := \{x_1, x_2, \ldots, x_n\}$ and P is the probability of the occurrence of the events x_i with the information content $\log_2(P(\Phi = x_i))$ for all i with $1 \leq i \leq n$. Due to the chosen base 'two', operations are performed with binary numbers and the information content is given in bits, i.e., the number of necessary (0,1)-states.

To now calculate the dependency on the coupled system $[X, Y] := [X(t), X(t+\tau)]$, we ask the following question: With what probability or uncertainty is the measurement of X to be evaluated if we have measured Y? To this end, we calculate $I(X, Y) := H(Y) - H(Y|X)$, where $H(Y|X)$ represents the so-called conditional entropy of Y given X. For understanding the *conditional* entropy, reference is made to the concept of *conditional probability*.

For the *conditional probability* (Sachs & Hedderich, 2006, p. 116) of Y given X, the following holds by definition: $P(Y|X) := \frac{P(X \cap Y)}{P(X)}$[27].

$I(X, Y)$ thus measures, in the *Shannon* sense, the amount of information that X contains about Y (Jumarie, 1990, p. 2).

Andrew *Fraser* and Harry *Swinney* propose a higher-dimensional generalised mutual information, the so-called redundancy, the first minimum of which needs to be determined. Initially, all pairs of values that are τ apart in the time series are formed (Fraser & Swinney, 1986).

To calculate the 'Mutual Information', the concept of conditional probability is now required. Using the above definition, the probabilities of $P((X = x_i) \cap (Y = x_i + \tau))$, that is, x_i and $x_i + \tau$ occurring together, are converted into the conditional probability $P((Y = x_i + \tau)|(X = x_i))$

by $P((Y = x_i + \tau)|(X = x_i)) = \frac{P((X = x_i) \cap (Y = x_i + \tau))}{P((X = x_i))}$.

---

[27] To better understand conditional probability, let's consider a simple example of a dice game. We choose a so-called *Laplace* dice, which is a fair dice where each of the 6 numbers has an equal chance of being rolled. Therefore, for event A ('rolling a number'), $A := \{a_1 = 1, a_2 = 2, a_3 = 3, a_4 = 4, a_5 = 5, a_6 = 6\}$ applies. Since the probability for each number is the same, the following holds: $P(A = a_i) = {}^1/_6$. Let X be the event: 'rolling the number 5'. Then the following applies: $X := \{x_1 = 5\}$. Furthermore, for rolling the number 5, the following applies: $P(X = 5) = {}^1/_6$. Let Y be the event: 'rolling an odd number'. Odd numbers on a dice are 1, 3, and 5, i.e., $Y := \{y_1 = 1, y_2 = 3, y_3 = 5\}$. Therefore, the probability of rolling an odd number is: $P(Y = y_i) = {}^3/_6 = {}^1/_2$. For the event that X and Y occur, the following applies: $X \cap Y = \{5\}$ and thus $P(X \cap Y) = {}^1/_6$. Therefore, the conditional probability of rolling a 5 given that an odd number is rolled is: $P(X|Y) = \frac{P(X \cap Y)}{P(X)} = \frac{{}^1/_6}{{}^1/_2} = \frac{2}{6} = \frac{1}{3}$. With a probability of about 33%, a fair dice will roll a 5 given that an odd number is rolled.

If one applies the calculation of this conditional probability to the *Shannon*- entropy, this results in the 'Mutual Information':

Definition (Mutual Information)
Let X and Y be time series of finite length. Then $I(Y,X)$ is understood as the mutual information or Mutual Information where:

$$I(Y,X) = -\sum_{i=1}^{n} \left(\frac{P((X = x_i) \cap (Y = x_i + \tau))}{P((X = x_i))} \right) \cdot \log_2 \left(\frac{P((X = x_i) \cap (Y = x_i + \tau))}{P((X = x_i))} \right)$$

As an estimate for the optimal 'Time-Lag' τ, the first minimum of the function of 'Mutual Information' applies. If, therefore, the information about a state at time $t + \tau$ is minimal due to the knowledge of the state at time t, a τ would be found that leads to the two time series X and Y being independent of each other.

For a more detailed explanation using slightly different terms, refer to the original work by *Fraser* and *Swinney* (Fraser & Swinney, 1986).

5.1.3.6 Special Features in the Reconstruction of Phase Spaces—The Determination of the Attractor Dimension: D_2

To reconstruct the attractor in phase space, a suitable τ, i.e., a suitable time delay coordinate, is first determined. Here, for example, the above-described 'Mutual Information' (Fraser & Swinney, 1986) can be used to calculate a suitable time delay. It measures the point in time at which temporal dependencies in the data become minimal.

In the next step, as briefly explained, the attractor should be embedded in a sufficiently high-dimensional phase space. This follows a simple algorithm. If, for example, a time series is given, then each data point forms an expression of the first dimension. The second dimension is formed by shifting each original data point by the found *Time-Lag*τ. The data thus obtained are again shifted by τ and so on.

In this sense, the calculation should be done for an embedding space that allows the determination of the actual dimension of the attractor D. For this reason, it is necessary to calculate the dimension of the attractor, for example, via the D_2. The somewhat complicated-looking formulas for this have already been mathematically considered and discussed in the background information in Sect. 4.1.2.7. One way to calculate the D_2 using the function proposed by Grassberger*Grassberger* and Procaccia*Procaccia* is possible via a simple limit formation (Grassberger & Procaccia, 1983, p. 346 ff.).

If the embedding dimension and thus ultimately the dimension of the phase space is chosen too small, then the attractor completely fills the phase space. This means that the dimension of the attractor determined via D_2 corresponds approximately to that of the phase space. However, this would suggest randomness, even though there may be no randomness at all.

To avoid this misinterpretation, the phase space must be made higher-dimensional by adding further dimensions with the help of the *Time-Lag*τ. This procedure should be repeated until the calculation of the D_2 shows saturation. That is, from a certain dimension of the phase space, the D_2 no longer increases significantly. As a rule of thumb, the embedding dimension should be chosen as $2D+1$ according to the corresponding theorem of Mañé (Mañé, 1981, p. 230 ff.), which is supported by Takens' theorem (Whitney, 1936, p. 655ff.; Takens, 1981, p. 370ff.; Kantz, 1994, p. 77) where Sauer et al. also consider $2D$ to be sufficient (Sauer et al., 1991, p. 580 ff.).

The saturation would then be an indication that a complex structure is present and the dimension of the strange attractor is thus determined. The saturation can be determined, for example, by a linear regression through the D_2 values of the highest embedding dimensions.

If, however, the D_2 continues to increase with increasing embedding dimension, this is an indication that the system flow is subject to a random process. But this would not prove any structure, so randomness and not complexity is present. The random noise thus fills the entire phase space.

However, there is now a non-trivial problem: It must be noted that the growth of the D_2 will eventually always come to an end, even in the absence of complexity, as the time series under consideration are finite. So if the termination of the algorithm, or the saturation, is due to the length or shortness of the time series, then ultimately little can be said.

Therefore, it could be that the structure is factually so high-dimensional that it cannot be proven as a complex structure due to a too small amount of data. However, it could just as well be that the whole thing is based on a random process.

For this reason, it is important that the time series have a corresponding length and the algorithm saturates (complex structure) or does not saturate (random process) before the data 'runs out'.

Unfortunately, there seem to be data that lead to saturation even though a random process is underlying (Strunk, 2009, p. 279).[28] This is allegedly less likely to occur with the usual assumed white noise than with coloured noise.[29] This malfunction of the D_2 could

---

[28] *Strunk* points out that "therefore, more specific surrogate data methods have been proposed that allow, for example, to exclude linear-stochastic processes. One method that makes this possible is the so-called FFT surrogate. By applying a Fourier transformation (FFT - Fast Fourier Transformation), randomisation of the phase angles and reverse transformation, only linear correlations remain in the data, while nonlinear ones are destroyed. Such FFT surrogates thus test for nonlinearity, which is a prerequisite for chaos" (Strunk, 2009, p. 279).

[29] Regarding the term 'white' or 'coloured' noise, the following should be said again: The term refers to the concept of light and colours. Physically, white noise contains all wavelengths and thus all (colour) frequencies. We perceive this mixture of frequencies as white light. Each frequency appears with the same probability. We have a scattered and thus random behaviour here.

Red light, for example, has longer wavelengths than white light. This means that, for example, the colour red has a lower frequency than the average (white). Pink noise is created, for example, by having a colour mixture that includes all frequencies, but emphasises red, i.e., has a slight level increase in the red range. This noise is also called $1/f$ noise. The noise power density increases inversely proportional to the frequency f. If the emphasis on long waves is even greater, for example, $1/f^2$ noise is present. This is also referred to as brown noise. Generally, one can speak of $1/f^x$ noise.

be related to the fact that coloured noise also corresponds to a stochastic normal distribution, but adjacent values, as already mentioned, are not stochastically independent (Castro, 1989, pp. 38 f.).

5.1.3.7 Special Features in the Reconstruction of Phase Spaces—Non-Overlap and Orthogonality

As we have seen in Sect. 5.1.3.6, proving complexity is fraught with a number of pitfalls that can cause significant problems in interpreting the results, with the decisive cause of misinterpretations being too short time series.

At this point, attention should be drawn once again to another special feature.

By determining the *Time-Lag* for example as the first zero crossing of the autocorrelation function or as the first minimum of the 'Mutual Information', a phase space is spanned whose axes are not correlated with each other.

This phase space may be topologically correct, but in terms of its visualisation, it could be erroneous. The example of the pendulum showed that depending on the choice of the *Time-Lag*, the result can be an ellipse of any shape instead of the desired circular motion.

'Topologically correct' means, for example, that in a complex deterministic dynamic system, trajectories must not intersect. This can be illustrated using the *Lorenz* attractor. If you map the *Lorenz* attractor in a two-dimensional phase space, the trajectories inevitably intersect. However, since the *Lorenz* attractor is a strange attractor, reflecting a complex system, the topologically correct space must be of higher dimension. Embedded in a three-dimensional space, the non-overlappingcan be guaranteed. Why is non-overlapping necessary in complex systems? Well, if the trajectory were to intersect in its course, then the system would be in the same state at different times. Since identical causes have identical effects (weak law of causality), the system would have the same future at different times. This would make the system periodic-ordered and not complex at all! The distinction from a random system also becomes clear here: In the case of randomness, the individual points of the system would not be in an ordered structure (whether this is periodic, quasi-periodic or complex), but they would be evenly distributed in the phase space (Greschik, 1998, p. 34 f.).

In addition to non-overlapping in strange attractors, to create a visually correct phase space representation, as explained, the criterion of orthogonality must be met.

To ensure this, a conceivable approach is provided by linear algebra, which deals extensively with vector spaces and their vectors (Fischer, 2014, p. 75 ff.).

If you were to translate white noise into music or sound, you would hear a high, uniform noise, as can be perceived, for example, when an FM radio station has no reception. 1/f noise, for example, sounds somewhat lower than white noise. It is more bass-heavy, as there is a stronger emphasis on the lower frequencies.

The idea is to consider the time series to be examined as vectors and to embed these vectors in a corresponding vector space (phase space). Since it can be assumed that complex deterministic structures should possibly be representable in mathematical functions, one could consider the vector space of all functions or mappings.[30]

Vectors can only be combined linearly (by adding a multiple of a vector). The following should now apply:

If a new vector is created using the described *Time-Lag* method, which, compared to the original vector and the existing vectors, fulfils not only the criterion of linear independence but also that of orthogonality, the next dimension is found. The search for further dimensions continues afterwards.

It should be noted again that the total number of dimensions is found when the constructed phase space is sufficient to fully represent the dynamics of the system. As long as the attractor fills the phase space, further dimensions should be sought.

When the dimension of the embedded dynamics no longer increases with an increase in the considered dimensions, the calculation can be considered complete (saturation). If such saturation does not occur, it is—subject to the problem cases presented in Sect. 5.1.3.6—a random process, as randomness can perfectly fill any phase space. In this sense, randomness is infinitely dimensional.

The dimensionality of the dynamics (attractor) does not necessarily have to coincide with the dimensionality of the phase space in which it is embedded. For example, a line still has the dimension one, even if it is embedded in a two- or three-dimensional phase space. Thus, the three-dimensional *Lorenz* attractor could also be embedded in a four-dimensional phase space. However, a three-dimensional phase space is sufficient here. For systems with an unknown dimension, it is advisable to choose a higher embedding dimension than the dimension at which the methods saturate.

This algebraic approach proposed here ensures that the representation of the phase space is also intuitively comprehensible (since orthogonal), as was clearly demonstrated by the example of the pendulum. In this context, methods such as the *Gram-Schmidt* orthogonalisation or orthonormalisation process could be interesting (Lipschutz, 1990, p. 283; Ott, 1994, p. 148).

However, it must be critically considered that while this consideration can theoretically work, real time series, unless they correspond to a sine curve, for example, can only be analysed with difficulty.

[30] It is easy to see that the set of all mappings forms a vector space: Let I be any set, K a field. $K^I = \mathrm{Abb}(I, K)$ is the set of all mappings from I to K. If $x, y \in K^I$, i.e., $x : I \to K$ and $y : I \to K$,, we define the necessary addition $x + y : I \to K$ by $(x + y)(i) := x(i) + y(i)$ and the necessary scalar multiplication ax, $a \in K$, $x \in K^I$ by: $(ax)(i) = a \cdot x(i)$. It is easy to see that the laws of a vector space apply. Thus, K^I is a K-vector space. Vectors are then mappings, e.g., $\mathbb{R}^{\mathbb{R}} = \mathrm{Abb}(\mathbb{R}, \mathbb{R})$ and $f : x \to \sin(x) \in \mathbb{R}$ (Liening, 2006a, p. 26 f.).

5.1.3.8 Special Features in the Reconstruction of Phase Spaces—Surrogate Test

We have seen in the previous sections that the complexity of the attractor can be determined by successive calculation of the D_2, unless there is a random process. This can be recognised by the fact that the entire phase space is filled. However, we have also seen that there are a number of other uncertainties that jeopardise the exact determination of complexity.

The methodology outlined nevertheless aims to identify complex order structures in data sets that appear random. To secure the results obtained with the methods shown against random processes, it is advisable to generate random sequences from the original time series. These are referred to as Random-Surrogate and offer, as *Strunk* says, "a clean statistical test against chance as the null hypothesis".

Such random or random surrogates no longer contain any dynamic order, as, as the name suggests, the data is arranged randomly, for example by simply shuffling it, with a multitude of random generators existing that can implement the necessary process. Any temporal dependencies in the data are thereby destroyed and white noise is generated. Due to the fact that a multitude of random surrogates can be generated from a data set, several can be used for the analysis, which *Strunk* recommends, for example, and which means that these "Random surrogates then form a characteristic value distribution (author), against which the characteristic value of the original time series can be statistically tested" (Strunk, 2009, p. 279).

To solve the already outlined problem, for example of excluding linear-stochastic processes, surrogates, so-called FFT or DFT-Surrogatefrom the existing time series are generated using *Fourier* transformations (concretised as 'Fast *Fourier*' or 'Discrete *Fourier*' transformation depending on the algorithm used), which consist of coloured random noise. *Strunk* describes the procedure as follows:

> First, a time series is Fourier-analysed and the function of the phase angle obtained is randomised. If a surrogate is generated from the spectral density function and the randomised phase angle function via a Fourier synthesis, it matches the original in terms of the frequency spectrum, but is based on a linear-stochastic process. Linear correlations remain in the data, whereas nonlinear ones are destroyed. A surrogate data test that uses such surrogates (again, a whole bundle per time series is generated) thus tests for nonlinearity, a prerequisite for chaotic dynamics (Strunk, 2004, p. 351).

This test can also be performed for several time series (Strunk, 2004, p. 352). Of course, it is not necessarily required. However, with the help of such a surrogate test, for example, the fractal dimension, which was calculated using the D_2, can be statistically significantly delimited against the random noise. The examination of the arithmetic means and the standard deviations of the original data compared to the surrogates usually already provides useful results. [31]

---

[31] In contrast to normal 'mixing', DFT-Surrogates only destroy the nonlinear dependencies through the randomisation of the phase angles, while linear dependencies remain. This has the advantage for our field of application, as also explained by *Strunk*, that one can specifically test for nonlinear

5.1.3.9 About the Use of *Lyapunov* Exponents for Empirical Research: D_2, PD_2, *Wolf-*, *Briggs-*, *Kantz-* and other Algorithms

After the phase space has been reconstructed, we have generated a statement about complexity with the calculation of the D_2.

Another method is the calculation of *Lyapunov* exponents to determine the complexity of trajectories. This method also requires a (re-)constructed phase space. As already explained several times, the *Lyapunov-* exponent λ measures the exponential divergence of neighbouring trajectories, which is why, as detailed in Sect. 4.2.2, λ results from $|\Delta v(t)| = |\Delta v(0)| \cdot e^{\lambda \cdot t}$ mit $\Delta v(0) = |v_0(0) - v_1(0)| \ll 1$.

Loistl and *Betz* recommend, after thorough examination of a multitude of algorithms, the method proposed by Keith *Briggs* for calculating the *Lyapunov* exponent, as it shows good convergence behaviour and is easy to handle (Loistl & Betz, 1993, pp. 64–80). However, *Briggs* points out a difficulty in his method:

> A weakness of the proposed method is that no estimate of the errors in the computed Liapunov exponents is obtained. This becomes a problem especially when the largest exponent is close to zero (Briggs, 1990, p. 31).

Therefore, this algorithm can only be considered meaningful based on the results presented by *Briggs* if the distance of the largest calculated *Lyapunov* exponent from the value zero is relatively large (Briggs, 1990, p. 29).

One of the most well-known and historically first algorithm is that of Alan *Wolf* et al., which also has some serious weaknesses (Wolf et al., 1985). Regarding the *Wolf* algorithm, *Rosenstein* et al. state:

> The algorithm by Wolf et al. (...) fails to take advantage of all the available data because it focusses on one "fiducial" trajectory. A single nearest neighbour is followed and repeatedly replaced when its separation from the reference trajectory grows beyond a certain limit. Additional computation is also required because the method approximates the Gram-Schmidt procedure by replacing a neighbour with one that preserves its phase space orientation. However (...) this preservation of phase-space orientation is unnecessary when calculating only the largest Lyapunov exponent (Rosenstein et al., 1993, p. 120).

Ultimately, the *Wolf* algorithm requires as little random component as possible, i.e., low noise in the data, as well as a precise embedding of the attractor in the phase space.

---

dependencies, while 'normal tests' could also respond to linear dependencies with simply mixed data. Unevenly distributed mixtures of random noise of different frequency bands may imitate certain properties of complex systems and therefore, for example, generate erroneous values when calculating the D_2. Especially for the test of such complexity characteristics, one needs more accurate surrogates than randomly mixed data (Strunk, 2004, p. 351).

However, in the literature one finds arguments that claim the exact opposite for normal white noise, namely that surrogates with randomised phase angles falsely show non-random structures, while simply randomised surrogates correctly identify the data as white noise (Rapp et al., 1994). In this respect, the FFT or DFT surrogates also seem to have their advantages and disadvantages.

Another possible problem is that the method already requires several thousand data points even for low-dimensional systems, which can lead to significant problems in the field of entrepreneurship, for example, when examining the subject 'young growth company', due to short time series. For high-n-dimensional systems, the necessary length of the data series even increases by 10^n (Strunk & Schiepek, 1994, p. 79). As simple as this algorithm may be to programme, it seems hardly suitable for practical use. *Loistl* and *Betz* found, for example, that despite "time series lengths of up to 50,000 points (logistic function with $r = 4$) (…) convergence of the approximated Lyapunov exponent towards the theoretically derivable value of ln 2 was hardly achievable" (Loistl & Betz, 1993, p. 78).

Ten Broek et al. point out that, for example, *Rosenstein's* algorithm is significantly more robust against smaller data sets compared to the *Wolf* algorithm. They were also able to demonstrate that the *Rosenstein* algorithm requires a computation time ten times shorter than the *Wolf* algorithm. When using a noise filter (Low-Pass Filter), the calculated *Lyapunov* exponent for the *Rosenstein* algorithm even increases with a fixed number of samples (TenBroek et al., 2007, p. 210). Thus, the results can gain in significance in the case that the error caused by the noise is known. The *Wolf* algorithm already shows that the results strongly depend on how long the period is and which period is considered. *Wolf* operates here with minimal distances ε at the beginning of each trajectory comparison and larger distances L_m, defined in advance, at which the algorithm stops. *Loistl* and *Betz* emphasise that this choice of ε and L_m is problematic (Loistl & Betz, 1993, p. 73). Ultimately, the criticism is related to the fact that the period to be considered is hardly determinable a priori without a closer knowledge of the system dynamics.

Therefore, *Rosenstein* et al. suggest initially choosing this period very large, storing it in between, and then determining through an analysis which period should be considered. *Rosenstein* et al. summarise their results as follows:

> The method follows directly from the definition of the largest Lyapunov exponent and is accurate because it takes advantage of all the available data. The algorithm is fast because it uses a simple measure of exponential divergence and works well with small data sets. In addition, the current approach is easy to implement and robust to changes in the following quantities: embedding dimension, size of data set, reconstruction delay, and noise level. Furthermore, one may use the algorithm to calculate simultaneously the correlation dimension (Rosenstein et al., 1993, p. 133).

It should be noted that regardless of the chosen method for determining the *Lyapunov* exponents (one usually restricts oneself to the largest *Lyapunov* exponent (LLE)[32] (Wolf et al., 1985; Rosenstein et al., 1993; Kantz, 1994) it is always assumed that the time series examined have a stationary character in terms of their complexity, as *Strunk* rightly emphasised in 2004 (Strunk, 2004, p. 389). Therefore, methods are still needed that can track changes in this complexity.

[32] 'LLE' stands for 'Largest *Lyapunov* Exponent'.

To calculate a time-related *Lyapunov* exponent, one could use the so-called PD_2 method ('Pointwise Dimension'), which is derived from the D_2 (Skinner et al., 1994). It must be considered here that the 'divergence' of two trajectories can only be measured over a period, an 'Evolution Time' (Wolf et al., 1985, p. 294), but not at a point in time.

The calculation of the PD_2 is initially carried out like the D_2. However, to determine the dimension, not all distances between all data points are recorded. Instead, individual reference points are defined, from which the distances to all other points are calculated. Then a D_2 is determined for each of these reference points. The calculation of the average over increasingly more reference points approaches the D_2. In fact, with this pointwise procedure, the D_2 can be determined relatively well with already few data points, although several hundred data points are still needed to obtain meaningful results for low-dimensional systems.

Strunk points out that with *Rosenstein's* algorithm, results can be expected that show a "sufficient reliability even for short time series" (Strunk, 2004, p. 389). He emphasises that for "empirical time series with an unknown generating system the calculation should be repeated for different window widths" (Strunk, 2004, p. 393). "If strong fluctuations are shown, either the window is chosen too small or the system actually shows constant changes in its chaoticity" (Strunk, 2004, p. 393).

In contrast to the D_2, the PD_2 provides a whole time series of data. This is particularly interesting when looking at phase transitions, so that time series in which phase transitions (spontaneous order-order, or order-disorder or disorder-order transitions) are suspected from the beginning of the investigation should be examined using the PD_2. Because the PD_2, as mentioned, is able to depict changes in dimensional complexity (Kowalik & Elbert, 1995, p. 478). *Strunk* points out that the PD_2 shows "an even better estimate for the dimensionality of the entire time series" (Strunk, 2009, p. 373) and that the sensitivity to noise and non-stationarity is lower (Strunk, 2009, p. 373).

The *Kantz* algorithm (Kantz, 1994), which also avoids the shortcomings of the *Wolf* algorithm, is based on the *Rosenstein* algorithm (Rosenstein et al., 1993). Comparable to the *Wolf* algorithm, a minimal ε ($\varepsilon_{\min}$) is defined from the outset, which indicates how far apart the reference point and the neighbouring point are at the beginning of a calculation. This prevents the trajectories under investigation from being far apart from the start. However, the method developed by Holger *Kantz* repeats the calculations, with the minimum initial distance $\varepsilon_{\min}$ being increased again and again. *Strunk* adds that an upper limit is set by a $\varepsilon_{\max}$. He notes:

> This results in a bundle of curve progressions in the plot of log ($\bar{\varepsilon}i$) vs. i. A linear area should then be recognisable in at least some curves. The quality of the identification of the scaling area can thus be improved overall (Strunk, 2004, p. 391).

Kantz's method exploits the exponential growth of small distances, which are measured in the one-dimensional space of the time series. Phase space embeddings are only used to distinguish between true and false neighbours, which is why the choice of an optimal embedding dimension is not essential in *Kantz's* algorithm (Kantz, 1994, p. 86).

Strunk has successfully implemented this algorithm in his GChaos-Software, where the number of calculation repetitions is referred to by him as 'Grid Resolution' and the distance between $\varepsilon_{\mathrm{min}}$ and $\varepsilon_{\mathrm{max}}$ is divided into as many sections as the 'Grid Resolution' specifies (Strunk, 2015).

5.1.3.10 Background Information: Complexity Measurement

i. Correlation Integral—D2

We have already discussed the dimension calculation in more mathematical detail in Sect. 4.1.2.7. One way to calculate the D_2 is to use the function proposed by by *Grassberger*and *Procaccia*:

$$C(l) := \lim_{N\to\infty}\left(\frac{1}{N^2}\sum_{\substack{i,k=1\\(i\neq k)}}^{N}\Theta(l-|X_i-X_k|)\right)$$ (Grassberger & Procaccia, 1983, p. 346).

The calculation of D_2 is then possible via a simple limit formation:

$$D_2 = \lim_{l\to 0}\frac{\log_2(C(l))}{\log_2(l)}.$$

Theiler, for example, calculates the D_2 for an n-dimensional phase space using the following correlation integral:[33]

$$C(w,N,l) := \left(\frac{2}{(N+1-w)(N-w)}\sum_{k=w}^{N-1}\sum_{i=0}^{N-1-k}\Theta(l-|X_i-X_{i+k}|)\right)$$ (Theiler, 1989, p. 1070)

The following applies, which is explained in more detail in the corresponding chapter of the theory part:

- n is the dimension of the phase space in which the attractor is embedded,
- l denotes the maximum distance between two points,
- N is the number of data points considered in the attractor,
- Θ is the Heaviside function with $\Theta(x) = 1$ for $x \geq 0$ and otherwise $\Theta(x) = 0$,
- $|X_i - X_{i+k}|$ describes the (Euclidean) distance between two points,
- w is the so-called 'Theiler Window', with $w > 0$, which ensures the 'exclusion' of neighbouring points to prevent spurious correlations (Theiler, 1987).

It should be added that the box dimension, which is explained in detail in the theory part, and the D_2 examined here again, are very similar in principle (exponential increase of boxes/points). However, the measurement is very different.

[33] In addition to the addition of the 'Theiler Window', it is particularly noticeable that the sums formed in the Theiler formula are multiplied by 2, i.e., explicitly doubled. This is because in Grassberger and Procaccia's way of adding, the differences $|X_i - X_k|$ are counted twice. Theiler's counting method, on the other hand, excludes these duplications. To obtain a comparable value to the D2 of Grassberger and Procaccia, he therefore multiplies the result by 2.

With D_2, the distances of the points are measured, i.e., the Euclidean distance between two vectors is calculated. This is relatively simple and in the next higher embedding dimension, even fewer measurements have to be made than before, as there are fewer points to consider due to the construction of time delay coordinates.

In the case of the box dimension, however, the n-dimensional space is divided by the reduction factor with the side length. Then each box has to be analysed and checked whether there is one or more points in it. The number of boxes that need to be checked increases exponentially with each additional dimension. And for each dimension, several runs with a smaller side length each have to be completed. The effort is therefore enormous with the box dimension, although the calculation of the D_2 looks more difficult at first glance when considering the formulas.

In addition, there is a geometric challenge: In a plane, two-dimensional boxes (i.e., rectangles or squares) are used. In a three-dimensional space, three-dimensional boxes. But what do these boxes look like in four- or higher-dimensional space? Thus, there is a lack of visualisation, although from an algebraic point of view, the idea of an n-dimensional box is simple.

ii. 'Pointwise Dimensionality'—*PD*$_2$

In this method proposed by James E. *Skinner* et. al, the D_2 is not directly determined. Instead, the $D_2$is determined as the average of numerous individual calculations (Skinner et al., 1994). A very clear description can be found in *Strunk,* who points out that starting "from individual reference points the distances to all other points are first determined and from this, a D2 is determined for each of the reference points using the known method (which, however, only applies to this reference point. An average over many reference points closely approximates the D2 and can be determined relatively well even for a few data points (the requirements are much lower than for D2 but here too several hundred to a thousand data points are necessary to obtain meaningful calculation results for low-dimensional systems)" (Strunk, 2004, p. 375).

So while for the D_2it applies that $D_2 = \lim_{l \to 0} \frac{\log_2 (C(l))}{\log_2 (l)}$, the PD_2 is defined as $PD_2 = \lim_{l \to 0} \frac{\log_2 (C(l,i))}{\log_2 (l)}$. The PD_2 thus builds on the correlation integral. Thus, $C(l,i)$ represents a pointwise correlation integral, "which gives a sort of time average over the whole signal providing a value for each time point of the signal and (â€¦ *l*, d. Verf.) is the distance reflecting the radius of the neighbourhood around a certain point (between 0 and 1)" (Světlák et al., 2010, p. 65). *Farmer* et al. but also *Grebogi* et al. point out that the PD_2 is independent for almost all i ("with respect to the natural probability measure on the attractor") (Farmer et al., 1983; Grebogi et al., 1988, p. 1712).

iii. The *Wolf* Algorithm

Let's assume that we have trajectories in a reconstructed phase space. For a given time series, we first construct an embedding and obtain a trajectory as a finite sequence of data points of dimension n with $v^{(n)}(t_k) = (x(t_k), x(t_k + \tau), x(t_k + 2 \cdot \tau), \ldots, x(t_k + (n-1) \cdot \tau))$

with $k \in \{1, 2, \ldots, m - 1 - n \cdot \tau, m - n \cdot \tau\}$. It is important that an exact calculation of the embedding dimension is carried out in advance of the analysis. The trajectory $v^{(n)}(t_k)$ is called reference trajectory (Peitgen et al., 1992, p. 362 ff.).

The *Wolf* algorithm (see Fig.5.20) tracks two closely located points over a certain period of time. If the observation trajectory is a certain distance measure away from the reference trajectory, the algorithm aborts (Wolf et al., 1985).

1. One chooses the closest point $z_0^{(n)}(t_0)$ to the first considered point of the reference trajectory $v^{(n)}(t_0)$. The distance of the two starting points is denoted by L_0; with $L_0 = |v^{(n)}(t_0) - z_0^{(n)}(t_0)|$, which can also be imagined as a distance vector $\overrightarrow{L}_0$.
2. The discrete development of the two points v and z is tracked over time until the distance between the two points exceeds a previously set value ε. This means, with increasing i, one calculates $L_0(i) = |v^{(n)}(t_i) - z_0^{(n)}(t_i)|$, until $L_0(i) > \varepsilon$. We denote this distance as L_0' and the point in time at which we measure L_0' we denote as t_1.
3. For the corresponding point on our reference trajectory, which we thus refer to as $v^{(n)}(t_1)$, we again look for a 'nearest neighbour' who is as close as possible to $v^{(n)}(t_1)$ and whose distance vector points in the same direction as the distance vector of L_0'. However, with noisy data, a minimal distance S_{min} must first be defined so that the starting point for the second trajectory is close, but not too close to the reference trajectory. We again calculate the distance between the two points $L_1 = |v^{(n)}(t_1) - z_1^{(n)}(t_1)|$. $\overrightarrow{L}_1$ should largely point in the same direction as $\overrightarrow{L_0'}$, i.e., the angle φ_1 between $\overrightarrow{L_0'}$ and $\overrightarrow{L_1'}$ should be minimal and not exceed a previously defined maximum angle φ_{max}. One then follows the course of the trajectories until the distance $L_1(i) = |v^{(n)}(t_i) - z_1^{(n)}(t_i)|$ again exceeds the value ε. We refer to the newly found distance as L_1'.

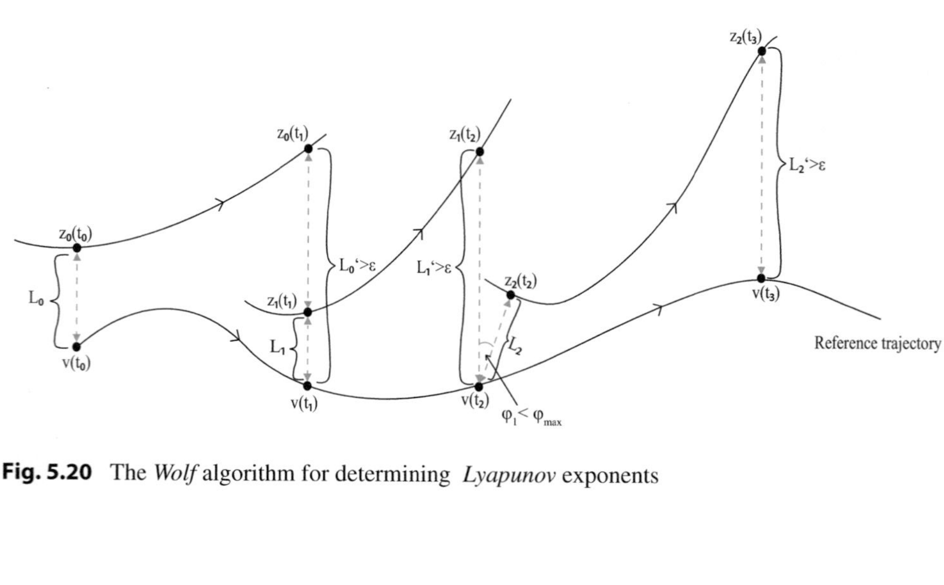

Fig. 5.20 The *Wolf* algorithm for determining *Lyapunov* exponents

4. Repeat this described process until the end of the reference trajectory.
5. The largest positive *Lyapunov* exponent can now be approximated from the following equation, where M represents the number of repetitions of the process described above: $L = \frac{1}{t} \cdot \sum_{k=1}^{M} \ln \frac{L_i'}{L_i}$ (Wolf et al., 1985, p. 295; Wolf, 1986, p. 283).[34]

Beyond the described algorithm, the *Wolf* method also offers the possibility to calculate the second and third largest *Lyapunov* exponents etc. (Loistl & Betz, 1993, p. 73), so that $\lambda_1 \geq \lambda_2 \geq \ldots \geq \lambda_n$. This provides the opportunity to demonstrate, for each direction in phase space, whether and how chaos or complexity in phase space is distributed and neighbouring trajectories diverge exponentially.

In practice, it has been shown that, as previously indicated, the *Wolf* algorithm for the *Lyapunov* exponent does not produce precise results.

One reason for this is that optimal neighbouring trajectories are not always available, and therefore one has to resort to suboptimal trajectories. Although one could omit areas of the reference trajectory for which no optimal neighbouring trajectories are available, the consequence would be a loss of information about the unstable direction of the trajectory.

Another point is the dependence of the initial distance L_0, i.e., the distance between the reference trajectory and a neighbouring trajectory, on the noise in the data. The initial distance must be above the noise level, otherwise noise-related fluctuations could be interpreted as deterministic divergence.

The correct choice of the embedding dimension n also plays an important role, as the *Lyapunov* exponent can be extremely overestimated, for example, with a too low embedding dimension, as trajectories can diverge because they simply do not represent neighbours in the 'true' phase space. A too high chosen embedding dimension is not so problematic from a theoretical point of view, but can also lead to problems in practice, as the minimum initial distance between the neighbouring trajectories increases with increasing embedding dimension. This can result in the scales of short distances no longer being investigated and the number of time steps until a new neighbouring trajectory needs to be searched for is reduced, which leads to larger error terms due to deviations in the directions of the distance vectors.

[34] In the theoretical part in Sect. 4.2.2 we saw that from the idea of exponential divergence of two neighbouring trajectories $\left|v^{(n)}(t_k) - z_0^{(n)}(t_k)\right| = \left|v^{(n)}(t_0) - z_0^{(n)}(t_0)\right| \cdot e^{L \cdot t}$ the calculation of the *Lyapunov* exponent L with $L = \lim_{t \to \infty} \frac{1}{t} \cdot \sum_{k=0}^{t-1} \ln\left|f'\left(v^{(n)}(t_k)\right)\right|$ can be derived. This is ultimately what *Wolf's* algorithm is based on, with *Wolf* using $\log_2$ (Wolf, 1986, p. 275).

iv. The *Briggs* Algorithm

The algorithm proposed by *Briggs* considers a polynomial of order d that is adapted to the trajectories under investigation (Briggs, 1990, p. 27 ff.). The high-order terms used in this context particularly take into account the almost always curved behaviour of the trajectories. After thorough analysis, *Loistl* and *Betz* conclude that the *Briggs* algorithm is "much more robust" (Loistl & Betz, 1993, p. 79) compared to the *Wolf* algorithm, an argument that is also attributed to the *Rosenstein* algorithm, but especially to the *Kantz* algorithm.

v. The *Kantz* and the *Rosenstein* Algorithm

To address the problem of noisy and high-dimensional data, *Kantz* has developed an alternative algorithm that is more robust to the problems mentioned above (Kantz, 1994). His method exploits the exponential growth of small distances measured in the one-dimensional space of the time series. Phase space embeddings are only used to distinguish between true and false neighbours, so the choice of an optimal embedding dimension is not crucial in the *Kantz* algorithm.

First of all, it should be noted that the exponential divergence only starts after a certain time, as any distance vector must first switch to the unstable direction. In addition, the divergence of the trajectories fluctuates along the trajectory. This means that the trajectories, after initially drifting apart, can indeed approach each other again in the course of time, with the fluctuations being given by the spectrum of effective *Lyapunov* exponents.

First, let's construct an embedding for a given time series $v^{(n)}(t)$ and again obtain a trajectory as a finite sequence of data points of dimension n with m time-delay coordinates:

$$\begin{aligned} v^{(n)}(t_k) &= (X(t_k), X(t_k+\tau), X(t_k+2\cdot\tau), \ldots, X(t_k+(n-1)\cdot\tau)) \\ &\text{und}\, k \in \{1, 2, \ldots, m-1-n\cdot\tau, m-n\cdot\tau\}. \end{aligned}$$

If $v^{(n)}(t)$ thus represents the temporal evolution of a trajectory, then one could determine the maximum *Lyapunov* exponent from an initial state $v^{(n)}(0)$ in a corresponding phase space by the following limit for almost all distance vectors $|v^{(n)}(0) - v_\varepsilon^{(n)}(0)|$ with a high probability using

$$\lambda_{\max} = \lim_{t\to\infty} \lim_{\varepsilon\to 0} \frac{1}{t} \left(\frac{\left|v^{(n)}(t) - v_\varepsilon^{(n)}(t)\right|}{\varepsilon} \right)$$

Analogously, the so-called *'maximum effective' Lyapunov* exponent is given by:
$\lambda_\tau(t) = \lim_{\varepsilon\to 0} \frac{1}{\tau} \left(\frac{\left|v^{(n)}(t+\tau) - v_\varepsilon^{(n)}(t+\tau)\right|}{\varepsilon} \right)$ mit $v^{(n)}(t) - v_\varepsilon^{(n)}(t) = \varepsilon\omega_u(t)$, where $\omega_u(t)$ is the local eigenvector associated with the maximum *Lyapunov* exponent $\lambda_{\max}$. The value of $\lambda_\tau(t)$ depends on the structure in the tangent space and is thus position-dependent, although it is approximately the same for all very closely neighbouring trajectories. By definition, the average value of $\lambda_\tau(t)$ along the trajectory is the *'true' Lyapunov* exponent.

For the calculation of the largest *Lyapunov* exponent, one considers any point on the time series consisting of m-dimensional time delay coordinates $v^{(n)}(t_k)$ with $k \in \{1, 2, \ldots, m-1-n\cdot\tau, m-n\cdot\tau\}$. Unlike the *Wolf* algorithm, one now considers not just *one* trajectory as close as possible to this point of the reference trajectory. Rather, all points within the ε neighbourhood of an environment U_ε (possibly an n-dimensional sphere) of $v^{(n)}(t_k)$ are considered as the start of neighbouring trajectories.

The distance between the reference trajectory $v^{(n)}(t_k)$ and a neighbouring trajectory $z_i^{(n)}(t_k)$ after a relative time span τ, relative to the time of the initial value, is defined by *Kantz* as $dist\left(v^n(t_k), z_i^{(n)}(t_k), \tau\right) := |v^{(n)}(t_k+\tau) - z_i^{(n)}(t_k+\tau)|$.

To measure the maximum *Lyapunov* exponent, a point in time t is fixed on the reference trajectory, and then *all* neighbouring trajectories $Z_i^{(n)}(k_k)$ within a ε neighbourhood U_ε are determined. Subsequently, the average of the distances between all neighbouring trajectories and the reference trajectory $v^{(n)}(t_k)$ is formed as a function of τ. To compensate for possible fluctuations in the distances, the average is logarithmised, resulting in the so-called *local* effective *Lyapunov* exponent[35]. To obtain the true *Lyapunov* exponent, this local effective *Lyapunov* exponent is averaged over all points in time t.

It can thus be summarised as: $S(\tau) = \frac{1}{T}\sum_{t=1}^{T} \ln\left(\frac{1}{|U_t|}\sum_{i\in U_t} dist\left(v^n(t_k), z_i^{(n)}(t_k), \tau\right)\right)$.

In contrast to the *Wolf* algorithm, the *Kantz* algorithm is simpler in that only the distances and not also the directions are compared. Thus, fewer parameters are needed. For comparison, remember that the *Wolf*-algorithm requires the embedding dimension n, an upper limit ε of the distances, beyond which a new neighbouring trajectory must be sought, a maximum angle $\varphi_{\max}$ and (for noisy data) a minimum distance $s_{\min}$ between the reference trajectory and the neighbouring trajectory. Fig. 5.21 illustrates the *Kantz* algorithm.

Furthermore, the statistical fluctuations in the *Kantz*-algorithm are significantly lower, as multiple neighbouring trajectories are evaluated for each point on the trajectory. By averaging over all U_ε along the entire time series, those trajectories that approach the reference trajectory as they move in the direction in which the attractor contracts are also taken into account. In contrast, the *Wolf*-algorithm would not include these trajectories in the consideration, as the vector difference in this area rarely reaches the upper limit at which a new neighbouring trajectory would have to be sought. The approach in the *Kantz*-algorithm also allows the calculation of the *Lyapunov*-exponent for (relatively) short time series. Moreover, *Kantz* has shown that the algorithm generally provides a

[35] In the calculation of the local effective *Lyapunov* exponent, fluctuations occur, given by the angle ϕ. Since these fluctuations are averaged out in the subsequent calculation of the true *Lyapunov* exponent, these fluctuations are not further discussed here. For further explanations, see Kantz (1994).

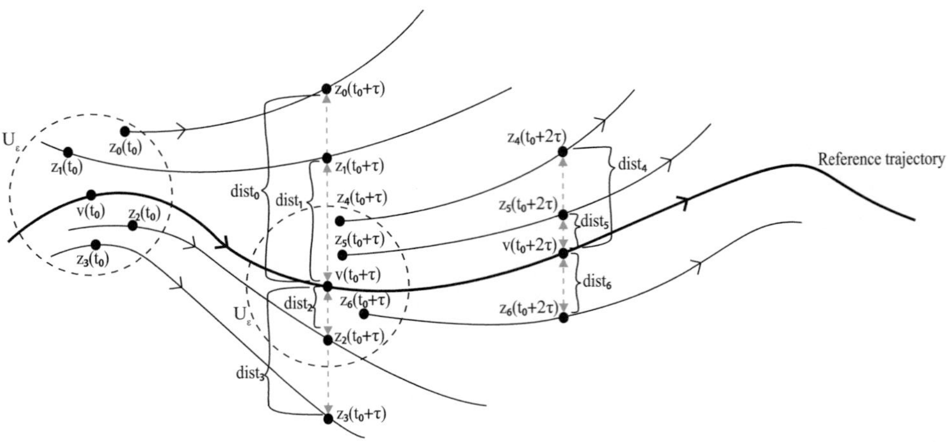

Fig. 5.21 *Kantz* algorithm for determining the *Lyapunov* exponent

robust result even with noisy data. Unlike the *Wolf*-algorithm, the examination of the scaling range of $S(\tau)$ can also determine the standard error of λ.

Rosenstein et al. have—as already explained—presented an alternative algorithm that essentially uses the same method to determine the maximum *Lyapunov*-exponent (Rosenstein et al., 1993). The main differences to the *Kantz* algorithm are that the distance between the trajectories is defined as a (maximum or Euclidean) norm in the embedding space, which slightly reduces the scaling range as the different delay coordinates are mixed. Furthermore, like the *Wolf*-algorithm, they use only *one* neighbouring trajectory per time point *t*, which can lead to larger statistical errors, especially with noisy data. Fig. 5.22 outlines the *Rosenstein*-algorithm.

Finally, in Fig. 5.23 we see a comparison of the three important algorithms of *Wolf, Rosenstein* and *Kantz*.

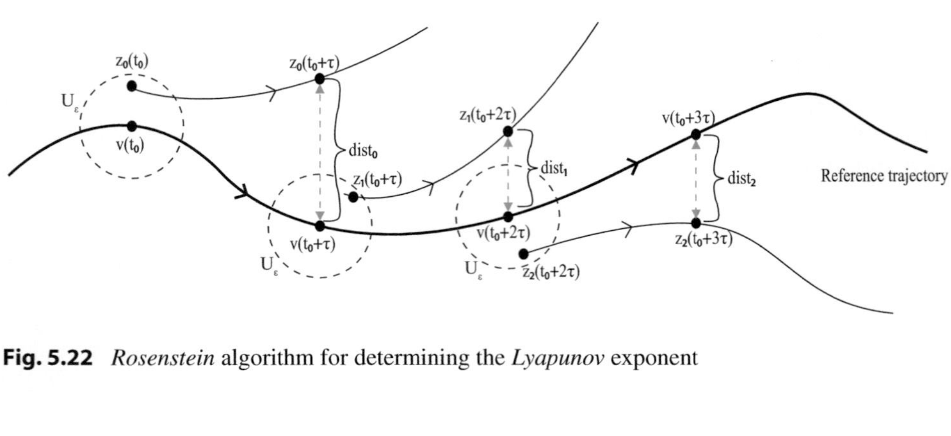

Fig. 5.22 *Rosenstein* algorithm for determining the *Lyapunov* exponent

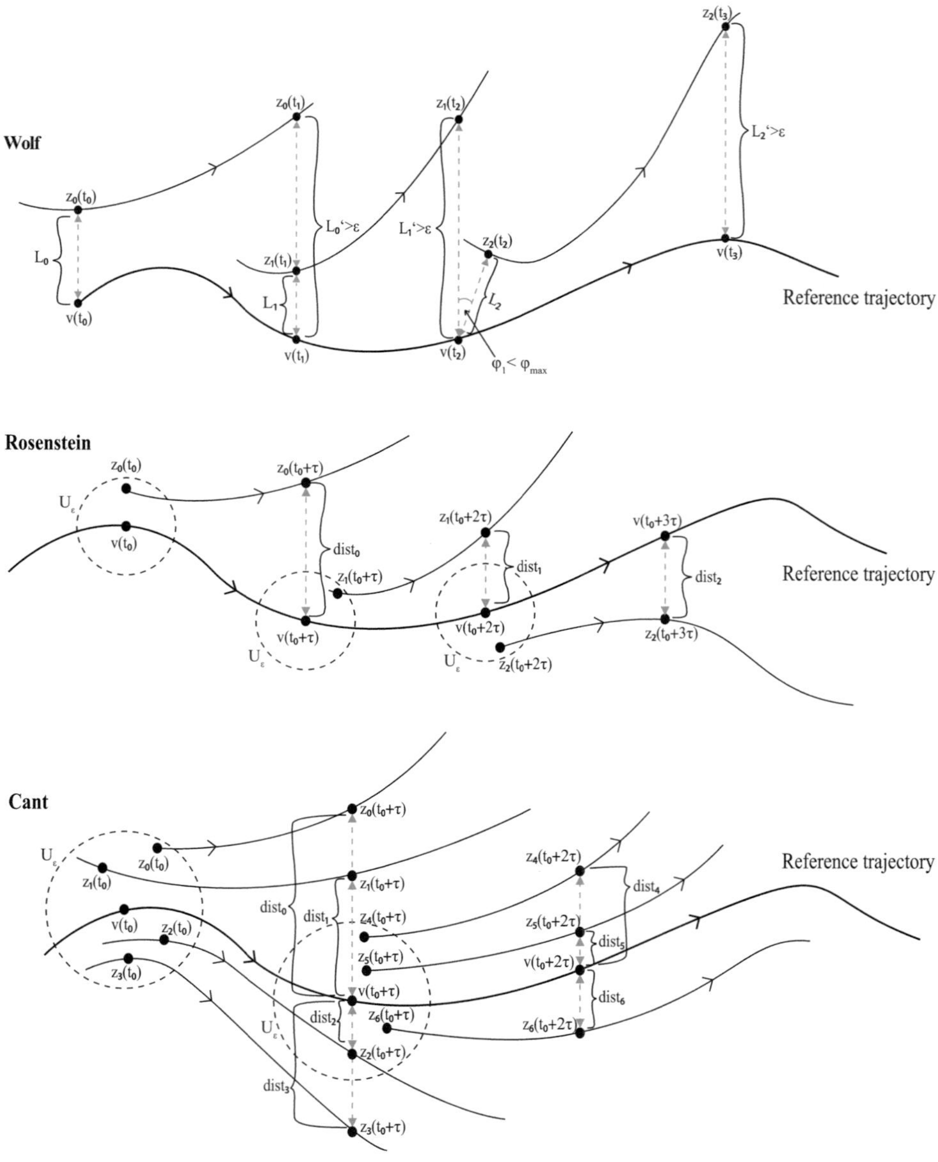

Fig. 5.23 *Wolf*-, *Rosenstein*- and *Kantz*-algorithm comparison

The different methods of complexity measurement presented are often applied to the topic of *Complex Systems* and Economics in empirical studies, as some selected examples will show in the following.

5.1.4 Examples of the Application of 'Classical' Methods in the Context of Empirical Studies

5.1.4.1 Macroeconomic Time Series, Such as GDP Time Series

There are numerous empirical studies on the topic of complex systems and economics, the origins of which can be traced back to the late nineteen eighties:

- For example, *Brock* and *Sayers* 1986 examined various *macroeconomic time series* of the USA among others by calculating *Lyapunov* exponents. The result of this study shows that the time series appear to be non-linear. However, no chaotic behaviour could be demonstrated (Brock & Sayers, 1988).
- *Frank* and *Stengos* also examined *macroeconomic data,* but from Canada in 1988. Based on the calculated *Lyapunov* exponents and the dimension of the proven attractors, no chaos could be demonstrated (Frank & Stengos, 1988).
- *Frank,Gencay* and *Stengos* starting from 1960, examined quarterly *Gross Domestic or Gross National Product developments* for Japan, Italy, Great Britain and Germany (Frank et al., 1988). Also in this study, the focus was on determining the dimension of the attractors and calculating the *Lyapunov* exponents. For Japan, for example, attractors with fractional dimension could be demonstrated. *Frank,Gencay* and *Stengos* note:

> Consideration of the dimensionality estimates alone might have left one inclined to interpret the findings as evidence of chaos in Japan (Frank et al., 1988, p. 1581).

However, it becomes clear at this point how important it is to examine the *Lyapunov* exponents in addition to the dimensionality of attractors. And so they continue:

> The results of the Lyapunov exponent estimates caution against such an interpretation (Frank et al., 1988, p. 1581).

Only negative *Lyapunov* exponents could be determined. And even with a regrouping of the data, only slightly positive *Lyapunov* values between 0.0012 and 0.0093 were found. Regardless of whether this rearrangement may be permissible, the values are much too small to make positive statements about the presence of chaos in the time series. The results for the other countries are no less disappointing if one expected chaotic trajectories. Overall, the authors note:

> None of these countries' national income would appear to be well interpreted as being chaotic (Frank et al., 1988, p. 1581).

However, the study showed that non-linearities occur in the gross domestic product developments of the respective countries, so it is appropriate to speak of a complex system, as understood in this book, in this context.

5.1.4.2 Price Developments

Schmidt and *Stahlecker* studied the changes in the *price index* for 22 sectors of the Federal Republic of Germany from February 1971 to December 1981 (Schmidt & Stahlecker, 1989). They were able to demonstrate positive *Lyapunov* exponents. They note the following about their research findings:

> In summary, it can be said that we have found evidence of chaotic behaviour in the sectoral time series we examined. However, the estimates found for (the maximum Lyapunov exponent, d. Verf.) are relatively small, in some sectors even almost zero (Schmidt & Stahlecker, 1989, p. 340).

Positive *Lyapunov* exponents indicate the sensitive dependence on the initial conditions of a system and, according to our definition of chaos (Sect. 4.5.1), are a crucial criterion for the presence of irregular fluctuations. However, since the positive *Lyapunov* exponents found in the study by *Stahlecker* and *Schmidt* are very small, the time series can only possibly be described as complex or chaotic, but certainly as unstable.

Holzer and *Precht* studied the *pig prices* in Bavaria for the period from 1957 to 1991. They were able to reconstruct 4 to 8-dimensional systems and demonstrate a weakly positive *Lyapunov* exponent (0.07) and a fractional dimension (3.6). Regarding the question of "whether pig prices have arisen from a random process or possess a complex dynamic that is not random," the authors conclude that "random behaviour can be ruled out" (Holzer & Precht, 1993, p. 157).

5.1.4.3 Exchange Rate Fluctuations

In 1990, *Kugler* and *Lenz* tested the non-linear dependence *exchange rate changes* using the *BDS* test proposed by *Brock, Dechert* and *Scheinkman* (Kugler & Lenz, 1990). They analysed weekly data from four currencies, Swiss Franc, DM, French Franc, and Yen, against the Dollar from the years 1979–1989. Significant non-linearities could be demonstrated for each of these currencies. The exchange rate fluctuations of the French Franc and the Japanese Yen against the Dollar may even exhibit chaotic traits. *Kugler* and *Lenz* critically note on the possible complexity:

> However, a final judgement cannot yet be made, as the dependencies could be conditioned by other non-linear stochastic models (Kugler & Lenz, 1990, p. 126).

5.1.4.4 Stock Price Fluctuations

An interesting field of empirical research is the development *stock prices*. According to the prevailing theory, stock price developments fluctuate independently of each other with a finite dispersion around a mean value, which represents an equilibrium resulting from linear relationships.

The state of financial market research can be summarised as follows (Weber, 2007), (Mandelbrot & Hudson, 2007):

- Stock prices are random and statistically independent ('Random Walk') (Fama 1965; Bachelier et al., 2006; orig: Bachelier, 1900).
- Stock prices follow the *Gaussian* bell curve (normal distribution).
- So far, standard indices such as the Dow Jones or DAX have shown a positive drift in the long term (25 years), i.e., despite short- and medium-term fluctuations, the long-term development is positive (Sharpe, 1963).
- In the long run, the market return is not beaten by any known 'active' investment strategy. As empirical studies repeatedly show, active investment strategies for private financial actors, such as 'stock-picking' (Barber & Odean, 2000), i.e., the selection of a few individual values, or market timing (Brinson et al., 1986), i.e., short holding periods and repeated portfolio reallocations, are particularly disadvantageous.
- The decisive factors for the financial investment return are risk (Markowitz, 1959) as well as cost and liquidity aspects.
- In addition to comprehensive portfolio calculations (Markowitz, 1959), the 'Capital Asset Pricing Model' (CAPM) allows, among other things, a simplified valuation of stocks (Sharpe, 1964)
- The *Black-Scholes* formula allows trading not only with stocks, but also with their volatility (measurement of market price risks), assuming continuity of price developments (Black & Scholes, 1973).

However, upon closer examination, the following three fundamental assumptions are increasingly being questioned:

1. Price changes are statistically independent,
2. they follow the *Gaussian* bell curve (normal distribution) and
3. continuity can be assumed in price developments (as found in all common models).

There are indications that these assumptions are not sustainable, as, for example, price jumps are by no means rare. There can be two reasons for this: Either the assumptions about the stochastic process, which overlays the deterministic conditions, do not apply, or the interrelated sequences of prices depend strongly on each other. A closer look at the second cause shows how these dependencies arise and how possible endogenous fluctuations are generated.[36]

Brock in 1988 examined a large number of stock prices and was able to demonstrate non-linear deterministic relationships. The underlying reconstructed attractor showed a fractional dimension.

[36] For comparison, see also the considerations that *Reszat* outlines in her essay 'Chaos in Exchange Rates'. Cf. Reszat (1993).

Scheinkman and *LeBaron* also examined stock prices in 1989 (Scheinkman & LeBaron, 1989). They pointed out that even simple non-linear deterministic systems can exhibit behaviour that mimics the results of stochastic systems. It has already been noted that special algorithms have been developed that allow a distinction between these types of systems. These methods have been applied by *Scheinkman* and *LeBaron* to stock price trends. The study shows that the 'random walk' theory is inadequate as it assumes stochastic independence between the data.[37] The results suggest rather that deterministic non-linearities play an important role in explaining stock price trends. This result was also demonstrated by *Thoma* in his 1996 study (Thoma, 2001, p. 47 ff.). *Thoma* states:

> Chaos research now also theoretically confirms what practitioners have known for a long time: The past continues to affect the future, and there are trends. Technical analysis, which exploits exactly this, is superior to a blind random selection (Thoma, 2001)

Sengupta and *Zheng* examined the development of eighteen different and grouped investment funds over a period of about five years in 1995 as part of empirical tests on chaotic dynamic behaviour (Sengupta & Zheng, 1995). Using three different test variants, they were able to show that the thesis of non-chaotic behaviour had to be rejected in many cases. They conclude their investigations as follows:

> Our tests show that chaotic instability cannot be excluded from some of the growth funds as the variance frontiers in such cases are likely very sensitive to initial conditions (Sengupta & Zheng, 1995, p. 299)

Mandelbrot is considered the founder of 'fractal geometry', which represents an important branch in the context of researching complex systems, as outlined in Sect. 4.1.2 of the second part of the book. He has applied his theory particularly in the field of financial market research. Fractals, as self-similar structures, can also be found in the price developments of the stock market: If you look at the graphical course of a stock price development without time specifications, it is impossible to determine at first glance whether the course of a day, a month or a year is depicted (Thoma, 2001, p. 5 ff.). *Mandelbrot* points out that the facts show something different in many respects than the common theories suggest:

1. Price changes are not independent of each other. If prices develop chaotically today, it is measurably likely that "they will move just as violently the next day" (Mandelbrot & Hudson, 2007, p. 37).

[37] According to the generally accepted theory, stock prices move as a 'Random Walk', i.e., real stock market developments can be described by normal distributions, as the rise and fall of prices are considered independent of each other and equally likely. However, this theory is beginning to falter due to insights from complexity science. An interesting presentation of this development can be found in: Thoma (2001).

2. Price changes are far from adhering to the bell curve. Thus, *Mandelbrot* and *Hudson* state: "From 1916 to 2003, the daily index changes of the Dow Jones are not distributed like a simple bell curve on graph paper. The outer ends flare up too high: too many large changes. According to the theory, the Dow Jones should change by more than 3.4% on 58 days during this period, but in reality it was 1001 days. The theory predicts six days with index jumps of over 4.5%, but in reality there were 366 days. And index changes of more than 7% should only occur once in 300,000 years, while the 20th century actually saw 47 such days" (Mandelbrot & Hudson, 2007, p. 38).
3. Thus, according to *Mandelbrot*, prices often do not develop continuously, but in jumps, as suggested by chaos theory or fractal mathematics. The approaches of *Bachelier, Markowitz, Sharpe* and *Black-Scholes* however, assume continuity, without which the formulas would not work (Mandelbrot & Hudson, 2007, p. 324). Ultimately, the assumption that price fluctuations follow the normal distribution (bell curve) leads to a systematic underestimation of risk.

5.1.5 Critical Examination of the 'Classical' Methods

Looking at the above results, it may initially seem disappointing from the perspective of the science of complex systems that there are no clearer indications of non-linear or chaotic behaviours. Upon closer examination of the results, one might suspect that disaggregated quantities are more promising for demonstrating irregular, chaotic system behaviour than aggregated macroeconomic quantities. It is possible that so much information is lost with aggregated quantities that it is no longer possible to demonstrate chaotic behaviour.

5.1.5.1 Reconstruction of the Phase Space

In practice, however, the problem may arise that the underlying time series, from which the phase space is reconstructed, are simply too short. Each additional dimension is ultimately determined by successively shifting the time series by τ until, through autocorrelation or 'mutual information', their independence from the original vector (the original time series) is established, so that the resulting time series spans another dimension of the phase space. With each of these processes, the generated time series shortens compared to the original time series, so the algorithm may stop due to the shortness of the time series. Thus, the dimension of the phase space may ultimately be chosen too small and the attractor may (erroneously) completely fill the phase space. This would suggest randomness, as we have discussed in detail, even though there may be no randomness at all.

To avoid this misinterpretation, the phase space must be made increasingly higher-dimensional by adding further dimensions with the help of the *Time-Lag*τ until the calculations yield a saturation. This would then be an indication that a complex structure exists and the dimension of the strange attractor is thus determined. However, if the dimension of the attractor continues to increase with increasing embedding dimension, this is an indication that the system flow is subject to a random process. But this would not allow any kind of ordered or complex structure to be demonstrated, so we can assume that the system is based on random processes. We have already pointed out that this is where a problem arises, because due to the finiteness of the time series, the algorithm always comes to an end (i.e., stops) even in the absence of complexity. But the stopping of the algorithm means that the time series is too short to ultimately make a qualified statement about complexity.

Therefore, it cannot be ruled out that due to a presumably very high dimensionality of the structure, it is not possible to meaningfully identify this structure due to a too small amount of data. It may be that the dynamics are highly complex, but in this sense have an order, albeit a complex one. However, it could just as well be that the whole thing is based on a random process.

Therefore, it is of great importance that the time series have a corresponding length and the algorithm saturates (complex structure) or does not saturate (random process) before the algorithm stops due to lack of data.

We have seen that there also seem to be data that lead to saturation, even though a random process is underlying, which may be related to a possible coloured noise in the data.

5.1.5.2 Fractals and Reality

A likewise non-trivial problem seems to exist in the construction of fractals. While aesthetically pleasing mathematical models of fractals can be constructed, one only analogises through a rough intuition that these fractals actually exist in reality.

Ultimately, this analogy formation naturally applies to any constructivist position. This does not contradict *Kant's* Critique of Pure Reason. He does say:

> That all our knowledge begins with experience, there is no doubt about that (Kant, 1995, p. 49).

All knowledge may indeed begin with experience, but it does not necessarily arise from it, *Kant* adds admonishingly. That such empirical knowledge, which has its sources in experience, thus is seen *a posteriori*, are not the only ones, he emphasises and refers to this other type of knowledge as that which is "independent of experience and all impressions of the senses" and calls it "knowledge a priori" (Kant, 1995, p. 49). Fractals have a connection to reality insofar as one can indeed get the impression that they can be found in various areas (see Sect. 4.1), thus they represent *a posteriori* knowledge. However, the mathematical visualisations of fractals are purely artificial and thus represent rather *a priori* knowledge, whose mathematical models exist completely detached from empirical knowledge.

We do not know reality, called "things in themselves" (*nuomena*) by *Kant*, and at most see their appearances (*phaenomena*) (Kant, 1995). Therefore, we cannot say whether the respective theory, which in the end is nothing more than a construction, is the correct one. However, we can certainly say that theory A has fewer contradictions than theory B.

It does not seem unproblematic to consider mathematical fractals as *a priori* knowledge on the one hand, and to be able to successfully determine dimensions, and on the other hand, to take a look at the world from a distance, so to speak, to generate empirical knowledge in the broadest sense, and then to say that this and that *a posteriori* recognised structure is a fractal.

In the end, we only see the shadows on the wall, cast by the real objects in the firelight, as illustrated by *Plato's* allegory of the cave.[38]

5.1.5.3 Lyapunov Exponents Under Criticism

Another problem is the values determined by *Lyapunov* calculations in the context of empirical studies, which may be positive, but very small. The closer the positive values approach zero, the less the "butterfly effect", which is supposed to be demonstrated, comes into play. As already noted, it is suspected that particularly noise in the data, caused by random influences and exogenous shocks, makes the proof difficult.

In any case, the empirical results do not unequivocally confirm the theoretical considerations about complexity. However, to conclude from this that applying the science of complex systems to economics and creating a complexonomics would be a failure considering the empirical results, would be premature and inadmissible. This conclusion is premature because the development of suitable methods and the conduct of empirical studies of this kind are still in their early stages. The conclusion is inadmissible because the examination of empirical data is associated with a not to be underestimated problem:

In open systems, as can be observed in economics, one must always assume that one will never find purely chaotic processes. Rather, the dynamic behaviours are overlaid by both exogenous disturbances and stochastic processes and influences. The elimination of this noise in the data is hardly possible. The proof of chaotic behaviour becomes even more difficult because so far only several hundred data points in a time series have been examined. In purely chaotic non-linear systems, this would be sufficient. However, in dirty systems permeated by noise, any result based on less than 1,000 values should be treated with the utmost caution.

An interesting approach has been suggested by *Sterman* (Sterman, 1989). He succeeded in generating chaos from the behaviour of decision-makers. To do this, he first

[38] *Plato* has *Socrates* say: "Imagine people living in an underground dwellingâ€¦ from childhood they are chained in this cave. They only look straight ahead; but from above and from a distance from behind, a firelight appears to them; but between the fire and the chained ones, a path runs above, along which a low wall is built. Along this wall people carry all kinds of equipment past Can such chained ones have seen anything else of themselves as well as mutually from each other than the shadows, which are thrown onto the wall of the cave opposite them by the effect of the fire? And furthermore: does the same not apply to the objects carried past? Throughout, therefore, the prisoners would accept nothing else as true than the shadows of the artificial objects" (Plato, 2010, p. 303).

developed two models and conducted experiments with decision-makers. Based on the experimental results, *Sterman* then estimated parameters for simple decision rules. The result was that he achieved good matches between the simulated and actual decision behaviour. In the models thus obtained, he was able to clearly demonstrate limit cycles, but also chaotic behaviour.

His analysis confirms the need to consider non-linear models in socio-economic systems, emphasising the need for empirical tests:

> Models (…) analysed with the tools of simulation and modern science and subjected to experimental test, offer the best hope to improve our understanding of the dynamics and evolution of social systems (Sterman, 1989, p. 175).

However, the criticism of the empirical results remains initially in all attempts to explain, as the findings cannot be argued away in the end.

5.2 Algorithmic Encodings as Alternative Complexity Measures?—Entropy Encodings and Other Measures

5.2.1 Resignation or Opportunity?

Due to the severe criticism of the classical complexity procedures and the sobering results of empirical studies, the question arises whether one should resign at this point or whether there might be a chance to research other methods that allow empirical investigation of complexity.

Indeed, there are such methods, algorithms that serve to process data series. Here, for example, sorting or compression algorithms can be mentioned. Until recently, they have never really been used in this context, the investigation of complexity.

5.2.1.1 Sorting Algorithms: From 'Bubble' to 'Quick' Sort

One possibility to investigate complexity would be to resort to common sorting algorithms like the 'Bubble' or the 'Quick-Sort'. The basic idea is that in a time series to be sorted, which is ordered, no exchanges need to be made to sort the data. The more complex the data is arranged, the greater the number of data exchanges should be, with a randomly arranged data series the number of exchanges is maximum. The same idea could in principle also be applied to the runtime of the used algorithm, so that a significant correlation between the complexity and the required sorting time of a data series could exist.

In literature, various sorting algorithms are now distinguished. At this point, we want to briefly discuss the typical classic methods such as 'Bubblesort', 'Shellsort', 'Quicksort', 'Mergesort' and 'Heapsort' (Sedgewick, 2002, p. 269–486), where a simple sorting method also represents 'Sorting by Selection'. The problem with this simple method, however, is that the number of comparisons and the number of swaps are almost independent of the complexity of the data, so this simple method is ruled out as a suitable algorithm for complexity measurement ($N^2/2$ comparisons and N swaps). With 'Sorting by Selection'[39] an average of $N^2/4$ comparisons are needed. The (half-)swaps vary between $N^2/4$ and twice that depending on the data set.

But what about a closer look at the sorting algorithms used in the literature (Sedgewick & Wayne, 2014; Güting & Dieker, 2013, p. 203 ff.; Nebel, 2012, p. 203 ff.)? Can they be used for the purpose of complexity measurement according to the above idea?

Let's first consider the relatively simple algorithm of 'Bubble-Sort'.[40] In the 'Bubblesort'Sorting algorithm method, the number of comparisons ($N^2/2$) and the number of swaps ($N^2/2$) in the average case is not much different from the complex case, so this method also does not seem suitable.

The 'Shellsort' method[41] is significantly more efficient than the ones mentioned before, but the runtime here is also not significantly dependent on the original data. This method is therefore also ruled out for complexity measurement.

One of the most common sorting algorithms is the 'Quicksort' algorithm, which is based on the 'divide and conquer' principle[42]. It is very fast and requires a runtime that

---

[39] The simple algorithm of 'Sorting by Selection' looks roughly like this when sorting a data series: Search for the smallest element in the data series and swap it with the element in the first position. Then search for the second smallest element in the data series and swap it with the element in the second position. Continue in this way until the entire data series is sorted (Sedgewick, 2002, p. 278).

[40] The also simple algorithm of 'Bubblesort', also 'Sorting by Swapping', looks roughly like this when sorting a data series: Continuously go through the data series and swap adjacent elements that are not yet in the desired order. Continue in this way until the data series is completely sorted (Sedgewick, 2002, p. 282).

[41] The algorithm of 'Shellsort' is a little more general than that of 'Sorting by Insertion': The latter algorithm works roughly as follows, if we want to sort in ascending order, for example: Take the next element from the data series and insert it before the previous element if it is smaller than the previous one. To this end, shift all larger data one position to the right and insert the selected element at the free position. This means that in 'Sorting by Insertion' only the adjacent elements are swapped, so that each element is moved a maximum of only one position. If sorted in ascending order and the smallest element is at the very back of the data series, it takes N steps with N elements to move it to the very front. In 'Shell-Sort', every h-th element is used for sorting. If this method is applied to a sequence of h-values ending with $h = 1$, the data series is finally sorted. On the way there, you get h so-called h-sorted files. This allows elements to be sorted over long distances initially, thus increasingly facilitating sorting for smaller h-values (Sedgewick, 2002, p. 290).

[42] The 'Quicksort' algorithm is based on the 'divide and conquer' principle. The algorithm for sorting a data series looks roughly as follows: Divide the data series into two halves and sort each half independently by repeatedly dividing the resulting halves. In the first step, any element, also called a partition element, is put in its place and then the data series is rearranged so that in ascending order, smaller elements are on the left and larger ones on the right of this partition element. Then the left and right parts are each sorted recursively in the same way, so that finally the entire data series is sorted (Sedgewick, 2002, p. 320).

is proportional to $N \cdot \log(N)$ to sort N elements in a data set. However, the algorithm has the disadvantage for our purposes that it can be very inefficient with certain simple data sets, i.e., it requires a very long runtime, in the worst case $(N^2/2)$ comparisons.

The 'Mergesort'-algorithm[43] requires approximately $N \cdot \log(N)$ comparisons regardless of the data and is therefore particularly suitable if you want to avoid a performance drop regardless of the data. However, this means that this method also appears unsuitable for our purposes.

The well-known 'Heapsort'-algorithm[44] is not suitable because it stably sorts N elements regardless of the specific data with $N \cdot \log(N)$ comparisons (Sedgewick, 2002, pp. 269–486).

The actual idea of using sorting algorithms for the purpose of complexity measurement has already been mentioned. Depending on the algorithm used, a significant correlation between the runtime of the algorithm on a specific data set and the complexity of the data set could theoretically be generated. Depending on the runtime, one could conclude, assuming knowledge of how the algorithm works, that a short runtime indicates ordered data and a long runtime indicates complex data. However, a reference system is always needed, as the runtime is extremely dependent on the length of the data set.

However, as we have seen, most good sorting algorithms are relatively invariant with respect to the specific data elements and thus not suitable for our purposes. Other sorting algorithms that are not stable and therefore show different sorting time behaviour depending on the complexity are not necessarily consistent in runtime, which can mean, for example, that even simple data sets have unfavourable runtimes, so even these algorithms are of little help for our purposes.

5.2.1.2 Compression Algorithms—Much Better

Another class of methods are the aforementioned compression algorithms. These are, for example, methods that can be described with keywords such as *Grammar Complexity, Kolmogorov-Sinai entropy* or *Permutation entropy* (Strunk et al., 2004, p. 481 ff.).

---

[43] 'Mergesort' can be seen as a complement to 'Quick-Sort', consisting of two recursive procedures and a mixing procedure ('Merge'). First, the data series is divided. Each part is sorted separately and then reassembled into a whole in a zipper-like process. The procedure is repeated until the entire data series is sorted (Sedgewick, 2002, p. 349 ff.).

[44] In the 'Heapsort' algorithm, the data series is converted into a binary tree. This 'heap' serves as a kind of intermediate storage, in which the data can be piled up and retrieved. The data series to be sorted is thus brought into such a branched structure (tree), in which each node has a maximum of two branches (binary). Then, from bottom to top and from left to right, the elements of the individual branches are swapped pairwise in such a way that the largest element is located at the node, until the largest element overall is at the top of the tree structure. This largest element is then removed from the binary tree and written into a (sorted) list. The element furthest to the right on the lowest level is moved up. This procedure is repeated recursively until the 'heap' is empty and thus all elements of the data series are sorted in the new list (Sedgewick, 2002, p. 390 ff.).

The idea behind these methods is to examine data series for complexity by trying to compress them (as losslessly as possible).

Example: Encoding of Images

Imagine two images. The first image was created by a master painter who has evenly painted a canvas the size of a 24'' screen with, for example, red paint. If you now photographed this canvas and wanted to display the image as losslessly and yet optimally space-saving as possible on a computer with such a 24'' screen, you would need relatively little information. The screen is divided into individual points, so-called pixels, e.g. 1280 × 1024 pixels. Since the screen must be uniformly red, you only need an encoding of the colour 'red'[45] and further the information that all pixels of the screen should be coloured red accordingly.[46] Thus, you could encode the image with one bit.

In the second image, we imagine a chimpanzee who, equipped with several pots of paint and brushes, paints a canvas of the above size. Given enough time, a very colourful, abstract image will be the result. After scanning, you can see that, for example, in the first pixel row of the screen the first 10 pixels are red, the next 100 pixels are green, the next 40 are black, etc. The second row is similar yet with different colour and sequences. That is, you do not have to provide a separate storage space for each pixel, but you can efficiently encode the colour information by noting that, for example, the colour 'red' now follows 10 times. It becomes clear that you need significantly more storage space for the second image than for the first image. In the most extreme case, you would actually have to provide a separate colour encoding for each pixel of the screen, i.e. for over 1.3 million pixels. To capture all colour nuances, you would assign a colour to each of these pixels, whose encoding could include values from 0–1024 or—to get an even more realistic image of the original—e.g. up to 65,535 encoding characters. Thus, a huge amount of storage space is needed for such a colourful, randomly created image. ◀

The example illustrates that for an image with high order, an encoding that requires very little storage space is needed. An image that appears very complex, on the other hand, will require an encoding that will be very storage-intensive. In other words: The first ordered image in the above example could be compressed very strongly in terms of computer-specific representation, the second complex image in the above example could be compressed less strongly.

[45] For example, for the RGB method to display any colours, an additive mixture of three primary colours: red, green, and blue is needed, for their encoding you can get by with a maximum of two 'bits', e.g.: red = 10, green = 01, blue = 11.

[46] This could be represented with one bit: 1 for everything in one colour, 0 for other.

We can also formulate this relationship in reverse: The more a data series can be compressed, the simpler and more ordered, and the less it can be compressed, the more complex and chaotic or even random it must be.

Data or information units often have parts of identical ‘characters’. Examples of this are, in addition to the images just discussed, in which there are areas of the same colour tones or colour patterns, e.g. texts that contain sequences of spaces or repeating combinations of letters. In pieces of music, one could imagine sequences of the same tones or sequences of tones. In number series, repetitions of number sequences etc. are conceivable.

For the compression of data for complexity investigations, you do not now have to develop new methods. Instead, you can rely on known algorithms. In relation to texts, for example, ZIP or similar methods would be suitable, in relation to graphics, for example, GIF, TIFF or JPEG, in relation to music, among others, MP3 or MP4. Whether these methods are actually suitable for measuring complexity would of course have to be examined more closely. The question of whether these methods do not react much more strongly to noisy data must also be considered.

A typical form of encoding is the run-length encoding (Run-Length Encoding (RLE)). Here, parts of repetitions, of patterns can be seen as a source for compression. Thus, sequences or areas can be represented by:

- ‘Byte’ (character)
- Identification byte (M-Byte)
- Length byte

Example: Encoding a string using the RLE method

Let the M-byte be the colon: ‘:’

Then the string abcdeeeeeeeeefghai can be encoded as: abcde : 9fghai

In this example, a compression of 44% (18:12 bytes) is thus achieved. ◀

Let’s consider another example with the RLE method:

Example: Encoding a string using the RLE method

Let’s consider the string: aaaaaaaaabbbbcccdddddd

What is the compression (%)?

The string can be losslessly compressed as follows: a:9b:4c:3d:6.

In this example, a compression of 45% (22:12 bytes) is therefore achieved. ◀

The RLE encoding (’Run Length Encoding’) is a very simple method. In this method, sequences of identical bytes are represented by a pair (character, number).

‘Run Length Encoding’ is particularly suitable for files with long sequences of identical characters, such as black/white graphics. For this reason, this method is often used for fax formats, in which very large white areas are only occasionally interrupted by black letters. Files with frequently changing bytes, on the other hand, are not well suited. In the worst case, the new file can even be twice as large as the original. A typical code is the so-called ASCII code[47], which provides for a uniform length of the code words. 256 characters are represented with 8 different sequences of 0 and 1 ($\log_2(256) = 8$ bits). However, the aim is now to allow code words of different lengths and to encode them according to the frequency of their occurrence. This method is called *entropy* encoding and is based on a form of encoding presented in information theory by Claude *Shannon*. Frequently occurring characters receive shorter code words and rarely occurring characters receive longer code words.

We are familiar with this type of encoding depending on the frequency of the occurrence of the characters, for example, from the Morse alphabet. Thus, the letter E, as a frequent letter, is encoded with 'short' and the less common letter Q with 'long long short long'.

In this context, the concept of entropy, (Greek Ηντροπια)[48] plays an important role, which we want to look at a little more closely in the next section.

5.2.2 Entropy as a Measure of Complexity

So what is time?
If no one asks me, I know;
if I want to explain it to someone on his question, I do not know.
(Augustine, 1983, p. 26)

Strunk points out that the methods associated with entropy do not explicitly address the phenomenon of chaos. He justifies this by stating that, on the one hand, chaos research is younger than the entropy approaches and, on the other hand, chaos is a phenomenon that can only occur in continuous dynamic systems. However, information entropy considers a discrete sequence of symbols (Strunk, 2009, p. 230). *Strunk* notes:

> Nevertheless, it can be shown that, for example, the *Grammar Complexity* is quite capable of identifying order structures in chaos. The method is therefore in line with the basic assumptions of chaos research, as it can expose chaos as deterministic dynamics (Strunk, 2009, p. 232).

---

[47] ASCII stands for 'American Standard Code for Information Interchange'. In computers, characters are often stored according to this encoding. Each character of the alphabet and some special characters are assigned a sequence of 8 bits = 1 byte.

[48] The term Ηντροπια or εντροπια is a coined word and is composed of: εν (*en*) = inside, τροπιη (*tropin*) = turn, reversal, where the entropy measure, as a measure for the irreversibility of an endogenous process, is denoted by the Greek capital letter H (*Eta*), i.e. the first letter of the word **E**ntropy or **Η**ντροπια.

Sturm describes the concept of entropy with the following illustrative story, which tangentially touches the field of thermodynamics, that discipline which represents a subfield of physics:

> Are you sitting at your desk with a steaming cup of coffee? Then I hope the following doesn't happen: You accidentally bump into the cup, it falls down and breaks, spreading the coffee on the carpet. This is annoying, but always possible. It can easily happen, and maybe it has already happened to you. Has the following also happened to you? The hot coffee on the carpet suddenly cools down. The energy released by this is used by the coffee to flow towards the cup, which also cools down and flies back onto the table with the coffee. Impossible, you say? Well, energetically speaking, not at all. Assuming that both the coffee and the cup cool down by 70° C, the energy released corresponds—roughly estimated—to 1000 times the energy needed to 'fly' back onto the desk. So it would be possible. But it is unlikely. So unlikely that it has never happened anywhere in the universe since the universe existed. So there must be another quantity besides energy that determines the 'course' of the universe. This quantity is called **entropy** (Sturm, 2003).

So there is a time arrow in thermodynamics! This means: Time is not reversible (irreversibility). The development of a system goes from a state of high order (unlikely state) to a (likely) state of high disorder (complexity).

> In the long run we are all dead (Keynes, 1923, p. 80)

says *Keynes* in an analysis of the quantity theory and its statement about the relationship between money supply and inflation rate.[49] Considering thermodynamics, one could specify:

> In the long run the world dies its heat death![50]

Normally, the world will eventually die a heat death. But what happens in the reverse case, in which the world would move towards a state of high order? *Hawking* describes this reverse case:

---

[49] *Keynes* says this to indicate that, for example, trusting in the self-healing powers of the market in the case of high unemployment can take a very long time, too long, and state intervention may therefore seem appropriate to combat the problem in a timely manner. He states about the truthfulness of the neoclassical approach: "Now, in the long run this is probably true (…) But this long run is a misleading guide to current affairs (…). Economists set themselves too easy, to useless a task if in tempestuous seasons they can only tell us that when the storm is long past the ocean is flat again" (Keynes, 1923, p. 80).

[50] A brief note on the term 'heat death': 'Heat death' refers to the theoretical state of the universe as a closed thermodynamic system, in which the total energy is evenly distributed to the matter. For example, mechanical work can be completely converted into heat, but heat cannot be completely converted into mechanical work.

(…) Now let's assume the opposite case, God decided that the universe should end in a state of high order, but it doesn't matter in which it begins. Then the universe would probably be in a disordered state at first. Consequently, the disorder would decrease over time. Shattered cups would reassemble and jump onto the table (Hawking, 1988).

And he correctly adds:

All people who observed such cups would live in a universe in which disorder decreases over time. I claim that such creatures would have a backward psychological time arrow. That is, they would remember events in the future, not events in their past. If the cup had shattered, they would not remember how it stood on the table, while if it stood on the table, they would remember that it lay on the floor (Hawking, 1988).

Hawking describes entropy by referring to the reading of his book. One could also have in mind the reading of this book as a representative example:

If you remember every word in this book, about two million units of information are stored in your memory: The order in your brain has increased by two million units. But while you have been reading the book, at least a thousand calories of ordered energy—in the form of food—have been converted into disordered energy—in the form of heat, which you have given off to the air through heat conduction and sweat. This will increase the disorder of the universe by about twenty million million million million units—so about ten million million times the increase in order in your brain. And this only applies if you remember *everything* that is in this book (Hawking, 1988).

So, heat is a form of energy. One could also say: heat is energy in disordered motion. The 'second law of thermodynamics' describes the most important property of entropy:

In a closed system, entropy never decreases.

While closed systems can spontaneously only develop in the direction of increasing disorder, in open systems, ordered structures can emerge from disorder through the possibility of exchange and energy supply. In this context, the idea of self-organisation plays an important role. So, the greater the entropy in a system, the greater the disorder and the smaller the entropy, the greater the order. Therefore, entropy can be seen as a measure of order!

5.2.3 Entropy in Information Theory—'Information Entropy'

5.2.3.1 Introduction to *Shannon* Entropy

For example, if we are looking for compression methods that are capable of compressing strings, we cannot avoid information theory. As already indicated, the concept of entropy in information theory also plays an important role:

The amount of information in a message can be measured by the number of characters needed to express the message in bits, (0,1)-symbols. The expected value over the information density of a source is measured and called entropy. For example, the so-called entropy coding is an algorithm to compress data without significant losses.

For the entropy calculation, we therefore need bits as well as expected values. If, for example, you want to represent 4 characters $\{z_1, z_2, z_3, z_4\}$ using a binary coding, you need at least 2 bits, since $2^2 = 4$ or $\log_2(4) = 2$:

$$\begin{aligned} z_1 &= 00 \\ z_2 &= 01 \\ z_3 &= 10 \\ z_4 &= 11 \end{aligned}$$

In the binary coding of 8 characters, you consequently need 3 bits, because $2^3 = 8$, or $\log_2(8) = 3$:

$$\begin{aligned} z_1 &= 000 \\ z_2 &= 001 \\ z_3 &= 010 \\ z_4 &= 011 \\ z_5 &= 100 \\ z_6 &= 101 \\ z_7 &= 110 \\ z_8 &= 111 \end{aligned}$$

Accordingly, for 16 characters you need 4 bits, because $2^4 = 16$ or $\log_2(16) = 4$, etc.

For the entropy calculation, we not only need the coding in bits, but also the relative frequency of the occurrence of a certain coding in a string as well as the concept of the expected value.

With the concepts of 'bits' and 'expected values', we can determine the information entropy. The specifically information-theoretical view of entropy, as already mentioned, goes back to Claude E. *Shannon*, whose fundamental essay was republished in 2001 (Shannon, 2001). Shannon developed this approach already at the end of the nineteen forties.[51] Information, in the *Shannon* sense, can be seen as a measure of uncertainty. The more characters you receive from a source, the more information you get and the more the uncertainty about what could have been sent decreases. Information is thus considered under the aspect of 'novelty value'. It follows the question of how likely the occurrence of the information is. Other aspects, such as the meaning of information for the recipient or sender, are excluded.

---

[51] This reference to the development of the *Shannon* concept is important when we later discuss the connection to complexity.

Therefore, information entropy can be interpreted as the average information content or average information density (expected value) of a symbol system.

The question arises whether this concept of information entropy corresponds with our developed concept of entropy as a measure of complexity? The term information *entropy* suggests this. Let's take a closer look at the information entropy:

A sender sends L symbols (or events) x_i, which occur with a probability $P(X = x_i)$, to a receiver. Each symbol occurs with a probability between 0 and 1, with the sum of all symbols occurring with a probability of 1. Before the symbol reaches the receiver, there is uncertainty. The greater the probability of the occurrence of this symbol, the lower the uncertainty or novelty value and vice versa. It is therefore obvious to take the reciprocal of the probability as the novelty or uncertainty value for the occurrence of the event x_i. However, in information theory, the logarithm to the base 2 of the probability is taken, i.e., $\log_2 \left({}^{1}/_{P(X = x_i)} \right)$, from which the required bits for encoding, now however depending on the probability of occurrence, result. Regardless of the occurrence or with equal distribution of probabilities, we would otherwise use $\log_2 (L)$ symbols for encoding. Since the functional equation

$$\log_a (x \cdot y) = \log_a (x) + \log_a (y) \text{ bzw. } \log_a \left(\frac{x}{y} \right) = \log_a (x) - \log_a (y)$$

generally applies[52] , it follows that

$$\log_2 \left(\frac{1}{P(X = x_i)} \right) = \log_2 (1) - \log_2 (P(X = x_i)) = -\log_2 (P(X = x_i)).$$

Interpreted as an expected value, the information entropy thus results as the sum of the probabilities, multiplied by the logarithm (to the base 2) of the respective probability of the total L considered symbols. We can therefore define:

Definition (Information entropy) Let X be a random variable with the set of values $W := \{x_1, x_2, \ldots, x_n\}$. P is the probability of the occurrence of the events x_i with the information content $\log_2 (P(X = x_i))$ for all i with $1 \le i \le n$. The (information) **Entropy H** (Eta) is understood as the expected value of the information content:

$$H(x) : -\sum_{i=1}^{L} P(X = x_i) \cdot \log_2 (P(X = x_i))$$

Furthermore, it is true that the information entropy $H(X) = 0$, meaning the uncertainty is minimal, when there is a symbol x_j that occurs with a probability of 1, thus certain, and all other symbols occur with a probability of 0, thus do not occur. $H(X)$ is also maximum $\log_2 (L)$, where L is the number of symbols, so:

[52] For justification or proof see: Forster (2004, p. 109 ff.).

$$0 \leq \mathrm{H}(x) \leq \log_2(L).$$

So how can we work with information entropy? Let's consider the German alphabet as an example.

Example: German Alphabet and Entropy

It consists of 26 characters, plus the three umlauts 'ä', 'ö' and 'ü' as well as the sharp s = 'ß'. Using binary encoding, with n = 26 characters, on average $\mathrm{H}_{soll} = \log_2(26) \approx 4{,}700$ bits per character are needed. If you calculate the actual entropy based on a German dictionary, you get $\mathrm{H}_{ist} \approx 4{,}099$ bits per character, as the relative frequency of the occurrence of the letters is not equal. This results in a redundancy of $\mathrm{R} = \mathrm{H}_{soll} - \mathrm{H}_{ist} \approx 0{,}601$ bits per character. The total redundancy is therefore: $\mathrm{R} \cdot \mathrm{n} \approx 15{,}625$ bits. If you divide the redundant bits by the average information content of an evenly distributed character, you get $^{(R \cdot n)}/_{\mathrm{H}_{soll}} \approx 3{,}32$. Thus, you could (theoretically) remove three letters from the German alphabet without loss of information. ◀

5.2.3.2 'Variable Length Coding' (VLC) and the *Shannon* Entropy

To better understand how information entropy works, let's consider a more detailed example.

Example: Student Attention

Professor *Lienzo* is giving a lecture on the topic of Business Model Canvas. He observes two students in his event. Every minute, he notes the degree of attention using a numerical code. The result is incorporated into the students' final module exam grade. This means

- 0 means both are sleeping,
- 1 means only the first one is sleeping,
- 2 means only the second one is sleeping, and
- 3 means both are listening.

Prof. *Lienzo* as a mathematician prefers to calculate in the binary system, thus preferring the digits 0 and 1. How can the four observations be encoded with these two digits? An obvious way is the binary code. So, two digits are written each time, so on average 2 bits are needed:

Listener observation

No.	Binary code	Observation
0	00	both are sleeping
1	01	A is sleeping
2	10	B is sleeping
3	11	both are listening

Is a more efficient encoding conceivable? If all four observations are equally likely, then this code is optimal. However, if they obey certain probabilities or relative frequencies h, then an encoding can be found that requires fewer bits on average.

Listener observation			
No.	Binary code	Observation	h
0	00	both are sleeping	0.500
1	01	A is sleeping	0.125
2	10	B is sleeping	0.125
3	11	both are listening	0.250

The trick is to encode frequent observations with fewer digits than rarer ones. This type of encoding is called 'Variable Length Coding' (VLC). First, such a code must be checked for validity. All possible observations are encoded. Is it also clearly determinable when the code of one observation ends and the code of the next observation begins? This would not be the case if such a code were the beginning of another, for example, if one observation were encoded with 01 and another with 010. In this case, separators would have to be introduced, which, however, would overwhelm the aforementioned mathematician.

Listener observation				
No.	Binary code	Observation	h	VLC
0	00	both are sleeping	0.500	0
1	01	A is sleeping	0.125	110
2	10	B is sleeping	0.125	111
3	11	both are listening	0.250	10

What about efficiency? The average number of bits per notation (expected value!) is $E(X) = \sum_{i=1}^{|L|} P(X = x_i) \cdot bit(x_i)$ with L = set of possible observations, $|L|$ the cardinality[53] of L, $P(x_i)$ probability of the occurrence of the random variable X, thus the x_i and $bit(x_i)$ = number of bits required to encode x_i.

For the simple binary code, the result is 2.0 bits per message. For the VLC, however, the result is: $E(X) = 0{,}500 \cdot 1 + 0{,}125 \cdot 3 + 0{,}125 \cdot 3 + 0{,}250 \cdot 2 = 1{,}75$ bits.

[53] The cardinality of a set refers to the number of elements in a set.

The VLC thus proves to be more efficient (provided one can work without separators).

To establish the connection to probability theory, we interpret the observation as a random experiment and thus the observed as a random variable X, which can take values from L, i.e., the set of possible observations.

Is there a lower limit to the average number of bits required for encoding? This lower limit can be found using the entropy of X.

The entropy of a random variable X is, as we know, defined as $H(X) := -\sum_{i=1}^{L} P(X = x_i) \cdot \log_2 (P(X = x_i))$

In the example of audience observation, the entropy is:

$$\begin{aligned} H(X) &= -(0{,}5 \cdot \log_2 (0{,}5) + 0{,}125 \cdot \log_2 (0{,}125) + 0{,}125 \cdot \log_2 (0{,}125) + 0{,}250 \cdot \log_2 (0{,}25)) \\ &= -(0{,}50 \cdot -1 + 0{,}125 \cdot -3 + 0{,}125 \cdot -3 + 0{,}25 \cdot -2) \\ &= 1{,}75 \end{aligned}$$

◀

The average (weighted) number of bits per notation (VLC) in the above example was 1.75. This also corresponds to the entropy H*(X)* calculated for the example.

This is no coincidence! By comparing the two terms for entropy and the number of bits, it becomes clear that the values are the same if each observation x is encoded with $-log_2(P(x))$, which corresponds to the minimum necessary bits for encoding.

▶ **Theorem**

The entropy H of a message source X is the lower limit of the average number of bits needed to encode x_i from L.

Furthermore, by encoding a message x with $[-log_2(P(x))]$ bits, one can get as close as possible to this limit. This expression denotes the smallest whole number that is greater than or equal to H.

A brief remark on the so-called prefix condition that is commonly required:

The problem to be solved in this context is that the use of code words of different lengths leads to the difficulty that sequences of code words are not necessarily uniquely decodable.

Example

Character	$P(x_i)$	Code 1	Code 2	Code 3
x_1	0.5	1	0	0
x_2	0.25	00	10	01
x_3	0.1	01	110	011
x_4	0.1	10	111	111

Code 1 ($x_1 = 1$, $x_2 = 00$, $x_3 = 01$, $x_4 = 10$) is the shortest of the three above encodings, but it is not unique:

Consider the sequence 0010100…

Beginning 00 = x_2, 10100 could mean:

$$1 = x_1$$
$$01 = x_3$$
$$00 = x_2$$

or

$$10 = x_4$$
$$1 = x_1$$
$$00 = x_2$$

or

$$10 = x_4$$
$$10 = x_4$$

This example makes it clear that unique and immediate decodability is required:

▶ **The Prefix Condition**

The prefix condition states: No code word may be the beginning of another code word!

5.2.3.3 Huffman Encoding for Generating Optimal Variable Length Codes

Let's now consider a simple algorithm that generates an optimal variable length code: The '*Huffman Code*'. The *Huffman* encoding is named after its developer David *Huffman* who first described this encoding method in the early 1950s (Huffman, 1952).

Optimal means that the average number of binary digits required for encoding is minimal and furthermore the code meets the prefix condition described above. The encoding follows a fixed procedure. *Huffman* says about the process:

> The procedure is applied again and again until the number of members in the most recently formed auxiliary message ensemble is reduced to two. One of each of the binary digits is assigned to each of these two composite messages. These messages are then combined to form a single composite message with probability unity, and the coding is complete (Huffman, 1952, p. 1099).

We want to look at the procedure using a simple example.

Example: Encoding of Letters

Let's consider the string: aaaaaaaaabbbbcccdddddd from the example of the RLE method. The string consists of the letters: a b c d and the RLE encoding resulted in:

$$a : 9b : 4c : 3d : 6$$

So we have a total of 22 characters, with the frequency of a being 9, of b 4, of c 3 and of d 6. The relative frequencies of their occurrence in the string are therefore, as illustrated in Fig. 5.24:

$$P(a) = 0{,}41, P(b) = 0, 18, P(c) = 0, 14, P(d) = 0, 27.$$

1. The two characters with the lowest relative frequency are now combined in a first binary tree. This means that here the two nodes P(b) and P(c) form the first level tree with the relative frequency P(cb) = 0.32, where the edge of the character with the smallest probability is assigned a 0 and the higher probability a 1, as Fig. 5.25 shows.
2. What remains are: P(a) = 0.41, P(cb) = 0.32, P(d) = 0.27.
The characters with the lowest frequency are now: d and cb, which together now give P(dcb) = 0.59, so that the *Huffman* tree takes the shape, as shown in Fig. 5.26.
3. What remains are the relative frequencies: P(a) = 0.41, P(dcb) = 0.59. Together they give a relative frequency of 1. This results in the representation in Fig. 5.27 for the *Huffman* tree.

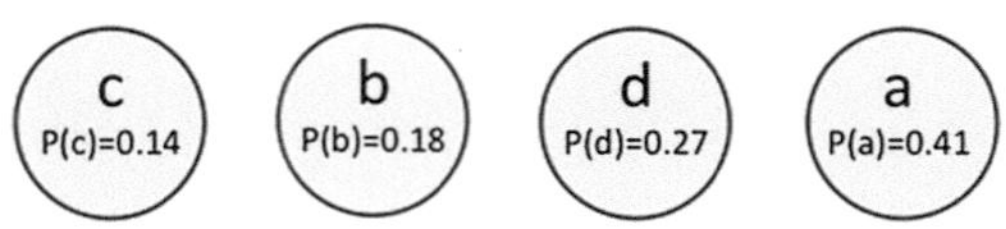

Fig. 5.24 Relative frequencies of the occurrence of characters in a string

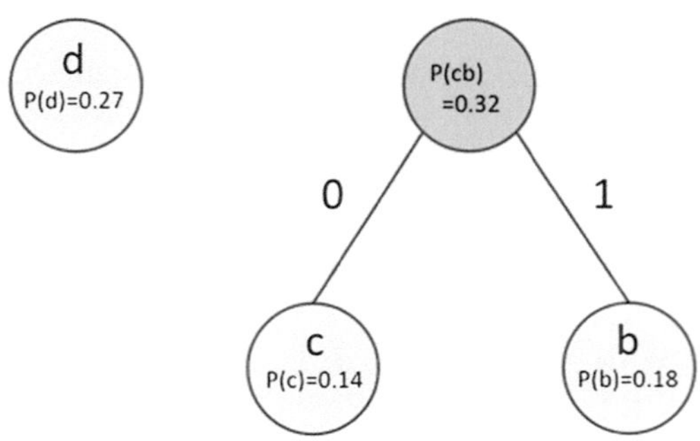

Fig. 5.25 *Huffman*-Tree 1st level

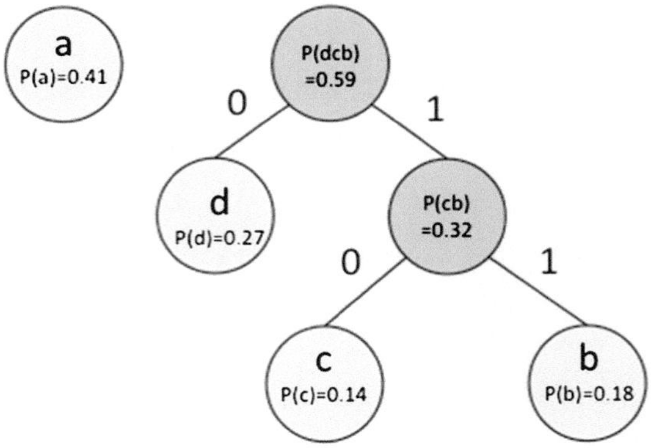

Fig. 5.26 *Huffman*-Tree 2nd level

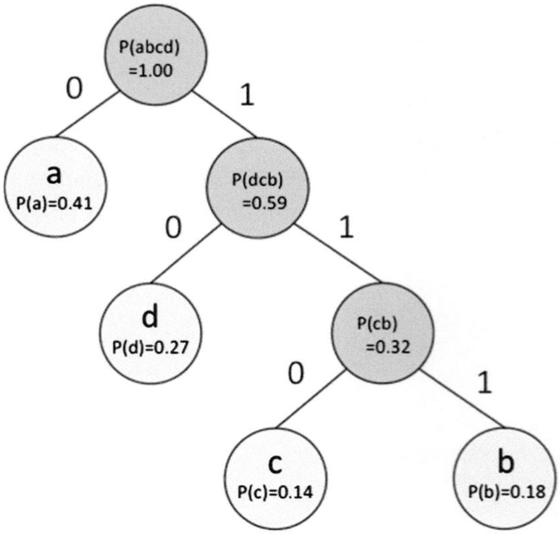

Fig. 5.27 *Huffman* Tree 3rd level

So the nodes with the lowest relative frequency are always combined.

4. The encoding can now be derived from the tree. To do this, the labels of the edges (0, 1) are strung together from top to bottom and assigned to the relative frequencies P(a) = 0.41, P(b) = 0.18, P(c) = 0.14, P(d) = 0.27. This results in the shortest code word W(a) = 0 for the most probable letter a with P(a) = 0.41, as Fig. 5.28 shows.
5. For d with P(d) = 0.27, W(d) = 10 results (see Fig. 5.29).
6. For c with P(c) = 0.14, W(c) = 110 results (see Fig. 5.30).
7. And for b with P(b) = 0.18, the encoding W(b) = 111 results (see Fig. 5.31). ◄

As the above example shows, frequently occurring symbols (in this case letters) are assigned shorter codes than those that occur less frequently. This shows the analogy to the

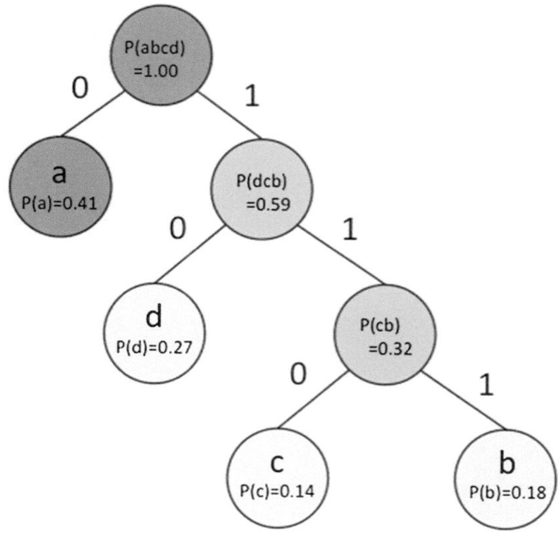

Fig. 5.28 Encoding of the character a

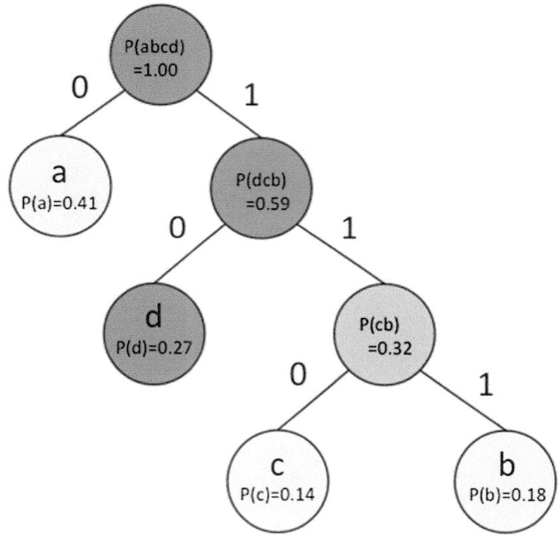

Fig. 5.29 Encoding of the character d

Morse alphabet, on whose principle the idea of the *Huffman*-encoding indeed goes back. The code for an 'e' for example, consists of only a single Morse character. Whereas to represent a rarely occurring character e.g. 'y', 4 Morse characters are necessary.[54]

[54]The encoding is also based on a kind of 'heapsort', so to understand it, you could also follow the notes on 'heapsort' in the chapter on sorting algorithms again.

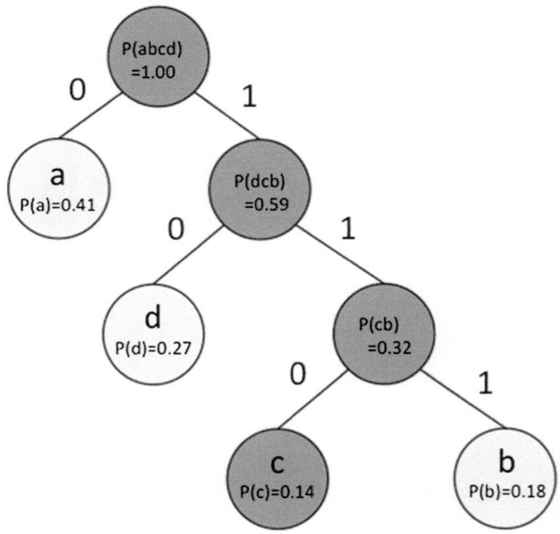

Fig. 5.30 Encoding of the character c

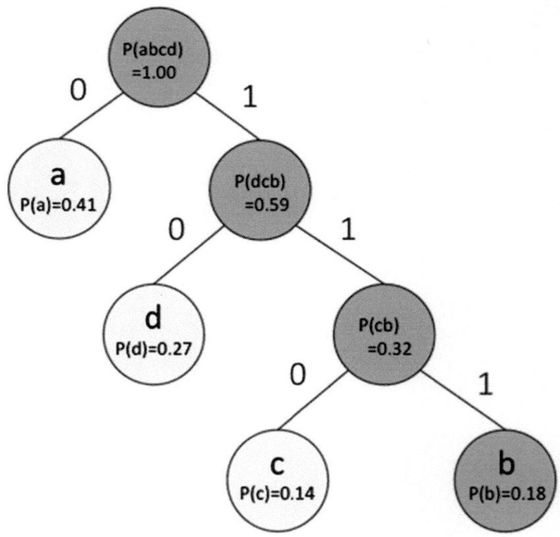

Fig. 5.31 Encoding of the character b

This method is also referred to as *entropy encoding*. Entropy encodings do not encode the data to be transmitted, but the symbols of the source. Entropy encodings work lossless.

The *Huffman*-encoding is an algorithm for generating an optimal code of variable length. Optimal means: The average number of binary digits required for encoding is minimal and the code meets the prefix condition. But what does this type of encoding mean for entropy?

Let's consider another example:

Example: *Huffman*-encoding of a character system of length 8, consisting of 4

Characters $\{a, b, c, d\}$:

$$X_1 = \{x_1 = a, x_2 = b, x_3 = c, x_4 = d, x_5 = a, x_6 = d, x_7 = c, x_8 = b\}$$

(equally distributed, but random)

$$X_2 = \{x_1 = a, x_2 = a, x_3 = b, x_4 = b, x_5 = c, x_6 = c, x_7 = d, x_8 = d\}$$

(equally distributed, but ordered)

$$X_3 = \{x_1 = b, x_2 = b, x_3 = c, x_4 = c, x_5 = b, x_6 = d, x_7 = a, x_8 = b\}$$

(unequally distributed and random)

and

$$X_4 = \{x_1 = a, x_2 = b, x_3 = b, x_4 = b, x_5 = b, x_6 = c, x_7 = c, x_8 = d\}$$

(unequally distributed, but ordered)

The following diagrams and codes result from the *Huffman* encoding:

For the equally distributed but random string X_1, Fig. 5.32 results with W(a) = 00, W(b) = 01, W(c) = 10 and W(d) = 11.

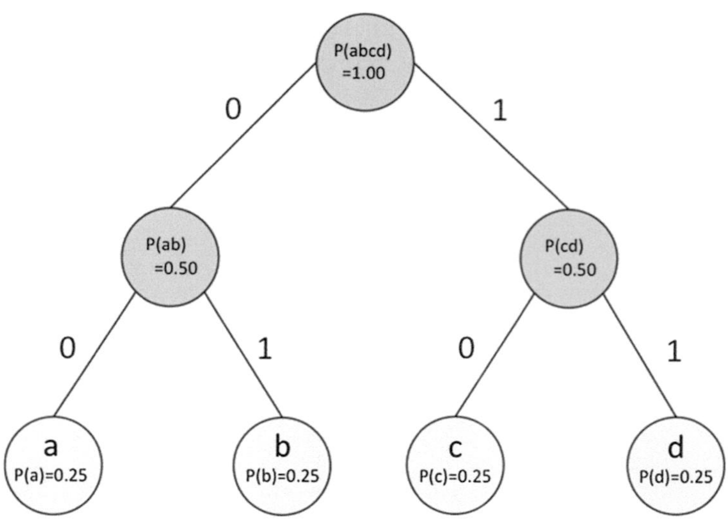

Fig. 5.32 Equally distributed, but random

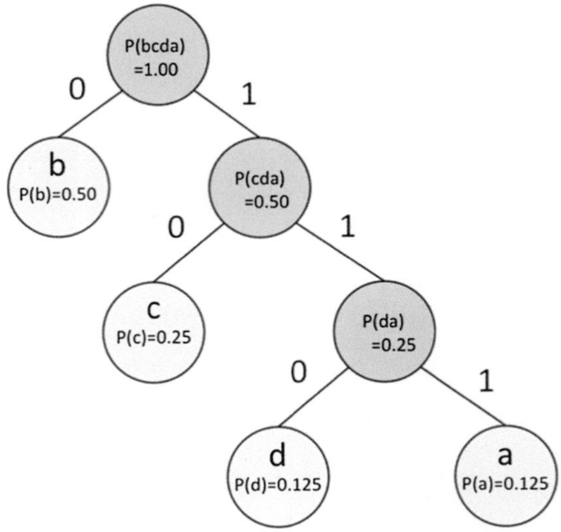

Fig. 5.33 Unequally distributed and random

For the equally distributed, but ordered string X_2, the same picture results as in the case of X_1, so again Fig. 5.32 with W(a) = 00, W(b) = 01, W(c) = 10 and W(d) = 11.

For the unequally distributed, but random string X_3, Fig. 5.33 results with W(b) = 0, W(c) = 10, W(d) = 110 and W(a) = 111.

For the unequally distributed, but ordered string X_4, the same picture results as in the case of $X_{3,}$ so again Fig. 5.33 with W(b) = 0, W(c) = 10, W(d) = 110 and W(a) = 111. ◀

We see that the equally distributed, but random string, has the same encoding as the equally distributed and ordered string. Furthermore, the unequally distributed and random string matches the unequally distributed, but ordered string, which cannot correspond to our concept of a complexity measure. If we now also calculate the entropy, the extent of the problem becomes even clearer.

Continuation of the Example

Let x_i be the i-th event and P the relative frequency. Then, for example, for the first string $X_1 = \{x_1 = a, x_2 = b, x_3 = c, x_4 = d, x_5 = a, x_6 = d, x_7 = c, x_8 = b\}$ with $n = 4$ characters:

$$x_1 = a \quad P(x_1) = \frac{2}{8} = \frac{1}{4}$$
$$x_2 = b \quad P(x_2) = \frac{2}{8} = \frac{1}{4}$$
$$x_3 = c \quad P(x_3) = \frac{2}{8} = \frac{1}{4}$$
$$x_4 = d \quad P(x_4) = \frac{2}{8} = \frac{1}{4}$$

This results in the entropy $H_X = -\sum_{i=1}^{n} P(x_i) \cdot \log_2 (P(x_i))$

$$= -\left(\frac{1}{4}\log_2\left(\frac{1}{4}\right) + \frac{1}{4}\log_2\left(\frac{1}{4}\right) + \frac{1}{4}\log_2\left(\frac{1}{4}\right) + \frac{1}{4}\log_2\left(\frac{1}{4}\right)\right) =$$

$$= -4 \cdot \left(\frac{1}{4} \cdot -2\right) = 2$$

So the entropy is $H_X = 2.0$ bits.

Overall, this results in:

$$X_1 = \{x_1 = a, x_2 = b, x_3 = c, x_4 = d, x_5 = a, x_6 = d, x_7 = c, x_8 = b\}$$

(equally distributed, but random), entropy: 2.0

$$X_2 = \{x_1 = a, x_2 = a, x_3 = b, x_4 = b, x_5 = c, x_6 = c, x_7 = d, x_8 = d\}$$

(equally distributed, but ordered), entropy: 2.0

$$X_3 = \{x_1 = b, x_2 = b, x_3 = c, x_4 = c, x_5 = b, x_6 = d, x_7 = a, x_8 = b\}$$

(unequally distributed, and random): entropy: 1.75

and

$$X_4 = \{x_1 = a, x_2 = b, x_3 = b, x_4 = b, x_5 = b, x_6 = c, x_7 = c, x_8 = d\}$$

(unequally distributed, but ordered): entropy: 1.75 ◄

It is easy to see that the above example reveals a major problem that we want to examine more closely in the following section.

5.2.3.4 Entropy Encoding and Complexity

The type of encoding described above, even though it is called entropy encoding, obviously does not correspond with the thermodynamic concept of entropy and the corresponding concept of complexity!

This is because the apparently more chaotic or complex string (e.g., X_3) has a lower entropy than the ordered one (e.g., X_2). However, since we consider entropy as a measure of disorder and thermodynamically, the higher the entropy, the greater the disorder, the *Shannon* concept of entropy, i.e., information entropy, contradicts the concept of entropy we use and which is physically secured!

Ultimately, this type of encoding therefore does not correspond with the concept of complexity, as *Shannon*entropy means '*uncertainty*'. This is obviously something different from chaos or complexity, which becomes particularly clear in the above example.

If you know that when rolling a dice each number is equally likely, the uncertainty about the next number to be rolled is maximum.

This applies in our character example for X_1 and X_2, i.e., for example, for the string$\{a, b, c, d, a, d, c, b\}$. But if you know, for example, that the character 'b' occurs much more frequently than the other characters, you expect the next 'rolled' character to be the letter 'b' and the surprise is small if 'b' also comes. You are less uncertain in your prediction (see $\{b, b, c, c, b, d, a, b\}$).

The order of the symbols does not matter here, and that is a problem with the *Shannon* method. The specific dynamics are not captured in the *Shannon* concept of entropy and the order of events or characters is not taken into account. And so the string $\{b, b, c, c, b, d, a, b\}$ with H_X= 1.75 Bit has the same information entropy as the string $\{a, b, b, b, b, c, c, d\}$, although the latter is clearly more ordered than the former.

Is there a solution to the problem outlined, without discarding the entropy approach, which we rewrite with the formula $H(X) := -\sum_{i=1}^{L} P(X = x_i) \cdot \log_2 (P(X = x_i))$?

5.2.4 'Permutation entropy' Versus 'Information Entropy'

To propose a solution for the problem outlined above within the framework of information theory, it 'merely' requires a modification or extension of the current approach. A solution to the problem can consist of considering finite strings within certain window widths instead of individual characters, in order to take into account the order of events on the one hand and the dynamics on the other.

This means that one looks at the frequency distribution of sequence patterns in certain sections (word lengths) to consider the order of events through the permutations occurring there.

Furthermore, the dynamics can be captured if a window is additionally implemented and run over the data set taking into account a fixed number of data points (word length):

In this case, the window moves through the time series and, for example, with a word length of 2, the smaller digit in the time series is assigned a 0, the larger one a 1 (rank pattern).

The method was first described in the first version (word length = n) without a window by Christoph *Bandt* and Bernd *Pompe* and was referred to as permutation entropy (Bandt & Pompe, 2002). For this, one considers a string $X = \{x_i\}_{1 \leq i \leq L}$ of length L and examines all permutations π of order n. This results in the definition of permutation entropy

Let's consider the example of a number series with 9 different numbers:

Definition (Permutation Entropy) Let$X = \{x_i\}_{1 \leq i \leq L}$ be a string of length L. We define H (Eta) for a word length $n \geq 2$ with: $H(n) := -\sum_{\pi_i \in S_n} P(\pi_i) \cdot \log_2 (P(\pi_i))$ with $S_n = \{\pi_i\}_{1 \leq i \leq \Pi}$ and

a) $\Pi = n!$ if $\forall i,j \in \mathbb{N}$ with $1 \leq i,j \leq L : x_i = x_j \Leftrightarrow i = j$ and

b) $\Pi \leq \sum_{i=1}^{n-1} \frac{n!}{(n-i)!} + 1$, if $\exists i,j \in \mathbb{N}$ with $1 \leq i,j \leq L \leq 3 : x_i = x_j \Leftrightarrow i \neq j$.

with $P(\pi_i) := \frac{|\{i|1 \leq i \leq L-n+1, \text{ für } \pi_i = (x_i,\ldots,x_{i+n-1})\}|}{L-n+1}$.

H is called permutation entropy and S_n is the associated permutation group[55].

Example: Permutation Entropy with word length $n = 2$ and $n = 3$

Let $X = \{x_1 = 5, x_2 = 7, x_3 = 10, x_4 = 2, x_5 = 8, x_6 = 9, x_7 = 3, x_8 = 4, x_9 = 6\}$ be.

a) If we now consider a word length n = 2, we get two conceivable permutations π ($2! = 2$) or a maximum of two patterns that can be represented by (0,1) or (1,0), where 0 is to symbolise the smaller and 1 the larger number. This assumes that the elements of the tuples considered here are different, otherwise (0,0) would also be conceivable.
   If we consider the case $x_i < x_{i+1}$, then we get six out of eight conceivable pairs of numbers in relation to X:
   (5,7), (7,10), (2,8), (8,9), (3,4), (4,6), which we each encode with $\pi_1 = (0{,}1)$, i.e. $P(\pi_1) = \frac{6}{8} = \frac{3}{4}$.
   For the case $x_i > x_{i+1}$ we get in relation to X
   (10,2), (9,3), which we each encode with $\pi_2 = (1, 0)$, i.e. $P(\pi_2) = \frac{2}{8} = \frac{1}{4}$.
   This results in: $\text{H}(2) := -\left(\frac{3}{4} \cdot \log_2\left(\frac{3}{4}\right) + \frac{1}{4} \cdot \log_2\left(\frac{1}{4}\right)\right) \approx 0{,}31 + 0{,}5 \approx 0{,}81$
b) If we encode the whole thing by choosing the word length $n = 3$, there are $3! = 3 \cdot 2 \cdot 1 = 6$ conceivable encodings for a maximum of 7 combinations of three.

In relation to $X = \{x_1 = 5, x_2 = 7, x_3 = 10, x_4 = 2, x_5 = 8, x_6 = 9, x_7 = 3, x_8 = 4, x_9 = 6\}$ the result for n = 3 is thus:

$\pi_1 = (0, 1, 2)$, thus $x_i < x_{i+1} < x_{i+2}$ applies to: (5,7,10), (2,8,9), (3,4,6), i.e. $P(\pi_1) = \frac{3}{7}$.

$\pi_2 = (0, 2, 1)$, thus $x_i < x_{i+2} < x_{i+1}$ does not apply to any event, i.e. $P(\pi_2) = 0$

$\pi_3 = (1, 0, 2)$, thus $x_{i+1} < x_i < x_{i+2}$ does not apply to any event, i.e. $P(\pi_3) = 0$

$\pi_4 = (1, 2, 0)$, thus $x_{i+1} < x_{i+2} < x_i$ applies to: (7,10,2), (8,9,3), i.e. $P(\pi_4) = \frac{2}{7}$

$\pi_5 = (2, 0, 1)$, thus $x_{i+2} < x_i < x_{i+1}$ applies to: (10,2,8), (9,3,4), i.e. $P(\pi_5) = \frac{2}{7}$.

$\pi_6 = (2, 1, 0)$, so $x_{i+2} < x_{i+1} < x_i$ applies to no event, i.e. $P(\pi_6) = \frac{0}{7}$

This results in: $\text{H}(3) := -\left(\frac{3}{7} \cdot \log_2\left(\frac{3}{7}\right) + 2 \cdot \frac{2}{7} \cdot \log_2\left(\frac{2}{7}\right)\right) \approx 0{,}52 + 1{,}03 \approx 1.56$ ◀

[55] The concept of a group comes from algebra. The associated group theory originated in the consideration of finite permutation groups. A group of permutations of a finite set with the execution in sequence as group linkage is then referred to as a permutation group. None other than Everiste *Galois*, the founder of the eponymous *Galois theory*, recognised the importance of permutation groups for the theory of algebraic equations (Meyberg, 1980, p. 26).

To capture the dynamics in the data set, a so-called window is introduced in addition to the considered word length, which—provided with a certain width (e.g. m characters)—is successively moved over the data set. For each window, the permutation entropy is calculated for a certain word length, e.g. $n= 2$.

Example: Permutation entropy with word length n = 2 and window width m = 5

Let $X = \{x_1 = 5, x_2 = 7, x_3 = 10, x_4 = 2, x_5 = 8, x_6 = 9, x_7 = 3, x_8 = 4, x_9 = 6\}$. With a window width of $m = 5$, we obtain the following five data sets for a string with 9 characters, for which we have to calculate the permutation entropy at a word length of e.g. n = 2:

$$X_1 = \{x_1 = 5, x_2 = 7, x_3 = 10, x_4 = 2, x_5 = 8\}$$
$$X_2 = \{x_2 = 7, x_3 = 10, x_4 = 2, x_5 = 8, x_6 = 9\}$$
$$X_3 = \{x_3 = 10, x_4 = 2, x_5 = 8, x_6 = 9, x_7 = 3\}$$
$$X_4 = \{x_4 = 2, x_5 = 8, x_6 = 9, x_7 = 3, x_8 = 4\}$$
$$X_5 = \{x_5 = 8, x_6 = 9, x_7 = 3, x_8 = 4, x_9 = 6\}$$

For $X_1 = \{x_1 = 5, x_2 = 7, x_3 = 10, x_4 = 2, x_5 = 8\}$ we get:
$\pi_1 = (0{,}1)$, so $x_i < x_{i+1}$ applies to: (5,7), (7,10), (2,8), i.e. $P(\pi_1) = \frac{3}{4}$.
$\pi_2 = (0{,}2)$, so $x_{i+1} < x_i$ applies (10,2), i.e. $P(\pi_2) = \frac{1}{4}$
This results in: $H_1(2) := -\left(\frac{3}{4} \cdot \log_2\left(\frac{3}{4}\right) + \frac{1}{4} \cdot \log_2\left(\frac{1}{4}\right)\right) \approx 0{,}31 + 0{,}5 \approx 0{,}81$
For $X_2 = \{x_2 = 7, x_3 = 10, x_4 = 2, x_5 = 8, x_6 = 9\}$ the result is:
$\pi_1 = (0{,}1)$, so $x_i < x_{i+1}$ applies to: (7,10), (2,8),(8,9) i.e. $P(\pi_1) = \frac{3}{4}$.
$\pi_2 = (0{,}2)$, so $x_{i+1} < x_i$ applies to: (10,2), i.e. $P(\pi_2) = \frac{1}{4}$
From this it follows: $H_1(2) := -\left(\frac{3}{4} \cdot \log_2\left(\frac{3}{4}\right) + \frac{1}{4} \cdot \log_2\left(\frac{1}{4}\right)\right) \approx 0{,}31 + 0{,}5 \approx 0{,}81$
For $X_3 = \{x_3 = 10, x_4 = 2, x_5 = 8, x_6 = 9, x_7 = 3\}$ the result is:
$\pi_1 = (0{,}1)$, so $x_i < x_{i+1}$ applies to: (2,8), (8,9), i.e. $P(\pi_1) = \frac{2}{4} = \frac{1}{2}$.
$\pi_2 = (0{,}2)$, so $x_{i+1} < x_i$ applies to: (10,2), (9,3) i.e. $P(\pi_2) = \frac{2}{4} = \frac{1}{2}$
From this it follows:$H_3(2) := -\left(2 \cdot \frac{1}{2} \cdot \log_2\left(\frac{1}{2}\right)\right) = 1$
For $X_4 = \{x_4 = 2, x_5 = 8, x_6 = 9, x_7 = 3, x_8 = 4\}$ the result is:
$\pi_1 = (0{,}1)$, so $x_i < x_{i+1}$ applies for: (2,8), (8,9), (3,4) i.e. $P(\pi_1) = \frac{3}{4}$.
$\pi_2 = (0{,}2)$, so $x_{i+1} < x_i$ applies for (9,3), i.e. $P(\pi_2) = \frac{1}{4}$
From this results: $H_4(2) := -\left(\frac{3}{4} \cdot \log_2\left(\frac{3}{4}\right) + \frac{1}{4} \cdot \log_2\left(\frac{1}{4}\right)\right) \approx 0{,}31 + 0{,}5 \approx 0{,}81$
For
$X_5 = \{x_5 = 8, x_6 = 9, x_7 = 3, x_8 = 4, x_9 = 6\}$ the result is:
$\pi_1 = (0{,}1)$, so $x_i < x_{i+1}$ applies for: (8,9), (3,4), (4,6), i.e. $P(\pi_1) = \frac{3}{4}$.
$\pi_2 = (0{,}2)$, so $x_{i+1} < x_i$ applies for (9,3), i.e. $P(\pi_2) = \frac{1}{4}$
From this results: $H_5(2) := -\left(\frac{3}{4} \cdot \log_2\left(\frac{3}{4}\right) + \frac{1}{4} \cdot \log_2\left(\frac{1}{4}\right)\right) \approx 0{,}31 + 0{,}5 \approx 0{,}81$ ◄

In summary, it can be said that the *permutation entropy* is a meaningful *measure of the disorder* of a system, as empirical studies by *Strunk* and *Mittelstädt* also demonstrate (e.g., Strunk, 2009; Mittelstädt, 2011).

This means:

- The lower the permutation entropy, the higher the order (self-organisation) and the adaptability of the system.
- The higher the permutation entropy, the lower the order (increase in complexity, up to (deterministic) chaos and randomness) and the lower the adaptability of the system.

5.2.5 'Grammar Complexity' as an Inverse Alternative to 'Permutation Entropy'

Another method is the '*Grammar Complexity*' (GC), where, as with permutation entropy, the sequence patterns of a data series are examined.

However, unlike permutation entropy, the GC is not a measure of disorder, but a *measure of order* (the result is inverse to permutation entropy).

In addition to the data series to be examined, random sequences are generated from the existing data (Random-Surrogate).

The GC then shows how complex the same data could be. Due to the additional random data, the data consistency increases, so that with a larger window width, the degree of order can be calculated more reliably than with permutation entropy (Strunk, 2009).

Example (GC)

Let's choose the same example of a string X:

$$X = \{x_1 = b, x_2 = a, x_3 = c, x_4 = b, x_5 = a, x_6 = c, x_7 = b, x_8 = a, x_9 = c, x_{10} = b, x_{11} = a, x_{12} = c\}$$

(based on: Strunk, 2009, p. 223 ff.)

First, pairs that occur more than once are searched for. These are replaced by another symbol (digit). If no more pairs are found that occur more than twice in the time series, triples are searched for (etc.) (Strunk, 2009, p. 224).

So:

$$\{bacbacbacbacbac\} = 15\,\text{Symbole}$$

Then:

$$\{0c0c0c0c0c\} = 10\,\text{Symbole} + 2\,\text{Symbole}$$

$$0 = \text{ba}$$

Then:

$$\begin{aligned} \{11111\} &= 5\,\text{Symbole} + 4\,\text{Symbole} \\ 0 &= \text{ba} \\ 1 &= 0\text{c} \end{aligned}$$

From this, then:

$$\begin{aligned} \left\{1^5\right\} &= 1\,\text{Symbol} + 4\,\text{Symbole} \\ 0 &= \text{ba} \\ 1 &= 0\text{c} \end{aligned}$$

This is the maximum compression of the data!

In the context of GC, the power and the number of symbols are now calculated together, with the remaining symbols and the logarithmised powers being added up, i.e.:$1 + 4 + \log_2(5) \approx 1 + 4 + 2{,}32 \approx 7{,}32$.

You can now compare this number with the original number 15 or with correspondingly generated random surrogates to see if the time series significantly differs from the random surrogates. ◀

5.2.6 'Recurrence Plots'—Return Diagrams

Rational numbers, formulated as decimal numbers, as described in 4.4.1.4, have a finite or infinite number of decimal places. The special thing here is that a pattern sets in at some point during the calculation of the decimal places and the sequence of digits repeats itself.

This is in contrast to irrational numbers, whose sequences of decimal places cannot be predicted from previous ones, regardless of how many of these digits or decimal places have already been calculated.

Most predictions that people make are based less on mathematical equations than on two simple facts: Firstly, the strong principle of causality, that similar causes show similar effects, so similar situations develop similarly, and secondly, that some of these situations occur over and over again.

The first fact has already been discussed (see, for example, 3.1.2.4), where it became clear that in complex systems this strong causality must be questioned when considering longer periods of time, as the butterfly effect comes into play here, so that the smallest changes in the initial conditions can have enormous effects in the further course. This effect can be measured using the calculation of *Lyapunov* exponents, etc.

The second fact, which has not yet been discussed, is also of enormous importance. *Marwan* et al. speculate that it is probably the reason why evolution has produced a memory. Because memory allows us to remember similar situations, make predictions, and thus survive. But remembering similar situations is only helpful if a system returns or recurs to earlier states. (Marwan et al., 2007: p. 241). *Marwan* et al. therefore rightly write:

"Such a recurrence is a fundamental characteristic of many dynamical systems." (Marwan et al., 2007: p. 241)

Recurrences can indeed be used to investigate the properties of many systems, from physics, electronics, population dynamics, epidemics and medicine, brain dynamics to financial markets. (Marwan et al., 2007: p. 241) Another interesting method is the so-called '*Recurrence Plots*'. A *Recurrence Plot* is another advanced technique of nonlinear data analysis. The term plot indicates that this is a graphical analysis method, while the expression '*Recurrence*' refers to a characteristic of complex systems. (Eckmann, 1987)

Secretly, *Eckman* et al. are considered the founders of *Recurrence Plots*, although recurrences were considered many hundreds of years ago. *Marwan* points out that the *Maya* calendar is an example in which the principle of recurrence, the *Recurrences*, is found as a basic idea (Marwan, 2008). Even though *Poincaré* referred to *Recurrences* in his work on the three-body problem, it was not until a hundred years later with the development of powerful computers that it was possible to carry out the computationally intensive investigations that are useful in the creation of *Recurrence Plots*, up to, as *Marwan* writes, "a pair-wise comparison of all possible combinations of pairs of a data series." (Marwan, 2008)

Instead of *Recurrence Plots*, we can also speak of Recurrence Diagrams.

This is primarily a graphical illustration of a dynamic system. A challenge, as we have seen, is that we reconstruct so-called phase spaces in order to investigate the corresponding trajectories of a dynamic system. If the phase space is two-dimensional, i.e., a plane, then one has a good view of the respective trajectory. This also works well in three-dimensional spaces.

One of the considered examples in the plane was based on the Logistic Equation. The attractor that arose in this phase space was an inverted parabola.

Another example considered was the *Lorenz* attractor, which was embedded in a three-dimensional space. Here, a simple climate model was considered, in which the butterfly effect became visible par excellence.

Even merely quasi-periodic systems, which stabilise on a three-dimensional torus and consisted of two intertwined cycles, could be very well illustrated. The problem with the illustration only arises when the phase space becomes higher-dimensional, as it then inevitably gets lost. We can imagine the system mathematically, but the illustration is no longer given from the fourth dimension onwards.

Simple examples have shown that a higher-dimensional phase space can be reconstructed relatively quickly from a time series, or must be reconstructed if one wants to adequately depict the dynamics of the system and the associated attractor. The exact process was described in this book.

In the presence of, for example, a ten-dimensional phase space, there is of course no visualisation at all.

In short: Graphical illustrations of trajectories can only be done in a maximum of three dimensions.

Otherwise, higher-dimensional spaces would have to be transferred into lower-dimensional spaces, similar to what is known from linear algebra: Just as a photo of an object in space can convey an impression of the three-dimensional object with a clever choice of perspective, a three-dimensional "photo" of a four-dimensional structure (with a clever choice of perspective) can give an impression of the four-dimensional structure. But, as indicated, the choice of perspective matters. The "camera" must be set so that all dimensions are captured by the perspective, or choice of camera location, on the object to be photographed. Mathematically, this is undoubtedly possible. However, the visualisation suffers with increasing dimension if the transformation always goes into the third dimension or even only the second dimension. And dimensions of 10 and more are not uncommon in phase spaces that map dynamic systems.

This is where *Recurrence* analysis comes in handy to illustrate such high-dimensional trajectories under a very specific question and to pour them into a two-dimensional image, into a matrix one could say, which is then graphically illustrated. The concept behind this is that during an analysis, times are discretely recorded and diagnosed when the phase space trajectories of the dynamic system approximately revisit the same area of the phase space as at some point in the past.

The challenge is the interpretation of the resulting images, as dynamic systems can show very different behaviour patterns. They can exhibit a high degree of self-similarity as ordered systems, so that the trajectories recur over time. In the simple case, think of the decimal places of rational numbers, where the digits repeat from a certain point, and thus a pattern becomes clear, in contrast to the decimal places of the equally determined irrational numbers, which do not allow pattern formation, as sequences of digits, no matter how long they are, never repeat.

Recurrence thus means that after a finite time you arrive at a point where everything repeats. In other words, in this context, recurrence means that the trajectory eventually arrives again at a (possibly high-dimensional) point in the phase space that has already been passed through. We can then diagnose a kind of periodicity. But the trajectory of the system can also run quasi-periodically or complexly, so that the same point is never reached again.

Nevertheless, in complex systems there are phases of intermittency, phases of calm and uniformity, where the trajectory of the dynamic system approaches a point in the phase space that has already been reached. These phases of intermittency are typical for complex systems and thus a characteristic of such.

Ultimately, order and chaos, simplicity and complexity are just two sides of a coin. In these intermittent phases, triadic cycles can also be observed again and again. The diagnosis of triadic cycles is also an indication of the presence of a complex system.

The complexity and phase transitions, which cause fundamental structural changes in the trajectories, can be determined, for example, using *Lyapunov* exponents. The *Recurrence* analysis now allows in the two-dimensional illustrative plane to distinguish these phases of complexity and recurrence from each other and to make them clear by technically showing the *Recurrence Plot* all the times at which the phase space trajectory of the dynamic system approximately visits the same area in the phase space.

As a simple example to illustrate the *Recurrence* analysis, the swinging of the pendulum of a pendulum clock may serve.

The example illustrated in 4.1.1.3 made it clear that the dynamics of the pendulum system can be sufficiently captured by two time series, a location series and a momentum series. It is even sufficient to capture only the location in a time series. The second series can be constructed from the first by a clever choice of a distance parameter. A uniformly, e.g., weight-driven pendulum, would lead to a location-time series that resembles a trigonometric function, e.g., a sine curve, which could be represented in a diagram, see Fig. 5.34.

Then each value could be plotted in an x-y diagram, where the x-coordinate represents the time axis. It is unmistakable that each function value on the y-axis of the diagram repeats after a finite time. If now each point in time from the present diagram t on the x-axis of a new diagram, the *Recurrence Plot*, is plotted against each point in time t on the y-axis, a pattern of repetitions is obtained. As soon as a repetition appears, it is marked with a black dot, otherwise the dot remains white.

Since all points in the diagram that plot t against t coincide with themselves, the diagonal is always marked in black. All other areas of the plot are determined by the repetition of the trajectory after a finite time, see Fig. 5.35.

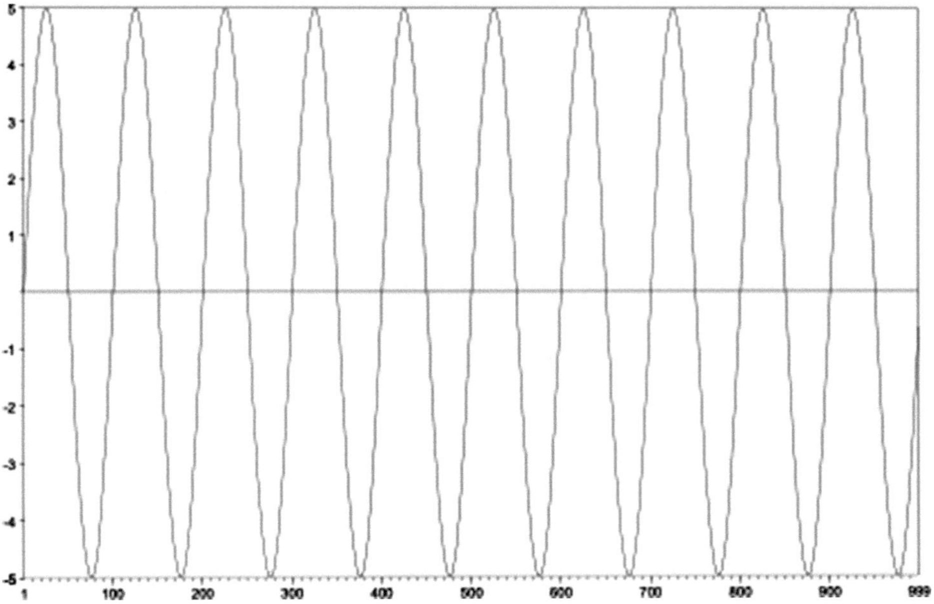

Fig. 5.34 Pendulum cycle sine curve

Fig. 5.35 Recurrence plot for the pendulum cycle—sine curve

The diagram can be constructed in such a way that it starts at the bottom left and ends at the top right. The black diagonal then also runs from the bottom left to the top right. In the present diagram, for example, we see that at an x-value of 100, the y-value of 1 is reached, but this also repeats at values such as 200, 300, 400, etc.

These periodic returns create diagonals in the *Recurrence Plot*. These regular patterns are an indication that there is an ordered system here.

The starting point of the investigation is therefore one or more (discrete!) time series. Subsequently, a phase space reconstruction is carried out using this/these time series, in which the embedded trajectory runs.

A distance limit, let's call it ε, is then set, which indicates how far a data point of the trajectory at time *i* should be from a data point at time *j* to be considered a value that indicates a repetition.

It may be that the trajectory does not touch directly again, but a distance can be defined beforehand that is considered close enough to speak of a return. We know this from trajectories whose cycles are "only" quasi-periodic, i.e., they approach arbitrarily closely but never fully reach. Such a system is very stable, as we have seen.

Since, especially in the complex case, trajectories never follow exactly the same path over time, this distance value is needed to define which value should be considered a "near repetition". The *Recurrence* value *R* is then referred to as 1 if the distance is less than ε, otherwise as 0.

Let X be the trajectory with $X =< v(t_1), v(t_2), \ldots, v(t_N) >$

$$R_\epsilon(i,j) := \begin{cases} 1, falls \| v(i) - v(j) \mid \leq \varepsilon \\ 0, \text{ sonst} \end{cases}, \text{mit } i,j \in \{t_1, t_2, \ldots, t_N\}$$

Then R is defined as: $R_\epsilon(i,j) := \begin{cases} 1, falls\|v(i) - v(j) \mid \leq \epsilon \\ 0, \text{ sonst} \end{cases}$, mit $i,j \in \{t_1, t_2, \ldots, t_N\}$

The temporal coordinate at which the values 1 now appear are then, for example, coloured black, the others white.

In the literature, another definition is often used, namely using the so-called *Heavy Side* function $R_\epsilon(i,j) := \Theta(\varepsilon - \|v(i) - v(j)\|)$.

with $\Theta(X) := \begin{cases} 1, & \text{falls } X \geq 0 \\ 0, & \text{sonst} \end{cases}$

The function has also been used here several times (see 4.2.2.7). It works analogously to what has already been described: If a certain distance is exceeded, the value is marked with 1, otherwise with 0, whereby the *Heavy-Side* function then refers to the value X, which of course can be nothing other than the difference between the distance ε and the distance between two points of the trajectory at different times $v(i)$ and v(j), which overall leads to the same result as before.

In the following, we will see examples that illustrate what the *Recurrence Plots* can look like.

The first example shows a random distribution, see Fig 5.36. A random distribution is also referred to as white noise. And now, if we plot the time points against each other, we can see both the diagonal of the same time points and the fact that the entire diagram

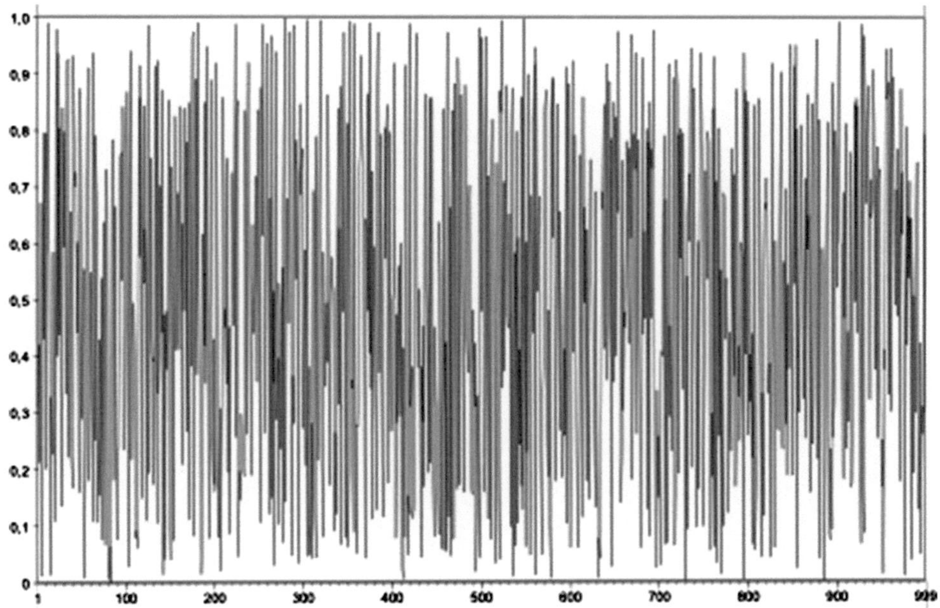

Fig. 5.36 Randomness—White Noise

is almost uniformly filled with black points. This uniform pattern of the filled diagram, see Fig. 5.37, indicates that the underlying dynamic system here must involve random processes.

If the system dynamics are periodic, as in the second example, see Fig. 5.38, where two different frequencies are intertwined, then one obtains a Recurrence Plot characterised by long and short lines, with the long lines reflecting the high and the short ones the lower frequency, see Fig 5.39.

The third example shows, for instance, a linear trend, as we know it from the *Logistic Equation* (Fig. 5.40). Unlike the random example, not the entire area is filled with points, but we have large white areas in the top left and bottom right. The strong accumulation of points along the diagonal is an indication of a certain trend (Fig. 5.41).

The next figure shows the complex system of the *Lorenz* attractor (Fig. 5.42).

The *Recurrence Plot* of the *Lorenz*-Attractor (Fig. 5.43) illustrates that this is a complex system in which the Butterfly Effect occurs repeatedly. This means that with slight minimal changes in the initial conditions, completely different results are obtained after a short time, with one trajectory staying in the left and the other in the right area.

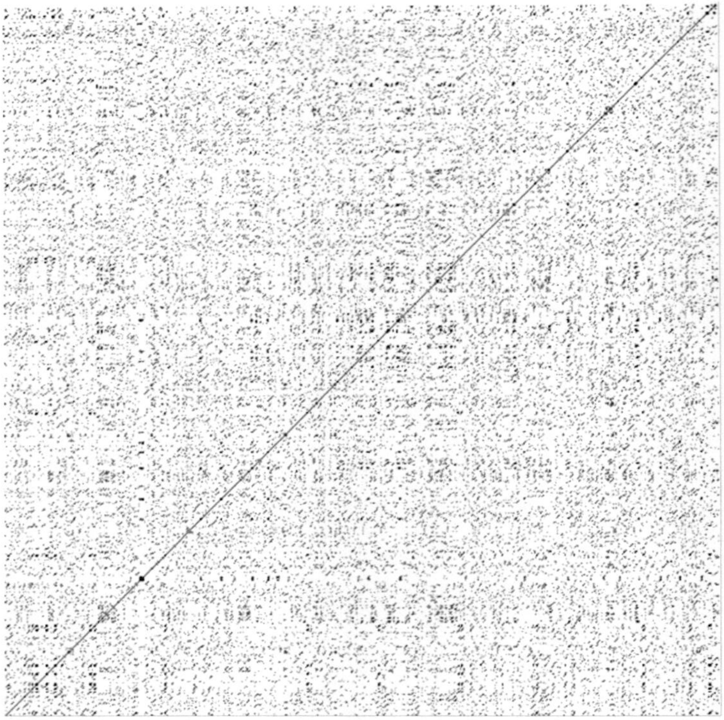

Fig. 5.37 Recurrence Plot for Randomness—White Noise

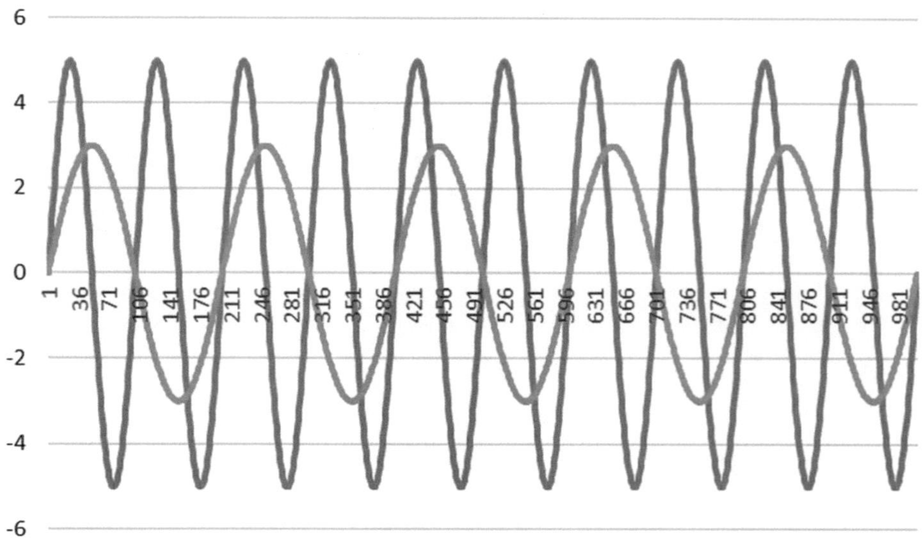

Fig. 5.38 Two Coupled Oscillations

On the one hand, we recognise the diagonal, but above all stripe patterns, which represent signs of intermittency and indicate that this is a complex system. However, it is not so easy to correctly interpret the *Recurrence-Plots* and it requires some experience.

But there are certain pattern types that can be observed and that allow classification, as the following table shows (Table 5.6).

***LOI**=Line Of Identity

Recurrence Plots thus allow a variety of interpretation possibilities depending on their graphic design. For example, if the observation is that something uniform is present, then the process is stationary. If there are white areas in the upper and lower areas, then the process is complex and has a trend. If there are interruptions within the black areas, i.e., white stripes appear, then this is an indication that phase transitions may have occurred. If a periodic pattern becomes visible, then this is a clear indication that we have quasiperiodic processes in front of us, as we have observed on the tori, etc.

In addition, there are a number of metrics that allow *Recurrence-Plots* to be analysed quantitatively, such as the *Recurrence-Density*, the *Recurrence-Determinism*, the *Recurrence-Intermittency* or the *Recurrence-Entropy*. In this context, we also speak of the *RQA* (*Recurrence Quantification Analysis*). (Marwan, 2007: p. 263 ff.)

Recurrence-Density:

$RR_\epsilon = \frac{1}{N^2}\sum_{i,j=1}^{N} R_\epsilon(i,j)$ The *Recurrence Rate* (RR) measures the number of *Recurrence* points in relation to the number of possible points, excluding the diagonal (LOI). It represents a measure of the density of recurrence points in the *Recurrence Plot*.

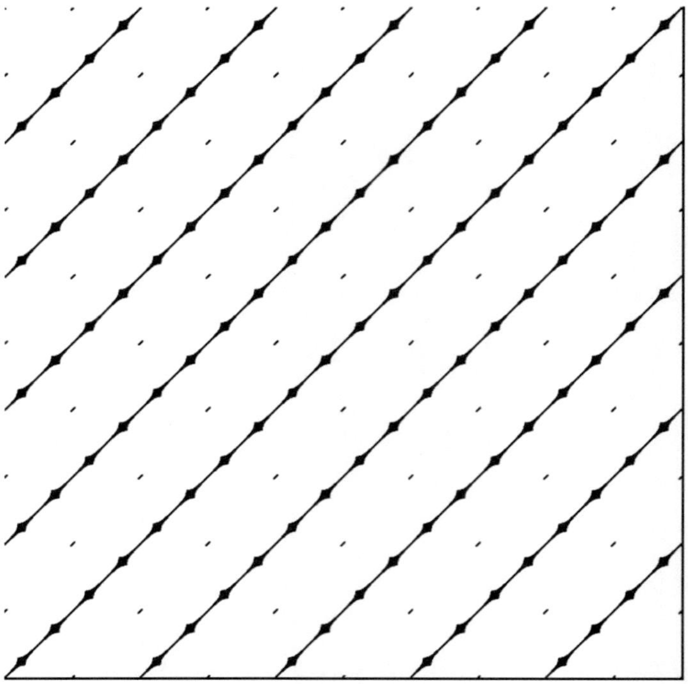

Fig. 5.39 Recurrence Plot: Coupled Oscillation

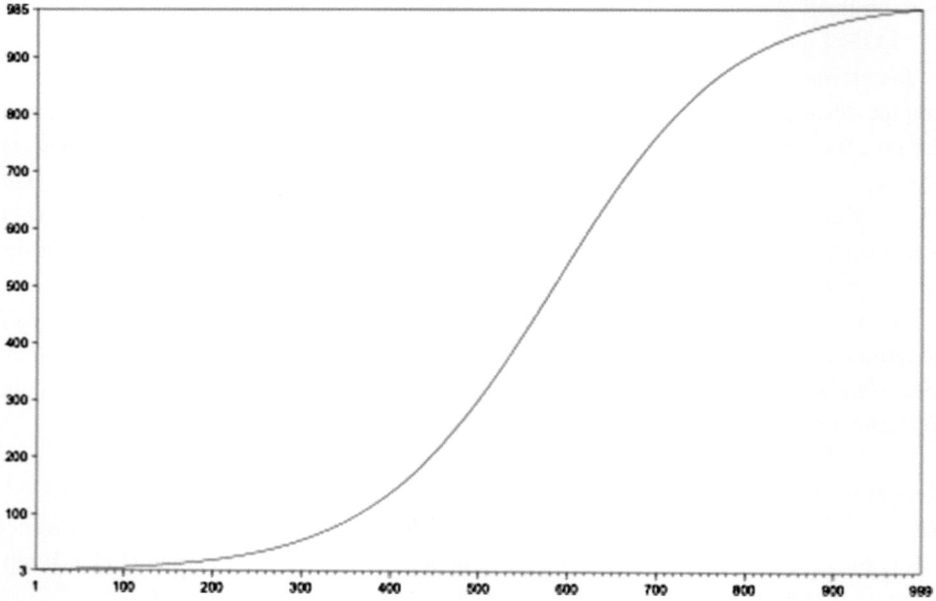

Fig. 5.40 Trend—Logistic Function

Fig. 5.41 Recurrence Plot for the Trend—Logistic Function

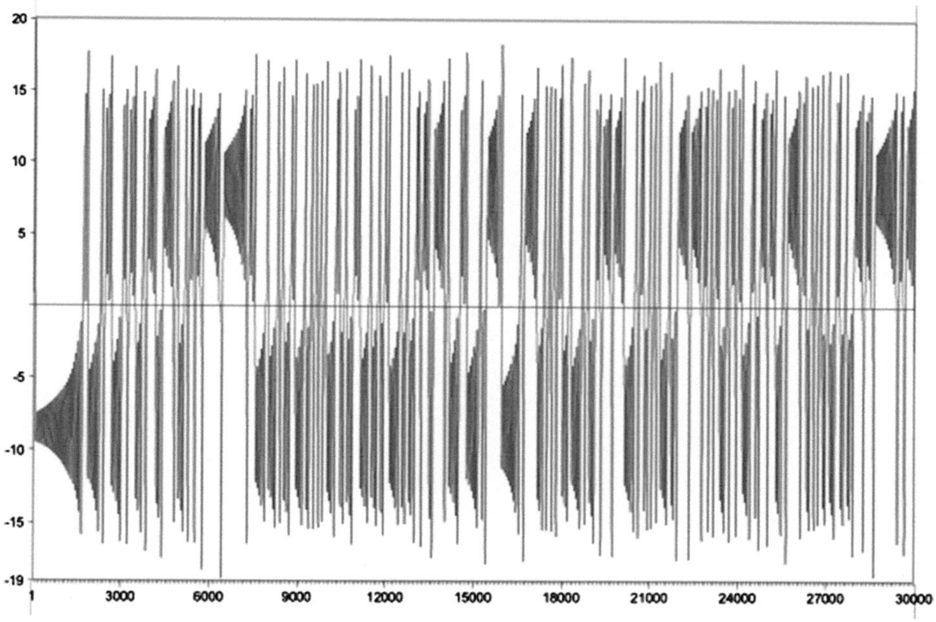

Fig. 5.42 *Lorenz* System—Data Series

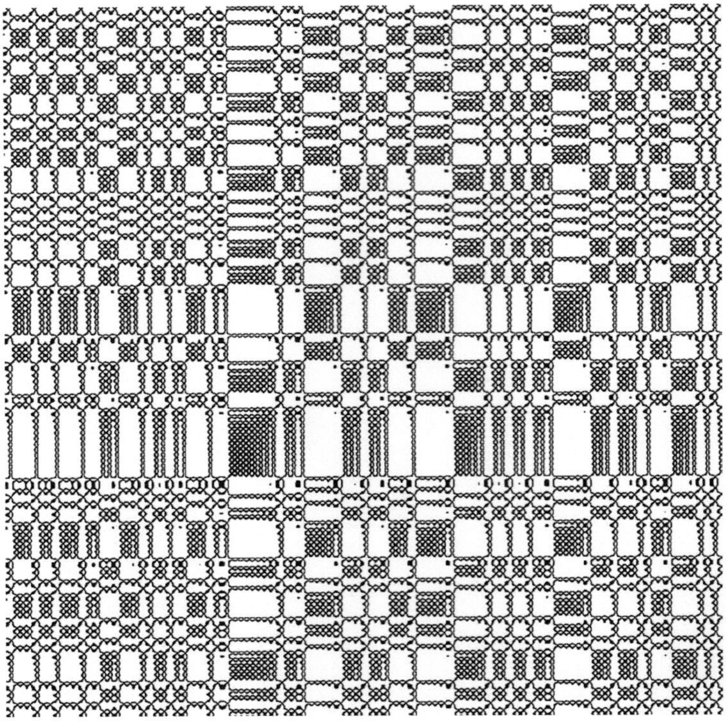

Fig. 5.43 *Lorenz* System—Recurrence Plot

Recurrence Determinism:

Strunk states: "Since diagonal lines indicate deterministic components, determinism (DET) is defined as the percentage of those *Recurrence* points that represent diagonal lines." (Strunk, 2019: p. 383)

Marwan points out that dynamic processes with complex behaviour cause no or very short diagonals, while deterministic processes cause longer diagonals and fewer single, isolated recurrence points (Marwan, 2008: p. 265).

In the following formula, l denotes the length of the diagonals and the frequency of occurrence of the diagonals of length l.

Thus, the ratio of *Recurrence* points that form diagonal structures (of at least lmin length) to all recurrence points is seen as a measure of the determinism (or predictability) of the system. (Marwan, 2008: p. 265). The longest line is the diagonal, the Line of Identity (LOI). This diagonal is understandably excluded.

$$DET = \frac{\sum_{l=1_{\min}}^{N} l \cdot h(\epsilon, l)}{\sum_{l=1}^{N} l \cdot h(\epsilon, l)}$$

Table 5.6 Recurrence Plots and their interpretations. *Source:* http://www.recurrence-plot.tk/glance.php?show_intro=1

Observations in Recurrence Plots	Interpretation
Uniformity	Process is stationary
Fading at the upper left and lower right corners	Non-stationarity—the process contains a trend or a drift
Interruptions (white stripes) occur	Non-stationarity; some states are rare or far from the normal state; transitions may have occurred
Periodic/quasi-periodic patterns	Cycles present; the temporal distance between periodic patterns (e.g., lines) corresponds to the period; long diagonal lines with different distances to each other reveal a quasi-periodic process
Single isolated points	Strong fluctuations; if only single isolated points occur, the process can be an uncorrelated random or even anticorrelated process
Diagonal lines (parallel to the main diagonal)*	The development of the states is similar at different times; the process could be deterministic; if these diagonal lines occur next to single isolated points, the process could be chaotic (if these diagonal lines are periodic, unstable periodic orbits can be found)
Diagonal lines (orthogonal to the main diagonal)	The development of the states is similar at different times, but with reversed time; sometimes this is a sign of insufficient embedding
Vertical and horizontal lines/clusters	Some states do not change or change slowly for some time; indication of laminar states
Long curved line structures	The development of the states is similar at different epochs, but with different speed; the dynamics of the system could change (but caution: this does not fully apply to short curved line structures)

Recurrence Intermittency:
Since vertical lines indicate intermittency, this laminarity (LAM) is defined here as "the percentage of those *Recurrence* points that form vertical lines." (Strunk 2019: 384). The verticals v should have a minimum length: **vmin**. With $h(v)$ the frequency, this time of the vertical lines, is meant.

$$LAM = \frac{\sum_{v=v_{\min}}^{N} v \cdot h(\epsilon, v)}{\sum_{v=1}^{N} v \cdot h(\epsilon, v)}$$

Recurrence Entropy:
The complexity of a *Recurrence Plot* is calculated using the *Shannon* information entropy definition H (Eta, like Entropy), where P here is intended to denote the relative

frequency of the individual lengths l of the diagonals. However, it is critical to distinguish between uncertainty and complexity, which we have considered in relation to *Shannon* entropy. (see Sect. 5.2.3.4). This results in approximately:

$$H = -\sum_{l=l_{\min}}^{N} P(l)\ \log_2(P(l))$$

Marwan pointed out a rather strange sign that the *Recurrence Plots* were on the verge of becoming widely known and accepted, referring to an April Fool's joke by the Australian office of the internet company *Google* from 2008. In a press release dated April 1, 2008, *Google* announced the introduction of a new search technology named *gDay*. This was supposed to be able to accurately predict future internet content. (Marwan 2008: p. 7)

> "Using Google's index of historic, cached web content and a mashup of numerous factors including recurrence plots and fuzzy measure analysis, *gDay* creates a sophisticated model of what the internet will look like 24 hours from now—including share price movements, sports results and news events." (Writers 2008)

Marwan's comment on this:

> "As we know, many things Google introduced turned out to be quite popular later." (Marwan 2008: p. 7)

5.3 JPEG as a Solution?—Transformation Encodings

5.3.1 *LZW*-Compression Algorithm (Lempel, *Ziv, Welch*)

The algorithm described by Jacob *Ziv* and Abraham *Lempel* is based on the fact that character strings can repeat in a data series (Ziv & Lempel, 1977). When a character string appears for the second time, it does not need to be transmitted again, but it is sufficient to transmit a pointer that refers to the place in the data series where the character string previously appeared. This algorithm was further developed several times and became known in 1984 by Terry *Welch* under the name *LZW*. In this encoding, sequences of individual bytes are searched for and then replaced by an indication of quantity and value. The *LZW* method thus searches for repeating character strings and replaces them with a reference to the identical character sequence, whereby the *LZW* refers not to a specific file position, but to the running number of an earlier character string. This approach allows a pointer of only a few bits to refer to much earlier character strings and finally to have a table that consists only of index entries.

The *LZW* compression algorithm therefore works with such an assignment table in which these references to the individual character strings are stored. The table is not stored in the actual file, but must be generated with each compression and decompression, whereby the data can consist of characters or numbers (Welch, 1984, p. 9 ff.).

This compression method is used by many graphic formats (e.g. GIF). In contrast to the *Huffman* method, which was explained in detail in Sect. 5.2.3.3 by encoding each source symbol, the *LZW* method combines entire symbol sequences into a new symbol each time.

5.3.2 Transformation Encodings

The fundamental challenge in this context can be described as follows:

- On a visual level: When looking at colour surfaces, there are often slight colour differences. These are often not perceived.
- On an audio level: Tones are not perceived at a certain volume and pitch when tones of greater volume cover them.
- On a textual level: Words are often not perceived in detail as a chain of characters when reading, but as a whole, which is why the meaning of the words is understood even when characters are omitted.

In transformation encodings, the original signals are broken down into their frequency spectrum[56] by transformation. The frequency spectra have different importance, for example in the area of colours and tones for perception. This can also be wonderfully transferred to empirical time series.

5.3.2.1 (Discrete) *Fourier* Transformation (FT and DFT)

The best-known transformation is certainly the so-called *Fourier* Transformation (Klingen, 2001).

Let's first look at the *Fourier* series expansion. Jean Baptiste *Fourier* proved that under certain conditions periodic functions f can be approximated by a sum of trigonometric functions such as cosine and sine. Ultimately, one switches from the spatial to the frequency domain, from the representation of real to mathematically complex values. If, for example, you pick out a position in an image in the spatial domain, you get the value of the pixel and its location. In the frequency domain, you get a multitude of amplitudes at this point. Thus, after the *Fourier* transformation, the spatial distribution of pixel values in an image becomes a frequency (oscillation width) and amplitude distribution (oscillation height).

---

[56] The frequency spectrum of a signal indicates the composition of the signal from different frequencies.

From the perspective of linear algebra, the *Fourier* Transformation is nothing more than a basis change from one basis[57] to another.

Linearly independent is a set of vectors exactly when none of these vectors can be represented as a linear combination (i.e., through addition and scalar multiplication) of the others. In other words: n vectors $v_i \in V$ and $\lambda_i \in K$ with $1 \leq i \leq n$ are called linearly independent if: $\sum_{i=0}^{n} \lambda_i v_i = 0 \Leftrightarrow \lambda_1 = \lambda_2 = \ldots = \lambda_n = 0$ (Liening, 2006a, p. 31 ff.).

A subset of m vectors $E = \{v_1, v_2, \ldots, v_m\}$ of a vector space V is called a *generating system* of a vector space V over a field K, if all vectors can be represented as linear combinations of the vectors from V, i.e., for any arbitrary vector $v \in V$ it holds: $v = \sum_{i=0}^{m} \lambda_i v_i$, with $\lambda_i \in K, v_i \in E$ with $1 \leq i \leq m$ (Liening, 2006a, p. 40 ff.).

For example, the three vectors $v_1 = \begin{pmatrix} 1 \\ 0 \end{pmatrix}, v_2 = \begin{pmatrix} 0 \\ 1 \end{pmatrix}$ and $v_3 = \begin{pmatrix} 0 \\ 2 \end{pmatrix}$ form a generating system of the vector space $V = \mathbb{R}^2$ over the field $\mathbb{R}$, thus a plane, since for any arbitrary vector $v \in V$ with $v = \begin{pmatrix} a \\ b \end{pmatrix} \in \mathbb{R}^2$, with $a, b \in \mathbb{R}$ applies:

$v = \begin{pmatrix} a \\ b \end{pmatrix} = a\begin{pmatrix} 1 \\ 0 \end{pmatrix} + \frac{b}{2}\begin{pmatrix} 0 \\ 1 \end{pmatrix} + \frac{b}{4}\begin{pmatrix} 0 \\ 2 \end{pmatrix} = a \cdot v_1 + \frac{b}{2} \cdot v_2 + \frac{b}{4} \cdot v_3$, i.e., any arbitrary vector $v \in \mathbb{R}^2$ can be represented or generated by a linear combination of the vectors from E = $\{v_1, v_2, v_3\}$.

A *basis* $B \subset V$ is thus a subset of vectors $v \in V$, for which applies: B is linearly independent and B is a generating system (Liening, 2006a, p. 42 ff.). into another basis. For this, we imagine polynomials as vectors. That the set of all polynomials forms a vector space over a field

K can be easily understood mathematically.[58] But this idea of the basis change can also be understood intuitively.[59] keep in mind.

---

[57] A finite-dimensional vector space is spanned by a finite set of vectors, so-called basis vectors. To qualify as basis vectors, these vectors must be linearly independent and form a generating system of the vector space.

[58] The set of all polynomials forms a vector space, because: Let I be any set, K a field. $K^I = Pol(I,K)$ is the set of all polynomials that each map a value range I to an image range K. If $f, g \in K^I$, thus $f, g : I \rightarrow K$, we define the necessary addition $f + g : I \rightarrow K$ by $(f + g)(x) := f(x) + g(x)$ and the necessary scalar multiplication $a \cdot f : I \rightarrow K$ with $a \in K, f \in K^I$ by: $(a \cdot f)(x) := a \cdot f(x)$. That the laws of a vector space such as associativity, existence of a neutral element, etc. apply here, can be easily understood. Thus, K^I is a K-vector space. Vectors are then polynomials, e.g. $\mathbb{R}^{\mathbb{R}} = pol(\mathbb{R}, \mathbb{R})$ with e.g. $f : x \rightarrow x^4 + 3x^3 - 2x + 1 \in \mathbb{R}$ (Liening, 2006a, p. 26 f.).

[59] A *basis change* is the transition from one basis of a finite-dimensional K-vector space V to another basis, so that, generally speaking, the coordinates of the vectors change. A basis change is also referred to as *basis transformation*. The basis change can be described by a basis change matrix, which can also be used to determine the coordinates with respect to the new basis.

So it is assumed that there are at least two different bases for a vector space, e.g., B and C. The basis change is then a one-to-one mapping from V to V (isomorphism) and thus each basis vector c_i

Normally, vectors are represented as directed lines in space. Thus, with respect to the x,y,z-axes with the coordinates (0,0,1), (0,1,0) and (1,0,0), the vector $a = \begin{pmatrix} 1 \\ 2 \\ 4 \end{pmatrix}$ can be clearly drawn into a three-dimensional coordinate system.

Instead of the described base with the vectors $B = \left\{ \begin{pmatrix} 1 \\ 0 \\ 0 \end{pmatrix}, \begin{pmatrix} 0 \\ 1 \\ 0 \end{pmatrix}, \begin{pmatrix} 0 \\ 0 \\ 1 \end{pmatrix} \right\}$ of such a vector space, whose three vectors are perpendicular to each other and span a three-dimensional (vector) space, theoretically other base vectors are conceivable. If, for example, a polynomial like $f(x) = x^2 + 2x + 3$ is considered as a scalar productf $f(x) = (3, 2, 1) \begin{pmatrix} x^0 \\ x^1 \\ x^2 \end{pmatrix}$, it quickly becomes clear that every polynomial can be formulated in this way. The polynomials differ in this specific notation only by the coefficient vectors, while the monomials[60] always remain the same. Thus, any polynomial can be uniquely identified by the respective coefficient vector. In the case of our example *f*(*x*) this is the vector $a = \begin{pmatrix} 3 \\ 2 \\ 1 \end{pmatrix}$.

For example, the function $g(x)$ with $g(x) = 2x^2 + 3x - 4$ can be written as: $g(x) = b \cdot \begin{pmatrix} x^0 \\ x^1 \\ x^2 \end{pmatrix}$ with $b = \begin{pmatrix} -4 \\ 3 \\ 2 \end{pmatrix}$.

The vectors a and b can now be graphically represented as directed lines (as the original concept of vectors) in a three-dimensional coordinate system, with the axes receiving the labels x^0, x^1 and x^2.

of the new basis $C = \{c_1, c_2, \ldots, c_n\}$ can be represented as a linear combination of basis vectors b_j of the original basis $B = \{b_1, b_2, \ldots, b_n\}$:$c_i = \sum_{j=1}^{n} a_{ji} b_j$, with $c_i \in C, b_j \in B, a_{ji} \in K$ and $1 \le i, j \le n$.
The basis change matrix, also called transformation matrix for the basis change from B to C, is obtained with the above scalars a_{ij}.

It is denoted by $T_C^B = \begin{pmatrix} a_{11} & a_{12} & \ldots & a_{1n} \\ a_{21} & a_{22} & \ldots & a_{2n} \\ \ldots & & & \\ a_{n1} & a_{n2} & \ldots & a_{nm} \end{pmatrix}$.

This matrix is square and invertible. The corresponding inverse matrix $\left(T_C^B\right)^{-1}$ describes the basis change from C back to B (Liening, 2006c, p. 51ff.).

[60] A monomial is a polynomial that consists of only one term, for example x^3. A 'normal' polynomial, e.g. a rational polynomial, on the other hand, consists of n summands and is of the form $p(x) = \sum_{i=0}^{n} \lambda_i x^i, \lambda_i \in \mathbb{R}$ mit $0 \le \mathrm{i} \le \mathrm{n}$.

Thus, in the end, every polynomial function can be imagined as a vector in a coordinate system, with a monomial base of x^0, x^1, x^2, etc. underlying it.

Regarding the base $B = \{x^0, x^1, x^2\}$, then *f*(*x*) and *g*(*x*) are uniquely determined by the vectors $a = \begin{pmatrix} 3 \\ 2 \\ 1 \end{pmatrix}$ and $a = \begin{pmatrix} -4 \\ 3 \\ 2 \end{pmatrix}$.

The idea with the *Fourier* transformation is now to make a basis change (Liening, 2006c, p. 47 ff.). This basis change arises from choosing a basis of sine and cosine functions with different frequencies instead of a basis consisting of monomials $B = \{x^0, x^1, x^2, \ldots\}$, e.g. $B = \{\sin(x), \cos(x), \sin(2x), \ldots\}$.

The dimension[61] of the spanned vector space can of course be arbitrarily larger than three, depending on the polynomial considered, as the above examples with *f*(x) and *g*(x) initially suggested.

The possibility of such a basis change becomes clear when one considers that on the one hand, sine and cosine functions can be represented as a sum of polynomials.[62] On the other hand, it is also conceivable in principle that under certain conditions[63] a polynomial can also be represented as a sum consisting of sine and cosine functions.

One could also say, viewed in this way, that the goal of the *Fourier* transformation is to approximate a real function through cosine and sine functions.

In the realm of mathematical complexity, there is a relationship between sine, cosine, and the exponential function.[64] This relationship can also be utilised here, so that after some transformations, the *Fourier* transformation takes approximately the following form: $F(\omega) = \int\limits_{-\infty}^{\infty} f(t)e^{-i\omega t}dt$ with $\omega \in \mathbb{R}$. Sine and cosine functions are periodic functions. It is easy to imagine that a periodic real function of the form $f(t) \in \mathbb{R}$ with the period T, i.e., $f(t) = f(t+T)$, can be approximated from a linear combination of these functions. What interests us is the question of whether non-periodic functions could also be decomposed into linear combinations of sine and cosine functions. Indeed, this is possible by transitioning from $T \to \infty$ and some further considerations.

---

[61] By definition, the number of basis vectors is the dimension of the vector space they span (Liening, 2006a, p. 46 ff.).

[62] The sine series is: $\sin(x) = \sum\limits_{k=0}^{\infty} (-1)^k \frac{x^{2k+1}}{(2k+1)!} = \frac{x}{1} - \frac{x^3}{3!} + \frac{x^5}{5!} - \ldots$, where:$k! := k \cdot (k-1) \cdot (k-2) \cdot \ldots \cdot 2 \cdot 1$. The cosine series is: $\cos(x) = \sum\limits_{k=0}^{\infty} (-1)^k \frac{x^{2x}}{(2k)!} = 1 - \frac{x^2}{2!} + \frac{x^4}{4!} - \ldots$.

[63] Polynomials can tend towards infinity, so: $\lim\limits_{x\to\infty} (f(x)) = \pm\infty$. Since sine and cosine are bounded functions, there are obviously limits to which polynomials such a representation is possible. Thus, for example, $\lim\limits_{x\to\infty} (f(x)) = 0$ would have to apply or *f* would also have to be a periodic function.

[64] It holds: $e^{ix} = \cos(x) + i\sin(x)$ mit $i^2 = -1$

The classic *Fourier* transformation is intended for time-continuous frequencies. For the more significant discrete time series for us, the comparable 'Discrete *Fourier Transformation*' (DFT) is suitable (Neubauer, 2012).

For large data sets, there is also the FFT, the 'Fast Fourier Transformation' (Rao et al., 2010).

Let's consider the visual area: Here, for example, frequencies describe how often colour and luminance (brightness components) change. The lowest frequency is the basic brightness and the basic colour tone. During compression, the coefficients with the greatest significance are encoded with greater accuracy than those with less significance. The coefficients with the least significance are completely suppressed. Therefore, the method is lossy. To better locate frequency bands, one can use (non-overlapping) windows over the time series, or function *f*, and apply the *DFT* to it. This is also referred to as *SWFT*, a 'Short-Window Fourier Transformation'. However, finding the right window width is not trivial here, as with the other methods presented. Here, too large windows have poor spatial resolution, too small ones have poor frequency resolution. To avoid these disadvantages of fixed windows, there is the so-called *DWT*, the 'discrete Wavelet Transformation'. Here, the analysis window is described by stretchable and compressible functions that can be variably adapted to the function during an analysis.

However, variable windows that adapt depending on the data series or function are not very helpful for our purposes of complexity measurement, as we are not looking for an optimal compression that is individually dependent on the time series, but for a fixed evaluation standard, and thus for an algorithm independent of the time series.

Other typical transformation encodings are the 'Differential Pulse Code Modulation' (*DPCM*), 'Vector Quantisation', or the 'Discrete Cosine Transformation' (Rao & Yip, 2000, p. 37 ff.). We want to take a closer look at the latter, as it avoids the journey through mathematical complexity unlike the *Fourier* transformation.

5.3.2.2 Discrete Cosine Transformation (DCT)

In the discrete Cosine Transformationavoids the path through the mathematically complex by making the sinus terms (provided with the factor i with $i^2 = -1$) disappear through a point-symmetrical continuation of the image (Rao & Yip, 2000, p. 117 ff.).

Let's consider a coloured image again. Since the human eye is not a perfect organ, it can, for example, resolve soft colour transitions much worse than slight differences in brightness. In this context, we speak of *low* spatial frequencies for colour differences that the eye resolves *better*, and *high* spatial frequencies for worse resolution. The analogy to the frequencies is related to the spatial resolution ability of the eye.

With certain colour differences, more distinguishable colour information can be accommodated (hence a high spatial frequency) than with other colour differences. The DCT now exploits this weakness of the human eye by filtering out the high spatial frequencies and encoding them poorly or not at all.

The DCT is based on the *Fourier* Transformation described in Sect. 5.3.2.1, which represents arbitrary signals as superposition of sine waves of different frequencies (oscillation width) and amplitudes (oscillation height). After the *Fourier* Transformation, a frequency and amplitude distribution is obtained from the local distribution of pixel values in an image.

Large, regular areas in the image are reflected in the low frequency components, fine details in the high ones. The majority of the visual information of an image with continuously distributed values lies in the range of low frequencies.

Compression takes place by now weighting the higher frequency components of the image less and setting the amplitudes to zero.

5.3.2.3 The JPEG Compression Algorithm

JPEG is a standardised and comparatively complex image compression method developed by the **J**oint **P**hotographic **E**xperts **G**roup. It is a composite method. Therefore, it seems interesting to take a closer look at the method because a number of interesting algorithms are used here. The data is compressed in five individual processes:

i. Data reduction (Down-Sampling),
ii. Discrete Cosine Transformation (DCT,
iii. Quantisation,
iv. Run-length encoding and the
v. *Huffman* Encoding.

The image quality depends on the compression rate. Let's consider, for example, the compression of an *RGB* colour image[65] using JPEG. In the first step i) in such image compression according to JPEG, the *RGB* colour images are transformed into a $YC_{fb}C_r$ space and the actual colour components C_bC_r (Chrominance : b = blue-yellow, r = red-green) are separated from the brightness information (Luminance)Y. For simplicity, we also write *YCC*. Since the human eye reacts relatively insensitively to rapid colour changes, a *coarser* sampling can take place without subjective loss of quality.

In step ii, the image is now divided into 8x8 blocks and the frequency spectrum[66] is calculated for each block using a DCT. The resulting 64 (spectral) coefficients per block

[65] Most colour images are encoded with one component each of the primary colours red, green, and blue (*RGB*), typically with 8 bits per component. Therefore, each pixel of an image consists of $3 \cdot 8 = 24$ bits, with the value range of each individual colour component thus covering 0,...,255, since $2^8 = 256$. For greyscale images, however, 1 bit per pixel is sufficient. For example, higher-quality greyscale images can comprise 8, 12, 14, or even 16 bits/pixel, which increases the value range of these greyscale encodings to a maximum of 0,…, 65535 (Burger & Burge, 2015, p. 12).

[66] The idea behind the frequency spectrum is that certain signals (time series, colours, tones) can be divided into a sum (possibly an integral) of different frequencies using a transformation (e.g., *Fourier* transformation). The frequency measures periodic repetitions, where, for example, oscillations can be represented sinusoidally or cosinusoidally. Such oscillations consist of several superimposed oscillations with different frequencies, which together form the frequency spectrum.

Table 5.7 Graphic format—GIF

Name	GIF
File extension	.gif
Colours	1-8 Bit
Compression	LZW
Comparison (Orig. 4.74 MB)	1.3 MB
Well suited for:	Images with areas of the same colour
Not suitable for:	Photorealistic motifs (low compression)
Advantage	Wide distribution, effective compression
Disadvantage	Maximum 256 colours
Note	Animated GIFs, transparent backgrounds, interlace effect

are quantised in a third step using a quantisation table, which effectively means that ultimately 'unimportant' information is removed, as it is divided by a definable quantisation factor and then rounded, with many values becoming zero. In general, especially high frequencies are quantised, which are important for the sharpness of the image, but their exact values are not so significant. In steps iv. and v., the quantised spectral components are further compressed losslessly using run-length and *Huffman* coding (Burger & Burge, 2015, p. 17).

In addition to the JPEG format, there are a multitude of graphic formats in the field of image compression, each equipped with different compression possibilities depending on their characteristics. The following are some selected graphic formats presented in an overview, with the compression capability illustrated using an image of 4.74 MB in size (Tables 5.7, 5.8, 5.9 and 5.10).

5.3.2.4 Audio Compression

Compared to image files, audio files are difficult to compress, as identical repetitions in music are only conditionally the case. But it is precisely these repetitions in the data series that algorithms such as *LZW*- or *Huffman*-encodings are based on.

First of all, audio files can of course be stored *uncompressed*. This is usually done in a *Wave* format. The most common Wave format is the *PCM* method, which is often equated with *WAV*. Here, the music signal is sampled point by point, translated into numbers (quantisation), transmitted in bits (digitisation), and finally stored. With a high frequency of the sampling rate, a pretty good equivalent to the original is obtained. Such a *Wave* file is usually the starting point for further compressions.

To compress the existing data material, the data is usually broken down into a noise and a music component in advance, with the noise component ideally corresponding to white noise. *FLAC* ('Free Lossless Audio Codec') or WavPack are examples of a *lossless compression*.

Since audio signals often have only a few redundant components, *lossy compressions* are often chosen in this area, including the well-known *MP3* method or also *AAC*

Table 5.8 Graphic format—PGN

Name	PGN
File extension	.pgn
Colours	Up to 24 Bit
Compression	LZW + Huffman
Comparison (Orig. 4.47 MB)	–
Well suited for	All types of image material
Not suitable for	Currently not readable everywhere
Advantage	Effective compression, many additional features
Disadvantage	Still relatively little spread
Remarks	New format specifically for the WWW, animations, transparent backgrounds

Table 5.9 Graphic format—JPEG

Name	JPEG
File abbreviation	.jpg, .jpeg
Colours	Up to 32 bit
Compression	Sampling, DCT, Quantisation, RLE, *Huffman*
Comparison (Orig. 4.47 MB)	1.62 MB, 0.23 MB, 0.05 MB (depending on setting)
Well suited for	Photorealistic motifs, archiving
Not suitable for	As a format for editing graphics, saving line drawings
Advantage	Wide distribution, powerful compression
Disadvantage	Lossy compression, not for B/W graphics
Note	Image quality depends on the compression rate

('Advanced Audio Coding'). The idea is to store sounds that are well heard by humans and filter out all others. For music lovers, the thesis is often that the sound quality deteriorates with *MP3*.

Comparable to the *JPEG* method, these compression algorithms also consist of several sub-algorithms, with the *Fourier*-transformation, the quantisation, and the *Huffman*-encoding playing an important role, with the special feature in audio signals being the consideration of a so-called psychoacoustic model that eliminates data irrelevant to the listener.

Table 5.10 Graphic format—TIFF

Name	TIFF			
File abbreviation	.tif, .tiff			
Colours	1-32 bit			
Compression	None	RLE	LZW	JPEG
Comparison (Orig. 4.47 MB)	4.47 MB	–	2.73	–
Well suited for	Any image material			
Not suitable for	Archiving, transport over networks			
Advantage	Universal format for all applications, effective compression possible			
Disadvantage	Complex structure			
Remarks	Multiple images in one file possible			

5.3.2.5 Background Information: Transformation Encoding

▶ i. Transformation Encodings—Preliminary Considerations

Preliminary note: Frequency, Amplitude, Phase Angle The ***frequency*** measures the periodic repetitions e.g. of trigonometric functions like sine or cosine, which oscillate between +1 and -1. The sine function, for example, completes exactly one period from the point $x = 0$ to $x = 2 \cdot \pi$. The function is therefore periodic with a period length of $T = 2 \cdot \pi$, i.e. $\sin(x) = \sin(x + 2k\pi)$, $k \in \mathbb{Z}$, $x \in \mathbb{R}$, where $\sin(0) = 0$. The same applies to the cosine function, but $\cos(0) = 1$.

An expression like $\cos(\omega_T x)$ describes the cosine function with the ***angular frequency*** ω_T at the point x. The relationship between angular frequency ω_T and 'normal' frequency Ω is: $\Omega = \frac{1}{T} = \frac{\omega_T}{2 \cdot \pi}$ or $\omega_T = 2 \cdot \pi \cdot \Omega$.

The same applies to $\sin(\omega_T x)$. For the associated angular frequency ω_T this applies in the case of $T = 2 \cdot \pi : \omega_T = \frac{2 \cdot \pi}{T} = 1$.

If you now multiply, for example, $\sin(\omega_T x)$ with a parameter a, so $a \cdot \sin(\omega_T x)$, the ***amplitude*** of the oscillation changes, so that the sine function oscillates between a and $-a$.

If you shift the sine function along the x-axis by a value φ, this is done by: $\sin(x) \to \sin(x + \varphi)$, where, derived from the consideration of sine and cosine in the unit circle, φ is referred to as ***phase angle***. For example, $\varphi = \frac{\pi}{2} = 90°$ results in $\sin(\omega_T x) = \cos\left(\omega_T x + \frac{\pi}{2}\right)$. We had already explained this relationship in the context of phase space reconstruction using the pendulum example. The representation of sine and cosine in the mathematically complex has illustrated the demonstrated relationship that sine and cosine, with a diameter of the circle of 1 (unit circle), stand at an angle of 90° to each other, i.e., perpendicular to each other, where the *Euler's* formulae$e^{ix} = \cos(x) + i\sin(x), \text{mit } i^2 = -1$ applies (Burger & Burge, 2015, p. 480 ff.; Liening, 2007, p. 30 ff.).

Fourier series development If you consider a real function *f*(*t*) in the interval from -*n* to *n* with the period T, i.e. *f*(*t*) =*f*(*t*+*T*), then the goal of the series development can be described in such a way that this function *f* should be approximated by the following sum:

$S_n(t) = \sum_{k=0}^{n} (a_k \cos(k\omega_T t) + b_k \sin(k\omega_T t))$ with $\omega_T = \frac{2 \cdot \pi}{T}$ and $k \in \mathbb{Z}$. Here, a_k and b_k must be determined in such a way that *f*(*t*) can be described as well as possible by $S_n(t)$.

To do this, one proceeds via the mathematically complex, using the *Euler* equation: $e^{ix} = \cos(x) + i\sin(x), \text{mit } i^2 = -1.$ It follows that $\cos(x) = \frac{1}{2}\left(e^{ix} + e^{-ix}\right)$, since $\cos(x) = \frac{1}{2}((\cos(x) + i \cdot \sin(x)) + (\cos(x) - i \cdot \sin(x)))$. Furthermore, $\sin(x) = \frac{1}{2i}\left(e^{ix} - e^{-ix}\right)$ applies, since

$$\sin(x) = \frac{1}{2i}((\cos(x) + i \cdot \sin(x)) - (\cos(x) - i \cdot \sin(x))).$$

This directly implies that

$\cos(k\omega_T t) = \frac{1}{2}\left(e^{ik\omega_T t} + e^{-ik\omega_T t}\right)$ and $\sin(k\omega_T t) = \frac{1}{2i}\left(e^{ik\omega_T t} - e^{-ik\omega_T t}\right)$.

Furthermore, it applies: $a_0 \cos(0) + b_k \sin(0) = a_0$.

Thus, the overall result from $S_n(t)$ is:

$$S_n(t) = a_0 + \sum_{k=1}^{n} \left(a_k \frac{1}{2}\left(e^{ik\omega_T t} + e^{-ik\omega_T t}\right) + b_k \frac{1}{2i}\left(e^{ik\omega_T t} - e^{-ik\omega_T t}\right)\right)$$

Therefore, it is:

$$S_n(t) = a_0 + \sum_{k=0}^{n} \left(a_k \frac{1}{2} e^{ik\omega_T t} + a_k \frac{1}{2} e^{-ik\omega_T t} + b_k \frac{1}{2i} e^{ik\omega_T t} - b_k \frac{1}{2i} e^{-ik\omega_T t}\right)$$

A slightly different summary of the terms results:

$S_n(t) = a_0 + \sum_{k=1}^{n} \left(\frac{1}{2} e^{ik\omega_T t}(a_k - ib_k) + \frac{1}{2} e^{-ik\omega_T t}(a_k + ib_k)\right)$, since $i^2 = -1 \Leftrightarrow \frac{1}{i} = -i$.

For $k \geq 0$ one defines: $c_0 := a_0, c_k := \frac{1}{2}(a_k - ib_k)$, and $c_{-k} := \frac{1}{2}(a_k + ib_k)$. This implies:

$S_n(t) = \sum_{k=-n}^{n} c_k e^{ik\omega_T t}$. A good approximation can be calculated for the coefficients c_k as follows: $c_k = \frac{1}{T} \int_{-T/2}^{T/2} f(t) e^{-ik\omega_T t} dt$ with $k \in \mathbb{Z}$ (Argyris et al., 2010, p. 70 ff.).[67]

Thus, we obtain a sequence of so-called partial sums, which we refer to as the ***Fourierseries*** of a function f with:

$\Im(t) = \sum_{k=-n}^{+n} c_k e^{ik\omega_T t}$ with $c_k = \frac{1}{T} \int_{-T/2}^{+T/2} f(t) \cdot e^{-ik\omega_T t} dt$ and the circular frequency $\omega_T = \frac{2 \cdot \pi}{T}$, where T represents the period of the function $f(t)$. For functions $f(x) \in \mathbb{R}$ in the domain $-\infty < t < \infty$ the actual (infinite) *Fourier* series results:

$f(t) = \sum_{k=-\infty}^{+\infty} c_k e^{ik\omega_T t}$ with $c_k = \frac{1}{T} \int_{-T/2}^{T/2} f(t) e^{-ik\omega_T t} dt$ and the angular frequency $\omega_T = \frac{2 \cdot \pi}{T}$.

(***Fourier*series**)
This *Fourier* series expansion thus allows the analysis or decomposition of a *periodic* function. In this process, every periodic function is decomposed into a weighted sum of sine and cosine functions, similar to a Taylor series expansion. The coefficients are the weights (Argyris et al., 2010, p. 76 ff.).

ii. Discrete Cosine Transformation (DCT)

Although the processed signals mathematically have real values, the basic *Fourier* transformation or the discrete *Fourier* transformation always produces mathematically complex values, as in addition to a real-valued cosine component, an imaginary sine component is always considered. One should remember the *Euler's* formula :$e^{ix} = \cos(x) + i \sin(x)$, mit $i^2 = -1$.*Burger* and *Burge* point out that there are

[67] The above approximation is related to the *Euler* equation and the fact that the coefficients a_k, b_k with $k = 0 \ldots n$ can be determined from the condition that for each n the mean square error $E^2 = \frac{1}{T} \int_{-T/2}^{T/2} (f(t) - S_n(t))^2 dt$ should be minimal. Since the trigonometric functions are orthogonal to each other in the mathematical complex, the real *Fourier* coefficients with $k = 1 \ldots n$ result: $a_0 = \frac{1}{T} \int_{-T/2}^{T/2} f(t) dt, a_k = \frac{1}{T} \int_{-T/2}^{T/2} f(t) \cos(k\omega_T t) dt, b_k = \frac{1}{T} \int_{-T/2}^{T/2} f(t) \sin(k\omega_T t) dt$, (Argyris et al., 2010, p. 77 f.).

"a number of spectral transformations (that, d. Verf.), which are quite similar in their properties to the DFT, but do not work with complex function values" (Burger & Burge, 2015, p. 535).

The cosine transformation is a well-known example of this (Burger & Burge, 2015, p. 543). In the discrete cosine transformation, the path through the mathematically complex is avoided by making the (with the factor *i* provided) sine terms disappear through a point-symmetric continuation of the image. "The trick of the DCT," according to *Burger* and *Burge*, "consists in halving all frequencies, which makes them closer together and thus doubles the resolution in the spectral space" (Burger & Burge, 2015, p. 536).

We therefore want to first deal with the DCT before we come to the more general *Fourier* transformation. To facilitate access, we start with the so-called one-dimensional DCT.

One-dimensional DCT While methods like JPEG etc. require the two-dimensional cosine transformation, the simpler one-dimensional transformation is initially helpful for understanding. The DCT can certainly not only be applied to images or pixels, but in the context of e.g. JPEG, it makes sense to discuss the DCT in the context of discrete pixels. Thus, one could consider an image as a two-dimensional collection of pixels. The image itself could thus be broken down into a multitude of individual image lines.

In a one-dimensional view, one could therefore imagine the application of the DCT to such an image line.

When viewed in one dimension, one could imagine, for example, a line or part of a line of length *n* from a two-dimensional image, where the values are denoted by *f* and numbered from i = 0…n, so that *i* denotes the position where the respective value is located: $f(i),\ i = 0\ldots n-1$.

The discrete cosine transformation now converts the above assignment into a discrete frequency-amplitude assignment. The amplitude is the maximum that the cosine takes in both positive and negative directions. The frequency indicates how often the course of the cosine function repeats. The function $f(i),\ i = 0,\ldots,n-1$ is thus interpreted as an overlay or sum of cosine waves of different frequencies. Generally, the one-dimensional DCT results in:

$$F(k) = \sqrt{\frac{2}{n}} C_k \sum_{i=0}^{n-1} \left(f(i) \cdot \cos\left(\frac{(2i+1)}{2n} k\pi \right) \right)$$

where:

- *F*(*k*) represents the amplitude of the cosine oscillation with the frequency at position k,
- *n* denotes, as described, the number of points considered,
- *k* is the number of the frequency in the considered row (spectral coordinate),
- *i* denotes the specific position in the row,
- *f*(*i*) represents, as described, the exact value at position *i* and

- C_k is a helper value, with $C_k = \begin{cases} 1/\sqrt{2} & \text{für } k = 0 \\ 1, & \text{sonst} \end{cases}$.

Since JPEG images are rasterised into 8 × 8 pixels, we also use $n = 8$ here.

This results in:

$$F(k) = \sqrt{\frac{2}{8}} C_k \sum_{i=0}^{8-1} \left(f(i) \cdot \cos\left(\frac{(2i+1)}{2 \cdot 8} k\pi \right) \right) = \frac{1}{2} C_k \sum_{i=0}^{7} \left(f(i) \cdot \cos\left(\frac{(2i+1)}{16} k\pi \right) \right)$$

For $F(0)$, for example, the following results:

$$F(0) = \frac{1}{2} C_0 \sum_{i=0}^{7} \left(f(i) \cdot \cos\left(\frac{(2i+1)}{16} 0\pi \right) \right) = \frac{1}{2} \cdot \frac{1}{\sqrt{2}} \sum_{i=0}^{7} f(i) = \frac{1}{\sqrt{8}} \sum_{i=0}^{7} f(i)$$

For the frequency, as we have seen: $\Omega = \frac{1}{T} = \frac{\omega_T}{2 \cdot \pi}$, where ω_T represents the angular frequency and T represents the period. This means here for the frequency Ω:

$$\cos(\omega_T x) = \cos\left(\frac{(2i+1)}{16} k\pi \right)$$
$$\Leftrightarrow \cos(\omega_T x) = \cos\left(\frac{k\pi}{8} (i + 0{,}5) \right)$$
$$\Rightarrow \omega_T = \frac{k\pi}{8} \Rightarrow \Omega = \frac{\omega_T}{2 \cdot \pi} = \frac{k}{16}$$

Thus, for the frequencies Ω_k from $k = 0 \ldots 7$:
$\Omega_0 = 0, \Omega_1 = \frac{1}{16}, \Omega_2 = \frac{2}{16} = \frac{1}{8}, \ldots, \Omega_7 = \frac{7}{16}$.

For example, for $k = 0$, the frequency is also 0, so there is no oscillation present and therefore with $F(0)$ the portion of all values of $f(i)$ that remains constant is described, which is why the value $F(0)$ is also referred to as ***DC coefficient*** (direct current) or DC coefficient. Ultimately, this means nothing more than that something like the average of $f(i)$ is formed here, which roughly explains the specific form determined above[68] $:F(0) = \frac{1}{\sqrt{8}} \sum_{i=0}^{7} f(i)$. All other $F(k)$ values are referred to as ***AC coefficients*** (alternate current) or AC coefficients.

Two-dimensional DCT In the two-dimensional case, the image data is rasterised in 8x8 pixel blocks, so we can denote the values with $f(i,j)$, with $i,j = 1 \ldots 7$ (see Fig. 5.44). For example, in greyscale images, each pixel is stored as a numerical value, usually using 8 bits, which allows greyscale levels between 0 and 255. A typical greyscale image with 640 × 480 pixels would therefore occupy about 300 KB of storage space. With 8 bits, however, colour images could also be encoded. This would allow 256 colours to be displayed.

---

[68] The difference to the average is that $\frac{1}{\sqrt{8}}$ instead of $\frac{1}{8}$ is in the formula.

Fig. 5.44 8x8 pattern

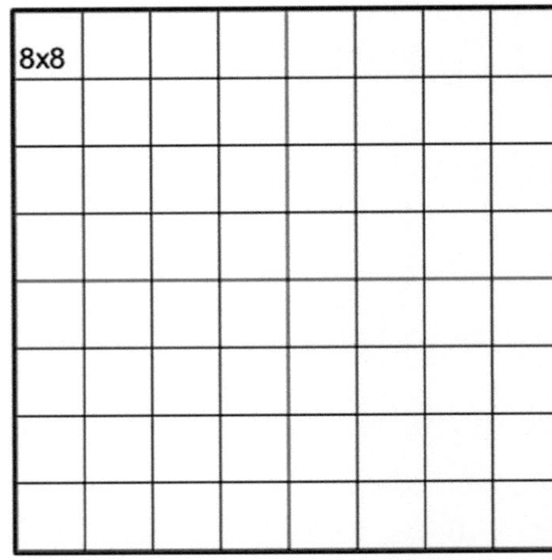

The coefficients are now calculated analogously to the one-dimensional case as follows, with two cosine functions instead of one, and two summands and two auxiliary factors C_i instead of one factor being considered:

$$F(k,l) = \frac{1}{4} C_k C_l \sum_{i=0}^{7} \sum_{j=0}^{7} f(i,j) \cos\left(\frac{(2i+1)}{16} k\pi\right) \cos\left(\frac{(2j+1)}{16} l\pi\right)$$

To transform this coefficient representation back into its original form, the already known auxiliary factors are needed:

$$C_i = \begin{cases} 1/\sqrt{2} & \text{für } i = 0 \\ 1, & \text{sonst} \end{cases}$$

where the $8 \times 8 = 64$ original values $f(i,j)$ are transformed into 64 DCT coefficients or amplitudes $F(k,l).F(0,0)$ is called AC coefficient, all others are referred to as DC coefficients denoted.

As an alternative to the two-dimensional cosine transformation, one could also first apply a one-dimensional DCT to each row of an image and then to each of the columns (Burger & Burge, 2015, p. 539 ff.).

With this encoding and decoding (codec), losses occur even without further treatment of the coefficients, as the required cosine or sine function can only be represented on computers with limited accuracy.

This also implies that this method is not iterable. That is, if you decode an image encoded using DCT and then re-encode it, you get a different result than with the first encoding.

As can be seen from the formulas, the calculation of the coefficients is quite extensive. For an 8 × 8 block, 63 additions and 64 multiplications are required. However, there are certainly fast algorithms for this. These take advantage of the symmetric properties of the formulas, among other things.

With modern hardware technology and effective floating-point arithmetic, acceptable implementations of the algorithm are possible.

iii. JPEG (Joint Photographic Experts Group)

JPEG is a composite method. The compression of the graphic data takes place, as mentioned, in several steps:

1. Data reduction (Sampling),
2. Discrete Cosine Transformation (DCT),
3. Quantisation,
4. Run-length encoding and
5. *Huffman* encoding.

The image quality depends on the adjustable compression rate.

1. Step: Data reduction Since the eye is not capable of distinguishing as many colour details as brightness differences, the colour information is reduced by omitting individual points.

This method is called *Sampling*.

The reduction is carried out separately in the horizontal and vertical directions. Thus, it is also possible to set different reduction rates for the different directions.

Let's look at the most common reduction rates (subsampling) in an 8x8 grid:

'1:1:1': For each brightness value, a value for the colour information is stored, resulting in the pattern shown in Fig. 5.45.

The conversion from *RGB* to YC_bC_r is done using an invertible transformation matrix, so the process is reversible:

$$\begin{pmatrix} Y \\ C_b \\ C_r \end{pmatrix} = \begin{pmatrix} 0{,}299 & 0{,}587 & 0{,}114 \\ -0{,}169 & -0{,}331 & 0{,}500 \\ 0{,}500 & -0{,}419 & -0{,}081 \end{pmatrix} \cdot \begin{pmatrix} R \\ G \\ B \end{pmatrix},$$

so that the weighting of the *RGB* components for the Luminance$Y$ is closely related to the Chrominance values C_b and C_r (Burger & Burge, 2015, p. 339 ff.).

Fig. 5.45 Pattern—'1:1:1'

YCC	*YCC*	*YCC*	*YCC*	*YCC*	*YCC*	*YCC*	*YCC*
YCC	*YCC*	*YCC*	*YCC*	*YCC*	*YCC*	*YCC*	*YCC*
YCC	*YCC*	*YCC*	*YCC*	*YCC*	*YCC*	*YCC*	*YCC*
YCC	*YCC*	*YCC*	*YCC*	*YCC*	*YCC*	*YCC*	*YCC*
YCC	*YCC*	*YCC*	*YCC*	*YCC*	*YCC*	*YCC*	*YCC*
YCC	*YCC*	*YCC*	*YCC*	*YCC*	*YCC*	*YCC*	*YCC*
YCC	*YCC*	*YCC*	*YCC*	*YCC*	*YCC*	*YCC*	*YCC*
YCC	*YCC*	*YCC*	*YCC*	*YCC*	*YCC*	*YCC*	*YCC*

Fig. 5.46 Pattern—'2:1:1'

YCC	*Y*	*YCC*	*Y*	*YCC*	*Y*	*YCC*	*Y*
Y	*Y*	*Y*	*Y*	*Y*	*Y*	*Y*	*Y*
YCC	*Y*	*YCC*	*Y*	*YCC*	*Y*	*YCC*	*Y*
Y	*Y*	*Y*	*Y*	*Y*	*Y*	*Y*	*Y*
YCC	*Y*	*YCC*	*Y*	*YCC*	*Y*	*YCC*	*Y*
Y	*Y*	*Y*	*Y*	*Y*	*Y*	*Y*	*Y*
YCC	*Y*	*YCC*	*Y*	*YCC*	*Y*	*YCC*	*Y*
Y	*Y*	*Y*	*Y*	*Y*	*Y*	*Y*	*Y*

Fig. 5.47 Pattern—'4:1:1'

YCC	*Y*	*Y*	*Y*	*YCC*	*Y*	*Y*	*Y*
Y	*Y*	*Y*	*Y*	*Y*	*Y*	*Y*	*Y*
Y	*Y*	*Y*	*Y*	*Y*	*Y*	*Y*	*Y*
Y	*Y*	*Y*	*Y*	*Y*	*Y*	*Y*	*Y*
YCC	*Y*	*Y*	*Y*	*YCC*	*Y*	*Y*	*Y*
Y	*Y*	*Y*	*Y*	*Y*	*Y*	*Y*	*Y*
Y	*Y*	*Y*	*Y*	*Y*	*Y*	*Y*	*Y*
Y	*Y*	*Y*	*Y*	*Y*	*Y*	*Y*	*Y*

'2:1:1': For two brightness values, one value for the colour information is stored (see Fig. 5.46).

'4:1:1': For four brightness values, one value for the colour information is stored (see Fig. 5.47).

Step 2: Discrete Cosine Transformation (DCT) This encoding method, which we have described in detail in the previous section, is a crucial step in the JPEG compression, where the process is reversible and therefore lossless. The result in this case are 8x8 blocks with the respective DCT coefficients.

As an example, we choose the following $f(i,j)$ coefficients as initial values:

$$f(i,j) := \begin{pmatrix} 110 & 86 & 74 & 63 & 52 & 40 & 34 & 30 \\ 76 & 74 & 66 & 56 & 46 & 36 & 29 & 25 \\ 67 & 64 & 56 & 47 & 38 & 30 & 23 & 20 \\ 56 & 51 & 46 & 38 & 30 & 22 & 17 & 14 \\ 44 & 42 & 36 & 29 & 22 & 15 & 10 & 7 \\ 37 & 33 & 28 & 22 & 14 & 8 & 4 & 2 \\ 29 & 26 & 21 & 16 & 10 & 4 & 1 & -1 \\ 26 & 23 & 19 & 14 & 7 & 2 & -1 & -3 \end{pmatrix}$$

The application of the two-dimensional discrete cosine transformation (DCT) then results in:

$$F(i,j) := \begin{pmatrix} 258 & 123 & 7 & 3 & 3 & 2 & 1 & 1 \\ 136 & 34 & 5 & 4 & 3 & 1 & 1 & 1 \\ 17 & 9 & 5 & 4 & 3 & 2 & 1 & 1 \\ 8 & 8 & 5 & 4 & 3 & 2 & 1 & 1 \\ 6 & 5 & 4 & 3 & 3 & 2 & 1 & 1 \\ 4 & 4 & 4 & 3 & 3 & 2 & 1 & 0 \\ 3 & 4 & 3 & 2 & 2 & 1 & 1 & 0 \\ 1 & 1 & 1 & 1 & 0 & 0 & 0 & 0 \end{pmatrix}$$

As can be easily seen, the application of the DCT has significantly simplified, or compressed, the original values.

Step 3: Quantisation The Quantisation is a particularly lossy method. From the linear progression of values, a step-like arrangement is formed. The quantisation factor is selectable and decides on the future file size and the quality of the recovered image.

For example, if a quantisation factor of 100 is chosen, then all values between -50 and +50 are represented by the value zero. Values over 50 up to and including 149 are represented by the value 1. Values that are greater than 149 and less than 250 are encoded with 2 etc.

Let's look at an example:

Example: Quantisation

Given is an 8×8 block with the following values:

$$F(i,j) := \begin{pmatrix} 258 & 123 & 7 & 3 & 3 & 2 & 1 & 1 \\ 136 & 34 & 5 & 4 & 3 & 1 & 1 & 1 \\ 17 & 9 & 5 & 4 & 3 & 2 & 1 & 1 \\ 8 & 8 & 5 & 4 & 3 & 2 & 1 & 1 \\ 6 & 5 & 4 & 3 & 3 & 2 & 1 & 1 \\ 4 & 4 & 4 & 3 & 3 & 2 & 1 & 0 \\ 3 & 4 & 3 & 2 & 2 & 1 & 1 & 0 \\ 1 & 1 & 1 & 1 & 0 & 0 & 0 & 0 \end{pmatrix}$$

The quantisation matrix with the corresponding quantisation factors is, for example:

$$Q(i,j) := \begin{pmatrix} 1 & 1 & 1 & 1 & 4 & 8 & 8 & 16 \\ 1 & 1 & 1 & 1 & 4 & 8 & 8 & 16 \\ 1 & 1 & 1 & 2 & 4 & 8 & 8 & 16 \\ 2 & 6 & 6 & 8 & 8 & 8 & 8 & 16 \\ 2 & 5 & 4 & 8 & 16 & 16 & 16 & 16 \\ 4 & 4 & 4 & 8 & 16 & 16 & 16 & 32 \\ 4 & 4 & 8 & 8 & 16 & 16 & 32 & 32 \\ 8 & 8 & 8 & 8 & 16 & 32 & 32 & 64 \end{pmatrix}$$

Now the DCT coefficients are divided by the quantisation matrix and then rounded to the nearest integer. The division is not to be confused with the inversion of matrices, but rather takes place element-wise.

$$qF(i,j) = \begin{pmatrix} 258 & 123 & 7 & 1 & 0 & 0 & 0 & 0 \\ 136 & 34 & 5 & 1 & 0 & 0 & 0 & 0 \\ 17 & 9 & 3 & 1 & 0 & 0 & 0 & 0 \\ 4 & 1 & 1 & 0 & 0 & 0 & 0 & 0 \\ 3 & 1 & 1 & 0 & 0 & 0 & 0 & 0 \\ 1 & 1 & 1 & 0 & 0 & 0 & 0 & 0 \\ 1 & 1 & 0 & 0 & 0 & 0 & 0 & 0 \\ 0 & 0 & 0 & 0 & 0 & 0 & 0 & 0 \end{pmatrix} \blacktriangleleft$$

Step 4: Run-Length Encoding The determined DCT values are now arranged in the next step in zigzag order, starting with the DC value, where the coefficients with high values are usually captured first and those with small values are further back. They are summarised by the already described run-length encoding (RLE encoding). The DC coefficient, i.e., the coefficient at the top left of the 8×8 block, which differs only slightly from those of adjacent blocks, is transmitted as a difference to the predecessor block. Then follow the AC coefficients, where the large number of zeros is now used by not having to store every AC coefficient according to the run-length encoding, but repetitions (especially) of zeros are summarised (Run Length Encoding). All zeros that are not followed by an AC coefficient with a value other than zero are omitted, so that significantly fewer than $8 \times 8 = 64$ values are considered. The idea of reducing the zeros leads to a slightly modified RLE procedure compared to the previously presented RLE algorithm, in which two symbols are now captured as general syntax:

Symbol 1	Symbol 2
(Runlength, Size)	Amplitude (DCT Coefficient)

The 'Runlength' captures the number of zeros that precede the DCT coefficient, i.e., the considered 'Amplitude', and 'Size' refers to the number of bits required for the binary encoding of the amplitude.

Fig. 5.48 Zigzag Order

$$\begin{pmatrix} 258 & 123 & 7 & 1 & 0 & 0 & 0 & 0 \\ 136 & 34 & 5 & 1 & 0 & 0 & 0 & 0 \\ 17 & 9 & 3 & 1 & 0 & 0 & 0 & 0 \\ 4 & 1 & 1 & 0 & 0 & 0 & 0 & 0 \\ 3 & 1 & 1 & 0 & 0 & 0 & 0 & 0 \\ 1 & 1 & 1 & 0 & 0 & 0 & 0 & 0 \\ 1 & 1 & 0 & 0 & 0 & 0 & 0 & 0 \\ 0 & 0 & 0 & 0 & 0 & 0 & 0 & 0 \end{pmatrix}$$

Example: Zigzag Order

Fig. 5.48 shows the zigzag capture of the quantised DCT coefficients from the above example.

If the DC coefficient of the previous block is, for example, 256, then the difference to our block is 2. To store the value 2, you need 1 bit and the symbol is 2, so you could formulate it approximately as follows: (1,2). For the AC values, two symbols are also used for encoding, but the first symbol contains two values: The run length of the symbol, i.e., the number of zeros that preceded the value, and the number of bits needed for encoding. For example, $AC_{21} = 17$ requires exactly 5 bits for encoding into a binary number, since $10001_2 = 1 \cdot 2^0 + 0 \cdot 2^1 + 0 \cdot 2^2 + 0 \cdot 2^3 + 1 \cdot 2^4 = 1 + 16 = 17$, so the encoding is ((0;5),17). The immediate number of zeros before the 17 is 0, 5 bits are needed for binary encoding, and the value is 17. Overall, for our example, the AC coefficients are:

((0;7),**123**), ((0;7),**136**), ((0;5),**17**), ((0;6),**34**), ((0;3),**7**), ((0;1),**1**), ((0;3),**5**) ((0;4),**9**),((0;3),**4**), ((0;2),**3**), ((0;1),**1**), ((0;2),**3**), ((0;1),**1**), ((3;1),**1**), ((0;1),**1**), ((0;1),**1**), ((0;1),**1**), ((0;1),**1**), ((0;1),**1**), ((0;1),**1**), ((0;1),**1**),((9;1),**1**), ((0;1),**1**),(0,0).

All values behind the last two AC coefficients not equal to zero (1) are zero and are no longer captured as described, so the total number of captured values is reduced from 64 to 24 + 1 = 25. The last 29 zeros are no longer captured, which is represented by an 'End of Block Symbol'. ◀

5. Step: Huffman Encoding This encoding forms the conclusion of the processing. Frequently occurring values are provided with a short code, rarely occurring values with a long code. To achieve this, the method uses, as already explained in detail, the different statistical probability of the occurrence of a source symbol to further reduce the amount of data. In the concrete application to the RLE values, both symbol 1 and symbol 2 are *Huffman* encoded. By stringing together the individual *Huffman* codes, you then get a (unique) binary code for the original 8 × 8 block.

iv. (Discrete) *Fourier* Transformation (FT and DFT)

Fourier Transformation(FT) "The general concept of 'frequencies' and the decomposition of oscillations into elementary, 'harmonic' functions," as *Burger* and *Burge* note, "originally arose in the context of sound, tones, and music." They further explain that the idea of "describing acoustic events on the basis of 'pure' sinusoidal functions is by no means unreasonable (appears, d. Verf.), especially since sinusoidal oscillations naturally occur in any form of oscillation" (Burger & Burge, 2015, p. 480).

To arrive at the *Fourier* transformation, let's reconsider the series development. With a slight reformulation, we get:

$$f(t) = \sum_{k=-\infty}^{+\infty} \frac{1}{T} F(k\omega_T) \cdot e^{ik\omega_T t} \text{ mit } F(k\omega_T) = \int_{-T/2}^{T/2} f(t) e^{-ik\omega_T t} dt \text{ und } \omega_T = \frac{2\pi}{T}$$

We obtain non-periodic functions *f* by extending the period indefinitely, so that it essentially never occurs, i.e., we consider the limit for $T \to \infty$. Furthermore, we replace $k\omega_T = k\frac{2\pi}{T}$ with ω and the difference between two successive ω values with $d\omega$, i.e., $d\omega = \frac{2\pi}{T}$.

When we then replace the sum with an integral, we get overall:

$$f(t) = \frac{1}{2\pi} \int_{-\infty}^{+\infty} F\omega \cdot e^{ik\omega_T t} d\omega.$$

Here, $F(\omega)$ is referred to as the ***Fourier*-Transformed**.

With the help of the *Fourier* transformation, the analysis of non-periodic functions is possible due to the above explanation, where of course *f* can also be periodic, as ultimately only the sum of *T*-periodic oscillations is formed.

It should be noted that different conventions exist for the choice of signs in the exponent and the factor in front of the integral. For example, sometimes frequencies 1/*T* are used instead of angular frequencies $^{2\pi}/_{T}$.

The following notation generally applies:

$f(t) = \frac{1}{2\pi} \int_{-\infty}^{+\infty} F\omega e^{i\omega t} \, d\omega$ or $F(\omega) = \int_{-\infty}^{+\infty} f(t) e^{-i\omega t} \, dt$ with $\omega \in \mathbb{R}$. (Argyris et al., 2010, p. 80 ff.).

Example

As a simple example, one could consider a rectangular function $f(x) \in \mathbb{R}$ with $f(x) = \begin{cases} 1, \text{falls} - 1 \leq \text{x} \leq 1 \\ 0, \quad \text{sonst} \end{cases}$ in view. Obviously, there can be no problems in calculating the integral, as the function is only non-zero around the value zero (constant). For $F(\omega) = \int_{-\infty}^{+\infty} f(t) e^{-i\omega t} \, dt$ the result is:

$$F(\omega)=\int_{-1}^{+1}1\cdot e^{-i\omega t}\,dt=\int_{-1}^{+1}e^{-i\omega t}dt=[-\frac{1}{i\omega}e^{-i\omega t}]_{-1}^{+1}=-\frac{1}{i\omega}e^{-i\omega t}-\frac{1}{i\omega}e^{i\omega t}$$

$$=-\frac{1}{i\omega}\left(e^{-i\omega}-e^{i\omega}\right)=\frac{1}{i\omega}\left(e^{i\omega}-e^{-i\omega}\right).$$

It is known that $\sin(x)=\frac{1}{2i}\left(e^{ix}-e^{-ix}\right)$. This relationship between the sine function and the exponential function obviously results from the often used *Euler's* formulae$e^{ix}=\cos(x)+i\,\sin(x)$, mit $i^2=-1$, because:

$$\frac{1}{2i}\left(e^{ix}-e^{-ix}\right)=\frac{1}{2i}((\cos(x)+i\cdot\sin(x))-(\cos(x)-i\cdot\sin(x)))=\frac{1}{2i}(2i\cdot\sin(x))=\sin(x).$$

So, taking this relationship into account, the result is:

$$F(\omega)=\int_{-1}^{+1}1\cdot e^{-i\omega t}dt=\frac{1}{i\omega}\left(e^{i\omega}-e^{-i\omega}\right)=\frac{2}{\omega}\cdot\frac{1}{2i}\cdot\left(e^{i\omega}-e^{-i\omega}\right)=\frac{2}{\omega}\cdot\sin(\omega).$$

Thus, for the rectangular function $f(x)$, the FT coefficients can be calculated in the context of the basis change using the simple formula $F(\omega)=\frac{2}{\omega}\cdot\sin(\omega)$. ◀

Autocorrelation and Power Spectrum When considering the *Fourier* transform of a real function, we see that it is generally mathematically complex, so we can split it into a real and imaginary part. That is, $F(\omega)=F_{\mathbb{R}}(\omega)+iF_{i\mathbb{R}}(\omega)$, as is true for any mathematically complex number: $z=x+iy$, with $i=1$ and x, y $\in\mathbb{R}$.

This means that: $F(\omega)=F_{\mathbb{R}}(\omega)+iF_{\mathbb{R}}(\omega)=a(\omega)\cdot e^{i\varphi(\omega)}$, where the amplitudes $a(\omega)$ are referred to as **Fourierspectrum** and $\varphi(\omega)$ as **phase angle**. The square of *a*, i.e., $a^2(\omega)$, is called **energy spectrum** (Argyris et al., 2010, p. 82).

So far, we have primarily used autocorrelation to determine the *time-lag* in phase space reconstruction. Using autocorrelation—i.e., the correlation of a function with itself $\left(corr(f,f)=\int_{-\infty}^{\infty}f(t)f(t+\tau)dt\right)$—insights can also be generated directly about complexity. In this context, it is interesting that the autocorrelation$a(\tau):=corr(f,f)$ and the energy spectrum $A^2(\omega)$ are mutual *Fourier* transforms (Argyris et al., 2010, p. 84).

The power spectrum$P(\omega)$ can be defined as the *Fourier* transform of the mean of the autocorrelation, $\overline{a}(\tau)$.

Argyris et. al therefore rightly point out that "Autocorrelation $a(\tau)$ and energy spectrum $A^2(\tau)$ or the averaged autocorrelation $\overline{a}(\tau)$ and power spectrum are equivalent representations of the same development process." (Argyris et al., 2010, p. 85). And further, they add: "Nevertheless, both forms of description highlight very different properties of the original signal: The autocorrelation reflects memory capacity and internal correlations of the system, while the power spectrum provides information about dominant fundamental frequencies" (Argyris et al., 2010, p. 85).

Discrete Fourier Transformation (DFT) If one does not need statements about time-continuous frequencies, the comparable "*Discrete Fourier Transformation* " (DFT) is suitable for our so important discrete analysis. From the *Fourier* series, not the integral explained above is obtained, but when considering 'only' a finite number of values *N*, the following results: $f(t) = \sum_{k=0}^{N-1} F(\omega_k)e^{it\omega_k}$ or $F(\omega_k) = \frac{1}{N}\sum_{t=0}^{N-1} f(t)e^{-it\omega_k}$ with $\omega_k := \frac{2\pi k}{N}$.

5.3.3 Complexity Studies

To conduct complexity studies, it is now conceivable to resort to the compression algorithms described above in selected examples.

5.3.3.1 Application of Image Compression Methods

For example, one could use the JPEG method or significant parts of it. One could first prepare the data series in such a way that, for example, each data point is encoded in such a way that a Discrete Cosine Transformation (DCT) can be applied. Subsequently, one would perform a run-length encoding and finally a *Huffman* encoding. In this way, any data series could be compressed using the JPEG algorithms. In the next step, one would perform a surrogate test by comparing the original compression with a compression of a random series generated from the time series (possibly FFT-surrogate[69]). With the help of this surrogate test, one can then examine the original time series for the degree of complexity, with the complexity being greater the smaller the difference in the compression of the original time series to the surrogate test (i.e., the compression of a random series).

In the simplest case, one could save a time series, for example, in a PDF file and then save it in JPEG or TIFF format using one of the usual routines provided by, for example, PDF programmes like *Adobe Acrobat*, and compare the Mbytes used there with a correspondingly stored surrogate test time series.[70]

5.3.3.2 Application of Audio Compression Methods

Alternatively, one could save the time series to be examined (uncompressed and lossless) in a wave file and then compress it using audio compression methods. Here too, as in Sect. 5.3.3.1, a surrogate test would be helpful to create a benchmark. The advantage of audio compression is also that there are a multitude of effective algorithms that can elim-

[69] It has already been pointed out that FFT surrogates serve to exclude linear-stochastic processes in particular.

[70] However, it would be more sensible to forego quantisation, as a lossy compression method may not necessarily be useful. If patterns are very similar (but not identical), they are equalised by such methods. Thus, information is lost and artificial structures are created. However, renouncing this means that one could not simply use JPEG, but would have to programme the individual compression algorithms individually to apply them.

inate the noise[71] in the data without damaging the dynamics of the source. Corresponding noise filters are available in software products like *Audacity, Adobe Audition,* etc.

5.3.3.3 Application of Text Document Compression Methods

A simple way to examine time series using compression methods is to save them as text documents and then compress them using one of the usual compression methods (e.g., ZIP, which is based on a variant of the LZW algorithm). Ultimately, entropy encodings or the *Huffman* code are used for compression, with lossless compressions being generated in contrast to transformation encodings. Here too, as in Sects. 5.3.3.1 and 5.3.3.2, a surrogate test would be useful to create a benchmark. However, this could also be problematic when considering that random time series to a certain degree are also compressible, as number sequences can also repeat there, so that erroneous results may occur. To this end, it could be helpful to generate a multitude of surrogates to somewhat limit this problem.

Overall, compression methods represent a possible alternative to previous methods, although their effectiveness for complexity studies still needs to be proven in many cases.

5.4 Third Conclusion—Numerous Methods for Determining Complexity

Summary of the Main Results

This chapter on the topic of empiricism has shown that simple statistical measures do not help to distinguish complexity from randomness, for example. This distinction and the degree of complexity are essential for the analysis of the data.

First of all, we had to clarify the question of the relationship between theory and practice to see what is realistically possible. Section 5.1 has made some contributions to this. Subsequently, we saw that there are numerous methods for determining complexity. In addition to traditional methods such as spectral analysis, autocorrelation, and the *BDS* test, the *Lyapunov* or dimension determination are particularly noticeable. Compared to the theory part, we were able to discuss the subtleties and thus the challenges that arise from the application of the methods in much more detail. In particular, the reconstruction of the phase space is a non-trivial undertaking, as we have seen. It became clear in Sect. 5.2 that there are interesting alternatives to the presented classical methods, such as the proven permutation entropy. But other compression algorithms, as became clear in Sect. 5.3, provided by LZW or JPEG, should not be excluded from the outset. Depending on the method, a number of challenges need to be considered, which concern the length of the time series, the degree of noisy data, etc.

[71] However, the question still needs to be clarified whether the noise in audio files is actually comparable to the noise in a time series.

Basis Attractor type	**Phase space behaviour** (3-dimensional representation)	**Time course**	**Range of services**	**Auto-correlation**	**Spectrum of the *Lyapunov*-Exponenten**	**Dimension** (z. B. $\boldsymbol{D_c}$)	**KS-Entropy**
Fixed-point tractor	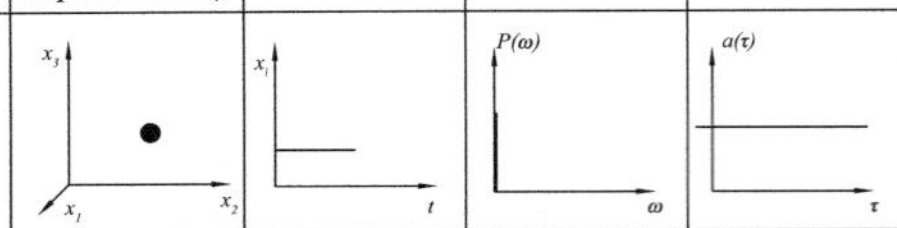				-,-,- general: -,-,-,...,-	**0**	**0**
Periodic Limit cycle	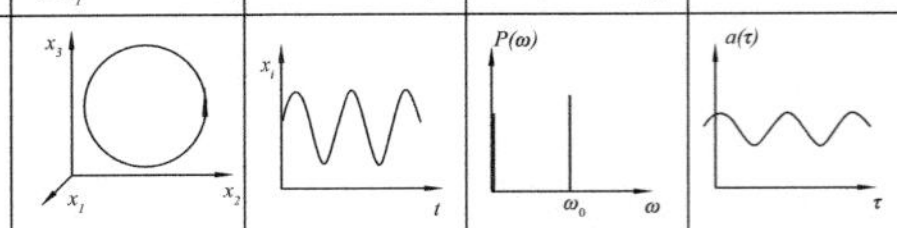				0,-,- general: 0,-,-,...,-	**1**	**0**
Stable *m*-torus-Attractor Quasiperiodicity	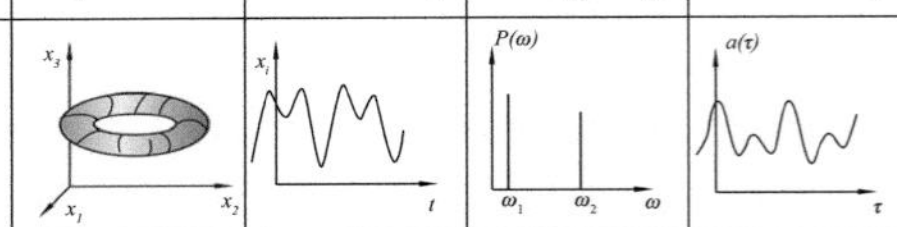				0,0,- general: 0,..,0,-,-..,- (0: *m*-fold)	**2**	**0**
Stranger Attractor Complex Behaviour	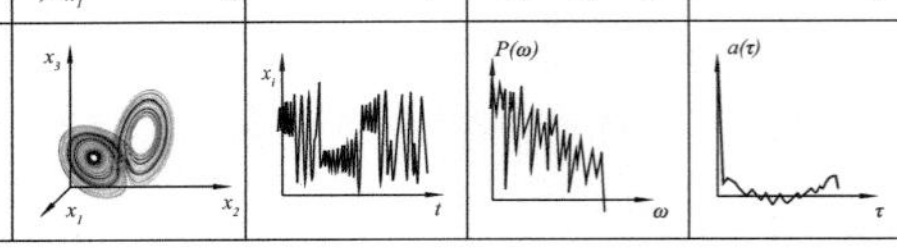				+,-,+ general: +,0,-,-,...,-	$\boldsymbol{2<D_c<3}$	$\boldsymbol{h(\sigma)>0}$

Fig. 5.49 Characterisation of different attractor types in three-dimensional phase space. (*Sources:* Loistl & Betz, 1993, p. 63; Argyris et al., 2010, p. 307)

Basis	**Phase portrait**	**Time course**	**Zip**	**PDF**	**JPEG**
Ordered series	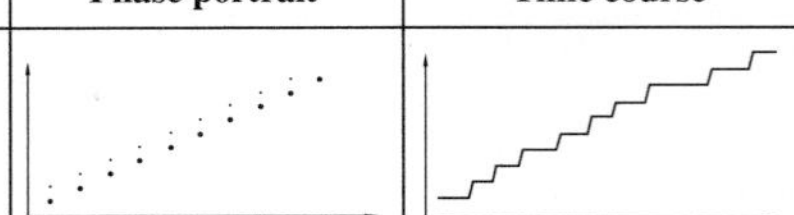		14 KByte (100 data) 21 KByte (1,000 Data)	- 89 KByte (1,000 Data)	770 KByte (100 Data) 7,444 KByte (1,000 Data)
Random series	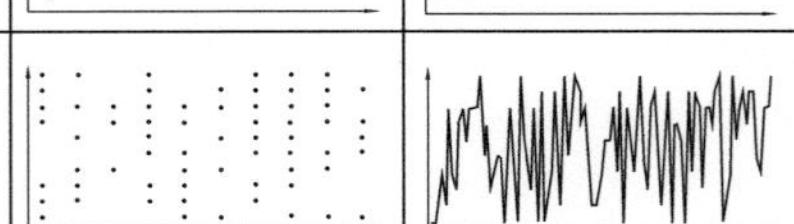		25 KByte (100 Data) 50 KByte (1,000 Data)	- 109 KByte (1,000 Data)	769 KByte (100 Data) 14,867 KByte (1,000 Data)
Root of 2	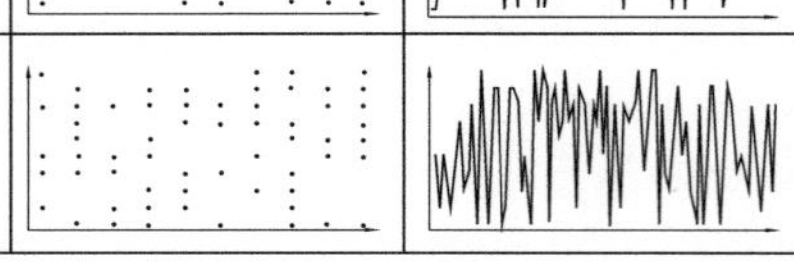		25 KByte (100 Data) 37 KByte (1,000 Data)	- 92 KByte (1,000 Data)	763 KByte (100 Data) 9,580 KByte (1,000 Data)

Fig. 5.50 Characterisation of different arrangements of root 2 in two-dimensional phase space

The two graphics Figs. 5.49 and 5.50 once again illustrate selected methods presented here in a rough overview.

5.5 Outlook

In the third and final part of the book, it is necessary to use the knowledge gained in the previous parts to present an entrepreneurship theory and the analysis of entrepreneurship processes from different perspectives, for example, to work out opportunities for acquiring entrepreneurial competence so that company foundations can succeed in a complex world.

References

Andersson, G. (1988). *Kritik und Wissenschaftsgeschichte. Kuhns, Lakatos' und Feyrabends Kritik des Kritischen Rationalismus*. Mohr.

Argyris, J., Gunter, F., Maria, H., & Rudolf, F. (2010). *Die Erforschung des Chaos—Eine Einführung in die Theorie nicht-linearer dynamischer Systeme* (2. edn.). Springer.

Augustinus. (1983). Die Zeit und die Ewigkeit (confessiones XI). In A. Müller (Ed.), *Erkenntnis- und Wissenschaftstheorie* (pp. 25–28). Aschendorffsche.

Bachelier, L. (1900). *Théorie de la spéculation*. Gauthier-Villars.

Bachelier, L., Davis, M. H. A., Etheridge, A. M., & Samuelson, P. A. (2006). *Louis bachelier's theory of speculation: The origins of modern finance*. Princeton University Press.

Bacon, F. (2014). *Neues Organon. Vollständige deutsche Ausgabe*. e-artnow.

Bandt, C. & Pompe, B. (2002). Permutation entropy—a natural complexity measure for time series. *In Physical Review Letters, 88*(17), 174102-1-174102-4.

Barber, B. M., & Terrance, O. (2000). Trading is hazardous to your wealth—The common stock investment performance of individual investors. *Journal of Finance, 55*(2), 773–806.

Black, F., & Myron, S. (1973). The pricing of options and corporate liabilities. *Journal of Political Economy, 81*(3), 637–654.

Brandes, W. (1985). *Über die Grenzen der Schreibtisch-Ökonomie—Die Einheit der Gesellschaftswissenschaften*. Mohr Siebeck.

Bräuer, K. (2002). *Chaos, Attraktoren und Fraktale*. Logos.

Briggs, K. (1990). An improved method for estimating Lyapunov-exponents of chaotic time series. *Physics Letters A, 151*(4), 1–2.

Brinson, G. P., Randolph, H., & Gilbert, L. B. (1986). Determinants of portfolio performance. *Financial Analysts Journal, 42*(4), 39–48.

Brock, W. A., Dechert, W. D., Scheinkman, J. A., & LeBaron, B. (1996). A test for independence based on the correlation dimension. *Econometric reviews, 15,* 197–235.

Brock, W. A., & Sayers, C. L. (1988). Is the business cycle characterized by deterministic chaos? *Journal of monetary economics, 22*(1), 11–14.

Burger, W., & Burge, M. J. (2015). *Digitale Bildverarbeitung—Eine algorithmetische Einführung mit Java*. Springer-Viehweg.

Casdagli, M., Eubank, S., Farmer, J. D., & Gibson, J. (1991). State space reconstruction in the presence of noise. *Physica D: Nonlinear Phenomena, 51*(1), 52–98.

Castro, I. P. (1989). *An introduction to the digital analysis of stationary signals*. IOP Publishing Ltd.

Eckmann, J. P., Kamphorst, S. O., & Ruelle D. (1987). Recurrence plots of dynamical systems. *Europhysics Letters, 4*(9), 973–977.

Fahrmeir, L., Künstler, R., Pigeot, I., & Tutz, G. (2007). *Statistik* (6. edn.). Springer.

Fama, E. F. (1965). *Random walks in stock-market prizes*. University Press.
Farmer, J. D., Ott, E., & Yorke, J. A. (1983). The dimension of chaotic attractors. *Physica D, 7D,* 153–180.
Feyerabend, P. (1986). *Wider den Methodenzwang*. Suhrkamp.
Fischer, G. (2014). *Lineare algebra* (18. edn.). Springer.
Forster, O. (2004). *Analysis 1* (7. edn.). Vieweg+Teubner.
Frank, M., & Stengos, T. (1988). The stability of canadian macroeconomic data in measured by the largest Lyapunov. *Economic Letters, 27*(1), 11–14.
Fraser, A. M., & Swinney, H. L. (1986). Independent coordinates for strange attractors from mutual information. *Physical Review A, 33*(2), 1134–1140.
Frank, M., Gencay, R., & Stengos, T. (1988). International Chaos? *European economic review, 32*(8), 1569–1584.
Grassberger, P., & Procaccia, I. (1983). Characterization of strange attractors. *Physical Review Letters, 50*(5), 346–349.
Greschik, S. (1998). *Das Chaos und seine Ordnung: Einführung in komplexe Systeme*. dtv—Deutscher Taschenbuch.
Güting, R. H., & Dieker, S. (2013). *Datenstrukturen und Algorithmen* (3. Aufl.). Springer.
Grebogi, C., Ott, E., & Yorke, J. A. (1988). Unstable periodic orbits and the dimensions of multifractal chaotic attractors. *Physical Review A, 37*(5), 1711–1725.
Glushkov, A. V., Khetselius, O. Y., Brusentseva, S. V., Zaichko, P. A., & Ternovsky, V. B. (2014). *Studying interaction dynamics of chaotic systems within a non-linear prediction method. Advances in neural networks, fuzzy systems and artificial intelligence* (21. edn., pp. 69–75). Wseas Pub.
Hawking, S. (1988). *Eine kurze Geschichte der Zeit*. Rowohlt.
Heil, J. von. (2000). *Einführung in die Ökonometrie* (6. edn.). Pearson Deutschland GmbH.
Holzer, C., & Manfred, P. (1993). Analyse der Schweinepreise mit Instrumenten der Chaostheorie. In E. Schulze, B. Petersen & H. Geidel (Hrsg.), *Berichte der Gesellschaft für Informatik in der Land-, Forst- und Ernährungswirtschaft* (5. edn.). GIL.
Huffman, D. A. (1952). *A method for the construction of minimum-redundancy codes*. Proceedings of the I.R.E. *40*(9), 1098–1101.
Hume, D. (2012). *Eine Untersuchung über den menschlichen Verstand*. Jazzbee.
Jumarie, G. (Hrsg.). (1990). *Relative information—theories and applications* (47. edn.). Springer.
Kant, I. (1995). Kritik der reinen Vernunft. In I. Kant (Hrsg.), *Werke in sechs Bänden* (Vol. 2). Könemann Verlagsgesellschaft mbH.
Kantz, H. (1994). A robust method to estimate the maximal Lyapunov exponent of a time series. *Physical Letters, 185*(1), 77–87.
Keynes, J. M. (1923). *Tract on monetary reform*. Prometeus Books.
Klingen, B. (2001). *Fouriertransformation für Ingenieur- und Naturwissenschaften*. Springer.
Knorr-Cetina, K. (2002). *Die Frabikation von Erkenntnis. Zur Anthropologie der Wissenschaft*. Suhrkamp.
Kowalik, Z. J., & Elbert, T. (1995). A practical method for the measurements of the chaoticity of electric and magnetic brain activity. *International Journal of Bifurcation and Chaos, 5*(2), 475–490.
Kuhn, T. (1996). *Die Struktur wissenschaftlicher Revolutionen*. Suhrkamp.
Kugler, P. & Carlos L. (1990). Sind Wechselkursfluktuationen zufällig oder chaotisch? *(Schweizerische) Zeitschrift für Volkswirtschaft und Statistik, 2,* 113–127.
Krämer, W. (2012). *So lügt man mit Statistik* (3. edn.). Piper.
Lakatos, I. (1974). Falsifikation und die Methodologie wissenschaftlicher Forschungsprogramme. In I. Lakatos & A. Musgrave (Hrsg.), *Kritik und Erkenntnisfortschritt* (pp. 89–190). Vieweg.

Lakatos, I., Worrall, J., & Currie, G. (1982). *Die Methodologie wissenschaftlicher Forschungsprogramme*. Springer.

Lenk, H. (1968). *Kritik der logischen Konstanten: Philosophische Begründungen der Urteilsformen vom Idealismus bis zur Gegenwart*. De Gruyter.

Liebert, W., Pawelzik, K., & Schuster, H. G. (1991). Optimal embeddings of chaotic attractors from topological considerations. *Europhysics Letters, 14*(6), 521–526.

Liening, A. (2006a). *Lineare Algebra I: Vektoren und Vektorräume*. Institut für Verbundstudien NRW.

Liening, A. (2006b). *Lineare Algebra II: Matrizen und Determinanten*. Institut für Verbundstudien NRW.

Liening, A. (2006c). *Lineare Algebra III: Lineare Gleichungssysteme*. Institut für Verbundstudien NRW.

Liening, A. (2007). *Analysis I: Folgen und Funktionen* (2. edn.). Institut für Verbundstudien NRW.

Lipschutz, S. (1990). *Lineare Algebra*. McGraw Hill.

Locke, J. (2012). *Über den menschlichen Verstand*. Jazzbe.

Lorenz, H. W. (1993). *Nonlinear dynamical economics and chaotic motion*. Springer.

Loistl, O., & Betz, I. (1993). *Chaostheorie: Zur Theorie nichtlinearer dynamischer Systeme*. Oldenbourg Wissenschaftsverlag.

Mandelbrot, B. B., & Hudson, R. L. (2007). *Fraktale und Finanzen. Märkte zwischen Risiko. Rendite und Ruin*. Piper.

Mañé, R. (1981). On the dimension of the compact invariant sets of certain non-linear maps. In D. Rand & L.-S. Young (Eds.), *Dynamical Systems and turbulance—lecture notes in mathematics* (pp. 230–242). Springer.

Markowitz, H. M. (1959). *Portfolio selection—efficient diversification of investments*. Blackwell.

Marwan, N. (2008). A historical review of recurrence plots. *European Physical Journal—Special Topics, 164*(1), 3–12.

Marwan, N., Romano, M. C., Thiel M., & Kurths J. (2007). Recurrence plots for the analysis of complex systems. *PhysicsReports, 438*, 237–329.

Meyberg, K. (1980). *Algebra* (2. edn.). Hanser.

Mittelstädt, E. (2011). Ökonomische Schulentwicklung: Wissensbilanzierung zum angemessenen Umgang mit Komplexität. In A. Liening (Hrsg.), *Komplexe Systeme und Ökonomie* (Vol. 3). Lang.

Müller, R. (1990). *Rauschen* (2. edn.). Springer.

Nebel, M. (2012). *Entwurf und Analyse von Algorithmen*. Vieweg+Teubner.

Neubauer, A. (2012). *DFT—Diskrete Fourier-Transformation*. Springer Vieweg.

Ott, E. (1994). *Chaos in dynamical systems*. Press Syndicate of the University of Cambridge.

Packard, N. H., Crutchfield, J. P., Doyne Farmer, J., & Shaw, R. S. (1980). Geometry from a time series. *Physical Review Letters, 45*(9), 712–716.

Peitgen, H.-O., Jürgens, H., & Saupe, D. (1992). *Chaos—Bausteine der Ordnung*. Klett-Cotta.

Platon. (2010). *Der Staat*. Anaconda.

Popper, K. (1995). *Objektive Erkenntnis* (3. edn.). Hoffmann & Campe.

Popper, K. (2004). *Auf der suche nach einer besseren Welt*. Piper.

Popper, K. (2010). *Die beiden Grundprobleme der Erkenntnistheorie: aufgrund von Manuskripten aus den Jahren 1930–1933* (3. edn.). Mohr Siebeck.

Rao, K. R., Kim, D. N., & Hwang, J. J. (2010). *Fast fourier transformation*. Springer.

Rao, K. R., & Yip, P. C. (2000). *The transform and data compression handbook boca raton*. Taylor & Francis Inc.

Rapp, P. E., Albano, A. M., Zimmerman, I. D., & Jiménez-Montano, M. A. (1994). Phase-randomized surrogates can produce spurious identifications of non-random structure. *Physics Letters A, 192*(1), 27–33.
Reszat, B. (1993). Chaos in den Wechselkursen. *WiSt, 3,* 146–149.
Rosenstein, M. T., Collins, J. J., & De Luca, C. J. (1993). A practical method for calculating largest Lyapunov exponents from small data sets. *Physica D, 65,* 117–134.
Sachs, L., & Hedderich, J. (2006). *Angewandte Statistik* (12. edn.). Springer.
Sauer, T., Yorke, J. A., & Casdagli, M. (1991). Ebedology. *Journal of Statistical Physics, 65*(3), 579–616.
Scheinkman, J. A., & LeBaron, B. (1989). Nonlinear dynamics and stock returns. *Journal of business, 62*(3), 311–337.
Schmidt, K., & Stahlecker, P. (1989). Gibt es Chaos im industriellen Sektor der Bundesrepublik Deutschland? *Jahrbuch für Sozialwissenschaft, 40,* 332–341.
Schwager, J. D. (2005). *Technische Analyse* (5. edn.). Finanzbuch.
Sedgewick, R. (2002). *Algorithmen in C++* (3. edn.). Pearson Education.
Sedgewick, R., & Wayne, K. (2014). *Algorithmen: Algorithmen und Datenstrukturen* (4. edn.). Pearson Education.
Sengupta, J. K., & Zheng, Y. (1995). Empirical tests of chaotic dynamics in market volatility. *Applied financial economics, 5*(5), 291–300.
Shannon, C. E. (2001). A mathematical theory of communication. *ACM Mobile Computing and Communications Review, 5*(1), 3–55.
Sharpe, W. F. (1963). A simplified model for portfolio analysis. *Management Science, 9*(2), 277–293.
Sharpe, W. F. (1964). Capital asset prices—A theory of market equilibrium under conditions of risk. *Journal of Finance, 19*(3), 425–442.
Skinner, J. E., Molnar, M., & Tomberg, C. (1994). The point correlation dimension: performance with nonstationary surrogate data and noise. *Integrative Physiological and Behavioral Science, 29*(3), 217–234.
Sterman, J. D. (1989). Deterministic chaos models of human behavior: methodological issues and experimental results. *System Dynamics Review, 4*(1–2), 148–178.
Strunk, G. (2004). *Organisierte Komplexität—Mikroprozess-Analysen der Interaktionsdynamik zweier Psychotherapien mit den Methoden der nichtlinearen Zeitreihenanalyse*. University of Bamberg, OPUS.
Strunk, G. (2009). Die Komplexitätshypothese der Karriereforschung. In A. Liening (Hrsg.), *Komplexe Systeme und Ökonomie* (Vol. 2). Lang.
Strunk, G. (2015). *GChaos—Nichtlineare Zeitreihenanalyse*. Springer.
Strunk, G. (2016). Es gibt nichts Praktischeres als eine gute Theorie. In H. Arndt (Ed.), *Das Theorie-Praxis-Verhältnis in der Ökonomischen Bildung* (pp. 17–29). Wochenschau.
Strunk, G. (2019). *Leben wir in einer immer komplexer werdenden Welt? Methoden der Komplexitätsmessung für die Wirtschaftswissenschaft*. Complexity Research, Forschung & Lehre Verlag.
Strunk, G., & Schiepek, G. (1994). *Dynamische Systeme—Grundlagen und Analysemethoden für Psychologen und Psychiater*. Asanger.
Strunk, G., Schiffinger, M., & Mayrhofer, W. (2004). Lost in transition? Complexity in organisational behaviour—the contributions of systems theories. *Management Revue, 15*(4), 481–509.
Sturm, G. (2003). Thermodynamik, Entropie und Quantenmechanik. Quanten.de Newsletter 2003 (Juli/August).
Světlák, M., Bob, P., Černík, M., Chládek, J., & Kukleta, M. (2010). Electordermal dimensional complexity and smoking. *Scripta Medica, 83*(1), 63–68.

Takens, F. (1981). Detecting strange attractors in turbulence. In D. A. Rand & L. S. Young (Eds.), *Dynamicals systems and turbulence—lecture notes in mathematics* (pp. 366–381). Springer.
TenBroek, T. M., van Emmerik, R. E. A., Hasson, C. J., & Hamill, J. (2007). Lyapunov exponent estimation for human gait accelcerations signals. *Journal of Biomechanics, 40,* 210.
Theiler, J. (1987). Efficient algorithm for estimating the correlaton dimension form a set of discrete points. *Physical Review A, 36*(9), 4456–4462.
Theiler, J. (1989). Estimating fractal dimension. *Journal of the Optical Society of America, 7*(6), 1055–1073.
Thoma, B. (2001). *Chaostheorie, Wirtschaft und Börse—Das neue Paradigma in den Wirtschaftswissenschaften*. Oldenbourg.
Weber, M. (2007). *Genial einfach investieren*. Campus.
Welch, T. (1984). A technique for high-performance data compression. *IEEE Computer, 17*(6), 8–19.
Whitney, H. (1936). Differentiable manifolds. *The Annals of Mathematics, 37*(3), 645–680.
Wittgenstein, L. (1963). *Tractatus logico-philosophicus: Logisch-philosophische Abhandlung*. Suhrkamp.
Wolf, A. (1986). Quantifying chaos with lyapunov exponents. In A. V. Holden (Ed.), *Chaos* (16. edn., pp. 285–317). Manchester University Press.
Wolf, A., Swift, J. B., Swinney, H. L., & Vastano, J. A. (1985). Determining lyapunov exponents from a time series. *Physica D, 16*(3), 285–317.
Writers, S. (2008). First in the april fools day press release stakes, is google. Retrieved 22.02.11.
Ziv, J., & Lempel, A. (1977). A universal algorithm for sequential data compression. *IEEE Transactions on Information Theory, 23*(3), 337–343.

Part III

Multiperspective—Entrepreneurship and Complexity

Entrepreneurship and Complexity

6

Contents

6.1 What is Entrepreneurship?—Trends and Controversies 450
  6.1.1 What is Entrepreneurship? 450
    6.1.1.1 On the Origin of the Term 450
    6.1.1.2 Entrepreneur versus Manager 455
    6.1.1.3 Entrepreneur—"Born or Made"? 459
    6.1.1.4 Different Entrepreneurship Classifications 459
  6.1.2 Current Trends and Controversies 461
    6.1.2.1 The Deterministic Belief in Feasibility and the *Laplacian* Demon 461
    6.1.2.2 Entrepreneurs between a Simple and Complex World 463
    6.1.2.3 *'Discovery-'* versus *'Creation-Theory'* 465
    6.1.2.4 The *Effectuation* Approach 469
    6.1.2.5 The *Bricolage* Approach 471
6.2 Development of a 'Synergetic Entrepreneurship Model' (SEM) 474
  6.2.1 Basics: Lineality versus Non-Lineality 474
  6.2.2 Synergetics as the Basis for the Complexity Science Discussion of Entrepreneurship 476
  6.2.3 The Extended Synergetic Model 479
  6.2.4 Basic Explanation of the Model 482
    6.2.4.1 The Embedding of the Analysis of Entrepreneurial Founding Processes in a Multi-Level Structure 482
    6.2.4.2 Closer Examination of the Three Levels of an Entrepreneurial Founding Process 485
    6.2.4.3 The Economic Perspective—Three Perspectives on Entrepreneurial Founding Processes 487
    6.2.4.4 Three Submodels, the Multi-Level Model, and Synergetics 488
References 490

A. Liening, *Complexity and Entrepreneurship*,
https://doi.org/10.1007/978-3-658-44032-9_6

6.1 What is Entrepreneurship?—Trends and Controversies

Whether we are managing in a time of change, or a time of uncertainty, or a time of revolution, or a time of chaos, we are leading organisations that have an increasing need to interoperate, exchange information, and make changes to adjust to their situations.
(Hite 2011, p. 290)

6.1.1 What is Entrepreneurship?

6.1.1.1 On the Origin of the Term

The domain "Entrepreneurship" is one of the younger fields of research in economics. When trying to approach the term, it becomes apparent that there is no uniform definition in the literature. First of all, it must be stated that there is not even a translation for the German language. The term could perhaps best be explained as "Entrepreneurship". However, since the term entrepreneurship is rarely associated with the solid merchant in everyday language, but rather with the exploitative capitalist, with a benevolent interpretation with the industrial captain, and ultimately generally with the CEO of a large corporation, this translation does not help further, especially since the CEOs of large corporations are ultimately only employees and by no means entrepreneurs or Entrepreneurs in the true sense of the word (Jacobsen, 2006, p. 27). Who thinks of the taxi driver with his own vehicle or the gardener with his small nursery when they hear the word entrepreneur (De, 2005, p. 16).

The introductory words show that they do not provide one thing: An idea of what Entrepreneurship is supposed to mean. The definitions range from action-oriented to characteristic- or attitude-oriented approaches. If we stick to the everyday language usage just mentioned, the entrepreneur and the associated discipline of entrepreneurship are often defined in terms of action.

▶ **(Narrow) Definition Entrepreneur**[1] An *Entrepreneur* is a person who runs a business on their own responsibility and direction. It is understood that behaviours such as courage, determination, and a certain willingness to take risks are dispositions that are necessarily associated with the successful[2] Entrepreneur (De, 2005, p. 17).

---

[1] This definition can be considered narrow because the term entrepreneur, regardless of whether he runs a business, can also mean a basic attitude that someone adopts when they are able to think and act entrepreneurially. Such a broader definition is then independent of whether someone runs a business. However, we stick to this narrow definition, as the yet to be developed "Synergetic Entrepreneurship Model" exemplarily refers to founding issues.

[2] At this point, there is a non-trivial question, namely what is meant by "Success". Is only the entrepreneur who achieves a correspondingly high ROI and generates company growth successful? Or can one also consider the entrepreneur who files for bankruptcy with his startup, but learns

The word Entrepreneur is borrowed from French[3] and was first used around 1730 by the economist Richard *Cantillon* for independent traders who buy goods without knowing at what price they can resell them (Cantillon, 1755). For *Cantillon*, an entrepreneur is therefore a person who pays a certain price for a product without knowing what the selling price will be, how environmental influences will change, or how the competition will behave, thus mentioning for the first time the willingness to take risks as an important characteristic of the entrepreneur (Cantillon, 1755). The original meaning is therefore in risk-bearing (intermediate) traders. Around 1920, Frank *Knight* referred to entrepreneurs who bet on changes in the markets and want to use these upheavals profitably as Entrepreneurs (Emmett, 1999). The ability of an entrepreneur to recognise favourable *opportunities* ('opportunities')[4] to recognise and use for themselves, thus becomes the central characteristic when the entrepreneur enters as a phenomenon in scientific discourse.

---

from the mistakes made and makes a new attempt, as successful? If the latter were true, however, the company's success would not be equated with the success of the entrepreneur. This is highlighted in a multitude of studies. For example, the characteristics and characteristics of an entrepreneur are compared with the success of the company and attempts are made to draw conclusions and statements about 'successful' entrepreneurs. However, it has been shown that it is more about behaviours than properties. *Gartner* describes the problem situation in such a way by asking: "Can one know the dancer from the dance?" (Gartner, 1988) For *Garland, Hoy* and *Carland* this question is essential, because one cannot understand the dance without the dancer and his way of dancing (Carland et al., 1988). In addition, there are also different aspects of success, such as continuation, reorientation, sale, closure of the company, generation of new shareholders etc. In parts, there is always a kind of ending in it, whereby this ending is not to be evaluated negatively in any way. Furthermore, as mentioned above, there is the aspect of learning. A failure can be at least as instructive for an entrepreneur as a success. Of course, this knowledge only comes into play with 'serial' entrepreneurs, as a person who only founds once cannot apply the learned knowledge after a failure (at least not with a foundation). Finally, an entrepreneur must be driven by more than just monetary success. If you compare employees and self-employed, on average employees earn more (in addition to the fringe benefits). This becomes even clearer if you calculate out the so-called 'Star-Performer'. Thus, for the evaluation of an entrepreneurial success, other key figures than purely monetary values must also be used (self-realisation, independence, design possibilities etc.). If you take up these points, in the end a company can have a failure, but the entrepreneur can be successful in his own right, or as *Sarasvathy* puts it: "Entrepreneurs can and do use both firm failures and firm success to increase the probabilities of their own success" (Sarasvathy, 2009, p. 130).

[3]The French term "entreprendre quelque chose" translates in German to "undertake something". The term "l'entreprise" means: "the company", or "the firm".

[4]The term 'opportunities' (Engl. 'opportunities') is discussed very intensively in the literature, so that when using it, one must at least be aware of the fact that this is a very multifaceted term, if one thinks only of the discovery approach ('opportunity recognition') and the emergence approach ('opportunity creation'), which we will deal with in more detail later (Fueglistaller et al., 2015, p. 37 ff.). The English term originates from the Latin 'oppurtunitas', which means 'favourable situation'. It is composed of the partial words 'ob' (before, in front of) and 'portas' (harbour), and in

It was particularly Joseph *Schumpeter,* who introduced the entrepreneur (in the role of entrepreneur) as a creative destroyer and supply-side enforcer of new factor combinations into economic science. *Schumpeter* was of the opinion that without dynamic, innovative people, no dynamic, innovative market economy is possible. A dynamic market economy needs initiative and creativity on the part of entrepreneurs, but also entrepreneurially thinking employees (intrapreneurs), in order to generate prosperity as a prerequisite for a modern welfare state (Schumpeter, 1912). In this respect, the domain of entrepreneurship can be divided into both StartUp and Corporate Entrepreneurship.

StartUps can be defined by four characteristics:

▶ **Definition StartUp** A StartUp is an enterprise that meets the following characteristics: A StartUp...

- is less than ten years old
- is (highly) innovative with its technology and/or business model
- shows significant employee and/or sales growth or aims for it (Ripsas & Tröger, 2015, p. 4)
- develops new products or services under conditions of extreme uncertainty (Ries, 2011, p. 27)

Blank and *Dorf* point out in their chapter "The Path to Disaster" of their "StartUp Owner's Manual" that a startup is not simply a small version of a large company (Blank & Dorf, 2012, p. 1). Ultimately, a startup is always also associated with the search for the 'right' *business model,* it is a kind of experiment and thus fundamentally differs from an established company.

The term entrepreneurship itself can be understood in several ways. *Morris* alone identifies seven different perspectives that one can have on entrepreneurship (Morris, 1998, p. 14) (Table 6.1).

---

its original meaning describes the favourable moment when a ship can enter a harbour (Brülhart. 2013, p. 1). In entrepreneurship, the term ultimately refers to a favourable situation in which, for example, new products or services can be distributed at higher prices than costs (Grichnik, 2006, p. 30 ff., Shane and Venkataraman, 2000).*Eckhardt* and *Shane* understand entrepreneurial 'Opportunities' more generally: "situations in which new goods, services, raw materials, markets and organising methods can be introduced through the formation of new means, new ends, or means-ends relationships" (Eckhardt & Shane, 2003, p. 336). To illustrate the meaning of this term, reference is made to a quote from *Brülhart*, who rightly emphasisses: "Without Opportunity no Entrepreneurship" (Brülhart 2013, p. 2).

Table 6.1 Seven perspectives on entrepreneurship. (Source: Morris, 1998, p. 14)

Creation of Wealth	Entrepreneurship involves assuming the risks associated with the facilitation of production in the exchange for profit
Creation of Enterprise	Entrepreneurship entails the founding of a new business venture where none existed before
Creation of Innovation	Entrepreneurship involves creating change by adjusting, adapting and modifying one's personal repertoire, approaches and skills to meet different opportunities available in the environment
Creation of Jobs	Entrepreneurship is concerned with employing, managing and developing the factors of production, including the labour force
Creation of Value	Entrepreneurship is a process of creating value for customers by exploiting untapped opportunities
Creation of Growth	Entrepreneurship is defined as a strong and positive orientation toward growth in sales, income, assets and employment

Creativity and creation are at the centre of these mentioned perspectives, with the descriptions not only targeting specific processes but also including the individual itself. If one wanted to classify the term entrepreneurship more closely, it could be seen as a certain way of thinking, but also as an activity or as a method to question previous stuck structures, or even as a scientific discipline. We will discuss the way of thinking and the associated entrepreneurship knowledge and entrepreneurial attitude in more detail later. *Volkmann* and *Tokarski* provide the following definition for entrepreneurship:

Definition Entrepreneurship as an activity or method Entrepreneurship is an activity/method that involves the following aspects:

- "Identification and use of entrepreneurial opportunities
- Innovation and novelty
- Resource acquisition and founding of a company/organisation
- Profit orientation taking into account appropriate risks and uncertainties" (Volkmann & Tokarski 2006, p. 5).

In this book, entrepreneurship is primarily understood as a scientific sub-discipline of business administration, which is why we use the following definition:

Definition Entrepreneurship as a discipline Entrepreneurship is a scientific sub-discipline of business administration that deals with the analysis of entrepreneurship processes (such as the identification of market opportunities, the development of business ideas and their implementation) as well as the development, research and evaluation of innovative, entrepreneurial methods.

Ultimately, there are a multitude of definitions just on the topic of "Entrepreneurship as a scientific discipline", and probably *Shane* and *Venkataraman* are right when they say:

> Entrepreneurship has become a broad label under which a hodgepodge of research is housed (Shane & Venkataraman, 2000, p. 217).

Frank points out that the term stands for a perspective that deviates from traditional business and management theory in several ways (Frank, 2009, p. 11). Accordingly, the focus is not only on existing companies, but often on business start-ups, so it is about the implementation of a start-up idea by a person or a team as a typical expression of entrepreneurial action, where the focus is primarily on an innovative start-up, i.e., the recognition or creation and enforcement of an entrepreneurial opportunity. Therefore, entrepreneurship is not so much about improving or optimising existing structures, but rather about creating new structures and processes in connection with entrepreneurial opportunities, with 'Opportunity Creation' or 'Opportunity Recognition' and Innovation being considered as strategic permanent tasks (Frank, 2009, p. 11).

Volkmann and *Tokarski* point out that the focus on business start-ups represents a very "narrow interpretation" of entrepreneurship (Volkmann & Tokarski, 2006, p. 13). A broader understanding of this term, on the other hand, refers to "the entire life cycle of a company (…), i.e., both newly founded, young and established companies as well as ultimately also established companies in crisis or in the process of restructuring" (Volkmann & Tokarski, 2006, p. 13).

The term *"Corporate Entrepreneurship"* thus illustrates in contrast to the term *"StartUp Entrepreneurship"* that the mentioned aspects of entrepreneurship can also come into focus in existing organisations or companies and do not only refer to start-ups.[5]

In economics, the construct of the entrepreneur was long neglected and only rediscovered in the Anglo-Saxon language area in the 1980s (Gibb et al., 1982). However, no uniform definition has yet emerged, partly due to an interdisciplinary influx of researchers. Entrepreneur or Entrepreneurship is usually referred to as "entrepreneurial spirit" or "entrepreneurship" in German-speaking countries, as already indicated (Blum & Leibbrand, 2001).*Mandl* and *Hense* understand this to mean entrepreneurial thinking and action. The associated competencies are becoming increasingly important in the development towards a knowledge society. This development towards a knowledge society is associated with buzzwords such as 'Industry 4.0', or 'Internet of Things', where the virtual world is networked with the real world (Mandl & Hense, 2004, p. 5 ff.). The

[5] Even in academia, entrepreneurship can be applied, as the term "Academic Entrepreneurship" suggests (Shane, 2004).

increased complexity of decision-making structures, an accelerated dynamic of change combined with the decreasing predictability of future developments, leads to a decentralisation of work, more autonomy, comprehensive task competence, increased interaction, more teamwork and a softening of rigid temporal and spatial boundaries of work.

Entrepreneurial thinking and action can be subdivided into the following four sub-competencies (competence bundles) according to *Mandl* and *Hense:* cognitive competencies, motivation-related competencies (self-initiative, goal-oriented action), social competencies, and organisational competencies (Mandl & Hense, 2004, p. 9). To ultimately understand the concept of the entrepreneur and his role, it is useful to compare him, for example, with the concept of the manager and—if possible—to differentiate him.

6.1.1.2 Entrepreneur versus Manager

To illustrate the distinction between the Entrepreneur and the Manager, Table 6.2 should serve, which clearly separates the key tasks of managers and entrepreneurs. *Intrapreneurs* are often seen, as with *Burns,* as a kind of combination of entrepreneurs and managers, although one should not go as far as *Pinochet,* who sees intrapreneurs merely as "… dreamers who act" (Pinochet, 1988, p. 7). *Burns* says:

> They are therefore likely to be hybrids, having to work hard to create entrepreneurial structures and cultures around them, but always having to communicate with more bureaucratic individuals in the organisation that employs them (Burns, 2013, p. 46).

Entrepreneurs must, if they want to shape an entrepreneurial process, be able to meet special requirements. These fundamentally differ from the tasks of a Manager or employee, as the comparison in Table 6.2 suggests. There are various concepts that

Table 6.2 Distinguishing between Managers and Entrepreneurs (Kuratko et al., 2011a, p. 13)

Manager	Entrepreneur
• Planning	• Having/developing visions
• Developing strategies	• Seeking opportunities
• Organising	• Creating
• Directing	• Initiating innovations
• Leading personnel	• Taking calculated risks
• Motivating	• Allocating/dividing/distributing resources
• Being responsible for the budget	• Being responsible for changes
• Evaluating	• Adaptive implementation of ideas
• Coordinating	
• Supervising	

define the competencies for entrepreneurs (Man et al., 2002; Mitchelmore & Rowley, 2010). These of course do not exclude the tasks of a manager, because an entrepreneur also has to deal with tasks that are more associated with management (exploitation), but it is the specific entrepreneurial tasks that make up the special requirements for an entrepreneur (exploration) (Wales et al., 2011).

For a manager, the central task is to exploit, implement, and execute a given opportunity or an existing product or service. These steps can be described with the umbrella terms *Execution* and *Administration*, whereas the tasks of an entrepreneur can be described more with the terms *Searching* and *Developing* (Osterwalder et al. 2014). Thus, it follows that an entrepreneur and a manager should have different specific competencies that they primarily need to fulfil.

The following examines the areas of competence that are relevant to an entrepreneur, as these are also mentioned repeatedly in the subsequent chapters. *Man* et al. list the areas of competence *opportunity, conceptual, interaction, organising, strategic* and *commitment competence*[6] , with the two areas of competence organising and strategic competence having a rather managerial focus according to the authors (Man et al., 2002).

Another list can be found in *Mitchelmore* and *Rowley*. They state for the area of entrepreneurial competencies that these include the *identification* and *definition of a market niche,* the *development of a suitable product or service for the targeted market,* the *generation of ideas,* the *observation of the environment,* the *recognition and realisation to seize opportunities, and* the *strategy formulation to seize opportunities,* (Mitchelmore and Rowley 2010). It is important to note at this point that managerial and entrepreneurial areas of competence are not clearly distinguishable from each other and, on the other hand, that the entrepreneurial and managerial areas of competence do not exclude each other, but result from the requirement environment. This means that—depending on the requirement environment (Exploitation versus Exploration)—both areas of competence have their justification.

It should be added that the presence of competencies *alone* does not yet answer the question of what *knowledge* is useful for an entrepreneur, and whether he believes the knowledge he has acquired to be true, can assert it and handle it responsibly. For example, competence training does not automatically lead to the entrepreneur being able to act entrepreneurially in a correct and responsible manner. Ultimately, this is what distinguishes an educated entrepreneur (Liening, 2015, p. 185).

[6] In the original English, these are referred to as 'opportunity competencies', 'conceptual competencies', 'relationship competencies', 'strategic competencies', 'organising competencies' and 'commitment competencies' (Man et al., 2002).

Probably Volker *Ladenthin* is not entirely wrong when he sharply criticises the topic "competencies" as a key word in educational policy and lists about four decisive points of criticism:

- Competence orientation means that learning prerequisites mutate into contentless learning objectives.
- Competence orientation means external control instead of self-determination.
- Competence orientation means *Taylorisation.*
- Competence orientation leads to arbitrariness (Ladenthin 2011).

So he *firstly* notes that learning prerequisites (the competencies mentioned) now become learning objectives (Ladenthin 2011, p. 2 f.). For example, the competence "ability to motivate", which as self-motivation is actually a prerequisite for acquiring content, becomes the goal of a training measure. Formulated as a competence goal, motivation, the will, becomes a contentless goal. A corresponding training measure would therefore be successful if the learner shows that he is motivated. And so *Ladenthin* critically notes:

> The competent learner is not the one who learns meaningful things, but the one who learns accepting (Ladenthin, 2011, p. 3).

The crucial thing for an entrepreneur, namely to pursue goals self-determined and self-responsible, and thus the free will, is thus undermined. For *Ladenthin,* this *secondly* approach is also the "most pronounced form of a theory of external control" (Ladenthin, 2011, p. 3), as competence trainings do not contribute to education, but model people, forcing them to learn something that the learner as an autonomous subject can no longer understand as an invitation to self-activity. But this is precisely a basic requirement in the field of entrepreneurship by definition.

Ladenthin points out *thirdly* that the idea of competence concepts is to "break down complex human actions into partial actions and thus make them learnable" (Ladenthin, 2011, pp. 3, 4), in order to then reassemble the partial competences into a whole (summativity). He rightly speaks here of the *Taylor*isation of humans (Ladenthin, 2011, pp. 3, 4). However, this fundamentally contradicts the findings of complexity sciences, as summativity is a central characteristic of the diametrically opposed *Laplacian* demon, and it contradicts the idea of entrepreneurship, as entrepreneurship is not about detailed specifications for performing tasks, exact definition of performance locations and performance times, and certainly not about extremely detailed and broken down work tasks, which are, however, characteristics of *Taylorism* (Hebeisen, 1999, p. 93 ff.).

In analogy to *Ladenthin's* argumentation, one could add that one would also have to play chess for some time to generate and/or strengthen competences, such as the ability to "generate ideas", "perceive opportunities", "be able to organise" and "think strategically", or what is often also mentioned in this context, "problem-solving thinking", "assessing people", "focussing on essentials", "motivation ability" etc. (Ladenthin, 2011, p. 3). But just because one can play chess does not mean that one is capable of acting as an entrepreneur. Such formal competences do not contribute to deciding which entrepreneurial contents are meaningful or not and thus do not necessarily make a person an entrepreneur.[7]

In short: Competences are undoubtedly necessary for entrepreneurship, no one can or should deny this, but on the other hand, and this is shown by the criticism of *Ladenthin,* a sole focus on competences neither creates Entrepreneurship knowledge nor an entrepreneurial attitude towards this knowledge, which, however, constitute the core of an entrepreneurial education, as we will see in more detail later.

Let's take another look at the managerial and entrepreneurial competence areas identified in the competence debate. *Sarasvathy* already states in 2001 that both the managerial (causal) and the entrepreneurial (effectual) area have their justification, depending on the challenges the person has to face (Sarasvathy, 2001a). Many years later, she therefore consistently formulates the following correlation:

> Causal problems are problems of decision; effectual problems are problems of design. Causal logics help us choose; effectual logics help us construct. Causal strategies are useful when the future is predictable, goals are clear and the environment is independent of our actions; effectual strategies are useful when the future is unpredictable, goals are unclear and the environment is driven by human action (Sarasvathy, 2009, p. 73).

From this it follows that both managerial and entrepreneurial approaches are important. If the two processes are carried out appropriately, once a company is established, the managerial or causal share will tend to increase and the entrepreneurial or effectual share will tend to decrease. However, the general rule is:

> Both causation and effectuation are integral parts of human reasoning that can occur simultaneously, overlapping and intertwining over different contexts of decisions and actions (Sarasvathy, 2009, p. 75).

Thus, it can be stated that when considering *entrepreneurial* processes and talking about the challenges of entrepreneurs, they must have competences that support an effectual and exploration-oriented process, but these alone are not sufficient to capture, for example, the content dimension. An effectual process mainly involves finding, testing, experimenting with and adapting ideas and implementing the results into a viable business model (Aulet, 2013).

---

[7] *Ladenthin's* arguments are worth considering, even if or precisely because he formulates pointedly: "A training camp of the neo-Nazis cannot be distinguished from training in elderly care from a competence-theoretical point of view" (Ladenthin, 2011, p. 6).

Methods that favour such a process include the *Business Model Canvas,* the *Lean StartUp Method* or *Customer Development,* which will be introduced later.

Extensive experience with economic-didactic and economic teaching/learning scenarios has shown that the didactic methods of the case study, the 'Business Game' and the experiment are particularly suitable for the development and learning of such competences (Liening, 2015). Therefore, these methods will be mentioned in a later chapter when it comes to the design of teaching/learning scenarios in entrepreneurial contexts.

6.1.1.3 Entrepreneur—"Born or Made"?

Often, in connection with the definition of the term entrepreneur, the question is asked: "Born or Made"? (Euler, 2012) So are characteristics such as determination, courage, drive, assertiveness, endurance, flexibility, etc., which are expected from an entrepreneur, innate or can they be learned? What about risk-taking, for example? Every start-up is also associated with risks, and the risk of failure. If this risk, which can be enormous depending on the necessary investments, did not exist, everyone could be an entrepreneur and everyone could achieve corresponding successes. Therefore, this specific characteristic is needed, the willingness to take calculated risks and to believe in one's idea with great self-confidence, without possessing too high a degree of *Overconfidence*-Bias or exhibiting other behavioural anomalies in excess. However, it must be emphasised that an entrepreneur is of course more and different than 'just' a risk-affine contemporary, as the above explanations regarding entrepreneurial competencies clearly show. But what about all the characteristics and behaviours of the entrepreneur? Are they ultimately innate?

So are you born an entrepreneur or are these characteristic traits and behaviours that can ultimately be worked out or acquired in educational processes? These questions alone suggest that there are a multitude of different concepts or schools in the field of entrepreneurship. The truth probably lies, as so often, in the middle. If someone is a rather fearful character from birth, then even the best training probably won't make an entrepreneur out of him. But a person with an interest in founding, who is perhaps endowed with a temperament tending towards 'normal' caution from birth, can probably be helped to develop entrepreneurial characteristics. Ultimately, one must actually also want to be an entrepreneur *want,* regardless of how much one or the other disposition has been pronounced from childhood.

6.1.1.4 Different Entrepreneurship Classifications

Building on *Cantillon*, one could now distinguish three schools of the dynamic entrepreneurial function. While the Chicago School around *Knight* refines the *Cantillon* position and distinguishes the named, but in his view always calculable risk, from an incalculable uncertainty by the entrepreneur (Knight, 1921), the German School, which was significantly influenced by Schumpeter's approach and is therefore also called the "*Schumpeterian* School", focusses on the entrepreneur's power of innovation in the economy (Schumpeter, 1912). In the Austrian School, for example, one can diagnose an expansion

Table 6.3 Entrepreneurship schools. (Based on: Ebbers, 2012, p. 116; Freiling, 2006, p. 15)

Entrepreneurship Schools	Ontology	Central Contents
Functional school (Gartner, 1993, 1995; Danhoff, 1949; Drucker, 1985)	Independent of individuals and thus cross-personal	Innovation, coordination, risk-taking, arbitrage
Personality-related school (Schumpeter, 1912; Faltin, 2008; Beaver, 2002)	Person-related	Innovative power, ingenuity, creativity, assertiveness, performance motivation, tolerance of ambiguity, judgement, knowledge of human nature
Founding-related school (Lichtenstein, 2000; De, 2005; Gartner, 1985)	Independent of individuals and thus cross-personal	Establishment of a new corporate identity
Behaviour-related school (Faschingbauer, 2013; Saßmannshausen, 2012; Holcombe, 2003; Cole, 1959)	Person-related (partly also cross-personal)	Self-interest, innovation, change, opportunity orientation and opportunity generation, positive attitude towards errors, proactivity

of entrepreneurial activity to all market participants in *Kirzner*, so that here the Entrepreneur can indeed be the employed, but entrepreneurially thinking and acting actor (Kirzner, 1978).[8]

In reference to *Kirzner's* considerations, one could also classify the schools according to aspects such as the question of a functional or personality- or behaviour-related approach.

Table 6.3 takes into account this form of classification in reference to *Ebbers* and *Freiling*.

However one wants to capture the discussion about the topic of entrepreneurship and contain the different arguments: Taking responsibility for oneself, instead of hoping for the state or society, seems to be a basic attitude that is often associated with the entrepreneur. It initially doesn't matter whether the associated entrepreneurial thinking takes place in the established company (Corporate Entrepreneurship) or in the company to be newly founded (StartUp Entrepreneurship).

Based on 75 Entrepreneurship definitions, *Morris* et al. have derived common keywords for the areas of Corporate and StartUp Entrepreneurship (Morris et al., 1994). However, although all these keywords apply to both Corporate and StartUp Entrepreneurship, the implied meanings of the words differ significantly for the two areas.

[8] It should not be concealed that some authors see other subdivisions in relation to the countries and, for example, count the *Schumpeterian* School to the German-Austrian School (Klapper, 2004, p. 129).

The keywords that can be found in more than a third of the definitions are:

- Starting, Founding, Creating (starting, founding, creating)
- New business, Creation of joint ventures (new business, venture creation)
- Innovation , new products, new markets (innovation, new products, new markets)
- Pursuit of opportunity (pursuit of opportunity)
- Risk-seeking, Risk management, Uncertainty (risk-seeking, risk-management, uncertainty)
- Profit-seeking, Personal benefits (profit-seeking, personal benefits)

When comparing these six commonalities of the definitions of relevance for the two areas, the deviations become clear (Kuratko et al., 2011b). Especially with regard to uncertainty, large differences and a wide range of what entrepreneurship (methods, tools, and theory) should cover and offer for Corporate Entrepreneurs or StartUp Entrepreneurs within an entrepreneurship process (like the resources offered, security, information, etc.) can be identified. Unlike in a StartUp, where every mistake can lead directly to a drastic change or the end of the company due to limited resources and entrepreneurial methods are in the foreground, the organisational resources in large organisations allow the use of management tools instead of real entrepreneurship tools within an entrepreneurship process.

Ultimately, there are very different types of entrepreneurs, but also start-ups: There are voluntary as well as involuntary Entrepreneurs, unplanned as well as planned start-ups; start-ups that follow an imitative start-up idea or those that improve a start-up idea or start-ups that have an innovative start-up idea as a basis (De 2005). The range is wide, the definitions varied. At least we were able to provide a first overview of the still ongoing discussion here. What trends, what controversies arise from the sometimes different definitions and uses of terms? We want to take a closer look at this in the next section.

6.1.2 Current Trends and Controversies

What gives us the extraordinary firmness of belief in causality,
is not the great habit of the sequence of events,
but our inability,
to interpret an event differently
than an event from intentions.
(Friedrich Nietzsche)

6.1.2.1 The Deterministic Belief in Feasibility and the *Laplacian* Demon

Gartner criticises the widespread deterministic belief in feasibility in the context of the entrepreneurship discussion, which we have already examined in detail in the first part of the book and which, historically, has strongly influenced economics as a whole over a long period of time (Gartner, 1995, p. 71 f.). *Saßmannshausen* emphasises in this context that *Gartner's* critical perspective corresponds with the emergence of the unpredictable (Saßmannshausen, 2012, p. 104). Ultimately, this debate shows that the hysteresis of traditional neoclassicism, based on classical mechanics, also prevails in the field of entrepreneurship. This in turn follows the "*Laplacian* Demon", which was discussed in detail in the first part of the book.

But let it be emphasised once again: The *Laplacian* Demon is that institution that has all the data of the universe, so that it could calculate future movements up to any point in time or also those of the past back to the earliest times. If the assumptions associated with the *Laplacian* Demon are valid, then it is merely a lack of information that hinders us from perfectly designing our StartUp rationally and foreseeing future developments.

The debate in the first part of the book also showed that in addition to the determinacy mentioned above, *Reversibility* or time reversibility prevails in mechanistic thought patterns. If, for example, the setup of a process, e.g. the setup of a specific logistics chain in the StartUp, was successfully completed, then this process can ultimately be reversed just as easily for process restructuring, should the principle of reversibility apply.

In addition to the points mentioned, the classical mechanics, as we know, not only follows the weak Law of Causality, according to which equal causes have equal effects and thus causality is invariant. Rather, mechanistic thinking also follows the *strongLaw of Causality*, which states that similar initial states always lead to similar results. Assuming that the strong law of causality is valid in the context of entrepreneurship, the following scenario could be imagined: If there were difficult challenges in a StartUp some time ago, which could be mastered by implementing a specific, sophisticated plan, then the same plan will also succeed in a future situation that, while not the same, presents a cetris paribus *similar* challenge.

We have pointed out that *Descartes* is considered one of the most important representatives of this mechanistic way of thinking. It is not an exaggeration to say that the basic concept of classical mechanics can be traced back to him. *Descartes* was particularly interested in the methods that allowed for secure, scientific knowledge. For this, he drew on logic and selected four rules from the multitude of prescriptions, which, in his view, constitute logic. We repeat here the second rule, which is of particular importance in this context. *Descartes* writes:

> The second, to divide each of the difficulties I would examine, into as many parts as possible, and as would be required to better solve them (Descartes, 1637/1990, p. 30).

So, if a problem is too complex to be solved all at once, it should be broken down into as many sub-problems as possible, which are then correspondingly small enough that each of these sub-problems can be solved individually. With this analytical view, it is implicitly assumed that *the whole consists of the sum of its parts.* We also called this principle *Summation.* If, for example, a complicated, seemingly insurmountable market situation, characterised by a multitude of challenges such as changes in consumer behaviour, new competitors, changed governmental conditions, new societal developments etc., threatens my startup, then according to the principle of summation, it should be possible to break down the overall situation into smaller, manageable individual problems, which can be tackled individually, to ultimately meet the great challenge.

We remember that *Descartes'* third rule states that scientific thinking is about "always arranging all my thoughts in a certain order when exploring the truth: starting with the simplest and most comprehensible, to gradually, step by step, arrive at the knowledge of the more difficult and complicated, and also to arrange things that do not naturally stand in such a sequence in a certain order" (Descartes, 1983, p. 35). Here too, it becomes clear that *Descartes* fundamentally believes it is possible to *break down complex things into a multitude of simple elements and reassemble them.*

We can thus reiterate that the entire worldview of classical mechanics, and ultimately also the idea of the *Laplacian* demon, is characterised by the focus on closed, simple, often linear systems, which therefore include the characteristics of

- determinacy,
- reversibility,
- (strict) causality,
- summation, and
- decomposability.

What is interesting in the context of the entrepreneurship debate is that this lineal-mechanistic worldview is in line with the approach referred to by Sara *Sarasvathy* as *Causation*, which is still widely spread (Sarasvathy, 2001a, p. 245).

This *Causation* approach, which follows the classical, mechanistic thinking, is evident, for example, in the demand for a focus on the creation of business plans etc. in the context of founding processes (Shane & Venkataraman, 2000; Venkataraman, 1997; Casson, 1982; Kihlstrom & Laffont, 1979).

6.1.2.2 Entrepreneurs between a Simple and Complex World

Opened the window to listen to the news,
but all I heard was the Establishment's Blues.
(Sixto Rodriguez)

When considering a startup process, one will traditionally identify four phases in the literature, ranging from the pre-startup phase, in which ideas are generated and concepts are developed and where entrepreneurship training may take place, through the actual startup phase, which focusses on planning and construction work, the early development phase, in which the actual start of the venture lies, up to the growth phase. They thus range from the decision to start up, the start of construction, the institutionalisation of the venture, to the successful breaking of the 'break-even' point. Figure 6.1 shows the individual phases of a startup in chronological order. *Volkmann* and *Tokarski* point out that typical phases such as maturity or degeneration phases are not addressed in this diagram, as the focus is on growth, which will be discussed in more detail in the next chapter (Volkmann & Tokarski, 2006, p. 401).

However, this lineal process is unlikely to occur in practice. The use of such a step-by-step understanding of a startup process is understandable from a systematic point of view, as all company phases and thus contents can be worked on in a structured manner and an entire startup process can be planned in an orderly manner. Thus, both the entrepreneur and stakeholders such as lenders get a structured insight into the company formation, but not a realistic one. The startup process, especially that of startups, however, requires methods and procedures that place complexity, iterativity, and flexibility at the centre (Lichtenstein et al., 2007; Frese, 2014). Thus, a number of authors conclude that entrepreneurship is a nonlinear and complex process (Sarasvathy, 2001a; Swanson & Zhang, 2011). As the findings from the field of complexity sciences show, developments within nonlinear processes are often characterised by uncertainty, risks, and entanglements, setbacks, and turbulence, in short, by complexity, which, however, can be interrupted by phases of randomness, but also simplicity, but can also overlap. Where there is randomness, there is uncertainty, where there is simplicity, there is clarity. Whether there is only uncertainty in phases of complexity ultimately depends on the methods used to analyse these phases. The methods largely determine whether it is possible to discover *structures* in the complex. Figure 6.2 is intended to suggest the different phases.

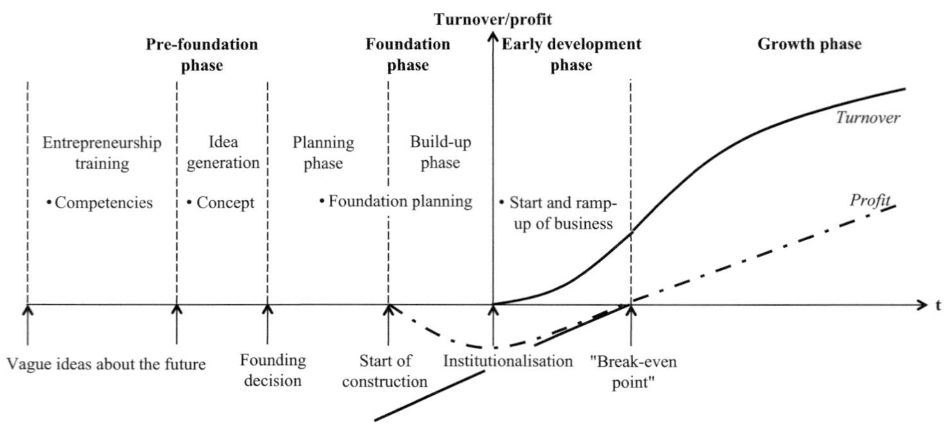

Fig. 6.1 Lineal phase model of a startup process. (Based on: Volkmann & Tokarski, 2006, p. 402)

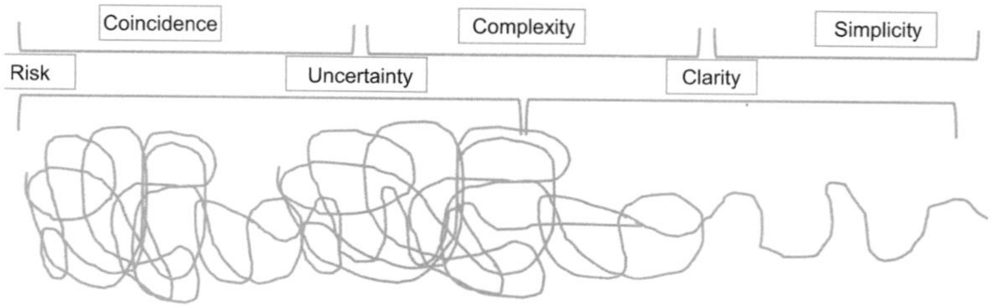

Fig. 6.2 Randomness, complexity, and simplicity

If we assume that we live in a lineal world, where similar causes have similar effects, then the world is simple, determined or predictable. But if everything is predetermined, then there is no room for spontaneity and creativity. Opportunities for new products, company formations, etc., viewed in this way, can only be found ('Opportunity recognition and discovery'). At least, one might think, and so *Lumpkin* and *Lichtenstein* attribute something very positive to this approach when they say:

> Opportunity recognition is the ability to identify a good idea and transform it into business concepts that add value and generate revenue (Lumpkin & Lichtenstein, 2005, p. 457).

In the underlying mindset of a lineal-causal world, the opportunities are always already present and thus exist independently of specific entrepreneurs. However, if the world is rather complex, non-linear and therefore only partially predictable, the future is thus open. Then there is room for individual creativity, for the creation of new things that were not there before, which can be surprising and whose emergence can only succeed with and through entrepreneurs ('Opportunity Creation') (Alvarez & Barney, 2007; Luksha, 2009).[9]

6.1.2.3 *'Discovery-'* versus *'Creation-Theory'*

If one follows *Alvarez* and *Barney,* then on the one hand there are obvious parallels between the *'Discovery Theory'* and the *Laplacian* worldview and in particular the aspect of strong causality and the assumption that one moves in *simple* (mechanistic) systems. On the other hand, there are apparent parallels between the *'Creation-Theory'* and the assumption of complexity, that is, entrepreneurship processes take place in complex systems or are permeated by complexity (Alvarez and Barney 2007).

---

[9]The reader may remember the 'mimesis debate' from the first part of the book, in which the development, starting with the possibility of exclusive imitation and finding, towards the possibility of spontaneity and creativity, was discussed as a result of a very long history of development on the way to modern scientific understanding (cf. Sect. 3.1.2.1).

Table 6.4 'Discovery-' versus 'Creation-Theory'. (Based on: Alvarez & Barney, 2007, p. 13)

	'Discovery-Theory'	'Creation-Theory'
Origin of entrepreneurial opportunities	… are present in the world, exist independently of entre-preneurs	… do not exist without an entrepreneur; are the result of emergence processes
Nature of entrepreneurs	Entrepreneurs differ from non-entrepreneurs particularly in terms of vigilance	Entrepreneurs can, but do not have to differ from non-entrepreneurs; differences are shown due to the results of the search; they are not the cause of the search
Basis of decision making	Risk	Ambiguity and uncertainty

Table 6.4 shows a comparison between the *'Discovery'*- and the *'Creation-Theory'*.

Fundamentally, the field of entrepreneurship can indeed be divided into these two main currents. On the one hand, there are scientists who assume that entrepreneurs recognise opportunities (*"Discovery-Theory", "Opportunity Discovery",* "Discovery Theory") (Askari, 2014; Venkataraman, 1997; Shane & Venkataraman, 2000; Mainela & Puhakka, 2009; Casson, 1982). On the other hand, there are scientists who hold the view that entrepreneurs create opportunities (*"Creation-Theory", "Opportunity Creation",* "Creation Theory") (Ahamat, 2013; Buenstorf, 2007; Alvarez, 2005). If we follow the assumption that opportunities are discovered, an entrepreneur 'only' needs to be able to conduct comprehensive market research to be successful. However, if the assumption is correct that entrepreneurial opportunities can be created and thus emergent processes in complex situations become important, then methods are needed that work in such complex situations and processes, that allow a high degree of flexibility, and that do not focus on planning, but at most on possibilities of control (Alvarez, 2005, p. 12).

With regard to the traditional, lineal-causal view, methods are needed that focus on planning and prediction. Linear methods such as business plans, SWOT analyses, five-year plans, etc. are used. These methods work excellently when the situations, structures, or processes in which we operate are of a lineal nature. However, if it turns out that the phases we are in are rather of non-lineal origin, if we are dealing with complexity instead of simplicity (in the sense of the *Laplacian* worldview), then these planning methods must fail, as the explanations in this book have made abundantly clear. If one follows the complexity approach, then an entrepreneur can be distinguished from a non-entrepreneur by the fact that he transforms a promising situation into an opportunity, which involves more than just market research. In such a conceived entrepreneurship process, the responsible person must deal with uncertainty (Sarasvathy, 2001a) and an unpredictable future (Dew et al., 2009). To understand such a complex Entrepreneurship process, it can be illustrated using an analogy as follows.

Example: Entrepreneurship—A Hiker's Analogy

A hiker stands on a path and can only see a few meters ahead due to fog. The hiker is unable to see where the 'journey' will end or who and what he will encounter on the 'journey'. He walks the path he can oversee, bravely, thoughtfully, and hopefully, without knowing what will come next (Liening et al., 2016). ◀

This image of the hiker can be applied to an Entrepreneur, who also has to find his way in an uncertain and unpredictable environment. The associated complexity also makes it impossible to plan very far in advance. Since basic management tools are based on forecasts and predictions, they may work in an organisation that is equipped with numbers and data about customers and is in calm times. However, for a real entrepreneurship process, which is characterised by uncertainty and complexity, new methods and understandings are needed (Dew et al., 2009; Brettel et al., 2012; Liening, 2013).

Thus, the entrepreneur needs special entrepreneurial tools and methods to be able to carry out the processes described above (Alvarez & Barney, 2007). For this purpose, non-lineal methods are more suitable. For example, the *Creation*-Theory does not focus on planning, but on possibilities of control and the creation of new things. In this context, there are a number of well-known entrepreneurship methods, such as *'Customer Development'*,*'Design Thinking'*,*'Business Model Canvas'*, the *'Value Proposition'* or for example the *'Lean*StartUp' approach, which we will discuss in more detail at a later point (Osterwalder & Pigneur, 2011; Ries, 2011; Plattner et al., 2009; Osterwalder et al., 2015; Blank & Dorf, 2012).

The *Creation* approach, in the sense that the conditions for the possibility of creating something new should not only exist but also be actively used, includes for *Kuratko* et al. in addition to the use of entrepreneurial methods, a number of central content aspects, such as the design of a company, the design of innovations, the design of change, job creation, wealth creation, value creation, and the creation of growth, which require special attention (Kuratko et al., 2011a).

Furthermore, we must acknowledge that not only success but also failure is part of entrepreneurship. The only important aspect in this context is that failure is 'successfully dealt with'. Already in the first part of the book, in chapter 2, it was pointed out that the one who has to lead a company into insolvency proceedings has already done something, that he has not capitulated in the face of the complexity of the world, but has seen the opportunities and tried to seize them or to quote *Lotter* once again:

> In a complex world, one must experiment, try out, dare to try. Soberly considered, every day is a bit of Waterloo: We fail our way forward (Lotter, 2014, p. 35).

Thus, it is about trying out, testing new technologies and potentials of markets. In this sense, a start-up is a kind of economic experiment that can succeed or fail. A common mistake in the context of failures or failures is that entrepreneurship performance is often equated with business success, which could be measured, among other things, using the EVA concept[10]. This often overlooks the importance of error and risk management. Thus, an entrepreneur's decision to stop an entrepreneurship process could well be considered a success if the ratio between uncertainty and resource use is no longer justified (Sarasvathy 2009). *Sarasvathy* correctly states:

> Firm failure can be an important input in entrepreneurial success: further, firm failures may actually contribute to productive novelty in the economy (Sarasvathy, 2009, p. 61).

She brings the topic of success or failure to the point when she writes:

> SUCCESS OR FAILURE OF THE FIRM ≠ SUCCESS OR FAILURE OF THE ENTREPRENEUR (Sarasvathy, 2009, p. 123).

In addition, as already mentioned, there are also various aspects of success, such as continuation, reorientation, sale, generation of new shareholders, etc. Here too, we sometimes always find a kind of ending, which is by no means to be evaluated negatively. Also, as also mentioned, the aspect of learning plays a not to be underestimated role here. From a failure of a company foundation, an entrepreneur can learn at least as much as from a successful foundation, if he uses what he has learned for new opportunities.

On the basis of the previous considerations, we can define the term "entrepreneur" in extension to *Venkataraman's* definition of entrepreneurship in a general version as follows (Venkataraman, 1997). Compared to the previous definition, this can be described as a broad definition, as no specific founding project has to be the basis.

▶ **(broad) Definition Entrepreneur** An *Entrepreneur* is a person who has entrepreneurship knowledge as well as an entrepreneurial attitude and corresponding competencies and who is thus able to create opportunities ('opportunities') and to commercialise them appropriately and responsibly through products and services.

Ultimately, this debate about the question of success and failure also shows that entrepreneurship needs its own methods and views, which can deviate from standard methods, e.g., for generating or controlling success. Various authors underline this view by rightly stating that entrepreneurship is a discipline in its own right and thus also needs its own

---

[10] We have already discussed the success of young growth companies in the first part of the book and introduced the EVA concept. As a reminder: EVA stands for 'Economic Value Added'. It is more than just a key figure. It takes into account both the demands of management and those of shareholders, as not only performance but also market value is calculated. The EVA results from the NOPAT (Net Operating Profit after Taxes (i.e., profit after taxes)) minus the capital required to generate the profit multiplied by the cost of capital.

methods and conditions (Sarasvathy & Venkataraman, 2011; Kuratko et al., 2015). Nevertheless, there is a particular lack of applicable methods in dealing with uncertainty and risk management.

When one thinks of the *Creation* theory as an interesting approach in the context of complexity, which confronts the *Laplacian* worldview, the term *"Effectuation"* already used in this context stands out. Sankaran *Venkataraman* notes on the significance of the 'creation' of 'opportunities':

> Historically, opportunities have been supposed to exist—and the entrepreneur either is alert to them (Kirzner, 1979) or somehow goes about "discovering" them (Hayek, 1945; Schumpeter, 1976). But the idea (…) is that entrepreneurial opportunities often have to be ***"created"*** (emphasis, the author) by using the entrepreneurial imagination to embody human aspirations in concrete products and markets (Venkataraman, 1997, p. 659).

The associated *Effectuation* approach will be briefly considered below.

6.1.2.4 The *Effectuation* Approach

> *In fact, to the extent that the future is shaped by human action,*
> *it is not much use trying to predict it –*
> *it is much more useful to understand*
> *and work with the people*
> *who are engaged in the decisions and actions*
> *that bring it into existence.*
> (Sarasvathy, 2001b p. 9)

Sarasvathy offers an interesting approach in entrepreneurship research, which convincingly confronts the idea of the *Laplacian* Demon (Sarasvathy, 2001a; Liening, 2013). The fundamental aspects of her *Effectuation* approach are succinctly summarised by *Saßmannshausen* as follows:

1. An acknowledgement of the importance of the unforeseen
2. a rejection of determinism
3. a—associated—reduced belief in feasibility and the recognition of external, unpredictable events, as well as
4. the abandonment of the dominant orientation towards the statistical average" (Saßmannshausen, 2012, p. 196).

In contrast to the *Causation* approach she named, *Sarasvathy* formulates the following analogy to explain her *Effectuation* approach:

> Imagine a chef assigned the task of cooking dinner. (…) the host asks the chef to look through the cupboards in the kitchen for possible ingredients and utensils and then cook a meal. Here, the chef has to imagine possible menus based on the given ingredients and utensils, select the menu, and then prepare the meal. This is a process of effectuation. It begins

with given ingredients and utensils and focusses on preparing one of many possible desirable meals with them (Sarasvathy, 2001a, p. 245).

Sarasvathy applies this analogy of cooking based on existing resources and not because of a specific menu idea to the *Effectuation* approach, which implies that *Effectuation*, unlike *Causation*, does not start with determined goals from which specific measures are derived to achieve them efficiently. Instead, the entrepreneur focusses on the development of new ideas and products as a goal of human endeavour, using the resources available to him and possibly his team, which exist at the individual, company, and market levels. Unlike a representative of the *Causation* approach, the *Effectuation* entrepreneur, also called an *Effectuator*, would not try to prepare for unpredictable events or try to avoid or overcome all unpredictability, but would instead use contingencies, opportunities that can arise spontaneously, and react flexibly to changes in the environment. While a representative of *Causation* would try to predict and plan an (uncertain) future according to the *Laplacian* worldview, an entrepreneur of the *Effectuation* approach would try to shape an unpredictable, complex future, consciously considering recursive structures, feedback loops, and turbulence (Sarasvathy, 2009). Or as *Sarasvathy* says:

An *effectual* logic is based on the premise: 'To the extent we can control the future, we do not predict it (Sarasvathy, 2009, p. 17).

Figure 6.3 illustrates this approach. The comparison between *Causation* and *Effectuation* reminds us of the economic principle in its two manifestations. While the minimum principle assumes achieving a given goal with as little effort as possible, the maximum

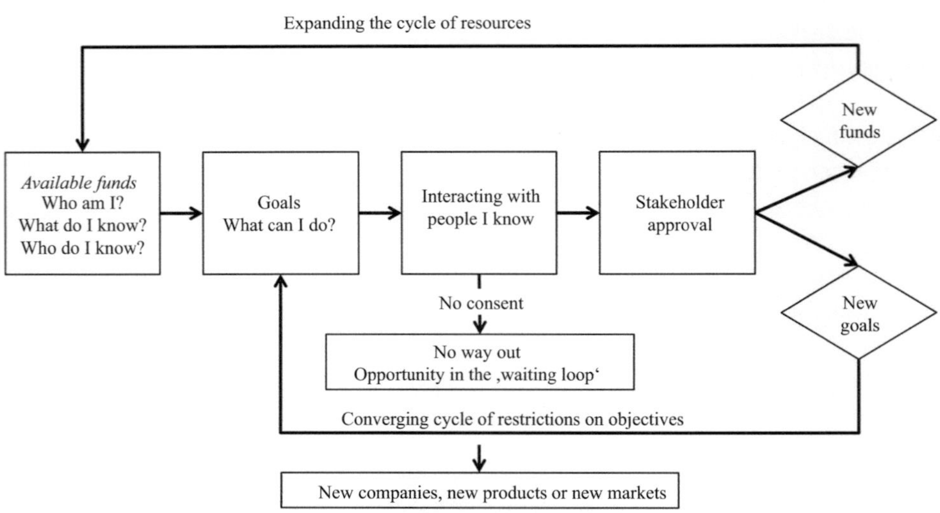

Fig. 6.3 Effectuation approach. (Based on: Sarasvathy, 2009)

principle assumes achieving the highest possible return with the available resources. The *Effectuation* approach is therefore more like the maximum principle, with the addition of feedback loops that underline the non-lineal character of the approach. Overall, it is not surprising when *Sarasvathy* writes:

> Effectuation is the inverse of causation (Sarasvathy, 2009, p. 16).

Figure 6.3 shows that *Effectuation,* as explained, begins with the *'given means',* that are available.

"How do I become a successful entrepreneur" is therefore the wrong initial question. From an effectual perspective, questions like these are crucial: Who am I, what can I do and what do I know, what do I want to be or become? What kind of entrepreneur could I become? What entrepreneurial activities can I sensibly start under the given conditions? What kind of business do I want to start? What resources are available to me and who do I know? (Sarasvathy, 2009, p. 61)

Within the concept, factors such as *'human imaginations'* and *'human aspirations'* also play an important role (Sarasvathy, 2001a, p. 249). In other words, as *Sarasvathy* once again clarifies the difference to *Causation*, it is about the following:

> (…) choosing between means to create a particular effect, versus choosing between many possible effects using a particular set of means (Sarasvathy, 2001a, p. 245).

Both, the *'means'* as well as the *'human aspirations',* change over time. The respective selected effects represent a function at the level of the (not only financial) acceptable loss or risk as well as the degree of control that the *Effectuator* can achieve from *Sarasvathy's* perspective through strategic partnerships.

These explanations make it clear that *Effectuation* is diametrically opposed to the *Causation* approach, but it is *by no means* a concept that exhibits characteristics such as "Anything Goes", "the Easy Way Out", "a Bunch of Traits", "a Recipe for Success" or even "Irrational and Intuitive" (Sarasvathy, 2009, p. 234 ff.).

6.1.2.5 The Bricolage Approach

At this point, a third keyword can be added alongside *Causation* and *Effectuation*: *Bricolage*.

Sometimes in the literature, this keyword is mentioned as another independent approach alongside *Effectuation*. Similar to effectual logic, available resources also form the starting point for perception to action in *Bricolage*, but with the peculiarity that Bricolage assumes an environment with scarce resources—this is not necessarily assumed in *Effectuation*. Both *Effectuation* and *Causation* can be placed close to the *Lean-Startup* approach (Fischer, 2012) and thus offer conceptual potential for the business model concept also discussed in this book.

Therefore, at least this approach, which was introduced by *Levi-Strauss* in 1966, should be briefly presented:

In his work "The Savage Mind", he explains how people create things out of nothing. For this, existing resources are utilised that are readily available and with which useful tools and structures can be constructed. Spontaneity and improvisation are therefore characteristic of Bricoleurs, who are opposed to a procedure oriented towards an ideal state. Therefore, *Bricolage* is particularly considered an important mode of action for entrepreneurs when they operate in a rather—one could say—meager environment, in which there is also a high degree of uncertainty and complexity (Levi-Strauss 1966).

To understand the "meager" situation, one could also describe Bricolage as the "Apollo 13" approach, referring to the dramatic mission at the time and the creative rescue of the astronauts.[11] Thus, the *Bricolage* approach is understood to mean trying to generate creative solutions under a high degree of uncertainty and with very scarce resources by reinterpreting the resources and putting them to new use.The following aspects are characteristic of *Bricolage* in the context of entrepreneurship according to (Baker & Nelson, 2005):

- the use of currently available resources (own abilities, the social environment, "ruins" of previous institutions from which new ones can be created, fragments of legal frameworks, organisational mechanisms, etc.), the empowerment of the existing, not immediately usable resources,
- the empowerment of the existing, not immediately usable resources,

[11] The Apollo missions from 1966 to 1972 were not only about reaching the moon, but also about landing on it. The Apollo 13 programme of 1970 was such a mission. However, the astronauts reported from the spacecraft 55 h after launch with the legendary words: "Houston, we've had a problem here" NASA (1970). "Detailed Chronology of Events Surrounding the Apollo 13 Accident." Retrieved March 17, 2022. The problem was that, among other things, an oxygen tank had exploded and the entire pipeline system next to it was also affected. The fuel cells, which were fed with oxygen from tanks to generate electricity and water, could only continue to work for a few more hours. Therefore, the mission had to be aborted as quickly as possible to return to Earth, as the crew was in extreme danger. In this context, the lunar module attached to the spacecraft played an important role because it became the "lifeboat" for the flight phase until just before entry into the Earth's atmosphere. The three astronauts thus switched from the actual spacecraft to this lunar module. Since the CO_2 filters of the spacecraft and the lunar module were not compatible, a necessary CO_2 adapter was missing, especially since the air (and also the water) was only sufficient for two days for two people. While Apollo 13 initially had to orbit the moon before it could start the return flight to Earth—three days were calculated for this—a team in the "Mission Control Center" in Houston, knowing what was on board, developed a construction manual to design a corresponding adapter from hoses, adhesive tapes, book covers, etc.; a sock is even said to have been used. This manual was transmitted to the astronauts and they actually constructed a corresponding CO_2 adapter for the lunar module with it and thus survived. Luzern, A. F. (2018). "A failure that became a case study." Retrieved March 17, 2022, Lorenzen, D. (2020). "Disaster at Apollo 13—The successful failure of a moon flight." Retrieved March 17, 2022.

- the permanent "making do", i.e., less strategic considerations about possible goal-means combinations than rather continuous engagement[12] and a shift of previously universally accepted boundaries and restrictions (e.g., with regard to the usability of production factors) by the *Bricoleur*

Imagination and the ability to improvise are therefore of particular importance for bricolage, as without them no transformation of the barren environment can take place. Such patterns of action are not only limited to the founding phase of startups but also occur in later phases, for example, by turning short-term, tactical improvisations into the strategic orientation of a company (Baker, 2003, p. 262ff.)

As far as the **market conditions** are concerned, the *Causation* approach tends to assume existing markets with lower uncertainties, whereas the *Effectuation* approach tends to target new markets characterised by higher uncertainty and dynamics. In the *Bricolage* approach, however, markets with very limited resources play a central role.

In terms of the **action situation,** the *Causation* approach clearly involves target specifications or the implementation of an ideal conception, while the *Effectuation* approach focusses on resource orientation. In the *Bricolage* approach, and here the similarity to *Effectuation* becomes apparent, it is also about existing resources and one's own abilities. In contrast to *Bricolage*, *Effectuation* does not presuppose resource scarcity.

Given the necessary **skills** of the entrepreneur, the *Causation* approach focusses on planning-anticipative skills, while in the *Effectuation* something like visionary imagination plays a role. In the *Bricolage* approach, however, the ability to rethink, to reinterpret the scarce resources available, is paramount.

In dealing with **risks** or **complex processes,** the *Causation* approach aims to predict future developments as precisely as possible through analyses and the collection of information. An effectual logic makes a conceptual separation between prediction and control, so that instead of prognostic procedures, small-step, controlled activities are in the foreground. A *Bricolage* logic is based on the fact of indeterminacy, it is about reducing risks through a new combination of resources.

In terms of **attitudes towards competitors,** the *Causation* approach sees competitors as competition, while in the *Effectuation* they are seen more as potential partners. Also in the *Bricolage* approach, the potential network that could arise from competitors is seen.

Regarding the **evaluation of opportunities,** in the *Causation* approach, success is measured by potential profit, while in the *Effectuation* approach, opportunities are rather measured by potential loss, whereas in the *Bricolage* approach, success is evaluated based on the available resources. (Baker, 2005; Fischer, 2012; Kriedel, 2017)

[12] *Baker* et al. point out that such action—although it can contain a contradiction between desire and reality—can lead to excellent, unanticipated results in the sense of an enterprise. Baker, T., & Nelson, R. E. (2005). "Creating Something from Nothing: Resource Construction through Entrepreneurial Bricolage " *Administrative Science Quarterly50,* 329–366.

As interesting as the *Effectuation* and *Bricolage* approaches may be, they lack a convincing quantifiable model that can both explain these entrepreneurship approaches and provide a convincing strategy for a successful entrepreneurship education model in the sense of a Homomorphy between content and learning approach[13] .[14] A potential solution lies in the doctrine of interaction, the theory of self-organisation or Synergetics, which we have already learned in detail.

The following will therefore develop a corresponding entrepreneurship model that is fundamentally aligned with the *Effectuation-*, *Bricolage-*, and *Creation* approach and thus meets the complexity of founding processes and their embedding in complex environments and processes. The aforementioned synergetics should take on the role of a tertium comparationis between the theory of entrepreneurship and the founding practice, between claim and learning, by creating a homomorphism between the individual areas. The model allows entrepreneurship processes to be transparently analysed from different perspectives (individual, organisational, macroeconomic).

6.2 Development of a 'Synergetic Entrepreneurship Model' (SEM)

Startups are inherently chaos.
As a founder you need to prepare yourself
to think creatively and independently,
because more often than not,
conditions on the ground will change so rapidly
that the original well-thought-out business plan becomes irrelevant.
(Blank 2009, p. 1)

6.2.1 Basics: Lineality versus Non-Lineality

The model of synergetic entrepreneurship explained below is exemplified by the topic "founding process".

In the previous Sect. 6.1, it became clear that, for example, in relation to startup entrepreneurship, the traditional conception of a founding process is thought of linealy, from

[13] The author does not claim that Effectuation or Bricolage could not be taught without further quantitative substantiation, and refers, for example, to a very interesting textbook written by *Sarasvathy* and *Read*: Sarasvathy and Read (2011).

[14] This is by no means to say that *Sarasvathy* and her colleagues only work qualitatively. On the contrary, very interesting empirical studies supporting the approach are conducted in the field of Effectuation (Sarasvathy, 2009: 240ff).

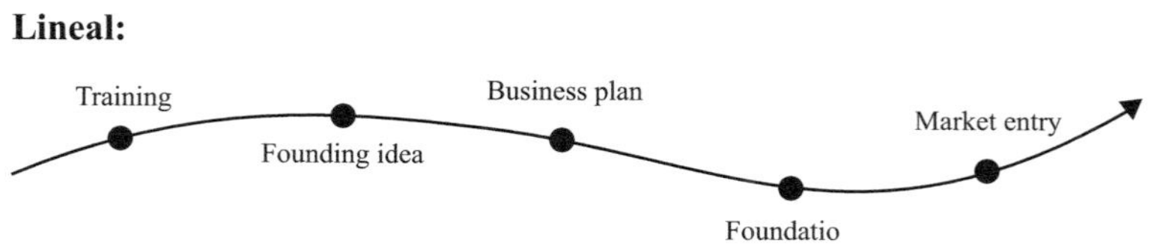

Fig. 6.4 Lineal-causal founding phases

the first idea through the actual founding to the ideally sustainable growth phase, as again illustrated in Fig. 6.4.

This lineal phase sequence can be imagined as follows: A potential founding team starts with entrepreneurship training out of interest due to an unclear future perspective, develops more concrete ideas regarding a founding, works out business plans etc., and finally founds a company. Then the company enters the market and generates growing revenues, so that the team moves from the actual founding phase to an ideally sustainable growth phase. It should be noted at this point that not every founding process starts with a training, but there can be many triggers. A similar phase sequence could also be drawn in the area of corporate entrepreneurship.

Different phases are also present in the concept presented here, the so-called "*S*ynergetic *E*ntrepreneurship *M*odel" (*SEM*). A central difference, however, is that the individual phases are deliberately not clearly separated from each other, so that, for example, concrete founding ideas can be developed as part of a corresponding economic-didactic concept[15] during entrepreneurship training and additional learning phases are integrated during the founding phase, as illustrated in Fig. 6.5.

Here, the overlaps of individual processes not only describe the events that can indeed be observed in reality. Rather, they also suggest a more efficient approach. The concept is therefore not just an *is*- concept found solely based on practical experience and theoretical considerations, but also a *should* concept, a suggestion of what a founding process could look like and what kind of education the entrepreneurs should bring or acquire. *Sarasvathy* hits the nail on the head when she states and asks:

[15] It should be noted that within economic didactics, the discipline of economics that deals with the content-related exploration of economic knowledge areas for non-economists, the topic of entrepreneurship education is gaining increasing importance. An example is one of the central annual meetings of the "German Society for Economic Education", where its members intensively and exclusively dealt with this topic and whose discussions resulted in a comprehensive conference volume under the editorship of the then chairman of the economic-didactic society, Prof. Dr. *Retzmann* (Retzmann 2012). Among the four sections of the society, there is explicitly the working group "Entrepreneurship Education" http://degoeb.de/index.php?page=_Sektionen.

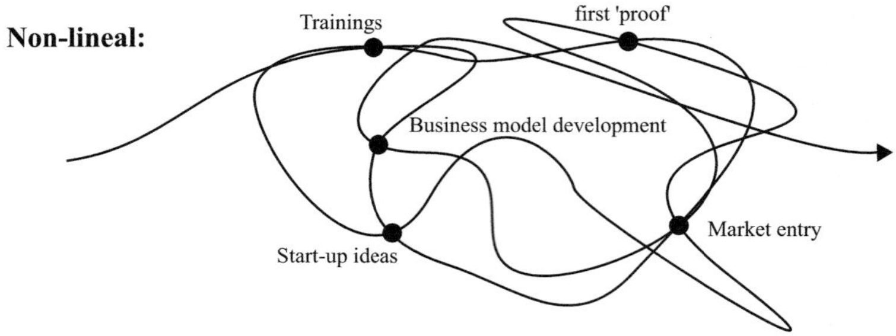

Fig. 6.5 Non-lineal founding phases

> Consider for example the fact that there are hundreds of new business schools being developed in India alone, with the growth rate of MBAs graduating each year increasing steadily. Similar trends hold in China and other developing countries. What are these students being taught about markets and economies and the entrepreneurship ethic? What should they be taught? What toolboxes are they provided with in building actual ventures and markets? (Sarasvathy, 2009, p. 307).

In the general formulation of a *should* concept to answer such questions, the model also sets different priorities compared to traditional lineal-causal concepts, so that here, for example, the focus is on business model developments using the 'Business Model Canvas' or a focus on developing an entrepreneurial attitude instead of, for example, the main development of a traditional business plan. Due to the overlap of the different identifiable processes, in this concept the actual market contact begins much earlier than in the lineal approach model, i.e., the first 'Proof of Concept' occurs much earlier, long before, for example, the legal form of the company is potentially established.

The overlaps in this new "*S*ynergetic *E*ntrepreneurship *M*odel" contribute to improving timelines, recognising misdevelopments early, exploring market opportunities in a timely manner, optimising product development with the help of customer contacts, but also making learning scenarios attractive and sustainable from a didactic point of view. This results in a non-lineal, complex model with numerous feedback loops, the application of which is associated with a high degree of dynamism, as will be further illustrated in the following chapters.

6.2.2 Synergetics as the Basis for the Complexity Science Discussion of Entrepreneurship

As pointed out in Sect. 6.1, there is also a controversy between complexity and simplicity in the entrepreneurship debate, as we have extensively discussed in this book. It became clear that, taking into account complexity, concepts such as the *'Creation'* theory, the *'Effectuation'* approach, etc., seem sensible, as they take into account the fact that the future is little predictable and thus uncertain. Ultimately, this debate reflects a departure from the belief in a deterministic, omnipotent, all-planning and controlling *Laplacian* demon and a turn towards a self-organisation shaped by calculated risk-taking and creativity in a world characterised by turbulence, leaps, and uncertainties. This does not mean that traditional approaches no longer have any justification. Especially in non-complex situations, processes, and structures, when the 'ship is in calm waters', they have achieved great success and must and should continue to be considered in the future. But the more complex the relationships become, the more the newer approaches should also be taken into account so that entrepreneurship processes can succeed.

In the second part of the book, in Chap. 4 ("Theory—Theoretical Approaches to Complexity"), an approach was emphasised that is referred to as the theory of self-organisation or synergetics. Due to its conception, synergetics can meet the associated requirements that relate to the understanding of complex structures, situations, processes, and environments, their empirical knowledge up to the corresponding actions in practice (Haken, 1977; Liening, 2014).

Since the concept of synergetics is fundamental for this third part of the book, we want to present some essential insights from the theory part again, albeit in slightly different words.

The basic idea, which synergetics has copied from nature, is simple to present. *Haken* points out that to transfer a structure to an object or to equip it with functions, we usually use the thought model of a sculptor who carefully chisels the smallest fragments from a marble block to create a head, for example. If we follow the example of nature, then synergetics contrasts with the *planning* organisation and *detailed* control of a system. Here, there is no 'sculptor' at work, to stay with the thought model. Rather, the principle of self-organisation applies. Here, the system, which consists of many parts, is only subjected to a few boundary conditions and it finds its structures and especially its functions itself. New things are created without an ordering hand, like the hand of a sculptor just described, but through self-organisation (Haken, 2006, p. 19 ff.; 2014, p. 39).

The term self-organisation here means that complex, open systems develop their structures without any *specific* external intervention (Haken, 1982). When new structures emerge through the interaction of the individual parts of the system, we can speak of emergence if the newly created quality of the emerging structure cannot be reduced to the original parts (Liening, 1999).[16] The idea of resorting to theories of self-organisation is not new, although synergetics has not been applied here so far. Theories of self-organ-

[16] It should be noted here that not every creation process necessarily has to be a self-organisation process. Instead, both phenomena (emergence and self-organisation) highlight different properties of a system and can exist independently of each other. For a deep distinction between the two terms, see De Wolf and Holvoet (2004).

isation have already been used in entrepreneurship research to identify relevant interdependencies within an entrepreneurship process (Lichtenstein et al., 2007; Lichtenstein, 2000).

For a deeper understanding of synergetics, we introduced, explained, and critically questioned the basic concept as well as the processes and terms in the theory part of the book. We want to repeat the most important aspects here again, initially apart from a concrete entrepreneurship reference, as synergetics is the decisive basis for the "Synergetic Entrepreneurship Model". At this point, it should be reminded that no less a person than *Haken* himself points out in the preface of this book that new perspectives on economics, which are vital for the entrepreneur or the field of entrepreneurship in an increasingly complex world, arise particularly from synergetics.

A basic prerequisite for the self-organisation process is that the system is an *open* multi-component system. As a self-organised system, it can only exist if there is a certain energy supply from the outside. This energy supply is unspecific. Just as the sun as an energy source enables plants to grow, this energy is not able to control, for example, the shape of the growing plant. But without solar energy, the plants die. Only open systems allow self-organised evolutionary structures in this sense; the other systems eventually extinguish.

The specific energy supply in the synergetic model is provided by the so-called *control parameters*, whose control influence, like the control influence of the sun on the plant, is rather unspecific. The fact that a certain plant grows from the seed is not due to solar energy, but without the sun, there would be no growth and therefore no plant. The control is at most specific in the sense that not every system reacts to every available control parameter (Manteufel & Schiepek, 1994). Ultimately, the control parameters do not determine the order structure, but they are able to influence the behaviour of the system elements at the *microscopiclevel* by controlling the intensity of the energy supply. In the process of self-organisation, the system elements build a pattern that becomes visible at the macroscopic *level* in the form of order parameters.

These *order parameters* ultimately form a dynamic pattern. The emerging order parameters successively enslave the elements of the microscopic level and force them into a coherent behaviour, which initially led to the order parameters.

Furthermore, there is an interaction between the order parameters and the control parameters. It is possible that once established patterns, such as the formation of a bird swarm, can destabilise again if the intensity of the control parameters, such as the wind, changes. Through the change of the control parameters and the resulting change in the energy supply, the system elements are stimulated and eventually end the coherent behaviour, leading to the disorganisation of the system and the dissolution of the order parameters. The system remains in a critical state, where it is highly sensitive to external disturbances. New order parameters emerge immediately, competing with each other until certain order parameters dominate all others and force the system elements into a specific coherent behaviour. From this, new behavioural structures can emerge.

However, predicting which of the behavioural possibilities will be built up is almost impossible. This is especially true when considering that the smallest random disturbances ("noise") in a destabilised system can determine which of the competing order parameters will dominate the others. These changes in the macroscopic patterns, caused by the change in control parameters, are called *phase transition* (Haken, 1975). As *Haken* notes, it is crucial that a system is only adaptable to new conditions when it is near instability, "where fluctuations can reveal new development possibilities" (Haken, 2014, p. 40).

Figure 6.6 illustrates the synergetics according to the theory part in overview.

6.2.3 The Extended Synergetic Model

In order for a transfer of synergetics to the domain of entrepreneurship to be possible, the basic model of synergetics must be slightly modified or extended. While the system elements that are modeled in the natural sciences (e.g., the atoms in the laser system) have simpler structures compared to entrepreneurship and the system as such is more clearly separated from the surrounding environment, the elements considered in the entrepreneurship area are much more complicated. From an effectual perspective, partnerships, i.e., the combination of several actors at the microscopic level, form completely new elements in the system and eventually emergently new order parameters, so that the dynamics at the microscopic level in this context are much more different and complex than, for example, in the laser.

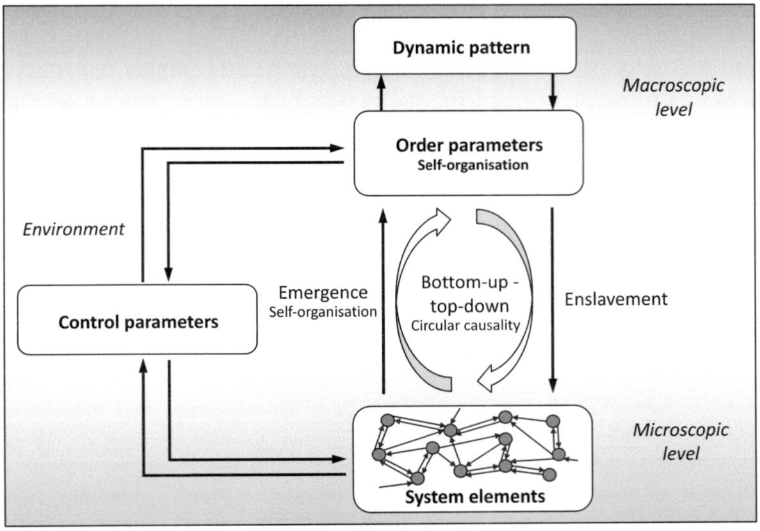

Fig. 6.6 Synergetic model. (Based on: Strunk & Schiepek, 1994, p. 27, see also: Strunk & Schiepek, 2006, p. 81)

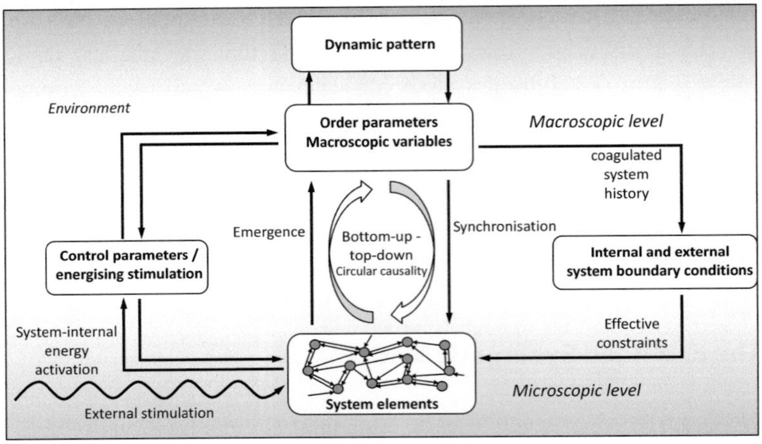

Fig. 6.7 Extended synergetics model. (Based on: Strunk & Schiepek, 2006, p. 81, see also Haken & Schiepek, 2010)

In short: If the laser already represents a complex phenomenon, then the field of entrepreneurship is even more complex.[17] The elements in the field of entrepreneurship are indeed more affected by internal and external constraints and interact with their environment to a greater extent. Therefore, the extended synergetics model by *Haken* and *Schiepek* or *Eckhard* et al. is used here, which takes into account the special influence of the environment as well as internal and external system constraints, as illustrated in Fig. 6.7 (Haken & Schiepek 2010; Eckert et al., 2005).

On the microscopic level, we find a multitude of interacting system elements. The environment represents the surroundings of the system and is highly dynamic, as it itself also consists of various self-organising systems, which in turn interact with the system on the microscopic level.

On the one hand, the environment is capable of sending stimulating signals to the system elements. It can also provide specific control parameters that are set by the dynamic conditions of the environment and activate the system elements, as well as bring about the emergence of order parameters or ultimately a new macroscopic pattern. On the other hand, conversely, the environment can be influenced or even determined by order parameters to a certain degree.

[17] Just considering a startup immediately brings the concept of complexity into play: Startups try to qualify themselves in dynamic environments. They aim to bring about innovations in the complex interplay of entrepreneurs, while significantly taking into account the constantly changing consumer and competitive conditions due to globalisation and the internet. Thus, each startup forms an open, dynamic subsystem that is embedded in a complex system environment.

In addition, the environment provides external system constraints that have a regulatory influence on the behaviour of the system elements.

Example: Potential entrepreneurs form the microscopic level, Part 1

In the case of considering potential entrepreneurs on the microscopic level, the environment could provide external constraints and even significantly influence their order parameters if it reflects, for example, the family environment or the financial basis. Possibly, these environmental conditions prevent potential entrepreneurs from initiating a startup. Alternatively, the environment, such as the family, may have the exact opposite effect, thus positively influencing the willingness to start a business. ◀

In addition to the external system constraints, there are internal constraints that are essentially based on the order parameters and the macroscopic patterns that were built up in the past. As soon as order parameters appear, they change the entire system behaviour and influence the probability of the occurrence of further order parameters in the future. This particularly increases the probability that order parameters with almost identical characteristics will occur. One can also speak of a coagulated or congealed system history, as all previously occurred order parameters are stored in the system and define the internal constraints, which in turn create the conditions for the emergence of new order parameters. The internal constraints are capable of influencing the functionality and interdependence of the system elements and determining the system framework.

Example: Potential entrepreneurs form the microscopic level, Part 2

Since potential entrepreneurs are able to exert some influence on their environment, they can also indirectly change the external constraints as imagined system elements of the microscopic level. However, these constraints change more slowly compared to the order parameter, which in turn changes more slowly than the system elements. ◀

As a final distinction from the original synergetic model (Fig. 6.6), the term 'enslavement' in the extended model is deliberately changed to 'synchronisation' (Fig. 6.7). The term 'enslavement' enslavement, which as already shown was introduced as a terminus technicus by *Haken* at the time to describe the behaviour of atoms, may provoke misleading associations in the human context. Therefore, as with *Eckert* et al., the term "synchronisation principle of synchronisation" is used (Eckert et al., 2005).[18]

[18] The renaming of the term enslavement to synchronisation is unlikely to receive *Haken's* approval. For example, Haken has clearly countered some sociologists who have criticised his concept of enslavement: "My opinion is rather contrary and has even changed over the years" (Haken, 2006, p. 25). Hermann *Haken*, who is personally acquainted with the author of this book and who has also written the foreword, may therefore forgive the author for using the term "synchronisation" here.

Up to this point, synergetics has been presented again as a theory that offers an explanatory approach to self-organisation and has been extended by some aspects that seem meaningful for the field of entrepreneurship. In the following chapters, the entrepreneurship process will now be explained as a self-organisation process in a synergetic way.

6.2.4 Basic Explanation of the Model

6.2.4.1 The Embedding of the Analysis of Entrepreneurial Founding Processes in a Multi-Level Structure

i. From the lineal phase model to the multi-level model

Let's consider the entrepreneurial process, as already mentioned, exemplarily in the context of startups. Classical business administration imagines a startup process, as we have seen, as a rather lineal process that is divided into at least four to five phases. The example of the traditional phase model illustrates this vividly, as we have seen in Fig. 6.1. It is noticeable that only the progress curves of sales and profit, i.e., two business key figures of a startup or its organisational level, are depicted. Thus, the insight into a startup process in this phase model is very limited, not only due to its lineality but also due to the limited information. However, it does provide a rough overview of the individual stages of the startup process.

But ultimately, if a "holistic"[19] , or let's say, comprehensive view of startups is to be taken, which considers both individual learning and decision-making processes, as well as specific business questions of a startup process and macroeconomic aspects of startups, it can be useful to expand or modify the traditional model in such a way that a multiperspective view can be adopted. But why is such a perspective useful?

In numerous works, *Fuller* and co-authors refer to the emergence process, which results from the interaction of different hierarchical levels (entrepreneur, company, and market) (Fuller & Warren, 2006; Fuller et al., 2004; Fuller & Warren, 2001). Also, in the

[19] The term "holistic" is put in quotation marks here because it should be used with some caution. Perhaps it should be exchanged for the term "comprehensive" for a better understanding of the above explanations, as there is a discussion of the terms "reductionism", "holism" and synergetics, with the holistic perspective being seen at the macroscopic level (Haken & Haken-Krell, 1992; Haken & Knyazeva, 2000). Thus, *Haken* and *Knyazeva* state: "Synergetics discovers universally valid laws of structure formation, self-organisation, and the evolution of complex systems and therefore belongs to the direction of universalism. It takes a mediating role between reductionism and holism" (Haken & Knyazeva, 2000, p. 21). And it continues: "While the holistic view focusses on macroscopic, unified properties of a system as the most important for our understanding of this system, the synergetic approach captures both levels, the macroscopic and the microscopic" (Haken & Knyazeva, 2000, p. 26).

context of success factor research in company startups, a traditional distinction is made between success factors at the individual, organisational, and environmental levels surrounding the companies (Gartner, 1985). *Phan* therefore rightly calls for the analysis of the startup process to be embedded in a multi-level structure that goes beyond the sole consideration of the founder person and considers the organisational and market level as essential determinants of the emergence process (Phan, 2004). Entrepreneurial activity is not exclusively limited to the creation of new companies by the merger of several founders, but also focusses on the dynamics with which companies compete with each other at a higher hierarchical level, the market level. *Phan* states:

> I see the direction of entrepreneurship research moving toward more multilevel theories on questions of emergence (Phan 2004, p. 620).

Overall, in contrast to the phase model, a multi-level model[20] is suggested, and we will examine the individual differentiations in more detail below.

ii. Three levels of startup processes

If we consider the above considerations and apply synergetics to the topic of entrepreneurship, then from a systemic perspective, *three levels* can initially be distinguished:

- the individual level
- the organisational startup level, and
- the macroeconomic market level

First Level Since we always take not only a complexity science perspective but also an economic one, regardless of the level of argumentation we are on, it is also useful here to start the structuring of the levels with a basic economic consideration: An economic perspective is initially always directed at the behaviour of individuals (as opposed to, for example, a collectivist view), as methodological individualism is one of the basic assumptions of the economic behaviour model, as was extensively explained in the first part of the book. Therefore, it is plausible that the *first* level describes the individual side of entrepreneurship.

Second Level If one focusses on entrepreneurship as exemplified here with the model to be presented, then it makes sense to include a *second* organisational founding level in

[20] It should be noted that the significance and development of models, in contrast to systems, was extensively discussed in the first part of the book in the chapter on model building and simulation of complex systems. We had there agreed with the definition of Niemeyer, who defines models as follows: "Models are material or immaterial systems that represent other systems in such a way that an experimental manipulation of the depicted structures and states becomes possible" (Niemeyer, 1977, p. 57).

the consideration, which goes beyond an individual perspective. This makes it possible to address questions that arise independently of the individual in the context of start-ups.

Third Level Finally, a successful start-up is always associated with market entry, whether start-ups take place in existing markets or even create new ones. In any case, these markets have effects and feedback on the development of a start-up and vice versa, so that a *third* explicit, especially macroeconomic consideration of the market level seems sensible.

iii. Three economic perspectives on start-up processes

These three levels outlined above can now be viewed from *three* different *economic perspectives*. If one assigns these three levels to sub-disciplines of economics, then one can identify

- an economic education perspective,
- a business economics perspective, and
- a macroeconomic perspective.

identify.

In this context, an economic education perspective can be applied to the individual level, a business economics perspective to the organisational level, and a macroeconomic perspective to the macroeconomic level.

First Perspective This assignment and division is useful because, first, the individual level is closely linked to individual economic learning and decision-making processes, as dealt with by economic education.

Second Perspective Secondly, the primary organisational founding level requires a business economics foundation, including innovative entrepreneurial methods.

Third Perspective Thirdly, the market level can be usefully viewed from an economic perspective, as such a perspective, detached from specific company issues, particularly considers markets, ranging from regional markets to global economic areas, thereby addressing questions related to the emergence of supply and demand, market equilibrium and disequilibrium, economic cycles, crises, and growth, etc.

It must be noted with a caveat that each perspective can only be 'relatively' clearly assigned to a level. Here are a few brief examples: Entrepreneurial methods can be found at the individual level in the context of entrepreneurship measures, where a business perspective can be useful. Furthermore, an economic didactic perspective could also come into play at the organisational level, as control parameters, as we will see, could include entrepreneurship education measures to stimulate the organisational founding level. A business perspective could also be helpful when considering the macroeconomic level, as, for example, growth in markets can also be viewed from this perspective.

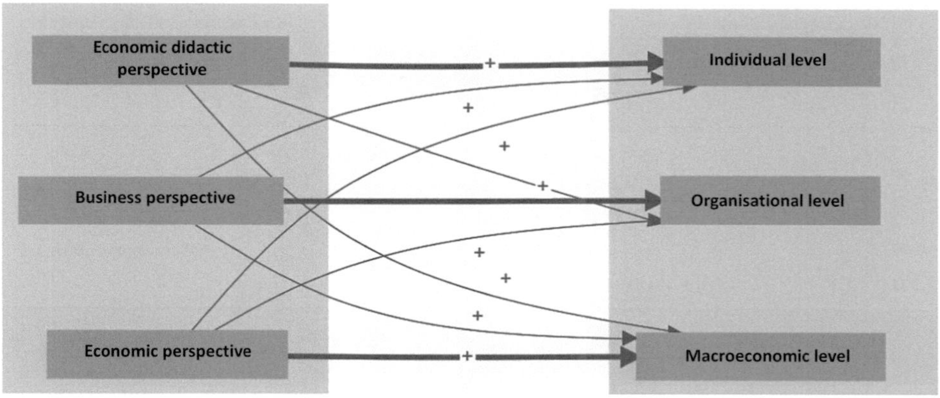

Fig. 6.8 Scientific perspectives on the three levels

The economic perspectives on the three outlined levels can also be referred to as a relation, which could be mathematically described as *bitotal* and *uniquely right*, although, as noted, other relations than those represented by the black arrows in Fig. 6.8 are conceivable.[21] They are symbolised by thin, light grey arrows.

6.2.4.2 Closer Examination of the Three Levels of an Entrepreneurial Founding Process

Figure 6.9 illustrates the individual levels from the perspective of the startup and their development over time, where the numbers on the x-axis merely symbolise the progression of time. Due to the temporal consideration, one can also speak of development lines that characterise the shares of the respective levels in the entire development process of a startup and thus add up to 100 on the y-axis.

At the beginning of a founding process, there is a possibly vague idea. The design of the concretisation of the idea initially takes place exclusively at the individual level. Therefore, the individual level also occupies the entire entrepreneurial process. As the idea matures, the organisational level comes into play at some point. What does the business model look like? Can the idea be realised? What costs are associated with the realisation? What profits can be expected? With which entrepreneurial methods can the

[21] A (binary) relation R can be mathematically defined in such a way that R reflects a relationship of elements of a set A to elements of another set B. One also writes: $R \subseteq A \times B$. R is called left total if $\forall a \in A \exists b \in B : (a, b) \in R$. R is called right total if $\forall b \in B \exists a \in A : (a, b) \in R$. R is called bitotal if R is left and right total. R is called uniquely right if $\forall (a, b) \in R \wedge (a, b) \in R \Rightarrow b = c$ (Liening, 2005a, p. 6 ff.). Note: The universal quantifier $\forall$ means: "For all …", the existential quantifier $\exists$ means: "There is (at least) one …", The symbol $\in$ means: "is an element of …" and the symbol $\subseteq$ means: "is a subset of …" (Liening, 2005b, p. 16 ff.).

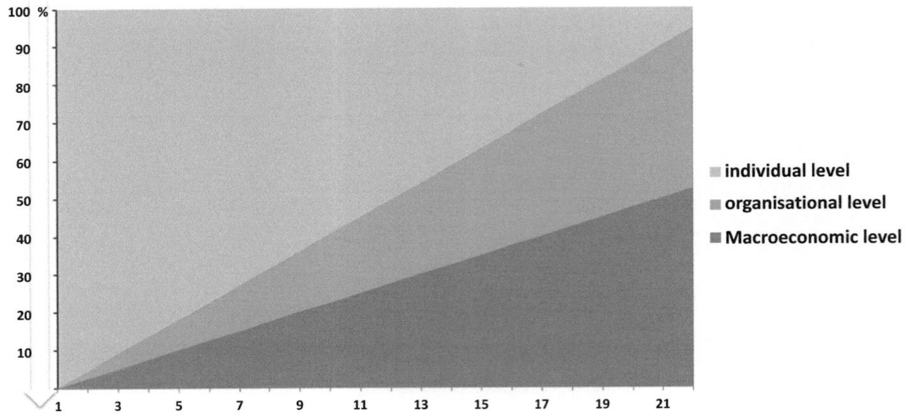

Fig. 6.9 The three levels of a linear entrepreneurial process

startup be designed? Thus, the share of the organisational level in the entrepreneurial process grows.

The more one discusses or elaborates on the business aspects, the more institutional and macroeconomic aspects are added. Can one rely on funding? What state support can be expected? What does the market or competition for the planned product look like? What is the optimal location? Is there a price binding considering the competition? How is the market developing? Are there turbulences, stagnations, growth or even decline? Market forces may increasingly affect the company. In the case of success, growth processes occur in the individual startups, which can create new markets, but can also overturn or grow existing ones.

So now the share of the macroeconomic level in the entrepreneurial process increases. At the same time, the focus on individual processes decreases, as the idea is now mature and it is essentially about implementing the idea. Adjustments to the idea are only of a marginal nature. Towards the end of the entire entrepreneurial process, the individual level only plays a subordinate role. Now it is a matter of consolidating and expanding the startup, taking into account the market economic level.

However, this classic view overlooks the nonlinear/complex processes within the levels. Therefore, a non-linear course as indicated in Fig. 6.10 would be more realistic. At the beginning, there is again the vague idea. However, while this idea is being worked out, external disturbances can already cause the individual level to be relegated in the entrepreneurial process. The cause could be new, external, previously unknown, or incorrectly assessed information from the environment regarding the costs for an item needed for the implementation of the idea, which forces, for example, the calculation of profitability to be prioritised, even though the idea is far from mature. If it turns out that this information can be taken into account, the design of the idea moves back into the foreground and the organisational aspects move back into the background.

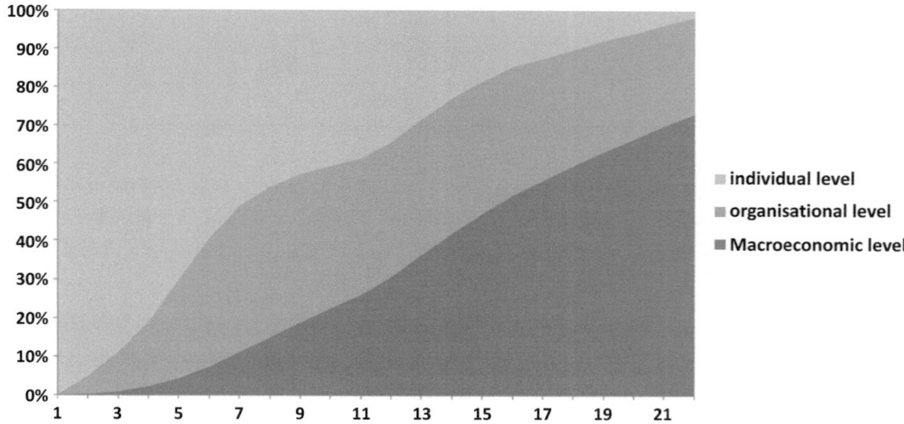

Fig. 6.10 The three levels of a non-linear entrepreneurial process

The same can also apply to the macroeconomic level. This can also be of interest earlier in time, for example, if a similar product comes onto the market during the concretisation of the idea and a market analysis is urgently necessary (increase of the macroeconomic level) to see whether the own idea could still be worthwhile (increase of the business level). Perhaps the competitive product also forces the idea to be fundamentally changed at the beginning to meet the competition, so that the individual level gains significantly in weight (increase of the individual level).

The entrepreneurial process does not necessarily have to proceed linearly in terms of the development of the individual levels. Changes to products under development, feedback loops, and setbacks may make it necessary to focus more on the individual level again, even though one is already quite far along in the organisational process.

Moreover, abrupt or sudden changes in the context of shocks or phase transitions are conceivable, as Fig. 6.11 suggests through the mathematically discontinuous and ultimately through all non-differentiable points in the development lines. A phase transition represents an abrupt change in order, which, for example, is caused by the departure of a co-founder, forcing one to suddenly take over and possibly revise the entire organisational level.

Each of these levels can also be considered from an economic perspective due to their focus, with the scientific perspectives largely correlating with the described levels.

6.2.4.3 The Economic Perspective—Three Perspectives on Entrepreneurial Founding Processes

The entire entrepreneurial process, which encompasses the three levels outlined, can be viewed and analysed from different scientific perspectives. For instance, the individual level can be illuminated from an economic educational perspective, as individual learning or educational processes are particularly prominent here. The actual founding pro-

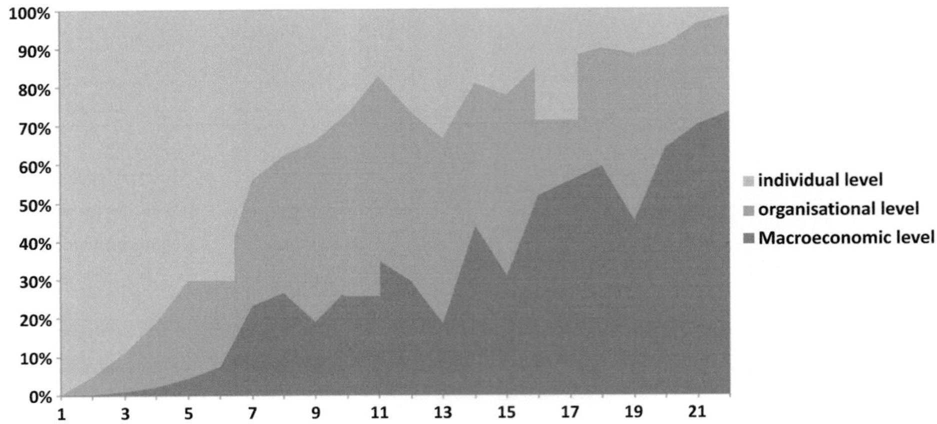

Fig. 6.11 Non-linear, abrupt course of the entrepreneurial process

cess, the second level, can be associated with an entrepreneurial business perspective, as the founding process raises essential questions about the selection and use of innovative business methods. For the third macroeconomic level, which specifically focusses on the growth process in the market, an economic perspective is particularly suitable.

Even if we ultimately have only a single entrepreneurial process from a possible first idea to generating economic growth through successful market entry, this process can still be meaningfully divided into three levels, each of which can be viewed from a different economic perspective, or as *Phan* puts it:

> Each level of analysis can be represented as a system of interdependent components (Phan, 2004, p. 619).

6.2.4.4 Three Submodels, the Multi-Level Model, and Synergetics

We want to take into account the above-outlined hierarchy in the construction of the synergetic model by mapping the three levels in three submodels. *Phan,* however, points out that a "holistic" view, which presupposes the overall embedding of the three individual levels in *one* overall model, is essential for a complete understanding. In this respect, the three submodels are also interconnected, depend on each other, and influence each other.

Such an overall picture makes sense, as, for example, one does not wait until a learning process, for instance, within the framework of a training course, is finished to initiate the actual founding process, but rather, various aspects (learning, founding, generating customers, creating growth, etc.) are consciously interwoven here.

It is therefore not surprising that *Phan,* who advocates a holistic view of several levels in an overall concept, states the following:

> Thus, entrepreneurship scholars cannot ignore the holistic and coevolutionary quality of the emergence phenomenon, even at lower levels of analyses. One cannot fully understand, for

> example, opportunity recognition as an emergence phenomenon, without being sensitive to its higher contexts—culture, institutional arrangements, and political—economic exigencies (Phan, 2004, p. 620).

Nevertheless, it should be pointed out that the three levels describe qualitatively different phenomena, which are viewed with different economic sub-disciplines. All three can be modeled using synergetics and are interconnected. However, since they are so different in content and form a hierarchy, it will be necessary to model the three levels separately from each other, taking into account the respective scientific perspective.

Based on the three outlined levels and the three economic perspectives on these levels, a multi-level model can be developed accordingly, consisting of three submodels of synergetic entrepreneurship, which are interconnected and influence each other, and are also referred to as three dimensions here.

Second Submodel Furthermore, there is a second level, namely the organisational level of a founding process, in which a multitude of decisions involving entrepreneurial business methods need to be made *(business level).* This level can therefore be viewed primarily from an entrepreneurial-business perspective. This perspective on the second level can significantly contribute to analysing and successfully shaping a complex founding process in a complex world. This level forms the basis for the second submodel.

First Submodel Firstly, there is the level that considers the individual, which follows the individual learning and action processes from a vague future idea to a concrete founding, and which particularly reflects the individual development in terms of a learning or even educational process *(individual level).* It can therefore be illuminated primarily from an economic educational perspective. This level forms the basis for the first submodel.

Third Submodel And thirdly, there is a level that focusses on the market and the growth of young startup companies in the context of complexity *(macroeconomic level).* It can be viewed primarily from an economic perspective, although, as already mentioned, business aspects can also be useful here. This level enables the third submodel.

These three submodels together form a multi-level model that is interconnected.

But why is synergetics, as one of the central theories of complex systems, so well suited to represent the individual dimensions beyond the arguments already mentioned many times? Ultimately, there is a

- synergetic and individual level Entrepreneurship Education , between
- synergetics and the organisational founding level, between
- synergetics and the market economy, in which companies compete and develop, but also between
- synergetics and the economic didactic perspective,
- synergetics and the business perspective, as well as between the
- synergetics and the economic perspective

each a *homomorphism*, a mapping that points to a structural similarity of the individual areas.[22]

This homomorphism consists in the similarities of the principles of freedom and self-determination as educational goals of an enlightened society, the self-organisation of companies in freedom and a liberal (possibly social) market economy, in which growth and competition lead to dynamic market equilibria due to self-organisation mechanisms, each associated with economic perspectives that are based on values and ideas such as freedom and self-organisation as basic categories. Viewed in this way, there are structurally no differences in relation to these basic principles between the three levels considered, associated with the respective perspectives and synergetics. This structural equality (except for the homomorphism) applies, although the elements considered of one level (e.g., an entrepreneurial learning process from the perspective of entrepreneurship education) differ from those of another level (e.g., the conditions of a perfect market from an economic perspective). This homomorphism between the mentioned levels and synergetics is ultimately another reason why entrepreneurship processes and the various levels, associated with the perspectives related to them, can be represented using synergetics.

References

Ahamat, A. (2013). *Entrepreneurial opportunity creation in the biotechnology industry in Malaysia*. University of Sheffield.

Alvarez, S. A. (2005). *Theories of entreneuship: Alternative assumptions and the study of entrepreneurial action*. Now.

Alvarez, S. A., & Barney, J. B. (2007). Discovery and creation: Alternative theories of entrepreneurial action. *Strategic Entrepreneurship Journal, 1*(1–2), 11–26.

[22]The term homomorphism originates from mathematics, which in this sense deals with mappings between two structures that are structure-preserving, and which perhaps better describe what is meant here than the term of the analogon. In the mathematical sense, one speaks of a *homomorphism* in relation to mathematical groups, if the following applies: **Definition** (Group Homomorphism): *Let G and H be two non-empty sets. With two types of connections* $(\times, \circ)$ *these sets should form mathematical groups:* $(G, \times)$ *und* $(H, \circ)$*. A mapping* $\varphi : G \rightarrow H$*is a (group) homomorphism then and only then, if for all elements x, y with* $x,y \in G$ *applies:* $\varphi(x \times y) = \varphi(x) \circ \varphi(y)$. So what is a homomorphism? A homomorphism is initially—as defined above—a term from mathematics. It describes a mapping or function between two sets, or let's say structures. The mapping completely and uniquely assigns elements from the second set to elements of the one set. The mapping is defined in such a way that it preserves structure. This means: If you find such a homomorphism between two structures, they are by no means necessarily the same, but the elements of one structure behave similarly to those of the other structure. Structurally speaking, there are no differences between the structures considered. This structural equality (except for the homomorphism) applies, although the elements of one structure can differ from those of the other structure and the respective rule for how to link two elements together can also be different in each of the structures considered.

Askari, H. (2014). *Opportunity Recognition als unternehmerische Aufgabe: Eine Analyse von Gründungschancen im Bereich der Roten Biotechnologie*. Josef Eul.

Aulet, B. (2013). *24 steps to success*. Wiley.

Baker, T., Miner, A. S., & Eesley, D. T. I. (2003). Improvising firms: Bricolage, account giving and improvisational competencies in the founding process. *Research Policy,32*, 255–276.

Baker, T., & Nelson, R. E. (2005). Creating something from nothing: Resource construction through entrepreneurial bricolage. *Administrative Science Quarterly, 50*, 329–366.

Beaver, G. (2002). *Small business, entrepreneurship and enterprise development*. Pearson Education.

Blank, S. (2009). Preparing for chaos—The life of a startup. Retrieved April 11, 2015, from http://steveblank.com/2009/04/29/startups-are-inherently-chaos/

Blank, S., & Dorf, B. (2012). *The startup owner's manual: the step-by-step guide for building a great company*. K&S Ranch.

Blum, U., & Leibbrand, F. (2001). *Entrepreneurship und Unternehmertum—Denkstrukturen für eine neue Zeit*. Gabler.

Brettel, M., Mauer, R., Engelen, A., & Küpper, D. (2012). Corporate effectuation: Entrepreneurial action and its impact on R&D project performance. *Journal of Business Venturing, 27*(2), 167–184.

Brülhart, A. (2013). *Opportunity recognistion and entrepreneurship education*. Josef Eul.

Buenstorf, G. (2007). Creation and pursuit of entrepreneurial opportunities: An evolutionary economics perspective. *Small Business Economics, 28*(4), 323–337.

Burns, P. (2013). *Corporate entrepreneurship. Innovation and strategy in large organisations* (3. Aufl.). Palgrave Macmillan.

Cantillon, R. (1755). *Essai sur la Nature du Comerce en General*. Institut Coppet.

Carland, J. W., Hoy, F., & Carland, J. C. (1988). Who is an entrepreneur? Is a question worth asking. *American Journal of Small Business, 12*(4), 33–39.

Casson, M. C. (1982). *The entrepreneur: An economic theory*. Martin Robertson.

Cole, A. H. (1959). *Business enterprise in its social setting*. Harvard University Press.

Danhoff, C. H. (1949). Observations on entrepreneurship in agriculture. In A. H. Cole (Ed.), *Change and the entrepreneur* (pp. 20–24). Cambridge.

De, D. A. (2005). *Entrepreneurship—Gründung und Wachstum von kleinen und mittleren Unternehmen*. Pearson.

De Wolf, T., & Holvoet, T. (2004). Emergence and self-organisation: A statement of similarities and differences. *Engineering Self-Organising Systems, 3464*, 1–15.

Descartes, R. (1637/1990). *Discours de la méthode*. Meiner.

Descartes, R. (1983). Abhandlung über die Methode. In A. Müller (Ed.), *Erkenntnis- und Wissenschaftstheorie* (pp. 33–46). Aschendorff.

Dew, N., Read, S., Sarasvathy, S. D., & Wiltbank, R. (2009). Effectual versus predictive logics in entrepreneurial decision-making: Differences between experts and novices. *Journal of Business Venturing, 24*(4), 287–309.

Drucker, P. (1985). *Innovation and entrepreneurship. Practice and principles*. Harper Business.

Ebbers, I. (2012). Zur Bedeutung der Entrepreneurship Eduation und der Gründungsperson an allgemeinbildenden Schulen—Eine wissenschaftsinterdisziplinäre Annäherung. In M. Schuhen, M. Wohlgemuth, & C. Müller (Eds.), *Ökonomische Bildung und Wirtschaftsordnung* (pp. 113–122). Lucius & Lucius.

Eckert, H., Schiepek, G., & Herse, R. (2005). Management Synergetischer Prozesse: Grundlagen und Ansatzpunkte für ein evidenzbasiertes Management von Veränderungsprozessen. *Zeitschrift für Systemdenken und Entscheidungsfindung im Management, 5*(2), 25–50.

Eckhardt, J. T., & Shane, S. (2003). Opportunities and entrepreneurship. *Journal of Management, 29*(3), 333–336.

Emmett, R. B. (1999). The economist and the entrepreneur. *History of Political Economy, 31*(1), 29–52.

Euler, M. (2012). Born or Made—Kann Entrepreneurship gelehrt werden? In T. Retzmann (Ed.), *Entrepreneurship und Arbeitnehmerorientierung* (pp. 66–76). Wochenschau.

Faltin, G. (2008). *Kopf schlägt Kapital—Die ganz andere Art, ein Unternehmen zu gründen*. Hanser.

Faschingbauer, M. (2013). *Effectuation—Wie erfolgreiche Unternehmer denken, entscheiden und handeln*. Schäffer-Poeschel.

Fischer, G. (2012). Effectuation, causation, and bricolage: A behavioral comparison of emerging theories in entrepreneurship research. *Entrepreneurship: Theory & Practice, 36*, 1019–1051.

Frank, H. (2009). *Corporate entrepreneurship* (2nd ed.). fakultas.wuv.

Freiling, J. (2006). *Entrepreneurship*. Vahlen.

Frese, T. (2014). *Entscheidungsfindung in jungen Unternehmen: eine empirische Untersuchung der Anwendung von Entscheidungslogiken*. Springer.

Fueglistaller, U., Müller, C., Müller, S., & Volery, T. (2015). *Entrepreneurship—Modelle, Umsetzung, Perspektiven* (4th ed.). Springer Gabler.

Fuller, T., & Warren, P. (2001). Small enterprises as complex adaptive systems: a methodological question? *Entrepreneurship & Regional Development, 13*(1), 47–63.

Fuller, T., & Warren, L. (2006). Entrepreneurship as foresight: A complex social network perspective on organisational foresight. *Futures, 38*(8), 956–971.

Fuller, T., Warren, L., & Argyle, P. (2004). Entrepreneurial foresight: A case study in reflexivity, experiments, sensitivity and reorganisation. In H. Tsoukas & J. Shepher (Eds.), *Managing the future: Foresight in the knowledge economy* (pp. 171–178). Wiley-Blackwell.

Gartner, W. (1985). A conceptual framework for describing the phenomenon of new venture creation. *AMR, 10*(4), 696–706.

Gartner, W. (1988). Who is an entrepreneur? Is the wrong question. *American Journal of Small Business, 12*(4), 11–32.

Gartner, W. (1993). Words lead to deeds: Towards an organisational emergence vocabulary. *Journal of Business Venturing, 8*, 231–239.

Gartner, W. (1995). Aspects of organizational emergence. In I. Bull, H. Thomas, & G. Willard (Eds.), *Entrepreneurship—Perspectives on theory building* (pp. 67–86). Pergamon Press.

Gibb, A. A., Eversley, J., & Ritchie, J. (1982). Aspirations and motivations of would-be entrepreneurs. In T. Webb, T. Quince, & D. Watkins (Eds.), *Small business research—The development of entrepreneurs* (pp. 47–61). Gower.

Grichnik, D. (2006). *International entrepreneurship—Entscheidungs- und Risikoverhalten von Unternehmensgründern und Venture-Finanziers in kulturellen Kontexten*. Duncker & Humblot.

Haken, H. (1975). Generalized Ginzburg-Landau equations for phase transition-like phenomena in lasers, nonlinear optics, hydrodynamics and chemical reactions. *Zeitschrift für Physik B Condensed Matter, 21*(1), 105–114.

Haken, H. (1977). *Synergetics. An introduction. Nonequilibrium phase transitions and self-organization in physics, chemistry and biology*. Springer.

Haken, H. (1982). Synergetics: Formation of ordered structures out of chaos. *Leonardo, 15*(1), 66–67.

Haken, H. (2006). Can synergetics be of use to management theory? In E. Brunner & T. Meynhardt (Eds.), *Selbstorganisation Managen. Beiträge zur Synergetik der Organisation* (pp. 19–30). Waxman.

Haken, H. (2014). *Entwicklungslinien der Synergetik. Wolfgang Tschacher. Forschungsberichte der Abteilung für Psychotherapie* (p. 14). Universität Bern.
Haken, H., & Haken-Krell, M. (1992). *Erfolgsgeheimnisse der Wahrnehmung. Synergetik als Schlüssel zum Gehirn*. Deutsche Verlags-Anstalt.
Haken, H., & Knyazeva, H. N. (2000). Synergetik: zwischen Reduktionismus und Holismus. *Philosophia Naturalis, 37*(4), 21–44.
Haken, H., & Schiepek, G. (2010). *Synergetik in der Psychologie: Selbstorganisation verstehen und gestalten* (2nd ed.). Hogrefe.
Hayek, F. A. von (1945). The use of knowledge in society. *American Economic Review, 35*(4). 519–530.
Hebeisen, W. (1999). *F. W. Taylor und der Taylorismus—Über das Wirken und die Lehre Taylors und die Kritik am Taylorismus*. vdf Hochschulverlag.
Hite, J. Jr. (2011). *Learning in chaos—Improving human performance in today's fast-changing volatile organizations*. Routledge.
Holcombe, R. (2003). The origins of entrepreneurial opportunities. *Review of Austrian Economics, 16*, 25–43.
Jacobsen, L. K. (2006). *Erfolgsfaktoren bei der Unternehmensgründung—Entrepreneurship in Theorie und Praxis*. Deutscher Universitätsverlag.
Kihlstrom, R. E., & Laffont, J. J. (1979). A general equilibrium entrepreneurial theory of firm formation based on risk aversion. *Journal of Political Economy, 87*(4), 719–748.
Kirzner, I. M. (1978). *Wettbewerb und Unternehmertum*. Mohr Siebeck.
Klapper, L. (2004). *The role of reverse factoring in suplier financing of small and medium sized enterprises*. Word Bank Policy Research Working Paper.
Knight, F. (1921). *Risk, uncertainty and profit*. University of Chicago Press.
Kriedel, R. (2017). *Systemkompetenz für Entrepreneure—Entwicklung der entrepreneurialen Systemkompetenz und eines Diagnoseinstruments*. Springer.
Kuratko, D. F., Hornsby, J. S., & Goldsby, M. G. (2011a). *Innovation acceleration: Transforming organizational thinking (Prentice hall entrepreneurship)*. Pearson.
Kuratko, D. F., Morris, M. H., & Covin, J. G. (2011b). *Corporate, innovation & entrepreneurship* (3rd ed.). Cengage Learning.
Kuratko, D. F., Morris, M. H., & Schindehutte, M. (2015). Understanding the dynamics of entrepreneurship through framework approaches. *Small Business Economics, 45*(1), 1–13.
Ladenthin, V. (2011). Kompetenzorientierung als Indiz pädagogischer Orientierungslosigkeit. *Profil, Mitgliederzeitung des Deutschen Philologenverbandes, 9*, 1–6.
Levi-Strauss, C. (1966). *The savage mind*. University of Chicago Press.
Lichtenstein, B. (2000). Emergence as a process of self-organizing—New assumptions and insights from the study of non-linear dynamic systems. *Organisational Change Management, 13*(6), 526–544.
Lichtenstein, B., Carter, N. M., Dooley, K. J., & Gartner, W. B. (2007). Complexity dynamics of nascent entrepreneurship. *Journal of Business Venturing, 22*(2), 236–261.
Liening, A. (1999). *Komplexe Systeme zwischen Ordnung und Chaos. Neuere Entwicklungen in der Theorie nicht linearer Systeme und ihre Bedeutung für die Wirtschaftswissenschaft und ihre Didaktik*. Lit.
Liening, A. (2005a). *Algebraische Strukturen*. Institut für Verbundstudien NRW.
Liening, A. (2005b). *Einführung in die Mathematik* (3rd ed.). Institut für Verbundstudien NRW.
Liening, A. (2013). Econoplexity: About the breakdown of Laplace's world view and the pretence of knowledge in economics. *Modern Economy, 4*(4), 305–319.
Liening, A. (2014). Synergetics—Fundamental attributes of the theory of self-organisation and its meaning for economics. *Modern Economy, 5*(8), 841–847.

Liening, A. (2015). *Ökonomische Bildung—Grundlagen und neue synergetische Ansätze*. Springer-Gabler.

Liening, A., Geiger, J. M., Kriedel, R., & Wagner, W. (2016). Complexity & entrepreneurship: Modelling the process of entrepreneurship education with the theory of synergetics. In E. Berger & A. Kuckertz (Eds.), *Complexity in entrepreneurship, innovation and technology research—Applications of emergent and neglected methods*. Springer Gabler.

Lorenzen, D. (2020). Unglück bei Apollo 13—Das erfolgreiche Scheitern eines Mondfluges. https://www.deutschlandfunk.de/unglueck-bei-apollo-13-das-erfolgreiche-scheitern-eines-100.html. Retrieved March 17, 2022.

Lotter, W. (2014). Wird schon schief gehen. *brandeins. Wirtschaftsmagazin, 11,* 35–44.

Luksha, P. (2009). Niche construction: The process of opportunity creation in the environment. *Strategic Entrepreneurship Journal, 2*(4), 269–283.

Lumpkin, T. G., & Lichtenstein, B. B. (2005). The role of organizational learning in the opportunity recognition process. *Entrepreneurship: Theory and Practice, 29*(4), 451–472.

Luzern, A. F. (2018). Ein Fehlschlag, der zum Lehrstück wurde. https://www.deutschlandfunk.de/unglueck-bei-apollo-13-das-erfolgreiche-scheitern-eines-100.html. Retrieved March 17, 2022.

Mainela, T., & Puhakka, V. (2009). Organising new business in a turbulent context: Opportunity discovery and effectuation for IJV development in transition markets. *Journal of International Entrepreneurship, 7*(2), 111–134.

Man, T. W. Y., Lau, T., & Chan, K. F. (2002). The competitiveness of small and medium enterprises: A conceptualization with focus on entrepreneurial competencies. *Journal of Business Venturing, 17*(2), 123–142.

Mandl, H., & Hense, J. (2004). *Lernen unternehmerisch denken. LMU- Forschungsbericht* (p. 169). Ludwig-Maximilians-Universität, Department Psychologie.

Manteufel, A., & Schiepek, G. (1994). Systemkompetenz. Orientierung und Handeln in komplexen Sozialsystemen. *Verhaltenstherapie und psychosoziale Praxis, 26*(2), 203–216.

Mitchelmore, S., & Rowley, J. (2010). Entrepreneurial competencies: A literature review and development agenda. *International Journal of Entrepreneurial Behavior & Research, 16*(2), 92–111.

Morris, M. H. (1998). *Entrepreneurial intensity: Sustainable advantages for individuals, organization, and societies*. Qourum Books.

Morris, M. H., Lewis, P. S., & Sexton, D. L. (1994). Reconceptualizing entrepreneurship: An input-output perspective. *SAM Advanced Management Journal, 59*(1), 21–21.

NASA. (1970). Detailed chronology of events surrounding the Apollo 13 accident. https://www.deutschlandfunk.de/unglueck-bei-apollo-13-das-erfolgreiche-scheitern-eines-100.html. Retrieved March 17, 2022.

Niemeyer, G. (1977). *Kybernetische System- und Modelltheorie: System dynamics*. Vahlen.

Osterwalder, A., & Pigneur, Y. (2011). *Business model generation*. Campus.

Osterwalder, A., Pigneur, Y., Bernarda, G., & Smith, A. (2014). *Value proposition design: How to create products and services customers want*. Wiley.

Osterwalder, A., Pigneur, Y., Bernarda, G., & Smith, A. (2015). *Value proposition design*. Campus.

Phan, P. (2004). Entrepreneurship theory: Possibilities and future directions. *Journal of Business Venturing, 19*(5), 617–620.

Pinochet, G. (1988). *Intrapreneuring. Mitarbeiter als Unternehmer*. Gabler.

Plattner, H., Meinel, C., & Weinberg, U. (2009). *Design-thinking. Innovation lernen—Ideenwelten öffnen*. FinanzBuch.

Retzmann, T. (Ed.). (2012). *Entrepreneurship und Arbeitnehmerorientierung*. Wochenschau.

Ries, E. (2011). *The lean startup: How today's entrepreneurs use continuous innovation to create radically successful businesses*. Portfolio Penguin.

Ripsas, S., & Tröger, S. (2015). *Deutscher startup monitor*. KPMG AG. 3.
Sarasvathy, S. D. (2001a). Causation and effectuation: Toward a theoretical shift from economic inevitability to entrepreneurial contingency. *Academy of Management Review, 26*(2), 243–263.
Sarasvathy, S. D. (2001b). *What makes entrepreneurs entrepreneurial?* (pp. 1–9). University of Washington School of Business.
Sarasvathy, S. D. (2009). *Effectuation—Elements of entrepreneurial expertise*. Edward Elgar.
Sarasvathy, S. D., & Read, S. (2011). *Effectual entrepreneurship*. Routledge.
Sarasvathy, S. D., & Venkataraman, S. (2011). Entrepreneurship as method: Open questions for an entrepreneurial future. *Entrepreneurship Theory and Practice, 35*(1), 113–135.
Saßmannshausen, S. P. (2012). *Entrrepreneurship Forschung—Fach oder Modetrend?*. Josef Eul.
Schumpeter, J. (1912). *Theorie der wirtschaftlichen Entwicklung: Nachdruck der 1. Auflage in 2006*. Duncker & Humblot.
Schumpeter, P. (1976). *Capitalism, socialism and democracy*. Harper and Row.
Shane, S. (2004). *Academic entrepreneurship—University spinoffs and wealth creation*. Edward Elgar.
Shane, S., & Venkataraman, S. (2000). The promise of entrepreneurship as a field of research. *Academy of Management Review, 25*(1), 217–226.
Strunk, G., & Schiepek, G. (1994). *Dynamische Systeme—Grundlagen und Analysemethoden für Psychologen und Psychiater*. Asanger.
Strunk, G., & Schiepek, G. (2006). *Systemische Psychologie—Eine Einführung in die komplexen Grundlagen menschlichen Verhaltens*. Elsevier—Spektrum Akademischer.
Swanson, L. A., & Zhang, D. D. (2011). Complexity theory and the social entrepreneurship zone. *Emergence: Complexity and Organization, 13*(3), 39–56.
Venkataraman, S. (1997). The distinctive domain of entrepreneurship research: An editor's perspective. In J. Katz & R. Brockhaus (Eds.), *Advances in entrepreneurship, firm emergence, and growth* (pp. 119–138). JAI Press.
Volkmann, C. K., & Tokarski, K. O. (2006). *Entrepreneurship: Gründung und Wachstum von jungen Unternehmen*. UTB.
Wales, W., Monsen, E., & McKelvie, A. (2011). The organizational pervasiveness of entrepreneurial orientation. *Entrepreneurship: Theory & Practice, 35*(5), 895–923.

The 'Synergetic Entrepreneurship Model' (SEM)

7

The real voyage of discovery consists not in seeking new landscapes, but in having new eyes.

(Marcel Proust)

Contents

7.1 The Individual Level: Focus on Entrepreneurship Education *(SEM1)* 498
7.1.1 Rough Sketch of the 'Synergetic Entrepreneurship Model 1': The Individual Level from an Economic Didactic Perspective *(SEM1)*...................... 498
7.1.2 The Elements of the System 503
7.1.2.1 Control Parameters 503
7.1.2.2 The Microscopic Level 515
7.1.2.3 The Macroscopic Level—Order Parameters...................... 516
7.1.2.4 Limitations 516
7.1.2.5 Environment 517
7.1.3 The Circular Causal Process 518
7.1.3.1 General Explanation of the Circular Causal Process 518
7.1.3.2 Order Parameters Arise through Self-Organisation and Synchronsation—The Importance of Phase Transitions 520
7.1.3.3 *'Nudges'* Can Support the Emergence of Appropriate Order Parameters that Favour a Justified Entrepreneurial Attitude................ 524
7.1.3.4 Measuring Complexity for Targeted Initiation of *'Nudges'* 526
7.2 The Organisational Level: Focus on Entrepreneurial Founding Processes *(SEM2)* 527
7.2.1 Rough Sketch of the 'Synergetic Entrepreneurship Model 2': The Organisational Level from a Business-Entrepreneurial Perspective *(SEM2)*............. 527
7.2.2 The Elements of the System 528
7.2.2.1 Control Parameters 528
7.2.2.2 The Microscopic Level 529

A. Liening, *Complexity and Entrepreneurship*,
https://doi.org/10.1007/978-3-658-44032-9_7

7.2.2.3 The Macroscopic Level—Order Parameters . . . 530
7.2.2.4 Limitations . . . 541
7.2.2.5 Environment . . . 542
7.2.3 The Circular Causal Process . . . 542
7.3 The Macroeconomic Level: Focussing on Market, Business Cycle, and Growth *(SEM3)* . . . 543
7.3.1 Rough Sketch of the 'Synergetic Entrepreneurship Model 3': The Macroeconomic Level from a Predominantly Economic Perspective *(SEM3)* . . . 543
7.3.2 The Elements of the System . . . 550
7.3.2.1 Control Parameters . . . 550
7.3.2.2 The Microscopic Level . . . 550
7.3.2.3 The Macroscopic Level—Order Parameters . . . 551
7.3.2.4 Limitations . . . 552
7.3.2.5 Environment . . . 552
7.3.3 The Circular Causal Process . . . 553
7.3.3.1 Business Cycle . . . 553
7.3.3.2 Dynamic Growth . . . 554
7.3.3.3 A Growth Model with Endogenised Human Capital Formation—Transmission Effects through Entrepreneurial Attitude . . . 561
7.4 Fourth Conclusion: Synergetic View of Entrepreneurship from Multiple Perspectives . . . 566
7.4.1 Brief Summary of the *SEM* Model and the Theories and Views Behind It . . . 566
7.4.2 *SEM1*—The Individual Level: Entrepreneurship Education as a Self-Organising, Complex Process . . . 570
7.4.3 *SEM2*—The Organisational Level: StartUp Foundations as a Synergetic Process Involving Specific, Ordering Business-Economic-Entrepreneurial Methods . . . 571
7.4.4 *SEM3*—The Macroeconomic Level: StartUps Support the Macroeconomic Growth Process through an Entrepreneurial Transmission Effect . . . 571
References . . . 572

7.1 The Individual Level: Focus on Entrepreneurship Education *(SEM1)*

7.1.1 Rough Sketch of the 'Synergetic Entrepreneurship Model 1': The Individual Level from an Economic Didactic Perspective *(SEM1)*

After an understanding of the underlying theories of entrepreneurship, and especially in the previous parts of the book of complexity and synergetics, has been developed, these theories are now merged into an entrepreneurship-synergetics model and presented, whereby we want to focus exemplarily on the topic of founding as one of the central entrepreneurship areas for the entrepreneurial area, as emphasised several times. However, it should not go unmentioned that especially the first of the three perspectives to be considered, which is illustrated by the so-called *SEM1,* has general validity with regard to entrepreneurship and is not only suitable for founding processes.

Through the 'Synergetic Entrepreneurship Model 1' new insights for the field of entrepreneurship, especially for the understanding of individual entrepreneurial learning

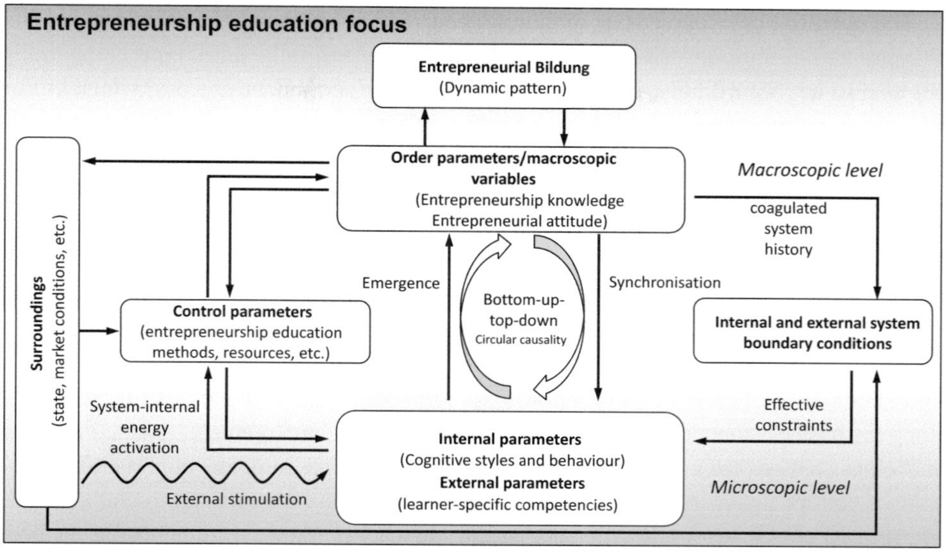

Fig. 7.1 The 'Synergetic Entrepreneurship Model 1': The economic didactic dimension of individual learning *(SEM1)*

processes and how such processes should be designed, could be derived (see Fig. 7.1). The fact that we start here with the *SEM1,* i.e. the individual perspective, and do not put the founding of the start-up, which is discussed in the *SEM2,* at the beginning, is not only due to a potentially chronological sequence, i.e. that every founding process ultimately starts with an individual decision. Rather, this is ultimately due to an economic view, which is also reflected in the entrepreneurial way of thinking, or as *Sarasvathy* formulates:

> The view from entrepreneurial expertise, however, turns the spotlight on the performance of the *entrepreneur,* sometimes in harmony with, sometimes in opposition to, the performance of the *firm* (Sarasvathy, 2009, p. 14).

While in some traditional readings the entrepreneur is seen as a means of founding and growing companies, from an entrepreneurial perspective the firm is rather the means (Sarasvathy, 2009, p. 14).[1]

[1] This view, by the way, as already mentioned, is in line with the basic economic behaviour model, which is based, among other things, on methodological individualism, which puts the individual and not a collective at the centre of consideration. Furthermore, *Sarasvathy's* focus on the entrepreneur also means that founding a company is just one way to act as an entrepreneur: "Firms are one way for entrepreneurs to achieve their aspirations. In other words, an instrumental view of the entrepreneur gets replaced by an instrumental view of the firm" (Sarasvathy, 2009, p. 61).

The potential development to an entrepreneur, of entrepreneurship knowledge and an entrepreneurial attitude, which includes the ability to not only think entrepreneurially, but also to act accordingly, is the result of a possibly permanent process, which culminates in an entrepreneurial education, or more aptly expressed with the difficult-to-translate German word: *Bildung*.

▶ **Entrepreneurship knowledge** We understand entrepreneurship knowledge to be those areas of knowledge that are linked to the topic of entrepreneurship. This includes traditional business knowledge areas as a basis and, very importantly and centrally, the newer entrepreneurial knowledge areas. The entrepreneurship discipline focusses on the latter.

In addition to the canon of classical business knowledge areas[2], which can be structured along the business functions (such as business management, procurement, production, sales, financing, storage, etc.), the entrepreneurial methods are of immense importance for the field of entrepreneurship, as they provide innovative possibilities for successful entrepreneurship processes beyond traditional business approaches. These entrepreneurial methods include, as already mentioned and examined in more detail later, the 'Customer Development', the 'Design Thinking' , the 'Business Model Canvas', the 'Value Proposition' or, for example, the 'Lean StartUp' approach. Since, as already mentioned, these newer methods in particular constitute the core of entrepreneurial insights, one could focus the area of entrepreneurship knowledge particularly on the associated entrepreneurial knowledge.

In this context, it must be considered that the above-mentioned knowledge areas enable one to make individual, situation-dependent, open to the future, sustainable, etc., and particularly appropriate decisions in the context of entrepreneurship. However, this also presupposes that one believes the insights gained to be true, i.e., can represent them from

[2]Traditional business knowledge areas include, for example, in the area of founding, basic insights into business management, which encompass the planning, control, and monitoring of companies. Furthermore, insights into the choice of a company's legal form, accounting and balance sheet analysis, cost accounting, marketing, logistics, and business performance indicators (systems), 'Balanced Scorecards' as well as traditional management techniques are among the basic business knowledge areas that are particularly relevant for founding issues (Wöhe & Döring, 2013).

Each of these areas includes interesting sub-areas. For example, in cost accounting, traditional full cost can be distinguished from partial cost or standard cost and process cost accounting, and newer cost accounting methods such as 'Target Costing' or 'Active Based Costing' are increasingly playing an important role. In management techniques, traditional creativity methods such as brainstorming, method 635 or the morphological method can be distinguished from decision-making techniques, utility analyses, cost comparison calculations, ABC or SWOT analyses or 'benchmarking'. In this context, basic business knowledge also includes, for example, knowledge management, which includes methods such as knowledge maps, 'Communities of Practices', 'Lessons Learned', 'Story Telling' or scenario techniques and also provides newer methods, such as knowledge accounting (Liening & Mittelstädt, 2008). Specifically, from a traditional business perspective, in the context of start-ups, additional areas, such as the creation of business plans, are added.

a rationally justified conviction, and is also capable of making not only appropriate but also 'correct' decisions. The question of the individual significance of a situation plays an important role here. The associated answer to the question of which solution is now the individually 'correct' one, however, cannot be answered within the knowledge of entrepreneurship due to the claim of value-free judgement of science. Science shows me what I can *do,* but not what I should *do!* The question of this should requires the ability to make value judgements and moral judgement ability[3] and in the context of start-ups, a canon of characteristics and behaviours commonly referred to as 'Entrepreneurial Spirit', entrepreneurship mentality, entrepreneurial mindset or entrepreneurial spirit. To find a common language, the term entrepreneurial attitude is used.

▶ **Entrepreneurial Attitude** Entrepreneurial attitude is defined here as a (valuing) attitude towards entrepreneurship knowledge, which makes it possible to claim validity for the knowledge on a rationally justified basis. Entrepreneurial attitude is the prerequisite for acting appropriately and responsibly at the same time in entrepreneurship contexts.

An entrepreneurial attitude therefore presupposes, on the one hand, that one believes in entrepreneurship knowledge. Believing in something means that one can largely rationally and intersubjectively justify the entrepreneurship knowledge and reorganise it for oneself against the background of one's own previous knowledge, experiences, and attitudes. This belief is closely linked in the context of attitude with valuing something, which on the other hand presupposes the ability to make value judgements, but also moral judgements, which in turn are the basis of responsible action. If both (believing in, valuing) apply, one is able to adopt an attitude towards entrepreneurship knowledge. This attitude is reflected in whether one considers one's own, newly ordered entrepreneurship knowledge to be so significant that one is able to articulate a claim to validity for this knowledge. An entrepreneurial attitude is shown, for example, in the willingness to take initiative, in the urge to shape, in conscious risk-taking, in high frustration tolerance and great perseverance, in the ability to criticise, in assertiveness, in creativity and the joy of creative shaping, but also in the acceptance of uncertainty and complexity.

This kind of attitude is finally also reflected in the ability to live principles of entrepreneurial expertise with conviction. Such principles also serve as the basis for the effectuation approach and are as follows:

[3] Ability to make value judgements means valuing and evaluating and thus being able to make judgements and decisions. Moral judgement ability ultimately means not deciding and acting based on any traditional values, but on a rational justification considering morality and ethics in a situation-specific manner. We use a definition of morality that ultimately refers to the result of rational evaluations in terms of validity-claiming determinations of meaning that is realised in action, thus showing a dynamic emergence process in the sense of theories of complex systems (Liening, 2015b, p. 149 ff.).

- *Bird-in-hand principle:* The starting point for decisions are the means, not the goals. Entrepreneurs start with their means.
- *Affordable-loss principle:* Before initiating a process, entrepreneurs define what they are willing to invest. This not only concerns financial aspects, but also time and effort.
- *Crazy-quilt principle:* Entrepreneurs continuously negotiate with their stakeholders. They do not stick to their first idea, but rather look for ways to make the best of their resources.
- *Lemonade principle:* Instead of avoiding contingencies and coincidences, they are appreciated by entrepreneurs. Surprises are therefore seen as an opportunity to get the idea moving.
- *Pilot-in-the-plane principle:* Entrepreneurs keep the process under control. They rely on facts that drive the entrepreneurship process, rather than relying on and exploiting external factors such as technology or socio-economic trends (Sarasvathy, 2009, p. 15 f.).

In this context of the discussion about knowledge and attitude, if one looks at entrepreneurship *Bildung* from an educational theory perspective, the question arises as to when one can consider a learner to be entrepreneurially "gebildet". By the way, there is no really good translation for the German word "Bildung" into English, where one speaks of "education", or into French, where one speaks of "formation". Both only touch on the meaning of the German concept of *Bildung* to a limited extent.

But what is meant by entrepreneurial *Bildung*? Well, the answer to this question is not, as one might suspect, that someone is educated if they have acquired a firmly defined canon of (fact) knowledge. Actually, the answer has already been given, so we can summarise here:

▶ **Entrepreneurial Bildung** A person can be described as entrepreneurially *gebildet* if they are able to design founding projects, but also entrepreneurship processes within established companies, with a high degree of independence, appropriately, responsibly, and confidently for themselves and others under uncertainty with moderate but determined risk-taking.

Entrepreneurial Bildung is thus reflected, for example, in the willingness to take initiative, the joy of creatively shaping opportunities, and openness to change as well as the willingness to take responsibility for oneself and others. These characteristics of entrepreneurial Bildung are important far beyond the mere founding process. Entrepreneurial Education is therefore not a measurable, firmly defined canon of knowledge components that someone has acquired. Rather, it is about the individually answerable question of the possibility of successfully shaping one's own life in the context of entrepreneurship processes by being able to act appropriately and responsibly at the same time.

If the goal of such thought-out entrepreneurship education is to familiarise as broad an audience as possible with entrepreneurship, because the associated entrepreneurial attitude is considered necessary and sensible for a successful life, then all educational measures begin with the support of generating that attitude associated with the entrepreneur. Whether this ultimately results in a founding process cannot be predicted in advance, but such measures can enable a climate of entrepreneurial thinking and action, which ultimately forms the basis for a successful founding process. Entrepreneurial Bildung ultimately includes the already described entrepreneurship knowledge and an associated entrepreneurial attitude. For this Bildung to emerge, it is necessary for the individual to access the technically sensible toolkit as far as possible and to recognise it as correct for themselves. Only then can they give validity to their ideas with a corresponding claim; only those who are convinced of something themselves can also convince others.

The complex entrepreneurial learning process associated with knowledge and attitude, which can culminate in dynamic entrepreneurial Bildung, can be explained by the theory of synergetics. As presented, the theory of synergetics differentiates between control parameters, order parameters, macroscopic and microscopic levels, the environment, and system constraints.

If one models the individual Entrepreneurship Education process based on this theory, the process begins with an external activation, which is realised, for example, by a motivating *Business Game*[4] (Control parameter). This impulse ignites an undirected change process in the learner (microscopic level), which (in the best case) leads to the emergence of an entrepreneurial attitude (macroscopic level). It is important to consider that the control parameter stimulates an unspecific process at the microscopic level. Therefore, it is impossible to predict the result of such a process at the macroscopic level in advance. The only way to influence the emergence process is to carefully configure the control parameter. In the case of Entrepreneurship Education measures, the goal is to bring about the corresponding entrepreneurial Bildung, which we have already discussed, and which includes both the area of knowledge and the area of attitude (Order parameter). For a deeper understanding, each part of the *SEM1* (see Fig. 7.1) is explained in detail in the following section.

7.1.2 The Elements of the System

7.1.2.1 Control Parameters

Control parameters can be individual and group-specific. However, the focus here, as already explained in this chapter, is on the individual person. In the case of Entrepreneurship Education (EE), the entrepreneurship learning parameters (Control parameter) can aim to address various aspects such as knowledge, motivation, or the individual's attitude.

[4] The 'Business Game' in particular allows, due to its playful and simultaneously simulative character, to actively simulate start-ups, to put oneself in the concrete role of a founder or founding team, to generate a start-up, to accompany and shape it through initial highs and lows, to play through various scenarios and to understand and experience founding experiences in many ways, without any real dangers arising.

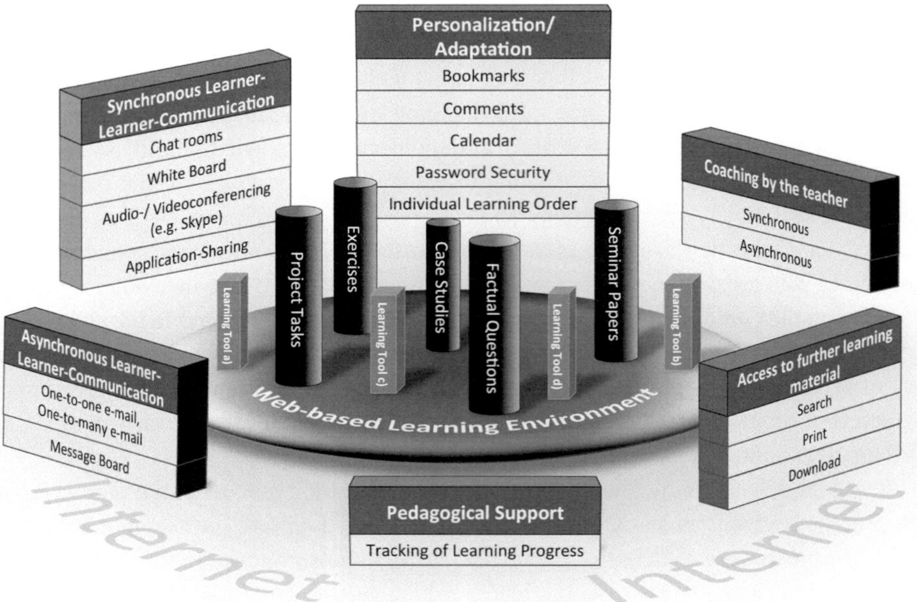

Fig. 7.2 Multimedia learning environment as control parameter

To function as a synergetic control parameter, the economic-didactic methods with which one wants to enable synergetic, entrepreneurial learning must create an incentive situation that offers the learner the opportunity to engage educationally with the entrepreneurship content. In fact, there are a number of very proven economic-didactic methods that support learning in this sense (Liening, 2015b; Young & Sexton, 1997; Euler & Hahn, 2007; Hindle, 2002; Fayolle & Gailly, 2008). These methods include, for example:

- Case Studies *(Case Studies)*
- Business & Simulation Games *(Business & Simulation Games)* and
- Classroom Experiments *(Classroom Experiments)*

These methods can be embedded in a multimedia learning environment, in which content learning tools and a variety of communication tools are provided, which also support collaborative learning, as illustrated in Fig. 7.2.[5]

[5] In the context of cooperative learning forms, all forms that are associated with "Web 2.0" are gaining in importance. "Web 2.0" can be illustrated with the expression "living internet" because the users actively shape, influence or even produce the content, instead of just "surfing" as before. In addition, "Web 2.0" stands for a new generation of users who largely move their everyday life

While case studies, for example, consider real cases, we are faced with two methods, *Business & Simulation Games* and *Classroom Experiments,* that enable learning in virtual or so-called micro-worlds. We have already discussed virtual and micro-worlds in detail in the first part of the book in Sect. 3.4 against the background of why they are particularly useful for understanding and analysing complex systems. We therefore want to briefly consider the above-mentioned methods due to their fundamental importance.

i. Case Studies

Let's start with the ***case study method*** (English *Case-Study-Method*) in reference to the works of *Liening* and *Paprotny* (Liening & Paprotny, 2005). The case study represents a possibility for motivating an entrepreneurial attitude and generating corresponding knowledge under the regulation of self-organised learning (Moog, 2001, p. 14).

What is a case study? A case study assumes a fundamentally exemplary situation that corresponds as closely as possible to reality and contains an economic problem. This should then—in the classic *Case-Study-Method*—be found, defined, and analysed for solution approaches by the learners themselves. Accordingly, alternative solutions should be allowed.

Variants of case studies In total, in addition to the classic *Case-Study-Method,* several basic variants of case studies can be distinguished, as shown in Table 7.1.

Use of Case Studies in Entrepreneurship Education Group work is suitable for solving a case study, within which the learners should make a meaningful and well-justified decision for problem-solving. For this, the groups receive more or less extensive situation descriptions, which contain information for problem analysis, problem synthesis, and decision-making. In this process, the learners go through a process that can ideally be divided into several phases (Liening & Paprotny, 2005, p. 7 f.).[6]

---

and professional life to the internet. The most important applications of "Web 2.0" are: Online communities, WIKIs (e.g. WIKIpedia, WIDAWIKI), virtual worlds (e.g. Second Life was very popular for a while), newsfeeds (e.g. RSS), blogs, podcasts, social tagging, folksonomies (Liening, 2010).

[6]A case study can be divided into six phases. They are:

i) In the *confrontation phase,* the learners are presented with the initial situation of the economic problem. Traditional situation descriptions in text form, supplemented by tables, diagrams, cartoons, etc., usually dominate here.

ii) At the beginning of the *information phase,* working groups are formed. The situation description and additional information are analysed in the groups to evaluate the presented problem situation and to create the prerequisite for a well-founded decision.

Table 7.1 Basic variants of case studies

Variant	Short description
Case-Study-Method	This is the classic form of the case study, where the focus is on the analysis of not immediately visible problems. The underlying situation descriptions often present very extensive cases that bundle and provide the necessary information for problem analysis, problem synthesis, and decision-making
Case-Problem-Method	This variant has a similar structure to the 'Case-Study-Method' with the difference that the problem does not have to be found but is given. Using the provided information, solution variants for the given problem are determined and a decision is made
Case-Incident-Method	This is a very time-consuming but very practical variant of the case study, where the case is only incompletely presented and the situation description does not contain all the necessary information for problem-solving. The focus is therefore on independent information research to support the decision-making process
Stated-Problem-Method	Unlike the aforementioned variants of the case study, no problems and solutions need to be defined. The problem, relevant information, and problem solution are given and put up for discussion. By carefully presenting both the process and the structure of the decision situation, learners should get as realistic an impression as possible and be encouraged to criticise the decision made and/or show alternative solution projections

This phase model results in the ideal-typical process of a case study, but it does not necessarily have to underlie every case study. With regard to the basic variants shown in the table above, the phases do not necessarily have to run in the order listed. In addition, some phases can be particularly short or very detailed, or even skipped (Liening & Paprotny, 2005, p. 8).

---

iii) In the *exploration phase,* the learners in their groups try to systematise, evaluate, and synthesise the provided information material and possibly the results of further research activities to show solution calculations for the evaluation of the advantages and disadvantages of different solution alternatives and to make an assessment.
iv) The end of the exploration phase marks the resolution phase, in which the participants make and justify a decision.
v) Depending on the basic variant, the case study can also include a disputation phase: If the groups have come to different results or decisions, the groups can present and defend their solutions in plenary. The discussion can be rounded off by bringing together the individual perspectives or by making a final decision.

vi) If a decision made in reality is available and accessible, the *collation phase* can optionally stand at the end of the case study processing, by presenting the original solution and comparing it with the group solutions (Liening & Paprotny, 2005, p. 7 f.).

Selection of Case Studies From the teacher's perspective, some criteria must be met when selecting the case study. For example, the presented case should reflect the complexity of a real start-up situation (situative representation). It should be ensured that the case does not contradict the scientific theories and models (scientific representation). In addition, the teacher should put themselves in the learners' position: Does the described case address the current and future entrepreneurial action situations (subjective significance)?

It should also be considered whether the case is tangible for the learners or whether it is too complex and therefore needs to be reduced (subjective comprehensibility).

Advantages and Disadvantages of Case Studies Like any method, the case study method also has advantages and disadvantages. Let's first look at the advantages:

The case study method addresses the already hinted entrepreneurial competence dimensions, such as *strategy formulation to seize opportunities perceptively,*. The technical competencies can be improved insofar as theoretical specialist knowledge and practical manifestations are related to each other. The learners jointly take responsibility for the results of the group work, thereby strengthening their social competence. Within the case study method, in addition to the actual method—the case study method itself—other methods can also be used. For example, the presentation of the results can take place as a role play, in which different positions are represented and defended, thereby promoting the ability to handle various methods confidently. Furthermore, the learners strengthen their decision-making ability and their argumentation skills. In addition, it is possible to differentiate within the tasks in the context of the case study method. Thus, learners can be individually promoted according to their level of knowledge. Depending on the extent to which the information for processing the case study is provided, other media can be used, for example in the form of independent internet research. This also gives the learners impulses for exploring facts. The case study method thus corresponds to a "modern" understanding of educational measures and is considered suitable for entrepreneurship education for the reasons described.

What are the disadvantages of this method? In addition to the very labour-intensive and time-consuming preparation for the teacher, one disadvantage certainly lies in the risk of overburdening the learners. Case studies deal with complex relationships and it can sometimes be difficult to adequately reduce the level of abstraction of the tasks. Moreover, the method is not suitable for all phases of a learning phase, as depending on the level of difficulty, a high level of prior knowledge is necessary, so that a case study can only be placed at the beginning of a longer, topic-related learning phase to a limited extent.

Developing Case Studies Anyone who wants to develop their own case studies must take into account a multitude of things. Traditionally, one follows the *'Harvard Business Method',* but here the *'Sherman Method'* is recommended, which, unlike the *'Harvard Method',* places value on the so-called 'Teaching Notes', which are particularly important for the design of a successful synergistic entrepreneurship education using case studies.[7] Regarding the 'Teaching Notes', which are intended to serve as inspiration for the developer, Herbert *Sherman* writes:

> Some teaching notes include a role-playing exercise and have the students enact their solution to what the students believe is the problem the case is highlighting. Others will use debate or game show formats, case related films, invite guest speakers to discuss the case, of even have a case analysis competition using outside judges. Some teaching notes include exercises related to the case epilogue, sort of a mini Part A/Part B case while others provide guidance for using the case as a take-home exam or an individual or group project (Sherman, 2004, p. 22).

ii. Business Games (Business & Simulation Games)

Next, we want to take a closer look at the simulation game method , a central economic didactic method for entrepreneurial teaching/learning processes, based on the explanations of *Liening* and *Kirchner* from the numerous *gaming* methods[8] . It also represents a possibility for entrepreneurship education under the regulation of self-organised learning (Liening & Kirchner, 2011).

> Tell me and I forget, show me and I remember, let me do it and I understand (Confucius, 551–479 BC).

---

[7] The renowned CASE Journal, co-edited by Herbert *Sherman,* is recommended reading for the interested reader. Information about this can be found on the website of the corresponding CASE Association (www.caseweb.org).

[8] In the context of didactic gaming methods, different types are distinguished: Adventure games are interactive computer and video games in which learners, for example, have to solve tricky missions and tricky cases. They are primarily developed by the gaming industry for the entertainment sector, but the didactic potential of such games is increasingly being recognised.

• In the context of *strategygames,* learners, for example, have to put themselves in the role of creating entire civilisations, the welfare of which depends on the ability to drive economic development, for example. Behind games that resemble a historical classic, complex economic simulations are often hidden.

• Furthermore, there are *computer-assisted role-playing games* that immerse the individual in a virtual world in which he or she takes on the role of individual game characters. For example, there are games that allow you to take on the role of the central bank president, who is to determine the monetary policy of a country in difficult times, or the federal chancellor, who with his economic policy should try to combat the tense situation on the labour market, etc. The design of characters and the assumption of roles are in the foreground.

• And finally, there are the *computer-assisted simulations* and *business games* that allow, for example, the management of a football club or the running of a production company to be as realistic as possible. Here, the *rule-based* game is crucial. Thus, in English, the term *game* is distinguished from *play,* the latter term specifically referring to the rule-free game. Originally conceived as on-site games, the internet is increasingly being used to, for example, compete globally against and with each other in the competition of simulated markets as part of *business games* (Liening, 2010).

The above quote shows that a fundamental motivation of business games, namely to strengthen the understanding of complicated learning content through active engagement, is based on a very old idea. Business games are not a new invention: as early as 3000 BC, there were primitive forms of the business game in China. These business games took on a very formal and abstract character over time. It is suspected that the game of chess originated from such business games (von Reißwitz, 1824).

Despite their long tradition, business games have not lost their relevance. On the contrary: rarely has the importance of entrepreneurship business games been as great as today, where the multimedia possibilities of new media (e.g. computer, tablet, smartphone and internet) offer a new dimension of this didactic approach, which enables learning especially in *virtual* start-up worlds with all their advantages (see in detail: first part of the book, Sect. 3.4.4).

In recent years, a trend towards internet-based learning and gaming can be observed. To enable learners to experience media-rich learning processes, computer-based business games are increasingly being used. In this context, new media offer unprecedented possibilities to comprehensively and interactively depict reality and integrate it into computer-based business games. The synthesis between business games and new media represents a promising connection (Liening, 2010).

Focus of the business game method Computer-based business games support the synergetic learning process. They offer the opportunity to imitate the activities of an entrepreneur in the sense of *genetic learning* (Wagenschein, 1975) to find assumptions, generalisations and specialisations. As in "real" life, the learner can embark on an entrepreneurial journey of discovery (*discovery learning* [Bruner, 1972]): Since the lecturers or the authors can present and formulate a well-defined learning environment, he can, for example, initiate a founding process without having to go through all the wrong turns and temporal dimensions of reality. This gives the learner the opportunity to perceive entrepreneurship not as a kind of "secret science" whose insights fall from the "sky", but as an exciting scientific discipline in which one can participate in the gain of knowledge by "re-discovering" it (Moog, 2001, p. 13).

The trend in economic didactic discussion is moving from pure theory reference to the integration of application orientation. With the help of computer-based business games, much more complex issues can be illustrated than would be possible with paper, ballpoint pen or book. For example, in the field of entrepreneurship, computer-based simulations can be used profitably to illustrate complex founding processes.

When using computer-based business games, learning content is acquired creatively and exploratively, not simply passed on, which is of immense importance for the attitude of an entrepreneur who discovers or creates opportunities. This type of learning is very much in line with the widely spread constructivist worldview of a strong intra-individual, self-created mental reality.

Business games, which are designed as computer-based simulation software, prepare better for practice than would be possible without the use of computer-based algorithms. On the one hand, learners can acquire more cross-content qualifications, such as capturing data series, interpreting environmental events, etc. On the other hand, the use of computer-based business games can contribute to promoting characteristics and behaviours, such as rationally justified risk-taking, responsibility, creative behaviour and ability to criticise, which are considered important aspects of entrepreneurial thinking and action, on a permanent basis (Liening et al., 2012; Auchter & Keding, 2004).

Learning cognitive strategies requires affective dispositions. Computer-based business games enable the achievement of affective goals such as self-confidence and self-esteem, and thus also the further development or consolidation of an individual-entrepreneurial personality structure of the learner. The learner is not guided, but can work out his knowledge himself with the help of the computer to solve practical tasks. The ability to work in a team, defend solutions, and practice and accept criticism is also promoted by this approach, as team work is supported by the possibilities offered by computer-based business game environments, which are essential for the successful founding of start-ups, for example.

General Information on the Method Compared to traditional business games, the inclusion of the medium 'computer' allows for a more detailed and complex replication of reality (Liening, 1999). This is made possible by using a mix of various modern media (such as videos or voice output) as well as the realistic replication or integration of applications or tools from everyday business life. For the representation of reality, it is necessary that the learners can move as freely as possible in an interactive decision-making space. This promotes that the participants can better identify with the role assigned to them, e.g. as an entrepreneur, and ultimately better understand and internalise the decisions and their effects on the environment simulated in the business game. In this way, learners can be adequately and practically prepared for complex situations in everyday business life.

Computer-based business games also pose risks. In an attempt to replicate the game situation as realistically as possible, the game developer strives to integrate as many variables, dependencies, and information into the game as possible. In this way, a 'black box' can emerge for the participants. Then, reflection and transfer of insights from the model to reality are hardly possible anymore. Instead, it is desirable to integrate the model assumptions into the business game in a comprehensible way for the learners (Capaul, 2009, p. 11). Accordingly, the target group and the intended learning objectives must be taken into account in the construction. The higher the performance of the group, the more accurately reality can be depicted without overwhelming the participants.

Example: Campus Career Competition—a computer-based business game

In the business game 'Campus Career Competition—CCC', up to six business years of a startup founded three years ago are simulated, which is in the process of establishing itself as a young growth company in the market. Three to five participants each take on the role of the company's board of directors, prepare a multitude of decisions and implement them. The teams are provided with information media such as an e-handbook, various 'association announcements' and current local and economic policy news, with the news being offered online as media-prepared *podcast* broadcasts. The respective chairman of the board enters the decisions made by the company management at the end of a business game year via an internet interface into a virtual 'management cockpit' via PC, tablet or smartphone, which transmits the data to the business game server. The associated computer software takes over the evaluation of the decisions and calculates their influences on the game situation. The analysis and result calculation takes into account the decisions of competitors, potential customers interested in the offered goods, as well as the general economic situation, which is sometimes characterised by turbulence in the labour market, changes in economic conditions, government interventions, etc. The results can be accessed via a web browser. In this way, several virtual years with 'ups and downs' are experienced and shaped. While at the beginning of the business game the formulation or further development of the respective business model as well as the formulation of operational, but also strategic goals are in the foreground, at the end of the business game a detailed evaluation and reflection of the decisions and the results of the individual game phases is crucial. ◄

Procedure of a computer-based business game Computer-based business games can be divided into three main phases: the introduction, simulation, and reflection phase. During the introduction phase, the lecturer presents the business game and the underlying model.

This is followed by the simulation phase, in which the learners carry out the business game. This phase begins with the analysis of the situation and the identification of the problem within the individual groups. For this purpose, the groups have appropriate information materials or possibilities for information procurement (e.g. via the internet) at their disposal. Subsequently, within the groups, there is an exchange of information, the search and consideration of decision alternatives, and finally the decision-making process. The decisions are entered into the computer programme of the business game. These inputs are evaluated by the computer and the consequences of the group's decision are communicated through corresponding computer outputs. Within the group, a reflection of the results of the business game period then takes place. Further business game rounds can then follow the same pattern.

After going through the scheduled business game rounds, the results and insights are reflected in the final reflection phase in the plenary.

Organisation of a computer-aided business game As a result of the computer taking over administrative tasks, the teacher, in the synergetic sense of a control parameter, assumes the role of a coach or moderator. In this role, they guide the learners through the three main phases: introduction, simulation, and reflection (Capaul, 2009, p. 8).

Due to the ever-increasing proportion of multimedia-intensive computer games (games) in the everyday life of learners, there is a risk that learners within the business game make decisions intuitively and hastily, enter them and do not reflect on them. At the end of the business game, the learners would have completed the game, but would not have understood the sense and purpose, nor reflected on their decision-making processes (Blötz, 2003, p. 21). Even if one follows an effectual concept instead of a causation approach, which relies on causality and planning, this by no means implies a 'muddling through', as we have already seen. Therefore, while it is significant to let the group dynamic processes run self-organised in the individual phases, a targeted reflection of the decisions made and their effects should take place after the business game. If problems arise within these group dynamic processes, the teacher must provide advisory support. Then, the use of the computer enables the promotion of self-organising activities. Such simulations often lead to radical changes in the way reality is understood, as we have already quoted *Sterman* (Sterman, 2000, p. 38).

Thanks to the computer programme's logging of input data and actions, and possibly keeping an individual learning diary that reflects and justifies the decisions after each business game phase, the lecturer can precisely evaluate the individual approach of the learners. This way, he can give the learners targeted, detailed feedback on their performance. In many programmes, learners are given feedback directly after the business game or even during the run. The *'Learning Feedback'* is thus accelerated and intensified.

In addition, the teacher is relieved by the automatic calculation of the results and the automatic exclusion of invalid entries by the participants. This gives him more time to supervise the learners. Overall, the administrative effort of teachers in computer-aided business games is significantly lower than in conventional business games, as many tasks are independently taken over by the business game programme.

In addition to the introduction to the computer-aided business game, the implementation and reflection, the teacher also has to consider many organisational things to successfully use computer-aided business games in the learning process:

- Are there licence rights that need to be considered?
- What system requirements and capacities does the business game require (technical and infrastructural conditions)?
- What is the existing media competence of the group (handling computers, internet etc.)?
- Are there accompanying materials that are not provided by the computer and are these necessary (manuals etc.)?
- Is the business game played offline or online?
- How many computers/tablets/smartphones are needed for implementation?
- Is there a possibility that groups can work on one or more computers and still exchange information without disturbing other groups?
- Can the learners handle all the information provided by the computer-aided business game, or does this need to be limited?
- Are there storage options within the individual game rounds?
- How much time is needed for the meaningful implementation of the computer-aided business game?

In conclusion, it can be stated that computer-aided business games are particularly well suited to enriching entrepreneurship education and making it more practical. They can depict complicated or even complex relationships, and in particular real-life processes, such as the design of a founding process, and simulate them in a learning environment to prepare learners as best as possible for practice. However, it must be considered that computer-aided business games can only depict sections of reality under certain aspects and criteria. Through the role as a coach, the teacher is able to support the learners individually. The automatic evaluation by the computer can also relieve the lecturer.

Computer-aided business games or *Business & Simulation Games* thus represent a future-proof synergetic method for learning, which can make learning processes interesting and cover a wide range of entrepreneurship content.

iii. Economic Experiments ('Classroom Experiments')

The challenges associated with the claim of self-organised learning can be met, for example, by focussing on *"EconomicExperiments"*, also referred to as *"Classroom Experiments"* in the context of learning processes. They are intended to contribute in a theory-guided, experimental, and exploratory way to enabling learners to engage creatively and self-organised with entrepreneurial issues, either individually or in a team (Perote et al., 2016).

However, economics as a whole (apparently) belongs to those sciences where experiments are rarely used. If one were to follow the common argument, the following could be asserted: The lack of experiments in economics is due to the fact that economics, i.e., business practice, has a high complexity that is difficult to reproduce through simple, controlled experiments. Furthermore, there are numerous exogenous shocks that significantly influence economic processes and that elude control in the form of experiments. Thus, economic phenomena are often only comprehensible, if at all, through very time-consuming experiments. Furthermore, for these very reasons, financial considerations often stand in the way of such experiments. Therefore, neither economics nor the corresponding entrepreneurship education measures belong to the experimenting domains (Schuhen & Weyland, 2011, p. 390; Liening, 2015b, p. 130 f.).

A key argument for these theses could be formulated in comparison with other sciences as follows: Unfortunately, in economics, it is not like in *Newtonian* Physics , where an apple (assuming knowledge of its circumference, weight, etc.) always falls to the ground with exactly calculable acceleration and speed as soon as it detaches from the tree.

However, looking at the past years, it is noticeable that despite the difficulties described above, experiments are increasingly being conducted in economics. Nobel Prizes have even been awarded for topics in experimental economics, so the topic is not as marginal as the above argument might suggest. Pioneers such as Daniel *Kahneman* who, together with Amos *Tversky,* made significant contributions to modern Behavioural Economics (Kahneman & Tversky, 1979).*Kahneman* received the Nobel Prize in 2002. The Nobel Prize was also awarded in 2002 to Vernon *Smith,* one of the most important representatives of experimental capital market research, who, inspired by the first experiments of his teacher Edward *Chamberlin,* developed further market experiments (Smith, 1962, 1975). One can also refer to Reinhard *Selten,* who already received the Nobel Prize in 1994 together with John F. *Nash* and John C. *Harsanyi* for groundbreaking contributions in game theory (Selten, 1965, 1982).

Their models of behavioural economics, decision-making or Game Theory are significant foundations and contributions to the field of Experimental Economics.

Therefore, it is not surprising that for several years now, the use of economic experiments has been increasingly recommended for learning processes, not least to utilise the aspect of "discovery journey" inherent in this method. With their help, it can be possible to integrate theoretically demanding economic topics into the learning process in a playful, experimental way (Gremmen & Potters, 1997; Becker & Watts, 1998; Jacobs, 2010).

In Germany, Hans-Jürgen *Schlösser* and his team from ZöBiS, the Centre for Economic Education at the University of Siegen, are leading in the field of "Economic Classroom Experiments" (see, for example, Schlösser et al., 2009 or Schlösser & Schuhen, 2011).

Economic experiments can be implemented using miniature systems. This allows experimental groups to trade with each other, participate in auctions, invest in simulated stock markets, shop in Potemkin businesses, or experimentally explore start-up situations, and ultimately act in a variety of situations (Beinhocker, 2007, p. 87). Accordingly, learners can study various economic and especially entrepreneurial behaviours as an experimental group themselves or as observers of experimental groups (Perote et al., 2016).

Regarding the peculiarities of economic experiments, which are characterised by uncertainties in the course and the result compared to simple physical experiments, *Schlösser* formulated in an interview as part of the project "Entrepreneurial Spirit into Schools" supported by the Federal Ministry of Economics:

> When you participate in an economic experiment, it's like being invited to dinner with cannibals. You don't know exactly whether you are part of the guests or part of the meal. You only find out during the course of the evening (Schlösser, 2014).

When experiments in the real system are unfeasible, ultimately experiments in real micro-worlds or simulations or role-playing games in virtual worlds are the only way to learn how complex systems work. An extreme alternative is rote learning (*rote learning*), which is based on the authority of the lecturer and the authority of the material, as *Sterman* rightly notes (Sterman, 2000, p. 38), and has little in common with self-organised learning aimed at entrepreneurial Bildung. *Perote, Vincente-Loerente* et al. rate the 'Classroom Experiments' for Entrepreneurship Education overall as an "interesting tool for teaching purposes", stating that the following characteristics can be achieved with 'Classroom Experiments':

> (…) autonomous learning, skills linked to the labour market and entrepreneurial activities, and continuous evaluation of knowledge and competencies (Perote et al., 2016, p. 12).

iv. Further Control Parameters: Motivation and Resources

In addition to such methods as described above, there are a multitude of other conceivable control parameters that can set appropriate incentives. Examples of these are *motivation* and *resources.*

Motivation The motivation of the individual can be promoted by lectures from people who have already founded a company (de Dios & Montero, 2003). Through their experiences (successful or not), the individual gets first-hand information about the field of entrepreneurship and the theoretical input becomes lively. In addition, the individual gets the opportunity to ask questions and get in touch with founders. Other motivational aspects can be addressed by awarding prizes or issuing performance points or grades for successful participation in an Entrepreneurship Education programme. This does not automatically lead to a better learning outcome, but a stronger confrontation with the topic takes place by achieving a higher goal (Liening et al., 2016).

Resources Through the availability of resources, such as rooms (for meetings or external collaboration), financial resources for creating or conducting *Business Games, Case Studies, Economic Experiments* or even for testing and producing products or services like the 'minimum viable product approach', as well as through consultations (to get advice for one's own idea), the potential entrepreneur obtains low entry barriers to attempt to start entrepreneurship processes (Liening et al., 2016).

The two areas mentioned are examples of further control parameters in the *SEM1.* The methods proposed earlier therefore also deal in particular with the knowledge aspect as an activation point, which triggers the emergence process of a corresponding attitude and ultimately an entrepreneurial Bildung (order parameter). Especially through the mixture of control parameters, such as the mentioned didactic, motivational and guiding resources, the individual is confronted with a larger number of entrepreneurship impulses (microscopic level) and the permanent occurrence of new order parameters becomes more likely.

7.1.2.2 The Microscopic Level

In the *SEM1,* the learning individual (the microscopic level) represents the system with its elements. Two aspects must be considered at the microscopic level: On the one hand, this includes the individual's prior knowledge, experiences, and cultural perspectives. On the other hand, it is learning and cognitive styles that determine how the individual acquires new knowledge, experiences, and cultural references. Each individual has different cognitive styles and cognitive behaviours (Riding & Rayner, 1998). Therefore, the control parameters must take into account that each individual is in different initial situations. Especially for an educational process, it is important to know how homogeneous or heterogeneous learning groups are in order to choose learning parameters accordingly (Liening et al., 2016).

7.1.2.3 The Macroscopic Level—Order Parameters

At the macroscopic level, the entrepreneurship education process aims to enable the individual to receive entrepreneurial Bildung. Through the control parameter(s), the constitution of the individual at the microscopic level changes. New information and experiences influence the old macroscopic pattern. Depending on how strong the old pattern is, new patterns emerge through the self-organisation process and compete with each other until one wins and dominates the other patterns. This means that new knowledge, experiences, or resources are considered with the understanding of the new pattern. Even if the resulting dominant, dynamic pattern, the emerging entrepreneurial Bildung, cannot be predicted, the appropriate use of learning parameters (control parameters) and external stimulations should increase the chance that an entrepreneurial Bildung is developed, which then becomes visible through entrepreneurial actions of the individual in various contexts (Liening et al., 2016).

The order parameter 'entrepreneurial attitude' can be considered as the gateway to the domain of entrepreneurship. An entrepreneurial attitude shows the reasoned acceptance and a deep understanding of the basics of entrepreneurship theory. A person who exhibits this attitude *knows* not only how to act, for example, according to the principles of entrepreneurial expertise, which also serve as the basis for the Effectuation approach and which we have already discussed (Sarasvathy, 2009, p. 15 f.), but is also *convinced* by them.

The necessary entrepreneurship knowledge as an order parameter shows that the corresponding technical expertise is present. Both order parameters can together only give the dynamic pattern of entrepreneurial Bildung.

For other people, the newly acquired entrepreneurial Bildung becomes visible, for example, when the people in the learning process apply methods and tools such as the Lean StartUp approach or the principles mentioned above. If the entrepreneurial attitude and the entrepreneurship knowledge are the active order parameters, then all new actions are synchronised by these parameters (see Fig. 7.1) (Liening et al., 2016).

It is obvious that there is not only *one* entrepreneurial attitude or *one* entrepreneurship knowledge. There can be infinitely many manifestations, depending on time, situation, and location with very different focusses, which appear as order parameters. Through didactically cleverly designed control parameters, there is the possibility that an entrepreneurial Bildung crystallises as a dynamic pattern, which takes into account the complexity and dynamics of an entrepreneurship process and deserves the designation 'Bildung'.

7.1.2.4 Limitations

There are two types of limitations, internal and external, that influence the system elements of the individual and often have a stabilising effect. The internal limitations consist of the coagulated system history. During a phase transition, the probability that patterns that have already emerged in the past will reappear is higher than the probability that other patterns will occur. Therefore, old patterns, such as perhaps linear understandings of a founding process that the individual has already learned, compete with new patterns that have arisen through influences of the current control parameters at the microscopic level. In addition, external constraints, such as a low number of credit points for entrepreneurship courses, a poorer reputation, poor grades, or high demands on employees in the market, influence the system elements at the microscopic level (individual).[9] Therefore, the control parameters, like the constraints, influence the microscopic level and thus the emergence of the order parameters (Liening et al., 2016).

External limitations, institutions, interaction processes, building architecture, etc., as well as the internal limitations, are difficult to change. Nevertheless, they can be influenced in the long term by the order parameters of the individual.[10] For the internal limitations, this means that due to newly developing patterns, more (and more suitable) patterns are available and the historical coagulated patterns lose importance. External constraints can also change due to long-term effects of entrepreneurial Bildung. For example, if entrepreneurs who have an entrepreneurial attitude have a good reputation within society, more people will want to become entrepreneurs themselves. This then also increases the demand for entrepreneurship courses. This results in a change in external constraints, such as an increase in the number of offered entrepreneurship courses, as the courses are more strongly supported by the public sector (Liening et al., 2016).

7.1.2.5 Environment

The environment encompasses several aspects, the commonality of which is that the individual cannot directly influence them. Although it is possible for these aspects to change over time, this process does not occur in the short term and is particularly not *directly* influenceable in the *SEM1* process. The environmental aspects must therefore be taken into account in the short term and treated as a given (Liening et al., 2016).

Examples of environmental aspects could be the public sector, organisations, and legal regulations. Overall, the environment represents all parts that are not within the individual's system (microscopic level) and that do not belong to the control parameter of the *SEM1,* but have an indirect or direct influence on the microscopic level. Thus, framework conditions, such as those affecting the education system, also play an important role. According to the German StartUp Monitor 2014, 81.2 % of German startup founders have successfully completed a degree (Ripsas & Tröger, 2014, p. 25). The 2015 study states:

---

[9] External constraints could further be divided into physical (such as financial resources) and non-physical (such as cultural characteristics) elements.

[10] *Neumann-Cosel* even considers it possible that constraints or boundary conditions can be based on order parameters and that the system can set these from within itself (von Neumann-Cosel, 2006, p. 154 f.).

> However, according to the founders, the German (university) education system has numerous deficits in terms of promoting and imparting entrepreneurial thinking and action (Ripsas & Tröger, 2015, p. 54).

Such statements suggest that, for example, the 'education system' as an environmental size could have a significantly greater positive influence on the willingness to found and the foundations themselves through modification of the curricula and other activities. Hardly any university sees itself as a founding university, and even in the context of the upstream school system of high schools and comprehensive schools, there has been a socio-political dispute for decades about the introduction of a 'business' subject, let alone that the topic of 'business ownership' or even entrepreneurship would be comprehensively addressed in further education schools (Liening, 2014).

7.1.3 The Circular Causal Process

7.1.3.1 General Explanation of the Circular Causal Process

After the various parts of the *SEM1* process have been explained, the comprehensive sequence of the model will be explained below. First of all, it is important to recognise that initially the only point at which lecturers could intervene within the *SEM1* process is the control parameter. This implies that there is initially no possibility of predicting which pattern or which order parameter will occur at the relative macro level.

We had already pointed out in the first part of the book (Sect. 3.4.4) that the distinction between 'single-loop-' and 'double-loop-learning' emphasises the preserving and stabilising aspect of learning processes (Argyris & Schön, 1978). It is initially most effective for an unhindered maintenance of the status quo if a *single-loop* is first used to respond to errors. *Single-loop-learning* is based on the basic assumptions and beliefs that have been successfully used in the past. Here, solutions for emerging problems are sought first. Each individual has a different starting situation (knowledge, attitude, motivation, and experience).

Only when these corrections are not sufficient, a *double-loop-learning* is initiated, in which important basic assumptions and beliefs that one has had so far become the subject and are changed if necessary. Therefore, it is important to provide a wide range of entrepreneurship learning parameters (control parameters) that allow the individual to question his previously acquired knowledge, his motivations and experiences, which represent the individual at the microscopic level and form the basis for the development of an order parameter at the macroscopic level. Questioning proven basic assumptions threatens central pillars of the previous, so such learning processes are sometimes only carried out against internal resistance. Because through the coagulated system history (old developed patterns in the individual) it is likely that new knowledge, new attitudes, new experiences will be evaluated by the old, already learned patterns. For example, a person who has already developed an understanding of entrepreneurship based on business plans instead of business models, on predictions instead of control, and on market research instead of Lean StartUp, will use these old patterns and not necessarily accept new patterns or supplement the old patterns with new aspects. Due to the coagulated system history, the chosen entrepreneurship learning parameters (control parameters) must therefore be well thought out and address as many aspects as possible at the individual level, so that a new mentality, a new attitude, can be stimulated and can emerge.

The questioning of previous order parameters by the individual influences the microscopic level, old patterns lose their validity and suddenly a new pattern develops, which, in the case of *SEM1,* for example, goes hand in hand with an entrepreneurial attitude.

Figure 7.3 illustrates as in the first part of the book the 'single-' and 'double-loop-learning' inherent in the circular causal process.

In the self-organising circular causal learning process shown, a new, emergent and dynamic structure emerges in the sense of synergetics and with the processes explained in its description, which can be described with the term entrepreneurial education. The associated entrepreneurship knowledge and the corresponding entrepreneurial attitude represent the order parameters in the synergetic sense, which order the multitude of individual pre-judgements, individual pre-knowledge, attitudes and opinions and help to a individually rationally justified understanding of entrepreneurship and its processes.

This dynamic structure of entrepreneurial Bildung is stimulated and enabled within the framework of a self-organising feedback process depending on the incentive situations, which are designed by the changeable control parameters (learning arrangements). Since the control parameters are also subject to feedback processes, they are constantly questioned and redesigned by the entire *SEM1* process, which ultimately, if successful, represents an educational process.

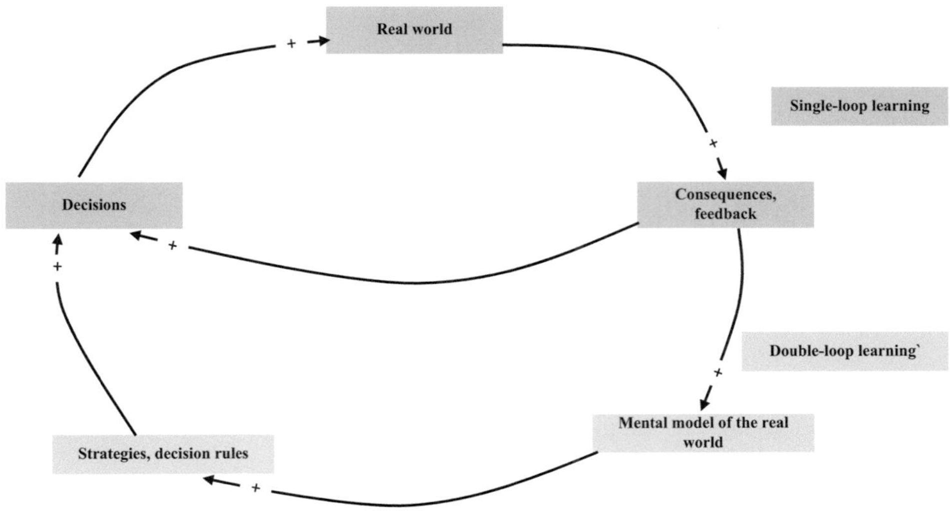

Fig. 7.3 Double-loop-learning. (Based on: Sterman, 2000)

7.1.3.2 Order Parameters Arise through Self-Organisation and Synchronsation—The Importance of Phase Transitions

The dynamic pattern of each individual's entrepreneurial education, which includes knowledge and attitude, is visible in the synergetic model at the macroscopic level as an order parameter in the form of entrepreneurship knowledge and an entrepreneurial attitude, by stimulating emergence and synchronisation processes at the microscopic level through the corresponding economic-didactic learning arrangements given by the control parameters, starting from pre-knowledge, pre-judgements, etc.

The transition from one state to another stable state, which ultimately contributes to the formation of order, can be vividly characterised in synergetics, as outlined in the second part of the book in Sect. 4.5, using the model of a ball rolling in a valley, and can be referred to as a *phase transition*.

We want to apply this image to entrepreneurship education and consider a simple example from the field of knowledge. To visually embed incorrect prior knowledge, which changes and leads to appropriate knowledge, into the synergetic concept, we use the image of the ball outlined above in the following example.

Example: Learning Business Models, but how?

The goal in the learning group is for each learner to know the concept of the business model and to understand the associated content by being able to differentiate it from other terms such as business plan, name examples, and apply it.

If all learners already had a technically correct understanding of what a business model is and why it is so valuable for the entrepreneurship process, the corresponding course for learning the content and use of business models would be unnecessary. Therefore, we exclude this case and assume that no one can specifically explain the idea and purpose of business models in the context of entrepreneurship. Of course, the synergetic process would also work if there were learners who had a correct understanding of business models and their application. But for the sake of simplicity, we also exclude this case in order not to have to discuss too many case distinctions. Thus, in the extreme case, there are only two cases:

Either everyone has a different (wrong) idea (case a) or everyone has the same, but wrong idea of business models and their significance (case b).

In case a), where everyone has a different or no idea, we find, from a synergetic point of view, only 'white noise' at the microscopic level, or—if we think of the example with the laser—white light (see Fig. 7.4). The state of the system 'knowledge about business models' would be maximally complex, as each learner believes to know something different. The answers to the question of what a business model is are therefore random and there is no order for this prior knowledge in the learning group.

In case b), a highly ordered system of prior knowledge would exist, although this pre-instructional knowledge would also be wrong.

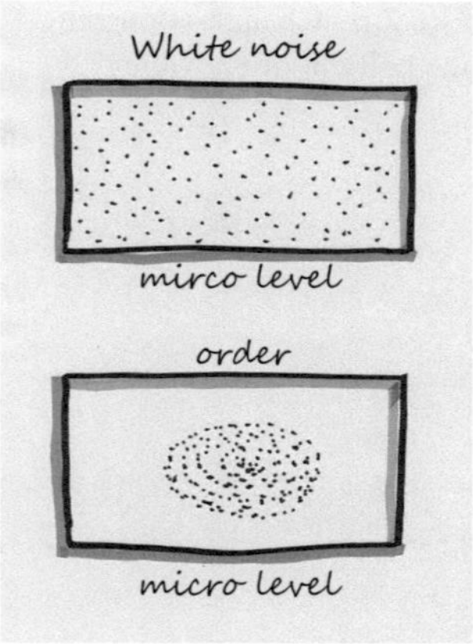

Fig. 7.4 'White noise' versus 'order': Microlevel

In practice, one would probably have a combination of the two cases.

Now let's consider any learner from the learning group. His knowledge is represented by a ball that is in a valley (see Fig. 7.5). This is meant to describe that the learner's prior knowledge can indeed be described as stable, albeit stably wrong. This means that other opinions do not quickly lead to giving up one's own ideas.

If one wanted to change the state of the ball, one would have to move the ball out of the stable valley with a lot of energy (see Fig. 7.6). This could happen by the teacher explaining the correct definition and the content to the learners. But as soon as this energy is removed, i.e., the teacher does not constantly insist on the application of this concept and motivates the learners to deal with it, the ball inevitably rolls back (see Fig. 7.7). We have already described this clinging to concepts once recognised as correct for oneself in both the first and second part of the book with the term *hysteresis*. This is a physical system inertia that we find in pattern formation also in our brains ('cognitive set'). The behavioural economist would speak here of "status quo bias". ◀

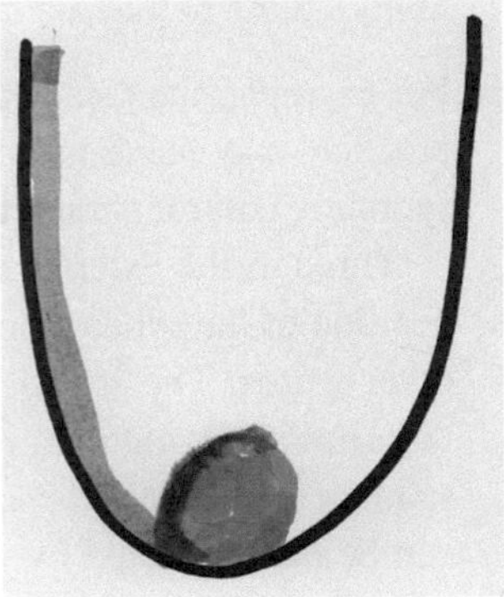

Fig. 7.5 Stable situation—'ball in the valley'

Fig. 7.6 Change—'pushing the ball out of the valley'

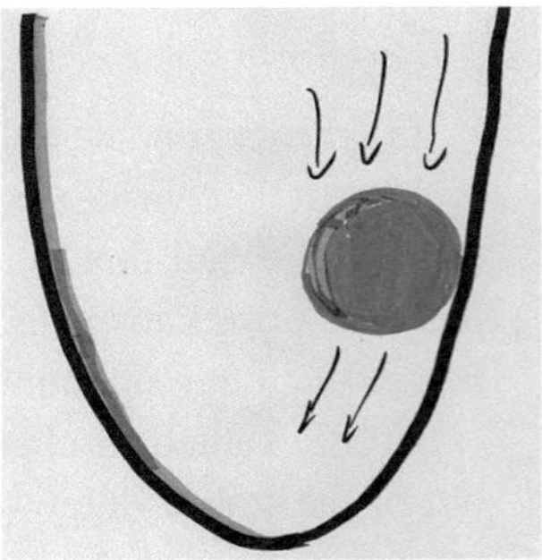

Fig. 7.7 Change—'Without permanent energy supply, the ball rolls back'

How can the sphere described in the above example be moved without having to constantly add energy from the outside? How can incorrect prior knowledge be sustainably changed into professionally correct knowledge from a synergetic perspective?

This is where the control parameter comes into play. The control parameter changes the sphere's environment as an external stimulus. However, it does not move the sphere itself.

Continuation of the example: Learning business models, but how?

For example, the use of a case study that describes the topic of business models in a practical way using a successful example of a founding process could act as a corresponding control parameter on the learning group.

Through the external stimuli, i.e., the active engagement with the case study, the position of the sphere can become unstable, i.e., the prior knowledge is questioned. In other words: The stability of the previous behaviour pattern gradually decreases. At the same time, external influences become more important. The system loses its old stability and becomes more and more a plaything of its environment. This behaviour can be demonstrated by an increase in complexity and is referred to as *critical fluc-*

tuation. At some point, the valley turns into a mountain and the sphere has the choice to roll down in any direction. The direction in which the sphere rolls can be triggered by a minimal disturbance. The flap of a butterfly's wing, one could say with reference to the 'butterfly effect' in complex systems, may be enough to make the sphere roll in one direction or another. Once the sphere has rolled down, it takes up a stable position in the next valley, which, with the right choice of case study and well-thought-out tasks, includes a comprehensive understanding of business models and their importance for entrepreneurship processes, as illustrated in Fig. 7.8. ◀

The above example makes the following clear: Through a learning arrangement that is based on the attempt of pure transmission of knowledge instead of rational reasoning and critical questioning, on rote learning instead of understanding and penetrating, etc., the sphere of prior knowledge and also of pre-judgements (if one wants to add the aspect of entrepreneurial attitude here) is indeed brought into another position desired by the teacher. However, this type of learning or teaching has nothing to do with self-determination, with one's own insight and knowledge, i.e., with sustainable learning and education. This is also immediately noticeable in that, after the course on the topic is over, after a short time many learners have forgotten everything or at least refrain from consistent application. The sphere rolls back into the initial situation. Here the 'status quo bias' is at work.

However, if the described economic-didactic methods are used as synergetic control parameters within the framework of entrepreneurship education, a situation is created that finds the 'sphere' on a mountain again. Where the sphere rolls, however, and this is the unsatisfactory thing about synergetics in relation to learning processes, is not really clear.

Through repeated synchronisation (circular process of the *SEM1*), combined with emergence, an understanding of business models crystallises among the learners in relation to the above example, which pushes aside all other ideas of business models. This *one* understanding *'enslaves'* the others in a synergetic sense and thus becomes the order parameter.

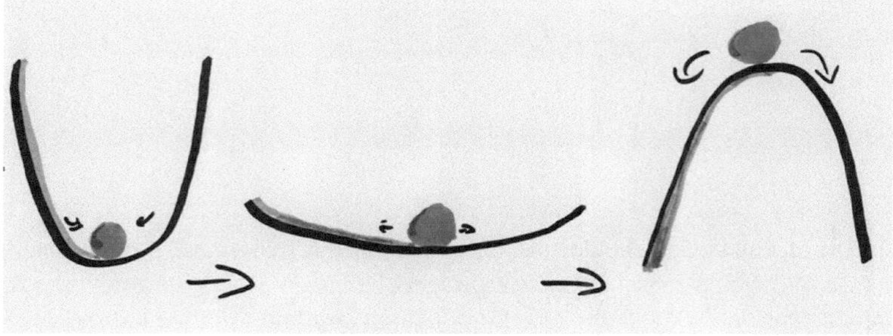

Fig. 7.8 Phase transition

Fig. 7.9 Phase transition—'Nudges'—Butterfly effect

Whether the order parameter that arises accordingly reflects the technically correct conception depends very much on how the control parameter possibly reacts to change processes and how it is possibly readjusted. Synergetics does not see the need for an additional intervention here, as it merely describes how self-organisation processes lead to the formation of order. It can therefore be described as value-free. Whether the resulting order parameter 'entrepreneurship knowledge about business models' is technically correct or not is therefore not decided by the fact that this knowledge has manifested itself as an order parameter. One could also say: The formation of order in synergetics is blind to the 'truth', or less pathetically formulated: The formation of order is content-neutral.

7.1.3.3 *'Nudges'* Can Support the Emergence of Appropriate Order Parameters that Favour a Justified Entrepreneurial Attitude

Within the context of Entrepreneurship Education, one cannot accept the blindness described above, as the goal is precisely to offer individuals the opportunity to explore as much as possible the technically sensible toolkit and to recognise it as correct for themselves. Therefore, the teacher has the responsibility to ensure that the rationally developed chains of argument do not drift into arbitrariness. If no other assistance as a control parameter seems possible, the teacher should trigger the butterfly effect, which occurs one way or another, through their commitment due to the impossibility of a final justification[11] as symbolically sketched in Fig. 7.9.

[11] Every element of knowledge should, insofar as it is meant scientifically, be rationally causally justified. In case of doubt, a causal chain of arguments builds up, which, however, can find no final end, since no one can seriously claim something like an absolute truth for themselves. Therefore, there is no final justification for any knowledge, at most a provisional justification or in case of doubt a commitment, or more neutrally formulated: an axiom. Only ideologies or religions provide

By consciously changing the control parameter with the purpose of giving learners the opportunity to act appropriately and responsibly, it does not in any way—and this is important—cause a manipulation of the learners. In an unstable state, a small nudge, a 'Nudge', is enough to point in the right direction. At this point, reference is made to the discussion of the concept of *'libertarian paternalism'* as used by Richard *Thaler*-Cass *Sunstein* et al. (Thaler & Sunstein, 2012; Neumann, 2013). They make it clear why 'Nudges' are not an exercise of force.[12] With the ideas of *Thaler* and *Sunstein*, the

something like a final justification. The sciences, but also democracies, lack the irrefutable 'true' starting or ending point, which is why ideologies such as Marxism are always argumentatively advantageous compared to liberal concepts, such as a democracy.

[12] Let it be repeated at this point: The obvious problem is that from an economic point of view, there is no real qualitative difference between paternalism (ultimately an exercise of force) and *libertarian* paternalism, as *Thaler* and *Sunstein* would have us believe. Ultimately, both those who favour paternalism and those who act as representatives of libertarian paternalism only manipulate prices by, for example, changing transaction costs. Consider the example of an American company that offers its employees health insurance that can be renewed annually by consent on the intranet. To promote the retention of insurance coverage at the end of the year, the company could now reverse the process so that the insured would have to actively cancel the insurance at the end of the year to lose coverage. This change in booking conditions is the 'Nudge', the push, intended to encourage employees to keep the supposedly sensible insurance. They still have the freedom of choice as before, but in the new situation, employees no longer need to take action to maintain insurance coverage. This increases the likelihood that the insurance will remain in place, as the act of canceling is more cumbersome than not having to act. Thus, given preferences, the behaviour of the actors changes, although the alternatives (insurance yes/no) remain the same.

If the state, for example, were to ban cigarette consumption for the sake of public health (this would then probably be strict paternalism), transaction costs and thus prices would increase enormously, as demanders would have to switch to a black market or this would first have to be established, but would also be established. In any case, paternalism also has alternatives, only the cost and thus price changes are possibly significantly higher compared to libertarian paternalism. The actual difference between paternalism and libertarian paternalism is therefore quantitative, not qualitative in nature. Therefore, it is difficult to draw a clear distinction between paternalism and that libertarian paternalism, between coercion (here: by the lecturer) and lightly nudged self-determined decisions, as suggested by libertarian paternalism. One could, for example, take a look at transaction costs to locate the boundary between libertarian and non-libertarian paternalism: Whenever the transaction costs of all alternatives change relatively, but, viewed absolutely, remain constant, libertarian paternalism would be present. But whenever the *absolute* transaction costs of all possible decisions (and thus their prices) are changed by intervention, the undesirable paternalism is present, which appears all the more questionable the more the transaction costs change absolutely, i.e. in total, through the intervention. But this measurement remains hypothetical for now, as it seems difficult to implement from analysis to evaluation. Therefore, it is the responsibility of the lecturer within the framework of specific training measures not to endanger the self-determination and self-organisation of the learners and to actually only assume the role of the "butterfly". Let us therefore assume responsible lecturers who pursue an entrepreneurial education process and not coercive measures, who promote the freedom of the individual and their ability to self-determine and who do not ultimately practice external determination under the guise of self-determination (Liening, 2010, p. 157 ff.).

synergetic concept can be supplemented, which explains all order formation processes as self-organisation processes, without thereby substantially endangering self-organisation.

If we apply the above considerations to the desired Entrepreneurship Education, this means that the learning arrangements are designed in such a way that, on the one hand, entrepreneurial education is possible through self-organisation, but on the other hand, the sphere (knowledge ,attitude), when it stands on top of the hill and could roll in any direction, is nudged in the 'right' direction by minimal 'pushes' (e.g., by changing the structure of a case study, through Socratic dialogues[13], through impulse lectures etc.) or inserts it into the learning process at the appropriate time.

The crucial question at the last point is how a lecturer, coach, consultant etc. knows when to intervene. To answer this question, complexity research with its empirical measurement methods is required, which we have extensively presented and analysed in Chap. 5 of this book and which are now being applied to Entrepreneurship Education.

7.1.3.4 Measuring Complexity for Targeted Initiation of *'Nudges'*

Indeed, one problem for the teacher is to recognise whether the learners are on the verge of a phase transition or not. Only then does it make sense to intervene using a 'nudge'. Ultimately, this is exactly what an experienced teacher who practices synergetic entrepreneurship education does every day, without necessarily being able to explain it in detail. This requires a great deal of experience and empathy, as the individual learning processes, which cannot be captured empirically with traditional statistics, require a deep understanding of the learner and his developments, which neither a novice nor a computer-assisted learning programme based on artificial intelligence can possess (Tschacher & Haken, 2011).[14] Learning and teaching are thus both complex undertakings.

However, as we have seen, there are now a number of empirical methods that could *support* the complex teaching and learning process, as they allow complexity in learning processes to be measured.

Complexity is greatest when the ball is on a mountain peak and least when the ball is in a valley (order). Order and complexity are thus two antipodes that can be measured using certain empirical methods. In addition to the method of bifurcation analysis

---

[13] During a Socratic dialogue, the teacher, in accordance with the Delphic demand 'Know thyself!', leads the learner to check the validity of his hypotheses, discover contradictions, and finally draw correct conclusions from known facts using certain heuristics (Wenger, 1987, p. 39; Stavemann, 2007, p. 9 f.). Leonard *Nelson* writes: "This art of forcing freedom is the secret of the Socratic method" (Nelson, 1970, p. 287).

[14] Especially in the context of learning processes, the support of computers, the internet, etc. is rightly demanded again and again. The years-long efforts to programme AI-based learning programmes that can ultimately replace a teacher have to be considered as failed from the nineteen sixties to this point. One reason for this is the lack of physical embodiment of the artificial learning system, the 'embodiment', which prevents a comprehensive understanding (Liening, 1992; Tschacher & Dauwalder, 2003).

that we have considered, the calculation of *Lyapunov* exponents or dimension calculation (e.g., D_2, PD_2 etc.) are among the most important traditional empirical methods of complexity science. We had worked out in the discussion that it was always difficult in the context of empirical studies to prove complexity solely on the basis of, for example, the calculation of *Lyapunov* exponents. However, other methods, which must partly be considered in combination, offer the possibility to compensate for this deficit. These include methods that can be described with keywords such as *Grammar Complexity*, *Permutation entropy* or *Transformation encodings* and which we have analysed in detail in the empirical part of the book.

However, the phase transitions to be measured can only be detected in sufficiently long and noise-free time series data, which—and this is the difficulty—must first be captured in this way.

Initial empirical measurements in the field of entrepreneurship education, however, suggest that this is a very powerful approach that can analyse such self-organising learning situations as we have described, in order to then set a 'nudge' that contributes to the entrepreneurial Bildung of the learner (Liening et al., 2013). Nevertheless, there is still a lot of research work to be done to obtain a tool for fine-tuning using 'nudges' that is easy for the teacher to handle and can be integrated into the learning process, which allows such *targeted* interventions that directly intervene in the described circular causal process without shaking the educational self-organisation process to its foundations. In the end, it is the preparatory work, the didactic conception of the control parameters, that is crucial for the success of entrepreneurship education. The necessary basic considerations for this were worked out here.

7.2 The Organisational Level: Focus on Entrepreneurial Founding Processes *(SEM2)*

7.2.1 Rough Sketch of the 'Synergetic Entrepreneurship Model 2': The Organisational Level from a Business-Entrepreneurial Perspective *(SEM2)*

Through the second model, the '*S*ynergetic *E*ntrepreneurship *M*odel 2' (*SEM2*), new insights for the field of entrepreneurship can be derived, as with the *SEM1*. However, since entrepreneurship can manifest in many ways (within established companies, as a basic attitude, in founding processes), the *SEM2* should also be exemplified using the example of a founding process. This is intended to contribute to the understanding of how founding processes work and how such a process should be designed. The founding of a company is the result of a long, complex process. This can be explained by the theory of synergetics. As presented several times, the theory of synergetics differentiates between control parameters, order parameters, macroscopic and microscopic level, the environment, and system constraints. If one models the founding process based on this theory, the process begins with an external activation, which is realised, for example, by a founding idea (control parameter). This impulse ignites an undirected change process among potential entrepreneurs (microscopic level), which (in the best case) leads to the emergence of startups (macroscopic level). From the potential founder collective at the micro level, order parameters are thus formed (a concrete idea, methods, …), which, by the way, do not necessarily have to include that a team ultimately stands behind the dynamic pattern. Sometimes the paths of founders also separate (so that possibly only one person remains), nevertheless, the one-man startup would not exist in this form without the initially "unordered human capital" of a group of potential founders. An alternative to the idea of a multitude of potential entrepreneurs at the microscopic level would be to depict the founding potential (financial resources, networks, ideas, human capital, etc.) in its multitude. This would avoid the discussion to what extent this is distributed to one or more persons and one would still be at the level of the founding process. Regardless of this, it is important to consider that the control parameter initiates a nonspecific process at the microscopic level. Therefore, it is also hardly possible here to predict the result at the macroscopic level in advance. The only way to influence the emergence process is to carefully configure the control parameter.[15] In the case of founding projects, the goal is to increase the probability of the occurrence of a startup (dynamic pattern) by initiating entrepreneurship education measures as control parameters, for example.

For a deeper understanding, each part of the *SEM2* (see Fig. 7.10) will be explained in detail in the following section.

7.2.2 The Elements of the System

7.2.2.1 Control Parameters

The control parameters from a business-entrepreneurial perspective, which provide the energy for entrepreneurial changes and ultimately for the founding process, can be diverse. A control parameter can also lie in entrepreneurship education, as in the previous perspective. It can aim to stimulate various aspects such as knowledge, attitude, motivation, or resources of potential entrepreneurs. But also founding ideas that potential entrepreneurs generate, or suggestions by friends, colleagues, etc., experiences in markets, etc. can contribute to encouraging people to think about founding and to pursue it concretely.

A specific control parameter could be a so-called *'Accelerator'*, whose energy can accelerate the founding process, as the name suggests. This specifically encourages interested parties to advance the development, elaboration, and implementation of a business

[15] But also in SEM2, one should not underestimate the possibilities of setting 'nudges' from the outside, small pushes in the 'right' direction, for example through targeted workshops on specific topics, as we have explained in detail in SEM1.

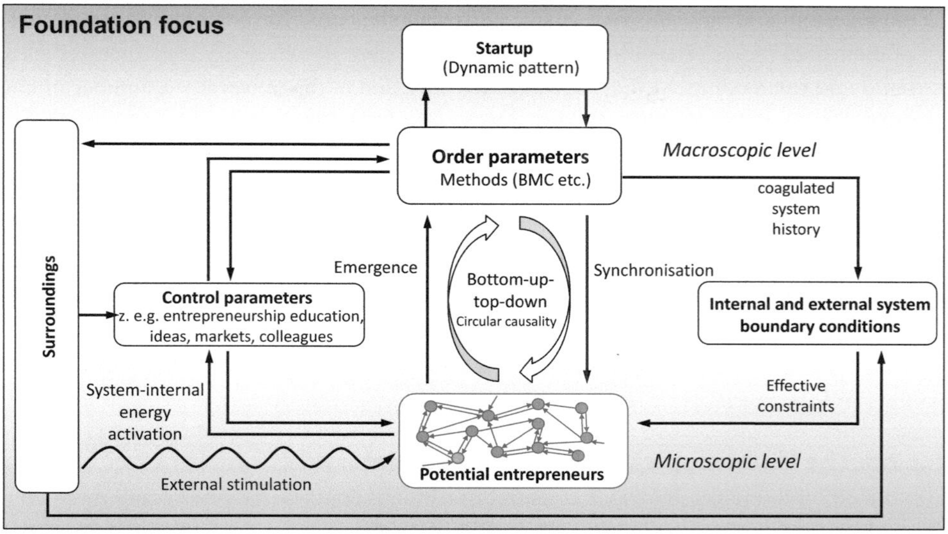

Fig. 7.10 The 'Synergetic Entrepreneurship Model 2': the Founding Dimension *(SEM2)*

idea. Entrepreneurs thus have the opportunity to actively apply and internalise entrepreneurial thinking and action. In this way, a business idea can be developed in collaborative teamwork and, in the best case, brought to market maturity. Comprehensive seminars and events as well as personal contacts could be provided as incentives.

7.2.2.2 The Microscopic Level

At the microscopic level of this model, potential entrepreneurs are located. The alternative case mentioned above, to instead represent the entrepreneurial potential in its diverse manifestations at the microscopic level, is not pursued further at this point, although this variant is conceivable as already emphasised. Thus, for the present case, it means that at the organisational level of the *SEM,* founding teams are exemplarily in focus, who self-organise. They create order parameters in an emergent cyclical process that synchronise the different ideas, approaches, etc. of the entrepreneurs at the microscopic level. Using the example of students at a university, we can illustrate such a situation that could exist at the microscopic level.

Example: Microscopic level at a university

On the one hand, we can imagine business students at a university who have a definite interest in founding a company and believe that they are capable of starting and running a company with the management skills they have acquired. However, they may lack (in addition to entrepreneurial knowledge) a brilliant idea of what the service or product of their venture could be. On the other hand, there are, for example, engineering students who have fantastic (product) ideas, for example, in the context of their final theses (Bachelor, Master, PhD, etc.), but do not really trust themselves to build and run a company. Furthermore, we may find at the university a number of students from cultural studies who presumably feel similar to the engineering students, who have created good ideas but have neither managerial nor entrepreneurial knowledge. In this hodgepodge of potential entrepreneurs, there is, synergistically speaking, disorder. ◀

A state of disorder, as described in the above example, is now stimulated from the outside by control parameters, and there is a gradual circular ordering process from which the order parameters gradually emerge, contributing to synchronisation at the microscopic level.

7.2.2.3 The Macroscopic Level—Order Parameters

Stimulated by the ideas, by concrete entrepreneurship courses, etc., more and more concrete ideas for founding a company crystallise. For example, in the context of the above university example, engineering and business students could come together to deal with their respective competencies with a concrete founding project. The concrete founding project in the form of business models, etc., gradually synchronises the different ideas of potential entrepreneurs. In particular, corresponding entrepreneurship education events can force the formation of order by contributing through a series of entrepreneurial methods to the design and development of a startup as a dynamic pattern. The entrepreneurial methods thus form the order parameters that gradually become visible at the macroscopic level and are reflected in the dynamic pattern of a startup. Several crucial methods can be identified here, which can form the central order parameters. The *Lean-StartUp* process, the business model, the *Customer Development,* the revenue model and the value proposition differentiation represent such entrepreneurial methods present. These methods enable dealing with uncertainty in complex systems, e.g., by early testing of customer and product groups. They allow a flexible as well as iterative building of the business model and are therefore, in addition to basic business knowledge such as accounting, cost accounting, financing, marketing, etc., of particular importance for the domain of entrepreneurship. Since the mentioned methods are not part of the classic business repertoire, they are briefly outlined below.

i. Lean StartUp

Introductory description*Lean StartUp* is a method developed by Eric *Ries* to help entrepreneurs experience as little resource loss as possible when starting a startup (Ries, 2011).

▶ **Definition (Lean StartUp)** The Lean StartUp method includes procedures that are supposed to help entrepreneurs improve the chances of success of their startups. The Lean StartUp is based on five principles:

1. "Entrepreneurs are everywhere (…)
2. Entrepreneurship is management (…)
3. Validated Learning (…)
4. Build-Measure Learn (…)
5. Innovation Accounting (…)" (Ries, 2011, p. 8 f.).

From the perspective of *Ries,* these five principles mean the following:

1. Entrepreneurs can be found not only in startups, but also in established companies, so the Lean Startup method can also work in established companies.
2. Startups are not just about innovative products, but represent organisations, so leadership skills are required that can deal with great uncertainty.
3. Startups are not just about the products and making money, but also about validated learning on how to build a viable business model through continuous experiments.
4. The central task of a startup is to transform ideas into products, measure customer reactions, and learn from the experiences whether the path is the right one, or whether something needs to be changed and how to accelerate associated feedback loops.
5. Finally, successes must be measured, milestones set, and tasks prioritised, which requires a new kind of accounting (Ries, 2011, p. 8 f.).

The *Lean Startup* method is ultimately based on the traditional *Lean Management,* the 'lean management' and the *Lean Manufacturing*.

The Lean Management and Lean Manufacturing approach contrast with the *Taylorism* or *Fordism* to original concepts of mass production and focus on a whole bundle of principles and methods that offer the possibility to design clearly defined functions, structures and processes of a company and even an entire value creation network with maximum efficiency and high degree of customisation (Pfeiffer & Weiss, 1994, p. 53 ff.). In the Lean Management approach, it is particularly important to focus on issues such as customer orientation, cost reduction and the economic use of resources, taking into account an integrated view of product and production factors (Gorecki & Pautsch, 2016, p. 6; Pfeiffer & Weiss, 1994, p. 57).[16]*Ries* points out that the principles of the associated Lean Manufacturing method include "utilising knowledge, the individual responsibility of each employee, reducing batch sizes, just-in-time production, inventory controls and accelerating cycle times". This leads to the "difference between value-adding activities and waste" and shows "how product quality can be increased from the inside out" (Ries, 2014, p. 23).

If one follows *Ries,* then according to him a startup is an institution where new products or services are developed under "conditions of extreme uncertainty" (Ries, 2011, p. 27).

[16] It should be noted that the focus on "cost reduction" can easily be misunderstood, as it was often misused by consulting firms for cost reduction programmes in the nineteen nineties (Gorecki & Pautsch, 2016, p. 9).

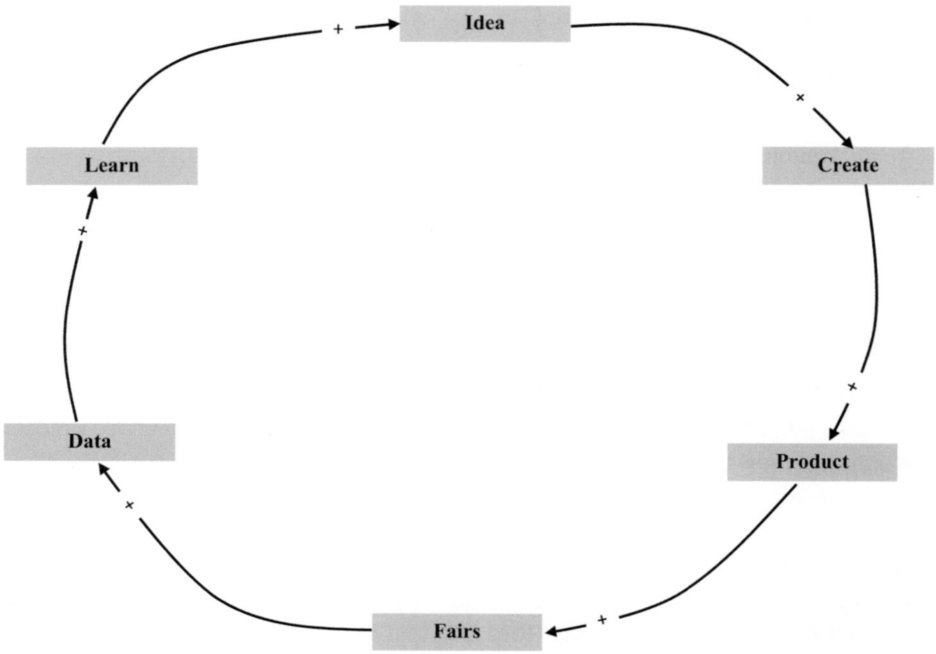

Fig. 7.11 Build-measure-learn feedback loop. (Based on: Ries 2011, p. 75)

Due to the extreme uncertainty, the risk of making wrong decisions is very high. To transform ideas into products, which *Ries* sees as the central task of a startup, potential customers interact with these (minimum viable) products, giving the startups information about how the potential customers perceive the product. To implement this, *Ries* has transferred the approaches of Lean Manufacturing (Ohno, 2013; Shingo, 1985) to the entrepreneurship domain. [17]

The Functioning of Lean StartUp *Lean* StartUp can be described by the *Build-Measure-LearnFeedback Loop*. Ries states:

> The fundamental activity of a startup is to turn products, measure how customers respond, and then learn whether to pivot or persevere (Ries, 2011, p. 9).

This is a continuous cycle that should be run through as quickly as possible at several stages, as illustrated in Fig. 7.11 (Ries 2011, p. 228).

---

[17] Further information on 'Lean Management' can be found in *Womack* et al. (Womack et al., 1990). The Toyota car production with approaches such as just-in-time production and constant improvement of products can be cited as the most famous example.

The individual steps always follow the above-mentioned basic premise of quickly understanding the customers. Customers can only be understood if they receive a concrete idea about the product or service. Therefore, a *Minimum Viable Product* (MVP), a minimal product, must be created so that potential customers can provide usable feedback. From this, measurable data are collected and learning insights derived. Based on these insights, the original idea is adjusted and the cycle is repeated (Ries, 2011, p. 118 ff.).

The Use of Lean StartUp The *Lean StartUp* approach, combined with its methods, can be understood as the basis for all processes of entrepreneurship. Similar to *Lean Manufacturing,* the *LeanStartUp*-Process serves as a basic attitude for all entrepreneurial processes. This basic attitude particularly highlights the differences to traditional business methods. Thus, the concept of progress is not measured by the production of high-quality goods, but progress here is understood as the aforementioned validated learning, the *Validated Learning,* (Ries, 2014, p. 25). It's about understanding, continuous change and adaptation, a learning concept that aims to identify and eliminate waste that impairs entrepreneurial thinking and action (Ries, 2014, p. 25). While long-term planning and anticipatory actions based on theoretical considerations and past-related data correspond to the traditional approach, the Lean StartUp approach focusses more on permanent change etc.[18]

ii. Customer Development

Introductory Description Many innovation processes aimed at starting a business lack a structured process in which the product idea is tested (Blank & Dorf 2012). The goal of such a process is to minimise the customer and market risk *(customer risk, market risk),* or from an effectual perspective, one should rather speak of uncertainty, in our reading of complexity (Blank & Dorf, 2012).

So in the context of Invention for example, it's not about solving engineers' problems in implementation, but about finding out whether there is a customer and a business model for a particular product. *Blank* and *Dorf* formulate this as follows:

> A startup is a temporary organisation in search of a scalable, repeatable, profitable business model (Blank & Dorf, 2012, p. xvii).

Ultimately, it's about the organised, structured search for a suitable business model, to test the hypotheses that one has regarding markets, customers, channels, pricing, etc., and to put them into practice, so that we, quoting *Blank* and *Dorf,* can define *Customer Development* as follows:

---

[18] In addition to the standard work by *Ries*, the works of *Maurya, Golthelf* and *Seiden* as well as *Croll* and *Yoskovitz* provide further insights (Ries, 2011; Maurya, 2012; Gothelf & Seiden, 2013; Croll & Yoskovitz, 2013; Ries, 2014).

Definition *Customer Development* "Customer Development is the process to organise the search for the business model" (Blank & Dorf, 2012, p. xxviii).

The Functioning of Customer Development In the context of *Customer Development*, valid data and information about the planned product should be generated early and structured. Or as *Blank* and *Dorf* put it:

> Instead of asking 'How many days to the beta test?' or, 'What's in our sales pipeline?' a startup's board and management team need to ask specific questions about results on its long list of tests and experiments to validate all components of its business model (Blank & Dorf, 2012, p. 12).

For this purpose, *Blank* and *Dorf* recommend four steps, as illustrated in Fig. 7.12 (Blank & Dorf, 2012, p. 22):

1. *"Customer Discovery"*—Discovering customers (see Blank & Dorf, 2012, p. 24 ff. and in particular: Blank & Dorf, 2012, p. 53 ff.)
   The first step is to capture the founders' ideas and formulate the hypotheses on which these ideas are based. On this basis, a plan is then created on how to test customer reactions to these hypotheses and how to turn the hypotheses into facts. *Blank* and *Dorf* summarise this as follows:

   > In a startup, the founders define a product vision and then use the customer discovery to find customers and a market for that vision (Blank & Dorf, 2012, p. 25).

2. *"Customer Validation"*—Validating customers (see Blank & Dorf, 2012, p. 27 ff.) and in particular: Blank and Dorf (2012, p. 277 ff.)
   In the second step, the insights supported by facts are transferred into a business model. It is checked whether this model can be implemented. If it is not feasible, one remains in the search phase and even starts again with step 1 in case of doubt. *Blank* and *Dorf* state:

   > Learning that a hypothesis is wrong is not a crisis (Blank & Dorf, 2012, p. 28).

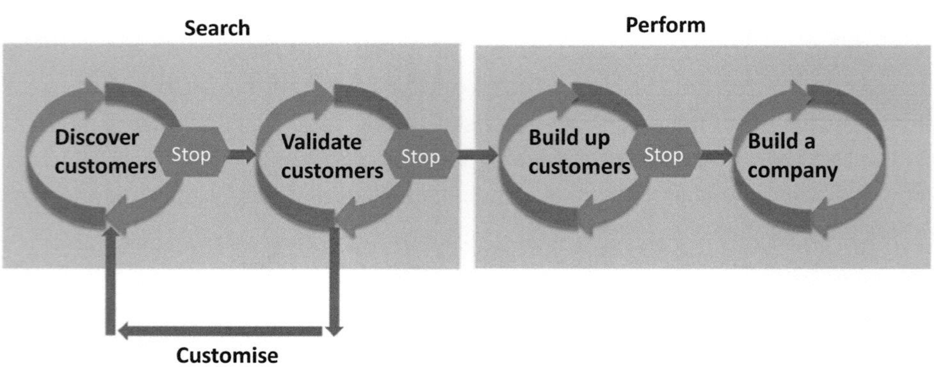

Fig. 7.12 Customer development process. (Based on: Blank & Dorf, 2012, p. 23)

Thus, in the search phase, everything can be adjusted or one sticks to the previous assumptions and tries to validate customers again. *Blank* and *Dorf* describe only an adjustment process (Blank & Dorfm 2012, p. 23). *Ries,* however, rightly notes that it can also be sensible to show some persistence and perseverance before adjusting one's idea *(Pivot or Persevere)* (Ries, 2011).

3. "*Customer* Creation"—Building customers (see Blank and Dorf 2012, p. 29)
   If it turns out that the hypotheses of the idea can be confirmed as facts in a business model by potential customers, one enters the phase of execution or implementation. Now markets (new market or existing market—see *Blue vs. Red Ocean*[19]) and customer groups are defined. It should be noted that the principle of hypothesis testing and resource-saving principles continue to be followed.
4. "*Company*-Building"—Building a company (see Blank & Dorf, 2012, p. 30)
   Once the 'Customer Creation' step is completed, the startup transitions to a sustainable enterprise. *Blank* and *Dorf* incidentally call the point at which a corresponding *Business Model* has been developed or found, the "Graduation Day" (Blank & Dorf, 2012, p. 30). Then begins the phase of scaling[20] and establishment. So, the fourth step is about the entrepreneur or the founding team developing and implementing a sustainable corporate structure based on the insights from the previous stages.

The Use of Customer Development First of all, two areas of application are distinguished in *Customer Development:* the physical and the digital world (Blank & Dorf, 2012, p. 71 ff.). Both areas require, for example, a different approach in the design of tests and customer groups, which is why the division seems sensible from the perspective of *Customer Development* (Blank & Dorf, 2012).[21]

The process of *Customer Development* seems to be of interest in principle to all entrepreneurs who want to implement an idea and develop a resource-saving and functioning

[19] Red Ocean strategy means to compete in an existing market with its competitors in a price and quality competition. Blue Ocean, on the other hand, means creating your own market by specifically differentiating the business model (Kim & Mauborgne, 2005).

[20] Scaling means being able to bring the company to rapid, exponential growth through investments (usually venture capital). This applies to only a few startups, but these are the ones that receive media attention and are therefore often cited as examples (Zalando, Facebook or LinkedIn). Special platforms, where growth does not necessarily entail additional effort (online platforms), are predestined for scalable business models. In contrast, service-based business models, such as consulting, are not infinitely scalable.

[21] It should be noted that we find a similar two-part process in *Osterwalder* et al. in the context of Value Proposition Design, where the distinction is not between the two markets, but between the customer profile (What does the customer understanding look like?) and the Value Map (What value does one want to create for the customer?) (Osterwalder et al., 2015).

business model. It is important to listen to the customers: "Get the customer to talk, not you," is therefore rightly stated by *Blank* and *Dorf* (Blank & Dorf, 2012, p. 204).[22]

iii. Business Models—*Business Models*

Introductory Description *Osterwalder* and *Pigneur* define a business model as follows:

▶ **Business Model** "A business model describes the rationale of how an organisation creates, delivers, and captures value" (Osterwalder & Pigneur, 2010, p. 14).

A business model thus describes the basic principle according to which an organisation creates, conveys, and captures value. However, there is no uniform understanding in the literature regarding a business model definition. There are, however, common areas that have been worked out by a literature review by *Schallmo* (Schallmo, 2013). These include the further development of existing or new companies or business areas, the creation of new mechanisms, for example by the novel combination of elements, the provision of new products or services, the satisfaction of customer needs, the creation of novel benefits, and the generation of revenues while differentiating from competitors.

Osterwalder et al. name nine relevant areas that make up a business model and can be divided into four categories (Osterwalder et al., 2005). These categories include the product (value proposition), the customer interface (target customers, delivery channels, relationship), infrastructure management (value configuration, key competencies, partner network), and financial aspects (revenues, costs). According to *Osterwalder* et al., the nine fields represent the central building blocks of a business model (Osterwalder et al., 2005, 2015).

The Functioning of a Business Model A business model initially serves as a common basis for discussion. For *Magretta*, business models are "at heart, stories—stories that explain how enterprises work" (Magretta, 2002, p. 87). *Kuratko* and *Audretsch* additionally note that these 'stories' address four basic questions:

1. Who is the customer?
2. What does the customer value?
3. How do we make money in this business?
4. What is the underlying economic logic that explains how we can deliver value to

[22] Further information can be found in addition to the mentioned literature sources at *Blank* and *Dorf, Osterwalder* et al. as well as at *Cooper* and *Vlaskovits* and furthermore at *Bartel* and *Barbarski* (Blank & Dorf, 2012; Osterwalder et al., 2015; Cooper & Vlaskovits, 2013; Bartel & Barbarski,2015).

customers at an appropriate cost? (Kuratko & Audretsch, 2009, p. 7).

Osterwalder and *Pigneur* comment on the central components of a business model:

> The nine business model Building Blocks form the basis for a handy tool, which we call the Business Model Canvas (Osterwalder & Pigneur, 2010, p. 42).

A business model thus presents a compelling story that explains how the startup works and is at the same time a flexible *planning tool.* The clarity and reduction of the company aspects to their actual core, which consists of the mentioned nine components of the business model, makes it possible to continuously incorporate current changes in the business model during the design and development phase. As outlined with the other methods, the business model represents the structure of the company with which the entrepreneur wants to enter the market. However, this is constantly adjusted until a final version emerges. Therefore, the *Business Model Canvas* (BMC) is used with sticky notes, on which only one aspect is noted at a time. Thus, when new insights are gained (through the verification of one's own hypotheses by tests), the corresponding sticky notes can simply be exchanged. Regarding the creation of a business model, *Magretta* accurately states:

> Creating a business model is, then, a lot like writing a new story (Magretta, 2002, p. 87).

The nine areas to be considered can be represented as shown in Fig. 7.13, using a business model 'canvas', a *Business Model Canvas.*

The Use of Business Models

Business Models are used in business and idea development. They serve to provide clarity about the current situation and to visualise the current or future situation of the company. Through visualisation, the entrepreneur gets the opportunity to clearly understand which aspects still need to be developed, clarified, checked, or changed. In contrast to a business plan, which consists of about eight to twelve parts depending on the structure[23], working with business models represents a reduction in the level of detail, which allows for continuous work.

Further information can be found in the mentioned literature sources by *Osterwalder* et al., *Schallmo* and for example by *Faltin* and *Ripsas* as well as *Bartel* and *Barbarski* (Osterwalder et al., 2005; Osterwalder & Pigneur, 2011; Schallmo, 2013; Faltin & Ripsas, 2011; Bartel & Barbarski, 2015).

[23] A business plan typically distinguishes between eight to twelve components, which in turn can be further subdivided in detail. With ten components, these are roughly as follows: 1) Executive Summary, 2) Business Idea, 3) Entrepreneurial Team, 4) Industry and Market Analysis, 5) Marketing and Sales Concept, 6) Market Entry Barriers, 7) Organisation, Management and Legal Form, 8) Financial and Cost Planning as well as Financing Sources, 9) Opportunities and Risks, and 10) an Implementation Plan (Bonnemeier, 2015; Vogelsang et al., 2015; Lutz, 2014).

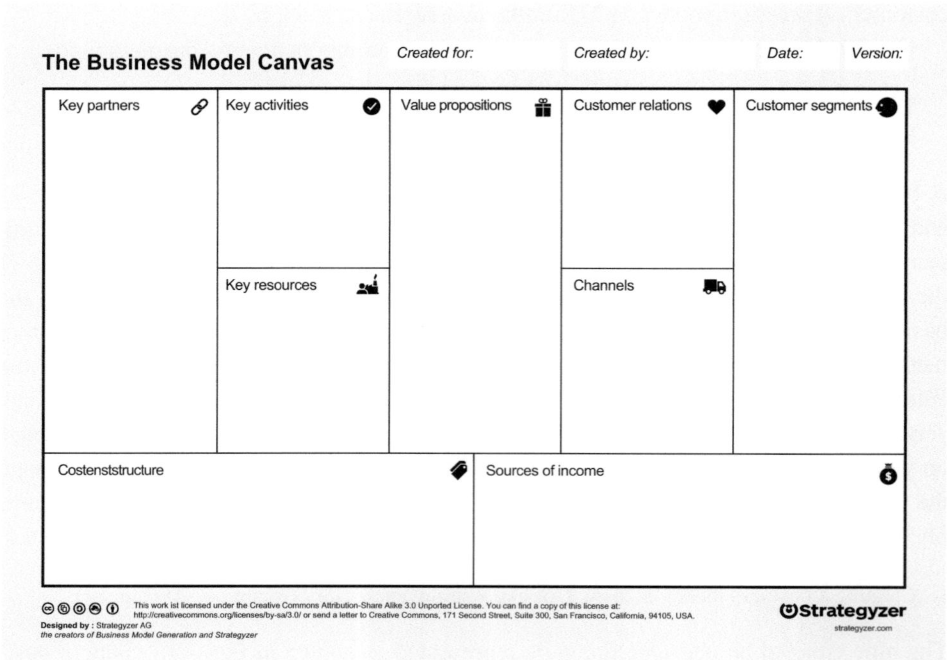

Fig. 7.13 Template of the business model canvas. (Source: https://strategyzer.com/, Osterwalder & Pigneur, 2011)

iv. Value Proposition Differentiation

Introductory Description*Kuratko* and *Audretsch* point out that scientifically, instead of differentiation, there is more talk of strategic renewal *('Strategic Renewal')* and in practice more of strategic Innovation*('Strategic Innovation')* (Hamel & Prahalad, 2013) or Value Innovation*('Value Innovation')* (Kim & Mauborgne, 2005) (Kuratko & Audretsch, 2009). Using the example of the work of *Kim* and *Mauborgne* and the term *Value Innovation* coined by them, it can be shown that the core lies in the differentiation of the company's value proposition *('Value Proposition')* (Kim & Mauborgne, 2005). They point out that there are two ways for companies to position themselves: On the one hand, by entering into a price and quality competition with their competitors *('Red Ocean')* or on the other hand, by creating their own market through targeted differentiation of the business model *('Blue Ocean')* (Kim & Mauborgne, 2005). By creating an independent market, one becomes more independent as a competitor and does not enter into a continuous competition and competitive situation. Or as *Chia* puts it:

> (…) rather than follow the logic of confronting competitors and attempting to out-perform them thereby creating a 'bloody' red ocean of competition, corporations ought to seek out new *blue oceans* of as-yet-untapped opportunities (Chia, 2011, p. 195).

The resources that would have to be invested in a continuous competitive spiral can thus be put into the individualisation and further development of one's own unique products or services. Often, a restructuring of the boundaries and markets of industries is the result (Kuratko & Audretsch, 2009).

The method of value proposition differentiation can therefore be defined as follows:

▶ **Definition (Value Proposition Differentiation):** Value proposition differentiation deals with tailoring the company's value proposition (promise of benefit) to the customers. This method is about accurately representing the benefit that a company promises its customers.

The Functioning of a Differentiation Model The differentiation strategy concerns both the area of costs and the value propositions for customers. The costs are altered, relative to competitors, by reducing or eliminating offers. The value proposition for customers is varied by removing or adding values for customers (Kim & Mauborgne, 2005). From this perspective, a four-field matrix with the areas of elimination, increase, reduction, and creation (Kim & Mauborgne, 2005) can be used to evaluate the company's own or existing business model in the market and thus differentiate based on the four areas. The goal is to create or enter a *Blue Ocean*. Two possibilities arise from this: on the one hand, this approach provides the opportunity to open up a new business model or a new market, on the other hand, it avoids a resource-intensive competition. *Kim* and *Mauborgne* write about this:

> What blue ocean strategy brings to life, however, is that the focus on the competition all too often keeps companies anchored in the red ocean (Kim & Mauborgne, 2015, p. xii).

The Use of Differentiation Models Differentiation models serve on the one hand for innovation development or strategic innovation orientation in established companies, on the other hand, they are helpful in the phase of idea development for the elaboration of the 'right' business model and customer groups. It becomes possible to differentiate oneself from potential competitors and thus implement the innovation process in a company with less resource use.[24]

v. Revenue Model

Introductory Description Mark *Johnson* as well as Oliver *Gassman* et al. introduce various types of revenue models (Johnson, 2010; Gassmann et al., 2013). These models are

[24] Further information can be found in the literature of *Kim* and *Mauborgne*,*Gassmann* and *Sutter* as well as *Hamel* and *Prahalad* (Kim & Mauborgne, 2005; Gassmann & Sutter, 2013; Hamel & Prahalad, 2013; Kim & Mauborgne, 2015; Gassmann et al., 2013).

referred to by them as business models, but at their core, they are about showing the various revenue opportunities of companies (Gassmann et al., 2013). Therefore, a revenue model can be defined as follows:

▶ **Definition Revenue model** A revenue model describes how a company generates revenue streams with its products and services. The method allows to find out what a company should ultimately focus on. The fit of the revenue model to the business model or the value proposition is of great importance.

Exemplary here are the so-called *Razor BladeModels*, which, as in the example of the wet razor, generate a so-called *Lock-in* effect through relatively cheap entry-level products. The use of this product results in a multitude of purchases, which, like the purchases of razor blades for the wet razor, arise from the use of the products. These are relatively expensive and bring the company recurring revenues.[25] Steven *Johnson* lists eighteen further variants (Johnson, 2010). *Gassmann* et al. even fifty-four (Gassmann et al., 2013). Essentially, it is about understanding *why* and *how* a company makes money. Sometimes limited products or services are given out for free *(Freemium),* but additional services can be purchased, another time products or services are offered without any additional service, where only the pure benefit without additional services is offered particularly cheaply *(No Frills).*

The Functioning of a Revenue Model A revenue model illustrates what a company needs to focus on. What are the biggest cost blocks and cost drivers? But above all, what are the central sources of revenue and how are these revenues generated? What are customers willing to pay for and where are the financial risks? (Gassmann et al., 2013, p. 24).

Through revenue models, companies have the opportunity, similar to the *BlueOcean* strategy, to differentiate themselves from each other. However, the revenue and business model must match. The interplay of the revenue and business model allows a company to be successful, assuming that all sub-areas can also be fulfilled.

The Use of Revenue Models Revenue models are used in the development of new business ideas. In the creation of business models, revenue models also play a significant role. New ideas *(inventions)* only become innovations when they are also exploited

[25] It should be noted again that upon closer examination, this is primarily not a business model, but essentially the revenue structure of a company. For a business model, in addition to the revenue structure, the components necessary for the implementation of the revenue structure are also considered (see section Business Model).

(exploitation), i.e., generate revenues (Roberts, 2007, p. 36 ff.). Thus, an innovation requires a suitable revenue and business model.[26]

The five entrepreneurial methods selected and outlined from a multitude of business-entrepreneurial procedures *(Lean* StartUp, *Customer Development, Business Models, Value Proposition Differentiation* and *Revenue Models)* can represent conceivable order parameters that become visible at the macroscopic level over time. The methods act as order parameters as they contribute to the successive synchronisation of the different ideas of potential entrepreneurs and ideally lead to the founding of a company and thus reflect in the dynamic pattern of this start-up.

7.2.2.4 Limitations

The presented methods as well as the start-up itself represent conceivable order parameters, which at the microscopic level turn potential entrepreneurs into factual entrepreneurs of a specific start-up and a specific idea.

Here too, there are two types of limitations, internal and external, which influence the system elements of potential entrepreneurs. The internal limitations consist of the coagulated system history. During a phase transition, it is more likely that patterns that have already appeared at a point in the past will appear more often than other patterns. Therefore, old patterns, which come about through order parameters such as the creation of a business plan as a classic business method and which have already been learned by the potential entrepreneur, compete with new patterns, which are expressed in order parameters, such as the *Business Model Canvas (BMC)*,, which have arisen from the stimuli of the actual control parameters at the microscopic level. In addition, external limitations[27] , such as the expectation of a bank that requires a business plan instead of a *BMC,* limited funding opportunities of the country, legal requirements for a company, income and corporate tax rates of the federal government, trade tax rates and commercial areas of the municipality or for example the competition in the market, influence the system elements of the microscopic level (potential entrepreneurs). Therefore, the limitations, just like the control parameters, influence the microscopic level.

External as well as internal limitations are difficult to change. Nevertheless, they can be influenced in the long term by the order parameters of the entrepreneurs. For the internal limitations, this means that due to newly developing patterns, more and subjectively better patterns are available and the historical coagulated patterns lose importance.

External limitations can also change due to long-term effects of the start-up. For example, if a newly founded company is successful in the market, more start-ups will try

---

[26] Further information can be found in the literature of *Johnsohn* and *Gassman* et al., as well as *Osterwalder* and *Pigneur* and *Aulet* (Johnson, 2010; Gassmann et al., 2013; Osterwalder & Pigneur, 2011; Aulet, 2013).

[27] External limitations could further be divided into physical (such as financial resources) and non-physical (such as cultural characteristics) elements.

the same path. The municipality, due to increasing tax revenues and decreasing unemployment, may designate additional commercial areas or even lower the trade tax rate to make the establishment and settlement more attractive for more entrepreneurs.

7.2.2.5 Environment

The environment encompasses several aspects. All have in common that potential entrepreneurs cannot directly influence them. It is possible that aspects change over time. However, this is not a direct process and in particular, it cannot be directly influenced in the *SEM2* process. Therefore, environmental aspects must be considered and treated as given.

Examples of environmental aspects could be the German Commercial Code (HGB), EU directives, the tax code, the Social Security Code (SGB), legal decisions, etc. But also questions concerning knowledge transfer, for example between universities and startups, are part of this. Thus, innovations from research institutions contribute significantly to the competitiveness of the national economy. According to the German Startup Monitor, 44.2 % of founders in Germany see a benefit from scientific findings from professional journals, studies or research files (Ripsas & Tröger, 2015, p. 59). But also established companies are part of the environment, which in turn have an influence on the founding events. For example, it can be diagnosed that the co-operation between established companies and startups is becoming increasingly important, as can be seen from the high number of incubators and corporate startup initiatives (Ripsas & Tröger, 2015, p. 55). Which environmental aspects are more likely to be considered restrictions can best be seen by how close they actually are to the microscopic level in practice.

Overall, the environment represents all parts that are not within the system of entrepreneurs (microscopic level) and that do not belong to the control parameter of the *SEM2*, but have an indirect or direct influence on the microscopic level.

7.2.3 The Circular Causal Process

After the different components of the *SEM2* process have been explained, the circular causal process will be briefly explained in the following. First of all, it is important to recognise that the only point within the *SEM2* process where one can intervene is essentially the control parameters, just like in the *SEM1*. This implies that there is no possibility of predicting which pattern or which order parameter will occur at the macroscopic level. Each potential entrepreneur has a different starting situation (knowledge, attitude, motivation, and experience). Therefore, it is important to provide a wide range of incentives (control parameters) that allow potential entrepreneurs to question or strengthen their predispositions and motives, which they represent at the microscopic level and which form the basis for the development of an order parameter at the macroscopic level, depending on their characteristics. Only the self-organisation process triggered here leads to new order parameters, which can ultimately lead to the founding of a company.

The order parameters in turn influence the entrepreneurs and thus contribute to the formation of order. Old patterns thereby lose their influence and a new pattern develops spontaneously and self-organisingly, in the case of *SEM2* a startup.

7.3 The Macroeconomic Level: Focussing on Market, Business Cycle, and Growth *(SEM3)*

7.3.1 Rough Sketch of the 'Synergetic Entrepreneurship Model 3': The Macroeconomic Level from a Predominantly Economic Perspective *(SEM3)*

Kuratko and *Audretsch* state, following Jean Babtiste *Say* and Joseph *Schumpeter*:

> The link between entrepreneurship and economic growth has a long tradition (Kuratko & Audretsch, 2009, p. 2).

And so it is not surprising when *Purle* writes:

> Young, rapidly growing companies have been proven to lead to the greatest employment growth (compared to established large companies) and are therefore particularly desirable from an economic and regional policy perspective. They accelerate structural change and at the same time mitigate the problems in regions with major structural change (Purle, 2004, p. 1).

With these words, *Purles* begins his work on "Managing Complexity in Young Growth Companies". But growth per se does not have to be good, as we have already pointed out in the first part of the book. We remember *Gharajedaghi,* whom we quoted with the words:

> One can easily grow by 'faking', or making lousy acquisitions (Gharajedaghi, 2006, p. 107).

Furthermore, when it comes to growth, for example, the speed is also important, as rapid growth of companies is associated with challenges that can lead to a crisis situation. Warren *Buffet* hits the nail on the head when he is quoted as follows:

> The worst business is one that grows quickly, needs significant amounts of capital to generate growth, and then makes little or no money (sla/n-tv.de, 2015).

If one leaves the business perspective and considers growth from an economic point of view, then the advantages of economic growth are undisputed (Smolney & Schneeweis, 1999). As it is accurately stated in the "Agenda for Development":

> Without economic growth, there can be no sustainable increase in private or public consumption, private or public capital formation, health, welfare, and security. Regardless of the social processes through which distribution decisions are made, the ability to do so is extremely limited in poor societies; economic growth promotes this ability (Boutros-Ghali, 1995).

In addition to the economic and economic policy advantages that young growth companies bring, there are also a multitude of endogenous reasons from a business perspective why young startups embark on a growth course (Fueglistaller et al., 2008, p. 451 ff.).[28]

Thus, one finds a number of empirical and theoretical discussions in the literature, which can be summarised in reference to *Purle* and cited as arguments "pro growth" for startups. The two following motives are considered the most important based on his literature study (Purle, 2004, p. 56 ff.):

- The survival probability of startups increases

To counter the risk of bankruptcy, growth is one way to avoid it. Ultimately, smaller companies are more sensitive to external "life-threatening" shocks, so the argument is that the probability of survival increases with size. However, it should be noted that too rapid growth can also be a threat to existence. "Everything in moderation" is also the motto here.

- Shareholder Value Orientation

Although the growth argument only indirectly states that this is also profitable, shareholder value orientation is seen as a motive for growth. It must certainly be taken into

[28] Despite all the justified euphoria associated with the advantages of young startups and their growth potential, one must also see the other side of the coin. The criticism associated with this is not directed against the positive statements as such, but is rather an extension to also consider the negative sides of startups, which must not be concealed, otherwise the topic appears like a *panacea*. Ted *Baker* and Friederike *Welter* therefore rightly emphasise: "We do not mean to suggest that entrepreneurship does not contribute to economic development. Of course it does!" (Baker & Welter, 2015, p. 9).

But often, for example, jobs in startups are characterised by low to no wages, low social benefits, lack of security, and lack of planning certainty. This means that people who are employed there initially make fewer investments than employees in established companies. In addition, they are often 'necessity founders', that is, they had no other choice but to start a company. Ted *Baker* points out these issues, and shows that entrepreneurship is often seen purely positively, but often also has negative aspects. Thus, *Baker* and *Welter* criticise governments for being too optimistic in this regard: "Governments and support organisations, always in need of means to grow and develop their own economies, have eagerly picked up the mantra of 'entrepreneurship is something good', contributing to employment, innovation, general wealth and wellbeing. Consequently, for decades now entrepreneurship has been perceived as something of a panacea for all kinds of economic problems (…). Name it, and entrepreneurship helps to solve it!" (Baker & Welter, 2015, p. 9).

There are also studies in the USA that the positive effects of entrepreneurship for an economy are not higher on average due to bankruptcies etc., especially when it is relative to the individual persons. Especially the *Unicorns* outshine many statistics. Here, the median or the variance and standard deviation would certainly be interesting in terms of numbers.

account that, for example, sales growth or an increase in the number of employees does not necessarily lead to an increase in profits. Ultimately, however, the basic idea here is that growth increases the company's value.[29]

Further mentioned, but rather secondary rated motives are:

- Employee motivation (individual promotion opportunities, participation in new things, etc.)
- Stabilisation of employment
- Economies of Scale (cost advantages with increased production in areas such as procurement, research and development, production, sales, financing, organisation, etc.)
- Economies of Scope (greater synergy effects between individual business areas, product lines, functional departments, etc.)
- Reputation (creation of a positive, successful perception)
- Negotiating power towards customers, suppliers, state, union, etc.
- Improvement of the ability to innovate
- Individual interests of the entrepreneurs (higher prestige, greater power, higher salaries, greater leeway, etc.) (Purle, 2004, p. 56 ff.)

If one follows, for example, the Lean-StartUp approach, then there are four primary ways that are crucial for sustainable growth (Ries, 2011, p. 208):

1. "Word of mouth"
   Most products have a natural degree of growth embedded, which is caused by the enthusiasm of satisfied customers, by sharing their enthusiasm for the product through word of mouth.
2. "A side effect of product usage"
   Fashion or status, such as luxury goods, increase their popularity through their use. Just the fact of seeing someone wearing the latest fashion or driving a special car can inspire us to want to acquire the product as well.
3. "Through funding advertising"
   Advertising entices customers to buy. As long as the cost of advertising a new customer, i.e., the marginal cost in this regard, is less than the corresponding marginal return achieved with the additional customer, the surplus (marginal profit) can be used to generate further customers. The larger the marginal profit, the presumably larger the growth. Thus, sustainable growth can arise from advertising measures.

---

[29] The principle of future orientation has a major influence on the valuation of young growth companies, which initially contribute a rather small value to the economy compared to their future development potential (Heinrichs, 2008, p. 1).

4. "Through repeat, purchase or use."
   Some products are repeatedly purchased by customers, e.g., through one-time subscriptions (e.g., with cable companies) or through repeated individual purchases (e.g., in grocery stores), so that growth can be generated in this way (Ries, 2011, p. 208).

Such sources of sustainable growth lead to feedback loops, which *Ries* refers to as *"engines of growth"* (Ries, 2011, p. 208).[30]

The range of types and strategies of growth in startups from a business perspective ranges from internal growth to external growth to cooperative growth. Internal growth refers to, for example, technology or customer orientation strategies, external growth to, for example, company takeovers, and cooperative growth to, for example, joint ventures, franchising, strategic alliances, with growth strategies including collaborative technologies also conceivable (Volkmann & Tokarski, 2006, p. 23).

If one now wants to take a *macroeconomic* perspective on entrepreneurship processes, taking into account a complexity science view, then the focus on evolutionary economics is appropriate, which in particular makes parallels to the analysis of complex systems clear (Liening, 1998, p. 211).[31] Moreover, Evolutionary Economics also opposes a

[30] *Ries* adds that in the negative case, startups would not starve, but drown. He means that while there would be millions of ideas on how to make a product even better, most of these ideas often only have marginal effects on success. Startups, according to *Ries,* therefore need to focus on the big experiments that lead to "validated learning". The "engines of growth" can help to focus on the important things (Ries, 2011, p. 209).

[31] According to *Witt,* an evolutionary theory is spoken of when three criteria are met, which can be described with the keywords "dynamic", "historical" and "self-transformation explaining" (Witt, 2002, p. 10): First, the theory is a *dynamic theory,* i.e., it opposes static or statically comparative views in economics. Because these views implicitly assume that one can abstract from the temporal dimension of economic action without the theory losing explanatory power. However, this is doubtful if the theory specifically aims at the laws of temporal change of economic phenomena. The theories of complex systems with their consideration of non-linear dynamic processes can offer an explanatory approach here. Secondly, the theory is based on the concept of *irreversibility,* i.e., it opposes attempts to develop dynamic theories that are 'without memory' and in which the prehistory can be neglected. One could speak here, in terms of synergetics, of taking into account frozen system history. And thirdly, the theory formulates hypotheses about the temporal behaviour of systems in which innovations occur, i.e., not exogenous, but *endogenous explanations* are used for changes or transformations. This means that the aspect of *self-organisation,* as also emphasised by synergetics, is inherent (Liening, 1998, pp. 212 f.; Witt, 1987, pp. 9 ff., 2002, p. 10).

These are three important criteria that the theories of complex systems repeatedly emphasise. The last criterion, which highlights the endogeneity of explanatory patterns, represents the specificity of an Evolutionary Economics as a subset of a more comprehensive science of complex systems. The basis of an Evolutionary Economics is *Schumpeter's* theory of economic development, which over time has been taken up, modified and supplemented by other economists.

reduction of complexity to lineal equilibrium processes and simple prediction models in the context of macroeconomic considerations. Thus, *Nijkamp* and *Reggiani* state about Evolutionary Economics:

> The evolutionary paradigm is recently coming to the fore in modern economic and social sciences as a reaction against conventional theories aiming to reduce many complex phenomena to an equilibrium projection, system predictability and hierarchical control (Nijkamp & Reggiani, 1993, p. 1).

Schumpeter, for example, puts forward three theses in his evolutionary design: First, the entrepreneurs, who can implement new combinations of resources or change existing organisational forms, decide how the evolutionary course[32] of an economy will be. Secondly, the necessary condition for this is a stationary phase of the economy, in which only the effects can be calculated that are associated with a change. And thirdly, the spread of an innovation wave is characterised by the "flock-like" appearance of entrepreneurs (Schumpeter, 1912).

These three theses connect *Schumpeter's* evolutionary design to a business cycle theory combined with growth effects, which can be embedded in our approach of a synergetic view of the market, in which dynamics and growth are generated on the markets through self-organisation processes.[33] The associated idea of "*Schumpeterian* growth" can be linked with considerations of modern growth theories.

---

[32] The current understanding of evolutionary processes was significantly influenced by *Darwin*, who laid the foundation with his 1859 book 'On the origin of species by means of natural selection'. He explained the process of evolution as a multi-stage process in which variation (i.e., random deviation) and selection (i.e., natural selection) result in mutual interaction. Variation creates different fitness or suitability (Darwin, 1859). The process of natural selection can then take place, which, according to *Nissen,* "must be understood less as selection of the best, but better as selection against the worst" (Nissen, 1997, p. 7).

[33] To gain an introductory understanding of the fundamentals of evolutionary economics, reference is made here to the theory of economic development according to *Schumpeter*, which we had highlighted as significant in the context of examining entrepreneurship schools.

The term 'innovation' is particularly noticeable in the criteria of evolutionary economics. However, evolutionary economics does not make any statements about the content of the innovations mentioned here, as this would contradict the nature of innovations. Instead, it discusses the factors for their occurrence, the conditions for their implementation, and the question of when and how transformation processes are initiated by them. But what should one understand by an innovation? Since *Schumpeter*, attempts have been made to separate two central aspects, that of invention and that of innovation, from each other (Witt, 1987, p. 17).

Schumpeter defines Invention as the invention and Innovation as the implementation or enforcement of the invention. *Schumpeter* considers this distinction important because for him these two terms are associated with different roles: theoretically, anyone can invent, but the enforcement of inventions is left to the entrepreneur. Innovation does not only mean the successful introduction of a new good or service, but possibly also the introduction of new processes and production

In connection with *Schumpeter's* approach, the term 'creative destruction' is used. "In the process of creative destruction", says *Neumann,* "old structures decay under the pressure of competition from innovations and at the same time new directions of production and new economic structures emerge with the innovations" (Neumann, 1984, p. 88). Here, the connection to our considerations becomes clear: order and complexity are two interrelated quantities. Complexity can arise from order without external influence. But order can also emerge from apparent lawlessness. And: *Schumpeter* defines 'development' as "such changes in the cycle of economic life (…) that the economy generates from within itself, only possible changes of the 'self-reliant', not driven by external impulse economy" (Schumpeter, 1912, p. 95). He thus speaks of an endogenous, self-organising explanatory component of the economic process, with the self-organising factor of change being the entrepreneur—in our modern language—formed with entrepreneurship knowledge and an entrepreneurial attitude. He is the 'creative destroyer' in *Schumpeter's* concept.[34] Even if *Schumpeter's* approach may be seen as linear causal or even reductionist in some respects, one must ultimately agree with *Louca* who states:

---

methods, the development of new procurement and sales markets, the generation of new sources of raw materials, and the reorganisation of companies (Schumpeter, 1912, p. 100 f.). Furthermore, the term 'entrepreneur' refers less to the profession than to a certain attitude: readiness for initiative, joy in creative design, foresight, and power drive characterise the entrepreneur. Creativity and inventiveness are left to the one who carries out inventions. The entrepreneur is able to make inventions real, to enforce them. Since pioneer profits are naturally only of short duration, it is not primarily profit that drives the entrepreneur, but rather the will to win, the desire to fight, the urge to shape. He is therefore also primarily curious and inquisitive, thus focussed on a temporal lead. The typical entrepreneur is anything but a hedonist. "He creates restlessly, because he cannot do otherwise …", proclaims *Schumpeter* (Schumpeter ,1912, p. 137). This incorporates psychological assumptions into his concept: they are exogenous assumptions. And the inventions are also explained exogenously. This suggests that on the one hand he appears committed to the neoclassical approach, a view that, among others, *Dopfer* also shares (Dopfer, 1990, p. 29). *Schumpeter* on the other hand distinguishes himself from contemporary, neoclassical equilibrium theories, based on *Marshall, Pigou, Walras* and others. He makes it clear that these theories contain nothing "that would indicate the possibility of development from within itself" (Schumpeter, 1912, p. 75).

[34] To summarise *Schumpeter's* arguments, one can agree with *Witt* who points out that *Schumpeter* sees the form and content of development in the implementation of new combinations. "By implementing new combinations," says *Witt,* "we understand the innovative reallocation of economic resources or the change of organisational forms, distinguished in five categories" (Witt ,1987, p. 37). These five categories are product innovations or differentiations in the quality of products, process innovations in the production and distribution area, the development of new sales markets, the development of new pre-product markets and new sources of supply, and changes in market or corporate organisations.

These changes result in significant adjustment problems. The innovations initially appear alongside the existing forms before they can be displaced by "outcompeting" (Witt, 1987, p. 36). This naturally presupposes that the entrepreneurs, the innovators, have sufficient financial means to implement their combinations. The banks provide the innovators with the necessary purchasing

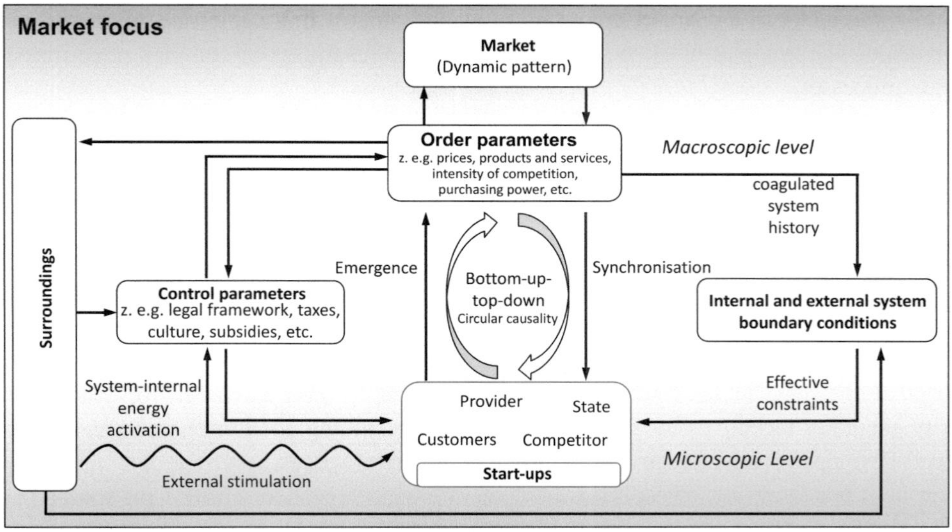

Fig. 7.14 The 'Synergetic Entrepreneurship Model 3': *An* example for the market dimension *(SEM3)*

> Schumpeter's theory was a system of self-generating complexity and instability, where the equilibrium concept really played only a very subsidiary role (Louca, 1997, p. 246).

For a deeper understanding, each part of the *SEM3* (see Fig. 7.14) will be explained in detail in the following section. It should be noted that the details in the model reflect only one of countless possibilities. Whether, for example, prices represent order parameters or external conditions depends, among other things, very much on whether the startups implement a Blue or Red Ocean strategy, and whether the companies are thus, for example, able to co-determine prices or whether they have to accept the prevailing prices on the market (quantity adjusters). In the latter case, prices would not be an 'order parameter', but an 'external boundary condition'. However, it could also be that prices nevertheless represent an order parameter because prices are only formed by the start-ups. Each individual company cannot dictate the price, but it emerges as an emergent

power through credit creation, as *Neumann* emphasises, to "detach production factors from their traditional uses" (Neumann, 1984, p. 88). Apparently, *Schumpeter* sees no problems in assessing the creditworthiness of the innovators, although the risk is borne by the lender and not the entrepreneur. *Witt* suspects that the "innovations and the possible 'founder profits' associated with them (...) seem to be so reliable or so high that the banks are willing to satisfy any credit demand of the innovators at the prevailing interest rate" (Witt, 1987, p. 37).

order parameter as a result of an extensive market process in the interplay of supply and demand. The first part of the book looked in detail at examples of complex price formation processes.

7.3.2 The Elements of the System

7.3.2.1 Control Parameters

The control parameter is never the sole starting point, but it provides the energy necessary to set something in motion at the microscopic level. In the case of examining the emergence of new startups in existing markets or the creation of new markets, legal frameworks or tax policies, for example, certainly play a role. If, for example, a city generates incentives for young companies by providing good infrastructure, such as well-developed roads, free and inexpensive commercial spaces, fast fibre optic lines, low business tax rates, etc., these measures can stimulate a positive climate for startups in the market. If, for example, a technology centre (TC) is established in a university town, which, with the help of attractive conditions and good infrastructure, such as individually tailored premises, personnel support[35], a comprehensive ICT basis, an organised knowledge and research transfer between TC and university, etc., contributes to startups being founded from the university, then this would be an example of such a control parameter that stimulates the market at the microscopic level.

7.3.2.2 The Microscopic Level

A conceivable starting point of a self-organising economic cycle is a phase of stagnation, which can be described by the neoclassical equilibrium theory. In this phase, highly qualified entrepreneurs with their startups appear on the market, bringing innovations to the market or even creating a new market. While *Schumpeter* only sees those entrepreneurs who use long-invented innovations, this model emphasises the role of the entrepreneur in the development of innovations, so that the research and development leading to the startups or taking place within the startups are also taken into account. The transition from the microscopic level to the macroscopic level shows that an emergent process is also seen, which leads to new products, for example, starting from the microscopic level.

While *Schumpeter* sees the role of the entrepreneur, or more generally the businessman, as the only decisive force, this model also emphasises the active roles of stakeholders. For

[35] Personnel support within the infrastructure of a technology centre can include consulting topics related to the establishment of a business model, legal formalities in the context of founding, choice of legal form and insurance, feasibility and economic viability of a business model, funding programmes, generation of equity capital, financing of assistant programmes, etc.

example, stakeholders such as customers are not portrayed as passive, non-innovative individuals whose needs are usually 'taught' by the production side. Because the motto 'What is sold is determined by us, the entrepreneurs' contradicts any modern market-oriented view, according to which not production determines what can be sold, but the market, the customers, the competition.[36] Therefore, the other stakeholders in this concept play an important active role.

7.3.2.3 The Macroscopic Level—Order Parameters

Due to the description of the microscopic level, not only startups but also customers, and other *stakeholders* such as the state, providers of intermediate or preliminary products, competitors etc., play an important role. These factors only lead to the emergence of order parameters, such as prices, products or services, on a macroscopic level from the microscopic level, which in turn could successively synchronise the microscopic level and form a market as a dynamic pattern.

Ultimately, it also depends on the respective market whether prices, quantities or the quality of the offered products emerge as order parameters. For example, consider a comparatively homogeneous good like cement: The price for cement is determined by demand, but also by the competition among cement producers. The current cement price is an important factor for the producers' decisions. Thus, many reduce their cement quantities at lower prices or invest in technology and infrastructure at higher prices. In this case, the price for the good is an order parameter that is formed by the activity in the market and simultaneously influences the activities of the cement producers.

In the market for mobile devices, it is important for manufacturers to be as innovative as possible and not to miss any trend. Apple, in particular, with its range of products and services (iMacs, MacBooks, iPads, iPhone, software) and the associated business model, is considered one of the market leaders that other companies in this market orient themselves towards. In this case, it is mainly not prices and quantities, but product quality and business model, with which Apple has established itself as an order parameter and which many other manufacturers orient themselves towards.

This leads to multiplier effects by those entrepreneurs or startups that assert themselves in the market, which reinforce the emergence and synchronisation until the dynamic pattern on the macroscopic level stabilises. In this dynamic development, the microscopic level is synchronised in such a way that entrepreneurs with their startups

[36] For a long time, companies have tried to manage costs and thus also calculate prices using full cost accounting. However, cost accounting is more of a long-term process, while price calculation is a very short-term process if you want to maintain the ability to react flexibly to the market. Only the introduction of partial cost accounting allows this flexibility, because by determining the variable costs, it defines a price floor above which prices can be flexibly adjusted to the market (Liening, 2002a, 2002b).

also get their turn, whose entrepreneurial competencies are less pronounced than those who previously set the process in motion on the microscopic level.

7.3.2.4 Limitations

Here too, system-internal and -external limitations can be identified that can impact the growth of young companies by directly targeting the microscopic level, but which can also be influenced by the order parameters. Internal elements include, for example, the number of employees, with questions about professional qualifications, company experience, and ultimately human capital etc., being significant. Furthermore, the proportion of departments, the range of products, product complexity (number, diversity, components, integration density etc.), the number of distribution channels, the number of shareholders, the number of subsidiaries or branches etc. influence the internal complexity of the company and can thus be counted among the internal boundary conditions that need to be considered (Purle, 2004, p. 108 ff.). External limitations include aspects such as the number and needs of customers in the market, the number of partners, the proportion of external services, the number of suppliers, the annual market growth, the number of competitive products, the number of new products in the market or the total turnover in the market. They influence the external complexity of the company (Purle, 2004, p. 108 ff.).

7.3.2.5 Environment

As a condition for economic upswing, *Witt* sees an economically stable environment, so that from a complexity science perspective, order and not complexity must be the prerequisite here.

> A necessary condition for the first, most skilled entrepreneurs in a swarm to introduce a major innovation is a state of circular flow where the economic situation is calculable (Witt, 2002, p. 14).

This includes, among other things, creating planning security, which can be ensured, for example, by reliable framework conditions provided by the state. These can be characterised, for example, by a reliable macroeconomic tax and financial policy, a security policy that protects property, permanent price level stability, etc.

Thus, the importance of the environment for young growth companies can be divided into environmental complexity or simplicity, environmental dynamics or stability, but also environmental pressure or liberality, with the frequency of changes in individual environmental elements, the extent and predictability of environmental changes in the dynamic process being of particular relevance. The pressure to adapt or the compulsion to react due to the scarcity of resources or legal regulations must be taken into account (Purle, 2004, p. 75 ff.). When considering the environment, the question of the complexity-environment mismatch must be asked, which arises because the implemented company complexity does not match the environmental requirements. If one follows *Purle,* such a mismatch can arise for different reasons:

1. The *perceived* environmental requirements do not (any longer) correspond to the *actual* environmental requirements. As a result, the company complexity implemented based on the perceived environmental requirements is oriented towards ‘wrong’ requirements.
2. The perceived requirements do indeed correspond to the actual ones, but the company is not able to implement them adequately within the framework of company complexity. This can happen, for example, when the company wants to implement too many different requirements at the same time (Purle, 2004, p. 307).

7.3.3 The Circular Causal Process

7.3.3.1 Business Cycle

On the one hand, in reference to *Schumpeter's* business cycle theory, the circular causal process describes a business cycle in which, as shown in Fig. 7.15, upswing, boom, downturn, and low point of the cycle alternate.

As described at the microscopic level, not only startups but also customers and other *stakeholders* such as the state etc. play an important role. Only in combination do they lead to the emergence of order parameters such as prices and goods at the macroscopic level, which in turn successively synchronise the market at the microscopic level. In a first phase, those startups that establish themselves on the market, as described, lead to multiplier effects that reinforce emergence and synchronisation until the dynamic pattern stabilises at the macroscopic level. In this process (during the upswing), entrepreneurs with their startups also come into play, whose entrepreneurial skills are less pronounced than those who previously initiated the process at the microscopic level. There is a “flocking appearance” (Schumpeter, 1912, p. 342) of entrepreneurs until no entrepreneurial skill is needed to enforce the innovations. The analogy to synergetics is vividly underscored by *Witt* when he says:

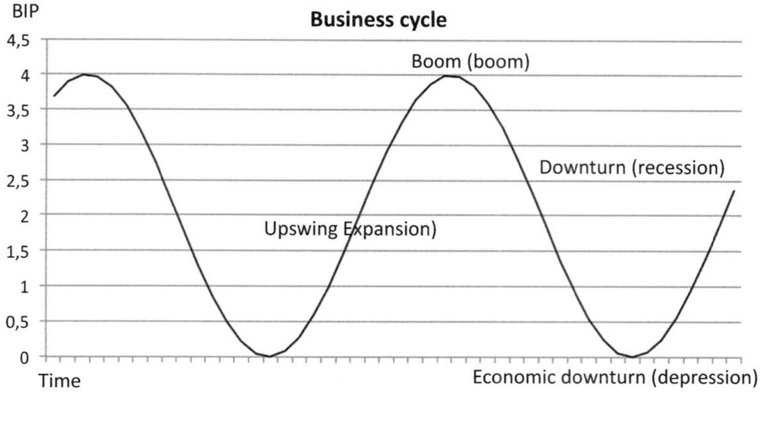

Fig. 7.15 Business cycle

> The analogue to Schumpeter's thesis of the 'flocking' appearance of entrepreneurs is the synergetic phenomenon of self-reinforcing expansion following the breakthrough of basic innovations (Witt, 1993, p. 33).

However, the notion that the "flocking appearance" of entrepreneurs is the *only* cause of economic upswing must be rejected. *Neumark* points out that this thesis is "exaggerated, not to say misleading (is, d. Verf.), even if one links it with the—at least system-immanent correct—view of the cyclical 'elimination of entrepreneurial profit'" (Neumark, 1984, p. 52).

In the phase of boom, when the innovations have become commonplace and overcapacities have formed, a price drop and thus a downturn sets in, which can lead to a low point in the cycle or a depression. The pioneer profits[37] are reduced and only those companies that best manage this phase can survive in the market.[38] Bankruptcies increase until only those startups that can handle this situation confidently remain active. A new stationary phase sets in. This new phase—and this is not clear in the simplified Fig. 7.15—is at a higher evolutionary level, as the achievements of the upswing spread throughout the entire economy, and the circular causal process begins anew (Liening, 1998, p. 216 ff.).

Thus, the cycle process contains not only the described business cycle but also a growth component, which will be examined in more detail below.

7.3.3.2 Dynamic Growth

i. The 'old' growth theory

The dynamic pattern that emerges at the macroscopic level of our synergetic model is not only subject to fluctuations within the framework of a business cycle, but is particularly characterised by dynamic growth, as is schematically represented in the overall

---

[37] When we discuss profits and profit maximisation in relation to our discussion of *Schumpeter's* evolutionary concept compared to neoclassical economics, it is difficult to see a contrast between the neoclassical approach to profit maximisation, as we have already discussed in the first part of the book, and the motivation of the entrepreneur. As *Neumann* emphasises: "The difference between Schumpeter's model and that of neoclassical economics is not that alternative objectives are postulated, but that the assumed possibilities for action differ" (Neumann, 1984, p. 89). And he further explains:

"The neoclassical model assumes a given technical knowledge and a given institutional framework. In Schumpeter's model, however, entrepreneurs seek to maximise their profit by pushing the boundaries of technical knowledge and by making institutional (organisational) changes" (Neumann, 1984, p. 89).

[38] In this context, the product life cycle model by *Hellbrück* is also interesting, who has expanded *Schumpeter's* business cycle model under the topic 'Synergetics and Market Processes' (Hellbrück, 1993).

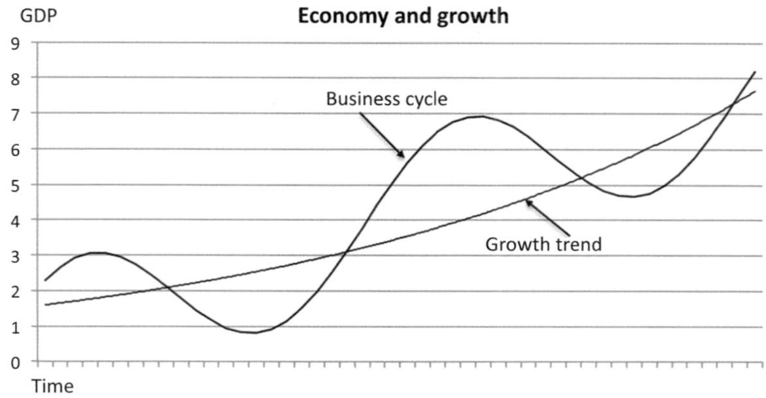

Fig. 7.16 Business cycle and growth

development in Fig. 7.16. Business cycle and growth processes together form a dynamic pattern at the macroscopic level in the synergetic model.

The growth theory has developed into one of the most dynamic and innovative areas of economics in recent years (Liening, 2008, p. 397). The central question it addresses is: How can the long-term development of economic systems be researched if changes in growth processes are not exogenous, but endogenous generated, if developments cannot be explained via linear cause-effect chains, if structural breaks are likely and equilibria are both rare and multiple, in short:

How do we investigate dynamic economic systems between order and complexity?

Mechanistic approaches, which significantly shape both *Keynesianism* and neoclassicism, do not answer this question (Liening, 2008, p. 398). This is certainly one reason for the economic policy irrelevance of the 'old' growth theory , which is Keynesian motivated based on the models of *Harrod* and *Domar* and neoclassically oriented towards the *Solow* model. The latter undoubtedly has a higher status in the economic discussion (Liening, 2008, p. 398).

Thus, *Solow* himself correctly states that the models of *Harrod* and *Domar* inaccurately reflect reality. These models are designed in such a way that an equilibrium growth rate is surrounded by centrifugal forces, so that one can speak of a "growth on the knife's edge" (Liening, 2008, p. 398). Even if one must consider the following words of *Solow* as exaggerated, the criticism of the instability of the model, combined with exponential growth effects, is not entirely unjustified:

> An expedition from Mars arriving on Earth, having read this literature, would have expected to find only wreckage of a capitalism that had shaken itself to pieces long ago (Solow, 1988, p. 308).

Indeed, it must be stated that in contrast to the post-Keynesian models, the neoclassical *Solow* model can be described as the 'peak' of the 'old' growth theory. This neoclassical model assumes that there is only one production sector, one good, no foreign countries, and no government activities. It is therefore, like the other growth models, a model with very restrictive assumptions. *Solow* notes on this:

> All theory depends on assumptions which are not quite true. That is what makes it theory (Solow, 1956, p. 65).

At the centre of the neoclassical growth theory is the production function. It is the central neoclassical instrument for theoretical analysis. The production function describes the relationship between input and output. The input consists of two production factors: labour L and capital K. The production function can therefore be generally described as follows: $Y = F(K, L)$, where Y symbolises the output (Solow, 1956, p. 66).

If we now consider the production function not two-dimensional, but one-dimensional for simplification, by looking at the output per labour force, the equation $Y = F(K, L)$ results under certain assumptions (constant scale returns): $Y/L = F(K/L, 1)$, or in other words: $y = f(k)$, where $y = Y/L$ represents the output per labour force and the capital per labour force is symbolised by $k = K/L$. Expanded by the possibility of technological progress, $Y = F(K, L \cdot A)$ results, where A symbolises labour efficiency. For $y = f(k)$, $k = K/(L \cdot A)$ is then the capital intensity, which is defined here as capital per head and labour efficiency.

A significant result of this theory is that given a predetermined savings rate and the identity of national savings and investment, the long-term growth rate of an economy is determined solely by the rate of population growth and the increase in average labour productivity or technological progress.

The factors that influence growth in the long term, such as population growth and technological progress, are exogenously given in this model. This also applies, for example, to the investment rate, which—and this is often criticised—has no sustainable impact on long-term growth. However, it must be emphasised once again that all relevant factors that can guarantee sustainable growth are considered exogenously from the outside (Liening, 2008, p. 398 f.).

ii. The 'New Growth Theory'

Based on the above considerations, an approach that interprets decisive determinants explaining long-term growth as exogenous variables can be seen as not particularly satisfying. *Ruschinski* notes on this:

> Technical or scientific achievements do not fall like manna from heaven, but are results of real economic actors. The aim of the theory of endogenous growth is therefore to provide a decision-theoretic foundation for sustained economic growth without having to resort to exogenous explanatory variables (Ruschinski, 1996, p. 53).

The question therefore arises as to how such an approach can be modified to become more realistic, so that a model emerges whose growth determinants understand growth as a self-organising process, which can also be described as complex and synergetic in our sense. The goal must be to describe a model that characterises growth processes (especially with regard to startups) not exclusively by smooth transitions, but rather allows discontinuities, eruptive changes, and turbulence. Only in this way can the economy be understood as a non-linear, dynamic, or complex system. From these and numerous other considerations, the 'New Growth Theory' arises (Liening, 1998, p. 269 ff., 2008, p. 399; Bloom et al., 2013; Grossmann & Helpman, 1994; Rivera-Batiz & Romer, 1991).

In this context, the 'New Growth Theory' can be seen as a stringent further development of the neoclassical growth theory (Ruschinski, 1996, p. 53). In particular, the works of Paul *Romer* should be noted, which have significantly shaped the growth theory discussion (Romer, 1986a, 1986b, 1990, 1994).*Romer,* who received the Nobel Prize in Economic Sciences in 2018 together with W. *Nordhaus,* names three important prerequisites for growth:

> The first is that technological change—improvement in the instructions for mixing together raw materials—lies in the heart of economic growth (…).
> The second premise is that technological change arises in large part because of intentional actions taken by people who respond to market incentives (…).
> The third and most fundamental premise is that instructions for working with raw materials are inherently different from other economic goods. Once the cost of creating a new set of instructions has been incurred, the instructions can be used over and over again at no additional cost (Romer, 1990, p. 72).

Technological change and progress, people who generate this progress in response to market incentives, and finally the assumption that knowledge about the processing of raw materials is to be distinguished from other goods, are therefore decisive for *Romer*. The question arises whether the *Schumpeterian* approach, which we pursue in our synergetic concept, is reflected or can be reflected in the models of *Romer*. *Romer* discusses his assumptions using the example of various growth theories, which correspond at one time with one premise, another time with another premise, and comes to the conclusion:

> The only way to accept all three premises (…) is to return to the suggestion of Schumpeter (1942) and explicitly introduce market power.

Therefore, it does not seem too daring to also refer to the new growth theory as "Neo-*Schumpeterian* Growth Theory", in which entrepreneurs and the start-ups they initiate play a significant role (Liening, 1998, p. 275).

Especially in a highly industrialised economy, where there are almost no raw materials available, good research and development results play an important role. However, this requires highly qualified entrepreneurs and employees in business and entrepreneurship who are determined to turn inventions into innovations. The endowment of an economy with human capital[39] is therefore a central aspect of modern economies.[40]

In reference to *Romer*, the neoclassical production function should be extended here by a factor that takes this aspect into account. This ultimately amounts to endogenising human capital in the growth model. This endogenisation represents a new quality in the discussion about growth theory, which can therefore also be referred to as 'Endogenous Growth Theory'.

For example, the assumption of an exogenously given technical progress is abolished. While the neoclassical growth theory assumed that technical and scientific achievements 'fall from the sky like manna', the new growth theory aims to endogenise key variables that are still of an exogenous nature in the neoclassical theory.

Lucas highlights the following effects that arise when integrating human capital development into an economic growth model:

> Introducing human capital into the model, then, involves spelling out both the way human capital affects current production and the way the current time allocation affects the accumulation of human capital (Lucas, 1988, p. 17).

To integrate these two effects into the current model, it is assumed that the rate of change of knowledge and skills is dynamic and dependent on capital accumulation.

It is assumed that the change in human capital *(h)* is always positive from a certain income per worker (here referred to as z) and increases over time in accordance with the law of returns with the monetary and physical capital per head, or more precisely per efficiency unit (see Fig. 7.17). It is plausible to assume that human capital stagnates in the medium term,[41] if the assumed minimum income per worker is undercut.[42]

---

[39] Here we want to understand human capital as a factor of production. By human capital we mean the abilities, skills and knowledge internalised in humans, which the individual has acquired through education, further education and experience. The term human capital is therefore closely linked to the concept of knowledge, competence and education. Human capital is increased by individuals increasing their knowledge and improving their competences through education, further education and practice/experience. See also: *Krämer* or *Donges* in the context of the debate about the non-word "human capital" of the year 2004 in: Halasz (2005).

[40] Factors of production such as labour and capital as well as technological progress lead to economic growth. This idea applies to industrial and service societies, but not to the knowledge society, as Horst *Siebert* emphasises, in which human capital becomes the decisive determinant of growth (Siebert, 2005).

[41] The assumption that knowledge stagnates rather than decreases at low income is in line with the idea that *Romer* represents. Thus, *Romer* states: "Knowledge does not depreciate" (Romer, 1986b, p. 1019).

[42] Our considerations start with a neoclassical growth model by *Solow,* which operates with very restrictive assumptions (one production sector, one good, no foreign countries, no state) (Solow, 1956). The model of *Solow* shows how savings, population growth, and technological progress

Fig. 7.17 Endogenous law of returns growth of human capital

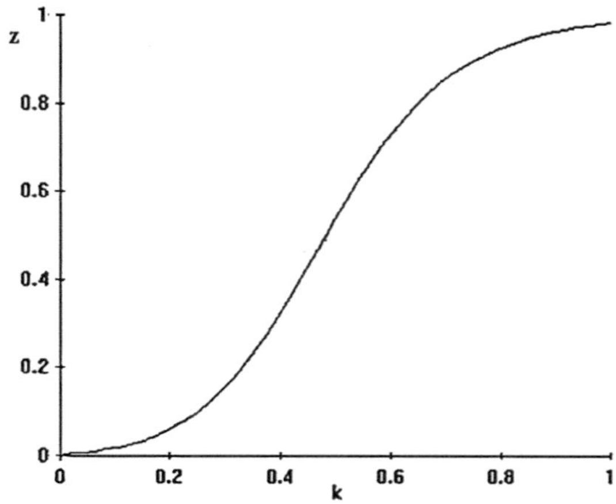

Overall, on the one hand, with higher human capital, respectively higher general knowledge and higher specific entrepreneurship knowledge, the possibility of a higher per capita income can grow and on the other hand, a higher per capita income can lead to

---

interact and influence the growth of production over time. The following model is based on the work of Richard *Day,* who already in 1982 gave pioneering impulses for the explanation of the emergence of chaos and complexity in growth models by modifying the neoclassical model based on *Solow* (Day, 1982). However, the model deviates from *Day's* proposal according to our considerations on technological progress. Our neoclassical starting model, in which the capital intensity per *efficiency unit* is calculated, is therefore:

(1) $k(t) = \frac{K(t)}{L(t) \cdot A(t)}$ and $k(t+1) = \frac{\sigma \cdot f(k(t)) - \delta \cdot k(t) + k(t)}{(1+\omega)(1+a)}$ mit

$K =$ Kapital, $L =$ Arbeiteinsatz, $A =$ Arbeitseffizienz, $\sigma =$ Sparquote, $\delta =$ Abschreibungsrate, $\omega =$ Wachstumsrate der Bev ö lkerung, $a =$ technologischer Fortschritt,

Where the work efficiency *A* depends on a variety of factors, such as education, knowledge level, and the skills of entrepreneurs and workers. The volume of work is therefore measured in *efficiency units*, which takes into account both the number of entrepreneurs and employees and the efficiency of each worker. For the per capita production function *f* for *f(k(t))* applies:

$f(k(t)) = B \cdot k(t)^{\beta}.$

The latter function also results from a common *Cobb-Douglas* production function$F$ with $F(L(t), K(t)) = B \cdot L(t)^{\alpha} \cdot K(t)^{1-\alpha}$, where then $\beta := 1 - \alpha$ is set and calculated per head (Cobb & Douglas, 1928).

Days model can be seen as a kind of special case of the above model (1) if one first excludes technological progress, secondly sets the depreciation $\delta = 1$ and thirdly adds a pollution term to the per capita production function *f*. For a better understanding of the model, see Liening (1998, p. 238 ff.). In this new model, technological progress is initially also explained exogenously by the parameter *a*, which represents the factor by which work efficiency changes, which in turn depends on the level of knowledge of the workforce. Thus, *a* can also be generally declared as the rate of the possibility of a higher (entrepreneurial) level of knowledge. This situation can therefore be interpreted from both directions, education or income.[43]

However, it cannot be easily transferred to the national economy as a whole. Assuming that there had been neither innovations nor technological changes in the last hundred years, then the population would still be driving carriages across the country and crossing the seas with sailing ships. One could promote human capital formation by enabling a larger proportion of the population to achieve a higher level of education. Or one could force (physical) capital accumulation by producing more sailing ships and carriages. But at some point, one would have to realise that the economic benefit, assuming diminishing marginal utility, is very low if an additional high school graduate drives an additional carriage (Liening, 1998, p. 279 f.).

In summary, this means that—from an economic perspective—a higher level of human capital does not per se lead to a higher national income or a (technological) progress. Rather, it is the innovation, creativity, inventive spirit, and the entrepreneurial mentality invoked by Schumpeter*Schumpeter* (Schumpeter, 1912) or the entrepreneurial attitude introduced by us, which leads to a higher standard of living (expressed in per capita income) with an increase in human capital. Therefore, in the context of human capital formation, *Entrepreneurship Education* can take on an important function to promote the corresponding entrepreneurial Bildung.[44]

Overall, the above considerations imply that in the present model it is implicitly assumed that there is a *'transmission effect'* between human capital and per capita monetary and physical capital, which can be triggered by terms such as entrepreneurial attitude or 'Entrepreneurial Spirit' (Liening, 2013, p. 99). In the context of the corresponding entrepreneurial education to trigger and support such an effect, an appropriate Entrepreneurship Education makes sense.[45] In this context, it is important to address

---

change of knowledge. This rate of change is now replaced by the endogenous human capital function h, so that the new model (2) results overall:

$$(2)\ k(t) = \frac{K(t)}{L(t)\cdot A(t)} \text{ and } k(t+1) = \frac{\sigma\cdot f(k(t))-(\delta-1)\cdot k(t)}{(1+\omega)(1+h(k(t))}, \text{ where}$$

$$h(k(t)) = \begin{cases} z(k(t)), \text{ falls } f(k(t)) \geq y^{\min} \\ 0, \text{ falls } f(k(t)) < y^{\min} \end{cases} \text{mit}_{z(k(t)} = \frac{1}{1+e^{\tau\left(y^{\min}-f(k(t))\right)}}$$

It is assumed that the change in human capital is always positive from a certain income and develops over time according to the law of returns with *k(t)*. It is plausible to assume that the level of knowledge stagnates in the medium term if the assumed minimum per capita income $y^{\min}$ is undercut.

[43]The yield law function course of $z(k(t))$ was depicted using the software *Maple*. In this example, $\tau = 10$, $y^{\min} = 0.6$ and in the production function $B = 1.0$ as well as $\beta = 0.7$ were set.

[44]*Ziesemer*, for example, assumes with reference to *Solow* that technical progress in general can hardly be stimulated and that it ultimately remains the result of entrepreneurial initiative, so that even well-intentioned state subsidies may only hinder progress (Ziesemer, 2007, p. 185).

[45]The direct connection between the macroeconomic and the individual level becomes visible at the latest in the above summary.

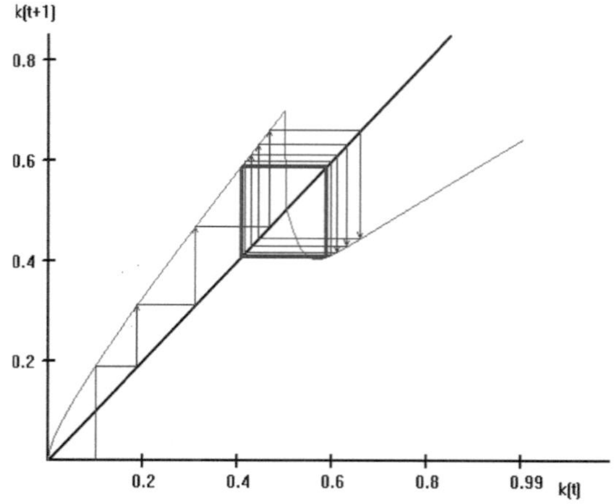

Fig. 7.18 Two-cycle attractor in the growth model with endogenised human capital formation

the significance of the value basis in addition to the knowledge base in the educational processes of entrepreneurs or intrapreneurs. Bildung in the form of Entrepreneurship Education promotes economic creativity, personal responsibility, decision-making ability, independence, and the ability to take responsibility for others. The focus should be on self-organised learning forms that link instruction with construction in a stimulating way and lead to entrepreneurial assessment, decision-making, and action skills through methods that activate learners (Liening, 2006). This can be seen as a central opportunity to positively reinforce the transmission effect.

7.3.3.3 A Growth Model with Endogenised Human Capital Formation—Transmission Effects through Entrepreneurial Attitude

The results of a simulation of the growth model outlined above are shown in Fig. 7.18.[46]

The parameters are chosen so that, ceteris paribus, only the endogenously defined human capital formation with its transmission effect can be considered as a cause for permanent growth.

For below-average values (< 0.5) of the capital intensity , i.e. the monetary and physical capital per head or per efficiency unit, human capital development stagnates, so that

[46] The savings rate here is 40 %, i.e. $\sigma = 0.4$. To simplify the analysis, the population growth rate is 0 %, so $\omega = 0$. The depreciation rate also applies $\delta = 0$. In the 'knowledge function' h, $\tau = 100$ and $y^{\min} = 0.5$ are set. In the production function, the level parameter $B = 0.7$ is set and the substitution parameter $\beta = 0.5$ is assumed. The reason for this can be found in the previous comments on the neoclassical model. It should be added that a change in the savings rate can at best explain a short-term change in economic growth, but by no means a permanent growth. In the original neoclassical model, it is primarily the exogenously defined population growth and the exogenously given technological progress that can explain permanent growth. In contrast to the neoclassical *Solow* model, in this model the technological progress is implicitly explained by the endogenous function for human capital formation.

one obtains undisturbed growth of the monetary and physical capital intensity (measured in efficiency units), provided that the per capita capital is below the steady state , the growth equilibrium, as is the case here.[47] When the critical point y^{min}, the minimum income required for an increase in the level of knowledge and degree of competence, is reached, human capital begins to grow according to the law of returns, which ultimately increases work efficiency, initially resulting in a decrease in monetary and physical capital intensity.

Given the parameter constellation, it is shown that an equilibrium is achieved at a certain initial value of capital intensity (0.1), which exhibits a two-cycle. This results from the fact that the critical value y^{min} is repeatedly undercut with the current parameter constellation, which leads to a stagnation of the level of knowledge and degree of competence. This leads to a short-term increase in monetary and physical capital intensity, as the work efficiency is now lower than before. However, this short-term increase causes the critical value to be exceeded and human capital to grow. Ultimately, this results in an increase in work efficiency and thus a short-term decrease in monetary and physical capital intensity, and so on.

This makes it clear that the growth effect caused by the endogenous explanation of human capital accumulation does not lead to a uniform increase in gross domestic product (GDP). Instead, fluctuations occur, which, as in the above parameter constellation, can lead to a uniform oscillation. Figure 7.19 shows this process in relation to the development of capital intensity over time.

At this point, it should be noted that the endogenisation of the level of knowledge and the degree of competence can result in an irregular development of monetary and physical capital per capita, in addition to a regular course like the one above.

In the bifurcation diagram , which is visualised in Fig. 7.20, the capital intensity *k(t)* is shown against the substitution parameter β of the production function. [48] This parameter indicates how strongly the factor of labour is substituted by the factor of (monetary and physical) capital in the production function.

It turns out that with increasing values of the substitution parameter of the production function, the development of the capital intensity is by no means stable, but is repeatedly interrupted by independent processes or irregular development courses.[49]

The bifurcation diagram shows that there are attraction areas at about $\beta = 0.5$ and $\beta = 0.9$, which are likely to be described as chaotic due to their structure. Figure 7.21

---

[47] The growth equilibrium is reached when, in the simplest case, investments and depreciations balance each other out. Then the amount of capital stock per worker will no longer change over time.

[48] As already explained, 'furca' in Latin denotes a two-pronged fork. A bifurcation, as we know, shows the qualitative change in the structure of a complex system. For example, a system whose trajectory converges to a point attractor can suddenly 'flip' into a two-cycle by changing a parameter.

[49] The parameters for the following figures are: $\sigma = 0.3$, $\omega = 0$, $\delta = 0$, $\tau = 100$, $y^{min} = 0.5$, B $= 0.7$ and $0 < \beta < 1$.

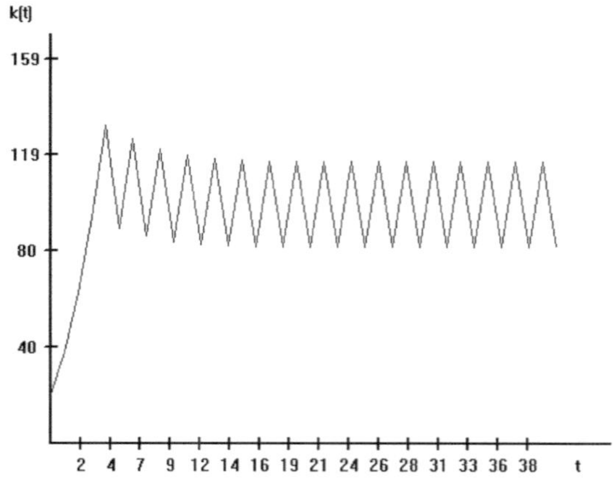

Fig. 7.19 Cyclical development of capital intensity in a growth model with endogenous human capital formation

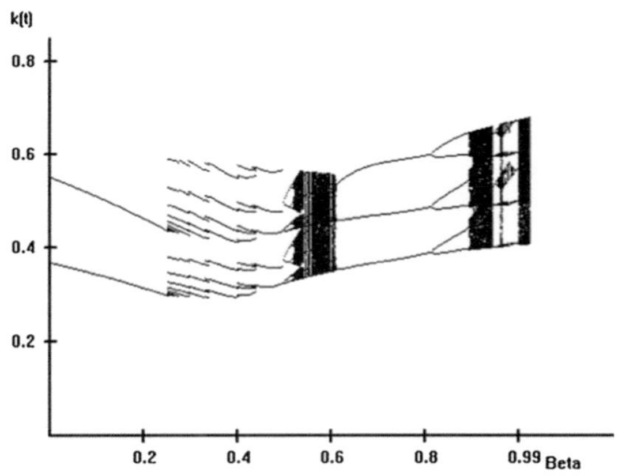

Fig. 7.20 Bifurcation diagram—growth model with endogenised human capital formation

illustrates one of these strange attractors at $\beta = 0.55$, where the development of capital per efficiency unit is shown.

The typical characteristic of strange attractors is that although one can say in which area the capital intensity moves, the exact location cannot be determined.

The butterfly effect fully comes into play here: Minimal deviations in the initial conditions lead to large differences in development after a short time.

Figure 7.22 shows the situation just explained over time. Here you can clearly see the irregular fluctuations, which do not suggest a regular pattern.

A more detailed analysis using the calculation of *Lyapunov* exponents for different β values confirms the suspicion that chaos arises over time. The *Lyapunov* exponent, as we have already discussed in detail, indicates how the trajectories of neighbouring initial values develop in relation to each other. As we know, the *Lyapunov* exponent is positive when neighbouring trajectories drift apart exponentially.

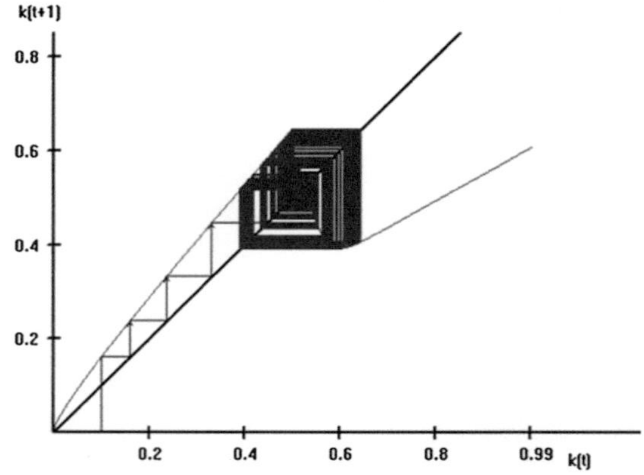

Fig. 7.21 Strange attractor—development of capital intensity in the growth model with $\beta = 0.55$

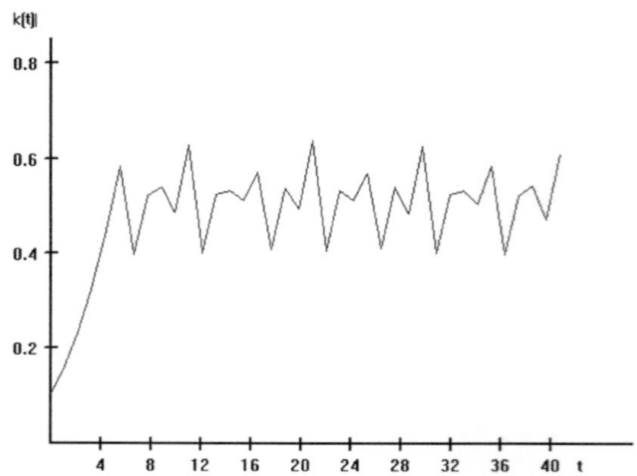

Fig. 7.22 Complex development of capital intensity in the growth model with $\beta = 0.55$

In Fig. 7.23, we see the diagram that shows the development of money and physical capital per capita in the calculation of the *Lyapunov* exponents for different β values. If we compare the *Lyapunov* diagram with the bifurcation diagram, it is clear that the chaotic areas assumed in the bifurcation diagram are indeed chaotic.

Finally, reference is made to Fig. 7.24, which illustrates a growth course for the total output of an economy generated using the developed model, with a significant driver of growth being the influence of endogenous human capital development. This causes, through the transmission effect that we have described with terms such as entrepreneurial spirit, entrepreneurial attitude or entrepreneurial spirit, a positive, even exponential growth trend, which, however, is interspersed with irregular phases.

Overall, it can be stated that the growth effect through human capital accumulation in the model developed here can lead not to a uniform increase in GDP, but to fluctuations, with processes of irregular development possibly occurring. Special importance is given to entrepreneurship education in this model, as it stands for the promotion of the required

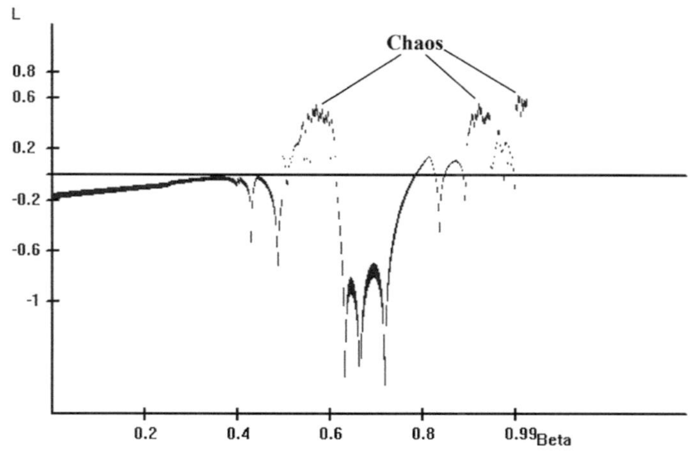

Fig. 7.23 *Lyapunov* diagram for the growth model with endogenous human capital formation

Fig. 7.24 Complex growth cycles—
Y(t) = F(K(t), L(t) · A(t))

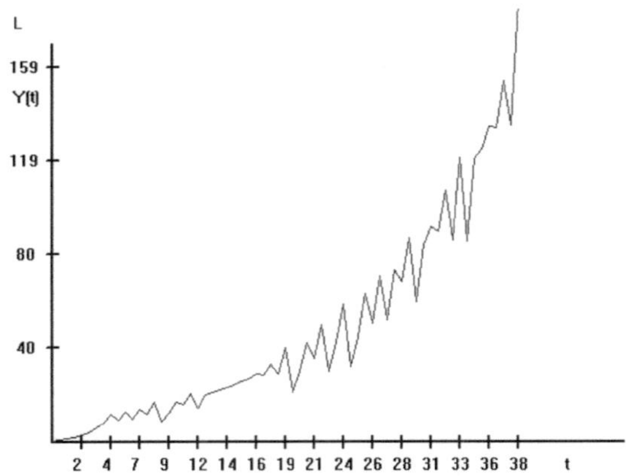

entrepreneurial attitude as a transmission effect between human capital and economic growth. Only this entrepreneurial transformation effect enables the necessary synergistic cyclical process with sustainable growth. Only in this way can a positive effect from human capital on economic growth occur within the framework of this model.

The analysis of the model also shows that the new concept does not necessarily have to lead to a complete break with the neoclassical view. Rather, there are starting points with the help of which neoclassical elements can be integrated into the new view as a special case through modification. Therefore, this theory is not substitutive, but rather complementary to the neoclassical view. Thus, as in the example presented, a link can be created from the neoclassical to the New Growth Theory.

It can be stated that, of course, one cannot expect such a relatively simple model as presented here to exactly reflect real conditions. Such expectations cannot be fulfilled by these models—if one follows the logic of complex systems. But with the help of these models, basic properties of non-linear economic systems can be illustrated. Furthermore, a closer analysis shows that such models allow a wide range of possibilities and explanatory patterns that far exceed the explanatory power of linear or lineal models. This indicates that the consideration of complex systems in economics is not only expedient, but necessary if one wants to leave behind the *Laplacian* demon of a linear-causal economic world. Overall, *Solow's* statement about the enlightening character of his models can be confidently transferred to the non-linear model considered and developed:

> I don't think that models like this lead directly to prescription for policy or even to detailed diagnosis. But neither are they a game. They are more like reconnaissance exercises (Solow, 1987, p. 105).

To save the neoclassical perspective, it can be noted that even in the presented model of dynamic, non-linear growth, taking into account entrepreneurial transmission effects, there is ultimately a philosophy of equilibrium. However, in such a model, the economic equilibrium in the sense of a growth equilibrium is not necessarily a *steady state,* to which the model inevitably runs out like a point attractor. Firstly, the horizon of equilibrium lies clearly in the future, and secondly, the corresponding attractor is rather 'strange' due to the non-linear dynamics and only effective if technological development, supported by human capital formation and an entrepreneurial transmission effect, continues to advance forcefully, thus ensuring appropriate economic growth. Zero growth or the absence of any economic growth in this model would lead to a permanent economic regression, which would ultimately threaten the prosperity and livelihoods of society.

This sounds quite plausible. If we were in an economy like the one that existed in the Middle Ages, for example, a low-level equilibrium could possibly settle into a point attractor without any further change, for example, in capital intensity. But in a complex economic world, as it has developed over the last 150 or more years, economic development is already non-linear and linked to the future with its technological innovations.

Thus, in conclusion, the synergetic cycle consists of a business cycle, which is completed by endogenous growth processes. In our model, the endogenous development of human capital, which triggers innovations and technological progress in the context of founding processes through an entrepreneurial transmission effect, and thus unfolds an accelerator effect in terms of growth and prosperity, is crucial.

7.4 Fourth Conclusion: Synergetic View of Entrepreneurship from Multiple Perspectives

7.4.1 Brief Summary of the *SEM* Model and the Theories and Views Behind It

The aim of this chapter was to model and present the topic of entrepreneurship within a multi-level structure with specific economic approaches based on synergetics, without reducing its complexity. Rather, the complexity of the topic was to be constructively accepted, with the area of startup entrepreneurship being considered as an example.

It is obvious that the model presented is based on the underlying assumption of what entrepreneurship should actually be. However, we have seen that there is no uniform definition of entrepreneurship in the relevant literature. Therefore, the term entrepreneurship was examined in more detail and classifications of entrepreneurship were made. Trends and controversies were discussed, which particularly highlighted the importance of the complexity science perspective.

The difficulty of formulating a generally binding definition for entrepreneurship also applies to the understanding of the three levels shown. When applying the presented *SEM* model, one should be aware that an explicitly entrepreneurial-complexity science perspective is represented here. All three levels, the individual, the organisational, and the macroeconomic, are considered meaningful in order to obtain a comprehensive picture of entrepreneurial-complex processes.

Thus, the *'Synergetic-Entrepreneurship-Model',* or *SEM,* consists of these three levels, which encompass a complex founding process from a multi-perspective economic view.[50]

As soon as entrepreneurs are on their way to acquiring an entrepreneurial education, and they succeed in implementing successful startups, the processes in the *SEM* can be marked as successful. The implementation is carried out using entrepreneurial-business methods that correspond to complexity and entrepreneurial ways of thinking. These startups are supported by the entrepreneurial transmission effect in the macroeconomic context by potentially triggering growth processes in markets. Overall, the three levels interact with each other: individual learning processes influence the startup events, successful startups enable sustainable growth processes. Conversely, economic growth can

[50] In the context of a very daring thought experiment, one could say that the *'Synergetic-Entrepreneurship-Model',* or *SEM,* consists of these three levels, which accompany an intertwined process along trajectories that in turn—if the process is successful—lead into a 'strange attractor'. As soon as a trajectory of the founding process moves into this strange attractor, the entrepreneurs are on their way to acquiring entrepreneurial Bildung, managing to implement successful startups using business-entrepreneurial methods that conform to complexity science thinking, with these startups triggering growth processes in the macroeconomic context, supported by the entrepreneurial transmission effect, which are largely based on economic reasons.

This idea, to ultimately conceive *SEM1–3* as three *dimensions* of a process that culminates in a strange attractor, only seems charming at first glance. It must be considered that the three levels ultimately describe qualitatively different phenomena. Each of these three levels can be modeled using synergetics and all three are hierarchically linked. However, *SEM 1–3* are so different in content and moreover to be seen in a hierarchy that they should be considered as three clearly distinguishable but interrelated levels according to our presentation. Therefore, the thought experiment of a comprehensive *SEM* in the context of a 'strange attractor' can actually only be classified as very daring. And so it remains here just a footnote on the edge of considerations ...

favour new startups, growth and startups can in turn initiate new, important individual education and learning processes etc.

A specific characteristic of the *SEM* is its synergetic foundation and the analysis of the processes including the synergetic terminologies. Only with such a theoretical basis is it possible to develop a complex, scientifically valid understanding of entrepreneurship and to further develop it. The assumption of complexity and self-organisation as important characteristics inherent in entrepreneurial processes suggested a theoretical foundation through the synergetics as a central sub-discipline of a science of complex systems.

Thus, the model offers new possibilities at various levels. Figure 7.25 shows the '*Synergetic* E*ntrepreneurship* M*odel*' with its three levels or dimensions and the connections between the levels at a glance.

In a certain way, the approach of a 'fractal' structure of the SEM is shown. Thus, the SEM1 can be imagined as an element at the micro level of the SEM2 and the SEM2 as an element at the micro level of the SEM3.

In terms of content, however, the SEM does not ultimately derive the only true path, regardless of whether the SEM is underpinned with the Effectuation, Bricolage or any other entrepreneurial approach, such as the Discovery or Creation approach, or perhaps even discusses the Causation approach. If you look at the organisational level (SEM2), for example, the customer benefit is often not immediately recognisable and it may take a long time to understand the customer at all. The first idea will certainly never be the one that is successful. You always have to test your ideas and possibly change them:

While one moves on safe paths with the *Causation* approach and has a lineal procedure in which one can think in cause-effect mechanisms and thus also make significant progress with the help of classic business methods, the *Effectuation* approach starts from the existing resources and the fact that one cannot be sure at the beginning in which direction everything will develop. There is no certainty about whether the idea one has will still be the same tomorrow. One does not know because new opportunities might arise due to the high degree of complexity, with the scarcity of resources adding to the difficulty from the perspective of *Bricoleurs*. While the *Causation* approach assumes that three conditions must be met, namely having a plannable future, being able to formulate fixed goals, and operating in a stable environment, these conditions are differently situated in the *Effectuation* approach. Here, the presence of complexity or an uncertain future is important. Therefore, it is not possible to calculate probabilities for future events. On the other hand, negotiable goals (Goal ambiguity) are to be mentioned as a condition. There are no fixed goals at the beginning, but these are gradually created, changed, and redeveloped by the actors. And the last condition would be to have a shapeable environment (Isotropy Environment) (Baker & Nelson, 2005; Fischer, 2012; Kriedel, 2017).

Ultimately, the temporal dimension also plays a role, which becomes clear in the SEM due to the embedded dynamic-temporal processes. While one is in a phase characterised by uncertainty in the immediate founding phase, certainty increases over time

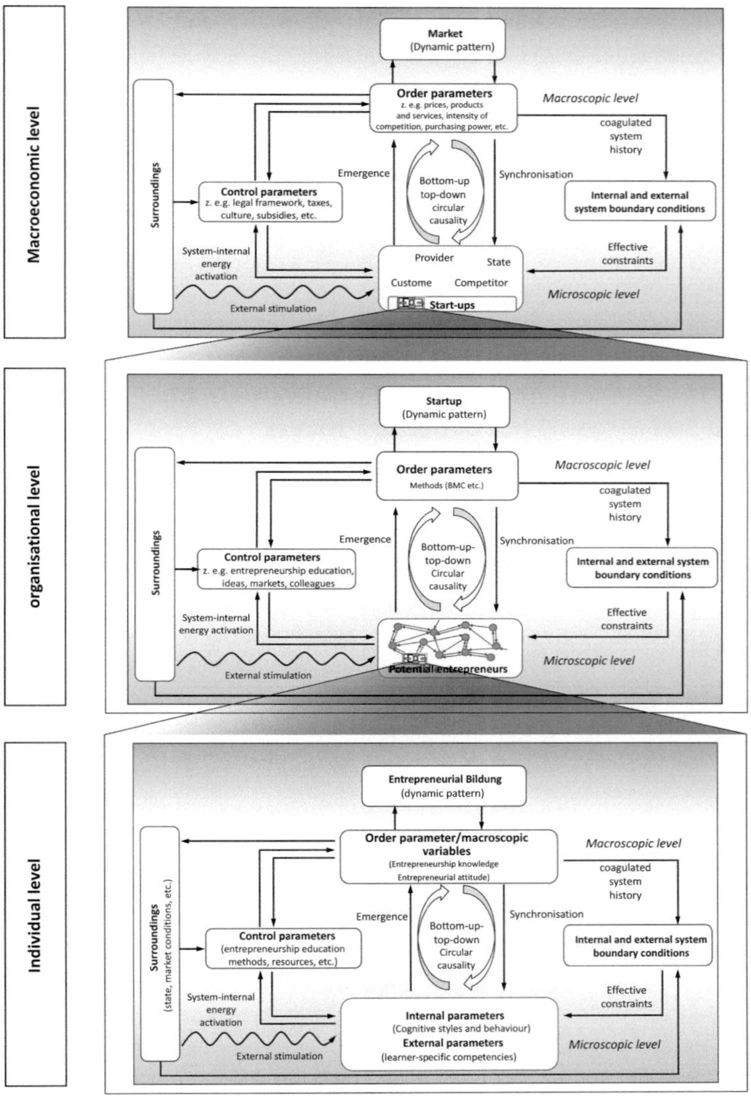

Fig. 7.25 *Synergetic* E*ntrepreneurship* M*odel* (*SEM*). (The final structure of the *SEM* presented here was critically questioned and refined in numerous workshops with the participation of Jan-Martin *Geiger*, Ronald *Kriedel*, Till *Sender* and Waldemar *Wagner*, the author's research team. For example, the creation of the *SEM1* was critically and constructively accompanied by *Sender*. The variants of the micro level of the *SEM2* are the result of extensive discussions with *Geiger*. The selection of entrepreneurial methods as order parameters of the *SEM2* are largely due to the numerous discussions with *Kriedel*. In particular, details of the *SEM3* were repeatedly critically questioned by *Kriedel* and *Wagner*, so that overall the results of the numerous discussions of the research team have flowed into the *SEM*. The graphic itself was implemented by Maximilian *Schimanski*, like many other graphics in this book)

and uncertainty decreases, so that, for example, *Causation* and *Effectuation* replace each other on the timeline, or as *Kriedel* rightly says:

> "With increasing duration of the existence of the products and services, knowledge about, for example, partners, customers, and distribution channels should increase. Thus, the effectual (entrepreneurial) action is replaced by a causal (managerial) action." (Kriedel, 2017: p. 45)

When considering these conditions, the *Bricolage* approach is indeed closer to the *Effectuation* than to the *Causation* approach. (Baker & Nelson, 2005; Fischer, 2012; Kriedel, 2017). Let's look at the individual levels of the SEM in summary next.

7.4.2 *SEM1*—The Individual Level: Entrepreneurship Education as a Self-Organising, Complex Process

First of all, the *SEM1* in the Entrepreneurship Education debate allows for the first time to model entrepreneurial learning processes as an explainable, transparent process. As already shown, effects through Entrepreneurship Education can differ depending on, for example, the structure of the internal and external parameters of the individual. The model takes such facts into account by considering the conceptual changes at the macroscopic level.

Secondly, the *SEM1* makes use of an economic-didactic approach. When talking about Entrepreneurship Education, economic-didactic dimensions and characteristics of Economic Education must be taken into account, whereby the consideration of Entrepreneurship as a complex process requires the integration of complexity and the resulting consequences.

Finally, within the entire *SEM1*, the individual elements of the Entrepreneurship Education process are to be considered separately and in their interaction transparently. Synergetics makes it possible to distinguish between the learning environment (Control parameters), which acts as a stimulus, as an incentive for learning, and the self-organised and individual learning process (circular process). *SEM1* shows, as we have seen in detail, why it is important to design the Learning environment with great caution. In addition, the model makes it possible to reflect separately on the order parameters, the microscopic level, the macroscopic level, and the constraints, without neglecting the system and the dependencies as a whole. Nevertheless, it should be mentioned that there is not always a clear separation of the parameters and the elements of the system and therefore there is still room for discussion about the correct classification, such as the distinction between control parameters and the environment-bound effects.

There is potential for further research, such as in relation to the phase transitions of the system and the possibility of recognising these phase transitions in time and influencing them in an entrepreneurial sense. It would be helpful for both teachers and learners to know at which point of phase development an individual is exactly in the learning process. Suggestions have been made for this—initially for teachers.

7.4.3 *SEM2*—The Organisational Level: StartUp Foundations as a Synergetic Process Involving Specific, Ordering Business-Economic-Entrepreneurial Methods

When viewed from a business perspective, the *SEM2* also allows for a processual view. Unlike in *SEM1,* where the focus was particularly on control parameters and the cyclical process with possibilities for intervention through 'nudges', in *SEM2* the importance of the macroscopic level, i.e., the ordering parameters, is elaborated. The ordering parameters that emerge here are by no means classic business methods such as *SWOT* analysis, *Business Planning,* cost comparison calculations, method 635, morphological method, utility analysis, *Balanced Scorecard* or traditional statistics, to name some important traditional methods also in the context of founding processes, although these proven methods certainly retain their validity and meaningfulness. However, the entrepreneurial methods , which can be described with keywords such as *Lean StartUp, Customer Development, Business Model* etc., and which appear suitable(er) in a complex, dynamic and turbulent environment to successfully accompany and shape founding processes, were highlighted. They contribute to taking an ordering, positive influence on founding events in the emergent founding process through repeated synchronisation and ultimately forming a StartUp as a dynamic pattern.

7.4.4 *SEM3*—The Macroeconomic Level: StartUps Support the Macroeconomic Growth Process through an Entrepreneurial Transmission Effect

SEM3 shows that the synergetic view of the macroeconomic dimension of founding processes is necessarily linked to the topic of economic growth. We did not rely on classic growth theories of Keynesian or post-Keynesian, nor on original growth theories of neoclassical interpretation. Instead, we rely on endogenous growth theory, which due to its approach reveals a homomorphism between growth theories and complexity theories in the sense of synergetics, as the term "endogenous" already suggests.

The importance of increasing human capital formation was emphasised. In this context, the special role of an entrepreneurial attitude was highlighted, which can trigger a transmission effect to generate innovations and technological progress for macroeconomic growth processes from increasing human capital formation, in order to ensure sustained (possibly increasing) prosperity, the "wealth of nation" (Smith, 1776), to guarantee.

The economic and technological developments of the last 150 years, unleashed by scientific insights and overall increased human capital formation, combined with technological progress, have created a world that on the one hand guarantees a high standard of living, but on the other hand has also produced ecological and economic challenges that must be solved. Only the solution of the challenges, which can easily be described with keywords such as global population growth, ageing of industrial societies, energy crises, climate catastrophe, long-term unemployment etc., will maintain or even improve the standard of living. However, this requires technological progress, innovations and thus corresponding economic growth. This presupposes, however, that there are more people who create or perceive opportunities ('opportunities') and make innovations by founding corresponding companies, asserting themselves in existing markets or even shaping new ones. In short, there is a permanent need for more entrepreneurs and more entrepreneurship.

References

Argyris, C., & Schön, D. (1978). *Organizational learning: A theory of action perspective*. Addison-Wesley.

Auchter, E., & Keding, M. (2004). The benefits of simulations in entrepreneurship education. In W. C. Kriz & T. Eberle (Eds.), *Bridging the gap. Transforming knowledge into action through gaming & simulation* (pp. 385–394). SAGSAGA.

Aulet, B. (2013). *24 steps to success*. Wiley.

Baker, T., Miner, A. S., & Eesley, D. T. I. (2003). Improvising firms: Bricolage, account giving and improvisational competencies in the founding process. *Research Policy,32,* 255–276.

Baker, T., & Nelson, R. E. (2005). Creating something from nothing: Resource construction through entrepreneurial bricolage. *Administrative Science Quarterly, 50*, 329–366.

Baker, T., & Welter, F. (2015). Bridges to the future—Challenging the nature of entrepreneurship scholarship. In T. Parker & F. Welter (Eds.), *The routledge companion to entrepreneurship* (pp. 1–18). Routledge.

Bandt, C., & Pompe, B. (2002). Permutation entropy—A natural complexity measure for time series. *Physical Review Letters, 88*(17), 174102-1–174102-4.

Bartel, D., & Barbarski, K. (2015). *Mit customer development durchstarten*. Guide Edition.

Becker, W. E., & Watts, M. (1998). Teaching economics: What was, is, and could be. In W. E. Becker & M. Watts (Eds.), *Teaching economics to undergraduates. Alternatives to chalk and talk* (pp. 1–10). Edward Elgar.

Beinhocker, E. (2007). *The orign of wealth: Evolution, complexity, and the radical remaking of economics*. Random House.

Blank, S., & Dorf, B. (2012). *The startup owner's manual: The step-by-step guide for building a great company*. K&S Ranch.

Blötz, U. (2003). *Planspiele in der beruflichen Bildung—Aktualisierter Planspielkatalog und neue Fachbeiträge*. Bundesinstitut für Berufsbildung.

Bloom, N., Romer, P., Terry, S., & Van Reenen, J. (2013). A trapped factors model of innovation. *American Economic Review, Papers and Proceedings, 103*(3), 208–213.

Bonnemeier, S. (2015). *Der Businessplan*. Beck.

Boutros-Ghali, B. (1995). Agenda für Entwicklung—Bericht des Generalsekretärs. Retrieved December 15, 2009 from http://www.un.org/depts/german/gv-sonst/adev/adev-3.html

Bruner, J. (1972). *Der Prozeß der Erziehung*. Berlin.

Capaul, R. (2009). Planspiele erfolgreich einsetzen. In A. Hohenstein & K. Wilbers (Eds.), *Handbuch E-Learning—Expertenwissen aus Wissenschaft und Praxis* (pp. 182–198). Deutscher Wirtschaftsdienst.

Chia, R. (2011). Complex thinking: Towards an oblicque strategy for dealing with the complex. In P. Allen, S. Maguire, & B. McKelvey (Eds.), *The SAGE handbook of complexity and management* (pp. 182–198). Sage.

Cobb, C., & Douglas, P. H. (1928). A theory of production. *The American Economic Review, 18*(11), 139–165.

Cooper, B., & Vlaskovits, P. (2013). *The lean entrepreneur*. Wiley.

Croll, A., & Yoskovitz, B. (2013). *Lean analytics: Use data to build a better startup faster*. O'Reilly Media.

Crowdsourcing, LLC. (2012). *Crowdfunding Industrie Report—Market trends, composition and crowdfunding platform*. Massolution. http://crowdsourcing.org

Darwin, C. (1859). *On the origin of species: By means of natural selection or the preservation of favoured races in the struggle for life*. Dover.

Day, R. H. (1982). Irregular growth cycles. *American Economic Review, 72*(3), 406–414.

de Dios, M. J., & Montero, I. (2003). *The motivational function of private speech: An experimental approach*. In Paper presented at the Biennial Meeting of the Society for Research in Child Development. Tampa, FL: Educational Resources Information Center. April.

Dopfer, K. (1990). Elemente einer Evolutionsökonomik. In U. Witt (Ed.), *Studien zur evolutorischen Ökonomik I* (pp. 19–47). Duncker & Humblot.

Euler, D., & Hahn, A. (2007). *Wirtschaftsdidaktik* (2nd ed.). Bern.

Faltin, G., & Ripsas, S. (2011). *Das Gestalten von Geschäftsmodellen als Kern des Entrepreneurship* (4th ed.). Working Papers.

Fayolle, A., & Gailly, B. (2008). From craft to science: Teaching models and learning processes in entrepreneurship education. *Journal of European Industrial Training, 32*(7), 569–593.

Fischer, G. (2012). Effectuation, causation, and bricolage: A behavioral comparison of emerging theories in entrepreneurship research. *Entrepreneurship: Theory & Practice, 36,* 1019–1051.

Fueglistaller, U., Müller, C., & Volery, T. (2008). *Entrepreneurship* (2nd ed.). Gabler.

Gassmann, O., Frankenberger, K., & Csik, M. (2013). *Geschäftsmodelle entwickeln—55 innovative Konzepte mit dem St. Galler Business Model Navigator*. Hanser.

Gassmann, O., & Sutter, P. (2013). *Praxiswissen Innovationsmanagement: Von der Idee zum Markterfolg* (3rd ed.). Hanser.

Gharajedaghi, J. (2006). *Managing chaos and complexity: A platform for designing business architecture*. Elsevier.

Gorecki, P., & Pautsch, P. R. (2016). *Lean management*. Hanser.

Gothelf, J., & Seiden J. (2013). *Lean UX: Applying lean principles to improve user experience*. O'Reilly Media.

Gremmen, H., & Potters, J. (1997). Assessing the efficacy of gaming in economic education. *The Journal of Economic Education, 28*(4), 291–303.

Grossmann, G. M., & Helpman. E. (1994). Endogenous innovation in the theory of growth. *Journal of Economic Perspectives, 8*(1), 23–44.

Haken, H., & Schiepek, G. (2010). *Synergetik in der Psychologie: Selbstorganisation verstehen und gestalten* (2nd ed.). Hogrefe.

Halasz, U. (2005). Humankapital: Wie viel ist unser Wissen wert? Blickpunkt Wirtschaft. Retrieved March 11, 2015 from http://www.blickpunkt-wirtschaft.de/detailseite/news/humankapital-wie-viel-ist-unser-wissen-wert. Zugegriffen: 11 März 2015

Hamel, G., & Prahalad, C. K. (2013). *Competing for the future*. Harvard Business Press.

Heinrichs, N. (2008). *Bewertung von Wachstums- und Startup-Unternehmen*. Diplomica.

Hellbrück, R. P. (1993). *Synergetik und Marktprozesse*. Physica.

Hindle, K. (2002). A grounded theory for teaching entrepreneurship using simulation games. *Business, Management and Accounting, 33*(2), 236–241.

Jacobs, H. (Ed.). (2010). *Ökonomie spielerisch lernen. Kompetenz gewinnen. Spiele, Rollenspiele, Planspiele, Simulationen und Experimente*. Wochenschau.

Johnson, S. (2010). *Where good ideas come from: The natural history of innovation*. Riverhead Hardcover.

Kahneman, D., & Tversky, A. (1979). Prospect theory: An analysis of decision under risk. *Econometrica, 47*(2), 263–291.

Kim, W. C., & Mauborgne, R. (2005). *Blue ocean strategy: How to create uncontested market space and make competition irrelevant.* Harvard Business Press.

Kim, W. C., & Mauborgne, R. (2015). *Blue ocean strategy, expanded edition: How to create uncontested market*. Harvard Business Press.

Kowalik, Z. J., Schiepek, G., Kumpf, K., Roberts, L. E., & Elbert, T. (1997). Psychotherapy as a chaotic process. Part II: The application of nonlinear analysis methods on quasi time series of the client-therapist interaction: A nonstationary approach. *International Journal of the Society for Psychotherapy Research, 7*(2), 197–218.

Kricks, K., Mittelstädt, E., & Liening, A. (2013). Schwellenkonzepte und Phänomenografie. Explorative Studie zur Messung von Unterschieden im ökonomischen Verstehen. *Zeitschrift für ökonomische Bildung, 2*, 17–41.

Kriedel, R. (2017). *Systemkompetenz für Entrepreneure—Entwicklung der entrepreneurialen Systemkompetenz und eines Diagnoseinstruments*. Springer.

Kuratko, D. F., & Audretsch, D. B. (2009). Strategic entrepreneurship: Exploring different perspectives of an emerging concept. *Entrepreneurship Theory and Practice, 33*(1), 1–17.

Liening, A. (1992). *Intelligente Tutorielle Systeme (ITS). Eine kritische Analyse unter besonderer Berücksichtigung ihrer Einsatzmöglichkeiten in der Wirtschaftsdidaktik*. LIT.

Liening, A. (1998). *Komplexe Systeme zwischen Ordnung und Chaos*. LIT.

Liening, A. (1999). Didaktische Innovationen—Neue Ansätze zur Entwicklung computergestützter ökonomischer Planspiele. In G.-J. Krol & K.-P. Kruber (Eds.), *Die Marktwirtschaft an der Schwelle des 21. Jahrhundert—Neue Aufgaben für die ökonomische Bildung?* (pp. 237–260). Hobein.

Liening, A. (2002a). *Kostenrechnung: Teilkostenrechnung, Plankostenrechnung und betriebswirtschaftliche Kennzahlen* (2nd ed.). Institut für Verbundstudien.

Liening, A. (2002b). *Kostenrechnung: Vollkostenrechnung—Von den Kostenarten bis zur Kostenträgerrechnung* (2nd ed.). Institut für Verbundstudien.

Liening, A. (2004). Die Bedeutung der ‚Neuen Medien' in der Didaktik der Wirtschaftswissenschaft unter besonderer Berücksichtigung der Darstellung ‚Neuer Technologien'. In H. J. Schlösser (Ed.), *Anforderungen der Wissensgesellschaft: Informationstechnologien und Neue Medien als Herausforderungen für die Wirtschaftsdidaktik* (pp. 1–61). Hobein.

Liening, A. (2006). iLearning—Ein synergetischer Ansatz zum selbstorganisierten Lernen im Rahmen ökonomischer Bildung. In E. Brunner & T. Meynhardt (Ed.), *Selbstorganisation Managen. Beiträge zur Synergetik der Organisation* (pp. 179–205). Waxmann.

Liening, A. (2008). Humankapital und Wirtschaftswachstum—Endogenisierung der Humankapitalbildung in nicht-linearen Wachstumsmodellen. In D. Lörwald, M. Wiesweg, & A. Zörner (Hrsg.), *Ökonomik und Gesellschaft, Festschrift zum 65. Geburtstag von Prof. Dr. Gerd-Jan Krol* (pp. 394–413). VS.

Liening, A. (2009). *Campus career competition—Management. Ein computergestütztes Planspiel. 12. überarbeitete Fassung*. Dortmund.

Liening, A. (2010). Computergestütztes Lernen. In H. May (Ed.), *Lexikon der Ökonomischen Bildung* (pp. 156–162). Oldenbourg.

Liening, A. (2013). Growth theory and endogenous human capital development: A contribution to the theory of complex systems. *Theoretical Economics Letters, 3*(2), 96–104.

Liening, A. (2014). Synergetische Wirtschaftsdidaktik: Ein kraf(f)tvoller Ansatz für die Ökonomische Bildung. In C. Müller, A. Liening, H. J. Schlösser, & M. Schuhen (Eds.), *Festschrift zum 80. Geb. von Dietmar Krafft* (pp. 55–74). Lucius & Lucius.

Liening, A. (2015a). *Campus career competition business game*. Dortmund, iLearning-Verlag.

Liening, A. (2015b). *Ökonomische Bildung—Grundlagen und neue synergetische Ansätze*. Springer-Gabler.

Liening, A., Geiger, J.-M., Kriedel, R., & Wagner, W. (2016). Complexity & entrepreneurship: Modelling the process of entrepreneurship education through the theory of synergetics. In E. Berger & A. Kuckertz (Eds.), *Complexity in entrepreneurship, innovation and technology research—Applications of emergent and neglected methods*. Springer Gabler.

Liening, A., & Kirchner, M. (2011). Computergestützte Planspiele. In T. Retzmann (Ed.), *Methodentraining für den Ökonomieunterricht II*. Schwalbach am Taunus. 45-67.

Liening, A., & Kriedel R. (2013). Entrepreneurship & Synergetic—The Dortmunder Entrepreneurship Model. In *Developments in economics education—Conference 2013, University of Exeter*.

Liening, A., Kriedel, R., & Wagner, W. (2015). Die Entrepreneurship School—Ein EXIST-Projekt im Rahmen von tu>startup. In J. Teichert, R. Ofianka, & A. Jendrosch (Eds.), *Universitäre Gründungsförderung. Abläufe, Akteure, Erfolge* (pp. 145–155). Waxmann.

Liening, A., & Mittelstädt, E. (2008). *Wissensmanagement*. Barmer Akademie.

Liening, A., Mittelstädt, E., & Strunk, G. (2012). Ist unternehmerische Kompetenz messbar? Komplexitätswissenschaftliche Ansätze zur Kompetenzmessung in Unternehmensplanspielen. In T. Retzmann (Ed.), *Entrepreneurship und Arbeitnehmerorientierung* (pp. 39–49). Wochenschau.

Liening, A., Mittelstädt E., & Wiepcke C., (2008). Enhancing empoyability of non-business graduates by economic education as a part of extracurricular studies. In *Proceedings of the 6th International Conference on Management, Athens Institute for Education and Research*.

Liening, A., & Paprotny C. (2005). Fallstudienarbeiten in der Ökonomischen Bildung. In *Dortmunder Beiträge zur Ökonomischen Bildung, 4*.

Liening, A., Strunk, G., & Mittelstädt, E. (2013). Transitions between lower and higher level management learning in times of crisis. Experimental study based on the theories of nonlinear dynamic systems within a business simulation game. *Nonlinear Dynamics, Psychology, and Life Sciences, 17*(4), 517–541.

Louca, F. (1997). *Turbulence in economics*. Elgar.

Lucas, R. E. (1988). On the mechanics of economic development. *Journal of Monetary Economics, 22*(1), 3–42.

Lutz, A. (2014). *Businessplan*. Linde.

Magretta, J. (2002). Wy business models matter. *Harvard Business Review, 80*(5), 86–92.

Maurya, A. (2012). *Running lean—Iterate from plan A to plan that works* (2nd ed.). O'Reilly Media.

Menn, A. (2010). *Schlaue Stoffe. Handelsblatt*. Retrieved March 8, 2015 from http://www.handelsblatt.com/technik/forschung-innovation/textilindustrie-schlaue-stoffe/3525750.html.

Meyer, J. H. F., & Land, R. (2006). Threshold concepts and troublesome knowledge: An introduction. In J. H. F. Meyer & R. Land (Eds.), *Overcoming barriers to student understanding: Threshold concepts and troublesome knowledge* (pp. 3–8). Routledge.

Moog, P (2001). Anforderungen an die Gründungsausbildung und Gründungsforschung dargestellt am Beispiel des Massachusetts Institute of Technology (MIT). In Institut für Mittelstandsforschung Bonn (Ed.), *Jahrbuch zur Mittelstandsforschung, Schriften zur Mittelstandsforschung* (No. 91, pp. 1–42). Deutscher Universitätsverlag.

Nelson, L. (1970). Die sokratische Methode, Vortrag, gehalten am 11.12.1922 in der Päd. Ges. in Göttingen. In P. Bernays, W. Eichler, & A. Gysin (Eds.), *Leonard Nelson—Gesammelte Schriften in neun Bänden*. Meiner.

Neumann, M. (1984). Schumpeter oder Keynes: Zwei komplementäre Perspektiven. In D. Bös & H.-D. Stolper (Eds.), *Schumpeter oder Keynes* (pp. 87–96). Springer.

Neumann, R. (2013). *Libertärer Paternalismus: Theorie und Empirie staatlicher Entscheidungsarchitektur*. Mohr Siebeck.
von Neumann-Cosel, A. (2006). *Change Management systemtheoretisch betrachtet: Ein synergetisches Handlungsmodell*. Dr. Kovac.
Neumark, F. (1984). Chancen einer Schumpeter-Renaissance. In D. Bös & H. D. Stolper (Eds.), *Schumpeter oder Keynes* (pp. 45–66). Springer.
Nijkamp, P., & Reggiani, A. (1993). *Nonlinear evolution of spatial economic systems*. Springer.
Nissen, V. (1997). *Einführung in evolutionäre Algorithmen: Optimierung nach dem Vorbild der Evolution*. Teubner Verlag.
Ohno, T. (2013). *Das Toyota-Produktionssystem* (2nd ed.). Campus.
Osterwalder, A., & Pigneur, Y. (2010). *Business model generation*. Wiley.
Osterwalder, A., & Pigneur, Y. (2011). *Business model generation*. Campus.
Osterwalder, A., Pigneur, Y., Bernarda, G., & Smith, A. (2014). *Value proposition design: How to create products and services customers want Hoboken*. Wiley.
Osterwalder, A., Pigneur, Y., Bernarda, G., & Smith, A. (2015). *Value proposition design*. Campus.
Osterwalder, A., Pigneur, Y., & Tucci, C. L. (2005). Clarifying business models: Origins, present, and future of the concept. *Communications of the Association for Information Systems, 16*(1), 1–25.
Perote, J., Vincente-Lorente, J. D., & Zuniga-Vicente, J. A. (2016). Classroom experiments: A useful tool for learning about economic and entrepreneurial decisions. In M. Peris-Ortiz, J. A. Gomez, F. Vélez-Torres, & C. Rueda-Armengot (Eds.), *Education tools for entrepreneurship* (pp. 1–14). Springer.
Pfeiffer, W., & Weiss, E. (1994). *Lean management: Grundlagen der Führung und Organisation lernender Unternehmen*. Schmidt.
Pöppel, K. G. (1990). Moralische Erziehung im Fachunterricht—Zur Einheit von Unterricht und Erziehung. In A. Regenbrecht & K. G. Pöppel (Eds.), *Moralische Erziehung im Fachunterricht*. Aschendorff.
Purle, E. (2004). *Management von Komplexität in jungen Wachstumsunternehmen*. Josef Eul.
von Reißwitz, G. H. R. J. (1824). *Anleitung zur Darstellung militärischer Manöver mit dem Apparate des Kriegsspiels*. Berlin.
Riding, R., & Rayner, S. (1998). *Cognitive styles and learning strategies: Understanding style differences in learning and behaviour*. David Fulton.
Ries, E., (2011). *The lean startup: How today's entrepreneurs use continuous innovation to create radically successful businesses*. Portfolio Penguin.
Ries, E. (2014). *Lean startup: Schnell, risikolos und erfolgreich Unternehmen gründen*. Redline.
Ripsas, S., & Tröger, S. (2014). *Deutscher startup monitor*. KPMG AG. 2.
Ripsas, S., & Tröger, S. (2015). *Deutscher startup monitor*. KPMG AG. 3.
Rivera-Batiz, L. A., & Romer, P. (1991). International trade with endogenous technological change. *European Economic Review, 35*(4), 971–1001.
Roberts, E. B. (2007). Managing invention and innovation. *Research Technology Management, 50*(1), 35–54.
Romer, P. (1986a). Economic growth. In D. R. Henderson (Ed.), *The concise encyclopedia of economics*. Liberty Fund.
Romer, P. (1986b). Increasing returns and long-run growth. *Journal of Political Economy, 94*(5), 1002–1037.
Romer, P. (1990). Endogenus technological change. *Journal of Political Economy, 98*(5), 71–102.
Romer, P. (1994). The origins of endogenous growth. *Journal of Economic Perspectives, 8*(1), 3–22.
Rudolf, M., & Müller, J. (2012). *Multivariate Verfahren* (2nd ed.). Göttingen.

Ruschinski, M. (1996). *Neuere Entwicklungen in der Wachstumstheorie*. Springer.

Sachs, L., & Hedderich, J. (2006). *Angewandte Statistik* (12th ed.). Springer.

Sarasvathy, S. D. (2009). *Effectuation—Elements of entrepreneurial expertise*. Edward Elgar.

Schallmo, D. R. A. (2013). *Geschäftsmodelle erfolgreich entwickeln und implementieren—Mit Aufgaben und Kontrollfragen*. Springer.

Schiepek, G., & Strunk, G. (2010). The identification of critical fluctuations and phase transitions in short term and coarse-grained time series—A method for the real-time monitoring of human change processes. *Biological Cybernetics, 102*(3), 197–207.

Schlösser, H. J. (2014). Die Kreativität der Lerngruppe ist es die die Lehrenden trägt—Interview mit Prof. Dr. Hans Jürgen Schlösser, Zentrum für Ökonomische Bildung (ZöBiS). Retrieved September 01, 2014 from http://www.unternehmergeist-macht-schule.de/DE/HilfenundTipps/Expertensicht/Interviews/Interview-Schloesser.html. Zugegriffen: 01. Sept. 2014

Schlösser, H. J., & Schuhen, M. (2011). Mit Ökonomischen Experimenten Wirtschaft erleben. In T. Retzmann (Ed.), *Methodentraining für den Ökonomieunterricht II* (pp. 57–74). Wochenschau.

Schlösser, H. J., Schuhen, M., Schäfer, A.-T., Niederschlag, S., & Macha, K. (2009). *Ökonomische Experimente*. Cornelsen.

Schuhen, M., & Weyland, M. (2011). „Marktwirtschaft" unterrichten—aber wie? *Gesellschaft • Wirtschaft • Politik (GWP),* (3), 387–398.

Schumpeter, J. (1912). *Theorie der wirtschaftlichen Entwicklung: Nachdruck der 1. Auflage in 2006*. Duncker & Humblot.

Selten, R. (1965). Spieltheoretische Behandlung eines Oligopolmodells mit Nachfrageträgheit: Teil I: Bestimmung des dynamischen Preisgleichgewichtes. *Zeitschrift für die gesamte Staatswissenschaft, 122*(2), 301–324.

Selten, R. (1982). Einführung in die Theorie der Spiele bei unvollständiger Information. *Information in der Wirtschaft, Schriften des Vereins für Socialpolitik, 126,* 81–147.

Sender, T. (2017). *Wirtschaftsdidaktische Lerndiagnostik und Komplexität—Lokalisierung liminaler Unsicherheitsphasen im Hinblick auf Schwellenübergänge*. Diss., Springer, Wiesbaden.

Sherman, H. (2004). Case research and writing: Three days in the life of professor moore. *Case Journal, 1*(1), 8–30.

Shingo, S. (1985). *A revolution in manufacturing: The SMED system*. Productivity Press.

Siebert, H. (2005). *Jenseits des sozialen Marktes*. Deutsche Verlags-Anstalt.

sla/n-tv.de (2015). Die gefährliche Spitze der Einhörner. Retrieved November 01, 2015 from http://www.n-tv.de/wirtschaft/US-Tech-Riesen-bereiten-Sorgen-article15791146.html?mobile=false. Zugegriffen: 01. Nov. 2015.

Smith, A. (1776). *An inquiry into the nature and causes of the wealth of nations*. The Modern Library.

Smith, V. (1962). An experimental study of competitive market behavior. *Journal of Political Economy, 70,* 111–137.

Smith, V. (1975). Experimental econonics: Induced value theory. *American Economic Review, Papers and Proceedings, 66*(2), 274–279.

Smolney, W., & Schneeweis, T. (1999). Innovation, Wachstum und Beschäftigung—Eine empirische Untersuchung auf der Basis des Ifo Unternehmenspanels. *Jahrbücher für Nationalökonomie und Statistik/Journal of Economics and Statistics, 218*(3–4), 453–472.

Solow, R. (1956). A contribution to the theory of economic growth. *The Quarterly Journal of Economics, 70,* 65–94.

Solow, R. (1987). *Growth theory—An exposition*. Oxford University Press.

Solow, R. (1988). Growth theory and after. *American Economic Review, Papers and Proceedings, 78*(3), 307–317.

Spiegel Online. (2016). Konzeptstudie GINA. Retrieved December 02, 2016 from http://www.spiegel.de/auto/fahrkultur/bmw-gina-ein-auto-mit-massgeschneiderter-textilkarosserie-a-1071856.html

Stavemann, H. H. (2007). *Sokratische Gesprächsführung* (2nd ed.). Beltz.

Sterman, J. D. (2000). *Business dynamics. Systems thinking and modeling for a complex world.* McGraw-Hill.

Strunk, G. (2019). *Leben wir in einer immer komplexer werdenden Welt? Methoden der Komplexitätsmessung für die Wirtschaftswissenschaft.* Complexity Research, Forschung & Lehre.

Strunk, G., & Schiepek, G. (2006). *Systemische Psychologie—Eine Einführung in die komplexen Grundlagen menschlichen Verhaltens.* Elsevier—Spektrum Akademischer.

Thaler, R. H., & Sunstein, C. R. (2012). *Nudge—Wie man kluge Entscheidungen anstößt* (2nd ed.). Ullstein Taschenbuch.

Tschacher, W., & Dauwalder, J.-P. (Eds.). (2003). *The dynamical systems approach to cognition: Concepts and empirical paradigms based on self-organization, embodiment, and coordination dynamics.* World Scientific.

Tschacher, W., & Haken, H. (2011). The transfer of principles of non-equilibrium physics to embodied cognition. In W. Tschacher & C. Bergomi (Eds.), *Implications of embodiment—Cognition and commuication* (pp. 75–88). Imprint Academic.

Vogelsang, E., Fink, C., & Baumann, M. (2015). *Existenzgründung und Businessplan.* Schmidt.

Volkmann, C. K., & Tokarski, K. O. (2006). *Entrepreneurship: Gründung und Wachstum von jungen Unternehmen.* UTB.

Wagenschein, M. (1975). *Verstehen Lehren. Genetisch—Sokratisch—Exemplarisch.* Beltz.

Wenger, E. (1987). *Artificial intelligence and tutoring systems. Computational and cognitive approaches to the communication of knowledge.* Morgan Kaufmann.

Witt, U. (1987). *Individualistische Grundlagen einer evolutionären Ökonomik.* Mohr Siebeck.

Witt, U. (1993). *Individualistische Grundlagen einer evolutionären Ökonomik.* Mohr Siebeck.

Witt, U. (2002). How evolutuionary is schumpeters theory of economic development? *Industry and Innovation, 9*(1), 7–22.

Wöhe, G., & Döring, U. (2013). *Einführung in die Allgemeine Betriebswirtschaftslehre* (13th ed.). Vahlen.

Womack, J. P., Jones, D. T., & Roos, D. (1990). *The: Machine that changed the world.* Simon & Schuster.

Young, E. J., & Sexton, D. L. (1997). Entrepreneurial learning: A conceptual framework. *Journal of Enterprising Culture, 5*, 223–248.

Ziesemer, B. (2007). *Eine kurze Geschichte der ökonomischen Unvernunft.* Campus.

Empirical Studies—The "Synergetic Entrepreneurship Model" in Practice

8

Contents

8.1 Studies Using Complexity Science Methods within the Framework of the "Synergetic Entrepreneurship Model" . . . 580
8.2 Studies on Phase Transitions and Complexity Measurements in the Context of SEM1 . . . 582
8.2.1 The 'Entrepreneurship Academy' as a Practical Implementation of *SEM1* . . . 582
8.2.2 The 'Synergetic Entrepreneurship Model' (*SEM*) and the Problem of Phase Transitions . . . 585
8.2.3 *'Business Gaming'* as a Practical Control Parameter of the 'Entrepreneurship Academy' . . . 586
8.2.4 Complexity Measurement for Determining Phase Transitions and Their Practical Consequences . . . 589
8.2.4.1 Learning Processes, Crises, and Complexity Measurements . . . 589
8.2.4.2 A Study from the Field of Business Gaming: "Learning from Crises—Complexity Measurements" . . . 589
8.2.4.3 Critical Examination of the Study Results . . . 598
8.2.5 Another Study from the Field of ***Business Gaming*** (Complex Stock Market Simulation)—in the Context of SEM1 . . . 599
8.3 Complex Dynamics of StartUps within the Framework of SEM2 . . . 603
8.3.1 The Business Game as an Environment for Observing Learning Processes at the Organisational Level . . . 603
8.3.2 An Example of Observing a Real Startup in the Founding Process . . . 604
8.4 Complexity Investigations within the Framework of SEM3 . . . 605
8.4.1 Complexity Science Investigations of Entrepreneurial Ecosystems . . . 605
8.4.1.1 Entrepreneurial Ecosystems in Research . . . 605
8.4.1.2 Objectives of the Study . . . 606
8.4.1.3 Approach to Complexity Science Data Analysis . . . 606
8.4.1.4 Results of the Complexity Science Analysis . . . 608
8.4.1.5 Conclusions from the Results of the Complexity Science Analysis . . . 609

A. Liening, *Complexity and Entrepreneurship*,
https://doi.org/10.1007/978-3-658-44032-9_8

8.4.2 Development of Business Start-ups in Germany 612
8.4.2.1 Company Founding in Germany 612
8.4.2.2 On the Empirical Methodology and Procedure 613
8.4.2.3 Results: Federal 613
8.4.2.4 Results: Federal States 614
8.4.2.5 Plausible External Events 619
8.5 Fifth Conclusion—Limitations in the Explanation of the Study Results and Perspectives 622
References 624

8.1 Studies Using Complexity Science Methods within the Framework of the "Synergetic Entrepreneurship Model"

Economics, as a real science, is based on two pillars: theory and practice. The theories should be coherent in themselves and complement existing theories. However, theories can only be considered (provisionally) valid if they also have empirical relevance. This means that it is essential to validate theories by examining them in practical examples. Therefore, empirical studies are needed to substantiate the understanding of entrepreneurship using the SEM in practice and its mode of operation. Only through empirical research is the second pillar of economics, practice, revealed. To take into account the complexity inherent in entrepreneurship, we rely on quantitative studies to apply the methods presented in this book to specific cases. To conduct empirical studies within the three SEM levels, we want to apply various methods, such as D_2, PD_2, the "Largest *Lyapunov* Exponent", the "Local Largest *Lyapunov* Exponent", the "BDS Test", or "Permutation Entropies" and *"Recurrence Plots"* and analyse the results. The methods were all described in Part II, Chap. 5. We have seen that certain prerequisites are necessary for this. Many of the methods mentioned are geometric in nature, which is why they require a phase space representation, like the methods for fractal dimensions or the determination of Lyapunov exponents, where the distances between the data points play an important role. While the methods based on a phase space representation require interval scale level, for example, permutation entropy can cope with ordinal scales. For the practical application of the described methods, it is also necessary to capture a certain minimum number of data points in order to obtain usable results. *Strunk* writes about this:

> "A period of time is always required to reach a result. If this is large, it can lead to blurring and erroneous calculation results. Some methods allow a very accurate quantification of complexity (*Lyapunov* exponents, fractal geometry), but require long observation times (many hundreds to several thousand measurement points) for this. Other methods are rather coarse-grained in the identification of order and chaos, but require far fewer data. Thus, the chosen method determines how many observation points are needed to perform a complexity analysis. At the same time, however, it also depends on the motive, i.e., the system, how often it is able to provide data points and how quickly it changes (stock price

> fluctuations in time series can experience relevant changes every minute, while climate changes should be measured in generations and geological changes represent adequate time scales in millions of years" (Strunk, 2019: p. 102).

D_2: To recognise the dimensionality of the attractor, the D_2 method can be applied. Depending on the phase space embedding, approximately 200–1000 data points are minimally needed. The rule is: The more complex the time series are, the larger is the dimension of the phase space embedding and the higher is the required number of data points.

PD_2: The PD_2, as we have seen in Chap. 5, is defined like the D_2, but represents a non-stationary extension. Since not all distances between all data points are used to determine the dimensionality, but "starting from individual reference points, the distances to all other points are first determined and from this, individually for each of the reference points, a D_2 is determined according to the known method, which then, however, only applies to this reference point and is therefore referred to as pointwise dimensionality (PD_2)" (Strunk, 2019: p. 255f.), the PD_2 can be determined for relatively few data points. Ultimately, it is less sensitive to noise than the D_2. Here too, however, at least 200–1000 data points are required. *Strunk* adds that the analysis "should succeed for 75 % of the data points" (Strunk, 2019: p. 260) in order for an interpretation to be justified. Largest *Lyapunov* Exponent: The *Lyapunov* exponent can be used to measure the initial sensitivity of a system, which is a necessary criterion for complexity. While the so-called Wolf algorithm requires at least 2000–5000 data points (Strunk, 2019: p. 313), for example, the *Rosenstein* and *Kantz* algorithms require only 100–500 data points (Strunk, 2019: pp. 326, 334). For the calculation of the Local Largest *Lyapunov* Exponent (LLLE), the *Rosenstein* and *Kantz* algorithms also require 100–500 data points to obtain significant results.

BDS Test: The BDS test, which is based on *Brock, Dechert* and *Scheinkman*, is used to examine the empirical data for the underlying dynamics. More precisely, the test can be used to verify the null hypothesis that a variable is identically and independently distributed. Thus, it tests for a random process. The rejection of the null hypothesis allows the conclusion that the dynamics underlying the empirical data could be based on deterministic chaos (Brock et al., 1996).

Entropy Calculations: Permutation entropy is a measure of the disorder of a system. This means that the lower the permutation entropy, the higher the order (self-organisation) and the adaptability of the system and vice versa: The greater the permutation entropy, the lower the order (increase in complexity, up to (deterministic) chaos and randomness) and the lower the adaptability of the system. While the *Shannon* entropy requires 5–30 data points (Strunk, 2019: p. 412), permutation entropies require slightly more data points. But compared to other methods, relatively few data points are also sufficient here to achieve significant results. According to Strunk, 20–400 data points are sufficient (Strunk, 2019: p. 439).

Recurrence Plots: The more *recurrences* are measured by the *RR*, the more repetitions are diagnosed, the greater the order in the system. Recurrence is a characteristic of ordered dynamic systems. In addition to a phase space embedding, at least 32 data points are required. Thus, this method requires significantly fewer data points than other described methods (Strunk, 2019: p. 387). Strunk points out that on the other hand, "the results from recurrence plots are also coarser and less differentiated (are, d. Verf.), as they are based on a dichotomisation of the comparison of data from different time periods" (Strunk, 2019: p. 387).

No matter how many examples we use and make available for empirical investigation, there are always only a finite number of examples from which no general validity of a theoretical construct, here the SEM, can be demonstrated. Therefore, a proof of the validity of a theory can never be achieved in a real science like economics, neither inductively (establishing a theory from practical examples) nor deductively (testing a theory on practical examples). Every theoretical approach, no matter how well thought out, is therefore only to be considered as provisional. However, if it has been formulated intersubjectively and rationally like the SEM, it must face falsifiability. The criterion of falsifiability is thus the basis on which the SEM also moves. If the empirical studies do not have explanatory power in relation to the SEM, we must question this theoretical approach. Otherwise, we interpret the results as a hopeful signal that we are on the right path. All calculations of the studies presented here were carried out with the GChaos statistical software, a C++ programme developed by Strunk to enable nonlinear time series analyses (http://www.complexity-research.com).

8.2 Studies on Phase Transitions and Complexity Measurements in the Context of SEM1

8.2.1 The 'Entrepreneurship Academy' as a Practical Implementation of *SEM1*

In order to promote the individual learning process with the aim of strengthening the entrepreneurial education of the individual and making a contribution to the generation of an entrepreneurial culture, and thus to illustrate the practical use of the 'Synergetic Entrepreneurship Model' (SEM), an 'Entrepreneurship School' was already founded at TU Dortmund in 2012 as part of the EXIST project 'tu-startup' funded by the Federal Ministry of Economics and the European Social Fund (Liening et al., 2015: 145).

The Entrepreneurship School was transferred and further developed into the Entrepreneurship Academy as part of the Excellence Award by the state of NRW.[1] This

[1] The Academy is embedded in the university-wide "Centrum for Entrepreneurship and Transfer" (CET). This CET was awarded the **Excellence Startup Centre.NRW** in 2019 and was provided with approximately 16 million euros for 5 years to design the expansion of the centre on a large

'Entrepreneurship Academy' is based on the basic assumption that it is often not the lack of knowledge that hinders the possibility or success of starting a business, but the problem of dealing with the complexity of a start-up process (Liening, 2013). The frequently used and still demanded by credit institutions and in start-up competitions 'Business Plan', as already described, represents a linear-causal representation of a business start-up. However, this neglects the challenge that a dynamic process peppered with various influencing factors (e.g., partners, suppliers, customers) and unpredictable events (e.g., development of sales figures, success of marketing, production difficulties) does not allow linearly depictable actions (Liening et al., 2015: 149). Assuming that the complexity is taken into account, the 'Business Plan' can therefore only be one component in the context of a start-up process, which is important for obtaining credit, and therefore has a promotional function and thus also a certain selection function, but otherwise only contributes to a limited extent to making the start-up process successful.

Therefore, in the teaching or learning units of the 'Entrepreneurship Academy', in addition to the 'Business Plan', dynamic, internet-based 'Business Gaming', 'Entrepreneurship Case Studies' or Entrepreneurship 'Class Room Experiments' are used and in particular current Entrepreneurship methods such as 'Business Model Canvas', 'Lean-Startup Management' or the 'Effectuation' approach are taught and worked out. The organisation of the methods mentioned as examples and their content design are named as control parameters in the sense of SEM1 and serve according to the synergetic paradigm as incentives for a self-organised learning process, so that the teachers

scale. In this context, the Academy was further developed and integrated as one of the important pillars of the CET. Thus, an interdisciplinary sensitisation and qualification programme is offered for members as well as employees of TU Dortmund and also interested individuals and companies in the region on the topics of entrepreneurship and business start-ups. In order for entrepreneurial thinking and action to grow and for successful products and services to emerge from ideas and technologies, students, graduates, and employees are supported with a comprehensive range of events. While internally the process is divided into three phases ("Understand", "Apply" and "Implement"), these are externally bundled, delimited, and clearly outlined under the term "educate" derived from the term "cetucate" and assigned to three products "**cetucate.THINK**", "**cetucate.ACT**" and "**cetucate.START**". The goal is to enable participants to implement their own ideas, create new opportunities, and accomplish innovations, with the result being the sustainable establishment of an entrepreneurial mindset.—**THINK** enables self-directed learning on a digital learning platform with the aim of working out basic entrepreneurial, but also classic business management content. - **ACT** offers the interlocking with the subject content in order to transfer the insights worked out in THINK to the respective discipline.—Behind **START** is a certificate programme that enables young people, after theoretical deepening within the framework of a practical project, to formulate a concrete business model or to submit a corresponding funding application (e.g., EXIST start-up scholarship). In 2021 alone, the CET had over 2500 participants in the corresponding events. And indeed, the further development and also the transformation of the centre's structure continues and thus remains very close to the needs of the target group, the potential StartUp teams.

in the 'Entrepreneurship School' in the synergetic sense are rather coaches and advisors than lecturers, who only intervene directly in the learning process through 'nudges'. The learning processes thus stimulated are pursued with the aim of enabling the participants to think and act entrepreneurially, and thus ultimately to prepare them for business start-ups (Liening & Kriedel, 2013).

This includes that the participants are encouraged to build their lives autonomously and to shape it responsibly according to self-chosen, rationally justified principles (Liening, 2014). Entrepreneurship Education as an entrepreneurial education process can only be a dialogical one in this understanding, which focusses both on the area of Entrepreneurship Knowledge and on the area of Entrepreneurial Attitude towards this knowledge. Such an entrepreneurial education process is "neither affirmation to a past, nor to a present, nor to a future system of norms" (Pöppel, 1990: 23), but a future-open, complexity-considering process. In the sense of a synergetically interpreted education process, this new, emergent and dynamic structure is created, whose order parameters include Entrepreneurship Knowledge and entrepreneurial attitude and can be described with entrepreneurial education. This structure is generated within the framework of a self-organising feedback process depending on the incentive situations, which are designed by the changeable control parameters. Since the control parameters are also subject to feedback processes, they are constantly questioned and redesigned by the synergetic process itself, with the processes in the Entrepreneurship Academy being consciously reflected on the SEM1 again and again (Liening, Kriedel et al., 2015: 150).

Thus, the 'Entrepreneurship Academy' corresponds both in its conception and in its practical implementation to the 'Synergetic Entrepreneurship Modell' (SEM1), thereby providing a first practical contribution to the design of a synergetic entrepreneurial education. However, it would be premature to make a final judgement on the success of the 'Entrepreneurship Academy' modeled after the SEM1. Much research work is still needed, especially with regard to evaluation and the attempt to falsify the SEM1. It should be emphasised that the 'Entrepreneurship Academy' is by no means a rigid structure that, once implemented, always functions according to the same patterns. The 'Academy' itself is also subject to a complex, dynamic learning process. Its everyday life is constantly critically questioned. This leads to the successive further development of the 'Entrepreneurship Academy', which thus moves on an open, dynamic development path.

In this development context, the question of *Sarasvathy* is very justified:

> "(...) is it enough to educate MBA students and potential entrepreneurs, or should entrepreneurship education pervade the population more widely and become part of high school and grade school curricular (...)?" (Sarasvathy, 2009: 307)

Anyone who follows the debate about the introduction of a subject "Economics" in general education schools knows that we are still more at the beginning of the discussion than that comprehensive solutions for the Federal Republic would be available (Liening, 2015b). But in the run-up to the 'Entrepreneurship Academy', for example, the 'Junior Entrepreneurship School'(JES), formerly 'Junior Business School', was created, which, among other things, contributes to giving secondary schools the opportunity to provide their students with entrepreneurial education (Liening et al., 2015: p. 154). As a response of the JES to the 'Fridays for Future' debate, a "Coding Seminar" was launched as another building block. Here, ideas are implemented that are offered as short-term formats for selected upper levels of general education schools. For example, in the JES, fine dust sensors are built and coded, combined with the task of developing business models on this topic. The business ideas are finally presented to a jury and the best ones are awarded. Thus, within the framework of this specific offer form, it is about questions of actively shaping the future with integrative approaches from technological and digital inventions using economic methods. It is not an exaggeration to say that the JES as a pre-university institution forms the foundation of the 'Entrepreneurship Academy' (Liening et al., 2015: 154). The 'Junior Entrepreneurship School' is, like the 'Entrepreneurship Academy', subject to a dynamic learning process. [2]It also works according to the SEM1. Overall, there is still a lot of research work to be done to present a universally valid solution approach based on the SEM1, which reaches from school, possibly via the university, into the everyday life of the entrepreneur. However, the first steps have been taken and the initial results are promising (Liening et al., 2008, 2015).

8.2.2 The 'Synergetic Entrepreneurship Model' (*SEM*) and the Problem of Phase Transitions

The 'Synergetic Entrepreneurship Model' (SEM) is largely based on the complexity science theory of synergetics. It explains, for example, how phase transitions occur, i.e. how order-order, order-disorder, or disorder-order transitions take place in a self-organised manner. Thus, the theory is able, for example, to explain how coherent, dynamic patterns can self-organise from a multitude of possibly very different, chaotic initial conditions. The SEM illustrates three levels. It becomes clear how entrepreneurship knowledge and entrepreneurial attitudes are developed on the complex individual level, how startups with innovative business-entrepreneurial methods are created on the organisational level, and how complex growth effects can be sustainably created on the macroeconomic level with the help of technology and innovation due to entrepreneurial transmission effects. Ultimately, the individual levels interact with each other or are intertwined.

---

[2]The "Junior Business School" has meanwhile (2020) been transformed into the "Junior Entrepreneurship School", whereby the integrated Junior Innovation Day (JID) is a regular highlight for pupils.

A crucial question is whether the point in time at which a corresponding change process, no matter on which level it may take place, can be recognised in advance. Because only then would it be possible to consciously and sustainably steer the development in a desired direction with the help of gentle interventions ('nudges'). And indeed, the empirical methods derived from the theories of complex systems offer a variety of approaches and procedures for investigating such phase transitions. We have presented and analysed these methods in detail in the empirical chapters of the second part of the book.

To illustrate the possibilities that exist here, the exemplary use of such methods will be demonstrated in the following. This will be done using the example of a learning environment that allows the creative development of a young startup in the context of a market exposed to economic turbulence and changing conditions.

We remember that on the individual level, control parameters such as *Business Games* are provided for the development of entrepreneurship knowledge and an entrepreneurial attitude. In order to include the founding and growth process and thus the outlook on the other two levels, a special software was developed that addresses these questions in the context of a *Business Game,* which is used here as a control parameter in the 'Entrepreneurship Academy'.

8.2.3 *'Business Gaming'* as a Practical Control Parameter of the 'Entrepreneurship Academy'

In addition to a multitude of learning environments, learning content and methods, the previously described method of *Business Gaming* is used within the framework of the Entrepreneurship Academy. The learning environment, which is intended to contribute as one aspect of the overall concept to strengthening entrepreneurial education, essentially consists of a computer- and internet-based business simulation game[3], which is connected to a *Moodle* learning platform (https://beopen.tu-dortmund.de) and is distributed via it (https://www.moodle.org).

The subject area of the *Business Game* is the textile industry, which was considered a victim of structural change and globalisation decades ago. Of the approximately 900,000 jobs at the beginning of the nineteen seventies, only about 116,000 remained, as reported by Handelsblatt (Menn, 2010). At the beginning of the book, it was pointed out that the collapse of industries such as the textile industry, which have significantly shaped entire regions, living conditions and attitudes to life, was often and primarily perceived as a

[3]The *Business Game* was initially conceived by the author as object-oriented *C++* software and then implemented in its current version as a distributed system based on Java2Enterprise-Edition (J2EE) and enriched with a multitude of multimedia elements. Object-oriented programming includes, among other things, the enormous advantage of scalability, e.g., regarding the number of startups, so that the *Gaming* can take place with 5 as well as with 50 companies.

crisis. Meanwhile, the situation in this industry has fundamentally changed due to innovative startups, so that today almost as much turnover is generated as in the past. As the already quoted Handelsblatt report accurately states:

> "The abundance of innovations testifies to the transformative power of an industry that was considered irretrievably lost in Germany ten years ago." (Menn, 2010)

Especially in the textile industry, which was believed to be lost, entrepreneurs in Germany have set out to innovatively combine the know-how of a high-tech industrial society with traditional textiles. The innovative range of products extends from electric textiles that produce electricity during the day and serve as street lamps at night, to special fabrics that can generate drinking water from air humidity, to fabrics for very large inflatable halls. Modern textiles generate heat, produce electricity, heal wounds. For example, the products range from fabrics for modern zeppelins, wings of wind turbines to car parts, such as airbags or panoramic roof linings of modern SUVs. The car brand BMW already presented a concept car named Gina in 2008, whose bodywork is completely made of a flexible fabric that allows the body shape to change depending on the driving speed to achieve the best aerodynamics (Menn, 2010; Spiegel Online, 2016) (Fig. 8.1).[4]

In the *Business Game,* such an open, dynamic and innovative textile market is represented, in which a multitude of companies (inter-)act. Depending on the number of participants, there is a certain number of already founded startups ('Baby-AGs'), whose board positions must be taken over by the learners in the role of entrepreneurs. A team of up to five people takes over one of these young growth companies. The focus of the *Business Game* is therefore not on founding, but on the first growth and development phases of young companies (Liening, 2009). In addition to the classic business aspects of a business simulation game (deepening financial accounting, cost accounting, balance sheet accounting, marketing, production), participants have the opportunity to get to know entrepreneurial decisions under uncertainty, complexity and dynamics in their interdependencies, to strengthen their own entrepreneurial spirit, and to engage in supplementary workshops with innovative entrepreneurial methods, such as the application of business models (Business Model Canvas etc.) or interesting financing options (Crowd Financing, funding opportunities through 'Business Angel', state, federal etc.).

In five to six game rounds (each round represents a business year), which are accompanied by the workshops outlined above, a multitude of decisions are made and entered online via a so-called *StartUp-Cockpit.*

These decisions are subsequently evaluated. The analysis and the calculation of results take into account the decisions of competitors, potential customers who are interested in the offered products, as well as the general economic situation, which is represented by tax rates, interest rates, press releases, and association announcements. In addition to

[4] Further information on innovative developments in the textile industry can be found, for example, on the homepage of the "European Centre for Innovative Textiles" (http://www.ceti.com).

Fig. 8.1 "StartUp Cockpit" of the business game

a quantitative analysis, a number of qualitative data are analysed, which are generated, among other things, by the evaluation of virtual learning diaries, in which the learners reflect on and justify their respective decisions promptly, i.e., immediately after entering the decisions into the *StartUp-Cockpit*.

In the form of video clips, different news broadcasts in German and English are offered via the Internet, reporting on current (virtual) developments in the region, in the labour market, but also on developments at the federal economic policy level and on international events that are directly or indirectly related to the immediate (simulation) situation. The simulation participants receive the results of the calculations, which result from their decisions and the developments in the market, the framework conditions, etc., in the form of balance sheets, profit and loss accounts, financial and market reports, details from cost accounting, both as full and as partial cost accounting, as well as general data on the overall economic development. These reports serve as the basis for the decisions of the next fiscal year.

At the end of the simulation, there is a general meeting of the respective StartUp-AG. In this, the boards (team of the respective StartUp) present their results as company management to the shareholders (all other participants who do not belong to the presenting StartUp) in a role-play and justify or explain them. While the first (last) game period can be seen as an extended (de-)briefing period, the actual action under uncertainty and incomplete information takes place in the three middle game periods.

8.2.4 Complexity Measurement for Determining Phase Transitions and Their Practical Consequences

8.2.4.1 Learning Processes, Crises, and Complexity Measurements

To measure phase transitions in learning processes, one can, for example, examine the emergence of learning opportunities. The question of whether a learner perceives a certain situation he is confronted with as relevant or critical enough to recognise it as a learning opportunity is a necessary prerequisite for successfully mastering challenges that may be associated with a crisis situation and thus for further self-development (Liening et al., 2012).

Friedrich August *von Hayek's* concept of *catallaxy*, the spontaneous formation of order, which we have already referred to in the introduction of the book, we find not only in real markets but also in simulated markets, as they arise and are designed in the context of a business simulation game. By intervening in the simulation game, which disrupts the complex development of (simulated) market events and leads to a temporary increase in complexity, a crisis situation and thus the desired learning opportunity can be created, which brings about a new spontaneous order. The participant's ability to perceive this new spontaneous order is, as already mentioned, the necessary prerequisite for dealing successfully with it. Thus, conclusions can be drawn from the action in a crisis situation about the abilities of the simulation game participants (Liening et al., 2012: p. 41).

8.2.4.2 A Study from the Field of Business Gaming: "Learning from Crises—Complexity Measurements"

i. **The Basic Assumption**

The following study was conducted by the author, Ewald *Mittelstädt*, and—regarding the crucial calculations of the results—by Guido *Strunk* (Liening et al., 2012, 2013).

Based on the considerations in the previous section, the following basic assumption arises:

> "Participants in the simulation game who are able to perceive the crisis as a learning opportunity show a higher complexity in their activities during the crisis and are more likely to be able to act successfully in the market after the crisis." (Liening et al., 2012: p. 41)

ii. **Participants—The Cohort Studied**

A total of 96 participants from TU Dortmund actively participated in the *Business Game* in the role of company executives. The average age was 24.7 years, 32.3 % were women, the average study duration of the participants was 3.7 years at the time of the implementation. The majority of the company boards consisted of teams of 5 people each. The empirical study was conducted in two seminars, one in the winter term 2008/09 with a total of 16 and the other in the summer term 2009 with 5 (virtual) StartUps (Liening et al., 2013: p. 529).

iii. **Examined Phases in the *Business Game***

In the study, the three middle game periods of the *Business Game* process outlined in the previous section, out of a total of five game periods, represent the examined phases 1 to 3. In phase 2 (third game period), a dramatic economic-didactic intervention is carried out, which can only be successfully managed by the participants making a qualitative change in behaviour regarding their entrepreneurial decisions. A "business as usual" approach would plunge the startups into a deep crisis (Liening et al., 2013: p. 527).

Firstly, in phase 2, the warehouses of a central supplier for domestic companies burn down, causing the costs for preliminary products to skyrocket.

Secondly, there is the announcement that an East Asian competitor with dangerously low dumping prices and equal product quality is massively penetrating the domestic market.

Both announcements trigger a crisis situation in the domestic market and pose enormous challenges to the young growth companies.[5] The participants receive the information in the form of "special broadcasts" from the "regional news studio", which are provided via the front-end system of the *Business Game*.

iv. **Multimedia Learning Platform for Generating Data Streams**

The front-end system of the *Business Game* is a multimedia learning platform. This refers to a software infrastructure for supporting electronic teaching/learning processes. Multimedia learning platforms provide opportunities for managing events, learners, teachers, and content, and offer an infrastructure for internet-based communication.[6] In

[5] The crisis can be intensified or mitigated by the game management through further predefined or spontaneously developed scenarios (Liening, 2015a).

[6] Administrative functions of such a learning platform include the recording and management of learners, the recording and management of teachers, and the management and presentation of events. From the teachers' perspective, these learning environments support the planning and management of events. An intuitive, self-explanatory user interface is used. Tutoring, tracking, evaluation, testing, and grading can be supported. For the learning processes, learning platforms can

this way, learners can communicate with other learners and lecturers independently of time and place using various asynchronous and synchronous forms of communication, such as the use of discussion forums, chat rooms, etc. (Liening, 2004).

The learning environment BEOpen (Business Education Open Source Platform) used here and already mentioned is such a multimedia learning platform. In addition to its role as a communication interface for the Business Game, it generates a multitude of data that can be used for empirical research purposes. For example, the following data are tracked and recorded:

- Persons (participant list, group list)
- Activities (Course-Views, Forum Views, Material-Views, Learning Logs, etc.)
- Administration (evaluations, statistics), also recorded are:
  - Latest activities (newly posted materials or interactive activities)
  - Latest news (new discussions)
  - Calendar (with global, group, course or participant dates)
  - Upcoming dates (task list from the calendar)
  - Online users (which course participants are currently logged in) etc.

The use of the multimedia learning platform thus enables the generation of data series that provide information about the participants' activities in the game, as every activity on the learning platform is documented (Liening, 2004).

From the multitude of activities, the *'Course-View'* and the *'Forum-View'* were examined in more detail. In the *Course-View,* the number of daily accesses during the implementation of the *Business Game* is recorded. In the *Forum-View,* the writing of discussion posts is counted. The time series data from the *Course-View* and the *Forum-View* are determined using the Time-Sampling-Method over the entire time course with a sampling frequency of one day. The recording of both variables over time serves to collect indicators for dealing with the simulation scenario and the crisis simulated therein (Liening et al., 2013: p. 531).

provide progress monitoring. In addition, further personalisations and the adaptability of the system to individual learning processes are conceivable. From the authors' perspective, who do not necessarily have to be identical to the teachers, learning platforms can support the development of learning materials by providing tools, for example, for the graphical creation of learning units. Furthermore, multimedia learning environments support different media such as texts, graphics, audios and videos, podcasts or, as in our case, the specific transmission of "news broadcasts" (Liening, 2015a).

v. **Selection of the dependent variable**

The dependent variable is the calculated 'Return on Investment' (ROI) of the young growth companies of the simulation game per game phase. Of all conceivable key figures, the ROI is very significant, as only a sufficient profit allows, for example, to pay appropriate wages, distribute sufficient dividends to equity providers, pay interest to debt providers and taxes to the state, make investments, maintain substance, open up new markets etc. In short, the ROI reflects the success of a company in a concise form, whereby this key figure itself can be the result of a comprehensive key figure system in which a multitude of key figures, starting with the return on sales and the capital turnover up to individual positions from individual cost centres, can be linked (Liening, 2002a: p. 37ff., 2002b, 14ff.).

The ROI in the present Business Game is recorded for the last day of the phase. The central *target size* of the experimental design is the "ROI of Phase 3".

vi. **Permutation entropy as a measurement method**

To illustrate the power of the methods for complexity measurement, only one method is used as an example, namely a method from the field of entropy codings, which we got to know in an empirical chapter in the second part of the book. Thus, the complexity measurement is carried out with the help of the so-called Permutation entropy.

This is based, as we have seen, on the *Shannon*-entropy, which is probably the most frequently used method for measuring the information content of a data series, but—as we have seen—also brings with it some problems that are overcome by permutation entropy (Bandt & Pompe, 2002). We have already seen that the *Shannon* approach only considers the frequency distribution of events, not the order in which the events occur. If, for example, one determines the frequency distribution of the letters of this book, the same *Shannon* information content always results, regardless of whether the letters form "meaningful" words and sentences or whether they are arranged randomly. However, the definition of complexity used here requires consideration of the arrangement. Complexity is in a tension between simple order (e.g., sorted arrangement of the characters of this book) and randomness (random arrangement of the characters). As we already know, permutation entropy, as a further development of *Shannon* entropy, precisely takes into account the arrangement of the characters in a time series by forming so-called words and combining several characters into a larger element. Permutation entropy transforms the words into simple sequences of numbers by replacing the numerical values of the word with rank orders. The lowest number in the word receives the digit 0, the next higher the digit 1, and so on. If a word with a word length of 6 is symbolised by the set $\{0, 1, 2, 3, 4, 5\}$, then the data series of raw values is strictly monotonically increasing. A set like $\{5, 4, 3, 2, 1, 0\}$ shows a strictly monotonically decreasing arrangement and the set $\{1, 0, 3, 2, 5, 4\}$ could be described as a 'zigzag' pattern. The original numerical values are irrelevant after this transformation. Now patterns can be counted in the transformed data and their frequency distribution can be used to determine the complexity of the data sequence according to the definition of *Shannon*. In this way, the complexity of two or more time windows can be compared with each other (Liening et al., 2013: p. 528f.)

As we have already emphasised in the corresponding chapter on empiricism, permutation entropy is a measure of disorder or complexity: the higher the entropy, the higher the complexity. Conversely, the lower the entropy, the higher the order. When a bifurcation or a phase transition occurs, it can be said for the observed system: It "is on the brink" (Strunk & Schiepek, 2006: p. 73). The behaviour of the system can abruptly tip into another pattern at this threshold. In this situation, the complexity in a local temporal environment is maximal. Conversely, such a phase transition can actually be measured using complexity calculations. In the second part of the book, we examined this in detail in a theory chapter. Recall Fig. 8.2, which exemplifies the relationship between complexity and bifurcation or phase transition, thus illustrating that the (local) maximisation of complexity and the increase in complexity can provide a clue to an impending phase transition (Fig. 8.2).

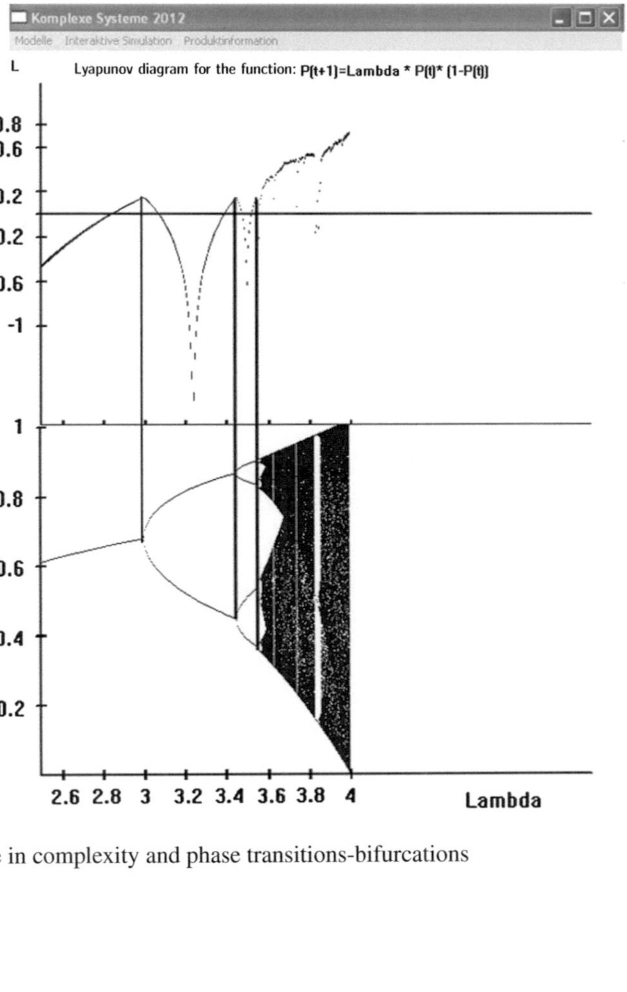

Fig. 8.2 Change in complexity and phase transitions-bifurcations

In the learning process, such a phase transition can also be compared to an 'aha' effect (pattern 'ignorance/misunderstanding' flips into pattern 'knowledge/understanding'). The insights that crossing such a learning threshold brings should, for example, help to better cope with the challenges one faces. In this context, the discussion about threshold concepts ('threshold concepts') is very promising for the interpretation of such phase transitions in learning processes (Meyer & Land, 2006; Kricks et al., 2013). With the help of permutation entropy, such complexity changes in the concrete simulation of the presented *Business Game* among the participants are to be identified, because permutation entropy is also suitable for demonstrating phase transitions in simulated systems (Bandt & Pompe, 2002; Schiepek & Strunk, 2006).

vii. **The Hypothesis**

As already mentioned, the central (dependent) variable of our experimental design is the "ROI in Phase 3". The central hypothesis is now as follows:

It is assumed that the ROI in Phase 3 is related to the learning process in Phase 2 and that this learning should be reflected in the increasing complexity due to dealing with the problems of Phase 2 (Liening et al., 2013: p. 532).

It is therefore suspected that the higher the complexity measured in Phase 2, the better the crisis should be managed and the higher the "ROI of Phase 3" should be. The "complexity in Phase 2" should therefore be a predictor, a predictive factor, for the "ROI in Phase 3", with a phase transition being indicated by the increase in complexity from Phase 1 to Phase 2 of the simulation game.[7] Results of various articles make it clear that this consideration can be well supported theoretically (Haken & Schiepek, 2010; Schiepek & Strunk, 2006; Kowalik et al., 1997)

Strunk now suggests testing this correlation hypothesis with a multiple regression model:[8] "As part of a Stepwise Forward Selection, the variables that serve to predict the ROI of Phase 3 are included in the model. Available are the complexity characteristics of the three phases, the ROI of Phases 1 and 2, and gender as a control variable. Furthermore, the frequency of activities of *"Course-View"* and *"Forum-View"* are included in the model as possible alternative explanations." (Liening et al., 2012: p. 44)

[7] Note: A change in complexity between Phase 2 and 3 is neither suspected nor can it be inferred from the course of the present experiment. It should also be noted that a phase transition is expected to result in a (local) maximum of complexity. However, this can only be stated after the crisis, as only then may the complexity decrease again.

[8] Since a simple linear regression only measures bivariate relationships between two variables, the multiple regression is suitable for the higher number of variables present here. The step-by-step approach ensures that the model is extended by another independent variable that increases the R^2 the most, and thus also improves the prediction the most.

Table 8.1 Key figures in Phase 1 and Phase 2. (Source: Liening et al., 2012: p. 45)

	Phase 1		Phase 2						
	AM	SD	AM	SD	N	T	d	p 1-sided	
Course-view	2.721	0.714	2.854	0.664	96	2.081	95	0.020	*
Forum-view	2.099	0.996	2.319	0.955	96	2.340	95	0.011	*

The following is now expected: The "complexity of Phase 2" is included in the model and, together with other variables, such as the ROI of the other phases, has a significant effect on the "ROI of Phase 3". The complexity values of Phase 1 and also of Phase 3 should not be relevant. The activity sums should also not be included. The probability for the inclusion of a variable is set at 0.05 and for the exclusion of a variable at 0.10 (Liening et al., 2013: p. 532).

viii. **Application and Results of Permutation Entropy**

First, permutation entropy is used to check whether the complexity differs between the phases. A slight increase in complexity from Phase 1 to Phase 2 is expected. The calculation of permutation entropy is done with a word length of 4 (Liening et al., 2013: p. 532).

On the one hand, considering synergetics, it is important that ultimately, due to a change in the complexity of relevant variables, a phase transition of the system under consideration can be presumed. On the other hand, complexity in the sense of permutation entropy means the presence of a high information content in the patterns of the time series examined. Complexity is therefore to be distinguished from a mere increase in activities.[9] A possibly hectic (i.e., random) response to the crisis does not solve any problems and therefore does not lead to a positive change in the ROI. Rather, a qualitative change in the behaviour of the participants and an associated learning process is required.

Indeed, the expected correlations emerge from the study, that according to the hypothesis, the increase in complexity is statistically significant both in the *Course-View* and in the *Forum-View,* as illustrated in Fig. 8.2 and Table 8.1 (Fig. 8.3).

The specific complexity calculations were carried out using the latest "GChaos" software version 18.8 from *Strunk* (http://www.complexity-research.com) available at the time of the study, who also interpreted the results accordingly (Table 8.1).[10]

AM: Arithmetic mean; SD: Standard deviation; N: Number of people, T: Test size, df: Degrees of freedom; p 1-sided: Significance value.

[9] This can also be well demonstrated statically in this study (Liening et al., 2013: 534).

[10] The further statistical tests were determined using SPSS 8.0.

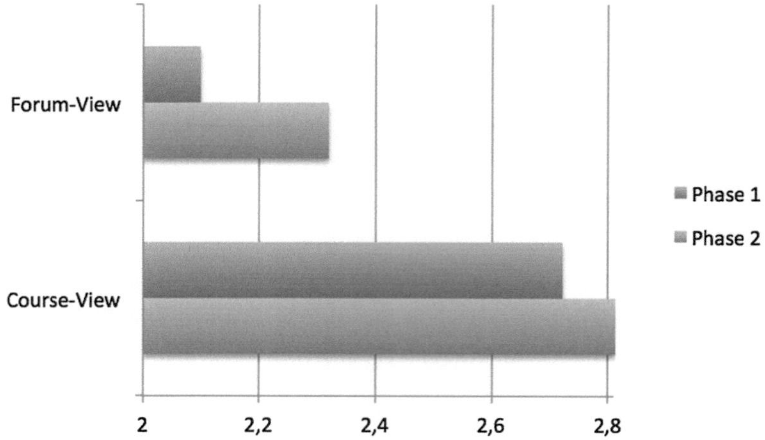

Fig. 8.3 Permutation entropy in the Business Game (in Bit). (Source: Liening et al., 2012: p. 45)

The results obtained show that the intervention in Phase 2 actually leads to an increase in the complexity of activities within Phase 2.[11]

ix. **Determination of dependent variables using stepwise, multiple regression with forward selection**

In addition to this complexity measurement, the relationship between the complexity and ROI variables should now also be measured. Here, a method of traditional statistics, regression analysis, is suitable. The question to be answered is therefore: Is there a dependency between the considered variables or does the relationship follow a random pattern? And what are the 'correct' independent variables[12] that need to be considered?

To answer these questions, the stepwise multiple regression is applied based on the mentioned suggestion by *Strunk*. This can be done as forward selection or backward elimination, where we choose the first variant. In the first step, the independent variable that correlates most strongly with the dependent variable is included in the equation. In the next step, the independent variable that has the highest partial correlation with the

[11] During the same period, the increase in activity in the *Forum-View* area is not significant (p-1-tailed = 0.244) and in the *Course-View* area it is significant (p-1-tailed = 0.041), but not as pronounced as for complexity. This confirms the already established assumption that complexity is somewhat dependent on the sum of activity, but is by no means identical to it. For detailed results of descriptive statistics and correlations, see Liening et al. (2013: 533).

[12] While the dependent variable is the "ROI in Phase 3", possible independent variables or predictors of the ROI of Phases 1 and 2 are the complexity of the *Course View* or *Forum* in Phases 1, 2 and 3, as well as the activity totals of the *Course View* or *Forum* in Phases 1, 2 and 3.

dependent variable is included. The second step is repeated until the addition of further variables does not increase the R^2 value[13] or all variables have already been considered (Liening et al., 2013: p. 532).

Course-View

The concrete implementation shows that the stepwise multiple regression with forward selection for the *Course-View* selects the following three variables from the available variables into the model for predicting the ROI of Phase 3: a) “ROI Phase 1”, b) “Complexity of Phase 2” and c) the “ROI of Phase 2” (Liening et al., 2012: p. 44). *Strunk* points out that the “ROI of Phase 2” does not correlate bivariately with the “ROI of Phase 3” and that the beta weight[14] has a negative sign, suggesting a suppression effect. This means that the addition of the Phase 3 variables increases the proportion of explainable variance, but they do not correlate with the criterion. Thus, the “ROI of Phase 1” and the "Complexity of Phase 2” remain in the model as directly interpretable influencing factors. This corresponds to the above assumptions (Liening et al., 2012: p. 46).

Forum-View

The stepwise Multiple Regression with forward selection for the *Forum-View* selects from the provided variables according to the same principle as the *Course View*. The same suppression effect[15] and the influence of the "ROI of Phase 1” are evident. The "Complexity of Phase 2”, this time measured for the *Forum-View*, is also highly significant. This also corresponds to the assumptions (Liening, Mittelstädt et al., 2012: p. 46). If one does not distinguish between *Forum-* or *Course-View* and both sources are tested within the framework of a stepwise model, the calculations using the GChaos software include the “ROI of Phase 1” and “Phase 2” (here too there is a suppressor effect) both

[13]The coefficient of determination, the R^2 value, measures the explained proportion of a dependent variable, indirectly also measuring the relationship between the dependent and independent variables (0 = no relationship, ..., 1 = maximum relationship). The measure increases with the number of independent variables, which is not relevant for us here (Sachs & Hedderich, 2006: 573).

[14]The beta weight is a standardised regression coefficient that results when all predictors involved in the multiple regression are z-standardised, where the z-value indicates how many standard deviations there are and in which direction (i.e., sign to be observed) a measurement value deviates from the mean (Rudolf & Müller, 2012: 393).

[15]A suppression effect occurs when independent variables (predictors) increase the predictive value of other predictors by compensating for irrelevant variable components of these variables (Rudolf & Müller, 2012: 399).

Table 8.2 Stepwise multiple regression for the ROI in Phase 3. (Source: Liening et al. 2013: p. 534)

Variable	B	SD	Beta	T	Sig
Intercept	−18.56	4.02		−4.62	0.000
ROI Phase 1	1.37	0.19	0.60	7.19	0.000
Complexity *Forum-View* (Phase 2)	3.07	0.93	0.28	3.32	0.001
ROI Phase 2	−0.25	0.09	−0.22	−2.67	0.002
Complexity *Course-View* (Phase 2)	2.82	1.31	0.18	2.15	0.034

R2=0.464
B: Regression weight; SD: Standard deviation; Beta: standardised regression weight; T: Test statistic; Sig: Significance.

complexity values of Phase 2, but not complexity indicators of the other phases or activity totals of the three phases, as can be seen from Table 8.2.

The forward selection thus shows that, according to the hypothesis, the ROI of Phase 3 significantly correlates with the complexity of the *Course-View* and the *Forum-View* in Phase 2 and the ROI in Phase 1.[16]

8.2.4.3 Critical Examination of the Study Results

Overall, due to the applied permutation entropy, combined with a stepwise multiple regression, the thesis is confirmed that participants in the *Business Game* who are able to actively perceive a (simulated) economic crisis in their (virtual) company as a learning opportunity, exhibit a higher complexity in their activities within the crisis and are more likely to be able to operate successfully in the market after the crisis. This perception of the crisis as a learning opportunity suggests that learning in a crisis situation is to be understood as a self-organisation process (Liening et al., 2012: p. 46f.). However, it should be noted that the complexity measurement does not make any statements about the content success. It was not investigated what the *Business-Game* participants actually learned. At least it can be assumed that what was learned was useful, as the ROI in Phase 3 was significantly higher for those participants whose activities previously showed a higher complexity in Phase 2 than in Phase 1. This research methodology or the developed measurement technology thus opens a wide door to subject-specific competence measurement.

[16] Although bivariate analysis has indeed shown the influence of other variables, these do not offer any additional variance explanation that could significantly improve the models reported here.

8.2.5 Another Study from the Field of *Business Gaming* (Complex Stock Market Simulation)—in the Context of SEM1

The empirical example outlined below, which culminated in the dissertation of Till *Sender* (Sender, 2017), is based on an extension of the described *Business Game*. The start-ups considered there are—as described—corporations, so-called baby corporations. The shares are traded on a (virtual) stock exchange, so that a stock market simulation exists parallel to the Business Game. The stock market simulation game is designed in such a way that it can also be carried out independently of the Business Game, with the company data always coming from the start-ups of the Business Game.

The extreme crisis situation that arises in the Business Game in the described Phase 3 does not pass the stock exchange without a trace, but also creates a crisis mood there.

In order to be able to evaluate the behaviour of the learners, who now individually trade the shares on this (virtual) stock exchange, in the previously described experimentally created phase of uncertainty from a complexity science perspective, to see whether potential change processes in the game behaviour during this uncertainty phase are accompanied by critical fluctuations, time series data suitable for complexity science methods were generated for this purpose. The associated **research question** is:

How can individual transition states be recognised as an essential part of learning processes?

The game behaviour of each individual player was recorded in the form of a *logbook* on a server, which documents every decision (stock purchase or stock sale) as well as every other action (e.g., information obtained) to the second. Furthermore, the simulation game experiment was accompanied by a *biofeedback*[17] by having selected test subjects measure their heart rate during the simulation game implementation, thereby generating time series data with several thousand data points that are directly related to individual game behaviour. Depending on the length of the time series, selected complexity science methods presented in this book (e.g., permutation entropy, PD_2) are used in the further course of the research process imitated by *Sender* to analyse the complexity courses of the generated time series from a synergetic perspective, as to how these enable

[17] For the *biofeedback*, a Nexus system from the provider Mind Media® was used, which can be used as a 4-channel system for physiological monitoring (muscle tension, heart rate, relative blood flow, skin conductivity, breathing) and also for neurofeedback (brain activity). In the present study, the system was used to record the blood volume pulse. The pulse is recorded via sensors attached to the earlobe or fingertip at a sampling rate of 128Hz and recorded using the associated software "BioTrace". This measurement also allows the recording of the heart rate. Mind-Media (2022). "BVP Sensor." Retrieved March 08, 2022.

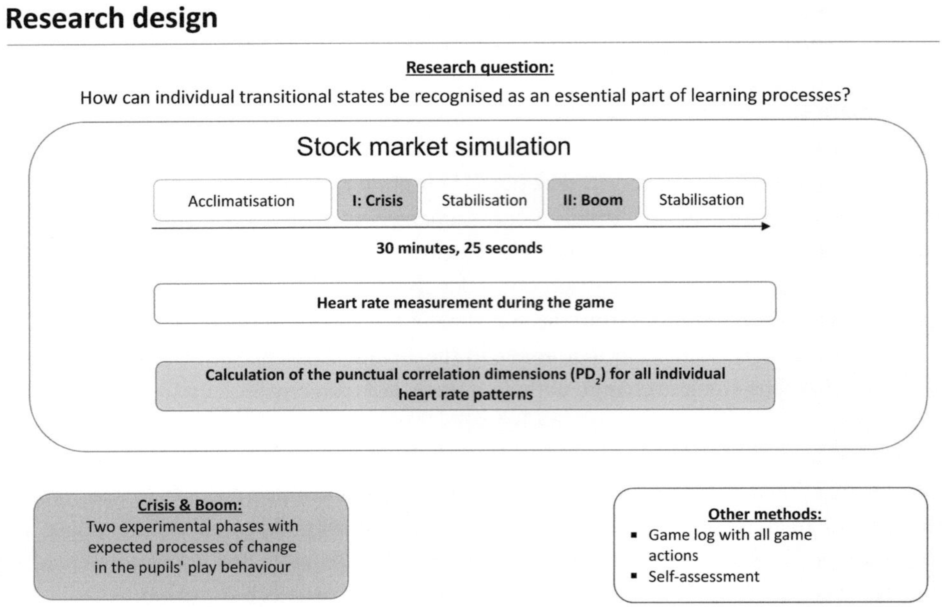

Fig. 8.4 Research design

monitoring of uncertainty phases with regard to phase transitions in student behaviour by demonstrating critical fluctuations.[18] (Fig. 8.4).

Thus, with the stock market simulation game, a learning environment was created in which behavioural changes of the participants could be expected during the game. In particular, two experimental game phases—a boom and a crisis—were conducted, in which the players were encouraged to "learn" new game behaviour in a time of changing market conditions.

In order to obtain process data of the individual learning processes, the stock market game was accompanied by a heart rate measurement during the game. Physiological process data such as the individual heart rate patterns are a valid data source for human thinking and action. All individual heart rate patterns were transformed into time series with the complexity of the heart rate by calculating the pointwise correlation dimension

[18] Till *Sender* is a former member of the author's research team and conducted this investigation as part of his dissertation.Sender, T. (2017). **Economic Didactic Learning Diagnostics and Complexity—Localisation of Liminal Uncertainty Phases with Regard to Threshold Transitions. (Diss.)**. Wiesbaden, Springer Verlag.

(PD_2). In this way, there was information about the complexity of the individual game course for every second of the game. The research focus was then on the suitability of the PD_2 as a nonlinear data analysis for detecting transitions in the game behaviour of the participants by focussing on changes in the dimension complexity. To ensure that the analysis really focussed on "important" changes, the game logbook with all game actions and a self-assessment of the players were used as external criteria.

Based on this research design, the suitability of the PD_2 measures was demonstrated by testing three hypotheses:

Hypothesis:

1. In destabilising game phases, the process data of the participants show increased complexity.
2. When the participants change their behaviour during the game, the complexity of the individual time series data increases.
3. An increased complexity in the individual process data is a predictor for individual game success (Fig. 8.5).

This exemplary time series of a participant provides insights into the nonlinear data analysis conducted in the study. In total, 30 heart rate patterns with 3650 data points each

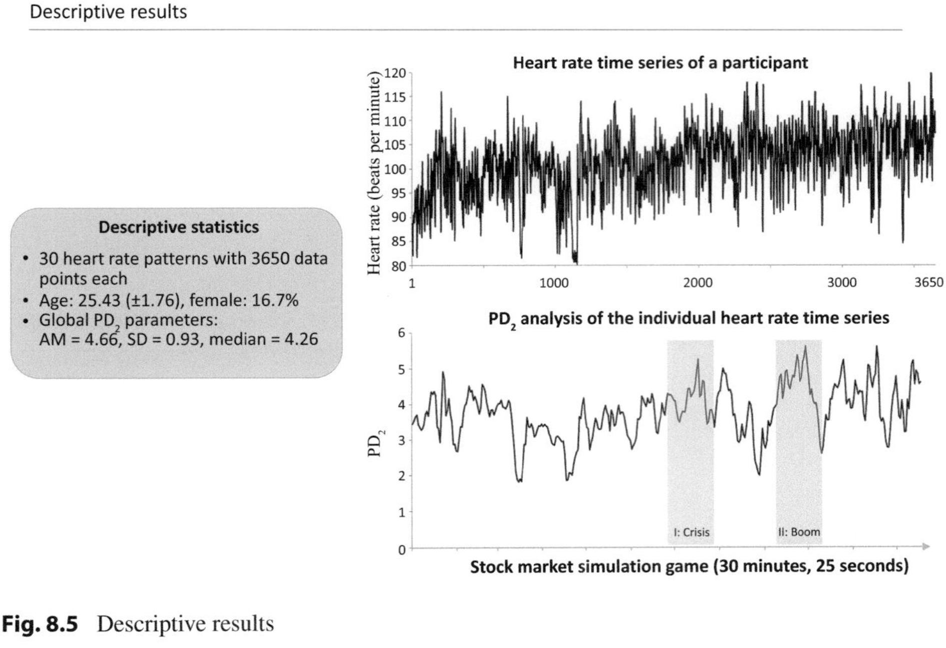

Fig. 8.5 Descriptive results

were collected and then transformed into PD_2 time series. The data analysis then zoomed into the experimental phases "crisis" and "boom", but also into other time segments where the game logbook or the statements of the participants in the self-assessment suggested a fundamental change in game behaviour (Fig. 8.6).

This is an overview of some of the most important results of the study. Regarding hypothesis 1, the data processed by the students actually show a statistically significantly increased complexity in the destabilising game phases "crisis" and "boom". To test hypothesis 2, individual time windows were located using the game logbook and self-assessment, in which the game behaviour of the students changed from one behaviour A (e.g., purchase order) to another behaviour B (e.g., sales order). These changes are accompanied by an intermediate stage with increased complexity, as the results on the slide underline. In addition, the individual PD_2 maxima in the individual time series, based on a correlation analysis and a regression analysis, proved to be statistically significant predictors for individual game success operationalised with the realised total assets in the game. In summary, the study underscores the diagnostic importance of complexity measures for monitoring individual change or learning processes. Limitations regarding the explanatory relevance follow directly from the relatively small sample size. Therefore, it is crucial that further research on the relationship between complexity and the learning process in economic learning environments be conducted to further substanti-

Hypothesis tests & results

Hypothesis 1

	before	Crisis	after	before	Boom	after
PD_2 (median)	4,27	**4,43**	4,23	4,17	**4,39**	4.38
Wilcoxon test	z =-1.16, p = .12		z =-1.70, p = .05*	z = -2.64, p = .00**		z =-2.13, p = .02*

N = 30

In the destabilising game phases "crisis" and "boom", the students' process data show a statistically significant increase in complexity.

Hypothesis 2

Based on the game log and the self-assessment, individual time windows were localised in which the students' game behaviour changed from one behaviour A (e.g. buy order) to another behaviour B (e.g. sell order). These changes are accompanied by an intermediate stage with increased complexity.

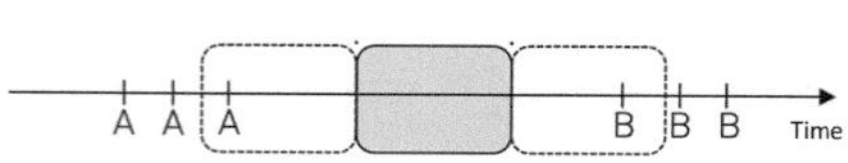

	A	between	B
PD_2 (median)	4,48	**4,58**	4,39
Wilcoxon test	z =-2.21, p = .01*		z =-2.52, p = .01**

N = 41

Hypothesis 3

Based on a correlation analysis and a regression analysis, the individual PD2 maxima were identified as statistically significant predictors of individual player success (i.e. the total wealth realised in the game).

Fig. 8.6 Hypothesis tests and results

ate the relationship shown. However, the relevance of the complexity methodology with regard to learning diagnostics was already evident in this small study (Sender, 2017, p. 229 ff.).

8.3 Complex Dynamics of StartUps within the Framework of SEM2

8.3.1 The Business Game as an Environment for Observing Learning Processes at the Organisational Level

SEM2 describes the genesis and development process of a startup within the 'Synergetic Entrepreneurship Model'. Strictly speaking, the first study already described in SEM1 is also a prime example for SEM2, as it essentially asks and answers the question of how startups get through crises, beyond the consideration of the individual learning process. Although the focus in SEM1 is on individual learning, the success of the (virtual) startup and mastering the described crisis in the Business Game ultimately depends on team performance. Therefore, it is not only about the individual learning process as described in SEM1, but also about the learning process at the organisational level of the startup. In this sense, it is not only the individuals who go through different learning opportunities: The entire team that forms the startup undergoes manifold learning opportunities. Since the number of participants with $N = 96$ was not very high, a quantitative complexity analysis aggregated to the respective startup hardly seems possible, especially since the results at the individual level, which can be assigned to the individual startups, allow clear conclusions for the organisational level:

Due to the applied permutation entropy, combined with a stepwise multiple regression, the thesis is confirmed that the individual learners in the *Business Game* are able to actively perceive a (simulated) economic crisis in their (virtual) company as a learning opportunity, so that they exhibit a higher complexity in their activities within the crisis and are thus better able to act successfully in the market after the crisis. Since the individual learners ultimately act in their teams and make decisions for the startup they lead, it can be concluded from the results that, when viewed in aggregate, those individually successful learning processes during times of crisis have a positive effect on the respective startup's market actions. This perception of the crisis as a learning opportunity to cope with a crisis situation in which a startup finds itself, thus suggests that successful learning as an organisation in a crisis situation can also be understood as a complex self-organisation process with phase transitions. Overall, the study confirms the thesis:

> "Organisations undergoing a phase transition during a crisis will be able to act more successfully on the market after the crisis" (Liening et al., 2013, p. 527).

In this respect, the first example of SEM1 has a not to be underestimated significance at the level of SEM2.

8.3.2 An Example of Observing a Real Startup in the Founding Process

The next investigation involves the application of the complexity science method known as *"Recurrence Plots"*. As described in SEM2, the founding processes of startups are often of a complex nature and involve dynamic jumps or phase transitions. Such dynamic jumps can be identified using various complexity science methods. In the present investigation, the method of *Recurrence Plots* is applied to time series data on the number of founding activities of a startup in the founding process to identify dynamic jumps in the founding process.

It should be reiterated that a *Recurrence Plot* is considered an advanced technique of non-linear data analysis and provides a visualisation to illustrate the recurrence of states of a dynamic system in phase space as a fundamental property of deterministic dynamic systems with respect to non-linearity and chaos.

For the analysis, data from a qualitative study by *Lichtenstein* et al. (2006) is used. It was prepared by Tim *Haarhaus*[19] and evaluated using GChaos. The results of the interviews with the founder of the startup *HealthInfo* (the startup was at the beginning of the founding process) were taken into account. The founder was interviewed by the researchers every two weeks from December 1998 to March 2001 about the founding activities carried out in the respective period. In addition, secondary data was collected, for example on the founder's expenses, further developments of the offered product, and produced materials for marketing. The examined founding activities were divided into 28 different categories.

In the context of the investigation carried out here, the method of Recurrence Plots was applied to the number of founding activities over time to identify possible dynamic jumps in the founding process. Based on the specifically created Recurrence Plots, several dynamic jumps in the founding process can be identified, which are particularly noticeable at observation points 16 and 17 (see Fig. 8.8). The white areas or bands in the Recurrence Plot indicate abrupt changes/dynamic jumps in the founding process. The white areas or bands thus overlap with periods of dramatically increased founding activity. This means that a particularly large number of founding activities must have occurred here (Fig. 8.7).

So how are the results of this small study to be interpreted? The pattern changes in the *Recurrence Plot* thus reveal dynamic jumps in the emergence of startups. These jumps, which are accompanied by a dramatically increased number of founding activities, may represent phase transitions in the development of the startup. This suggests that the startup assumed a qualitatively different state (in the sense of a new identity) during the identified dynamic jumps. We can see from this that the tactical organisation of the startup has changed significantly and abruptly several times during the founding process.

[19] Tim *Haarhaus* was a member of the author's research team and has developed these calculations as part of the chair's projects.

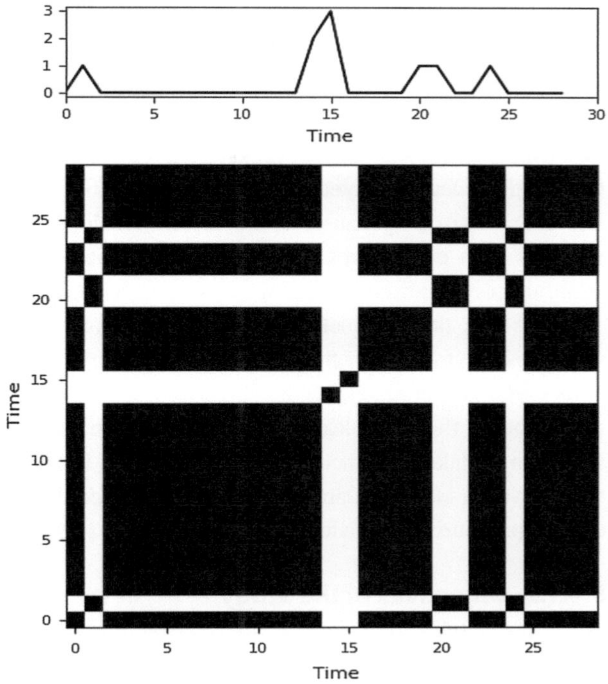

Fig. 8.7 Recurrence Plot for the number of founding activities (fortnightly) of HealthInfo. (Figure created with tool by Arwan et al., 2007)

8.4 Complexity Investigations within the Framework of SEM3

SEM3 focusses within the 'Synergetic Entrepreneurship Model' on the design and creation of new markets, on economic developments and economic growth.

8.4.1 Complexity Science Investigations of Entrepreneurial Ecosystems

8.4.1.1 Entrepreneurial Ecosystems in Research

The first study mentioned in the context of SEM3 refers to the development of the entrepreneurial ecosystem in Singapore from January 1970 to May 2018 at the macroeconomic level. It is the result of a study by *Haarhaus, Strunk* and *Liening* (2020), which was significantly initiated and implemented by *Haarhaus* and therefore rightly culminated in his dissertation (2022). Entrepreneurial ecosystems can be perceived as combinations of interconnected organisations, institutions, actors, and actions that are arranged in such a way that they facilitate and maintain entrepreneurial activities in regional environments (Haarhaus et al., 2020). The concept of entrepreneurial ecosystems represents an emerging field of research, with the focus so far mainly on describing the main components of various ecosystems (Roundy, 2018).

It was found that existing research predominantly applies a static framework for examining entrepreneurial ecosystems, thus neglecting that ecosystems are constantly evolving (Alvedalen, 2017, Kuckertz, 2019). Furthermore, entrepreneurial ecosystems have so far been portrayed as structures consisting of entirely or partially separate parts and characterised by causal or linear relationships between the actors (Roundy, 2018), whereas such ecosystems, as *Roundy* et al. note, actually "emerge from nonlinear and dynamic combinations of sets of variables" (Roundy, 2018: p. 7).

Therefore, there is increasing agreement that evolutionary, time-related perspectives are necessary to explain the emerging and complex dynamics of entrepreneurial ecosystems (Haarhaus et al., 2020).

Although the complex and evolutionary nature of entrepreneurial ecosystems is increasingly taken into account in the literature to adequately capture their development, there is still a lack of quantitative empirical evidence for the assumed complex dynamics of entrepreneurial ecosystems (Haarhaus et al., 2020).

8.4.1.2 Objectives of the Study

The present study therefore attempts to empirically quantify the development of entrepreneurial ecosystems. The described methods of Pointwise D_2 (PD_2), the BDS test, and *Local Largest Lyapunov Exponents* (LLLE) are applied to the empirical case of Singapore's entrepreneurial ecosystem. The present study underpins the idea of a complex and nonlinear development of entrepreneurial ecosystems and answers the call for further empirical studies in this area (Haarhaus et al., 2020).

To conduct the study, archived time series data on the monthly establishment of new companies were used, which come from the Singapore Statistical Office. The establishment of new companies was used as a proxy for measuring ecosystem dynamics, as the establishment of new companies is seen as the result of the interaction between various interest groups and elements (Gartner, 1985; Cavallo, 2019) and thus adequately represents the entire entrepreneurial activity in regional agglomerations. Singapore's entrepreneurial ecosystem consistently ranks among the strongest and most efficient entrepreneurial ecosystems worldwide (StartupGenome, 2018). As shown in Fig. 8.9, 581 sample months (and thus data points) of the establishment of new companies were recorded during the investigation period (Haarhaus et al., 2020) (Fig. 8.8).

8.4.1.3 Approach to Complexity Science Data Analysis

Considering the current sketches of the development of the entrepreneurial ecosystem as a dynamic and nonlinear process, the assumption of stationarity for entrepreneurial ecosystems may not be appropriate. Therefore, it might be more accurate to assume non-stationary changes during the development of entrepreneurial ecosystems. Such critical transitions are typically expected over long observation periods, e.g., when studying

Fig. 8.8 Raw time series of the establishment of new companies, 1970/1 to 2018/5 (Haarhaus et al., 2020: p. 3)

business cycles and economic dynamics (Hamilton, 1989; Chen, 1996). In this regard, methods were applied here that do not require stationarity of the underlying time series to reveal the temporal dynamics of entrepreneurial ecosystems. Before applying the three measures described below, the raw data of the time series were transformed into *logarithmic returns,* as described in 5.1.2.2 (see Fig. 8.6), to obtain a realistic representation of the system's internal dynamics and to eliminate strong seasonal or trend effects (Haarhaus et al., 2020) (Fig. 8.9).

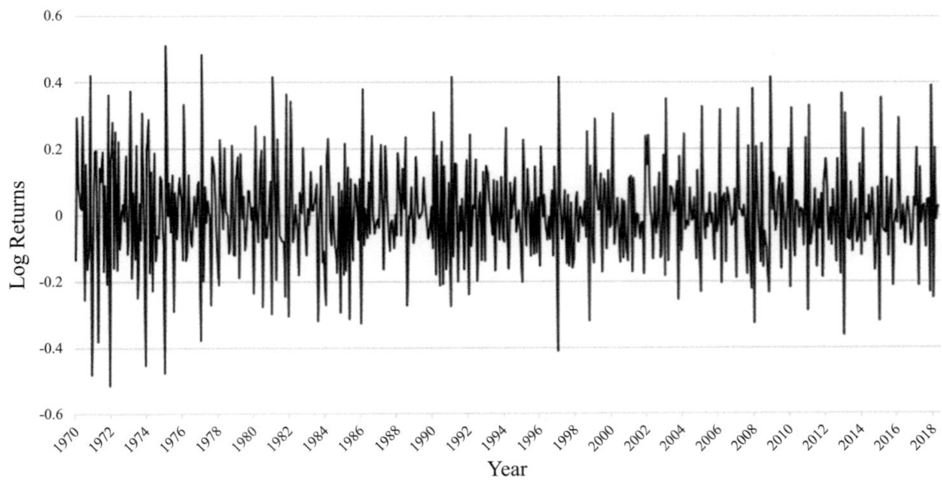

Fig. 8.9 Time series of logarithmic returns (Haarhaus et al., 2020: p. 4)

The PD_2 is a modification of the correlation dimension D_2 and shows pointwise changes in a system's dimensional complexity. It thus provides estimates of how many independent system elements influence the process dynamics, how many independent behaviours a system can show at certain times, and thus quantifies the number of degrees of freedom required to describe a system (Haarhaus et al., 2020). While the D_2 focusses on the static structure of the underlying data and estimates the complexity of the overall process, the PD_2 represents the changes in complexity over time. Relatively high values of the PD_2 indicate a temporarily high number of degrees of freedom of the system, which in turn suggests a complex system dynamics (Haarhaus et al., 2020).[20]

To assess whether the time series under investigation is nonlinear, which is considered a characteristic feature of a complex system, the BDS test is used. It identifies, as described in 5.1.3.1 vi), nonlinear serial dependencies in a time series. In this study, the null hypothesis was tested so that the logarithmic returns of the observed time series are independently and identically distributed—in other words—random. At the significance level of 5 %, the two-sided critical value for the BDS test is ± 1.96, which means that the null hypothesis is rejected if the BDS statistic is greater than 1.96 or less than -1.96. If the hypothesis is rejected, it can be assumed that there is an ordered structure instead of pure randomness in the time series, which indicates a nonlinear dependency in the logarithmic returns of the series. [21]

A positive *Lyapunov* exponent indicates the exponential divergence of two trajectories starting with similar initial values, implying the system's sensitive dependence on initial conditions and thus deterministic chaos.

While the LLE is used to investigate chaos at a global or macroscopic level and requires data stationarity, the LLLE allows the local, microscopic capture of transient process dynamics in certain periods, even if the system is not stationary.

8.4.1.4 Results of the Complexity Science Analysis

Since the PD_2 calculation provides valid results for 100 % of the 534 data points that can effectively be used for the analysis, all examined processes are suitable to be interpreted

---

[20] Crucial for the execution of the PD_2 algorithm is the setting of the embedding dimension (m), which is defined as the number of dynamic variables required to describe the system attractor. Based on comparable approaches used in the literature, the choice of the embedding dimension (m) here is between 19 and 33. The size of the Theiler window was set to 1. The PD_2 calculation provides valid results for 100 % of the 534 data points that can effectively be used for the analysis, thus exceeding the recommended threshold of 75 %. Haarhaus, T., Strunk G., & Liening A. (2020). Assessing the complex dynamics of entrepreneurial ecosystems: A nonstationary approach. *Journal of Business Venturing Insights, 14*.

[21] Since particularly time variations in the nonlinear dynamics should be captured to track the development of the entrepreneurial ecosystem, the BDS test was applied within a moving window of 80 data points. Ibid.

not as stochastic processes, but as ordered dynamics. The PD_2 has an arithmetic mean of 5.46 (± 0.95), which indicates chaos in the time series data. Figure 8.11 illustrates the development of the PD_2 dimensionalities over time and shows the changes in the complexity of the entrepreneurial ecosystem of Singapore (Fig. 8.10).

The development of the entrepreneurial ecosystem of Singapore shows profound non-stationarities and can be divided into different time periods. At the beginning of the measurement period (1971–1974), the dimension complexity reaches its peak with a PD_2 value of 9.7, indicating the critical instability of the system.

Then, from 1974 to 1995, the PD_2 value decreases until it reaches a minimum of 4.1. In the following years, the PD_2 moves between relatively low values of 4.3–6.2. Interestingly, during the time when the overall complexity of the system decreases and stabilises at moderate levels, several abrupt increases in the PD_2 measure are observed throughout its development. Such local peaks of the system's dimension complexity can be observed at PD_2 values of 6.6 (December 1981), 6.2 (June 1991), 5.6 (June 1998), and 6.2 (December 2007) (Haarhaus et al., 2020).

The calculation of the LLLE and the BDS test show comparable results, as the corresponding figures illustrate (Figs. 8.11, 8.12 and 8.13).

8.4.1.5 Conclusions from the Results of the Complexity Science Analysis

It was investigated whether noticeable changes in the PD_2 or LLLE trends can be attributed to plausible external events. The focus was on the factors that typically represent the main influencing factors for the founding events in the literature. Indeed, for most peaks

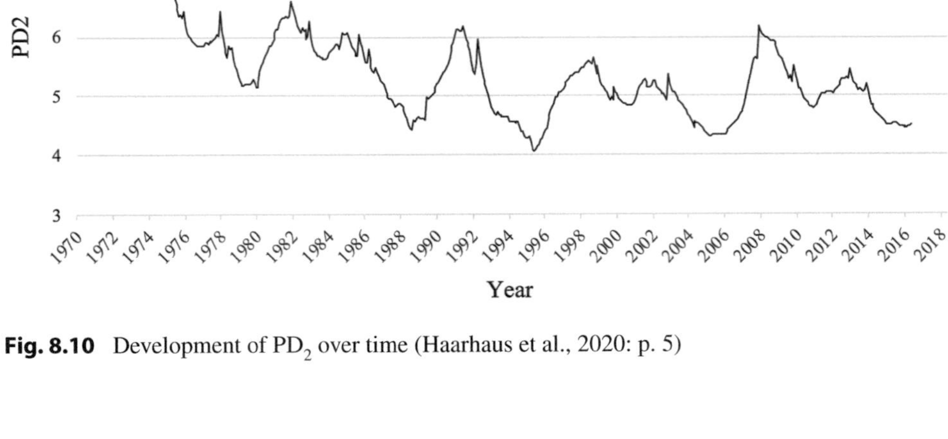

Fig. 8.10 Development of PD_2 over time (Haarhaus et al., 2020: p. 5)

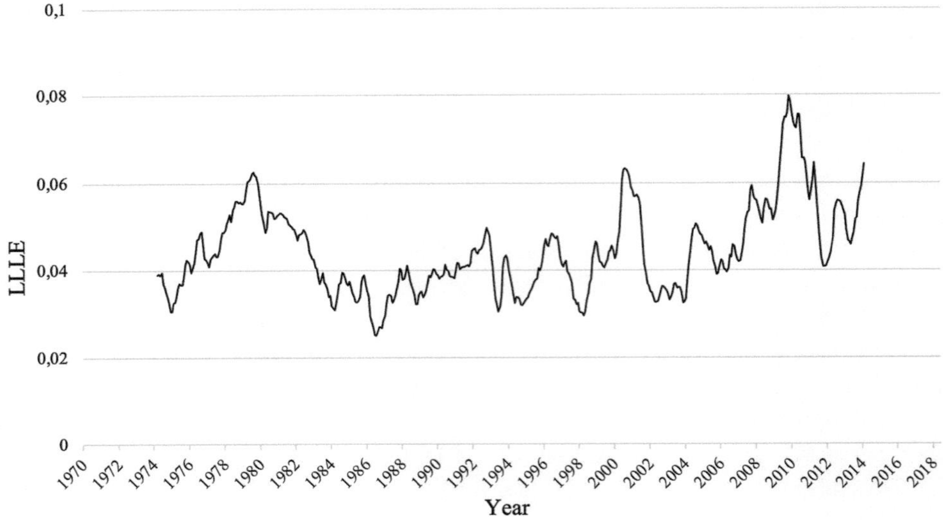

Fig. 8.11 LLLE over time (Singapore) (Haarhaus et al., 2020: p. 7)

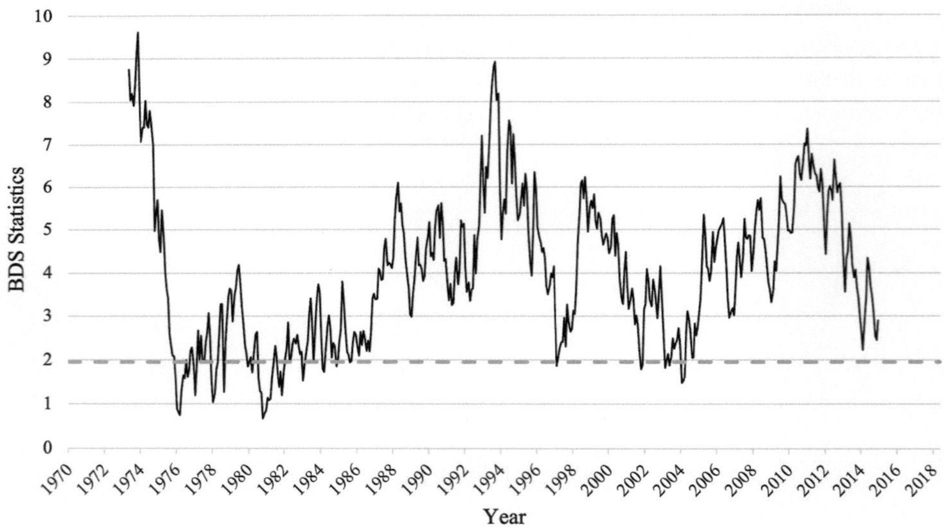

Fig. 8.12 BDS over time including peaks (Singapore) (Haarhaus et al., 2020: p. 6)

in the PD_2 or LLLE trends, conclusive external events could be identified that could explain the observed fluctuations, although these are initially only conjectures (Haarhaus et al., 2020) (Fig. 8.13).

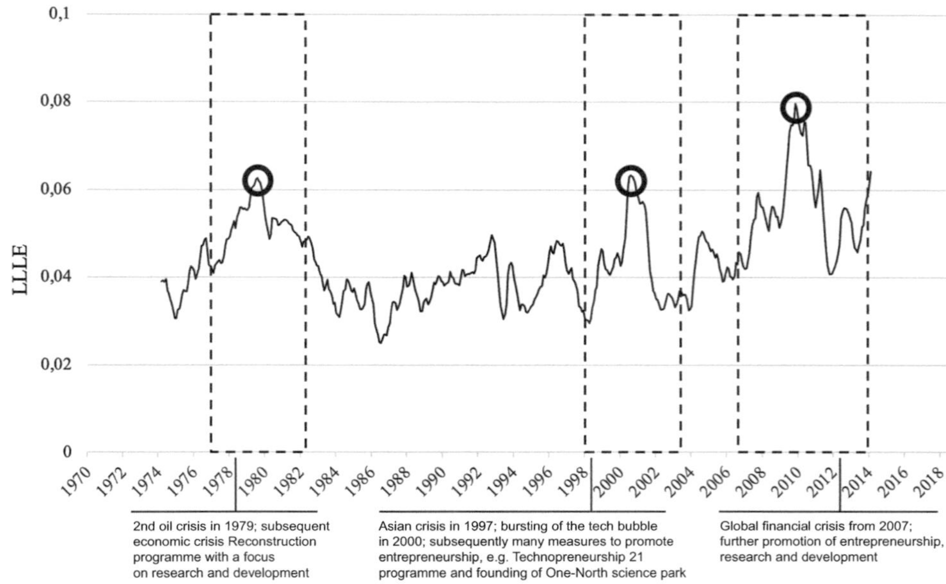

Fig. 8.13 LLLE over time (Singapore)—Peaks

For example, the 2nd oil crisis fell into the phase between 1987 and 1982, followed by an economic reconstruction programme with a focus on research and development.

Another peak can be diagnosed in the phase between 2000 and 2003. This may show the effects of the Asian crisis in 1997 or the bursting of the tech bubble in 2000. During this period, numerous measures were taken to promote entrepreneurship, e.g., the "Technopreneurship 21 Programme". The Singapore government pursued a dual approach to promoting entrepreneurship in the technology sector. The primary goal was to create a favourable climate for businesses and investments. Secondly, students were to be immersed in the domain of technology and innovation to spark their interest.

Another example is the establishment of the "One-North Science Park", which encompasses the fields of biomedicine, information and communication technology (ICT), and the media industry with the aim of creating a global "talent hub" and a knowledge-based economy.

In the phase with the last major peak between 2008 and 2014, the effects of the global financial crisis from 2007 can be seen. During this period, further promotion of entrepreneurship and research and development followed.

Overall, the development of the entrepreneurial ecosystem in Singapore appears as a **chaotic process,** in which an initial phase of critical instability is followed by a sustained phase of order formation, which in turn is characterised by repeated chaotic fluctuations. There are phases of greatly increased complexity or chaos that coincide with important historical events in Singapore's development. The peaks indicate **phase transitions**. Due to the chaotic nature of the system, the long-term development of Singapore's entrepreneurial ecosystem cannot be **exactly planned** or **predicted**. It could be inferred from this that the focus of politics and economy should therefore be on creating favourable conditions within the entrepreneurial ecosystem, thus enabling self-organisation (focus on flexibility and willingness to experiment).

Upon closer examination of the activities, especially in times of the peaks shown, Singapore proves to be a successful example of self-organisation of an entrepreneurial ecosystem. Certain **control parameters** (e.g., foreign direct investments, promotion of start-ups, research funding) seem to stimulate activities at the **micro-level** of the entrepreneurial ecosystem. Newly formed order structures become visible as **dynamic patterns** (e.g., in the form of new industries, innovative research fields) and synchronise the rest of the system behaviour. Complexity science methods thus make it possible to investigate the development of such systems and to identify turning points or phase transitions. (Haarhaus et al., 2020)

"Our findings suggest that conventional methods, which rely on linear cause-and-effect models, do not seem appropriate for studying the complex dynamics of EEs" (Haarhaus et al., 2020: p. 8)

Therefore, in the context of further research in the field of entrepreneurial ecosystems, methods should be used that explicitly take into account non-linearity and complexity, such as qualitative comparative analysis (QCA) or dynamic network modeling. In addition, it is necessary to more precisely determine which factors actually trigger complex dynamics of ecosystems and the timing associated with susceptibility to change should also be examined more closely. Under the conditions of non-linearity and thus sensitivity to minimal disturbances, the timing of an intervention could significantly determine whether the development of an entrepreneurial ecosystem transitions into an ordered or chaotic state. (Haarhaus et al., 2020: p. 8)

8.4.2 Development of Business Start-ups in Germany

8.4.2.1 Company Founding in Germany

The following presented study refers to the development of company founding in Germany and the peculiarities that influence the founding events, such as general economic crises, economic upswings, etc.

The study was conducted by the author and—as far as the decisive calculations of the results are concerned—by Tim *Haarhaus*[22]. It represents a complexity science analysis using Pointwise Dimensionality (PD_2) and local largest Lyapunov exponents (LLLE).

[22] Tim *Haarhaus* was a member of the author's research team and developed these calculations as part of the chair's projects.

The developments of company founding in Germany as a whole and divided into the 16 federal states were examined.

The underlying data are the monthly trade registrations from January 2006 to February 2020 (each at federal and state level); Source: Trade report statistics, available at www-genesis.destatis.de (as of June 2020).

8.4.2.2 On the Empirical Methodology and Procedure

The methods used were the presented PD_2 and *Lyapunov* calculations. The Pointwise Dimensionality (PD_2) is used to measure time-related changes in the dimensional complexity of the system and the local largest Lyapunov exponents (LLLE) to measure changes in the butterfly effect during the observation period (chaoticity), as explained in detail in chapter 5.1. Both methods were applied to the *log-Returns* of the time series data.

First, the development at the federal level is presented. Then we look at the presentation of the development at the state level. For clarity, the federal states were divided into four groups of 4 states each based on the number of trade registrations in the respective states in January 2020.

Presented are the development of the absolute trade registrations per month, the course of the PD_2 as well as the course of the LLLE (for the federation, the *log-Returns* are additionally shown.) To realistically assess the meaningfulness, it is important to know that relatively few data points are available (< 200). While e.g. with the *Rosenstein* as with the *Kantz* algorithm for calculating the LLLE 100-500 data points can be sufficient (Strunk, 2019: p. 334), with the *Wolf* algorithm you would need at least 1,000 data points to achieve meaningful results (Strunk, 2019: p. 313). Before application, however, one definitely needs a D_2 to not choose the phase space embedding too high dimensionally (Strunk, 2019: p. 334).

Only from over 200 points do we have secure results in relation to the D_2. Since only 170 data points are available here, the meaningfulness of the results is limited. Therefore, the results of this study can only be used for rough orientation to identify basic changes in dynamics. The PD_2 seems to work better in this context than LLLE, as the results appear more coherent. Furthermore, the methods used are sensitive to the choice of parameter settings.

8.4.2.3 Results: Federal

(Figures 8.14, 8.15, 8.16 and 8.17)

The results regarding the data examined overall in the Federal Republic of Germany show that the number of monthly business registrations at the federal level is decreasing. Furthermore, the PD_2 value fluctuates between 2.8 and 3.6, which indicates chaos in time series data. Upon closer inspection, we see local peaks in the PD_2 in the years 2008, 2011 and 2016, suggesting increased complexity or instability of the system at these points in time. The LLLE value fluctuates between 0.03 and 0.09, so this method also considers the development as a chaotic process. The LLLE values show significantly increased chaos in 2009, 2011 and 2016.

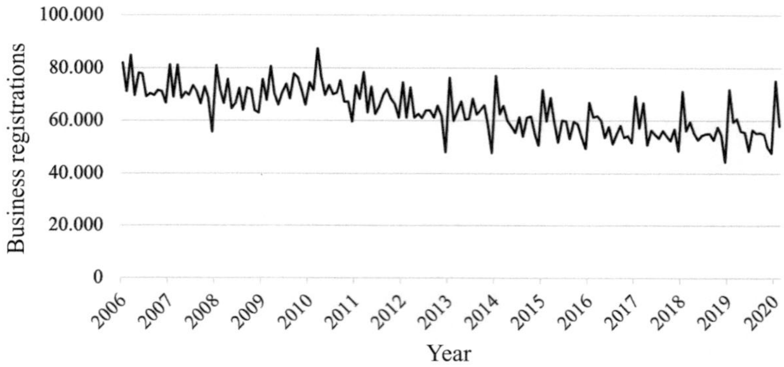

Fig. 8.14 Business registrations in Germany (01/20)

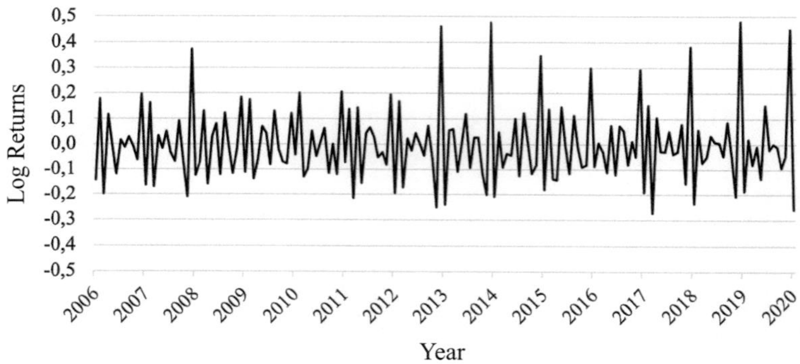

Fig. 8.15 Log-Returns of business registrations in Germany

8.4.2.4 Results: Federal States

The figures show the business registrations as well as the PD_2 and LLE courses for the federal states grouped by 4 states each, this grouping is intended solely for clarity. The first group includes NRW, Bavaria, Baden-Württemberg and Hesse (Figs. 8.18,8.19 and 8.20).

The second group includes Lower Saxony, Berlin, Rhineland-Palatinate and Saxony (Figs. 8.21, 8.22 and 8.23).

The third group includes Schleswig-Holstein, Brandenburg, Hamburg, and Thuringia (Figs. 8.24, 8.25 and 8.26).

The fourth and final group includes Saxony-Anhalt, Mecklenburg-Western Pomerania, Saarland, and Bremen (Figs. 8.27,8.28 and 8.29).

The PD_{2-}values fluctuate between 1.1 and 7.0, so they are consistently positive, which can be interpreted as an indication of chaos in time series data.

The highest complexity is recorded for Berlin, the lowest complexity for Bremen. In some federal states, the PD_2 development runs almost parallel and at a similar level,

Fig. 8.16 PD_2 over time (Federal)

Fig. 8.17 LLLE over time (Federal)

which suggests robustness of the results. In some federal states, the development of the PD_2 values deviates significantly from the development in the other federal states at times (see Bavaria and Hamburg). It would be interesting to identify the causes of abrupt changes in complexity here.

LLLE values fluctuate between −0.02 and 0.65, so the development in most federal states can be considered a chaotic process. The highest chaos is recorded for Bremen. A strong positive outlier in the monthly business registrations in 2018 could be the cause here. The development of the LLLE values for the individual federal states runs less

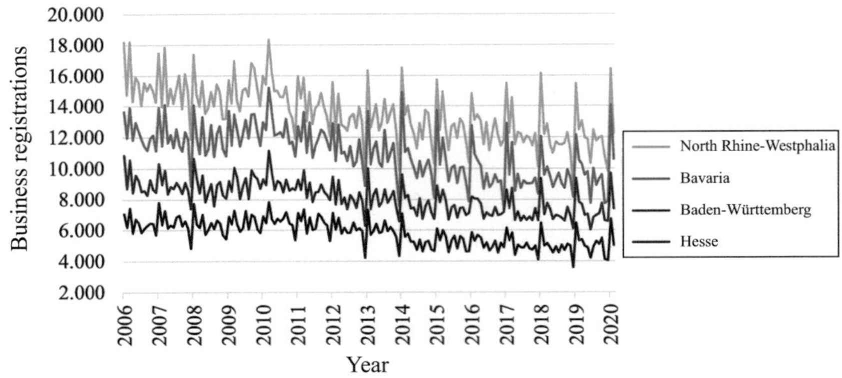

Fig. 8.18 Business registrations in NRW, Bavaria, Baden-Württemberg, Hesse

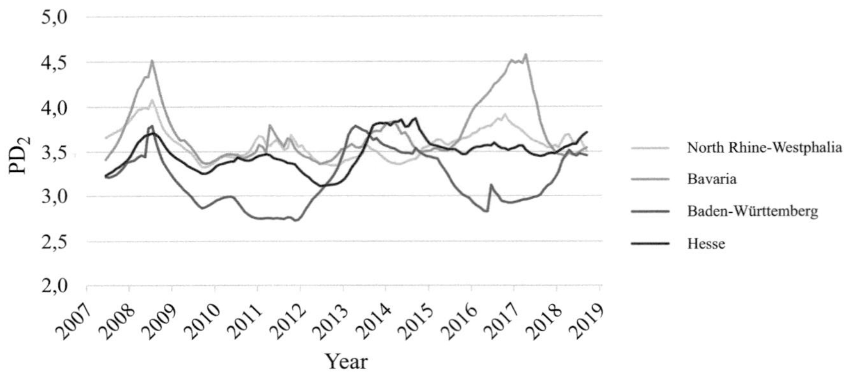

Fig. 8.19 PD_2 over time (NRW, Bavaria, Baden-Württemberg, Hesse)

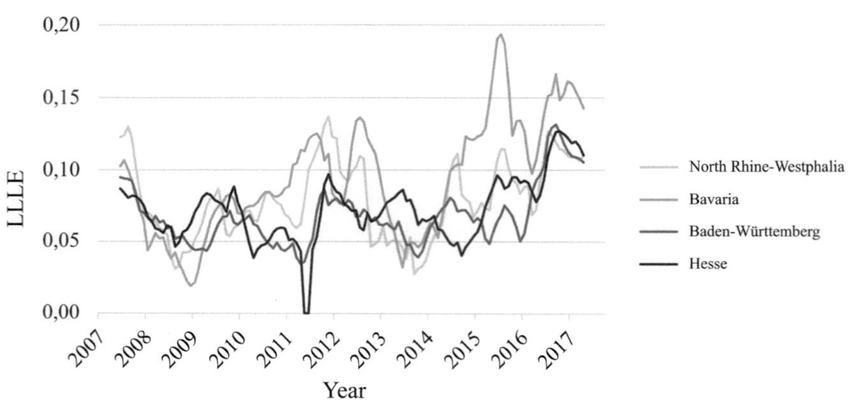

Fig. 8.20 LLLE over time (NRW, Bavaria, Baden-Württemberg, Hesse)

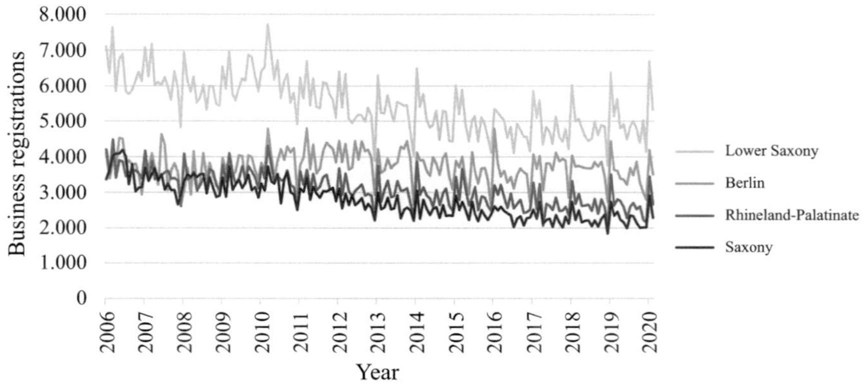

Fig. 8.21 Business registrations in Lower Saxony, Berlin, Rhineland-Palatinate, Saxony

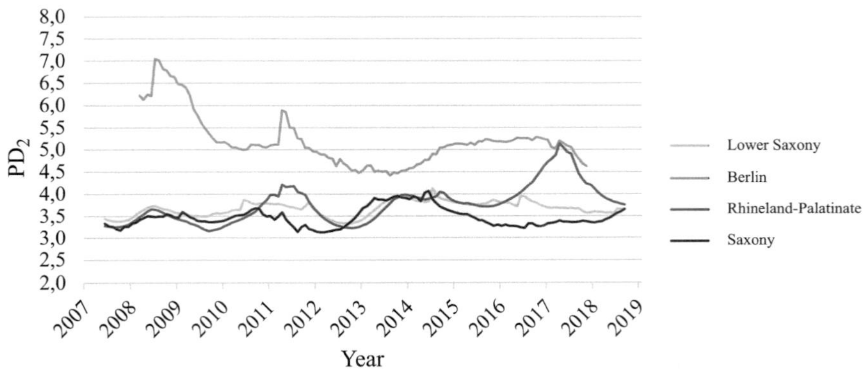

Fig. 8.22 PD_2 over time (Lower Saxony, Berlin, Rhineland-Palatinate, Saxony)

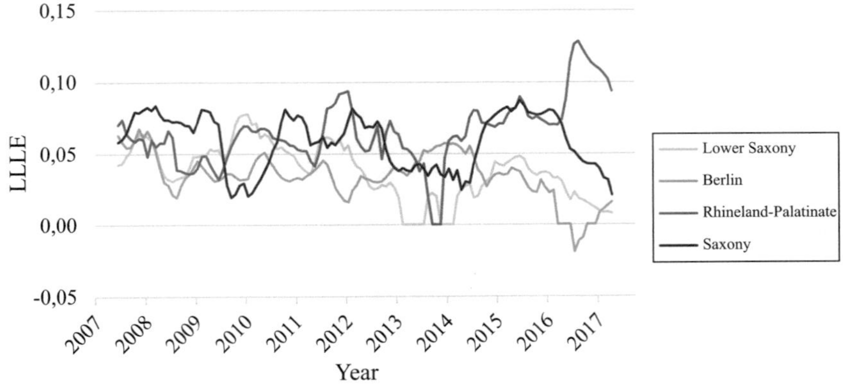

Fig. 8.23 LLLE over time (Lower Saxony, Berlin, Rhineland-Palatinate, Saxony)

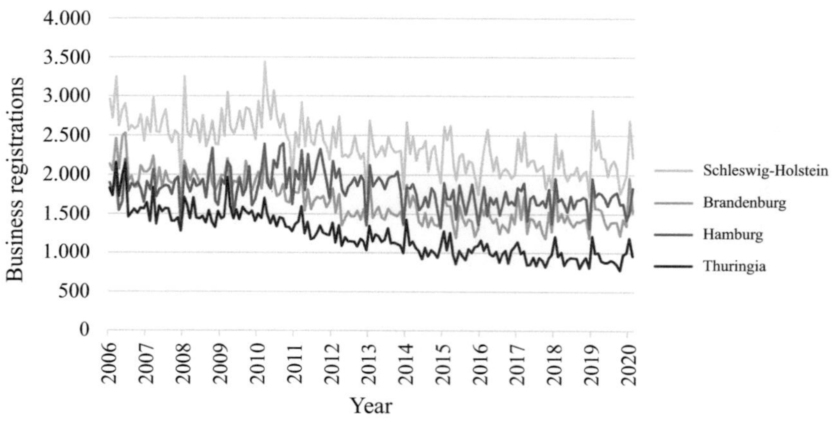

Fig. 8.24 Business registrations in Schleswig-Holstein, Brandenburg, Hamburg, Thuringia

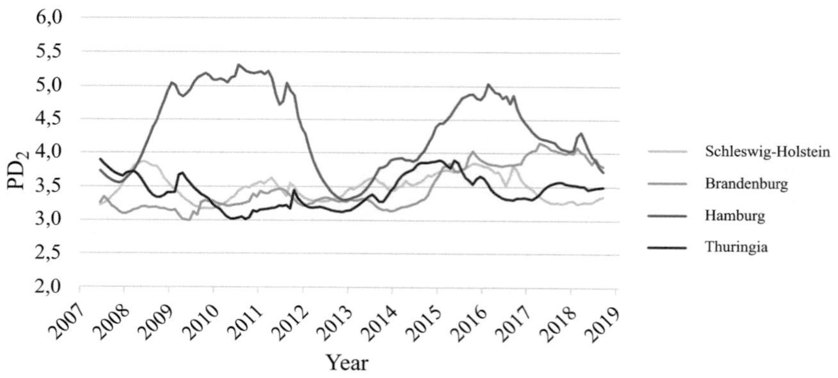

Fig. 8.25 PD_2 over time (Schleswig-Holstein, Brandenburg, Hamburg, Thuringia)

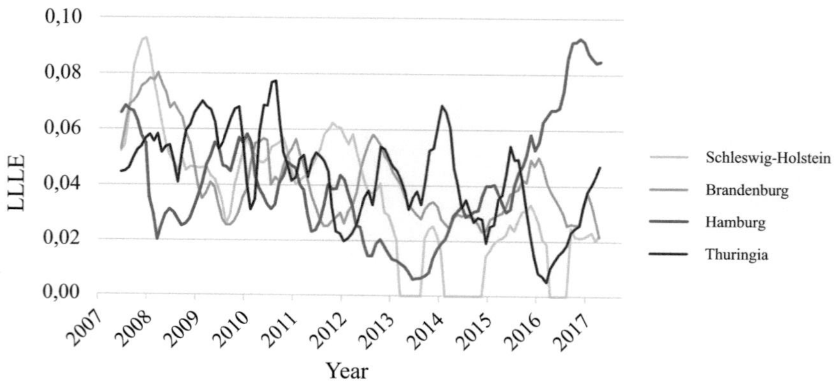

Fig. 8.26 LLLE over time (Schleswig-Holstein, Brandenburg, Hamburg, Thuringia)

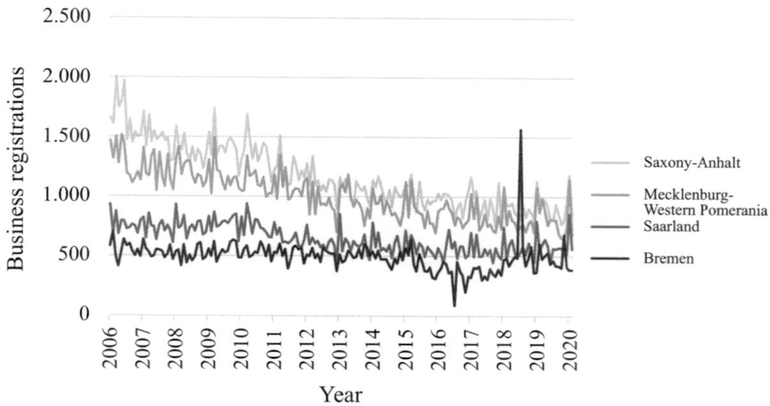

Fig. 8.27 Business registrations in Saxony-Anhalt, Mecklenburg-Western Pomerania, Saarland, Bremen

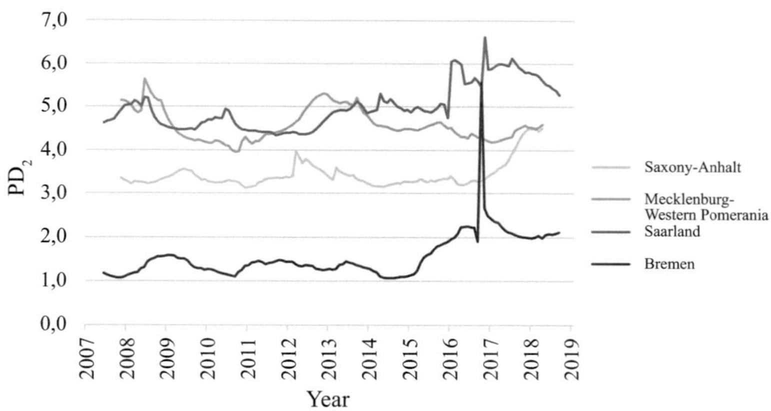

Fig. 8.28 PD_2 over time (Saxony-Anhalt, Mecklenburg-Western Pomerania, Saarland, Bremen)

parallel than the development of the PD_2 values. Nevertheless, there are sometimes very similar developments of chaos, which speaks for robustness of the results. Local peaks of the LLLE values indicate temporarily significantly increased chaos.

8.4.2.5 Plausible External Events

It was further investigated whether noticeable changes in the PD_2 or LLLE trends (at the federal level) can be attributed to plausible external events. The focus was on the factors that typically represent the main influencing factors for the founding of companies in developed countries in the literature. These include macroeconomic factors such as

Fig. 8.29 LLLE over time (Saxony-Anhalt, Mecklenburg-Western Pomerania, Saarland, Bremen)

economic growth, unemployment rate, and population growth. Indeed, for most peaks in the PD_2 or LLLE trends, plausible external events could be identified that could explain the observed fluctuations (with the emphasis on could!) (Fig. 8.30).

For example, the global economic crisis falls into the environment of the peaks in 2008/2009, where economic performance in Germany dropped rapidly, and the number of business registrations also fell sharply (Fig. 8.31).

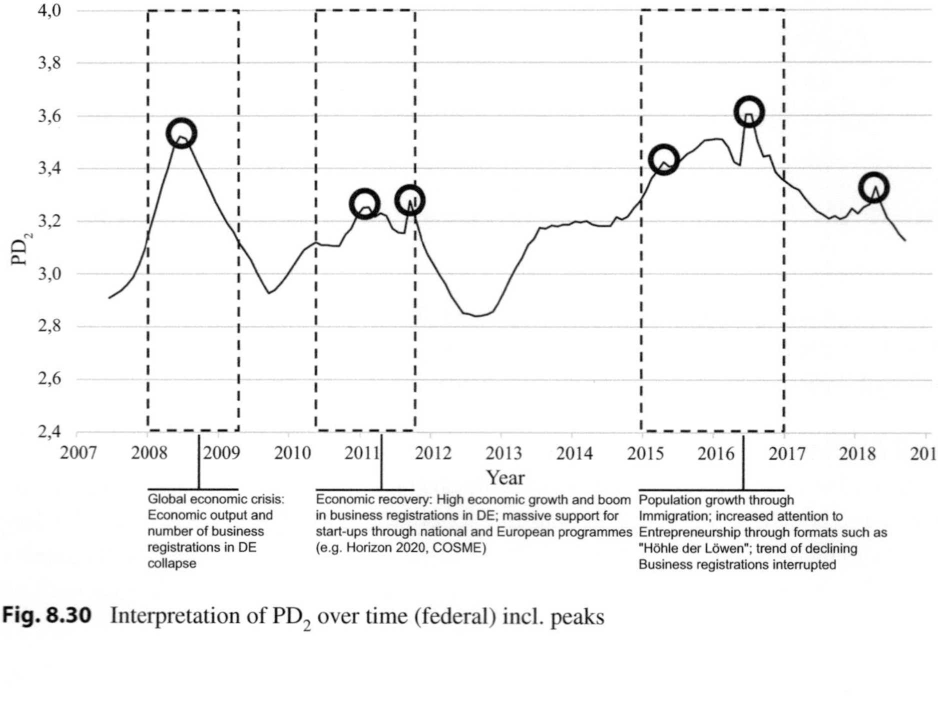

Fig. 8.30 Interpretation of PD_2 over time (federal) incl. peaks

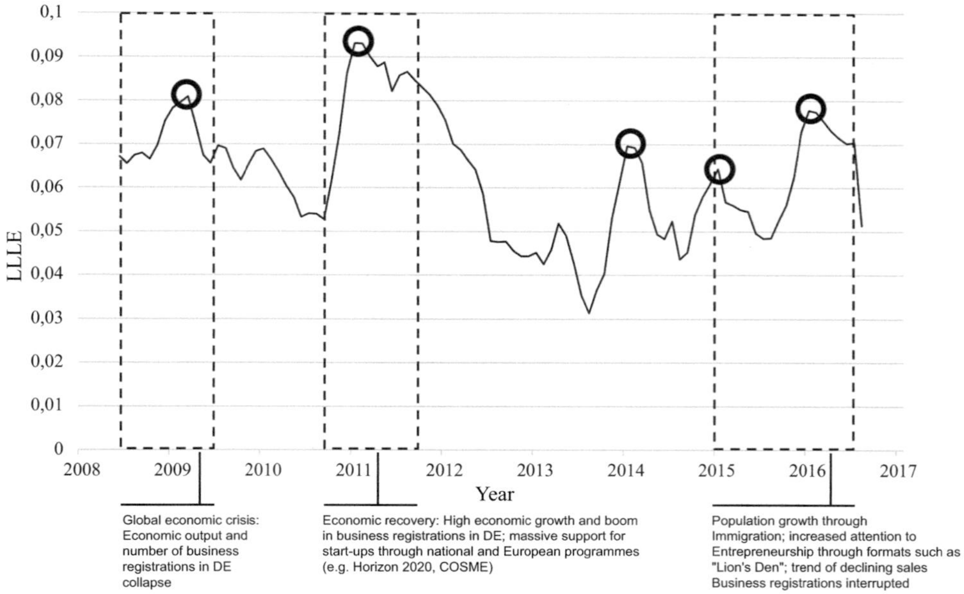

Fig. 8.31 Interpretation of LLLE over time (federal) incl. peaks

The environment of the peaks in 2011 was marked by a very strong economic recovery after the crisis. Economic growth in Germany was very high, and there was a boom in business registrations. In addition, from 2010/2011 onwards, there was massive support for start-ups through national and European programmes (e.g. Horizon, 2020, COSME).

Different factors fall into the environment of the peaks in 2015/2016. On the one hand, there was massive population growth in Germany from 2015 onwards due to the refugee crisis. On the other hand, there was increased media attention to the topic of entrepreneurship, for example through the TV show "Die Höhle der Löwen", which was broadcast in Germany from the end of 2014.

From 2015 onwards, the trend of declining business registrations was interrupted, and the number has since stabilised at a relatively constant level.

Overall, the development at both the federal and state levels appears to be a **chaotic process,** in which phases of critical instability and phases of order formation alternate. There are phases of greatly increased complexity or chaos, which coincide with important historical events in the development of the Federal Republic. The peaks here provide indications of **phase transitions**. The long-term development of business start-ups cannot be **exactly planned** or **predicted** due to the chaotic nature of the system.

8.5 Fifth Conclusion—Limitations in the Explanation of the Study Results and Perspectives

The crux of scientific work is ultimately that empirical results have a multitude of limitations in their explanation. Even if, for example, in the last presented study there are presumably correlations between the peaks and the events in the temporal environment, it must be pointed out that these are only presumed correlations, which by no means necessarily have to represent causalities. Although the described external events can be assigned retrospectively and the relationships also appear plausible, the findings are undoubtedly not empirical evidence. Instead, it is also conceivable that the identified external events are coincidentally in the environment of the peaks.

In this respect, one must also think about the difficult relationship between causality and correlation, as it can easily lead to confusion. The renowned statistician Walter *Krämer* pointed out the following example: It was found on the New Hebrides that there is a high correlation between the number of lice and the health of the people. For a long time on this island chain in the South Pacific, the prejudice persisted that one could promote health by having as many lice as possible. But the cause-effect chain is exactly the other way around: "It's not the lice that drive away the disease, but the disease that drives away the lice" (Krämer, 2012: p. 174f).

On the other hand, one must beware of spurious correlations. For example, one could easily demonstrate a positive correlation between the ROI and the number of employees. But to conclude from this that the more people you hire, the greater the ROI will be, is an obvious fallacy, as at least a third highly correlated characteristic, such as the qualification of the employees, the organisation of production, etc., was overlooked in the observed characteristics.

Krämer lists a multitude of examples where in reality only spurious correlations exist and moreover, there is no causal relationship, even though some believe this: "Starting with the storks, whose number is highly positively correlated with the births in Germany, through the number of unmarried aunts of a person and the calcium content of his skeleton (negative correlation), hay fever and wheat price (negative correlation), shoe sise and legibility of handwriting (positive correlation), education and income (positive correlation) to the proportion of foreigners and crime (positive correlation), a wide range of a misunderstood or intentionally misused concept of correlation is spanned," adding, as *Krämer* adds, that "the births and storks don't matter. Although these are indeed closely correlated in some areas, no one therefore believes that the stork brings the children. The positive correlation of the proportion of foreigners and crime in the municipalities of the Federal Republic is more dangerous; here, statistics may only support a popular but false prejudice, as large municipalities attract both foreigners and criminals" (Krämer, 2012: p. 172). If we consider this last example, it becomes clear that the analysis lacks at least one crucial background variable such as the 'municipality size', so that here too there is only a spurious correlation and that neglecting such sizes can lead to a non-trivial interpretation problem. And the more data can be processed faster and faster, the more correlations become visible, which in the end only represent spurious correlations, i.e. nothing more than "noise" in the data.

If one wants to identify a potentially rewarding area of investigation in the context of complexity measurements from the breadth of the entrepreneurship field, one could certainly name a multitude of examples ad hoc.

For example, if we look into the area of start-up financing, the relatively young form of crowd-funding stands out. The area is interesting in the context of complexity issues at first glance, because it is often translated as swarm financing in German. If we remember that the theory part of the book equated synergetics with swarm intelligence, it becomes clear that this could be a rewarding object of investigation from the perspective of complexity methodology, as swarm behaviour can be excellently described by synergetics.

For crowd-funding, various platforms can be distinguished, which are labeled with keywords such as Equity-Based Crowdfunding, which is also titled Crowd-Investing in German, Lending-Based, Donation-Based and Reward-Based Crowdfunding etc. (Crowdsourcin, 2012: p. 11ff.).

Ultimately, Crowd-Funding or Swarm Financing means that a multitude of micro-investors lend their money directly to, for example, StartUps or entrepreneurs. The area is little regulated or regimented by the state and ultimately an expression of high self-organisation. Upon closer inspection, it becomes obvious that the concept of swarm financing, comparable to the SEM, could be excellently described and analysed using synergetics.

A crowd-funding platform is ultimately a place where there is a higher volume of data, as these, by definition, live from the participation of many users. For example, based on a suggestion by *Wagner*, it would be conceivable to log the data on user participation in a project over the course of the transfer period. The resulting time series (number or amount of payments per unit of time) could then be used for complexity measurement, in order to draw conclusions about the success or development of the project, which could be as follows:

- If the complexity is particularly high or particularly low in the first third of the project, the probability is very high that the project will reach or not reach the financing target.
- News that is published during the collection period and brings with it high complexity fluctuations or changes is considered particularly credible by users and has a positive influence on the amount of funds collected at the end.
- If the complexity was low during the entire collection period, the probability that the project will be a success is higher than for a project whose complexity is high (with comparable payment volume and collected final amount). The basic idea here is that users who consider an idea to be very good and realistic support the project directly, while uncertain users only provide funds with a delay. Thus, the complexity could provide a statement about the general assessment of the users towards the project.

Overall, the results obtained in the course of the present empirical investigations make it clear that in combination with the empirical methods of complexity measurement, there is enormous potential for shaping entrepreneurial processes. However, it is also evident that research in this area is still 'in its infancy'. In conclusion, however, it can be stated that in addition to already established qualitative models, approaches of a quantitative, theory-based perspective are shown, whose initial results in the context of the SEM suggest exciting and worthwhile possibilities for further development in the field of entrepreneurship in science and practice.

References

Alvedalen, J., & Boschma, R. (2017). A critical review of entrepreneurial ecosystems research: Towards a future research agenda. *European Planning Studies, 25*(6), 887–903.

Bandt, C., & Pompe, B. (2002). Permutation entropy—A natural complexity measure for time series. *Physical Review Letters, 88*(17), 174102-1–174102-4.

Brock, W. A., Scheinkman, J. A., Dechert, W. D., & LeBaron, B. (1996). A test for independence based on the correlation dimension. *Econometric Reviews, 15*, 197–235.

Cavallo, A., Ghezzi, A., & Balocco, R. (2019). Entrepreneurial ecosystem research: Present debates and future directions. *Entrepreneurial Management, 15*(4), 1291–1321.

Chen, P. (1996). *Trends, shocks, persistent cycles in evolving economy: Business cycle measurement in time-frequency representation*. Cambridge University Press.

Cosme (2021): https://eismea.ec.europa.eu/news/introducing-cosmes-services-smes-and-start-ups-2021-04-27_en

Crowdsourcing, L. (2012). *Crowdfunding Industrie Report—Market trends, composition and crowdfunding platform*. Massolution. crowdsourcing.org

Gartner, W. B. (1985). A conceptual framework for describing the phenomenon of new venture creation. *Academy of Management Review ,10*(4), 696–706.

Haarhaus, T., Strunk G., & Liening, A. (2020). Assessing the complex dynamics of entrepreneurial ecosystems: A nonstationary approach. *Journal of Business Venturing Insights, 14*, e00194.

Haken, H., & Schiepek, G. (2010). *Synergetik in der Psychologie: Selbstorganisation verstehen und gestalten* (2nd ed.). Hogrefe.

Hamilton, J. D. (1989). A new approach to the economic analysis of nonstationary time series and the business cycle. *Econometrica, 57*(2), 357–384.

Horizon (2020): https://digital-strategy.ec.europa.eu/en/news/startup-europe-growth-h2020-projects

Kowalik, Z., Schiepek, G., Kumpf, K., Roberts, L., & Elbert, T. (1997). Psychotherapy as a chaotic process. Part II: The application of nonlinear analysis methods on quasi time series of the client-therapist interaction: A nonstationary approach. *International Journal of the Society for Psychotherapy Research, 7*(2),197–218.

Krämer, W. (2012). *So lügt man mit Statistik*. Piper Verlag.

Kricks, K., Mittelstädt, E., & Liening, A. (2013). Schwellenkonzepte und Phänomenografie. Explorative Studie zur Messung von Unterschieden im ökonomischen Verstehen. *Zeitschrift für ökonomische Bildung, 2*, 17–41.

Kuckertz, A. (2019). Let's take the entrepreneurial ecosystem metaphor seriously! *Journal of Business Venturing Insights, 11*, e00124.

Lichtenstein, B. B., Carter, N. M., Dooley, K. J., & Gartner, W. B., (2007). Complexity dynamics of nascent entrepreneurship. *Journal of Business Venturing* , *22*(2), 236–261. https://doi.org/10.1016/j.jbusvent.2006.06.001.

Liening, A. (2004). Die Bedeutung der ‚Neuen Medien' in der Didaktik der Wirtschaftswissenschaft unter besonderer Berücksichtigung der Darstellung ‚Neuer Technologien'. In H. J.Schlösser (Ed.), *Anforderungen der Wissensgesellschaft: Informationstechnologien und Neue Medien als Herausforderungen für die Wirtschaftsdidaktik* (pp. 1–61). Hobein.

Liening, A. (2009). *Campus career competition—Management. Ein computergestütztes Planspiel.* 12. überarbeitete Fassung.

Liening, A. (2013). Growth theory and endogenous human capital development: A contribution to the theory of complex systems. *Theoretical Economics Letters, 3*(2), 96–104.

Liening, A. (2014). Synergetische Wirtschaftsdidaktik: Ein kraf(f)tvoller Ansatz für die Ökonomische Bildung. Festschrift zum 80. Geb. In K. von Dietmar, C. Müller, A. Liening, H. J. Schlösser, & M. Schuhen (pp. 55–74). Lucius & Lucius.

Liening, A. (2002a). *Kostenrechnung: Teilkostenrechnung, Plankostenrechnung und betriebswirtschaftliche Kennzahlen.* (2nd ed.). Institut für Verbundstudien NRW.

Liening, A. (2002b). *Kostenrechnung: Vollkostenrechnung—Von den Kostenarten bis zur Kostenträgerrechnung.* (2nd ed.). Institut für Verbundstudien NRW.

Liening, A. (2015a). *Campus career competition business game.* Dortmund, iLearning-Verlag.

Liening, A. (2015b). *Ökonomische Bildung. Grundlagen und neue synergetische Ansätze.* Springer.

Liening, A. et al. (2008). Enhancing empoyability of non-business graduates by economic education as a part of extracurricular studies. Proceedings oft the 6th International Conference on Management, Athens University, 07-10 July 2008, Athen.

Liening, A., & Kriedel, R. (2013). *Entrepreneurship & Synergetic—The Dortmunder Entrepreneurship Model. Developments in Economics Education—Conference*, University of Exeter. Economicsnetwork.ac.uk

Liening, A., Kriedel, R., & Wagner W. (2015). Die Entrepreneurship School—Ein EXIST-Projekt im Rahmen von tu>startup. In J. Teichert, R. Ofianka, & A. Jendrosch (Eds.), *Universitäre Gründungsförderung* (pp. 145–156). Waxmann.

Liening, A., Mittelstädt, E., & Strunk, G. (2012). Ist unternehmerische Kompetenz messbar? Komplexitätswissenschaftliche Ansätze zur Kompetenzmessung in Unternehmensplanspielen. In T. Retzmann & Schwalbach/Ts. (Eds.), *Entrepreneurship und Arbeitnehmerorientierung* (pp. 39–49). Wochenschau.

Liening, A., Strunk, G., & Mittelstädt, E. (2013). Transitions between lower and higher level management learning in times of crisis. Experimental study based on the theories of nonlinear dynamic systems within a business simulation game. *Nonlinear Dynamics, Psychology, and Life Sciences, 17*(4), 517–541.

Marwan, N., Romano, M. C., Thiel, M., & Kurths, J. (2007).Recurrence plots for the analysis of complex systems.*PhysicsReports, 438*, 237–329.

Menn, A. (2010). *Schlaue Stoffe. Handelsblatt, Verlagsgruppe Handelsblatt.* GmbH & Co. KG.

Meyer, J. H. F., & Land, R. (2006). Threshold concepts and troublesome knowledge: An introduction. In J. H. F.Meyer & R. Land (Eds.), *Overcoming barriers to student understanding: Threshold concepts and troublesome knowledge* (pp. 3–8).

Mind-Media. (2022). BVP Sensor. Retrieved March 08, 2022. https://www.mindmedia.com/de/produkte/biofeedback-gerate/.

Pöppel, K. G. (1990). *Moralische Erziehung im Fachunterricht—Zur Einheit von Unterricht und Erziehung. Moralische Erziehung im Fachunterricht. A. R. u. K. G. Pöppel* (pp. 27–48). Aschendorff.

Roundy, P. T., Bradshaw, M., & Brockman, B. K. (2018). The emergence of entrepreneurial ecosystems: A complex adaptive systems approach. *Journal of Business Research, 86*, 1–10.

Rudolf, M., & Müller, J. (2012). Multivariate Verfahren (2. Aufl.). Göttingen.

Sarasvathy, S. D. (2009). *Effectuation—Elements of Entrepreneurial Expertise*. Edward Elgar.

Sachs, L., & Hedderich, J. (2006). Angewandte Statistik (12. Aufl.). Springer.

Sender, T. (2017). *Wirtschaftsdidaktische Lerndiagnostik und Komplexität—Lokalisierung liminaler Unsicherheitsphasen im Hinblick auf Schwellenübergänge*. Diss., Springer.

StartupGenome. (2018). Global Startup Ecosystem Report. Succeeding in the New Era of Technology.https://startupgenome.com/

Strunk, G. (2019). *Leben wir in einer immer komplexer werdenden Welt? Methoden der Komplexitätsmessung für die Wirtschaftswissenschaft*. Complexity Research, Forschung & Lehre.

Strunk, G., & Schiepek, G. (2006). *Systemische Psychologie—Eine Einführung in die komplexen Grundlagen menschlichen Verhaltens*. Elsevier—Spektrum Akademischer.

Spiegel Online. (2016). Konzeptstudie GINA. Retrieved 21 pm, 2022, from http://www.spiegel.de/auto/fahrkultur/bmw-gina-ein-auto-mit-massgeschneiderter-textilkarosserie-a-1071856.html

Part IV

Final Considerations

9 Conclusion

Contents

9.1 About the First Part of the Book 630
9.2 About the Second Part of the Book 631
9.3 About the Third Part of the Book 632
9.4 Concluding Remarks 635
References 636

Butterflies are extremely fleeting, graceful creatures. They are born, silently follow their limited tiny needs, and disappear unnoticed again. Perhaps into another world.

(Murakami, 2012, p. 149)

Demands on our Thinking At the beginning of the book, the question was raised as to what demands must be made on our thinking if the world in which we live, as exemplified, no longer drifts along like a sluggish slow river, but is characterised by turbulence, leaps, and entanglements. Especially an entrepreneur who wants to penetrate new markets, move old ones, or even create new ones, will quickly face the challenge that the traditional lineal-causal methods for analysis and decision-making no longer help in such complex situations, structures, and processes, and we apparently reach limits with our rationality.

In view of the Papillon spiral formulated in the introduction (Fig. 9.1), the three central parts of the book were formulated according to a spiral, the degree of mathematisation and complexity of which changes, starting from a simple verbal formulation, through first mathematical precisions, to a high level of abstraction and understanding.

A. Liening, *Complexity and Entrepreneurship*,
https://doi.org/10.1007/978-3-658-44032-9_9

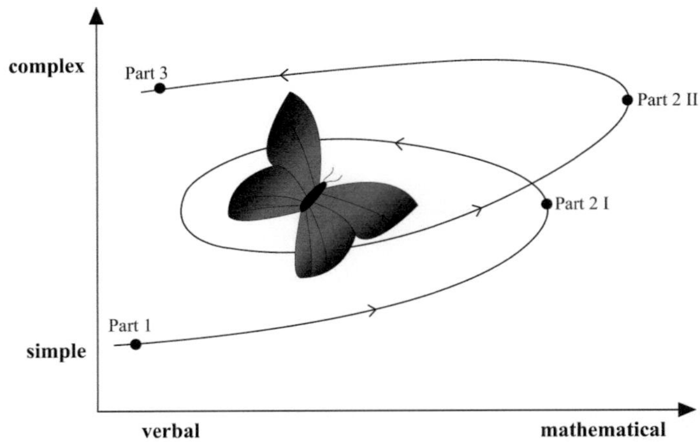

Fig. 9.1 The Papillon Spiral. (Since we are on the last pages of this book, it can be mentioned at this point that the term "complex" in the context of a book should rather be put in quotation marks.)

9.1 About the First Part of the Book

Behavioural and other anomalies obstruct a clear view The first part of the book explored the question of whether we, as neoclassical economics assumes, actually think and act as a rational **Homo Oeconomicus**. That rational action is necessary in the economic world and especially in the experimental situation of a startup process may be undisputed. But it became clear that people even in simple situations, which are considered lineal, continuous, and uniform, make systematic errors (possibly). Even in these simple lineal contexts, which include specific situations, processes, or structures, people can be subject to **perception, processing, evaluation,** and **behavioural anomalies**. How much more then must decisions and actions be questioned when acting in complex contexts. The observable strategies, ranging from 'trial and error' to 'simplicity', help only very limited. Traditional business methods seem to fail where **complexity** arises.

History shows a strong adherence to lineal-causal ways of thinking A look at history has shown why economics in particular has been so deeply and for so long entrenched in mechanistic, lineal ways of thinking, the resulting methods and models, and—let's not hide it—has been very successful in many cases. The message of traditional economics was: If people behave rationally and have sufficient information, possibly also sufficient good software and hardware, the economy is as predictable, planable, and calculable as a mechanical clockwork. The associated ***Laplacian* worldview** has, however, developed cracks and has been questioned.

The ***Papillon,*** the butterfly, may represent an image for the change of mind associated with the questioning, which allows distinguishing simple from complex systems and which allows recognising that seemingly random developments in the end may have nothing to do with chance, but rather with the right methods structures can be recognised that would not even be guessed with conventional approaches.

Especially an entrepreneur, who is usually recommended to create a *Business Plan* designed for several years as a central tool, quickly realises that he needs other and better methods, as the half-life of the forecasts in his *Business Plan* often shrinks faster than he would have ever guessed. Lineal, traditional methods, which only satisfy a strong law of causality, according to which similar causes lead to similar effects, have little in common with a reality characterised by complexity, entanglements, abrupt changes, and unpredictable events.

Considering dynamic systems supports the understanding of complexity To understand a **dynamic system** as simple, complex, or random, one must first know what a system is, what characteristics it has, and how **modeling** and **simulations** can help understand complex systems. These questions were discussed in detail, the concept of system was extensively discussed, and the consideration of system archetypes contained initial hints for dealing with complexity.

It turned out that without a scientifically sound basis, the topic cannot really be understood. In this context, it became clear once again that economics ultimately rests on two things: a coherent theory and a (however verifiable) reference to empirical reality. Therefore, both theories and empirical methods were discussed in the next part of the book.

9.2 About the Second Part of the Book

Theories explain complexity Through the examination of strange attractors, fractals, fractional dimensions, *Lyapunov* exponents, and bifurcation diagrams, we have learned the basics of ***chaos theory*** and ***fractal geometry*** in Part II of the book, which form the theoretical basis for understanding complexity.

In addition to other theoretical foundations such as the ***catastrophe theory***, the ***synergetics*** was particularly discussed, which as a theory of self-organisation can explain phase transitions, such as order-order, disorder-order, or order-disorder transitions, even when, or precisely when, no one is able to control these change processes from the outside.

Only these theoretical foundations enable us to define a scientific concept of complexity. In this context, it became clear that although complexity can be generated by a computer, it is by no means a phenomenon limited to it. Deterministic chaos and complexity are not merely 'Ignis Fatuus', as one might have suspected, but exist in reality. It was pointed out that despite the difficulty of distinguishing complexity from chance, and the fact that complexity, interpreted synergistically, arises from self-organising processes, there are possibilities to influence the emergent process of the creation of the necessary order parameters through 'Nudges'. Control would be too strong a word here, but influencing complexity seems possible in economic and social processes. However, this requires knowing where one is in a complex process, whether, for example, a phase transition is imminent or not.

Empirical methods enable the detection of complexity To recognise whether a phase transition in a complex system is imminent, whether complexity is present at all, and if so, whether this complexity is increasing, remaining the same, or decreasing, one needs **empirical methods,** with the help of which one can investigate complex systems for exactly these and other questions. In the empirical chapter, we saw that there are a multitude of such methods, starting with the phase space reconstruction, from the D_2 -PD_2 measurement of **dimensions,** the determination of ***Lyapunov* exponents**, the execution of **spectral analyses**, the application of **entropy encodings** such as the permutation entropy or comparable to the 'Grammar Complexity', up to various **transformation encodings** or **compression algorithms**. They complement, one could say enrich, the traditional statistical methods with the possibility to investigate complexity. All empirical complexity methods have advantages and disadvantages and it often requires the application of several of these methods to understand what is happening in a system and where the trajectories are located. Only more precise knowledge and a good understanding of our world enable us to make meaningful, rationally justifiable decisions to successfully cope with uncertainty and complexity. Of course, there is still a lot to explore, especially the new ideas added in the theory section, e.g. the use of various compression algorithms for complexity measurements, still harbour exciting development paths.

9.3 About the Third Part of the Book

Under the keyword "Multiperspective—Complexity and Entrepreneurship", different perspectives were taken in the third part of the book.

The "Synergetic Entrepreneurship Model" (SEM) makes entrepreneurial processes transparent In the last part of this book, the so-called "Synergetic Entrepreneurship Model" *(SEM)* was introduced, which is based on the complexity scientific considerations of the other two parts and was considered on three levels, an individual, an organisational, and an economic level, whose complex processes could be detailed and transparently disclosed in the sense of a 'White Box'.

Significance of Entrepreneurship Trends and Controversies An introduction to the topic of entrepreneurship, taking into account the different trends and controversies, provided an insight into this perspective, which is only partially familiar to traditional business administration.

It became clear that synergetics, as a subfield of the science of complex systems, presents an interesting opportunity to describe entrepreneurship processes as complex processes. For each of the three levels, the **synergetics** scheme was suitable for illustrating the self-organising processes inherent in them.

The Individual Level (SEM1) The first, the individual level of the model, was primarily concerned with **Entrepreneurship Education.** Here, an economic-didactic concept was presented, which is based on synergetics as one of the essential theories of complex systems and shows a specifically complexity-scientific approach to the theory of an *Entrepreneurship Education*. An understanding of *Entrepreneurship Education* was developed that does not understand learning as adaptation, as affirmation to the world. Rather, the goal of successful *Entrepreneurship Education* was understood as the opportunity to generate an **entrepreneurial education**, which includes both entrepreneurship knowledge and an entrepreneurial attitude. Since education presupposes freedom and entrepreneurship implies freedom, in a homomorphic synergetic process of self-organisation, a corresponding *Entrepreneurship Education* and its inner workings in relation to individual questions, decisions, and actions could be illustrated.

The Organisational Level (SEM2) The business field of entrepreneurship should serve as one of the innovative areas of business administration to open up newer approaches as the second level of the *SEM*. Here, it was about the organisational level in the context of complex founding processes, taking into account a business-entrepreneurial perspective. The task was to introduce newer entrepreneurial methods such as the *Business Model Canvas* and explain them in the context of the founding process. Here too, according to synergetics, the founding process was interpreted as a self-organising process.

The Macroeconomic Level (SEM3) Finally, the focus of the considerations was on the companies after the founding phase and their macroeconomic significance. Young growth companies with their innovative power were examined from the economic perspective of an endogenous economic growth theory, and the influence of the science of complex systems was explained within the framework of the third level of the *SEM*. An attempt was made not to contrast the inclusion of complexity-scientific findings with traditional neoclassicism, but to explain it as a fruitful complement to it. In this context, it became clear in terms of model theory that technological innovations and growing human capital, both linked by a transmission effect of an entrepreneurial attitude, can lead to sustainable success, growth, and prosperity through self-organisation, with turbulences and frictions not being excluded, but endogenously explainable and understandable in the present model.

A first 'Proof of Concept'—The use of empirical methods successfully demonstrates possibilities The empirical studies, which can be considered a first 'proof of concept', illustrate the application potential of complexity science methods for investigating entrepreneurial phenomena.

Without going into detail on all studies again, the connection to the individual levels of the **Synergetic Entrepreneurship Model (SEM)** will be briefly demonstrated using selected examples.

For instance, the empirical examples in the area of **SEM1** showed how **learning** itself can be perceived **as a self-organisation process**. Accordingly, learning is influenced by **control parameters**, but starting from the **micro level**, orders are realised on the **macro level** in a self-responsible manner, which become visible as learning successes and henceforth guide action. Using the **permutation entropy** or the **PD_2**, learning no longer has to be seen as a black box. The time series analysed with these methods indicate **phase transitions** and clearly show that impending learning successes are measurable even before a successful learning process occurs, even before the learners themselves know, so that small nudges can lead to phase transitions in formative processes.

The examination of a specific startup (*"HealthInfo"*) can be understood as an example of a consideration of the **SEM2**, with the diagnosed phase transitions being indicators of changing business processes. For example, the first white bar (see Fig. 8.7) in the diagnosed *Recurrence* plot is an indication of a **control parameter** that has influenced the startup's founder. Accordingly, the founder may have been open to new ideas in this phase, which have triggered corresponding activities for the first time. Furthermore, the *Recurrence* plot indicates the formation of a **dynamic pattern** on the **macro level**[1], so that here, for example, the business model becomes clearly visible for the first time. Overall, it is also possible to observe on the organisational level of entrepreneurial phenomena how complexity science repertoire (here: *Recurrence* plots) can be used to investigate self-organised structure genesis.

Various empirical studies were also assigned to the **SEM3**, such as the indications of the diagnosed phase transitions of the entrepreneurial ecosystem of Singapore. The development of the ecosystem is a successful example of the **self-organisation** of a market. Certain **control parameters** such as political interventions or foreign investments seem to influence the **micro level** of the ecosystem and stimulate new system behaviour. Thus, the micro level also reorganises itself, represented for example by financial actors, founders, universities, research institutions etc. As a result, a system behaviour could develop in the sense of the **SEM3** that is associated with a changed founding dynamic. This could mean that new industries, new markets, new industries or new research areas have unfolded in such a way that they eventually become visible on the **macro level** as **dynamic patterns**, with the phase jumps being identified by means of ***Lyapunov*** exponents, **BDS-** test or **PD_2** etc.

[1] The formation of the order pattern specifically occurs as visible in Fig. 8.7 in period 15, where a particularly large white bar becomes visible.

It is the self-organised genesis of entrepreneurial structures that constitute the central interest of the SEM—whether on an individual, organisational, or macroeconomic level. This is accompanied by an elaborate complexity science method repertoire, which needs to be adapted depending on the system being considered, as was clearly demonstrated in the studies presented. This opens up new spaces for entrepreneurship research to investigate the emergence of structures that are rightly perceived in scientific discourse as "complex" or "non-linear"—from initial ideas to entire economic sectors.

9.4 Concluding Remarks

The results clearly show that the application of empirical complexity methods as a whole has enormous potential for shaping entrepreneurial processes. However, in the concrete application of empirical methods, it has not only become clear that we are indeed still at the beginning of research in this area, but also that the inclusion of classical statistical methods, such as multiple regression analysis, can be a helpful addition. It became clear that there are numerous possibilities, which hold exciting options not only for scientific further development, but also for concrete practical implementation.

In relation to all three parts of the book, the words already quoted from Robert *Solow* will probably be justified when he states:

> I don't think that models like this lead directly to prescription (…) or even to detailed diagnosis. But neither are they a game. They are more like reconnaissance exercises (Solow 1987, p. 105).

In this sense, we are on a reconnaissance mission with complexity science theories and empirical methods, a "reconnaissance mission" that takes place in a mining operation, from which, hoping for *Serendipity,* the unexpected and hitherto undiscovered can be brought to light as truth. Therefore, it remains only to emphasise:

The fields "Entrepreneurship & Complexity" are not only wide, but also largely unexplored and we are the "reconnaissance researchers". If the analogy to the mining operation does not appeal, perhaps the comparison of the "reconnaissance mission" with an adventure journey across the open sea can be accepted. In this context, all those are reminded of the proverb attributed to the writer and adventurer André *Gide* (Mitchell 2009, p. 303):

> One doesn't discover new lands without consenting to lose sight of the shore.

Theories of complex systems deprive us of the illusion that we could meticulously control our economic fate, whether on an individual, organisational, or macroeconomic level, and always have a safe shore in sight. But the theories and methods presented give us powerful levers and navigation instruments to successfully accompany entrepreneurial processes. And these are particularly necessary in uncertain times, in which also the revitalisation and further development of artificial intelligence (AI), combined with an explosion in its use, is enabling completely new business models.

McKelvey rightly emphasises that it is time to help entrepreneurs, especially in the early start-up phase, which is characterised not by equilibrium states but by order creation processes, and therefore to use complexity sciences with their diverse theories and modeling approaches for this purpose (McKelvey 2004, p. 337). He states:

> Entrepreneurship is about order creation not equilibrium. It is time to put more emphasis on helping entrepreneurs, at the initial start-up phase, deal with adaptive tensions, critical values, phase transitions, and coevolving causalities (McKelvey 2004, p. 337).

The suggestion remains from this book to deal more intensively with the questions raised, the theories, methods, and models discussed and developed, even if the safe shore occasionally gets out of sight on the way to the undiscovered land.

As a motivation, a remark from the German Chancellor from the year 2022 may serve, who stated in the foreword for the "German StartUp Monitor":

> We need "creative startups and their far-sighted investors, who set impulses with entrepreneurial spirit and inventiveness. Innovative approaches in the circular economy help us to use resources sustainably. With the help of artificial intelligence, many processes can be organised more efficiently and resource-saving. Also, the further development in other important areas—such as quantum technologies, cyber security, space travel, hydrogen, and new materials—creates many opportunities for value creation in Germany. To take advantage of them, we need startups that are founded here, can grow and scale here." (Federal Association of German Startups e. V. (Ed.), 2022, p. 2)

References

McKelvey, B. (2004). Towards a complexity science of entrepreneurship. *Journal of Business Venturing, 19,* 313–342.

Mitchell, M. (2009). *Complexity.* Oxford University Press.

Murakami, H. (2012). *1Q84.* btb – DuMont.

Bundesverband Deutsche Startups e. V. (Hrsg.) (2022). *Deutscher StartUp Monitor 2022 – Innovation – gerade jetzt.* Berlin.

Solow, R. (1987). *Growth theory – an exposition.* Oxford University Press.

Outro—Excerpt from a Travel Report 10

A touch of serendipity
A little stroke of luck.

(Robert Plant, 2014)

… "Have we landed in a subspace rift?" "No, Leonard," I replied. "We are in a cave under the island." "We've been in such a cave before," Leonard noted, "remember, we talked about education and Plato's allegory of the cave. That was during our last holiday here on the island of Borkum." "I know," I said, "and believe it or not, it's the same cave as on our last holiday. It's the mountain mine."[1]

"No, not the mountain mine again," Leonard retorted in shock, "I filled it in."

"Perhaps the heavy rain has undermined the island and thus exposed the mountain mine again. It's like in the times of the dwarf Alberich, who forced all the Nibelungs to mine for gold in the mountain mine with the help of the ring he forged from the Rhine gold." "Oh, you've listened to too much Wagner," Leonard remarked.

He looked around the cave after his eyes had adjusted to the darkness and asked:

[1] This is a reference to the end credits of a book on synergetic economic education, which deals with challenges to economic education in the context of complex systems (Liening, 2019).

A. Liening, *Complexity and Entrepreneurship*,
https://doi.org/10.1007/978-3-658-44032-9_10

"What are all these cables doing here? Aren't those speaker cables?" "That's just the imagination of our neighbour, who recently founded a company for extravagant speaker cables, the HCC Ltd., the Hifi-Cave-Cable StartUp." "He is truly an entrepreneur, as you like to call such people," Leonard interrupted me. "True, but let's not digress," I said and continued: "Our speaker cables on the hi-fi system not only improve the sound of the music because they have a cross-section of almost two centimetres and are made of very specific rare metal, but especially because they have been stored here in the cave for almost fifty years, shielded from environmental influences and yet exposed to a strong magnetising effect of the earth's core."

Leonard looked at me in astonishment and said: "That's nonsense, lazy voodoo magic." "Tell that to the neighbour," I commented on Leonard's thoughtless remark.

"The long storage enriches the cables with complexity through an emergence process," I explained. "More precisely, these cables can perfectly reproduce the complexity of a piece of music. The complexity of the original source is largely preserved."

Leonard thought for a moment and said: "But nowadays it's always about reducing complexity, not preserving it. The books on your shelves are full of it." "That's all nonsense, dear Leonard. Not that I don't actually have half a cabinet full of such books, but ultimately all authors think they need to simplify the world. And they strive for a reduction of complexity not to make the world more understandable, but because they think they need to underchallenge people by offering mental savings, or should I better say, savings offers, because they trust them less than they can generally be trusted. Maybe we should hold an auto-da-fé and banish these books to the basement. Anyway: To transmit, for example, the analogue complexity of good music pieces, you need such good cables as are stored and matured here."

"But how do you know if the cables we have at home, which also come from this cave, do justice to the complexity of, for example, Wagner's Rhine gold?" Leonard asked. "That is indeed a good question," I replied, "and not easy to answer.

First of all, you have to record and digitise the music that comes out of the speakers through the cables. This requires excellent recording devices that can record the music vibrations in question as accurately as possible with as little background noise or other noise as possible.

And then comes the trick:

We store the music using a context-free, lossless algorithm that keeps the information to be stored as low as possible. And the more the algorithm compresses the music, the less complex it can be.

For example, if you were to digitally store a piece of music that consists of only one tone, you would need very little information to be stored: the tone and its duration. The corresponding file that would contain such a piece of music would therefore be very small.

The more intertwined and dynamic the music, however, the more information needs to be stored, the larger the file that encompasses the piece of music. And the larger the file, the more complex the music."

"But what is the standard by which I measure the complexity of a piece of music and thus the quality of the cables? Suppose a music file requires 10 megabytes of storage space. What does that specifically say about the complexity of the piece or the cables? That doesn't tell you anything," Leonard objected. "You're right," I said. "But we have several options to evaluate the complexity of the piece of music and thus the quality of the cables."

"For one," I continued, "we could make a relative evaluation:

Take, for example, the renunciation motif from Wagner's Ring of the Nibelung. A fantastic music sequence, full of dynamism and esprit. It first appears when one of the Rhine daughters reveals the magic of the Nibelung gold, which gives infinite power, by singing:

'Only he who renounces the power of love, only he who banishes the joy of love, only he achieves the magic to force the gold into a ring.'

Woglinde, the singing Rhine daughter, is surely guided by a certain naivety towards the dwarf Alberich, who is looking for their love, not knowing that he would actually go so far as to renounce love.

So let's capture this exciting, highly dynamic motif by first playing the music through our cave cables over our high-end speakers, and then saving the sequence using the chosen compression algorithm into a first file. Next, we take another pair of cables and repeat the procedure. If the second saved file is smaller than the first, it would suggest that our cables are better, as they led to a greater complexity of the music played back.

On the other hand, we could find a kind of orientation anchor, or surrogate, for the chosen piece of music by randomly shuffling the recorded music to achieve a random distribution of tones.

So far, we have agreed on the following: The more complex a piece of music is, the larger is the music file in which it is stored compressed. However, if the music tones follow each other randomly, the complexity is also maximal in a certain way. But here we would no longer speak of complexity, but of randomness, as in this case any structure has been lost. With any kind of complex piece of music, however, we would always assume some kind of structure, however intertwined it may be. In randomness, however, everything is noisy.

The saved compressed file of a musical random process should therefore be maximally large, as no pattern would be recognisable that would allow compression. The respective deviation to the stored and compressed, original piece of music thus serves us as a measure of complexity, where the rule is:

The smaller the measured value, i.e. the distance, the more complex the music.

Et voilà, we can judge the quality of our cables."

"But it could also be," Leonard countered, "that because of the simple music we have chosen, we see nothing or always measure a maximum value." "Yes, you're probably right and we really need highly dynamic music - like Wagner for example." "You and your Wagner," grumbled Leonard, "I would go for Frank Zappa, David Bowie or maybe The Cure - for old times' sake, which you talk about too often." "Well," I admitted, "you have to experiment a bit until you find the right music."

"But couldn't it also be," Leonard objected, "that the measured distance is so small because the playback is noisy due to the poor quality of the cables? Then you would not have measured high complexity in reality, but only randomness, i.e. noise. But based on your interpretation, you would assume that the cables are of particularly high quality, whereas in fact the opposite could be true."

"Oh dear, I hadn't thought of that, dear Leonard," I admitted, "so we need a noise filter that eliminates the random sequences in our playback and of course an audiophile source, so that it is excluded that the noise already comes from the music piece out of the speakers."

"But the usual noise filters just cut off the highs a bit at the end. They do reduce the noise, but the dynamics are also lost and thus the complexity," Leonard noted. "Yes, we need a very tricky noise filter that eliminates the noise but at the same time retains the dynamics and complexity of the piece of music. Such a thing already exists, but it doesn't make the procedure any easier."

"You know what," Leonard said after a longer silence, "we'll make it easier. I decide to believe our neighbour, the entrepreneur, that he is right and our cables have gained in quality through the fifty years down here in the cave. Believing that is not very scientific, but it doesn't spoil the prices, if everything was just voodoo, as I originally assumed and in the end probably even our entrepreneur thinks, even if he would never admit that for the sake of his Hifi-Cave-Cable company."

"I think it was serendipity, a happy coincidence, that we are back in the mountain mine. This way we were able to look at some open complexity questions from a slightly different perspective. It is precisely the change of perspective that leads us out of a general hysteresis in which we linger day by day and shows us new ways." "You're right," Leonard replied, "I see the exit from the mountain mine right in front of us. We are free!"

References

Liening, A. (2019). *Ökonomische Bildung – Grundlagen und neue synergetische Ansätze* (2. edn.). Springer-Gabler.

MIX
Papier aus verantwortungsvollen Quellen
Paper from responsible sources
FSC® C105338

If you have any concerns about our products,
you can contact us on
ProductSafety@springernature.com

In case Publisher is established outside the EU,
the EU authorized representative is:
Springer Nature Customer Service Center GmbH
Europaplatz 3, 69115 Heidelberg, Germany

Printed by Libri Plureos GmbH
in Hamburg, Germany